2

organizational
change

This book is dedicated to our partners, Bertha, Heather, and Steve.

2

organizational
change

An Action-Oriented Toolkit

Tupper F. Cawsey | **Gene Deszca** | **Cynthia Ingols**
Wilfrid Laurier University | *Wilfrid Laurier University* | *Simmons College*

Los Angeles | London | New Delhi
Singapore | Washington DC

Los Angeles | London | New Delhi
Singapore | Washington DC

FOR INFORMATION:

SAGE Publications, Inc.
2455 Teller Road
Thousand Oaks, California 91320
E-mail: order@sagepub.com

SAGE Publications Ltd.
1 Oliver's Yard
55 City Road
London EC1Y 1SP
United Kingdom

SAGE Publications India Pvt. Ltd.
B 1/I 1 Mohan Cooperative Industrial Area
Mathura Road, New Delhi 110 044
India

SAGE Publications Asia-Pacific Pte. Ltd.
33 Pekin Street #02-01
Far East Square
Singapore 048763

Acquisitions Editor: Lisa Cuevas Shaw
Editorial Assistant: MaryAnn Vail
Production Editor: Eric Garner
Copy Editor: Kim Husband
Typesetter: C&M Digitals (P) Ltd.
Proofreader: Dennis W. Webb
Indexer: Molly Hall
Cover Designer: Anupama Krishnan
Marketing Manager: Helen Salmon
Permissions Editor: Karen Ehrmann

Printed in the United States of America

Library of Congress Cataloging-in-Publication Data

Cawsey, T. F.

Organizational change : an action-oriented toolkit/ Tupper F. Cawsey, Gene Deszca, Cynthia Ingols. — 2nd ed.

p. cm.

Rev. ed. of: Toolkit for organizational chang /Tupper Cawsey, Gene Deszca. c2007.

Includes bibliographical references and index.

ISBN 978-1-4129-8285-6 (pbk.)

1. Organizational change. I. Deszca, Gene. II. Ingols, Cynthia. III. Cawsey, T. F. Toolkit for organizational change. IV. Title.

HD58.8.C39 2012

658.4'06--dc22   2011001691

This book is printed on acid-free paper.

13 14 15 10 9 8 7 6 5 4 3

Brief Contents

Detailed Contents

Preface to the Second Edition

Since the publishing of the first edition of this text, the world has been turned upside down by the global financial crisis and a major recession. These events and their consequences are still unfolding—a massive credit crisis, followed by unprecedented worldwide government stimulus spending, followed by sovereign debt crises followed by . . . ??? These events have shaken all organizations, big or small, public or private. They have also made us, your authors, much more aware of the extreme influence of the external environment on the internal workings of an organization. As we point out in our book, even the smallest of firms have to adapt when banks refuse them normal credit.

Our models have always included and often started with events external to the organization. We have always argued that change leaders need to scan their environments and be aware of trends and crises in those environments. The events of the past two years have led us to emphasize this even more. Managers must be sensitive to what happens around them and then react quickly.

A corollary of this is that organizations need a response capability that is unprecedented. If you are a bank, you need a capital ratio that would have been unprecedented a few years ago. If you are a major organization, you need to build in flexibility into your structures, policies, and plans. If you are a public-sector organization, you need to be sensitive to how capricious granting agencies or funders will be when revenues dry up. In today's world, organizational resilience and adaptability gain new prominence.

Further, we are faced with a continuing reality that change is endemic. All managers are change managers. All good managers are change leaders. The management job involves creating, anticipating, encouraging, and responding positively to change. This has been a theme of this book which continues. Change management is for everyone. Change management comes from the middle of the organization as much as from the top. It will be those key leaders who are embedded in the organization who will enable the needed adaptation of the organization to its environment. **Middle management will be key change leaders.**

In addition to the above, we have used feedback on the first edition to strengthen the pragmatic orientation that we had developed. The major themes of action orientation, analysis tied with doing, the management of a nonlinear world, and the bridging of the "knowing–doing" gap continue to be central. However, we have tried to shift to a more user friendly, action perspective. As a result, some theoretical material has been shifted to chapter appendices and out of the main text. Some of our models have been clarified, perhaps even simplified, to make them more accessible to the reader.

As we stated in the preface to the first edition, our motivation for this book was to fill a gap we saw in the marketplace. Our challenge was to develop a book that not only gave prescriptive advice, "how-to-do-it lists," but one that also provided up-to-date theory without getting sidetracked by academic theoretical complexities. We hope that we have captured the management experience with change so that our manuscript assists all those who must deal with change, not just senior executives or organization development specialists. Although there is much in this book for the senior executive and organizational development specialist, our intent was to create a book that would be valuable to a much broader cross section of the workforce.

Our personal beliefs form the basis for the book. Even as academics, we have a bias for action. We believe that "doing is healthy." Taking action creates influence and demands responses from others. While we believe in the need for excellent analysis, we know that action itself provides opportunities for feedback and learning that can improve the action. Finally, we have a strong belief in the worth of people. In particular, we believe that one of the greatest sources of improvement is the untapped potential to be found in the people of the organization.

We recognize that this book is not an easy read. It is not meant to be. It is meant as a serious text for those involved in change—that is, all managers! We hope you find it a book that gets pulled from your shelf when you need to lead change and you want help thinking it through.

With this second edition, we want to welcome Cynthia Ingols, our new co-author. Cynthia brings a wealth of experience from the nonprofit world of organizations. She also further sensitizes us to gender issues in organizations. Welcome, Cynthia.

Your authors,
Tupper, Gene, and Cynthia

Acknowledgments

We would like to acknowledge all who have helped to make this book possible. Our students, who suffered through its growing pains cheerfully, have been a source of inspiration. The managers that we have known have provided insights, case examples, and applications while keeping us focused on what is useful and relevant. Several colleagues have provided guidance and feedback along the way that have helped us test our logic and develop our thinking.

Our research assistants have provided valuable assistance. Jamie Moffatt and Oliver Winkler assisted with the search for relevant research articles, reports of change initiatives, and websites of interest.

We give special thanks to Jenna Toplin. She searched for articles, sat in on our conference calls, provided valuable input on the draft manuscript from a student/ practitioner's perspective, and then read the entire manuscript one last time, catching problematic areas. She did all these tasks while remaining a delight to work with. Thank you, Jenna.

Of special note, our partners Bertha, Heather, and Steve tolerated our moods, our myopia to other things that needed doing, and the early mornings and late nights spent over the keyboard. They helped us work through ideas, and they encouraged us when frustration with the manuscript brewed and the ideas and words wouldn't come.

Our editors at SAGE have been excellent. They moved the project along and made it easy. Thank you, Lisa Shaw and MaryAnn Vail.

Finally, we would like to recognize the reviewers who provided us with valuable feedback on the first edition. Their constructive, positive feedback and their excellent suggestions were valued.

George Vukotich/Roosevelt University, John E. Sawyer/University of Delaware

Christopher J. L. Cunningham/The University of Tennessee at Chattanooga

Our thanks to all who made this book possible.

CHAPTER 1

Changing Organizations in Our Complex World

Nothing endures but change.

—Heraclitus (540 BC–480 BC)

CHAPTER OVERVIEW

- The chapter defines organizational change as "planned alteration of organizational components to improve the effectiveness of organizations."
- The orientation of this book is to assist change managers or potential change leaders to be more effective in their change activities.
- The social, demographic, technological, political, and economic forces affecting change today are outlined.
- Four change roles found in organizations are described: change initiators, change implementers, change facilitators, and change recipients and stakeholders. The terms *change leader* and *change agent* are used interchangeably and could mean any of the four roles.
- Four types of organizational change are discussed: tuning, adapting, reorienting, and recreating.
- The difficulties in creating successful change are highlighted, and then some of the characteristics of successful change leaders are described.

Our world is filled with organizations. We put our children into day-care organizations. We work at for-profit or not-for-profit organizations. We rely on organizations to deliver the services we need: food, water, electricity, and sanitation. We depend on health organizations when we are sick. We use religious organizations to help our spiritual lives. We assume that most of our children's education will be delivered by formal educational organizations. In other words, organizations are everywhere. Organizations are how we get things done.

And these organizations are changing—adapting to meet the shifting demands of their environments. What exactly is organizational change? What do we mean when we talk about it?

Defining Organizational Change

When we think of organizational change, we think of major changes: mergers, acquisitions, buy-outs, downsizing, restructuring, the launch of new products, and the outsourcing of major organizational activities. We can also think of lesser changes: departmental reorganizations, installations of new technology and incentive systems, shutting particular manufacturing lines, or opening new branches in other parts of the country—fine-tuning changes to improve the efficiency and operations of our organizations.

*In this book, when we talk about organizational change, we refer to planned alterations of organizational components to improve the effectiveness of the organization. Organizational components are the organizational mission and vision, strategy, goals, structure, processes or systems, technology, and people in an organization. When organizations enhance their effectiveness, they increase their ability to generate value for those they serve.**

The source of the change is often ambiguous. Was the change internally or externally driven? In winter 2010, McDonald's Corp. announced that it was going to nearly double its number of franchises in China by 2013.[1] What drove this change? The executives are taking action, but only because of the explosive growth potential they see in the Chinese market. The driver of change can come from both the internal and external environment. It is essential for managers to be sensitive to the organization's environment and adapt to those changes.

Note that, by our definition, organizational change is intentional and planned. Someone in the organization has taken an initiative to alter a significant organizational component. This means a shift in something relatively permanent. Usually, something formal has to be altered. For example, a new customer relations system may be introduced that captures customer satisfaction and reports it to managers; or a new division is created and people are allocated to that division in response to a new organizational vision.

Simply doing more of the same is not an organizational change. For example, increasing existing sales efforts in response to a competitor's activities would not be classified as an organizational change. However, the restructuring of a sales force into two groups (key account managers and general account managers) would be, even though this restructuring could well be in response to a competitor's activities and could lead to increased sales.

---

*Organizational change and Organizational development are often seen as very similar. A discussion of the evolution of these concepts can be found in Appendix 1.1 at the end of this chapter.

Some organizational components, such as structures and systems, are concrete and thus easier to understand when contemplating change. For example, assembly lines can be reordered. The change is definable and the endpoint clear when it is done. Similarly, the alteration of a reward system or job design is concrete and can be documented. The creation of new positions, subunits, or departments is equally obvious. Such organizational changes are tangible and thus can be easier to make happen.

When the change target is more deeply imbedded in the organization and is intangible, the change challenge is magnified. For example, a shift in organization culture is difficult to engineer. A change leader can plan a change from an authoritarian to a more participative culture, but the initiatives required to bring about the change and the sequencing of those initiatives are trickier to get a hold of than more concrete change initiatives. Simply announcing a new strategy or vision does not mean that anything significant will change. As someone said, "You need to get the vision off the walls and into the halls"[2]. A more manageable way to think of such a culture change is to identify concrete changes that reinforce the desired culture. If management alters reward systems, shifts decision making downward, and creates participative management committees, then management increases the likelihood that it will create cultural change over time. Sustained behavioral change occurs when people in the organization understand, accept, and act. Through their actions, the new vision or strategy becomes real.[3]

The focus of change needs to be considered carefully. Often, managers choose concrete tangible changes because they are easiest to plan for and can be seen. For example, it is relatively easy to focus on pay and give monetary incentives in an attempt to address employee morale. But the root cause of these issues might be managerial styles or processes—much more difficult to recognize and address. In addition, intervening through compensation may have unanticipated consequences and actually worsen the problem. An example of this can be found in the story box: "Change at a Social Service Agency."

CHANGE AT A SOCIAL SERVICE AGENCY

In a mid-sized social service agency's family services division, turnover rates climbed to more than 20%, causing serious issues with service delivery and quality of service. The manager of the division argued that staff were leaving because of wages. According to him, children's aid societies' wages were higher and staff left to join those organizations. Upon investigation, senior management learned of morale problems arising from the directive, noninclusive management style of the manager. Instead of altering pay rates, which would have caused significant budgetary and equity problems throughout the organization, senior management replaced the manager and moved him to a project role. Within months, turnover rates dropped to less than 10% and the manager decided to leave the agency.[4]

In this example, if the original analysis had been accepted, turnover rates might have declined since staff may have been persuaded to stay for higher wages. But the agency would be facing monetary issues and would have had a festering morale problem!

In summary, the focus of this book is on **organizational change as a planned activity designed to improve the organization's effectiveness.** Changes that are random (occur simply due to chance) or unplanned are not the types of organizational change that this book will explore. Similarly, changes that may be planned but do not have a clear link to attempts to improve organization effectiveness are not considered. That is, changes made solely for personal reasons—for personal gain, for example—fall outside the intended focus of this book.

The Orientation of This Book

> *There is a story of two stone cutters. The first, when asked what he was doing, responded, "I am shaping this stone to fit in that wall." The second, however, said, "I am helping to build a cathedral."*

The jobs of the two stone cutters might be the same, but their perspectives are dramatically different. The personal outcomes of satisfaction and organizational commitment will likely be much higher for the visionary stone cutter than for the "just doing my job" stone cutter. Finally, the differences in satisfaction and commitment may well lead to different organizational results. After all, if you are building a cathedral, you might have the motivation to stay late, to take extra care, to find ways to improve things, and to help others when help is needed.

In other words, the organizational member who has a grander perspective on his or her contribution and on the task at hand is likely to be a better, more satisfied employee. As a result, we take a perspective that encourages change leaders to take a holistic perspective on the change and to be widely inclusive in letting employees know what changes are needed and are happening.

If employees have no sense of the intended vision and see themselves as "just doing a job," it is likely that any organizational change will be difficult to understand, be resisted, and cause personal trauma. On the other hand, if employees "get" the vision of the organization and understand the direction and perspective of where the organization is going and why, they are more likely to embrace their future role—even if that future means they leave the organization.[5]

This book is aimed at those who want to be involved in change and wish to take positive action. We encourage readers to escape from passive, negative change recipient positions and to move to more active and healthy roles—those of change initiators, facilitators, and implementers. Readers may be in middle-manager roles or may be entering management. Or they may be leaders of change within an organization or a subunit. The book is also intended for the informal leaders in organizations who are driving change, sometimes in spite of their bosses. They might believe that their bosses "should" be driving the change but don't see it happening, and so they see it as up to them to make change happen regardless of the action or inaction of their managers.

This book has an action, "how to do it" emphasis. Nothing happens unless we, the people, make it happen. As one wag put it, "The truth is—the cavalry aren't coming!" There will be no cavalry charging over the hill to save us. It is up to us to make the changes needed. At the same time, this "how-to" orientation is paired with a focus on developing a deep understanding of organizations. Without such an understanding, what needs to be changed, and what the critical success factors are, change efforts will be much more difficult. This twin theme, of knowing both what to do and how to do it, underpins the structure of this book and our approach to change.

Change capability has become a core managerial competence. Without change management skills, individuals cannot operate effectively in today's fluctuating, shifting organizations.[6] Senior management may set the organizational direction, but, in this decentralized organizational world, it is up to managers and employees to shift the organization to accomplish the new goals and objectives. To do this, change management skills are paramount.

Change management is often more difficult than we anticipate. We believe, as does Pfeffer, that there is a Knowing–Doing gap.[7] Knowing the concepts and understanding the theory behind organizational change are not enough. This book is designed to provide practicing and prospective managers with the tools they will need to be effective change agents.

Environmental Forces Driving Change Today

Much change starts with shifts in an organization's environment. For example, government legislation dealing with employment law pushes new equity concerns through hiring practices. Globalization means that production and other parts of the organization (e.g., customer service's call centers) can be outsourced and/or moved around the world, making an organization's competition worldwide rather than local. New technologies allow purchasing to link to production within the supply chain, changing forever supplier–customer relationships. Concerns over global warming, sustainability, and environmental practices give rise to new laws, standards, and shifts in consumer preferences for products and firms that exhibit superior environmental performance. A competitor succeeds in attracting an organization's largest customer and upsets management's assumptions about the marketplace. Each of these external happenings will drive change.

Sometimes organizations are caught by surprise by environmental shifts, while other organizations have anticipated and planned for new situations. For example, management may have systems to track the perceived quality of its products versus its competition's. That benchmarking data might show that its quality is beginning to lag behind that of a key competitor. This early warning system allows for action before customers are lost. Toyota had such systems in place, but management appears to have responded inadequately.

DID TOYOTA KNOW ABOUT THE SAFETY DEFECTS?

Misreading the Environment

On April 5, 2010, the U.S. government's transportation department stated it would seek $16.4 million from Toyota for not notifying the government about potential accelerator pedal problems. "In taking the step, federal authorities are sending the strongest signal yet that they believe the carmaker deliberately concealed safety information from them."[8]

Did Toyota know about these deficiencies and respond by denying they existed and covering up? If so, this is an example of an inappropriate organizational response to environmental stimuli.

This book is not the place for an in-depth treatment of all of the various trends and alterations in the environment. However, we will highlight below some of the important trends to sensitize readers to their environments. Today, organizations find themselves influenced by fundamental forces: changing social, cultural, and demographic patterns; spectacular technological achievements that transform how we do business; concerns about the physical environment and social responsibility that are producing demands for changes in our products and business practices; a global marketplace that sends us competing worldwide and brings competition to our doorsteps; political and legal forces that have the potential to transform the competitive landscape; continued political uncertainty in many countries that has the potential to introduce chaos into world markets; and economic turmoil that rocked the world economy in 2008, 2009, and 2010.

YOU NEED TO UNDERSTAND
THE RISKS OF NOT UNDERSTANDING
YOUR ORGANIZATIONAL ENVIRONMENT!

The financial crisis of 2008 occurred because banks failed to comprehend the risks they took with asset-backed securities and other derivatives. Incentive systems drove bankers to take on excessive risks for excessive profits. They denied the evidence presented to them, and when the bubble burst, the results were catastrophic. For example, when warned by his chief risk officer, who proposed shutting down the mortgage business in 2004, the head of Lehman threatened to fire him! This rush for profits drove many banks. Chuck Prince, the head of Citigroup at the time, just before the credit markets seized up in August 2007, said: "As long as the music is playing, you've got to get up and dance. We're still dancing."[9]

Clearly both bankers misread the ethical and business implications of what was going on inside their firms.

The Changing Social, Cultural, and Demographic Environment

The social, cultural, and economic environment will be dramatically altered by demography. Demographic changes in the Western World mean that aging populations will alter the face of Europe, Canada, and Japan. The financial warning bells are already being sounded. Even before the huge government deficits of 2009 and beyond, Standard and Poor's predicts that the average net government debt-to-GDP ratio for industrialized nations will increase from 33% in 2005 to 180% by 2050, due to rising pension and health care costs[10], if changes are not undertaken.

Although the United States will age slightly, Europe will face a dependency crisis of senior citizens requiring medical care and pension support. By 2050, the median age in the United States is projected to be 36.2 versus 52.7 in Europe. The United States will keep itself younger through immigration and a birth rate that is close to replacement level.[11] Even with this influx, the U.S. governmental debt-to-GDP ratio is expected to grow to 350% of GDP by 2050, due mainly to pension and health care costs.[12] Europe's population is projected to peak in 2015 at around 400 million, while the United States passes that number in 2020 and continues to grow thereafter.

Throughout the world, fertility rates are falling and falling fast.[13] In 1974, only 24 countries had fertility rates below replacement levels. By 2009, more than 70 countries had rates below 2.1. In some countries, the swings are dramatic. The fertility rate in Iran dropped from 7 in 1984 to 1.9 in 2009, a huge shift.

Some see a close tie between female education, fertility rates, and economic growth. When economies are poor, the fertility rate is high and there are many young dependents relying on working adults for sustenance. When fertility rates drop, there is a bulge of people, meaning the ratio of working adults to dependents increases, leading to surplus (relatively) wealth. When this bulge ages, dependent, nonworking seniors become a larger percentage of the population. As discussed above, this has happened and is happening in Europe and Japan. China and India are examples of nations with relatively small numbers of dependents relative to their working populations.[14]

Although these demographic shifts appear far in the future, the economic implications for organizations are significant. Imagine 400 to 500 million relatively wealthy Americans and the impact that will have on global economic power, assuming that pension and health care challenges are effectively managed. Consumer spending in emerging economies is expected to more than double from $4 trillion to more than $9 trillion in the next 10 years.[15] Also imagine the impact of a graying Europe and Japan's declining workforce.* Some estimates put the fiscal problems in providing pensions and health care for senior citizens at 250% of national income in Germany and France.[16]

Pension costs can become a huge competitive disadvantage at the company level as well. At General Motors, there were 2.5 retirees for every active worker

---

*Already, the impact of the graying of Europe is seen as the governments of Germany and France meet significant resistance as they attempt to reduce retirement and unemployment benefits for their citizens.

in 2002. These so-called "legacy" costs were $900 per vehicle at that time due to pension and health care obligations. These costs were estimated to have risen to $1,600 by 2005 and $1,800 by 2006.[17] At the same time, an aging population provides new market opportunities—who would believe that the average age of a Harley-Davidson purchaser is 52![18] Companies appear to be ill prepared to deal with this aging population.[19]

Other demographic issues will provide opportunities and challenges. In the United States, Latinos will play a role in transforming organizations. The numbers of Latinos jumped from 22.4 million to 35.3 million during the 1990s, and at 12.5% of the population, they are the largest ethnic/racial group in the United States.[20] Significantly, the largest growth often is in "hypergrowth" Latino destinations, which have seen an increase of more than 300% in Latino populations since 1980. This growth will continue due to the economic activity in these areas, and one of the outcomes will be an imbalance of Latino males and females. In the non-Latino population, the ratio of males to females is 96:100. In the Latino population, this switches to 107:100 and to 118:100 in the hypergrowth destinations (peaking at 188:100 in Raleigh, N.C.).[21] While the specific implications for businesses are unclear, the general need for response and change is not. Notions of cultural norms (including those around English literacy) and markets could be shattered by such demographic shifts.

With aging populations, organizations can expect pressures to manage age prejudice more effectively. Subtle discrimination based on age will not be acceptable. Innovative solutions such as those by Joe Pesce will be welcomed. (See the boxed insert.)

THE AGING WORKFORCE AT THE BAYCREST

"There is no mandatory retirement age at Baycrest (a large geriatric care facility in Toronto, Canada), where roughly 35 of the center's 2,000 employees are now over 65, said Mr. Pesce, vice president of human resources.

Mr. Pesce is putting together a list of "retiree alumni"—a pool of retired employees who might be willing to come back on a part-time or temporary basis as needed—and is also looking at other ways to make Baycrest a more elder-friendly workplace.[22]

Clearly, Joe Pesce has become a change initiator in this important area of demographic change.

Our assumptions about families and gender will continue to be challenged in the workplace and marketplace of the future. Diversity, inclusiveness, and equity issues will challenge organizations with unpredictable results. For example, the liberal initiatives in California are now subject to backlash, according to Diamond: "Immigration, affirmative action, multilingualism, ethnic diversity—my state of California was among the pioneers of these controversial policies and is now pioneering a backlash against them."[23] Signs of this were apparent in the heated debates that occurred in the United States in 2006 concerning legislation related to illegal or undocumented immigrants and workers. Some jurisdictions have begun implementing laws that discriminate against specific religious groups.[24] Organizational diversity will continue to be an area of concern for business leaders.

As the nature and variety of relationships change, organizations will have to respond. Flexible employment systems will be vital to attract and keep the knowledge workers of the future. Already, multinational corporations, such as IBM, view workforce diversity management as a strategic tool for sustaining and growing the enterprise.[25]

Finally, concerns over global warming, the degradation of the environment, sustainability, and social responsibility have escalated societal pressure for change at the intergovernmental, governmental, firm, and community levels. Accountability for what is referred to as the "triple bottom line" is leading firms to issue audited statements that report on economic, social, and ecological performance with the goal of sustainability in mind.[26] Pictures of BP's oil well gushing millions of gallons into the Gulf of Mexico, oil-coated pelicans, drought, extreme heat, labor exploitation, and disappearing ice masses are reinforcing the message that action is urgently needed. These pressures will intensify in the years ahead.

New Technologies

In addition to responding to demographic changes in the workplace and marketplace, organizations and their leaders must embrace the trite but true statements about the impact of technological change. Underpinning technological change is the sweeping digitization of information. The quantity of data available to managers is soaring. One estimate reports an increase of data collected from 150 billion gigabytes of data collected in 2005 to 1,299 billion gigabytes in 2010.[27] Massive amounts of data are available. How can management interpret such data into useful information that will help organizations stay effective? *Data mining* has become a common phrase to describe this transformation of data into information. Executives examine mounds of data to understand customers: who switched to a competitor; who buys what and why at their stores; how to position a new marketing campaign to attract a desired segment of customers; and how to use customers' feedback to improve products or services. Many firms have created a senior executive position, chief information officer, to handle this new area. The following list of technologies suggests the breadth of future changes:

- Software that writes its own code, reducing human error;
- Health care by cell phone;
- Vertical farming to save space and increase yield;[28]
- An implantable syringe-on-a-chip that will inject minute quantities of drugs at precise intervals over months.[29]

Wieners claims that there will be eight technologies that will change the world:

- Biointeractive materials that will provide high-tech sensors for living systems;
- Biofuel production plants where genetically engineered crops produce fuel to replace coal and oil;

- Bionics—artificial systems to replace lost or disabled body parts;
- Cognitronics where there are interfaces between the computer and the brain;
- Genotyping where we classify people based on their genetics;
- Brute-force R&D where powerful computers crunch data to identify and test random solutions for positive results;
- Molecular manufacturing that builds complex structures atom by atom; and
- Port-a-Nukes that will provide portable, safe, nonpolluting nuclear power.[30]

Technology has woven our world together. The number of international air passengers rose from 75 million in 1970 to 142 million in 2000. The cost of a 3-minute phone call from the United States to England dropped from more than $8 to less than $0.36 from 1976 to 2000, and the number of transborder calls in the United States increased from 200 million in 1980 to 5.2 billion in 1999.[31] The emergence of VoIP (voice over the Internet protocol) is poised to disrupt long distance telephone markets dramatically, reducing the cost of international calls to pennies per minute—or zero if one has the right equipment. At the same time, security concerns related to viruses and hacking are raised.[32] On a business-to-business level, supply chains are woven together and software allows them to operate effectively and be responsive to the marketplace.[33]

With the World Wide Web, high school students can have access to the same quality of information that the best researchers have! At the same time, the technology that has made the world small has also produced a technological divide between haves and have-nots that has the potential to produce social and political instability.* Lack of access to clean water, sufficient food, and needed medication is less likely to be tolerated in silence when media images tell people that others have an abundance of such resources and lack the will to share. Technology transforms relationships. For example, blogging is commonplace; more than 12% of U.S. newlyweds met online in 2005.[34]

Our purpose is not to catalogue all new and emerging technologies. Rather, our intent is to signal to change leaders the importance of paying attention to technological trends and the impact they may have on organizations, now and in the future. As a result of these forces, product development and life cycles are shortened and managers must respond in a time-paced fashion. Competitors can leapfrog organizations and drop once-market leaders into obsolescence through a technological breakthrough. The advantages of vertical integration can vanish as technical experts in one segment of the business drive down the costs and then migrate the technology through outsourcing to other segments that have not anticipated such changes. The watchwords for change leaders are to be aware of technological trends and to be proactive in their consideration of how to respond to organizationally relevant ones.

---

*The effects are not straightforward, as shown by the move of MIT's media lab to create a $100 laptop computer for disadvantaged youth in Africa, Asia, and around the world (see http://laptop.media.mit.edu).

Political Changes

The external political landscape of an organization is a reality that change leaders need pay attention to and figure out how to engage. Even the largest of multinationals has minimal impact on the worldwide alteration of national boundaries and the focus of governing bodies.[35]

The collapse of the Soviet Empire gave rise to optimism in the West that democracy and the market economy were the natural order of things, the only viable option for modern society.[36] With the end of communism, there was no serious competitor to free-market democracy and the belief existed that the world would gradually move to competitive capitalism with market discipline. The American hegemony would rule the world.

Of course, this optimism was not realized. Nationalistic border quarrels (India–Pakistan, for example) continue. Some African countries have become less committed to democracy (Zimbabwe and the Sudan). Nation-states have dissolved into microstates (remember Yugoslavia?). While American power may be dominant worldwide, September 11, 2001 (9/11) demonstrated that even the dominant power cannot guarantee safety. Non–nation states and religious groups have become actors on the global stage. The Middle East and Central Asia continue to be in turmoil, creating political and economic uncertainty. At the same time, the markets of China and India are on a tear.[37] They led the world out of the 2007–2008 crash.

As organizations become global, they need to clarify their own ethical standards. Not only will they need to understand the law, they will also have to determine what norms of behavior they will work to establish for their organizational members. Peter Eigen, chairman of Transparency International, states: "Political elites and their cronies continue to take kickbacks at every opportunity. Hand-in-glove with corrupt business people, they are trapping whole nations in poverty and hampering sustainable development. Corruption is perceived to be dangerously high in poor parts of the world, but also in many countries whose firms invest in developing nations. . . ."[38] This political corruption becomes imbedded in organizations. Transparency International finds bribery most common in public works/construction and arms and defense as compared with agriculture.[39] The accounting and governance scandals of 2001 to 2002 (Enron and WorldCom) created a demand for both new regulation and an emphasis on ethical role models. Some companies, Hewlett-Packard for example, have responded by demanding that they and everyone in their supply chain adhere to a set of specified ethical standards. Further, they are committed to working with their suppliers to ensure they reach these standards.[40]

The politics of globalization and the environment have created opportunities and issues for organizations. The United States's Obama administration appears committed to the introduction of new green energy initiatives. The desire to reduce America's dependence on foreign oil has meant subsidy programs for new, clean energy initiatives and opportunities for businesses in those fields. Some organizations are restructuring themselves to seize such opportunities. For example, Siemens has reorganized itself into three sectors—industry, energy, and health care—to focus on megatrends.[41] The Kyoto Accord will change the costs of operating for businesses in nations that sign on to the Accord. At the same time, they may develop new technologies that will bring profits in the future. Senge from MIT argues that the new environmentalism will be driven by innovation and will result in radical new technologies, products, processes, and business models.[42]

The politics of the world are not the everyday focus of all managers, but change leaders need to understand their influence on market development and attractiveness, competitiveness, and the resulting pressures on boards and executives. A sudden transformation of the political landscape can trash the best-laid strategic plan. Successful change leaders will have a keen sense of the opportunities and dangers involved in global, national, and local political shifts.

The Economy

In 2007, the world economy crashed into financial crisis and appeared headed for a 1930s depression. Trillions of dollars of asset-backed paper became valueless, seemingly overnight. Investors and pension funds lost 20% of their value. Global stock markets shrank by $30 trillion, or half their value.[43] The American housing market, which provided an illusory asset base, collapsed and led to the credit crisis. Firms that were chastised for having too much cash on hand and were seen as missing opportunities suddenly became the survivors when credit vanished. At the individual firm level, the economic crisis led to layoffs and bankruptcies. Firms saw their order books shrink and business disappear. Entire industries, such as the automotive industry, were overwhelmed and perhaps would have vanished if not for government bailouts. An example of the impact on one small firm is shown in the boxed insert: The Impact of the 2007–2009 Recession on a Small Business.

THE IMPACT OF THE 2007–2009 RECESSION ON A SMALL BUSINESS

Serge Gaudet operates a wholesale/retail drapery and window blind business in the small Canadian town of Sturgeon Falls, Ontario. The world economic crisis suddenly became real when banks would no longer extend him credit. In his words, "I had signed orders, contracts in hand, and my bank refused my line of credit so that I could buy the inventory. How was I to finance this deal? I had the contract and it was with a government hospital. Surely, this was credit worthy? What else could I do?"

Mr. Gaudet managed through the crisis by negotiating newer, tougher terms with his bank. But the lack of credit was not his only problem. "Normally, I bid on requests for proposals and win a reasonable percentage of them," he reported. "Suddenly, there was nothing to bid on. Nothing. Every institution that was going to buy blinds was waiting—waiting for government aid that was very slow in coming. It was touch and go whether I could last until new contracts came in."

> Mr. Gaudet's story is typical of the situation faced by many small businesses as they struggled through the economic crisis of 2007–2009. Many did not survive. Those that did were able to do so because they had low overhead and debt.[44]

Governments responded to the economic crisis with Keynesian abandon. G20 countries ran huge deficits as governments tried to stimulate their economies out of recession. America's federal deficit hit 10% of GDP in 2009, and the overall debt will continue to grow for many years into the future. One prediction suggests that America's debt will stabilize at 70% of GDP in 2014, but this would require trimming $200 billion from federal spending.[45] By December 2010, economists were talking about a slow recovery, particularly in America. The world's output in 2009 probably shrank by more than 1%, the first time it actually shrank since 1945.[46] Economists predicted that America's recovery would be weak and Europe's would be almost nonexistent, but China's would have an 8.6% GDP growth and 11.1% investment growth.[47] Clearly, there has been a shift in the economic order of the world.

The lessons for organizations from the economic crisis center around risk management and capacity building. In a world where everything is interconnected, organizations need to be able to respond quickly. In order to do so, organizations need the capacity to weather such challenges. Ideally, organizations will incorporate the mechanisms to anticipate these challenges into management and leadership. In many situations, this will not be possible and organizations will rely on their ability to change as the environmental shifts.

Toolkit Exercise 1.1 asks you to consider the implications of the environment on an organization you are familiar with.

The Implications of Worldwide Trends for Change Management

The economic globalization of the world, the demographic shifts in the Western world's population, technological opportunities, and the upheaval and political and economic uncertainties form the reality of organizational environments. Predicting specific short-run changes is a fool's errand. Nevertheless, change leaders need to have a keen sense of just how these seemingly external events impact internal organizational dynamics. "How will external changes drive strategy and internal adjustments and investments?" has become a critical question that change leaders need to address.

Barkema suggests that macroenvironmental changes will change organizational forms and competitive dynamics and, in turn, lead to new management challenges.[48] (Table 1.1 summarizes Barkema's article.) He describes three macro changes facing us today: digitization of information; integration of nation states and the opening of international markets; and the geographic dispersion of the value chain. These are leading to the globalization of markets. This globalization, in turn, will drive significant shifts in organizational forms and worldwide competitive dynamics.

Table 1.1 New Organizational Forms and Management Challenges Based on Environmental Change		
Macro Changes and Impacts	*New Organizational Forms and Competitive Dynamics*	*New Management Challenges*
Digitization leading to: • faster information transmission • lower-cost information storage and transmission • integration of states and opening of markets • geographic dispersion of the value chain All leading to globalization of markets.	Global small and medium-sized enterprises Global constellations of organizations (i.e., networks) Large, focused global firms All leading to: spread of autonomous, dislocated teams; digitally enabled structures; intense global rivalry and running faster while seeming to stand still	Greater diversity Greater synchronization requirements Greater time-pacing requirements Faster decision making, learning, and innovation More frequent environmental discontinuities Faster industry life cycles Faster newness and obsolescence of knowledge Risk of competency traps where old competencies no longer produce desired effects Greater newness and obsolescence of organizations

Source: Adapted from Barkema, H.G., J.A.C. Baum, & E.A. Mannix, "Management Challenges in a New Time", *Academy of Management Journal.* Vol. 45, #5, 916–930.

The early decades of the 21st century suggest accelerated change in comparison to the latter part of the 20th century. Diversity; synchronization and time-pacing requirements; decision making; the frequency of environmental discontinuities; quick industry life cycles and in consequence product and service obsolescence; and competency traps all suggest greater complexity and a more rapid organizational pace for today and tomorrow. Barkema argues that much change today deals with mid-level change—change that is more than incremental but not truly revolutionary. As such, middle managers will play increasingly significant roles in making change effective in their organizations in both evolutionary and revolutionary scenarios.

Four Types of Organizational Change

Organizational changes come in many shapes and sizes: mergers, acquisitions, buy-outs, downsizing, restructuring, outsourcing the human resource function or computer services, departmental reorganizations, installations of new incentive systems, shutting particular manufacturing lines or opening new branches in other parts of the country, and the list goes on. All of these describe specific organizational changes. The literature on organizational change classifies such changes into two types, episodic or discontinuous change and continuous change. That is, change can be dramatic and sudden—the introduction of a new technology that makes a business obsolete or new government regulations that immediately shift the competitive landscape. Or change can be much more gradual, such as the alteration of core competencies of an organization through training and adding key individuals.

Under dramatic or episodic change, organizations are seen as having significant inertia. Change is infrequent and discontinuous. Re-engineering programs are examples of this type of change and can be viewed as planned examples of injecting significant change into an organization. On the other hand, under continuous change, organizations are seen as emergent and self-organizing where change is constant, evolving, and cumulative.[49] Japanese automobile manufacturers have led the way in this area with *kaizen* programs focused on encouraging continuous change.

A second dimension of change is whether it occurs in a proactive, planned, and programmatic fashion or reactively in response to external events. Programmatic or planned change occurs when managers anticipate events and shift their organizations as a result. For example, Intel anticipates and appears to encourage a cycle of computer chip obsolescence.[50] As a result, the organization has been designed to handle this obsolescence. Alternately, shifts in an organization's external world lead to a reaction on the part of the organization. For example, the emergence of low-cost airlines has led to traditional carriers employing reactive strategies, such as cutting routes, costs, and service levels in an attempt to adapt.[51]

Nadler and Tushman combine these two dimensions in a useful model illustrating different types of change (see Table 1.2). They define four categories of change: tuning, adapting, redirecting or reorienting, and overhauling or re-creating.

Tuning is defined as small, relatively minor changes made on an ongoing basis in a deliberate attempt to improve the efficiency or effectiveness of the organization. Responsibility for acting on these sorts of changes typically rests with middle management. Most improvement change initiatives that grow out of existing quality-improvement programs would fall into this category. **Adapting** is viewed as relatively minor changes made in response to external stimuli—a reaction to things observed in the environment such as competitors' moves or customer shifts. Relatively minor changes to customer servicing caused by reports of customer dissatisfaction or defection to a competitor provide an example of this sort of change, and once again, responsibility for such changes tends to reside within the role of middle managers.

Redirecting or reorienting involves major, strategic change resulting from planned programs. These frame-bending shifts are designed to provide new perspectives and directions in a significant way. For example, a shift in a firm to truly develop a customer service organization and culture would fall in this category. Finally, **overhauling or re-creation** is the dramatic shift that occurs in reaction to major external events. Often there is a crisis situation that forces the change—thus, the emergence of low-cost carriers forced traditional airlines to re-create what they do. Likewise, the credit crisis bankrupted General Motors and forced a complete overhaul and downsizing of the company.

Table 1.2   Types of Organizational Change[52]

	Incremental/Continuous	Discontinuous/Radical
Anticipatory	**Tuning** Incremental change made in anticipation of future events Need is for internal alignment • Focuses on individual components or subsystems • Middle management role • Implementation is the major task • E.g., a quality improvement initiative from an employee improvement committee	**Redirecting or Reorienting** • Strategic proactive changes based on predicted major changes in the environment • Need is for positioning the whole organization to a new reality • Focuses on all organizational components • Senior management creates sense of urgency and motivates the change • E.g., a major change in product or service offering in response to opportunities identified
Reactive	**Adapting** • Incremental changes made in response to environmental changes • Need is for internal alignment • Focuses on individual components or subsystems • Middle management role • Implementation is the major task • E.g., modest changes to customer services in response to customer complaints	**Overhauling or Re-creating** Response to a significant performance crisis • Need to reevaluate the whole organization, including its core values • Focuses on all organizational components to achieve rapid, systemwide change • Senior management creates vision and motivates optimism • E.g., a major realignment of strategy, involving plant closures and changes to product and service offerings, to stem financial losses and return the firm to profitability

Source: Adapted from Nadler D. A and M. Tushman. "Organizational Frame Bending: Principles for Managing Reorientation", *Academy of Management Executive.* Aug 89, Vol. 3 Issue 3, p 196.

The impact of the change increases as we move from minor alterations and fine tuning to changes that require us to reorient and re-create the organization. Not surprisingly, reorienting and re-creating an organization is much more time consuming and challenging to lead effectively. They also have a greater impact on individuals who must reorient themselves. Regardless of difficulty, the financial crisis and recession of 2008–2009 have forced companies to react. While there are no data that we know of, anticipatory organizational change does not seem to be sufficient given the dramatic shift in the global business environment. It was not planning that helped firms to survive—it was a sense of awareness and adaptive capacity that allowed firms to respond and survive the crisis.

An examination of the history of British Airways provides a classic example of a single organization facing both incremental and discontinuous change while both anticipating issues and being forced to react.[53]

BRITISH AIRWAYS: STRATEGIC AND INCREMENTAL CHANGE

Todd Jick's case study describes the crisis of 1981. British Airways' (BA's) successful response in the 1980s was revolutionary in nature. During that period, BA revolutionized its culture and its view of the customer with outstanding results. In the 1990s, BA entered a period of slow decline as the systems and structures at BA became increasingly incongruent with the new deregulated environment and the successful competitors that were spawned by that environment. Since then, major upheavals in international travel have pushed BA into a reactive mode and the results of management's attempts to develop new strategies are unclear. A strike in the summer of 2003 created more uncertainty for the firm.[54] The dramatic rise in oil costs during 2007 and 2008 forced BA to cut costs and implement a merger with Iberia. These strategic moves to cut costs were matched by more gradual incremental internal actions to limit the wages of cabin staff to match those of its competitors.[55]

Nadler and Tushman raise the question: "Will incremental change be sufficient or will radical change be necessary in the long run?" Suffice it to say that this question has not been nor can it ever be answered. However, the Japanese provided a profound lesson in the value of incremental, daily changes. Interestingly enough, it was a lesson the Japanese industrialists learned from North American management scholars such as Duran and Deming. If one observes employee involvement and continuous improvement processes effectively employed,[56] one also sees organizational team members that are energized, goal directed, cohesive, and increasingly competent because of the new things they are learning. Such teams expect that tomorrow will be a little different from today. Further, when more significant changes have to be embraced, these teams are likely to be far less resistant and fearful of them because of their earlier experiences with facilitating change within group structures. Organizational change is part of daily life for them.

Many think of incremental/continuous change and discontinuous/radical change as states rather than a perspective or a spectrum of change size. From the organization point of view, a departmental reorganization might seem incremental. However, from the department's perspective, it will seem discontinuous and radical. As Morgan puts it:

A mythology is developing in which incremental and quantum change are presented as opposites. Nothing could be further from the truth . . . True, there is a big difference between incremental and quantum change when we talk of results (but) incremental and quantum change are intertwined. As we set our sights on those 500% improvements, remember they're usually delivered through 5, 10, and 15% initiatives.[57]

The perception of the magnitude of the change lies in the eye of the beholder. Incremental changes at the organization level may appear disruptive and revolutionary at a department level. However, as noted earlier, those who are accustomed to facing and managing incremental change on a regular basis will likely view more revolutionary changes in less threatening terms. Those who have not faced and managed change will be more likely to view even incremental changes as threatening in nature.

Organizational members need to learn to accept and value the perspectives of both the adaptor (those skilled in incremental change) and the innovator (those skilled in more radical change).[58] As a change agent, personal insight regarding your abilities and preferences for more modest or more radical change is critical. The secret to successful organizational growth and development over time lies in the capacity of organizational members to embrace both approaches to change at the appropriate times and to understand that they are, in fact, intertwined.

Planned Changes Don't Always Produce the Intended Results

To this point, it is clear that change—even radical reconstruction—is becoming a necessary prerequisite to organization survival. However, successful change is extremely difficult to execute. Many types of change initiatives have failed: reengineering, total quality management, activity-based costing, joint optimization, strategic planning, network structures.[59] If change leaders were to fully consider these failure rates when designing interventions or acquisitions, fear would trump action. As one manager put it, "The opportunity has turned out to be 10 times what I thought it would be. The challenges have turned out to be 20 times what I thought they were"![60]

Unfortunately, inaction and avoidance are no solution. Maintenance of our organization's status quo typically does not sustain or enhance competitive advantage, particularly in troubled organizations. Delays and half-hearted efforts that begin only after the problems have become critical increase costs and decrease the likelihood of a successful transformation. As Hamel and Prahalad put it: "No company can escape the need to re-skill its people, reshape its product portfolio, redesign its process, and redirect resources."[61] Organizations that consistently demonstrate their capacity to innovate, manage change, and adapt over the years are the ones with staying power.[62]

Hamel and Prahalad believe that restructuring and re-engineering, on their own, do little to increase the capabilities of the firm. These two Rs increase profitability and can enhance competitiveness but "in many companies . . . re-engineering (and restructuring) . . . are more about catching up than getting out in front."[63] Hamel and Prahalad argue that companies need to regenerate their strategy and reinvent their industry by building their capacity to compete.

Radical solutions both terrify and fascinate managers. Often managers are comfortable with relatively small technological fixes as the source of products, services, efficiency, and effectiveness. However, they tend to fear interventions that seem to reduce their control over situations, people, and outcomes. When organizations embrace technology but not people, they pay a steep price. They reduce the likelihood that the change will produce the desired results and they fail to take advantage of the collective capacity of organizational members to improve operations, products, and services. To say the least, this practice is extremely wasteful of human capacity and energy, causing them to atrophy over time. And recent evidence suggests that true productivity increases come only when the forms are reorganized, business practices reformulated, and employees retrained. Investment in infrastructure alone is insufficient.[64]

Table 1.3 highlights common sources of difficulty that change initiators, implementers, and facilitators face when attempting to implement planned changes. There are many external factors that can frustrate or divert progress in unanticipated and undesirable directions, but this table does not address these. This table focuses on ways in which change leaders can act as their own worst enemies, self-sabotaging their own initiatives. They stem from predispositions, perceptions, and a lack of self-awareness. The good news is that they also represent areas that a person can do something about if he or she becomes more self-aware and chooses to take the blinders off.

Managers play a critical role in creating successful change. The roles they adopt will often be critical in developing successful change strategies. Too many will accept a passive change recipient role. Our view, however, is that it is much better to become action oriented and be part of the change team. The roles of change leader or change agent, change implementer or change facilitator are healthier than

---

Table 1.3 Common Managerial Difficulties

In Dealing With Organizational Change

1. Managers are action oriented and assume other rational people will see the inherent wisdom in the proposed change and will learn the needed new behaviors. Or managers assume that they will be able to replace recalcitrant employees.

2. Managers assume they have the power and influence to enact the desired changes and they underestimate the power and influence of other stakeholders.

3. Managers look at the transition period as a cost, not an investment.

4. Managers are unable to accurately estimate the resources and commitment needed to facilitate the integration of the human dimension with other aspects of the change (e.g., systems, structures, technologies).

5. Managers are unaware that their own behavior, and that of other key managers, may be sending out conflicting messages to employees and eventually customers.

6. Managers find managing human processes unsettling (even threatening) because of the potential emotionality and the difficulties they present with respect to prediction and quantification.

7. Managers simply lack the capacity (attitudes, skills, and abilities) to manage complex changes that involve people.

8. Managers' critical judgment is impaired due to factors related to overconfidence[65] and/or groupthink.

a more passive change recipient role. Our next section will outline these roles and some of the implications of adopting them.

Organization Change Roles

Without a sense of vision, purpose, and engagement, it is easy to become the passive recipient of change. As a passive recipient, you see yourself as subject to the whims of others, as relatively helpless, perhaps even as a victim. As a passive recipient, your self-esteem and self-efficacy may feel as if they are under attack.[66] Your perception of power and influence will diminish and you will feel acted on. Years ago, Jack Gordon talked about aligning employees. That is, once top management has decided on the strategic direction, employees need to be aligned with that direction. We cannot help but think that if you are the recipient of change, "being aligned" just won't feel very good.[67]

Who are the participants in organization change? Many employees will step up and make the change work. They will be the change implementers, the ones making happen what others, the change initiators, have pushed or encouraged. Or we could be on the receiving end of change, change recipients. Some will play a role in facilitating change—they won't be the ones responsible for implementing the change, but they will assist initiators and implementers in the change through their contacts and consultative assistance. Or a person might be the change initiator or champion, framing the vision for the change and/or providing resources and support for the initiative.

Of course, one person might play multiple roles. That is, a person might have a good idea and talk it up in the organization (change initiator); take action to make the change occur (change implementer); talk to others to help them manage the change (change facilitator); and, ultimately, be affected by the change too (change recipient). **In this book, we use the terms** *change leader* **and** *change agent* **interchangeably.** Change initiators, change implementers, and change facilitators represent different roles played by the change leader or change agent. At any given moment, the person leading the change may be initiating, implementing, or facilitating. Table 1.4 on page 22 outlines the roles that people need to play in organization change.

Change Initiators

Change initiators get things moving, take action, and stimulate the system. They are the ones constantly seeking change to make things better. They identify the need for change, see the vision of a better future, take on the change task, and champion the initiative. Change initiators may face considerable risk in the organization. To use a physical metaphor, action creates movement, movement creates friction, and friction creates heat! And creating heat may help or hurt one's career. Change agents need to take calculated actions and be prepared to undertake the work needed to create and support the powerful arguments and coalitions to effect change in organizations from the top or the middle of the organization.

Change initiators will find useful aids for change in this book. We, as authors, cannot supply the passion and powerful vision needed by initiators, but we can point out the requirements of successful change: planning, persuasion, and perseverance. And we can provide frameworks for analysis that will enhance the likelihood of successful change.

Change initiators need to be dogged in their desire and determination. Those who succeed will earn reputations for realistic, grounded optimism, for a good sense of timing, and for not giving up. If nothing else, the opposition may tire in the face of their persistence. Better yet are those who have the uncanny ability to creatively combine with others into a coalition that turns resisters into allies and foot draggers into foot soldiers for change.

Change Implementers

Many would-be and existing managers find themselves as change implementers. Others, including their bosses, may initiate the change, but it is left to the implementers to make it work. This role is critical. Pfeffer argues that effectiveness doesn't come from making the critical decision but rather from managing the consequences of decisions and creating the desired results.[68] As he says, "If change were going to be easy, it would already have happened." The change implementer's role is important and needed in organizations.

Change implementers will find much in this book to assist them. They will find guidance in creating and increasing the need for the changes that change initiators are demanding. They will find tools for organizational diagnosis and for identifying and working with key stakeholders. And they will find concepts and techniques to improve their action plans and implementation skills.

At the same time, we encourage and challenge change implementers to stay engaged, to stay active, and to initiate change themselves. Oshry identifies the dilemma of "middle powerlessness" where the middle manager feels trapped between tops and bottoms and becomes ineffective as a result.[69] Many middle managers transform their organizations by recognizing strategic initiatives and mobilizing the power of the "middles" to move the organization in the direction needed.

Change Facilitators

Today's complex organizational changes can fail because parties lock into positions or because perspectives get lost in personalities and egos. In such cases, an outside view can facilitate change. Change facilitators understand change processes and assist the organization to work through change issues. As such, they sometimes formally serve as consultants to change leaders and teams. However, many of those who act as change facilitators do so informally, often on the strength of their existing relationships with others involved with the change. They have high levels of self-awareness and emotional maturity and are skilled in the behavioral arts—using their interpersonal skills to work with teams or groups.

In this book, change facilitators will discover conceptual frameworks that will help them to understand change processes. With these frameworks, they will be able to translate concrete organizational events into understandable situations and so ease change. And their knowledge will provide change perspectives that will allow managers to unfreeze their positions.

Change Recipients

Change recipients are those who find themselves on the receiving end of change. Their responses will vary from active resistance to passivity to active support, depending upon their perceptions of the change, its rationale, and its impact. When people feel acted upon and with little or no voice or control in the process, dissatisfaction, frustration, alienation, absenteeism, and turnover are common responses to demands for change.[70]

This book provides guidance that will help recipients to better understand what is happening to them and their organizations. Further, it will identify strategies and approaches that will help them to take an active role and increase the amount of control they have over organizational events.

Regardless of your role in the organization, change recipient, change implementer, change initiator, or change facilitator, this book contains useful tools. Change recipients will understand what is happening to them and will learn how to respond positively. Change implementers will develop their capacity to use tools that increase their effectiveness, and change initiators will learn to take more effective actions to lever their change programs. Change facilitators will find themselves with new insights into easing organizational change.

Table 1.4 Managerial Roles and Organization Change	
Roles	*Role Description*
Change leader or change agent	The person who leads the change. He/she may play any or all of the initiator, implementer, or facilitator roles. Often, but not always, this person is the formal change leader. However, informal change leaders will emerge and lead change as well. (Note: In this book, *change leader* and *change agent* are used interchangeably.)
Change initiator	The person who identifies the need and vision for change and champions the change.
Change implementer	The person who has responsibility for making certain the change happens, charting the path forward, nurturing support, and alleviating resistance.
Change facilitator	The person who assists initiators, implementers, and recipients with the change management process. Identifies process and content change issues and helps resolve these, fosters support, alleviates resistance, and provides other participant with guidance and council.
Change recipient	The person who is affected by the change. Often the person who has to change his or her behavior to ensure the change is effective.

Gary Hamel of Harvard talks about "leading the revolution"—anyone can play the change game. Anyone can seek opportunities, ask questions, challenge orthodoxies, and generate new ideas and directions![71] And in doing so, individuals from virtually anywhere in an organization (or even outside of it) can become change leaders. Change leaders foment action. They take independent action based on their analysis of what is best for the long-term interests of their organizations, and they recognize the many faces of change and the crucial next steps necessary to meet their long-term change goals. Finally, they recognize who needs to play what roles in order to advance needed change. As such, at different points in time they fulfill the roles of change initiator, implementer, and facilitator, depending upon the needs of the situation, their skills and abilities, and their beliefs about what is required at a point in time to advance the change.

Toolkit Exercise 1.2 asks you to think about change roles and your reactions to them.

The Requirements for Becoming a Successful Change Leader

Successful change leaders balance keen insight with a driving passion for action. They have that sensitivity to the external world described above and will be skilled anticipators of that world. They have a rich understanding of organizational systems—their system in particular and the degree to which continuous or strategic changes are appropriate. They understand themselves and their influence and image in their organizational context. They have special personal characteristics—a tolerance for ambiguity, emotional maturity, self-confidence, comfort with power, a keen sense of risk assessment, a need for action and results, and persistence grounded in reasoned optimism and tenacity. Finally, while they are curious and have a strong desire to learn, they also have a deep and abiding distrust of organizational fads and recognize the negative impact of fad surfing in organizations.[72] Change leaders who see the world in simple, linear terms will have more difficulty creating effective change.[73]

Change leaders understand the rich tapestry that forms the organizational culture. They understand the stakeholder networks that pattern organizational life. They recognize the impact and pervasiveness of organizational control systems (organizational structures, reward systems, measurement systems). They know and can reach key organizational members—both those with legitimate power and position and those with less recognizable influence. And they understand which tasks are key at *this* point in time given *this* environment and *this* organization strategy.

Successful change leaders know their personal skills, style, and abilities and how those play throughout the organization. Their credibility is the bedrock on which change actions are taken. Because change recipients will be cynical and will examine how worthy the leaders are of their trust, change leaders must be aware of their personal blind spots and ensure these are compensated for whenever needed.

Change leaders also embrace the paradoxes of change:

They are involved in both driving change and enabling change. Change leaders understand the need to persist and drive change through their organization. Without such determination, organizational inertia will slow change and other organizations will race ahead. At the same time, change leaders recognize that getting out of the way might be the most helpful management action to be taken. When those around a manager are following a passion, the best thing might be to help in whatever way possible or to provide resources to make things happen.

They recognize that resistance to change is both a problem and an opportunity. Change resistance happens in planned change. Overcoming such resistance is frequently necessary to make progress. However, change leaders recognize that there are often good reasons for resistance—the person resisting is not just being difficult or oppositional, he or she often knows things or has perspectives that cast doubt on the wisdom of change. Change leaders need to recognize this and work actively to overcome this paradox.

Good change leadership focuses on outcomes but is careful about process. Far too often, change programs get bogged down because a focus on results leads change implementers to ignore good process. At the same time, too much attention to process can diffuse direction and lead to endless rituals of involvement and consultation. Good change leaders learn how to manage this balance well.

Change leaders recognize the tension between getting on with it and changing directions. The environment is always changing. Leaders can always modify their objectives and respond to the environment. But if this is done repeatedly, they never settle on a design and direction and as a result will fail to get things done. Keeping the focus on the overall long-term direction while making adjustments can make sense. The trick is to understand and balance this tension.

Change leaders understand the need to balance patience and impatience. Impatience may prove very helpful in overcoming inertia and fear, generating focus, energizing a change, and mobilizing for action. However, patience can also prove a valuable tool in reducing tension and establishing focus and direction, by providing time for people to learn, understand, and adjust to what is being proposed.

Finally, today's change leader knows that in today's global competition, what matters is not the absolute rate of learning but rather the rate of learning compared to the competition. And if your organization doesn't keep pace, it loses the competitive race.

Critical Questions When Considering Organization Change

This chapter ends with a highlighting of the critical questions that are valuable to ask about change. The questions can serve as checkpoints in the change process that need to be tracked—from environmental awareness to planning, implementation, and preparation for next phases. Generalizations in matters related to change can prove difficult to apply to specific situations, but the following questions should provide guidance:

1. What is the environment telling you prior to, at the beginning, during, and following the implementation of the change? In particular:

    a. What is the broader environment telling you about future economic, social, and technological conditions and trends?
    b. What are your customers or clients (both inside and outside the organization) telling you?
    c. What are your competitors doing and how are they responding to you?
    d. What are the partners within your network doing and how are they responding to you?
    e. What do the people who will potentially be the leaders, managers, and recipients of change want and need?

2. Why is change needed? Who sees this need?

3. What is your purpose and agenda? How does that purpose project to a worthwhile vision that goes to the heart of the matter?

4. How will you implement and manage the change?

    a. How will you resource the change initiative?
    b. How will you select and work with your change team?
    c. How will you work with the broader organization?
    d. How will you monitor progress so that you can steer and alter speed and course, if necessary?
    e. How will you ensure that you act (and are seen to act) ethically and with integrity?

5. What have you learned about change and how can you remember it for the future? How can you pass on what you learned?

6. Once the change is completed, what comes next? The completion of one change simply serves as the start point for the next.

That's it. It's an evolving list, and its further development will come as readers think about the contents of this book and practice change. This book will help change agents deploy their ideas, see what works when, where, why, and how, and learn as they go.

The Outline of This Book

In this chapter we have introduced organizational change and our orientation to that change. Throughout the book, we take an applied action orientation, encouraging readers to embrace change to make things happen. To facilitate this, we will lay out a sequence of steps and tools that systematically lead people to successful organizational change.

The book focuses on two underlying dimensions of change management: what to change and how to change. Knowing what to change is situation specific, and managers must work hard to develop the sophisticated understanding of what needs doing. While knowing how to change will depend on the situation, there is a body of knowledge about change management that can be applied in most situations.

This book uses a framework based on Nadler and Tushman's model and Beckhard's work. Nadler's congruence model provides us with a framework for understanding what to change. Beckhard gives us the sequence for change and focuses on how to change. Beckhard's model outlines the basic steps in change: initiating the change, planning the change, doing the change, measuring and confirming the change, and finally celebrating success and preparing for the next change. Appendix 1.2 outlines these steps.

Chapter 2 begins this by providing Beckhard's process model for change. This model focuses on how change agents can think about change: the need for change, the gap between what exists and what is desired, and the action steps necessary to close that gap. Chapter 3 deals with what needs to change by providing organizational models that give us a better understanding of organizations. Nadler's model is central to this chapter and focuses on "what is out of alignment and needs changing?" Chapter 4 deals with both the need for change and the creation of a compelling change vision. Chapters 5, 6, 7, and 8 expand this understanding by examining organizational structures and systems, stakeholders and change recipients, and then change leaders. Chapter 9 takes these insights to develop logical, systematic action plans. Finally, Chapter 10 focuses on the measurement of change to enable us to better manage the change process, consider what changes have been accomplished, and help identify what is needed next.

Summary

This chapter defines organizational change as a planned alteration of organization components to improve the effectiveness of the organization. The forces that drive change today are classified under social, demographic, technological, economic, and political forces. Environmental shifts create the need for change in organizations and drive much organizational change today. Four types of organizational change—tuning, reorienting, adapting, and re-creating—are outlined. Finally, the nature of change leaders is discussed and some of the paradoxes facing them are examined.

This chapter outlines the change roles that exist in organizations: change initiator, change implementer, change facilitator, and change recipient. Change leaders or change agents could be any of the four roles, initiator, implementer, facilitator, or recipient.

Finally, the chapter outlines the underlying framework of the book: how to change and what to change.

Glossary of Terms

Organizational change—For the purposes of this book, organizational change is defined as a planned alteration of organizational components to improve the effectiveness of the organization. By organizational components, we mean the organizational mission and vision, strategy, goals, structure, process or system, technology, and people in an organization. When organizations enhance their effectiveness, they increase their ability to generate value for those they are designed to serve.

The open systems view of organizations looks at the web of structures, systems, and processes that underpin the organization. They are interrelated and affect one another and are also influenced by what happens in the external environment in which they are situated.

Organizational development is based in psychology and focused on bringing about organizational improvement, with primary attention to human factors.

Roots of change—Organizational development perspective

Small-group training focuses on creating change by improving self-awareness and the group's dynamics.

Survey research and feedback uses the analysis and feedback of sophisticated surveys, combined with employee participation, to create the need for change.

Action research encourages the use of action, based on research, in continuous cycles. In essence, one learns by doing, followed by observation, doing, and more learning.

Sociotechnical systems change focuses on the interaction between the sociological and technical subsystems of the organization and describes change in more holistic terms.

Change management is based in a broad set of underlying disciplines (from the social sciences to information technology), tends to be strategy driven, with attention directed to whatever factors are assessed as necessary to the successful design and implementation of change.

Change initiator—the person who identifies the need and vision for change and champions the change.

Change implementer—the person responsible for making certain the change happens, charting the path forward, nurturing support, and alleviating resistance.

Change facilitator—the person who assists initiators, implementers, and recipients with the change management process. Identifies process and content change issues and helps resolve these, fosters support, alleviates resistance, and provides other participants with guidance and council.

Change recipient—the person who is affected by the change. Often the person who has to change his or her behavior to ensure the change is effective.

Change leader or change agent—these two terms are used interchangeably in the text to describe those engaged in change initiator, implementer, or facilitator roles. All those involved in providing leadership and direction for the change fall within their broad coverage.

Macro changes—large-scale environmental changes that are affecting organizations and what they do.

Incremental/continuous changes—organizational changes that are relatively small in scope and incremental in nature. They may stem from the fine tuning of existing practices or represent an incremental adaptation to environmental changes.

Discontinuous/radical changes—changes that are broad in scope and impact and that may involve strategic repositioning. They usually occur in anticipation of or reaction to major environmental changes and are discontinuous in that they involved changes that are *not* incremental in nature and are disruptive to the status quo.

END-OF-CHAPTER EXERCISES

TOOLKIT EXERCISE 1.1

Analyzing Your Environment

Select an organization you are familiar with. What are the key environmental issues affecting your organization? List these and their implications for the organization.

Political Factors   Implications

Economic & Ecological Factors   Implications

Social Factors   Implications

Technological Factors   Implications

TOOLKIT EXERCISE 1.2

Change Roles in Your Organization

Pick an organization that you are familiar with—an organization you have worked for either full-time or part-time, a school you have attended, or a voluntary association you know such as a baseball league.

Who plays what change roles in the organization? How do individuals work at those roles? What are the consequences of their roles? How do individuals achieve effective change? Take a moment to identify people in your organization who play each of the roles: change recipient, change initiator, change facilitator, and change implementer.

What roles do you play? Think of a time when you have been involved in change. What role did you play? How comfortable were you with each of those roles?

Think back on your personal organizational history. When did you fill the role of:

Change initiator? _____

Change implementer? _____

Change facilitator? _____

Change recipient? _____

How did each of these roles feel? What did you accomplish in each role?

Appendix 1.1: The Roots of Organizational Change

Managers have long voiced an interest in improving their organizations. Writings on the topic can be found throughout recorded history. Early religious texts provide many examples of advice and action related to enhancing effectiveness (e.g., Moses's actions related to the Diaspora from Egypt and the advice of major religious figures on how life should be led). Likewise, early philosophers such as Plato offered advice on how change should be promoted and managed (e.g., "One of the penalties for refusing to participate . . . is that you end up being governed by your inferiors").[74]

> The founder of the Han Dynasty, Liu Bang (256–195 BC), attributed his success at defeating his opponent and founding his Dynasty to his policy of using the right people in the right position. He said: "In strategic planning of warfare Chang Liang is better than I; in logistics administration for the battlefield Shoa is better than I; and in deployment of a million troops to win the battles Han Sin is better than I. All three of these people are elite. I can look for their strength and put it to work. That's why I could be the founder of a new Dynasty."[75]

Liu Bang's thinking is similar to that of many managers: They are concerned with making their organization effective and they are focused on improving their position or role within that organization.

Modern thinking about organizational change has its roots in organization development.[76] French and Bell describe four stems of organization development:

- the small-group training stem, which focused on creating change by improving self-awareness and the group's dynamics,
- the survey research and feedback stem, which intervened with sophisticated surveys and analysis to create the need for change,
- the action research stem, which encouraged the use of action, based on research, in continuous cycles (in essence, learning by doing, followed by observation, doing, and more learning), and
- the sociotechnical stem, which focused on the interaction between the sociological and technical subsystems of the organization and described change in more holistic terms.

Worren and others have differentiated organization development from change management.[77] Table 1.5 outlines this shift according to Worren.

The field of organizational change has developed to become more integrative and strategic. There is a shift from considering personal and group outcomes to organizational ones. Organizational change is broader based and action often requires a change team to make change happen. Organizational change is focused on the business—using an understanding of human relationships to improve organizational results.

The rapid growth in the volume of formal research about organizational change is a relatively recent phenomenon, and the volume of literature on organizational change is overwhelming.* Despite this literature, management's ability to deliver successful change is modest at best. One study reports that 7 of 10 change efforts fail to achieve their intended results; for major corporate systems investments: 28% are abandoned before completion, 46% are behind schedule or over budget, and 80% are not used in the way intended or not used at all after 6 months.[79]

Table 1.5 Organizational Development versus Change Management (according to Worren et al.)		
	Organizational Development	*Change Management*
Underlying theory and analytical framework	Based primarily on psychology. Individual/group functioning	Includes principles and tools from sociology, information technology, and strategic change theories. Individual/group functioning and systems, structures, work processes (congruence model)
Role of change agent	Facilitator or process consultant	Content expert (organization design and human performance) and process consultant. Member of cross-functional team, which includes strategists and technologists. Part of project organization, which includes client managers/employees
Intervention strategies	Not directly linked to strategy. Focus on one component at a time. Normative–re-educative (change attitudes to change behavior)	Driven by strategy. Simultaneous focus on several components (strategy, human resources, organization design, technology). Action-oriented (change behavior before attitudes)

From Worren, Nicolay, Keith Ruddle, and Karl Moore. "From Organizational Development to Change Management," *The Journal of Applied Behavioral Science*. Vol. 35, No. 3, Sept 1999, p. 280.

*A Google search yielded more than 110 million hits; Ask.com, 7.5 million hits; Harvard Business School site, 1,024 hits; Proquest Search, 15,530 articles; Fast Company web search, 3,120 hits.

Appendix 1.2: A Summary Checklist for Change

Initiating change

- Understanding the need for change
- Creating the perception of need for change
- Developing the powerful vision for change

Planning change

- Having an organization model
- Differentiating how to change and what to change
- Structures and systems: approval of change, facilitating and hindering change, developing adaptive structures for change
- Informal systems: resistance to change, power dynamics, the role of perceived impact, force fields, stakeholders (commitment, adaptiveness)
- Recipients: reactions (negative, ambivalent, positive), recipients' adaptation (anticipation, denial, anger, acceptance)
- Change agents: leading and managing, change agent types, change teams

Doing the change

- Engaging others
- Developing the activity plan
- Contingency planning
- Commitment planning
- Communicating the change
- Managing the transition

Measuring and confirming the change

- Measuring the change
- Changing the measures over the life of the change project

Celebrating success and preparing for the next change

- Recognizing achievements and enjoying the successes
- Review of the change process and developing new learnings
- Anticipating and planning for the next wave of change

Notes

1. Fung, F. (2010, March 31). McDonald's sets plan for China. *Wall Street Journal.*

2. A version of this quote can be found on p. 55 in Wheatley, M. J. (1994). *Leadership and the new science.* San Francisco: Berrett-Koehler.

3. Miles, R. H. (1997). *Leading corporate transformation.* San Francisco: Jossey-Bass.

4. Personal experience of the authors.

5. Appelbaum, S. H., Henson, D., & Knee, K. (1999). Downsizing failures: An examination of convergence/reorientation and antecedents—processes—outcomes. *Management Decision, 37*(6), 473–490.

6. The Conference Board of Canada. (2000, November). 2000 change management conference: Increasing change capability. See also Higgs, M., & Rowland, D. (2005). All changes great and small: Exploring approaches to change and its leadership. *Journal of Change Management, 5*(2), 121–151.

7. Pfeffer, J., & Sutton, R. (1999). Knowing "what" to do is not enough: Turning knowledge into action. *California Management Review, 42*(1), 83–108.

8. Maynard, M. (2010, April 5). U.S. is seeking a fine of $16.4 million against Toyota. *New York Times.*

9. How to play chicken and lose. (2009, January 22). *The Economist.*

10. Sovereign creditworthiness could be undermined by age-related spending trends. (2006, June 5). *Standard and Poor's.* Retrieved from www.standardandpoors.com.

11. Half a billion Americans? (2002, August 22). *The Economist.*

12. Sovereign creditworthiness could be undermined by age-related spending trends. (2006, June 5). *Standard and Poor's.* Retrieved from www.standardandpoors.com.

13. Falling Fertility. (2009, October 31). *The Economist,* pp. 29–32.

14. Falling Fertility. (2009, October 31). *The Economist,* pp. 29–32.

15. Davis, I., & Stephenson, E. (2006). Ten trends to watch in 2006. *McKinsey Quarterly; The Online Journal.* Retrieved from http://www.mckinseyquarterly.com/article_print. aspx?l2=18&L3=30&ar=1734.

16. Davis, I., & Stephenson, E. (2006). Ten trends to watch in 2006. *McKinsey Quarterly; The Online Journal.* Retrieved from http://www.mckinseyquarterly.com/article_print. aspx?l2=18&L3=30&ar=1734.

17. Revell, J. (2002). GM's slow leak. *Fortune, 146*(8), 105; Why GM's plan won't work—and the ugly road ahead. (2005, May 9). *Business Week Online.* Retrieved December 2010 from http://www.businessweek.com/magazine/content/05_19/b3932001_mz001.htm; Maynard, M. (2008, March 7). GM to freeze pension plan for salaried workers. *New York Times business section.* Retrieved December 2010 from http://www.nytimes.com/2006/03/08/automobiles/08auto.html.

18. Marketing to the old. (2002, August 8). *The Economist.*

19. The silver tsunami. (2010, February 4). *The Economist.*

20. Suro, R., & Singer, A. (2002). Latino growth in metropolitan America. Center on Urban & Metropolitan Policy and The Pew Hispanic Center, The Brookings Institution.

21. Suro, R., & Singer, A. (2002). Latino growth in metropolitan America (Table 4, p. 9). Center on Urban & Metropolitan Policy and The Pew Hispanic Center, The Brookings Institution.

22. Galt, V. (2002, October 16). What am I, chopped liver? *Globe and Mail,* p. C1.

23. Diamond, J. (1999). *Guns, germs and steel.* New York: W. W. Norton, p. 322.

24. Scott, M. (2010). Red flag on Quebec niqab ban. *Gazette:* Montreal, Quebec.

25. Thomas, D. A. (2004). Diversity as strategy. *Harvard Business Review, 82*(9), 98–109.

26. Savitz, A. W., & Weber, K. (2006). *The triple bottom line: How today's best-run companies are achieving economic, social and environmental success—and how you can too.* San Francisco: Jossey-Bass.

27. The data deluge. (2010, February 25). *The Economist.*

28. The next disrupters. (2007, September). *Business 2.0.*

29. The Technology Quarterly. (2002, September 21). *The Economist.*

30. Wieners, B., (2002, June). 8 technologies that will change the world. *Business 2.0,* p. 79.

31. Yergin, D., & Stanislaw, J. (2002). *The commanding heights: The battle for the world economy* (p. 405). New York: Touchstone.

32. Mullen, R. (2005, March 11). Security issues lurking beyond voip's cost saving promise. *Silicon Valley/San Jose Business Journal.* Retrieved from http://www.sanjose.bizjournals.com/sanjose/stories/2005/03/14/smallb3.html.

33. Violino, B. (2004, July). Fortifying supply chains. *Optimize,* pp. 73–75. Retrieved from http://www.optimizemag.com/article/showArticle.jhtml?articleID=22101759.

34. Op Cit. Davis, I., p. 2.

35. Others believe otherwise. Note the protests whenever the WTO meets, for example.

36. False Heaven. (1999, July 29). *The Economist.*

37. Farrell, D., Khanna, T., Sinha, J., & Woetzel, J. R. (2004). China and India: The race to growth. *McKinsey Quarterly, Special Edition,* 110–119.

38. Transparency International Secretariat. (2002). Transparency international corruption perceptions index 2002. 10585 Berlin, Germany: Ott-Suhr-Allee 97–99.

39. Transparency International Secretariat. (2002). Bribe payers' index. 10585 Berlin, Germany: Otto-Suhr-Allee 97–99.

40. Lawrence, A. (2007, Winter). Hewlett-Packard and a common supplier code of conduct. *Case Research Journal.*

41. Siemens sees green tech driving economic growth. (2009, August). *Industry Week.*

42. Senge, P., & Carstedt, G. (2001). Innovating our way to the next industrial revolution. *Sloan Management Review, 42*(2), 24–38.

43. Where have all your savings gone? (2008, December 4). *The Economist.*

44. Personal communication with one author.

45. Stemming the tide. (2009, November 19). *The Economist.*

46. The hard slog ahead. The world in 2010. (2009, December). *The Economist.*

47. Not so fast. The world in 2010. (2009, December). *The Economist.*

48. Barkema, H. G., Baum, J. A. C., & Mannix. (2002). Management challenges in a new time. *Academy of Management Journal, 45*(5), 916–930.

49. Weick, K. E., & Quinn, R. E. (1999). Organizational change and development. *Annual Review of Psychology, 50,* 361–386.

50. Savyas, A. (2005, March 8). Intel points to convergence. *Computer Weekly,* p. 12.

51. Lam, J. (2005, March 1). Continental sets tentative accords for cutting costs. *Wall Street Journal* (Eastern edition), p. A2.

52. Nadler, D., & Tushman, M. (n.d.). Organizational frame bending: Principles for managing reorientation. *Academy of Management Executive, 3*(3), 196.

53. Jick, T., & Peiperl, M. (2003). *Changing the culture at British Airways and British Airways Update, 1991–2000.* In T. Jick & M. Peiperl, *Managing change* (pp. 26–44). New York: McGraw-Hill Higher Education.

54. One strike and you're out: British Airways. (2003, August 2). *The Economist*, p. 64.

55. Flight plans: BA and Iberia take a step closer to becoming one of the world's biggest airlines. (2010, April 8). *The Economist online.* Retrieved from http://www.economist.com/node/15872745; and Maintaining altitude: BA's cabin staff appear to be fighting a losing battle. (2010, March 25). *The Economist.*

56. An interesting comparison of TQM and employee involvement is contained in Lawler, E. E. III. (1994). Total quality management and employee involvement: Are they compatible? *Academy of Management Executive, 8*(1), 68–76.

57. Drawn from Morgan, G. (1994, June 28). Quantum leaps, step by step. *Globe and Mail*, p. B22.

58. Kirton, M. J. (1984). Adaptors and innovators—Why new initiatives get blocked. *Long Range Planning, 17*(2), 137–143; Tushman, M. L., & O'Reilly, C. A. III. (1996). Ambidextrous organizations: Managing evolutionary and revolutionary change. *California Management Review, 38*(4), 8–30.

59. The life cycle of interventions is readily apparent in the management literature. First comes the concept, accompanied or followed closely by examples of successful implementation. Next are cautionary notes, examples of failure, and remedies. As the luster fades, new approaches emerge in the literature and the process recurs, hopefully building upon earlier learning. For example, see Miles, R. E., & Snow, C. C. (1992). Causes of failure in network organizations. *California Management Review, 34*(4), 53–72.

60. Helyar, J. (1998, August 10). Solo Flight. *Wall Street Journal.* Quoted in T. Jick, *Managing change* (p. 503). New York: McGraw-Hill Higher Education.

61. Hamel, G., & Prahalad, D. K. (1994, October). Lean, mean and muddled. *Globe & Mail Report on Business Magazine*, 54–58.

62. Voelpel, S. C., Liebold, M., & Streb. (n.d.). The innovation meme: Managing innovation replicators for organizational fitness. *Journal of Change Management, 5*(1), 57–69.

63. Hamel, G., & Prahalad, D. K. (1994, October). Lean, mean and muddled. *Globe & Mail Report on Business Magazine*, 54–58.

64. The New "New Economy." (2003, September 13). *The Economist*, p. 62.

65. Russo, J. E., & Shoemaker, P. J. H. (1992). Managing overconfidence. *Sloan Management Review, 33*(2), 7–18.

66. Van Yperen, N. W. (1998). Informational support, equity and burnout: The moderating effect of self-efficacy. *Journal of Occupational and Organizational Psychology, 71*, 29–33.

67. Gordon, J. (1989, February 13). Employee alignment? Maybe just a brake job would do. *Wall Street Journal.* As reported in T. Jick. (1993). Managing change. Homewood, IL: Irwin.

68. Pfeffer, J. (1995). Managing with power: Politics and influence [video]. Executive Briefings. Stanford, CA: Stanford Videos.

69. Oshry, B. (1990). Finding and using a manager's power to improve productivity. *National Productivity Review, 10*(1), 19–33.

70. Mishra, K. E., Spreitzer, G. M., & Mishra, A. K. (1998). Preserving employee morale during downsizing. *Sloan Management Review, 39*(2), 83–95.

71. Hamel, G. (2000). *Leading the revolution.* Boston: Harvard Business School Press.

72. Shapiro, E. C. (1996). *Fad surfing in the boardroom: Managing in the age of instant answers.* Cambridge, MA: Perseus.

73. Higgs, M., & Rowland, D. (2005). All changes great and small: Exploring approaches to change and its leadership. *Journal of Change Management, 5*(2), 121–151.

74. Plato, 427 BC–347 BC. Retrieved from www.wikiquote.org.

75. Chenglieh, P. (1985). In search of the Chinese style of management. *Malaysian Management Review, 20*(3). Retrieved from http://mgv.mim.edu.my/MMR/8512/851210. htm.

76. French, W., & Bell, C. (1995). *Organization development* (5th ed., Chapter 3). Englewood Cliffs, NJ: Prentice Hall.

77. Worren, N., Ruddle, K., & Moore, K. (1999). From organizational development to change management. *Journal of Applied Behavioral Science, 35*(3), 273–286.

78. Miller, D. (2002). Successful change leaders: What makes them? What do they do that is different? *Journal of Change Management, 2*(4), 359–368. See also Higgs, M., & Rowland, D. (2005). All changes great and small: Exploring approaches to change and its leadership. *Journal of Change Management, 5*(2), 121–151.

79. Miller, D. (2002). Successful change leaders: What makes them? What do they do that is different? *Journal of Change Management, 2*(4),359–368. *See also* Higgs, M., & Rowland, D. (2005). All changes great and small: Exploring approaches to change and its leadership. *Journal of Change Management, 5*(2), 121–151.

CHAPTER 2

Change Frameworks for Organizational Diagnosis

"HOW" to Change

Change is.

CHAPTER OVERVIEW

- This chapter differentiates between **HOW** to create organizational change, its process, and **WHAT** should be changed, the content. Change leaders must understand both.
- A modified version of Beckhard and Harris's change management process is developed in depth. The model asks: (1) What is going on in the organization? (2) Why change? (3) What is the gap between the existing and desired states? (4) How do we close this gap? and (5) How do we manage during the transition phase?
- These explicit models will help change leaders articulate their implicit models of how organizations work and how to change their organizations.

S weeping demographic changes, technological advances, geopolitical shifts, and pressures to be sensitive to our physical environment are combining with concerns for security and organizational governance to generate significant pressure for organizational change. Awareness of the political, economic, sociological, and technological (PEST) aspects of any organization's external environment forewarns the need to pay attention to such factors. Furthermore, it alerts managers to attend to their organizations' relevant environmental contexts and to decide whether they need to take some action as a result.

McDonald's is one of many organizations scanning its environment and making decisions about changes to its products as a result of changes in its environment. The recession of 2008 to 2009 put pricing pressure on the restaurant business. McDonald's responded with a continuous stream of new products. Since 2004, it has introduced the snack wrap, several salads, specialty coffees, and, most recently, the Angus burger, a 1/3-lb. burger.[1] These product innovations have led to store sales increases and improved profits. More recently, McDonald's has embraced the "green movement" (in a small way) by placing charge points for electronic vehicles in one store. One trend that will challenge McDonald's creativity is the "eat local" movement where consumers are encouraged to eat locally grown foods. With McDonald's thousands of stores worldwide and its emphasis on worldwide uniformity of products, it is difficult to picture how local foods can be incorporated.[2]

To make these product decisions, McDonald's managers had to evaluate environmental shifts and assess their relevance to the organization's strategy and the probability of its continued effectiveness. The healthy food trend meant that McDonald's needed different products and different approaches to developing and sustaining its markets. McDonald's executives examined these trends and decided that product changes were necessary. If one takes the McDonald's example and generalizes it to all managers, then changes in the external environment provide the important clues and cues for change leaders. Diagnosing and understanding those clues and cues provides the basis for the vision and direction for change.

In this chapter, we focus on the process of organizational change. **How** might a change agent think about making change happen? The chapter sets forth frameworks that can help a change agent understand organizations and how to approach the change challenge. These frameworks, or models, provide explicit if somewhat simplified views of organizations. Using the models makes it easier to understand how organizations work. With this understanding, change is easier to plan and promote.

Each person has ideas about how organizations work. For some, this *model* is explicit—that is, it can be written down and discussed with others. However, many managers' views of organizational functioning are complex, implicit, and based on their personal experiences. Deep knowledge and intuition, so-called tacit knowledge, about the functioning of an organization is invaluable. However, such knowledge or intuition is intensely personal, often difficult to communicate, and almost impossible to discuss and challenge rationally. As a result, this book takes an explicit approach. This chapter and the next will provide ways to articulate unspoken models of how organizations work and to use several models to think systematically about how to change an organization.

Appendix 2.1 summarizes some of the literature on the types of change models that managers hold, often implicitly. These models guide and direct managers' assumptions and actions when creating change.

Differentiating How to Change
From What to Change

The complexity of change can be simplified somewhat by recognizing that there are two distinct aspects of change that must be addressed in any change-management situation. Managers must decide both **HOW** to change and **WHAT** to change. In this chapter, we look at **how** to change using a version of Beckhard and Harris's model of change. Then, in Chapter 3, we develop an appreciation of **what** to change, describing Nadler and Tushman's congruence framework. Also in Chapter 3, we outline Sterman's systems dynamic model, Quinn's Competing Values Model, Greiner's model of organizational growth, and Nadler and Tushman's differentiation of incremental and strategic change.

The example below highlights the difference between the **HOW** and **WHAT** of change.

Exercise: Imagine that you are the general manager of a major hotel chain and you received the following customer letter of complaint:

A LETTER OF COMPLAINT

Dear Sir:

As a customer of yours, I wanted to provide you with our experiences at ATMI, your London, England, hotel.* I have reflected on my experience and decided to provide you with feedback—particularly given your promise on your website—the Hospitality Promise Program.

My wife and I arrived around 10 P.M. after a flight from North America and the usual tiring immigration procedures, baggage check, and finding our way to your hotel. The initial greeting was courteous and appropriate. We were checked in; the desk person asked if we wished a room upgrade. After I clarified that this would cost money, I declined that proposal.

We then went to our room on the 3rd floor, I believe, and discovered it was a disaster, totally not made up. I phoned the switchboard and was put through to reception immediately. There were profuse apologies and we were told that someone would be up immediately with another key.

Within 5 minutes, someone met us with a key to a room on the 5th floor, a quick, fast response. However, when we got to the new room, it was not made up!

Again I phoned the switchboard. The operator said, "This shouldn't have happened. I will put you through to the night manager." I said that was not necessary, I just wanted a room. However, the operator insisted and I was put

*The hotel name is disguised.

(Continued)

(Continued)

through to the night manager. Again, there were profuse apologies and the manager said, "This shouldn't have happened, I will fix this and get right back to you." I indicated that I just wanted a room—I didn't want the organization fixed, just a room. The manager repeated, "I will get right back to you."

We waited 5, 10, 15 minutes. Inexplicably, the manager did not return the call even though he said he would.

Finally, around 20 minutes later, I phoned switchboard again. I said we were waiting for a room and that the night manager had promised to call me back. The operator said, "This is probably my fault as I was doing work for the assistant manager." I did not and do not understand this part of the conversation but again, I was told that they would call right back. Again, I repeated that "I just need a room."

I waited another 5 minutes—it was now 11 P.M. and we were quite tired—there was no return phone call.

My wife and I went down to reception, waited, and after a brief time were motioned forward by the person who registered us initially. I explained that we needed a room. He said "You were taken care of. You got a room." I stated that "No, I did not have a room, I just had two rooms that were not made up and we needed a clean one for the night."

Again there were profuse apologies. The reception person then said "Excuse me, just for a moment, so I can fix this." I said "Really, I just would like a room." The person at the reception desk went around the corner and began to berate someone working there. This went on for several minutes. He then returned to his station, called me forward again, apologized again, and located a third room for us. As well, he gave us coupons for a complimentary breakfast.

This third room was made up. It was "more tired" than the previous rooms but it was clean and we were delighted to find a spot to sleep.

In the middle of the night, as is the norm in many places, the invoice was delivered to our room. To our surprise, a £72 charge was added to the price of the room for a "room change."

Of course, early the next morning, I queued up to discuss this charge. The same reception person was still on duty. He motioned me forward and then immediately left to open up all the computer stations in the reception area. He had a tendency to not make eye contact. This may have been a cultural phenomenon or it may have been his dismay at having to deal with me again. I cannot say.

I showed him the invoice. He said, "Oh, there will be no charge for that room." I said that I was concerned as the invoice did show the charge. He said, "It is taken care of." I said "Regardless, I would like something to prove that there would not be another charge to my credit card." After one further exchange and insistence on my part, he removed the charge from my invoice.

My wife and I had a pleasant breakfast and appreciated it being complimentary.

> We thought that you would want to know of our experience. Customer service is a critical part of the hospitality industry and I am certain that ATMI would wish feedback on experiences such as these.
>
> I am interested in such things and look forward to your reply.
>
> Yours truly,

The list of things done poorly and the organizational issues that exist at this hotel are extensive. Identifying this list of **WHAT** needs attention is relatively easy. The desk clerk has twice assigned rooms that were unmade. This implies system issues—the system to capture the state of the rooms is either nonexistent or not working. One wonders if there is a quality-control person signing off on rooms. There are managerial issues—a manager promises to get back to a customer and doesn't. There are organizational culture issues—the excuses by the switchboard operator and yelling by the reception person. There are further system issues or customer service problems as indicated by the £72 charge for a room change. There are some service training issues—the responses by the receptionist were variable. He was quick to send up a second room key but left the customer standing while he turned on computers. He was reluctant to reverse the extra room charge. There is some hint that there might be other cultural issues that are pertinent. Perhaps you could list more things that are organizationally wrong.

However, it is not clear **HOW** the general manager should proceed with needed changes. First off, how accurate is the letter? Can the general manager accept it, or does he have to investigate? Assuming the letter reflects the experiences of more than one unhappy customer, then the general manager still faces the "how" question. If the computer system for tracking room availability does not exist, then it is relatively simple to create and install one. However, if the system exists but is not being used, how does the general manager create change? Closer supervision might work, but who can do that and who will pay for it? Even more difficult are the organizational and other cultural issues. The norm among employees appears to be to make excuses and to "berate" others when things go wrong. A manager can tell employees that these behaviors are inappropriate, but how does one persuade employees not to respond abusively? And how will the general manager know if and when the changes are implemented? Is there a system in place to track customer and employee satisfaction? Are these several systems worth the cost they impose on the organization?

Clearly, managers must know what needs to change. However, how to go about making change happen requires careful thought and planning. The models provided below help you think about change and how to make it happen.

How to Change: The Processes

As suggested above, many leaders know what they need to achieve, but they just don't know how to get there. An examination of competitors' initiatives and accomplishments will often provide cues as to what is needed, but moving one's own organization to successfully addressing these benchmarks is difficult.

Why is it so difficult to accomplish change?

One of the common causes lies in practices that have proven effective in the past and that are no longer appropriate; this can be called the "failure of success." Organizations learn what works and what doesn't. They develop systems that exploit that knowledge and establish rules, policies, procedures, and decision frameworks that capitalize on previous successes. Further, they develop patterned responses (habits), assumptions, attributions, and expectations that influence the ways they think about how the world works.[3] These beliefs and ingrained responses form a strong resistant force, which encourages organizations and people to maintain old patterns regardless of feedback or input suggesting that they are no longer appropriate. In many respects, this is where the questions of what to change and how to change intersect.

Charles Handy describes some of these dilemmas by examining the pattern of success over time.[4] As he so aptly describes, too often "by the time you know where you ought to go, it's too late" (p. 50). He describes a "sigmoid" curve that outlines where one should begin changing and where it becomes obvious that one needs to change (see Figure 2.1). This curve depicts the outcomes or outputs of a system as a curve that increases during early-stage development and growth phases, flattens at maturity, and shifts into decline over time. Consider the path tracked by successful technological innovations. Once an innovation demonstrates its value to key early adopters, then sales take off. As others see the benefits of the innovation, they begin to adopt it as well. Patents and proprietary knowledge provide some protection, but over time competitors launch similar

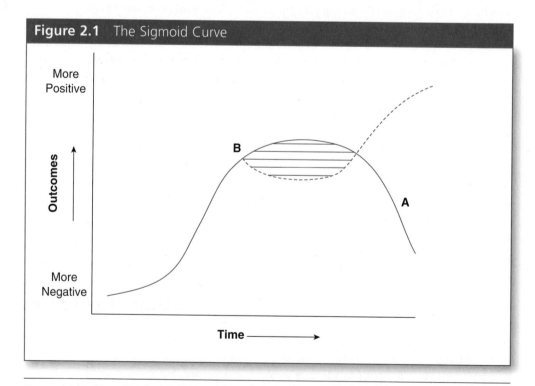

Figure 2.1 The Sigmoid Curve

Source: Adapted from: Handy, C., *The Age of Paradox*. Boston, MA.: Harvard Business School Press, 1994, p. 50.

products, profit margins become squeezed, and sales growth slows due to increased competition and the level of market saturation. This leads to a flattening of the curve, referred to as the maturity phase. Decline follows as the market becomes increasingly saturated and competitive, and this decline accelerates with the arrival of a new, disruptive innovation that attracts customers away from the existing product. Think of what happened to the VCR players when DVD players arrived on the scene, and consider how prices have fallen for DVD players in the face of competition. A similar process may happen with online video streaming making DVDs obsolete.

The time to introduce change is at point B when the system is growing. The dilemma is that in the short run, the costs are likely to be greater than the benefits. It is only when the new changes are adopted and the system is working well that the outcomes' curve turns upward again. One dilemma is that the costs of change are real and include adding people and shifting production lines, while the benefits of change are uncertain. Managers believe the changes will improve productivity and profits, but that may not occur. By holding off investing in change, an organization may improve its profits in the short run. However, if conditions change and the organization fails to adjust in a timely fashion, executives can quickly find themselves lagging behind their competitors, scrambling to adapt, and running to catch up. If management waited too long, then an organization may find it impossible to do so.

By the time the system reaches point A, the need for change is obvious, but it may also be too late for the organization to survive without experiencing significant trauma. Positive planned change needs to be commenced sooner in the process— before things deteriorate to a crisis or disaster stage. Unfortunately, change typically comes with costs that appear to lessen the positive outcomes in the short run. As many know, convincing anyone that they should incur short-run costs for long-run benefits is a difficult selling task, particularly if things are going well. This is depicted as the shaded space between the solid and dotted lines beginning at B in Figure 2.1. The costs of change appear certain and are tangible. But the benefits are uncertain and often vaguely defined. The time after point B is a time of two competing views of the future, and people will have difficulty abandoning the first curve (the one they are on) until they are convinced of the benefits of the new curve. In concrete terms, creating change at point B means convincing others about the wisdom of spending time and money now for an uncertain future return.

Knowing how to change is difficult because identifying and demonstrating the need for change is not obvious. If a system appears to be working, why on earth change for an unproven new one that promises—but cannot be assured—of something better? Many people, for example, have experienced adopting new technologies or approaches that fail to deliver on explicit or implied promises. Is it, then, any wonder that employees are skeptical about new proposals?

Sixty years ago, Kurt Lewin[5] wrote about the problem of how to bring about change. He described a three-stage model of change:

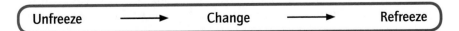

Unfreeze ⟶ Change ⟶ Refreeze

Lewin stated that we need to understand the situation and system as a whole as well as the component parts that make up the system. Before change can occur, an unfreezing process must happen within that system. This focuses on the need to dislodge or upend the beliefs and assumptions of those who need to participate in the change and engage in systemic alterations to the status quo. The unfreezing process might occur because of some crisis. For example, a major government cutback to a funded social service agency or new competitive products that are attacking the major profit producers of a private enterprise might be sufficient shocks to these organizations to "unfreeze" the patterns. In both examples, the balance in the system must be disrupted or broken in order to permit conditions for change to develop. Some top managers even talk about "creating a crisis" in order to develop the sense of urgency around change.[6]

When this unfreezing occurs, the systems and the people who are embedded in those systems become susceptible to change. Systems and structures, beliefs, and habits become fluid and thus can shift more easily. (Appendix 2.2 applies the Lewin model to the hotel case above.)

Beckhard and Harris's Change-Management Process

A second model of **how** to change is outlined by Beckhard and Harris.[7] (See their modified model in Figure 2.2). The change process begins with an assessment of why change is needed. Following the recognition of the need for change, change leaders are faced with the task of defining and describing a desired future state in contrast to an organization's present reality. A desired future state allows leaders to identify the gap between the present and the future and how they propose to close that gap. The discussion of how to get from the present to a desired future state represents the action or implementation stage. The final step in the change process is to manage the transition. As presented, this model provides a framework that the authors have modified and used to organize this book. Beckhard and Harris built on the work of Kurt Lewin described above.

According to Beckhard and Harris, the first step in change is an initial organizational analysis. Here the forces for and against change are analyzed and understood. A thorough understanding of the organization and its stakeholders will assist in this analysis. (See Chapter 3 of this book for frameworks to analyze organizations.)

The second step in the change process involves both determining the need for change and creating a powerful change vision. Chapter 4 of this book deals with this: "Building and Energizing the Need for Change"

Many assume that the need for change is easily recognizable, obvious, and evident from the environment. Often this is the case. If bankruptcy threatens or if profits have plummeted, then people in the organization likely will feel things must change. However, people may not accept the need or believe that they need to change—they may believe that it is the other person or department that is the problem. Or the falling profits are bad luck. However, we the authors believe that organizations are as they are because things are working. If people were really dissatisfied with the situation, they would recognize the need for change and begin searching for corrective action. If they accept the status quo and don't want to

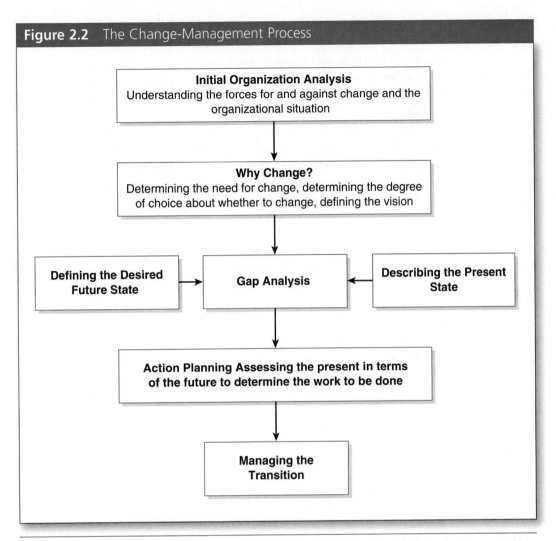

Figure 2.2 The Change-Management Process

Source: Adapted from : Beckhard, R., & R. T. Harris, *Organizational Transitions: Managing Complex Change.* Reading, MA.: Addison-Wesley, 1987.

change, they are likely relatively satisfied; not dissatisfied to the point of searching for options; believe that nothing can be done; or believe that the costs of changing are greater than the benefits. For example, many workers at Walmart have voiced unhappiness about such things as pay levels and hours of work for years, but most have never taken the steps required to unionize. The costs and risks seem to have been viewed as too high relative to the potential benefits.[*]

It is important to understand that the perception of the need for change is exactly that—a perception. And just because executives hold that perception does not imply that others will hold it or agree. Executives often think that other people simply do not understand the situation. Thus, if one explains things

---

[*]One of the risks is that Walmart will close the store that unionizes. The closing of the Jonquiere, Quebec, store is an example of this. You can find more on this at http://www .economist.com/displaystory.cfm?story_id=3706455.

persuasively, then the other person will change his or her mind. That might work. It is just as likely that other people have different objectives, experiences, assumptions, and beliefs that lead them to a different view of the situation. As a result, it is dangerous to assume that there is an alignment in goals. Employees may see no need for change or may believe that others might have to change, but they will not need to.

Managers sometimes make the mistake of assuming that once they are convinced, others will easily understand and be convinced as well. Even if others in the organization can be persuaded, this ignores the lag that will occur as the message about change moves through the organization. For example, senior managers may well be aware of a significant competitor's threat, such as a new product or service delivery model that will hit the market soon. Executives begin to respond with change plans. However, most employees will not have any awareness of what the competitor is doing. From the employee's perspective, things are fine. In fact, employees are likely busy meeting current product demand and are unaware of new products introduced by competitors. This lag in information requires change managers to present data through multiple communication channels to employees, persuading them of the importance of changing now and not continuing with previous patterns, procedures, and products.

The description and analysis of the present state and the definition of the future state leads to a **gap analysis**—an image of the differences in specific terms. Too often, an analysis results in nonhelpful gaps. For example, a manager might conclude that morale is low. This description does not lead easily to action plans. Instead, the root causes of the morale issue need to be understood. Why is morale low? Is it the pay system? Is it management's style? Is it working conditions? Each of these descriptions is more powerful and useful in moving to change and each suggests a different course of action. In Chapter 3, several frameworks are described to develop a sophisticated checklist for organizational diagnosis. If the diagnosis is wrong, it is likely that one will take inappropriate action. The gap analysis allows change leaders to clearly address the question of *why* change is needed. The analyses of formal and informal dimensions of the organization, the various stakeholders, the recipients of the change, and the change agents themselves (Chapters 5 to 8) help to complete an understanding of the situation and the gaps that need attention.

Beckhard and Harris talk about "getting from here to there" and "managing during the transition state." This involves action planning and implementation. These topics are dealt with explicitly in Chapter 9. While action planning often appears linear and straightforward, the reality is usually different. Unfortunately, in today's complex organizations, most change is neither linear nor straightforward. Managing change while operating the organization is like remodeling an airborne plane. Transition management, however, is the important study of doing just that. Understanding the success of the particular organizational changes we are trying to achieve depends on our ability to measure such change. In Chapter 10, we examine the difficulty and necessity of change measurement and suggest how change agents can manage this area.

Application of the Beckhard and Harris Model

The hotel case written earlier in this chapter offers an opportunity to apply the Beckhard and Harris model to an organization that appears to need to change.

Why Change?

The general manager who received the above letter might have very good reasons for not responding and changing. The hotel might be in the midst of a computer systems modification and be overwhelmed with this change. Or the general manager may have a tracking system that indicates that most hotel guests are very satisfied and that this is an unusual occurrence. Or the general manager may have cost objectives and view change as leading to increased costs. Or the general manager might see herself as exiting the organization and believe that change efforts could have an adverse impact on her career.

Even if the general manager accepts the need for change, the employees might not. At this point in time, they know nothing about the letter. They may feel that their performance is good and no change is needed. They might have a department manager who doesn't follow up on directives and, thus, they could believe that no action is necessary. Or they might be new to their jobs and be poorly trained in customer service. The challenge for the change leader is to articulate "why change" to key stakeholders in ways that they will understand and move them to positive actions. Gap analysis and visioning are important tools in addressing this challenge.

Gap Analysis of the Hotel

The present state of the hotel has several dimensions that could be addressed. The following gaps might exist:

- A gap in information between room readiness and the information that the desk clerk has
- A gap between what the hotel's managers say they will do and what they actually do
- A gap between the appropriate bill and the bill given to the customer
- A gap between the desired interpersonal relationships between employees and customers and that which exists
- A gap between the desired handling of hotel guests and that which occurs

Each of these gaps could require different action plans for change. And careful analysis might demonstrate that there is an underlying issue that needs to be dealt with. For example, if the organization's culture has evolved to one that is not focused on customer care and relationships, the individual gaps might be difficult to correct without a systematic approach. This gap analysis, then, needs to be used by change leaders to frame the vision for the change. This vision plays a critical role in helping others understand the gap in concrete terms by contrasting the present state with the desired future state.

Getting From Here to There

Here, the specific actions needed for the change are noted. Several planning tools can be used (see Chapter 9). If the general manager in the hotel case decided that the issue to be tackled is computer systems, then the transition plan might include the following steps:

- Discuss the need for change, the gap analysis, and the vision for change with involved staff to develop a consensus concerning the need for action.
- Form a users' task force to develop the desired outcomes and usability framework for a new computer system.
- Contact internal information systems specialists for advice and assistance on improving the hotel's information system.
- Identify the costs of systems changes and decide which budget to draw on and/or how to fund the needed system's changes.
- Work with the purchasing department to submit a "request for proposal," promoting systems' suppliers to bid on the proposed system.
- Contact Human Resources to begin staffing and training plans.

This example list lays out the actions needed to accomplish the change. In Chapter 9, tools will be identified that help in planning. For example, there are tools to assign responsibilities for different aspects of projects and others for contingency plans.

In Chapter 9, tools illustrate how to manage during the transition. Organizations usually don't stop what they are doing because they are changing! In the hotel, for example, rooms will need to be made up, allocated, and assigned while the information system is being modified. In particular, receptionists will need to ensure a seamless transition from the old to the new system. In many system changes, parallel systems are run until the bugs in the new system are found and corrected. Hotel receptionists need to be trained on the new system. How and when that will be done in this transition is part of the managerial challenge during the transition state.

The final aspect of the model deals with the measurement of change and the metrics used in that measurement. How will the general manager know that the changes implemented are working? Managers can measure inputs easily, such as the number of hotel receptionists who are trained on the new system. But management will also need to track the number of times rooms are misallocated. This is a more difficult problem because the staff could be motivated to prevent such a system if the results could put the staff in a negative light.

Models, such as the Beckhard and Harris one, improve change managers' abilities to plan and implement organizational change. This model provides a straightforward framework that lays out a linear process for change. At the same time, the model risks having change managers oversimplify the challenge. Cause–effect analysis is complex because organizations are nonlinear, complex entities. An overreliance on straightforward linear thinking can lead to errors in judgment and unpleasant surprises. Organizations are more surprising and messier than people often assume. The subsequent chapters of this book, particularly Chapter 3, will help change leaders avoid thinking simplistically.

Coordination and control of change appears straightforward using Beckhard and Harris. The reality is that organizations often undertake multiple change projects simultaneously. For example, a factory may be shifted toward a focused factory system while a continuous improvement process is being developed and while other parts of the organization are being restructured. Different managers are working on different change projects to make things better. Under such complexity, control is difficult and likely involves multiple layers of authority and systems.

The models of Chapter 3 suggest the need for complex thinking and anticipatory ways to avoid negative surprises. Nevertheless, outlining clear stages in the change process by using Beckhard and Harris or a similar model assists in logical diagnosis.

Toolkit Exercise 2.1, at the end of this chapter, asks you to interview a manager who has been involved with change and find out how he or she went about it.

Summary

This chapter differentiates **what** to change from **how** to change and uses the Beckhard and Harris model to explicitly consider how to change. Successful change management requires attention to both process and content. To focus on this, the chapter differentiates **what** needs to be changed from **how** change should be accomplished.

A modified version of the Beckhard and Harris model is presented as a process model that will help change leaders to plan how to make organizational changes. The model forms the framework for this book, and the chapter sequence is laid out using the model. Beckhard and Harris's model is elaborated, and the hotel case presented early in the chapter is analyzed to demonstrate the use of the Beckhard and Harris model.

Glossary of Terms

PEST

PEST factors—the political, economic, social, and technological environmental factors that describe the environment or context in which the organization functions.

The How and What of Change

The **How** of change relates to the process one uses to bring about change.

The **What** of change relates to the assessment of what it is that needs to change—in other words, the content of the change.

Sigmoid Curve

The sigmoid curve describes the normal life cycle of something. If we think of it in terms of a product or service, the initial or lag phase is the time at which it attempts to gain traction through market acceptance. Once it becomes accepted, a period of growth occurs, characterized by acceleration, and then deceleration as the market becomes more competitive and it reaches maturity. As competition mounts and the market becomes saturated, decline ensues. Decline can also be precipitated by the arrival and acceptance of a superior product or service. The only things that will differ are the slope and height of the curve and the time required to get to different points on the curve.

Lewin's Model of Change: Unfreeze → Change → Refreeze

Unfreeze—the process that awakens a system to the need for change—in other words, the realization that the existing equilibrium or the status quo is no longer tenable

Change—the period in the process in which participants in the system recognize and enact new approaches and responses that they believe will be more effective in the future

Refreeze—the change is assimilated and the system reenters a period of relative equilibrium

Beckhard and Harris's Change Management Process

Organizational analysis—the stage in the process used to understand the forces for change and the reasons why the organization is performing as it currently does

Why change—the stage of the process in which the need for change is determined and the nature of the change or vision is characterized in terms others can understand

Gap analysis—the identification of the distance between the desired future state and the present state at which the system operates

Action planning and transition management—the stage of the process in which plans are developed for bridging the gap between the current mode of operation and the desired future state and the means by which the transition will be managed. Managers also need to consider how to measure change and what measures will be used to help identify where the organization is and the level of success achieved.

END-OF-CHAPTER EXERCISES

TOOLKIT EXERCISE 2.1

Interview a manager who has been involved in change in his/her organization. Ask the person to describe the change, what he or she was trying to accomplish, and what happened?

After the interview, describe the processes of the change. That is, **HOW** did the managers work to make things happen? Who did they involve? How did they persuade others? What resources did they use?

As well, describe **WHAT** was being changed. Why were these things important? How would it help the organization?

Which was more important: how things were changed or what was changed?

Be prepared to share the results of your interview with others.

Appendix 2.1: Models of Change

Van de Ven and Poole categorize four types of change models that managers use implicitly when thinking about change.[8] These models are: life-cycle, evolutionary, debate-synthesis, and goal-setting.* In other words, many of the assumptions that managers make about change can be captured by these four types. **Life-cycle** change models assume that there is a prescribed series of steps or stages that must happen. The metaphor of a biological organism helps to explain the concept. Biological entities are born, grow, mature, decline, and die. Organizations can be viewed similarly. Under a life-cycle perspective, change involves natural, linear steps and is beyond the control of the changing entity. That is, change happens.[9] An organization starts as an entrepreneurial venture, grows, becomes mature, and eventually declines under this model.

Evolutionary change is based on Darwin's notions of survival. The conflict between types results in a natural selection process as the organism adapts to its environment. This recurrent competition notion can be seen in some of the literature describing organizational populations and survival rates.[10] Venture capital firms often operate under these assumptions. They know they must fund a number of start-ups. Many or most start-ups will fail, but the few that are significant successes make up for the failures. The conflict between North American automakers and the Japanese ones can also be seen in this context.

Debate-synthesis models suggest that there are opposing sides, which are in conflict. When the conflict is resolved, synthesis equilibrium is established until another conflict arises. An example in an organization could be the conflict between an older and younger generation in a family business. Eventually, a younger generation takes over. This new stability lasts until a further conflict occurs. Other examples could involve departments with conflicting goals or the organization itself with goals that collide with other organizations' intentions.[11]

Goal-setting change involves defining gaps between where the organization is and where you want it to be, setting goals, taking action to reduce those gaps, and measuring the results to identify new gaps. Since this book is oriented around planned organization change, much of the content, particularly the action planning

---

*Goal setting is named *teleological* in the literature. Debate-synthesis is called *dialectic*.

chapter, relies heavily on goal-setting-related themes. Because of environmental changes, there is a recurring pattern of goal setting followed by action.[12] Many performance management systems are based on a "gap-analysis/goal-setting/action" frame.

These frameworks capture how organizations change, or at least how we think about such change. The personalities of many managers often lead them to follow a goal-setting frame. Their need for power and achievement drives them to action to close perceived gaps in performance and effectiveness. Life-cycle and evolutionary change have an element of fatalism (what will happen will happen) about them, which does not fit easily with an active hands-on approach to change.

While the goal-setting model is simple and appealing, Higgs and Rowland found in one study that having a simple, linear model of change is not as effective as having a more complex view.[13] They claim that there is "relatively clear evidence to support the view that recognition of the complexity of change is important to the formulation of effective change strategies."[14] In this chapter, we move from a relatively simple model of change, Lewin's, to a more complex one, a modification of Beckhard's model.

While the analysis of the change is complex and often emergent, the type of actions that change leaders can take can be categorized fairly simply into eight sets:

- changes in mission/purpose;
- redefinition of strategy;
- shifts in objectives or performance targets;
- alterations in organization culture, values, or beliefs;
- organizational restructuring;
- technology changes;
- task redesign; and
- changing people.[15]

Changes in mission/purpose and strategy involve a realignment of the organization with its environment. Alterations in the organization culture, values, or beliefs (including its informal systems and processes) might just be a shift in the internal workings of the organization but could also be in response to environmental demands. Organizational restructuring includes the redesign of formal systems and processes and is perhaps the most common perspective on organizational change where new reporting relationships are developed. Technology changes and task redesign are changes inside the organization affecting how the work is accomplished. People can be changed either by altering key competencies, shifting attitudes, values, and/or perspectives, or through adding and/or removing key people from the organization. These broad categories of action suggest simplicity. We caution change leaders against assuming this, as the dynamic nature of the organization and its components make it far from simple.

Appendix 2.2: Application of Lewin's Model of Change

To illustrate Lewin's model, refer to the Letter of Complaint, pages 41–42, and examine the comments below.

Unfreeze

Will this letter of complaint be sufficient to "unfreeze" the general manager and move her to action? If this is a single letter, it is highly unlikely that change will occur. If complaints are common for this hotel, this might be seen as just one more letter in a pile—background noise in running the hotel. The letter suggests that this might be an airport hotel in London, England. The location of the hotel might be such that customer service shortfalls might not make a difference to occupancy rates, whereas minimizing costs would be crucial to the hotel's profitability. In all the above scenarios, no unfreezing would take place.

However, this letter may represent an initiative that captures managerial attention and promotes action. The general manager might be facing declining occupancy and view this letter as a signal of where problems may lie. A comparison with other hotels on measures of profitability and customer satisfaction might demonstrate a dramatic need for change that the letter foreshadowed. In this situation, the general manager's views on the existing system are more likely to be unfrozen, and she would be ready to change.

Note that the unfreezing must take place at many levels. The general manager might be ready for change, but the person at the reception desk might think things are just fine. His perceptions need unfreezing as well! The integration and interdependence of systems and people require us to think about the unfreezing of the organizational system as a whole.

Change

Assume that the general manager accepts the need to improve the specific system that indicates that rooms are ready. She must now decide on what needs to be changed to bring about the needed improvements. She could begin by using the options mentioned earlier in this chapter. For example, she could hire a quality-control person who is charged with inspecting and certifying all rooms before they are entered into the system as "ready to use." Some computer programming may need to be done so that rooms are flagged when they are ready or not ready, and the quality-control person might be given responsibility for managing that flag subsystem. The quality-control person will have to be recruited, hired, and trained if they cannot promote an appropriate person from within. Once the room-quality system has been designed and needed procedures are in place, all receptionists will have to be trained. This change could be a participatory process with the involvement of staff, or the general manager could have it designed and order its implementation. The change process would be reasonably complex, involving a number of people and systems.

During this phase, there would be considerable uncertainty. The new system could well be ready before the quality-control person is hired and trained. Or the reverse—the person may be hired and trained but the room-quality system is not ready. Employees might see opportunities to improve what is being proposed and make suggestions regarding those improvements. Regardless of the specifics, the system would be in flux.

In addition to a quality-control person alternative, many other possible solutions exist—some may be much more participative and job enriching than the above. The questions the general manager must answer are which alternatives will be selected, why, and how they will be implemented (who will do what, when, where, why, and how).

Refreeze

Once the changes are designed and implemented, employees will need to adapt to those changes and develop new patterns and habits. The new flag system will alter how those at reception and in housekeeping do their work. They may informally ask the quality-control person to check certain rooms first as these are in higher demand. The general manager will follow up to see how the system is working and what people are doing. New reporting patterns would be established, and the quality-control person might begin passing on valuable information to hotel maintenance and housekeeping regarding the condition of particular rooms. At this point, the system settles into a new set of balances and relative stability. With this stability comes refreezing, as the new processes, procedures, and behaviors become the new "normal" practices of the organization.

What do we mean by this notion of relative stability and predictability that comes with refreezing? It stems from the observation that organizational systems, composed of tasks, formal systems, informal systems, and individuals, develop an interdependent state of balance over time called homeostasis. Perturbations or shifts in one part of the system are resisted, or swings away from balance are countered and balance is regained. As suggested earlier, managers may introduce change initiatives only to have those initiatives fail because of existing systems, processes, or relationships that work against the change. Planned changes in structures and roles may be seen as decreasing the power and influence of informal groups, and these groups may react in complex ways to resist change. For permanent change, a reconfiguration is needed and new points of balance or homeostasis developed.

The image of a spider's web can help to picture the phenomenon. That is, view the organization as a complex web of systems, relationships, structures, assumptions, habits, processes, and so forth that become interconnected and interdependent over time. Altering one strand of the web is not likely to significantly alter the pattern or overall configuration. What is needed is a breaking of many interconnected items—the "unfreezing" in Lewin's terms.

This simple model has stood the test of time. Change agents find it useful both because of its simplicity and because it reminds us forcefully that you can't expect change unless the system is unfrozen first! We may need other, more complex models of the organization to be able to think through what must be unfrozen and changed, but Lewin forces us to recognize the rigidity that comes with stability and interconnectedness within existing systems, relationships, and beliefs.

However, several concerns prevent us from wholeheartedly embracing this model. First, the model suggests that change is simple and linear. The reality is that change tends to be complex, interactive, and emergent. Second, the creation of the need for change deserves more attention. It is not merely moving individuals away from their assumptions that is required. Rather, they need to have a vision of a future desirable state. Finally, the model implies that refreezing is acceptable as a frame of mind. This seems problematic. In today's rapidly changing world, organizations find that pressures to adapt mean they are never "refrozen"—and if they are, they are in trouble. However, at one level, leaders know that without a degree of refreezing, that is, some stability, efficiency is impossible. Without stability, it is difficult to establish coherence of direction and purpose. Each organizational member could claim primacy of direction for his or her local area without regard for an overarching vision (particularly as they do know local conditions best). On the other hand, organizations that freeze too firmly may fail to thaw when new markets and customers appear. They may refuse to incorporate feedback in making useful changes. Continuous improvement programs may appear faddish, but they reflect a realistic view of what is needed for a dynamic environment because they enhance an organization's adaptive capacity. Thus, there is concern with the image created by the word *refreeze*, as this is likely too static a condition for our long-term organizational health.[*]

---

*In discussions with managers and students, we often find the phrase "regelling" to have some appeal as a compromise between total fluidity and excess rigidity.

Notes

1. Arnoff, M. (2009, September 14). The challenges for McDonald's top chef. *Business Week.*

2. Schwartz, A. (2009, July 6). First "green" McDonald's to offer ChargePoint EV charging stations. *Fast Company.*

3. Schull, D. (1999). Why good companies go bad. *Harvard Business Review, 77*(4), 42–52.

4. Handy, C. (1994). *The age of paradox.* Boston: Harvard Business School Press.

5. Lewin, K. (1951). *Field theory in social science.* New York: Harper and Row.

6. A recent discussion of Lewin's contribution can be found in Rosch, E. (2002). Lewin's field theory as situated action in organizational change. *Organization Development Journal, 20*(2), 8–14.

7. Beckhard, R., & Harris, R. T. (1987). *Organizational transitions: Managing complex change.* Reading, MA: Addison-Wesley.

8. Van de Ven, A. H., & Poole, M. S. (1995). Explaining development and change in organizations. *Academy of Management Review, 20*(3), 510–540.

9. Szamosi, L. T. (1999, June). *A new perspective on the organizational change process: Developing a model of revolutionary change and a measure of organizational support for revolutionary change* (Unpublished PhD thesis). Carleton University, Ottawa, Ontario.

10. Carroll, G., & Hannan, M. T. (1989). Density delay in the evolution of organizational populations: A model of five empirical tests. *Administrative Science Quarterly, 34*(3), 411–430.

11. Szamosi, L. T. (1999, June). *A new perspective on the organizational change process: Developing a model of revolutionary change and a measure of organizational support for revolutionary change* (Unpublished PhD thesis). Carleton University, Ottawa, Ontario.

12. Burke, W. W. (2002). *Organization change: Theory and practice.* London: Sage.

13. Higgs, M., & Rowland, D. (2005). All changes great and small: Exploring approaches to change and its leadership. *Journal of Change Management, 5*(2), 121–151.

14. Op cit, p. 144.

15. Part of this categorization is drawn from Robbins, S., & Langton, N. *Organizational behavior* (3rd ed.). Toronto: Pearson Education Canada.

CHAPTER 3

Change Frameworks for Organizational Diagnosis

"WHAT" to Change?

> *There is nothing as practical as a good theory.*
>
> —K. Lewin

CHAPTER OVERVIEW

- Change leaders need to understand both **HOW** to go about change (the process of making the change) and **WHAT** changes need to be made (the content of those changes). Understanding **WHAT** needs to change is the focus of this chapter. Knowing **WHAT** to change depends on your skill in organizational diagnosis.
- Change leaders' success in determining what needs changing requires them to have a clear organizational framework they can use for analysis. They need to understand how complex and interactive organizational components are, how analysis can occur at different levels, and how organizations and their environments will shift over time.
- This chapter outlines the Nadler and Tushman's Congruence Model, which provides an organizational framework to assist change agents to analyze organizations. The Nadler and Tushman model is used in this text because it balances the complexity needed for organizational analysis and the simplicity needed for action planning and communication.

(Continued)

(Continued)

- The complexity of organizations is highlighted by Sterman's Dynamic Modeling View. It helps one to think of the nonlinear and interactive nature of organizations.
- Quinn's Competing Values Model provides a framework that bridges individual and organizational levels of analysis.
- Organizational changes over time are highlighted by Greiner's Phases of Organizational Growth Model.
- Complexity theory is introduced to highlight the interactive, time-dependent nature of organizations and organization change.

In Chapter 2, we considered **HOW** to change. That is, we outlined a process approach to effective change. In this chapter, we deal with the content of change, or **WHAT** to change. Differentiating the process from the content is sometimes confusing, but the rather unusual example below will highlight the difference.

Bloodletting is a procedure that was performed to help alleviate the ills of mankind.... In the early nineteenth century adults with good health from the country districts of England were bled as regularly as they went to market; this was considered to be preventive medicine.[1]

The practice of bloodletting was based on a set of assumptions about how the body worked—bloodletting would diminish the quantity of blood in the system and thus lessen the redness, heat, and swelling that was occurring. As a result, people seemed to get better after this treatment—but only in the short term. The reality was that they were weakened by the loss of blood. As we know today, the so-called science of bloodletting was based on an inaccurate understanding of the body.

It is likely that bloodletting professionals worked to improve their competencies and developed reputations based on their skills in bloodletting. They worked hard at the **HOW** aspects of their craft. Advances in medicine prove that they did not really understand **WHAT** they were doing.

The importance of **what** to change is highlighted by the story of Magna International.

MAGNA INTERNATIONAL CHANGES DIRECTION

Magna International, a $22 billion revenue company, designs, develops, and manufactures automotive components and vehicles primarily for sale to original equipment manufacturers worldwide. Magna International Inc. had for more than 10 years spun off divisions when they reached sufficient size for an initial public offering. This was based on the assumption that focusing on special parts and components achieved efficiencies and higher profits. Clearly, by 2004, these assumptions were incorrect. As Magna shifted to making complex modules and entire vehicles, the need for coordination soared. But coordination was increasingly difficult given the independence of each spun-off division.[2]

Magna's executives transformed their organization from 1994 to 2004. They may have been good at **HOW** they did things, but by 2004 there were concerns that **WHAT** to change had shifted. Magna's approach was increasingly out of alignment with what was needed in the marketplace. The company reorganized and increased coordination across divisions. By 2010, Magna had continued its strategy of making entire vehicles. The increased coordination seemed to be working. As the automotive market rebounded after the 2008 recession, Magna faced choices about expansion. Its senior executives decided to choose one developing nation, and the Russian market became its choice. To implement this plan, Magna approved the appointment of Siegfried Wolf as chairman of the GAZ Group, a Russian automaker. Magna plans on entering this market in its early stage of development and sees Russia as "a spectacular growth opportunity."[3] Only time will tell if Magna's diagnosis was correct and if **WHAT** they did was appropriate.

Bruch and Gerber differentiate the **WHAT** and the **HOW** in a leadership question—"What would be right?"—and a management question—"How do we do it right?"[4] They analyzed a strategic change program at Lufthansa that took place from 2001 to 2004. This program generated more than €1 billion in continuing cash flow. The **HOW** questions focused on gaining acceptance of the change: focusing the organization, finding people to make it happen, and generating momentum; and the **WHAT** questions were analytical, asking what change was right, what should be the focus, and what can be executed given the culture and situation. Bruch and Gerber concluded that a focus on implementation was not sufficient. A clear grasp of the critical needs, the change purpose or vision, was also essential.[5]

Underlying one's understanding of what needs to change in an organization are assumptions and beliefs about organizations and how they work. In the example that began the chapter, barber-surgeons believed that the body consisted of humours that needed to be in balance. Bloodletting could restore that balance. Today's physicians have a more complex, science-based, systemic view of the body. The parallel is clear. Determining **WHAT** should change in an organization relies heavily on the models we have of how organizations work and the practitioner's skill in using the models to identify appropriate and necessary changes.

Nadler and Tushman's model (see Figure 3.4 on page 79) provides a conceptual framework for organizations.* The model, explained below, allows one to explicitly consider the key components of any organization and sharpen one's understanding of how an organization works and how well it fits with its environment. In this chapter, there are other conceptual models that highlight the need to understand organizational dynamics, the level of analysis in an organization, and how organizations shift over time. All of these models help change agents to understand the underlying patterns of causation within an organization. Market intelligence gathering, news reports, benchmarking studies, and the like can be excellent sources for ideas, but they are not a substitute for the careful thinking and detailed organizational analysis that are needed. As Kurt Lewin said: "Nothing is as practical as a good theory."

---

*The Nadler model is just one of many frameworks that help in analysis. However, the focus for this book is on helping change leaders to be effective rather than helping them to understand the differences and intricacies of many models. Two other frameworks are introduced in appendices for Chapter 2.

In Chapter 2, the Beckhard framework for the change-management process was presented. In this chapter, we modify the Beckhard framework to concentrate on the initial organizational analysis, and a deeper gap analysis as shown in Figure 3.1. The gap analysis tools are discussed in more detail in Chapters 5, 6, 7, and 8.

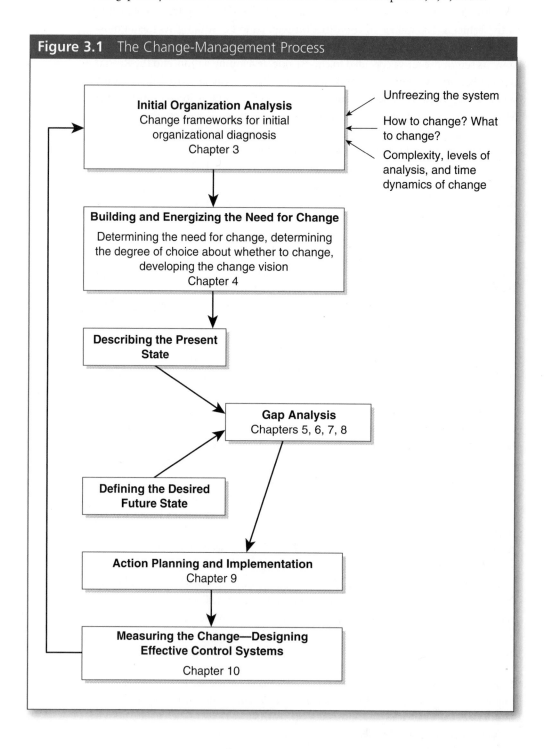

Figure 3.1   The Change-Management Process

Figure 3.1 allows change leaders to combine the **what** of change with the **how** of change. As well, Figure 3.1 links the chapters of the book to the **how** and **what** of change. The modified Beckhard model can be viewed as the vertical axis of Figure 3.1, and the Nadler and Tushman model can be used as a framework for gap analysis. The Nadler and Tushman model becomes the horizontal axis, focusing on the difference between the desired future state and the present reality.

A Systems Approach to Organization Analysis

In this book, the Nadler and Tushman model is used as a framework to assist in structuring change leaders' thinking and improving the quality of their analysis. The Nadler and Tushman model has a reasonably complete set of organizational variables and presents them in a way that encourages straightforward analysis. It specifically links environmental input factors to the organization's components and outputs. As well, it provides a useful classification of internal organizational components while showing the interaction between them. The Nadler and Tushman model is one example of many open systems models.

Regardless of the model, organizations are assumed to interact with their environments in a complex and dynamic way. This **open systems perspective** is based on the following assumptions:[6]

- Open systems exchange information, material, and energy with their environments. As such, a system interacts with and is not isolated from its environment.
- A system is the product of its interrelated and interdependent parts and represents a complex set of interrelationships rather than a chain of linear cause–effect relationships.
- A system seeks equilibrium, and one that is in equilibrium will only change if some energy is applied.
- Individuals within a system may have views of the system's function and purpose that differ greatly from the views held by others.
- Things that occur within and/or to open systems (e.g., issues, events, forces) should not be viewed in isolation but rather should be seen as interconnected, interdependent components of a complex system.

The adoption of an open systems perspective allows managers to identify areas of misalignment and risk. Open systems analysis helps practitioners to develop a rich appreciation for the current condition of an organization and the plausible alternatives and actions that could be considered for improvement. For example, when systems have been isolated from the environment for extended periods of time, they risk becoming seriously incongruent with the external environment.[7] Or, if an environment changes rapidly, the results can prove disruptive and, in some cases, disastrous for an organization. Consider what happened with the credit crisis of 2008, the deregulation of electrical utilities[8] in the United States in the late 1990s, the impact of the fall of the Berlin Wall on existing East German organizations in 1989, or the impact of the removal of protective tariffs on North American garment manufacturers.[9] Each of these led to significant disruption and change for specific organizations. Disruptions can shake organizations to their foundations, but they also have the potential to sow the seeds for renewal (hence the term *creative destruction*, coined by Joseph Schumpeter[10]).

In summary, organizations should not be analyzed as if they exist in a bubble, isolated from the environment.

The Nadler and Tushman Congruence Model for Organizational Analysis

Nadler and Tushman[11] provide a conceptual scheme that describes an organization and its relationship to its external environment. The model focuses on how the organization's parts fit or don't fit.[12] An adaptation of their model is depicted in Figure 3.2. This model is used as a framework for this book. Inputs are transformed to outputs, and the feedback links make the model dynamic and the components highly interdependent.

Figure 3.2 Nadler and Tushman Organizational Congruence Model

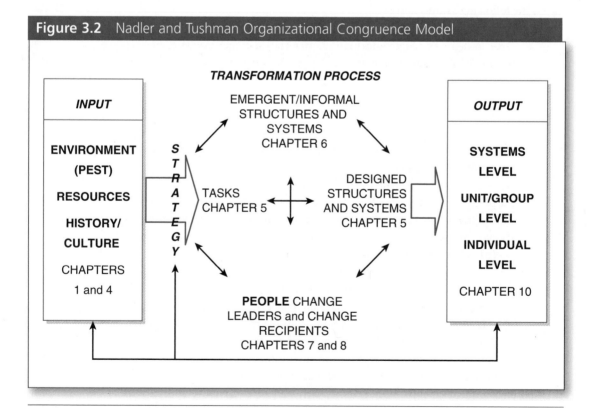

Source: Adapted from Nadler, D.A. & M.L. Tushman, "Organizational Frame Bending: Principles for Managing Reorientation," *Academy of Management Executive*, 1989, Vol. 3, #3, 194–204.

The major components of the model are:

The External Environment, History, and Resources of the Organization

These include the competitive situation faced by the organization, the trends in society, and other environmental factors that have an impact on the organization's ability to be effective and efficient. The history of the organization provides insights into the organization's culture and its emergent structure. Finally, the human, technological, and capital resources available also impact an organization's strategy, and, ultimately, its outputs. In thinking about what to change, all of these inputs may be sources of opportunity and constraint. Chapters 1 and 4 address these factors and they recur as themes throughout the book.

For change leaders, an ability to understand the organization's environment and the implications for action in the organization is a central change skill.

The Strategy

An analysis of the organization's competencies, strengths, and weaknesses, in light of the environmental threats and opportunities, leads to the strategy that the organization decides to pursue. Strategic choices lead to the allocation of resources. Sometimes the strategy is consciously decided. At other times, it is a reflection of past actions and market approaches that the organization has drifted into. When there is a gap between what leaders say their strategy is and what they do (i.e., the actual strategy in use), one needs to pay close attention to the strategy in use. Chapter 4 considers strategy, and it is a theme that recurs in later chapters of the book.

For change leaders, the change strategy is a critical focus of their analysis. What are the purposes and objectives of the planned change in the context of the organizational strategy?

The Tasks

In order to carry out the strategy, a set of tasks is defined. Some of these tasks are *key success factors* that the organization must execute in successfully implementing its strategy. An organization's tasks may be described in a very discrete way, listing, for example, the duties of a particular position, or, at the polar extreme, the basic functions such as marketing, production, and so on that the organization performs in its transformation processes. Chapter 5 deals with how the work is formally organized.

In change situations, change leaders should think through the necessary shifts in key tasks in order to carry out the change initiative. This will assist in developing a specific gap analysis.

The Designed Structure and Systems

This includes any formal structure or system that management creates to produce desired outcomes. Once the tasks are identified and defined, they are grouped to form reporting relationships, the formal organizational chart of roles, responsibilities, departments, divisions, and so on. The purpose of a structure is to enable efficient and effective task performance. The systems of an organization are the formal mechanisms that help the organization accomplish its tasks and direct the efforts of its employees. These include an organization's human resource management systems (recruitment and selection, reward and compensation, performance management, training and development); information systems; measurement and control systems (e.g. budget, balanced scorecard); production systems; and so forth. Chapter 5 deals with designed systems and structures.

Change leaders need to understand how the formal systems and structures can be used to facilitate or impede change. Often formal systems, such as budgeting systems, can be used to gather resources for change.

The Informal Organization

The informal relationships among people and groups in the organization and the informal way things get done form the emergent/informal structure. While managers define the tasks necessary to accomplish the strategy and then structure those tasks in formal ways, many things occur that are unplanned or unanticipated. For example, friendly relationships between individuals often ease communications, groups form and provide support or opposition for the accomplishment of tasks, and individuals adapt procedures to make things easier or more productive.* The informal system will include an organization's culture, the norms or understandings about "how we do things around here," values (e.g., about the importance of customer service), beliefs (for example, about why the organization is successful), and managerial style (a "tough boss" style, for example). Culture is a product of both the organization's history and its current organizational leadership. It acts as a control system in the sense that it defines acceptable and unacceptable behaviors, attitudes, and values and will vary in strength and impact, depending upon how deeply held and clearly understood the culture is. Other elements of the informal organization that are important to analyze when considering how to create change include power relationships, political influence, and decision-making processes. Chapter 6 deals with informal systems and structures.

Change leaders need to recognize the groups and relationships that can facilitate or block change. Identifying those factors and dynamics is a critical activity.

People

The people in an organization perform its tasks using both the organization's designed and emergent systems and structures. It is important that the knowledge,

---

*For an interesting perspective on the informal system, see either Hutt, M., et al. (2000). Defining the social network of a strategic alliance. *Sloan Management Review, 41*(2), 51–62 or Krackhardt, D., & Hanson, J. R. (1993). Informal networks: The company behind the chart. *Harvard Business Review, 74*(4), 104–111.

skills, and abilities of each person match what the organization needs. Understanding the individuals in the organization and how they will respond to the proposed change will be significant in managing the change situation. The role of stakeholders and change recipients is discussed in Chapter 7.

Within every organization, certain key individuals are critical to its success. Often we think of the formal leaders as those who are most important in terms of accomplishing the mission, but others may be crucial. These people might have special technical skills or might be informal leaders of a key group of employees. People such as these, acting as change leaders, are described in Chapter 8.

Change leaders need to understand the impact of proposed changes on the organization's employees. Further, they need to identify key leaders in the organization who can facilitate the needed changes.

The Outputs

The outputs of an organization are the services and products it provides to generate profitability or, especially in the case of public-sector and nonprofit organizations, to meet other goals. Additional outputs are also important: the satisfaction of organizational members, the growth and development of the competencies of the organization and its members, and customer satisfaction (to name just three). These outputs need to be defined and measured as attentively as profitability, return on investment (ROI), or numbers of clients served. The success of the organization in producing desired outputs becomes part of the inputs to the organization and pressures to modify the change strategy. Chapter 10 focuses on the measurement of change.

Change leaders need to recognize that "what gets measured is what gets done." They need to select key measures that will track the change process.

In their work, Nadler and Tushman make three critical assumptions. First, the system is dynamic. This means that a diagnosis will change over time with different concerns and objectives. Second, the "fit" or congruence between components is significant in diagnosing why the organization performs as it does. And third, the better the fit among organizational components, the more effective the organization. The organizational change challenge is to align the system components to respond to changing external and internal conditions.

The System is Dynamic

If an organization's environment shifts, so must a diagnosis. For example, when inflation was running at 1,100% per year in Brazil,[13] the influence of financial executives soared because financial management played a pivotal role in sustaining firms. When inflation slowed and stabilized in the range of 10 to 20%, power shifted away from finance and toward sales, marketing, and production. If the internal organization alters significantly, a diagnosis must also change. While this may seem like a statement of the obvious, it often goes unobserved in practice. Managers develop patterns of thinking about organizational performance that serve them well, but over time these patterned approaches may impair their ability to see when conditions change. As a result, the assumptions managers make about how things work may come to be just plain wrong!

The "Fit" Between Organizational Components Is Critical

A change agent needs to understand the various components of an organization and how they fit together and influence one another. For example, executives in an organization who restructure and ignore the informal groupings do so at some risk. Or, if managers create structures to fit several key people and then those people leave, there will be a significant loss of fit between the structural component and the key people within Nadler and Tushman's model. In our earlier example of Magna International, the fit between Magna's strategy and the external environment had been strained as the environment shifted. Magna's strategy of decentralizing operations and spinning them off into independent companies became incongruent with the need for coordination among units. As a result, Magna had to alter its strategy and repurchase those same independent companies.

Organizations With Good Fit Are More Effective Than Those With Poor Fit

Nadler and Tushman argue that effective organizations have excellent "fit" or "congruence" between components. Further, they argue that the strategy needs to flow from an accurate assessment of the environment and respond to the changes occurring in that environment. Similarly, the strategy fits the organization's capabilities and competencies. If all of these are not aligned reasonably, the strategy will fail or be less effective. Inside the organization, the four components (tasks, designed structure and systems, emergent structure and systems, and people) must fit each other. For example, if an organization hires motivated, highly skilled individuals and assigns them routine tasks without challenge or decision-making opportunities, those individuals will likely be bored. There will be a lack of fit and productivity will suffer. Or, if the strategy demands the adoption of new technology and employees are not provided with the necessary training, fit is lacking. There can be a lack of fit between the emergent structure of the organization and other components. Within categories, elements might not fit. For example, an organization might decide to "empower" its employees. If it fails to adjust the reward system, this lack of fit could easily lead to a failure of the empowerment strategy.

Overall, lack of fit leads to a less effective organization. Good fit means that components are aligned and the strategy is likely to be attained.

For many managers, the notion of fit is easiest to understand as they follow the flow from strategy to key tasks to organizing those tasks into formal structures and processes to accomplish the desired objectives. This is a rational approach to management and appeals to one's logic. At the same time, the reality of organizations as represented by the needs of individuals and by the informal structures that exist often means that what appears to management as logical and necessary is not logical to employees. Managerial logic is viewed by employees as against their interests or unnecessary. Peters recognizes the importance of the so-called nonrational aspects of organizations.[14] He argues that managers should tap into the power of teams to accomplish results, that individuals can be challenged to organize themselves to accomplish tasks. Thus, while fit is easiest to picture in logical terms, change agents need to consider it in terms of the informal system and the key individuals in the change process.

In a typical scenario, changes in the environment require leaders to rethink the organization's strategy. This, in turn, results in changes in key tasks and how managers structure the organization to do those tasks. In developing a new strategy and in redesigning an organization's systems and structures, managers need to become aware of and understand the influence of key individuals and groups.

Nadler and Tushman's Congruence framework helps practitioners in three ways. First, it provides a template to assist in an organizational analysis. Second, it gives one a way of thinking about the nature of the change process—environmental factors tend to drive interest in the organization's strategy, which, in turn, propels the transformational processes. These, then, determine the results. Third, the congruence framework emphasizes that, for organizations to be effective, a good fit among all elements in the process is required from environment to strategy through to the transformation process. Fit is also necessary within the transformation process; this is a constant challenge for incremental change initiatives such as continuous improvement programs. An emphasis on the internal fit between organizational components often focuses on efficiency. An emphasis on the external fit between the organization and its environment is an effectiveness focus.

An Example Using the Nadler and Tushman Congruence Model

Over the past several years, Dell Computers has transformed itself. Dell made its name by selling low-cost computers directly to customers. The company was renowned for an efficient supply chain that allowed it to receive payment for its computers before it incurred the cost of building them. The Dell story, below, outlines its attempt to reorient itself.

DELL COMPUTERS REORIENTS ITSELF[15]

For years, Dell focused on being the low-cost, efficient producer of computers. As one report put it, "Dell long stuck with its old playbook of cranking out PCs as efficiently as possible." Dell had focused on making the computer a commodity and sold online using generic parts. Dell focused on optimizing the business it already had while the market shifted. Its competitors, Hewlett-Packard, IBM, and others, marketed newer, sleeker laptops with better Internet capabilities using retail stores for distribution.

In 2007, Michael Dell returned as CEO after 3 years of relative distance from operations. Since then, he has replaced his senior management team,

(Continued)

(Continued)

added new products and services, and focused on what customers want. One of his first moves was to hire Garriques from Motorola, who broke with Dell's tradition of only selling directly to customers. As well, new products were developed and Dell was restructured around its customers. However, the marketplace was changing radically as smartphones and similar products became the hot new focus.

The troubles for Dell had begun when the market shifted. Corporate growth lessened and the consumer sector flourished. As well, developing markets overseas became critical, markets that were less willing to buy over the Internet and use direct delivery. Additional processing power became less critical and consumers demanded special features and more attractive machines. Clearly, Dell saw the need to alter what it was doing. A diagnosis of what would work had led to an overhaul of the company.

After taking over, Michael Dell responded to the marketplace. He set up mechanisms to get customers' input. He shifted Dell's distribution strategy to sell in retail outlets. This required a shift in mindset for Dell managers, as they had to have new distribution systems and manage their relationships with retailers. New machine designs were created and new hardware, including smartphones, was offered. Dell began selling mini-notebooks to appeal to overseas markets. And the company responded to changes in the corporate sector by providing systems solutions, not just computers.

To implement his strategy, Michael Dell installed a new senior management team. One of his first moves was to hire Ron Garriques, the executive who introduced Motorola's Razr phone, as head of Dell's consumer business. Garriques stopped work on the Mantra, a standard line of Dell products. As well, he stopped the introduction of Dell specialty stores and developed relationships with retailers. Design became a new, central focus.

Michael Dell also brought in Brian Gladden from GE. Gladden believed that Dell needed to be restructured, that its systems and processes were not sophisticated enough for a company of its size. One major move was to shift the focus of Dell to its external markets by organizing around those markets, such as consumers, corporations, small- and mid-sized businesses, and governments and educational buyers.

Culture change was encouraged to shift Dell to a more responsive, flexible company. Group leaders had clear financial targets but were given significant responsibility in how to achieve these targets.

New products were developed and Dell began selling the world's thinnest notebook. Design emphasized style and "tech appeal." Smartphones were in the planning stage.

Dell's financial performance has improved. Has it changed quickly enough to meet market demands? Will it be able to match the design flair of Apple? Time will tell.

By 2007, Dell Computers was no longer fitting its external environment. During its rapid growth years, Dell provided unrivalled service to the markets. Corporations wanted reliable equipment with good prices and excellent service. Dell provided this with Internet ordering and fast delivery. It streamlined its manufacturing and distribution systems. Orders led to production, which created product demand from Dell suppliers. Speed of production became critical in order to minimize the delay between customer order and shipment to that customer. Relationships with the market were with customers, not retailers. While major clients (governments, etc.) had clout, as long as Dell delivered quality products and provided good technical service, the clients were satisfied. The key tasks, to use Nadler and Tushman's terminology, were production and distribution.

During this growth phase, Dell's organization was aligned well with its market. Internally, the production orientation fit those market needs. Systems were designed for efficiency and simplicity. There was no need for retail management. Inventories were minimized as Dell built to order. Finances were simple because customers paid as they ordered and before Dell incurred the costs of production. Dell's management team excelled at getting efficiencies from this system, and the results showed for many years.

As the market shifted, the Dell organization became increasingly out of sync with the marketplace. Dell's strategy was no longer a good fit as the marketplace shifted away from corporate demand to consumers, from machine power to design, from hardware to software and the Internet, from America to developing nations. The clean, straightforward organization that Dell had built could not meet the more complex market expectations.

Note how Michael Dell responded. All components of the company changed. First, the strategy shifted. Design was emphasized. Retailers became key parts of the distribution network. Product variety increased. With that strategic shift, the key success factors or critical tasks changed. Design became more important. Management of retail distribution became crucial and introduced an entirely new set of skills at Dell. As the product range increased, skills in the introduction and timing of new products became more important. To manage this, the company was reorganized into four divisions, each focused on one major customer segment. Financial systems would need to be overhauled to manage this complexity. New formal and informal networks were established as the company's focus changed. Key executives were replaced by others with the skill sets demanded by this new strategy. In short, a new state of congruency was developed so that the internal operations fit the strategy better.

Dell's reorganization provides an excellent example of how the Nadler and Tushman model and that model's notions of congruency can be used to help to understand and analyze organizations. These efforts to introduce new key people, redesign organizational systems, modify the company's strategy, and alter the product mix have shown superb initial success and may reverse Dell's slide—at the time of the writing of this book, it is too early to tell. However, it is clear that the steps taken have improved the congruence between key variables in at least the short term, and the results are showing this. The question is whether the shift in the marketplace to the smartphone will make Dell's efforts too little too late.

The Nadler and Tushman model enables a change agent to think systematically about the organization. It serves as a checklist to ensure practitioners consider the critical components that must be matched with the strategy and environmental demands. Since the system is dynamic, the environment, the people, the competition, and other factors change over time, and part of that change is due to how the components interact with each other. Second, the fit between organizational components is critical. Dell Computer's products, organization, systems, and culture had become misaligned with the new environment. Finally, organizations with good fit are more effective than those with poor fit. The moves that Michael Dell made improved the fit and led to a turnaround in sales and margins.

Like any living entity, an organization survives by acting and reacting effectively to its external environment. Unless it adjusts with appropriate changes to its strategy, it reduces its capacity to thrive. When one part of the organization is changed, then other parts also need to adapt to maintain the congruence or fit that leads to effectiveness. Michael Dell and his new management team have begun the realignment at Dell Computers. Whether Dell and his team made enough savvy changes for the long term will be demonstrated by the company's future performance. Critical to this will be Dell's ability to innovate and change in the face of shifts in its environment.

Evaluating the Nadler and Tushman Congruence Model

Are the assumptions made by the Nadler and Tushman congruence model reasonable ones? For example, should strategy always dictate the organization's structure and systems? While that is the one of the traditional views of strategy, it is not unusual to see the reverse where changes in the structures and systems (the transformational process) drive alterations to strategy. For example, Yetton and his colleagues showed that changes in information technology produced changes in strategy as the organization learned about and took advantage of new technology.[16] Thus, the implied direction of the Nadler and Tushman model is appropriate, but any analysis must recognize how dynamic and interactive the factors are. For many change agents, particularly those in middle management, the strategy of their organizations will be a given and their role will be to adapt internal structures and systems. Alternatively, change agents may attempt to influence the strategy directly (e.g., participation in a strategic task force) and/or indirectly (initiate activities that lead to the development of new internal capacities that make new strategies viable).

Has the importance of fit been overstated? Probably not. For example, in an investigation into the mixed results achieved by total quality management (TQM) initiatives, Grant, Shani, and Krishnan found that "TQM practices cannot be combined with strategic initiatives, such as corporate restructuring, that are based on conventional management theories. The failure of one or both programs is inevitable."[17] Thus, they found that the strategy, the structure, and new TQM processes need to fit with each other. More recently, as a result of September 11, 2001, the U.S. government created a new superintelligence agency to control the dozen or so intelligence agencies. However, reports that have emerged suggest that the new intelligence czar has none of the levers needed to do his job: The formal structure has been created, but not the systems and processes that are necessary to give him leverage to be successful.[18] In both of these examples, a lack of alignment undermines the efforts to effectively change these organizations.

The need for change may not always be identified by looking at an organization's environment. Problems surface in a variety of ways. There might be problems in the organization's outcomes, indicating that some aspect of performance needs to be addressed. Further, there is the question of the magnitude of the change. The organization may decide to change its strategy, its culture, or some other core element. Generally, the more fundamental the change, the more other elements of the organization will need to be modified to support the desired change. For example, a change to an organization's culture often creates a domino effect, requiring multiple changes to its structure, systems, and people.

Finally, does better fit always mean more effectiveness? This depends upon the measure of effectiveness. In the short run, fit might mean increased profits as the organization reduces costs and becomes efficient. However, an innovation measure might show that fit has led to declining creativity. It can be argued that in the long run, tight congruence in a stable environment leads to ingrained patterns inside the organization. Individuals and organizations develop systems and structures, as they should, but these can lead to ritualized routines and habits. Such patterns can be change resistant and can be hugely ineffective when the environment changes. Dell Computers suffered from this prior to Michael Dell's reintroduction in 2007. A similar argument would hold: If the pace of change is rapid, then an overemphasis on congruence can lead to a static analysis. In a rapidly changing environment, approximations are appropriate: Don't make it perfect, get it acceptable and move on. Nevertheless, for most analytical purposes, the assumption that an increasing fit is a good objective is appropriate.

As with other congruence or alignment-oriented models, the Nadler and Tushman model must deal with the criticism that "too much emphasis on congruence potentially (could have) an adverse or dampening effort on organizational change."[19] The key lies in balancing the need for flexibility and adaptability with the need for alignment. This balance point shifts as environmental conditions and organizational needs change. To emphasize the dynamic nature of organizations, this chapter next examines Sterman's Systems Dynamics Model.

Toolkit Exercise 3.1 asks you to use the Nadler and Tushman model to assess an organization you are familiar with. The purpose is to develop your comfort in using this as an analytic tool.

Dynamic Organizational Systems—Sterman's Systems Dynamics Model[20]

Perhaps it is a statement of the obvious, but successful change agents will have a dynamic and complex view of organizations. In March 2009, General Motors and Chrysler were bankrupt. These same automobile firms invested billions of dollars in new plants and equipment in 2010. Change can be rapid and complex and change leaders (and their mental models) need to recognize this.

As discussed, Nadler and Tushman's Congruence Model focuses more on alignment than on the dynamic nature of systems. In contrast, Sterman's model, below, focuses on the interplay of dynamic forces of the environment, managerial decisions, and actions of others. Sterman believes that managers should handle increased complexity by increasing the number of variables that they consider. The dynamic nature of the variables and the interactions among the variables over time may lead to counterintuitive results.

Sterman argues that managers often take a linear view of the world—a rational, causative model where managers identify a gap between what is and what is desired, make a decision, and take action, expecting rational results. If sales are low, for example, management might increase advertising, thinking that sales will flow. However, because of complex, interactive, nonlinear dependent variables, this linear view can be inaccurate and limiting. What management may get are counterintuitive results that are often policy or change resistant. If Company A, for example, increases its advertising, then Companies B, C, and D may increase their advertising as well. The result may be increased costs and static revenues. Managers may fail to anticipate the side effects of their decisions and how their actions lead to competitive responses that neutralize their first round of actions (see Figure 3.3 Sterman's Systems Dynamics Model).

Consider the following example. Managers change the incentive structure for employees, anticipating that this will lead to higher productivity. However,

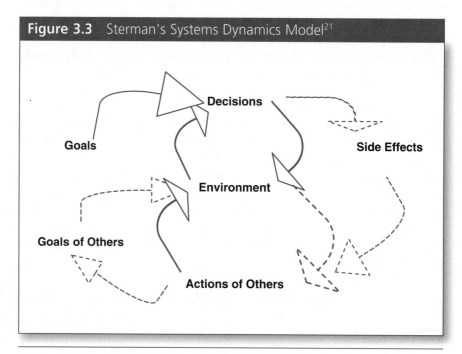

Figure 3.3   Sterman's Systems Dynamics Model[21]

Source: Copyright ©2001, by The Regents of the University of California. Reprinted from the *California Management Review,* "Systems Dynamic Modeling", Sterman, J., Vol. 43, No. 4, Summer, 2001. By permission of The Regents.

employees might see increased productivity as leading to layoffs (if we produce more, they will need fewer of us), and thus resist increasing outputs. Or employees will begin to focus on quantity and neglect crucial quality concerns. This, in turn, creates negative customer reactions that cause management to create new control systems around quality. Such control systems take additional paperwork and effort that increase costs and potentially defeat the original objective of increasing productivity.

According to Sterman, many of the issues result from time lags and delays, inventories and buffer stocks in the system, and attribution errors. Thus, in our above example, employees may increase their efforts to generate new sales as the result of the changed rewards. However, there could be a significant lag before sales increase. Some sales cycles take months and even years before producing results. Thus, management's initial observation might be that the change in the reward system did not work. Small changes in demand may get exaggerated because of inventory buffers that automatically adjust. And finally, humanity's need to attribute cause might mean that managers assume causal links that don't exist.

Sterman's model heightens the awareness of the complexity involved with change and the challenges involved in developing alignments that will produce desirable results in the short and long term and not result in unpleasant surprises. As such, Sterman's model builds on the work of Argyris and Schön,[22] identifying the importance of organizational analysis through double loop and triple loop learning.* It is also consistent with the work of Senge[23] on how organizations should be designed and managed in order to enhance organizational learning, innovation, and change.

In Figure 3.3, the decisions lead to side effects as well as intended effects. These interact with the environment and the goals of others to create a more complex set of responses than were anticipated.

At McDonald's at the beginning of the twenty-first century, management decided to increase the number of corporate-owned stores and decrease costs. In the short term, this led to improved results: higher sales and improved profits. However, it also led to a decreased focus on store cleanliness. With more stores, overall revenues increased. With less time and effort focused on cleanliness, operating costs decreased and, in turn, increased profits. However, over time, customers became aware of the lack of cleanliness and stopped going to McDonald's. These unintentional side effects created more pressure for short-term profits due to a decline in sales. The cycle would repeat until management became aware of this self-defeating cycle.[24]

---

*Single loop is essentially adaptive learning within the organization's operation. Internal data are assessed and modifications are made, but the original objectives are not questioned. Double loop goes beyond making incremental modifications and challenges the assumptions, standards, policies, values, and mode of operation that gave rise to the standards and objectives. Triple loop learning extends this analysis and exploration of possibilities further and questions the underlying rationale for the organization and why it exists.

When a firm lowers its prices to increase market share and profitability, management may do so without thinking through the implications of its decisions. Its actions may lead to competitor responses that lower prices further and sweeten sales terms and conditions (e.g., no interest or payments for 12 months or improved warranties) in an effort to respond to its competitors and win back market share. Thus, the planned advantages coming from the price cuts may end up adding a few new sales, shrink margins, condition customers to see the product in primarily price terms, and lock the organization into a price-based competitive cycle that is difficult to escape.[25]

Sterman cautions managers to avoid the trap of thinking in a static, simplistic way. Increasingly, successful managers are resorting to systems thinking and more complex, nonlinear modelling to improve their diagnostic skills. *The Economist* argues, "Better understanding is the key" to improved productivity.[26]

In doing a diagnosis, managers need to recognize their assumptions and values that underlie their implicit understanding of organizational dynamics and the nature of the environment and the market place. Picture marketing people in a meeting with operations or R&D people and you can imagine the value clashes. Marketing people are often externally oriented while operations people are concerned with internal dynamics. A model by Quinn helps to frame these issues and points to the value of a diversity of perspectives when approaching organizational and environmental analysis.

Individual Versus Organizational Analysis

Levels of Organizational Systems: Quinn's Competing Values Model

How managers think about organizations will largely determine what they think needs changing. The level of analysis that a manger examines can range from the individual to team/department to organizational level. A psychologist, for example, analyzes individuals and small groups and suggests changes at that level. In contrast, an economist uses econometric models to analyze on the organizational or societal level. Quinn provides a model that bridges the individual and organizational levels and encourages change agents to think about the interaction between the systems at both of these levels.[27]

Quinn's Competing Values model outlines four frames relevant to organizations. Each frame is based on a set of values and assumptions about the organization and how it works. Quinn argues that two dimensions underlie and help define these four frames: an internal-external dimension and a control-flexibility dimension. That is, underlying the perceptions of organizations are assumptions about the importance of the inside versus the outside of the organization and the need for control versus the need for adaptability. Plotting these two dimensions forms four quadrants, each of which provides a different "frame" or view of the organization. The Competing Values Model is portrayed in Figure 3.4.

As a manager, do you think about the organization in internal terms and how it operates? Or do you think of the organization's environment and the fit between that environment and the organization? Do you focus your attention on how the organization adapts and changes? Or is your emphasis more on ensuring that the direction is under control and that people do what is needed? Quinn argues that these dimensions form the four value orientations: Open Systems View, Rational Economic View, Internal Process View, and Human Resources View. Further, he states that while all orientations are needed in an organization, each person will tend to operate from one quadrant more than the others. As well, because the values underlying each quadrant are in conflict, individuals will have difficulty having a "natural" perspective from more than one quadrant. Individuals will tend to adopt one set of internally consistent values and find their views in conflict with or competing with those individuals with perspectives from other quadrants.

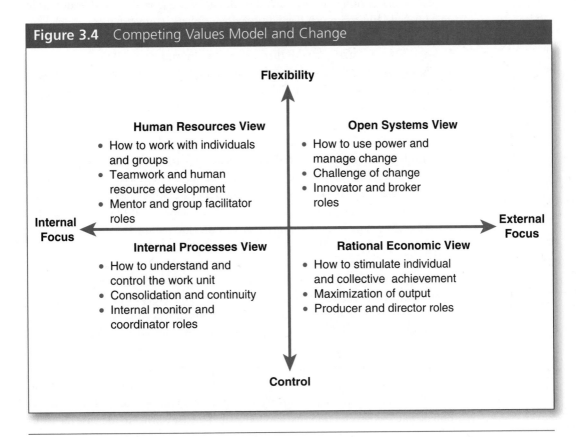

Figure 3.4   Competing Values Model and Change

Source: Quinn R. E. et all. (2003). *Becoming a master manager* (p. 13). New York: John Wiley & Sons.

One of the strengths of Quinn's model is that it links individual and organizational levels of analysis. That is, managers can examine an organization's processes and determine whether they are focused on external adaptation, internal adaptation, and so forth. At the same time, Quinn suggests managerial skills that are needed for each quadrant. To increase the focus on a quadrant, one needs to have managers develop the competencies needed and design systems to reinforce those skill behaviors. Of specific interest to change leaders are those skills that help with change processes. (See Chapter 8 on change leaders for more on this.)

Quinn labels the internal/flexibility quadrant the Human Resources view of organizations. Similarly, the external/flexibility quadrant is the Open Systems view, the external/control quadrant is the Rational Economic view, and the internal/control quadrant is the Internal Process view. Each of these quadrants can be associated with a particular way of thinking about organizations with roles that managers need to play and skill sets managers can learn that enable them to play the roles.[28]

Every organization needs to attend to all four quadrants to know what is going on internally while also understanding its external environment. It needs to control its operations and yet be flexible and adaptable. At the same time, too much emphasis on one dimension may be dysfunctional. That is, organizations and leaders need to be flexible, but too much flexibility can bring chaos. Conversely, too much control can bring rigidity and paralysis. In the end, organizations need to balance these in ways that are congruent with their external environmental realities.

Each quadrant provides a value orientation needed in organizations and suggests managerial roles and skills that will support those value orientations. For example, Quinn argues that innovator and broker roles are needed in the Open Systems quadrant. The innovator roles demand an understanding of change, an ability to think creatively to produce change, and the development of risk taking. The broker role involves the development and maintenance of a power and influence base, the ability to negotiate solutions to issues, and the skills of persuasion and coalition building. Care must be taken not to be trapped into adopting one view and ignoring alternate perspectives. Too much focus on internal stability led IBM to miss the PC revolution for many years. Too much focus on the external world led many dotcoms to spin out of control in the technology boom of the early 2000s.

Quinn's model can be used in several ways: to characterize an organization's dominant culture, to describe its dominant tasks, to portray the focus of its reward systems, or to describe a needed shift in task emphasis or in the types of people that it must recruit. To refer again to the Dell example, the company was striving to become more consumer oriented while maintaining its production efficiencies. Because these two value orientations are not joined easily, change leaders will know that the concurrent development of these two initiatives will require careful management.

As a second example, a newly appointed CEO discovered that Intuit had an "employee-centric culture." In his view (and using Quinn's model), their orientation or value set was too internal and too adaptable. He moved to increase the focus (i.e., increased control) on critical variables based on his view of external realities. Thus, in Quinn's terms, he emphasized the rational, goal-achievement value set and, through this process, shifted employees' focus.

Quinn's model provides both a framework that bridges individual and organizational levels of analysis and a framework to understand competing value paradigms in organizations. While these perspectives are useful, they suggest a relatively static situation, not a dynamic one that Sterman argues for. In particular, Quinn's framework does not encourage managers to consider possible changes that occur in organizations over time. Greiner's model, described below, provides a framework for predicting the stages of change that occur within organizations over time as they grow from entrepreneurial ventures to multidivisional, multinational entities.

Organizational Change Over Time

Greiner's Model of Organizational Growth

As discussed in Chapter 1, the magnitude of organizational changes can vary markedly—from small, evolutionary changes to large, revolutionary ones.[*] Evolutionary shifts are, by definition, less traumatic for organizational members and less disruptive to the organization. Since they typically involve small, incremental shifts in existing systems and behaviors, they are easier to plan and execute. However, they may not be what the organization needs in order to maintain health and vitality. For incremental, evolutionary change, the challenge might be convincing people of the need and tweaking systems and processes to reinforce the desired outcomes. For disruptive, revolutionary change, the issue may well be keeping the organization operating while making significant alterations to how the organization views the world, its strategy, and how it goes about transforming inputs into outputs that its customers desire.

Greiner believes that organizations pass through periods of relative stability, punctuated periodically by the need for radical transformations of practices.[30] During the periods of relative stability, organizations tend to be in equilibrium, and evolutionary approaches to change are adopted in order to incrementally improve practices. Then a crisis occurs, such as the rapid growth of the enterprise, and the crisis demands revolutionary change. In the "crisis of leadership" stage, the founding leader of an entrepreneurial adventure may be pushed aside for the hiring of professional managers. Greiner describes these alternating periods of evolutionary and revolutionary change as natural as an organization grows over time.[†] Figure 3.5 outlines Greiner's model.

---

[*]The determination of the size of the change is of course dependent upon organization level and perspective. An incremental change according to a CEO may well be viewed as transformational by the department head that is directly affected by the change.

[†]Eisenhart believes that organizations can force incremental change by "time pacing"—setting up targets and deadlines that require regular periodic change. See Brown, S., & Eisenhart, K. (1997). The art of continuous change: Linking complexity theory and time-paced evolution in relentlessly shifting organizations. *Administrative Science Quarterly*, *42*(1), 1–34, or Eisenhardt, K., & Tabrizi, B. N. (1995). Accelerating adaptive processes: Product innovation in the global computer industry. *Administrative Science Quarterly*, *40*(1), 84–110.

Figure 3.5   Greiner's Five Phases of Organizational Growth

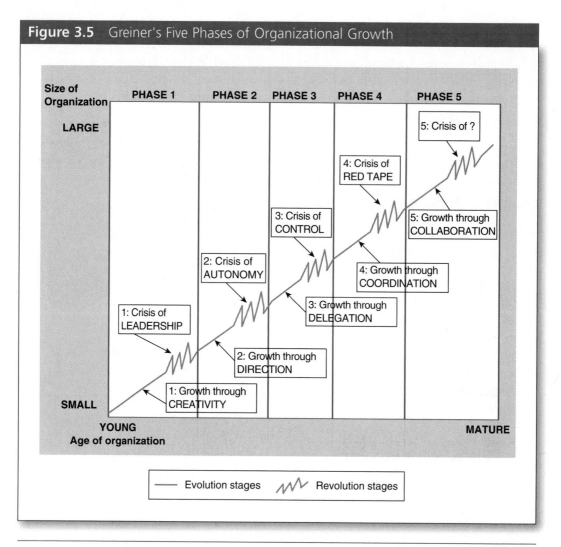

Source: Reprinted with permission from "Evolution and Revolution as Organizations Grow" by Larry Greiner in *Harvard Business Review,* July-August 1972.

In Greiner's view, over time, managers will change their views on how to operate a business incrementally. These become less effective as the business becomes increasingly less congruent with its internal and external realities. (In Nadler and Tushman's terms, the organizational strategy and/or the transformational components—task, formal organization, informal organization, and people—become increasingly out of sync with the environment.) Once the pressure builds sufficiently, it produces the need for more radical transformations of the organization. Pressures build until a breaking point is reached and change is forced.[31] This relatively rapid and discontinuous change over most or all domains of organizational activity is referred to by Greiner as the revolutionary change period.[32]

As shown in Figure 3.5, Greiner outlines a model of typical stages of growth in an organization. He suggests that these patterns are progressive and logical as the organization grows. Greiner is prescriptive in that he claims the organization must pass through these crises in order to grow and develop. The transitions may be caused by a variety of issues: the death of the founder; the need for a functional organization to develop specialties; the emergence of disruptive market forces and/or technologies; the need to decentralize into divisions to keep closer to the customer; and, finally, the need to become more flexible to enable the organization to use the potential of all employees.

This framework is appealing because of its logic and simplicity. However, the model is suggestively prescriptive. Not all organizations follow Greiner's patterns. In today's world, a small entrepreneurial venture may become a global competitor of reasonable size by using the Internet and collaborating with partners around the world. In other words, organizations need not develop as Greiner claims. The model does not seem open to the possibility of the broker organization, one that makes money by connecting organizations to each other. Nevertheless, the framework is valuable in highlighting many of the crises faced by organizations and in relating those crises to the growth stages of the organization. The model reinforces the notion of the competing values that managers must keep in an appropriate state of dynamic tension. For example, as managers move from the crisis of autonomy to growth through delegation, there should be a shift in values and perspectives, from control to flexibility in Quinn's terms.

In the Dell example, the company shifted from a control and functional specialty stage to one where the company was organized into relatively autonomous divisions focused on customer segments. While Greiner's model suggests that certain tensions predominate during different growth phases, such tensions might not vanish. As such, Dell will continue to struggle with the previously successful efficiency focus that its managers held.

While Greiner's model is prescriptive, it captures many of the issues faced by organizations both in growth and in dealing with the human side of organizational change. Too often, managers are trapped by their own perspectives. They fail to recognize that regardless of who is right, others will see things differently and have different criteria to judge potential outcomes. An important key in identifying what to change is to embrace multiple perspectives, recognizing that each comes with its own biases and orientation on what needs to be done. By developing an integrated, comprehensive assessment process and being conscious of one's own biases and preferences, the change leader is likely to achieve a holistic understanding of what change will produce the necessary alignment for organizational success.

Organizations as Complex Entities

Complexity Theory

Many models of organizational change rely on a gap analysis as the description of what needs to change,[33] just as this book does. While this has the advantage of simplicity, change agents need to move beyond this to recognize the importance of interdependence and interrelationships.[34] This chapter began by describing organizations as open systems, and frameworks have been presented for analysis that can account for the dynamic, multilevel, time-dependent nature of organizations. As well, change leaders have been encouraged to recognize that different situations require different levels of analysis, and the appropriate analytic tools are dependent on that level. The importance of moving away from seeing change in primarily simple, rational, cause-and-effect terms should not be underestimated. Change leaders must learn how to cope with complexity and chaos as realities.

Another branch of organizational theorists argues that organizations are complex, paradoxical entities that may not be amenable to managerial control. In this theory, called complexity theory, Stacey[35] identifies the following as the underlying propositions of complexity theory (adapted below):

- Organizations are webs of nonlinear feedback loops that are connected with other individuals and organizations by webs of nonlinear feedback loops.
- These feedback systems can operate in stable and unstable states of equilibrium to the point at which chaos ensues.
- Organizations are inherently paradoxical. On one hand, they are pulled toward stability by forces for integration and control, security, certainty, and environmental adaptation. On the other hand, they are pulled toward instability by forces for division, innovation, and even isolation from the environment.
- If organizations give into the forces for stability, they become ossified and change impaired. If they succumb to the forces for instability, they will disintegrate. Success is when organizations exist between frozen stability and chaos.
- Short-run dynamics (or noise) are characterized by irregular cycles and discontinuous trends, but the long-term trends are identifiable.
- A successful organization faces an unknowable specific future because things can and do happen that were not predicted and that affect what is achieved and how it is achieved.
- Agents within the organization can't control, through their actions, analytic processes or systems and controls, the long-term future. They can only act in relation to the short term.
- Long-term development is a spontaneous self-organizing process that may give rise to new strategic directions. Spontaneous self-organization is the product of political interaction combined with learning in groups, and managers have to pursue reasoning through the use of analogy.
- It is through this process that managers create and come to know the environments and long-term futures of their organizations.

Some complexity theorists would argue that the managed change perspective that underpins this book is fundamentally flawed. They would do so because it focuses on management of complexity and renewal through environmental analysis and programmatic initiatives that advance internal and external alignment, and through them the accomplishment of the goals of the change. Those who adopt a complexity perspective would view the change leader's job as one of creating conditions and ground rules that will allow for innovation and efficiency to emerge through the encouragement of the interactions and relationships of others.

Advocates believe this approach can unleash energy and enthusiasm and allow naturally occurring patterns to emerge that would otherwise remain unseen (i.e., they self-organize into alignment). Vision and strategy are still valued by complexity theorists because they can supply participants with a sense of the hoped-for direction. However, they are not viewed as useful when they attempt to specify the ultimate goal.

A close review of the complexity ideas, though, shows that this perspective is not far from the one advocated by this book. This book adopts an open systems perspective and argues that the environment is characterized by uncertainty and complexity and that organizations are more likely to be successful over time if they develop adaptive capacities. This means that openness to new ideas and flexibility need to be valued and that organizations need to learn how to embrace the ideas, energy, and enthusiasm that can be generated from change initiatives that come from within the organization. The book recognizes the value that teams (including self-managed teams) can contribute to successful change, from needs assessment to the development of initial ideas and shared vision through to strategy development and implementation. Further, it acknowledges that too much standardization and reduction of variance could drive out innovation. Finally, it notes that greater uncertainty and ambiguity gives rise to greater uncertainty over how things will ultimately unfold, thereby highlighting the importance of vision and strategy as directional beacons for change initiatives as opposed to set directives or rules.

An important idea that comes from complexity theory is that small changes at key points early on can have huge downstream effects. But can one predict with any certainty where those changes and leverage points will be or what downstream results will emerge as the result of actions we take today? Often the answer is no. Motorola likely had no clear idea where wireless technology would take the world when it began work on cellular phone technology in the 1960s. Likewise, Monsanto probably had little sense of the magnitude of the marketplace resistance that would build for genetically modified seeds when its research and development program was initiated in the 1980s.

We may not be able to predict precisely what will transpire over the long term, but we can make complex and uncertain futures more understandable and predictable if we do our homework in an open systems manner; look at data in nonlinear as well as linear terms; engage different voices and perspectives in the discussion; and rigorously consider different scenarios and different approaches to envisioning what the future might look like.

When organizations do this, they are likely to get a sense of what is possible from a visionary, directional, and technological perspective. Further, through the engagement and involvement of many, change leaders are in a strong position to initiate change with a shared sense of purpose. They are also more likely to have identified critical actions and events that must occur and where some of the potentially important leverage and resistance points exist. As a result, they are more aware of how things may unfold and are in a stronger position to take corrective or alternative action as a result of their ongoing monitoring and management of the process.[36] As well, change agents will recognize the importance of contingency planning as unpredictable, unplanned events occur.

It may not be possible to predict absolute outcomes. However, it is possible to generally predict where an organization is likely to end up if it adopts a particular strategy and course of action. The identification of the direction and the initial steps allow an organization to begin the journey. Effective monitoring and management processes allow leaders to make adjustments as they move forward. The ability to do this with complex change comes about as the result of hard work, commitment, a suitable mindset (e.g., openness and flexibility), skills and competencies, appropriate participation and involvement, access to sufficient resources, and control and signaling processes. In the end, the authors of this book subscribe to the belief that "Luck is the intersection of opportunity and preparation."[37]

Summary

In this chapter, change agents learned about four different organizational models that will help them to develop a well-grounded sense of **what** needs to change in their organization. This book uses the Nadler and Tushman model as its main framework. The model focuses on achieving congruence among the organization's environment, strategy, and internal organizational components to achieve desired outcomes. In addition, it helps managers categorize the complex organizational data that they must deal with. It examines both the formal and informal aspects of organizations. Finally, it fits neatly into a process approach to organization change, helping to merge the **WHAT** of change with the **HOW** of change.

While the book relies on both the Nadler and Tushman's framework and the Beckhard model, change leaders must be particularly sensitive to the dynamic nature of organizations, to the need for multiple levels of analysis, and to the shifts that organizations make over time. Sterman's, Quinn's, and Greiner's models are presented to reinforce these perspectives. As well, we discuss complexity theory. This theory challenges a simple goal-oriented approach that many change managers might take and encourages an emergent view of organizations.

Change leaders must recognize the assumptions and biases underlying their analysis and whether the assumptions they make limit their perspectives on needed change. Their diagnosis should recognize the stage of development of the organization and whether it is facing evolutionary, incremental change, or, at the other end of the change continuum, more revolutionary, strategic change. By developing an in-depth and sophisticated understanding of organizations, change leaders will appreciate what has to be done to enhance the organization's effectiveness.

Glossary of Terms

The How and What of Change

The **How** of change relates to the process one uses to bring about change.

The **What** of change relates to the assessment of what it is that needs to change—in other words, the content of the change.

Open Systems View of Organizations

The Open Systems view of organizations considers the organization as a set of complex, interdependent parts that interact with the environment to obtain equilibrium.

Models of Organizations:
Nadler and Tushman Model

The Nadler and Tushman model views organizations as composed of internal components (tasks, designed structures and systems, emergent structures and systems, and people). The model states higher effectiveness occurs when the organization is congruent with its strategy and environment. This model forms the framework for this text.

Sterman's Systems Dynamics Model

Sterman's model describes organizations as interactive, dynamic, and nonlinear as opposed to the linear, static view that many individuals hold of organizations.

Quinn's Competing Models Framework

Quinn's model describes organizations as based on competing values: flexibility versus control and external versus internal. These two dimensions lead to four competing views of organizations: the human resource view, the open systems view, the rational economic view, and the internal processes view.

Greiner's Model of Organization Growth

Greiner's model hypothesizes that organizations move through five states of growth followed by five stages of crisis.

Complexity Theory

Complexity theory argues that organizations are webs of nonlinear feedback loops that connect individuals and organizations that can lead to self-organization and alignment between parts.

END-OF-CHAPTER EXERCISE

TOOLKIT EXERCISE 3.1

Analyzing Your Organization
Using Nadler and Tushman's Model

1. Use the congruence model to describe your organization or an organization you are familiar with. Categorize the key components of the environment, strategy, tasks, formal system, informal system, and key individuals. What outputs are desired? Are they achieved?

2. Is the strategy in line with organization's environmental inputs? Are the transformation processes (the key tasks, the formal organization, the informal organization, and the key individuals) all aligned well with your organization's strategy? How do they interact to produce the outputs?

3. When you evaluate your organization's outputs at the organizational, group, and individual levels, do you see anything that might identify issues that your organization should address?

4. Are there some aspects of how your organization works that you have difficulty understanding? If so, identify the resources you can access to help with this analysis.

Appendix 3.1: Other Models of Organizational Analysis

While this book uses the Nadler conceptual scheme to assist us in analyzing organizations, there are many other models that are available. Three of these are presented in this appendix.

A. The McKinsey 7-S Model

One way of thinking about organizational components and their alignment with the environment can be found in the McKinsey 7-S model. It was developed by Peters and Waterman when they were consultants with McKinsey, a consulting firm with a strong, positive global reputation.[38] Table A3.1 describes the components of the model.

Table A3.1	Components of the 7-S Model
Strategy	A plan or course of action undertaken in response to or in anticipation of changes in the external environment. It leads to the allocation of the organization's finite resources to reach specific goals.
Structure	How people and the work are formally organized. It relates to the nature of the formal hierarchy, reporting relationships, and other design factors that go into the formal structure (e.g., span of control, degree of centralization).
Systems	The formal and informal processes and procedures used to flow information and facilitate decision making and action.
Style	How the managers behave (their style, what they pay attention to, how they treat others) in the pursuit of organizational goals. At a more macro level, it means the nature and strength of the culture (norms, shared beliefs and values) that develop over time and influences behavior.
Staff	How human resources are developed and categorized over time.
Shared Values	Longer-term vision and shared values that shape what organizational members do and the destiny of the firm.
Skills	The dominant attributes and distinctive competencies that exist in key personnel and the organization as a whole.

The seven elements in the model vary in the ease with which they can be understood and evaluated. Structures, systems, and strategy are normally easier to track because they tend to leave a visible trail (e.g., organization charts, documents detailing policies and systems, strategic plans, and implementation strategies). However, there is always the question of whether such data reflect the actual practices of the firm. One of the reasons that actual practices differ from what is espoused often lies in the influence that the other *S*s in the model have upon what occurs—the skills, staff, style (managerial style and culture), and the shared values and superordinate goals of the organization.

The underlying thesis of the model is that organizational effectiveness is a function of the degree of fit achieved among these factors and the environment. When organizations experience change, the degree of fit is affected and the challenge of change management is to make changes so that high levels of fit among the seven elements can be achieved.

Changes to one of the components can affect all the other components. Therefore those implementing change need to understand these components as an interconnected set of levers. For example, if changes are being made to the information system in order to make the organization more customer responsive, those making such changes need to carefully consider the implication on the other components and be prepared to manage the change in a more holistic fashion. Making changes to one of the components while ignoring the implications on the others is a recipe for failure. Enhancing internal and external congruence or alignment is the key to developing organizational effectiveness (See Figure A3.1).

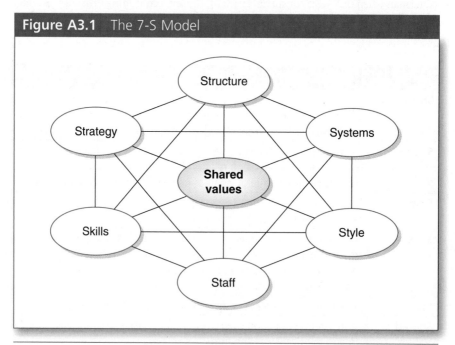

Figure A3.1   The 7-S Model

Source: Reprinted from Business Horizons, Vol. 23, Waterman, R. Jr., "Structure is not Organziation", pp. 14–26, Copyright 1980, Elsevier.

The 7-S approach to organizational analysis tells us first to think about the external environment and the alignment of the key organizational dimensions.

The environment does not appear as a variable in the model. However, the author's use of the model suggest that the organization should be considered as embedded in the environment. Second, it assists in identifying areas of strong alignment and support and areas of misalignment or nonalignment that will need to be addressed in order to increase the prospects for success. It does not emphasize the informal side of organizations—the politics and power and connections between people based on trust and friendships. Additionally, while it focuses on the interactions between components, it does not explicitly address organizational outcomes.

Table A3.2 provides a template for thinking about change and the components of the 7-S model.[39] First, one must address the question of why is change needed. This may be triggered by competitor actions, public complaints, or the fact that organizational members are no longer happy with how the organization is performing. When change is undertaken, the table helps the change leader to identify where congruence and incongruence exist and consider what options are available. Then the impact is considered on other variables. When a change leader uses this model, the goal is to develop a change approach that will lead to high levels of congruence among all the organizational factors and the environment, because this will result in heightened organizational performance.

Applying the Magna Corporation example (from earlier in the chapter) to Table A3.2, the analysis would show that the alignment between its strategy and structure had slipped. The decentralized structure did not fit the strategy requirements of making entire vehicles. Only by creating new coordinating mechanisms could Magna regain alignment. A second example would be the gap between what employees perceived to be the authoritarian management style of many corporate executives and the organization's espoused values of the importance of people and their development.

As the situation changes, the analysis must change as well. Environmental and organizational analysis and alignment represent an ongoing challenge that is facilitated by openness to new ideas, experimentation, organizational learning, and the capacity to implement and refine.

Table A3.2 Identifying Areas of Alignment and Misalignment That Will Need to Be Managed and Actions That Need to Be Taken

	Environment	Style	Shared Values	Skills	Staff	Systems	Structure	Strategy
Strategy	Degree of Alignment:							
Structure								
Systems								
Staff								
Skills								
Shared Values								
Style								
Environment								

The 7-S model provides change agents with a checklist of critical variables that need to be analyzed. It focuses on their connectedness and the need for alignment between variables. However, the role of the environment is implicit. The model does not suggest a flow from environmental variables to organizational ones, which then lead to performance outcomes. As well, while the model emphasizes interconnections and congruence, it does not suggest cause–effect relationships, which lead to increased understanding by change agents.

B. The Burke-Litwin Causal Model

Another model that can be used to analyze organizational situations is the Burke-Litwin causal model.[40] The Burke-Litwin model contains variables similar to other open-system models. However, it seeks to address more directly the question of change management. As Burke notes, the combination of double-headed arrows and multiple variables creates a messy, complex picture—however, it is one that is also reflective of the reality that those interested in change must deal with (see Figure A3.2).

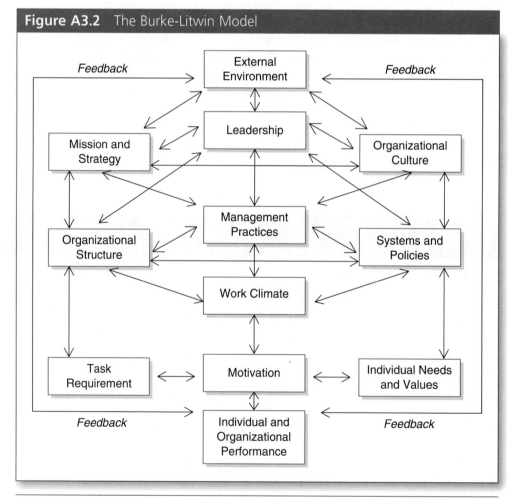

Figure A3.2 The Burke-Litwin Model

Source: Burke, W.W. *Organizational Change: Theory and Practice.* Copyright 2002 by SAGE Publications. Reprinted by Permission of SAGE Publications.

Variables located in the top half of the model (environment, leadership, mission and strategy, and organizational culture) are identified as the *transformational factors*. Changes to these organizational factors are seen as likely caused by interactions with the external environment. Initiatives in this area are difficult to manage because they challenge core beliefs and assumptions about the organization and what it should be doing. They entail significantly new behavior by organizational members and major alterations to other variables in the model. However, when fundamental reorientation and re-creation are a necessity, they may represent the only viable approach to organizational rejuvenation and long-term success.[41]

The remaining variables are identified as the *transactional factors* because they are more directly involved in the day-to-day activities of the organization. Changes of an incremental or evolutionary nature can occur without necessarily triggering changes in the transformational factors. We see this in ongoing quality-improvement initiatives, management-development programs, work realignment, and other incremental interventions aimed at refining and improving internal practices in order to enhance fit and, therefore, performance.[42]

As Burke notes, transactional factors can also, at times, be used to help trigger changes of a more transformational nature. For example, organizational assessments that lead to alterations in reward systems, team management processes, or a new product/service initiative may trigger questions about culture and strategy. This creates awareness of the need for transformational changes that then could migrate back to other transactional factors. Collins reports that transformations in companies that went from "good to great"[43] often began their journey by trying to sort out how to better align their internal systems and processes with their customers. They ended up with transformational changes through having the right people engage in disciplined evaluations, followed by a disciplined, steady committed course of action.[44] As noted elsewhere in this book, an understanding of timing, trigger points, catalysts, and leverage can be used to stimulate self-assessment, organizational learning, and change that has proven very difficult to initiate, energize, and implement.

The Burke-Litwin model enriches our conceptual map of the organization. It provides a complex set of variables that will help explain organizational dynamics. By separating variables into transformational and transactional, the model gives us a way of examining the impact of changes of different variables. However, this complexity makes it more difficult to keep track of all variables and develop clear action plans. Additionally, while the model does have both the environment and individual/organizational performance as variables, these are viewed as just two of the 12 variables. As a result, there is no apparent flow from environment to organization to performance.

Both the 7-S and the Burke-Litwin Model are useful analytical tools. The choice of model is often one of personal preference—both can help a change agent. However, because of the limitations that we see in the 7-S model and the Burke-Litwin model, this book relies on the Nadler and Tushman model as it offers a relatively complex organizational analysis while maintaining an action focus.

Notes

1. Seigworth, G. (n.d.). A brief history of bloodletting. Retreived from http://www.pbs.org/wnet/redgold/basics/bloodlettinghistory.html.

2. Magna reverses strategy, plans to take parts subsidiaries private. (2004, October 26). *Globe and Mail*, p. B1.

3. Keenan, G. (2010, April 8). Magna tightens ties with Russian auto maker. *Globe and Mail*.

4. Bruch, H., & Gerber, P. (2005). Strategic change decisions: Doing the right change right. *Journal of Change Management, 5*(1), 99.

5. Bruch, H., & Gerber, P. (2005). Strategic change decisions: Doing the right change right. *Journal of Change Management, 5*(1), 98.

6. Stacey, R. D. (2003). *Strategic management of organisational dynamics: The challenge of complexity*. Englewood Cliffs, NJ: Prentice Hall.

7. See Holling, C. S. (1987). Simplifying the complex: The paradigms of ecological function and structure. *European Journal of Operations Research, 30*, 139–146; and Hurst, D. K. (1995). *Crisis and renewal: Meeting the challenge of organizational change*. Boston: Harvard Business Review Press.

8. Hegazy, Y. (2003). Value in troubled energy markets. *Energy Markets, 8*(7), 38–41.

9. See, for example, Bender, R., & Greenwald, R. (Eds.). (2003). *Sweatshop USA: The American sweatshop in historical perspective*. Routledge, London, UK; or Foo, L., & Fortunato, N. (2003, October). Free trade's looming threat to the world's garment workers. *Asian Labor Update*. Retrieved from http://digitalcommons.ilr.cornell.edu/cgi/viewcontent.cgi?article=1000&context=globaldocs.

10. Schumpeter, J. (1942). *Capitalism, socialism and democracy*. New York: Harper & Row.

11. Nadler, D. A., & Tushman, M. L. (1977). A diagnostic model for organizational behavior. In J. R. Hackman, E. E. Lawler, & L. W. Porter (Eds.), *Perspectives in behavior in organizations* (pp. 85–100). New York: McGraw-Hill.

12. Nadler, D. (1987). The effective management of organizational change. In J. W. Lorsch (Ed.), *Handbook of organizational behavior* (pp. 358–369). Englewood Cliffs, NJ.: Prentice Hall.

13. McManamy, R. (1995). Fourth quarterly cost report: South America—Hyperinflation dying off. *ENR, 235*(26), 43–45.

14. Peters, T., & Waterman, R. H. (1982). *In search of excellence*. New York: Harper & Row.

15. Material for the Dell story was drawn from Dell's do-over. (2009, October 26). *Business Week, 4152*, 36; and from Take two: Michael Dell pioneered a new business model at the firm that bears his name. Now he wants to overhaul it. (2008, May 1). *The Economist;*

and retrieved February 2010 from the Dell website, http://content.dell.com/ca/en/corp/about-dell-investor-info.aspx.

16. Yetton, P. W., Johnson, K. D., & Craig, J. R. (1994). Computer-aided architects: A case study of IT and strategic change. *Sloan Management Review, 35*(4), 57–68.

17. Grant, R. M., Shani, R., & Krishnan, R. (1994). TQM's challenge to management theory and practice. *Sloan Management Review, 35*(2), 25–36.

18. Gates, R. (2003, September 3). How not to reform intelligence. *Wall Street Journal,* p. A16. See also Flynn, S., & Kirkpatrick, J. J. (2005). *The Department of Homeland Security: The way ahead after a rocky start.* Written testimony before a hearing of the Committee on Homeland Security and Governmental Affairs, U.S. Senate, Washington, DC.

19. Burke, W.W. (2002). *Organization change: Theory and practice* (p. 191). Thousand Oaks, CA: Sage.

20. Sterman, J. (2001). Systems dynamic modeling. *California Management Review, 43*(4), 8–25.

21. Adapted from Sterman, J. (2001). Systems dynamic modeling. *California Management Review, 43*(4), 13.

22. Argyris, C., & Schön, D. (1996). *Organizational learning II: Theory, method and practice.* Reading, MA: Addison-Wesley.

23. Senge, P. (1990). *The strategy.* London: Doubleday/Century Business.

24. Adapted from Gogoi, P., & Arndt, M. (2003, March 3). McDonald's hamburger hell. *Business Week.*

25. Rao, A. R., Bergen, M. E., & Davis, S. (2000). How to fight a price war. *Harvard Business Review, 78*(2), 107–116.

26. Boosting productivity on the shop floor. (2003, September 12). *The Economist,* p. 62.

27. Quinn, R. E. (1991). *Beyond rational management.* San Francisco: Jossey-Bass.

28. See Quinn, R. E., et al. (1990). *Becoming a master manager.* New York: Wiley.

30. For a detailed treatment of this topic, see Weick, K. (1999). Organizational change and development. *Annual Review of Psychology;* Romanelli, E., & Tushman, M. L. (1994). Organizational transformation as punctuated equilibrium: An empirical test. *Academy of Management Journal, 34,* 1141–1166; and Gersick, C. G. G. (1991). Revolutionary change theories: A multilevel exploration of the punctuated equilibrium. *Academy of Management Review, 16,* 10–36.

31. Strebel, L. (1994, Winter). Choosing the right change path. *California Management Review,* 29–51.

32. Greiner, L. (1998, May–June). Evolution and revolution as organizations grow. *Harvard Business Review,* 55–67.

33. Beckhard, R., & Harris, R. T. (1987). *Organizational transitions: Managing complex change.* Reading, MA: Addisson-Wesley.

34. Mitleton-Kelly, E. (2003). The principles of complexity and enabling infrastructures. In Mitleton-Kelly, E., *Complex systems and evolutionary perspectives of organisations: The application of complexity theory to organisations.* London: London School of Economics Complexity & Organisational Learning Research Programme, Elsevier.

35. Stacey, R. D. (1996). *Strategic management and organizational dynamics* (2nd ed.). London: Pittman.

36. Noori, H., Deszca, G., Munro, H., & McWilliams, B. (1999). Developing the right breakthrough product/service: An application of the umbrella methodology, Parts A & B. *International Journal of Technology Management, 17,* 544–579.

37. Letterman, E. (n.d.). Retrieved December 2010 from http://thinkexist.com/quotation/luck_is_what_happens_when_preparation_meets/11990.html.

38. Waterman, R. Jr., Peters, T., & Phillips, J. R. (1980). Structure is not organisation. *Business Horizons, 23*(3), 14–26; Pascale, R., & Athos, A. (1981). *The art of Japanese management.* London: Penguin; and Peters, T., & Waterman, R. (1982). *In search of excellence.* New York, London: Harper & Row.

39. Effective change in higher education. Retrieved from http://www.effectingchange. luton.ac.uk/approaches_to_change/index.php?content=default (now defunct).

40. Burke, W.W. (2002). *Organizational change: Theory and practice.* Thousand Oaks, CA: Sage.

41. Nadler, D. A., & Tushman, M. L. (1989). Organizational frame bending: Principles for managing reorientation. *Academy of Management Executive, 3*(3), 194–204.

42. Evans, J. R. (1997). Critical linkages in the Baldrige Award criteria: Research models and educational challenges. *Quality Management Journal, 5*(1), 13–30.

43. Collins, J. (2001). *Good to great: Why some companies make the leap…and others don't.* New York: HarperBusiness.

44. Webber, A. (2001). Good questions, great answers: An interview with Jim Collins. *Fast Company*, p. 90.

CHAPTER 4

Building and Energizing the Need for Change

You never want a serious crisis to go to waste.

—Rham Emanuel, President Obama's Chief of Staff[1]

CHAPTER OVERVIEW

This chapter asks the question "Why change?"

- It develops a framework for understanding the need for change based on making sense of external and internal organizational data and the change leaders' personal concerns and perspectives.
- The chapter describes what makes organizations ready for change and provides a questionnaire to rate an organization's readiness.
- It outlines how change leaders can create awareness for change.
- Finally, the chapter outlines the importance of the change vision and how change leaders can create a meaningful vision that energizes and focuses action.

In Chapter 2, we discussed the concept of unfreezing as a precondition to change. How can an organization and its people move to something new if their current mindset and response repertoire are not open to alternative paths and actions?

> You are in a large auditorium filled with people when suddenly you smell smoke and someone yells, "Fire!" You leap to your feet, exit the building, and call 911.

This situation above is straightforward. A crisis makes the need for change clear and dramatic. It demands an immediate response and the required action is understood—even more so if the institution has taken fire-safety planning seriously. Most people know the key actions: Where to exit? How to avoid panic? Who should be notified? Who should do the notifying?

However, in many situations, the need for change is vague and appropriate action is unclear. For example, even in an emergency, if there have been no "fires" for some time, people may have become complacent and warning systems might be ignored or broken and action plans forgotten. A parallel to this might explain the lack of action with the mortgage meltdown in the United States in 2007. Some economists and financial experts had raised alarms as early as 2003[2] (including the FBI in 2004[3]) over flawed financial practices and regulations. However, their warnings about the need to regulate mortgage lenders were ignored. The prevailing perspective within the Bush Administration was that regulations needed to be minimized because they got in the way of free markets and the generation of personal wealth. Before the meltdown, the need for change was evident to only a few people.

Past experiences may cause people to become not only complacent but also cynical about warnings. If false alarms have been regular occurrences, people will come to ignore them. If employees are told that there is a crisis when similar alerts in the past have proven to be false alarms, they will tend to discount the warning. If people are busy and they don't want to be sidetracked, they won't prepare for events that they think aren't going to happen. Remember the press reports concerning the H1N1 flu pandemic in the summer and fall of 2009 and how they changed by the winter of 2010? In the fall, there was a sense of panic, with people lining up overnight to get inoculated. By February, journalists were writing that the World Health Organization (WHO) had overstated the threat, as they had with Bird Flu. As such reports multiply and become the fodder for water-cooler and Internet conversations, will the public take WHO warnings as seriously next time[4]? When leaders cry "wolf" too often, who will take them seriously when the threat is real? Even trained professionals can miss obvious cues, as in the story below.

> A few years ago, my father was in intensive care, hooked to a heart monitor. Shortly after I arrived to visit him, the emergency alarm went off, but no one responded. I ran for help but was told not to worry—the alarm goes off all the time—just hit the reset button. The health care professionals had clearly adjusted their behavior to discount false alarms, but needless to say, I was left feeling anything but secure concerning the quality

of the system designed to monitor the need for change in my dad's treatment (G. Deszca).

Change agents need to demonstrate that the need for change is real and important. Only then will people unfreeze from past patterns. This is easier said than done. From 2008 through to the winter and spring of 2009, General Motors (GM) struggled to convince the United Auto Workers Union (UAW) that they needed significant financial concessions to survive. The UAW initially took the position that GM had signed a deal and should live up to it. However, the collapse of consumers' demand for automobiles in the summer of 2008 led to fears of bankruptcy. Political pressure from the U.S. and Canadian governments on both GM and the UAW escalated in the wake of bailout requests. As a result of this pressure, the UAW abandoned its position that "We have done our share." Concessions followed during the next 9 months, covering everything from staffing levels, pay rates, and health care benefits to pensions.[5] When it comes to raising alarms concerning the need for change, it is sometimes tough to know when and how to get through to people. With GM, it took going to the edge of the precipice and beyond. They had to go bankrupt!

Many change-management programs fail because there is sustained confusion and disagreement over (a) why there is the need for change and (b) what needs changing. Ask organization members—from production workers to VPs—why their organization is not performing as well as it could and opinions abound and differ. Even well-informed opinions are often fragmentary and contradictory. Individuals' perspectives on the need for change depend on their roles and levels in the organization, their environments, perceptions, performance measures and incentives, and the training and experience they have received. The reactions of peers, supervisors, and subordinates as well as an individual's own personality all influence how each person looks at the world. When there has been no well-thought-out effort to develop a shared awareness concerning the need for change, then piecemeal, disparate, and conflicting assessments of the situation are likely to pervade the organization.[6]

People often see change as something that others need to embrace and take the lead with. One hears: "Why don't they understand…;" "Why can't they see what is happening;" or "They must be doing this intentionally." But stupidity, blindness, and maliciousness are typically not the primary reasons for inappropriate or insufficient organizational change. Differences in perspective affect what is seen and experienced. As the attributions of causation shift, so too do the beliefs about who or what is the cause of the problems and what should be done.[7]

In terms of the change management process, the focus of this chapter is on the "why change" box contained in Figure 4.1. To address this, change leaders need to determine the need for change and the degree of choice available to them and/or the organization about whether to change. Further, they need to develop the change vision. Without these in hand, they are in no position to engage others in conversations about the path forward.

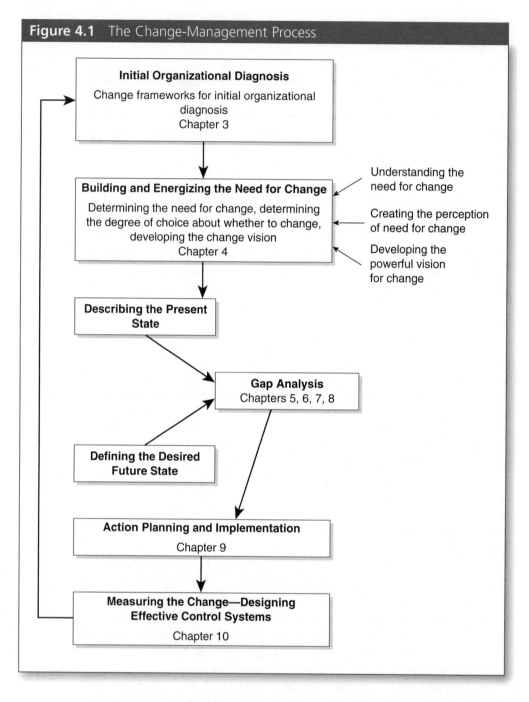

Figure 4.1   The Change-Management Process

This chapter asks change leaders, be they vice presidents or line operators, to seek out multiple perspectives as they examine the need for change. There is typically no shortage of things that could be done with available resources. What, then, gets the money? What is the compelling reason for disrupting the status quo? Are there choices about changing and, if so, what are they? In many cases, it is not clear that change is needed. In these cases, the first step is for leaders to make a compelling case for why energy and resources need to be committed to a particular vision. Addressing these concerns advances the unfreezing process, focuses attention, and galvanizes support for further action.

But recognizing the need and mobilizing interest are not sufficient—a change leader also needs to communicate a clear sense of the desired result of the change. Change leaders do this by creating a compelling vision of the change and what life will look like after it is implemented. This approach to creating momentum is the focus of the latter half of this chapter.

Developing a Knowledge for the Need for Change

The change process won't energize people until they begin to understand the need for change. People may have a general sense that things are amiss, but they will not mobilize their energies until the need is framed, understood, and believed. An organization may have amassed data on customers, production processes, suppliers, competitors, organization financials, and other factors, but nothing will happen until someone takes the information and communicates a compelling argument concerning the need for change. Advancing the change agenda is aided by being able to address the following questions:

DEVELOPING AN ASSESSMENT OF THE NEED FOR CHANGE

1. **What do you see as the need for change and the important dimensions and issues that underpin it?** How much confidence do you have in your assessment and why should others have confidence in that assessment? Is the appraisal of the need for change a solid organizational and environmental assessment, or is it a response to your personal needs and beliefs?

2. **Have you investigated the perspectives of internal and external stakeholders?** Do you know who has a stake in the matter and do you understand their perspectives on the need for change? Have you talked only to like-minded individuals?

3. **Can the different perspectives be integrated in ways that offer the possibility for a collaborative solution?** How can you avoid a divisive "we/they" dispute?

4. **Have you developed and communicated the message concerning the need for change in ways that have the potential to move the organization to a higher state of readiness for and willingness to change?** Or have your deliberations left change recipients feeling pressured and coerced into doing something they don't agree with, don't understand, or fear will come back to haunt them?

The challenges at this stage for change leaders are to develop the information they need to assess the situation, develop their views on the need for change, understand how others see that need, and create awareness and legitimacy around the need for change when a shared awareness is lacking. To make headway on these questions and challenges, change leaders need to seek out and make sense of external data, the perspectives of stakeholders, the internal data, and their own personal concerns and perspectives (Figure 4.2 outlines these factors).

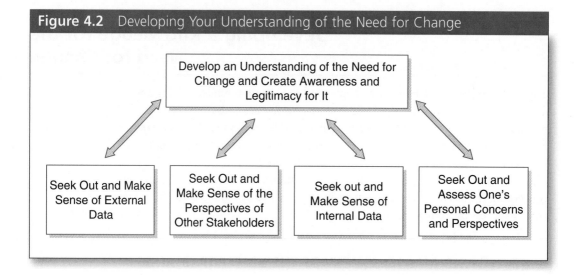

Figure 4.2 Developing Your Understanding of the Need for Change

Seek Out and Make Sense of External Data

Change leaders should scan the organization's external environment to gain knowledge about and assess the need for change. Getting outside one's personal perceptual box helps to avoid blind spots that are created by "closed-loop learning"*.[8] Change agents may make incremental improvements and succeed in improving short-term results. However, change leaders may not be doing what is needed to assess the risks and opportunities and to adapt to the environment over the long term.[9] Executives tend to spend too little time reflecting on the external environment and its implications for their organizations.[10]

An organization that is experiencing an externally driven crisis will feel the sense of urgency around the need for change. In this case, the change initiator's task will be easier.[11] This crisis can be used to mobilize the system and galvanize people's actions. Without this, many within the organization may not perceive a need for change even though the warning clouds or the unaddressed opportunities may be keeping the change leader awake at night.

---

*Closed-loop learning is learning that focuses on current practices and perspectives rather than developing a deeper understanding of the complex interactions underpinning the situation.

The value of seeing organizations as open systems cannot be underestimated. This analytic approach and the learning it promotes play an important role in the development of awareness, improved vision, and flexibility and adaptability in the organization.[12] Often the question becomes for the change leader: "Which external data do I attend to?" A change agent can drown in information without a disciplined approach for the collection, accumulation, and integration of data. Consider how complex the innocuous-sounding task of benchmarking can become.[13] The absence of a disciplined approach to data gathering may mean that time is wasted; that potentially important data go uncollected or are forgotten; or the data are never translated into useful information for the organization.

Some sources for data will be concrete (trade papers, published research, and news reports), while others will be less tangible (comments collected informally from suppliers, customers, or vendors at trade shows). Data collection can take a variety of forms: setting aside time for reading, participating in trade shows and professional conferences, visiting vendors' facilities, and/or attending executive education programs. Just as important, the change leader should recruit others to collect information, record it, and then review it systematically and in a timely fashion that makes it accessible and useful. Working without awareness of the external environment is the equivalent of driving blind. And yet it happens all the time. For a variety of reasons, ranging from a heavy workload to complacency to arrogance, organizational leaders can be lulled into relying on past successes and strategies rather than investigating and questioning. In so doing, they risk failing to develop an organization's capacity to adapt to a changing environment.[14]

Seek Out and Make Sense of the Perspectives of Stakeholders

Change leaders need to be aware of the perspectives of key internal and external stakeholders and work to understand their perspectives, predispositions, and reasons for supporting or resisting change. This will inform change agents' assessment of the situation and allow them to frame their approaches in ways that incorporate many stakeholders into the vision.

Externally, these stakeholders may include suppliers, bankers, governmental officials, customers, and alliance and network partners. Internally, the stakeholders will include those individuals who are directly and indirectly affected by the change. If the change involved a reorganization of production processes, the internal stakeholders would include production supervisors, employees, union officials, human resources (recruitment and training implications), finance (budget and control processes), sales and marketing (customer service implications), IT (information implications), and engineering managers.

The point of view of the person championing the need for change will likely differ from the perspectives of other stakeholders. What is interesting and important to those stakeholders will vary, and this will affect what data and people they pay attention to and what they do with the information. If the change leader hopes to enlist their support or at least minimize their resistance, the leader needs to capture and consider their perspectives and the underlying rationale.[15] Particular stakeholders may still remain ambivalent or opposed to the change, but not seeking them out and listening is likely to make things worse. Why create resistance if you don't have to?

All of this highlights the importance of doing preparatory analysis and having a purposeful discussion, if possible, with affected stakeholders and those who understand their perspectives and can potentially influence them. It will increase the change leader's awareness and sensitivity to the context, inform and strengthen the analysis, and indicate blind spots and alternative explanations and paths.

CHANGE VISION AT AN INSURANCE FIRM

When a North American insurance firm acquired one of its competitors, the senior manager in charge of integrating the acquisition was determined to have every employee understand the need for change, the new vision, and its implications. On the day the deal was announced, she made a live presentation (along with the CEO and other key officials) to employees at the head office of the acquisition and streamed the meeting live to all of the acquisition's branch offices and facilities, as well as into the parent organization. She honored the acquisition's senior management team, who were present, communicated the reasons for the acquisition and its implications for change, took questions, and encouraged employees to contact her with questions or concerns. She set up a special website and phone line to answer questions in a timely and direct manner and followed this with visits to all the offices, key customers, and suppliers over the next 2 months. She held two additional town-hall meetings with employees over the next year to communicate the status of integration activities and reduce anxiety.

An integration team from the acquiring firm was deployed to the acquired firm the day the deal was announced. After introducing themselves and their mandate, specific initiatives were commenced with staff to align key systems and processes and develop strategic and tactical plans. Leaders from the integration team visited key groups at all levels in the acquired organization to discuss the need for change, to discuss their current position in the marketplace, and to review how the roles and responsibilities were currently organized. Integration team members communicated what they knew, listened hard, and made firm commitments to get back with answers by specific dates. The integration team honored those commitments, including the communication of the new organization's strategic and tactical plans and clarification of each person's employment status, within 90 days of the acquisition. Like the senior manager responsible for the integration of the acquisition, the integration team communicated candidly, listened, and adjusted to assessments of the need for change and the strategic path forward, based upon what they learned. The team's approach tapped into the emotional needs of "acquired" employees, reducing their anxieties, instilling hope for the future, and illustrating that their views and concerns were heard. Employee surveys, low absentee and turnover rates, and performance data confirmed this.[16]

The change agents for the insurance firm did their homework when developing and communicating the need for change. They openly engaged stakeholders in dialogue, listened and responded with care and consideration, and then proceeded to the next stage in the change process. Too many executives underestimate the need for communication. There is never too much top-level communication and support, but there is often too little listening. A rule of thumb for managers is to talk up a change initiative at least three times more than you think is needed![17] One change leader states that messages need to be communicated 17 times before they get heard![18]

Seek Out and Make Sense of Internal Data

It is no surprise that change leaders need to pay careful attention to internal organizational data when developing their assessment of the need for a particular initiative. Change agents who command internal respect and credibility understand the fundamentals of what is going on within a firm. Change leaders need to know what can be inferred from internal information and measures, how these are currently being interpreted by organizational members, and how they may be leading the firm down the wrong path. Some of this will be in the form of so-called hard data—the sort that can be found in the formal information system and that is often numeric (e.g., customer retention and satisfaction, service profitability, cycle time, and employee absenteeism). Other valuable information will be soft data, the intuitive information gathered from walking the halls and plant floor and having discussions with critical stakeholders. For example, do employees generally pick up litter such as candy wrappers, or is that task left exclusively to the janitorial staff? The former often indicates widespread pride and feelings of ownership in an organization.

Seek Out and Assess Your Personal Concerns and Perspectives

"Know thyself" is a critical dictum for change leaders. Change agents need a good understanding of their strengths and weaknesses, attitudes, values, beliefs, and motivations. They need to know how they take in information and how they interpret and make decisions. They need to recognize their preferences, prejudices, and blind spots. As change agents expand their self-awareness, they are freer to ask questions and seek help when they need it.[19]

> "I think it's a combination of how self-aware people are and how honest they are. I think if someone is self-aware, then they can always continue to grow. If they're not self-aware, I think it's harder for them to evolve or adapt beyond who they already are."
>
> Tony Hsieh, CEO, Zappos.Com, Inc.[20]

During the Cuban Missile Crisis, Collins and Porras report that Kennedy was incredibly comfortable with expressing what he did not know and asking many questions before passing judgments.[21] This led to informed decision making that may have saved the world from World War III. Many change leaders have difficulty publically owning the fact that they do not have all the answers and demonstrating a real interest in listening and learning.

Whenever we, the authors, work with university student groups who are attempting organizational change, we caution them not to assume that their perspectives are held by all. Students often fail to understand their own biases and needs and how they differ from those of others involved in a change initiative. They believe that they understand the situation and know what must change; this attitude can create significant barriers to accomplishing the change objectives. The strength of their concerns combined with their lack of self-awareness creates blind spots and causes them to block out dissenting perspectives. When students talk to stakeholders, they may receive polite responses and assume that this implies a commitment to action. Statements such as "That's an interesting approach" are taken as support rather than as neutral comments. Students' inability to read subtle cues leads them astray.

In an extreme attempt to protect himself and his followers from his personal shortcomings and cult-like reputation, Nehru, one of the founding fathers of modern, independent India, used an alias when he wrote the following about himself in a prominent publication in 1937. The backdrop was the struggle for independence from Britain, which was achieved 11 years later.

> What lies behind that mask of his, what desires, what will to power, what insatiate longings? Men like (Nehru) with all their capacity for great work, are unsafe in democracy...every psychologist knows that the mind is ultimately a slave to the heart and logic can always be made to fit in with the desires and irrepressible urges of a person...(Nehru's) conceit is already formidable. It must be checked. We want no Caesars.[22]
>
> —Nehru writing in the press about himself, using an alias.

Nehru's deep commitment to India's independence did not blind him to how his own ego and the burgeoning hero worship that he was experiencing might impair the goal of a democratic India that would need an electorate that exercised thoughtful discourse and informed decision making. As such, he publicly noted the trend toward hero worship and its intoxicating impact on himself and his followers.

This section asks change leaders to consider their readiness for leading a change initiative and the roles that they will play in the process. It asks change agents to assess their skills, abilities, and predispositions to assess and guide the change. In Chapter 8, change agents will again be asked to look in a mirror and assess their predispositions toward various change-agent roles.

Toolkit Exercise 4.1 asks you to consider a specific situation you are familiar with and develop an assessment of the need for change.

The Organization's Readiness for Change

Understanding the need for change and creating a vision for change are closely linked. Diagnosing where an organization is in the present moment is a prerequisite for figuring out its future direction. Beckhard and Harris argue that addressing the question "Why change?" is a necessary precondition to being able to define the desired future state or the vision. If the question of "Why change?" is never meaningfully addressed, no one should expect the emergence of any sense of a shared vision. The answer to "Why?" is a prerequisite to the "What?" and the "How?" of change.

While dissatisfaction with the status quo by senior managers is certainly very helpful in advancing change, it is unlikely to be a *sufficient* condition.[23] Spector argues that the creation of dissatisfaction among others is needed. This dissatisfaction can be developed by sharing competitive information, benchmarking the organization's performance against others, challenging inappropriate behaviors through highlighting their impact, developing a vision for the future that creates frustration with the present state, and simply mandating dissatisfaction if one has the clout. Being dissatisfied with the status quo helps to ready the organization for change. That readiness depends on previous organizational experiences, managerial support, the organization's openness to change, its exposure to disquieting information about the status quo, and the systems promoting or blocking change in the organization.

Change initiators may understand the need for change, but other key stakeholders may not be prepared to recognize that need. Newspaper accounts of the failure to react in time are all too common (e.g., Chrysler in the auto industry[24], Kmart in retailing[25], Hollinger in media[26]). Though a litany of reasons are offered in the press, two common themes emerge: (1) Management failed to attend to the warning clouds that were clearly visible well in advance; and (2) when management took actions, they did too little too late. Past patterns of success can lead to active inertia (doing more of the same), flawed environmental scanning and assessments, and other factors that will be discussed later in the chapter that sabotage organization members' capacity to successfully adapt.[27]

An organization's readiness for change is determined by the previous change experiences of its members, the flexibility and adaptability of the organizational culture, the openness, commitment and involvement of leadership in preparing the organization for change, and member confidence in the leadership. It is also influenced by the organizational structure, the information, reward, and measurement systems, resource availability, and the organization's flexibility and alignment with the proposed change.[28] This theme goes back to Chapter 3's discussion of the Nadler and Tushman model and the importance of alignment. Readiness is advanced when organizational members can see how the new alignment will produce better outcomes and believe that realignment can be achieved. An organization's readiness for change will influence its ability to both attend to environmental signals for change and listen to internal voices saying that change is needed.[29]

Previous experiences affect the receptiveness to future change. If organizational members have experienced more gain than pain from past change initiatives, they will be more predisposed to try something new. However, there is also the risk that they may resist changes that divert them from initiatives that have worked in the past.

If previous change experiences have been predominantly negative and unproductive, employees tend to become disillusioned and cynical ("we tried and it didn't work" attitude).[30] However, under the right conditions, this situation may produce increased resolve concerning the need for change. (Reactions to past change experiences will be discussed further in Chapter 7.)

Writers regularly report that the development and maintenance of top management's support is crucial to change success.[31] If senior managers are visibly supporting the initiative, are respected, and define and tie their success to the change initiative, then the organization is likely to be receptive to change. However, it is not unusual to find differences of opinion concerning change at the senior management level, so a lack of unanimous support is a reality that many change leaders must navigate. Perhaps more troubling situations than the lack of visible support occur when senior management assures change agents of support but fails to provide it at crucial moments and engages in passive forms of resistance.

Organizations that have well-developed external scanning mechanisms are likely to be aware of environmental changes. Structures and systems that encourage the collection of benchmark data will provide evidence to support the need for change and will help make an organization ready for change.[32] If the culture supports environmental scanning and encourages a focus on identifying and resolving problems rather than "turf protection," organizations will be more open to change.

READYING AN ORGANIZATION FOR CHANGE

Armenkis and his colleagues[33] identified factors that signal an organization's readiness for change. Their list includes:

1. The need for change is identified in terms of the gap between the current state and the desired state.

2. People believe that the proposed change is the right change to make.

3. The confidence of organizational members has been bolstered so that they believe they can accomplish the change.

4. The change has the support of key individuals the organizational members look to.

5. The "what's in it for me/us" question has been addressed.

Holt was concerned about an organization's readiness for change and developed a scale based on four beliefs among employees: They could implement a change, the change is appropriate for the organization, leaders are committed, and the proposed change is needed.[34] Judge and Douglass were also interested in calibrating an organization's readiness for change and utilized a rigorous approach to identify **eight dimensions related to readiness:**

1. Trustworthy leadership—the ability of senior leaders to earn the trust of others and credibly show others how to meet their collective goals

2. Trusting followers—the ability of nonexecutives to constructively dissent or willingly follow the new path

3. Capable champions—the ability of the organization to attract and retain capable champions

4. Involved middle management—the ability of middle managers to effectively link senior managers with the rest of the organization

5. Innovative culture—the ability of the organization to establish norms of innovation and encourage innovative activity

6. Accountable culture—the ability of the organization to carefully steward resources and successfully meet predetermined deadlines

7. Effective communications—the ability of the organization to effectively communicate vertically, horizontally, and with customers

8. Systems thinking—the ability of the organization to focus on root causes and recognize interdependencies within and outside the organization's boundaries.[35]

Table 4.1 contains a readiness-for-change questionnaire. It reflects the questions and issues raised in this section and provides another method for stimulating a change leader's thinking about estimating an organization's readiness for change.[36] By considering what is promoting and inhibiting change readiness, change agents can take action to enhance readiness—a change task in and of itself. For example, if rewards for innovation and change are seen to be lacking, or if employees believe they lack the needed skills, steps can be taken to address such matters. This is essentially what was done at Capital One Financial. There, change readiness was consciously developed, aligned with supportive systems and structures, and then put to use as a source of competitive advantage.[37] Developing change readiness is an important matter in both public[38] and private organizations.

Creating Awareness of the Need for Change

When an organization is open to change, thinking individuals will still want to critically assess the evidence concerning the need for change. The change leader may experience blanket resistance and defensiveness or may experience more localized opposition. Individuals may recognize the need for change in some

Table 4.1 Rate the Organization's Readiness for Change

Readiness Dimensions	Readiness Score
Previous Change Experiences	
1. Has the organization had positive experience with change?	If yes, Score +1
2. Has the organization had failure experience with change?	Score −1
3. What is the mood of the organization: upbeat and positive?	Score +1
4. What is the mood of the organization: negative and cynical?	Score −2
5. Does the organization appear to be resting on its laurels?	Score −1
Executive Support	
6. Are senior managers directly involved in sponsoring the change?	Score +2
7. Is there a clear picture of the future?	Score +1
8. Is executive success dependent on the change occurring?	Score +1
9. Has management ever demonstrated a lack of support?	Score −1
Credible Leadership and Change Champions	
10. Are senior leaders in the organization trusted?	Score +1
11. Are senior leaders able to credibly show others how to achieve their collective goals?	Score +1
12. Is the organization able to attract and retain capable change champions?	Score +1
13. Are middle managers able to effectively link senior managers with the rest of the organization?	Score +1
14. Are senior leaders likely to view the proposed change as generally appropriate for the organization?	Score +2
15. Will the proposed change be viewed as needed by the senior leaders?	Score +2
Openness to Change	
16. Does the organization have scanning mechanisms to monitor the environment?	Score +1
17. Is there a culture of scanning and paying attention to those scans?	Score +1
18. Does the organization have the ability to focus on root causes and recognize interdependencies both inside and outside the organization's boundaries?	Score +1
19. Does "turf" protection exist in the organization?	Score −1
20. Are the senior managers hidebound or locked into the use of past strategies, approaches, and solutions?	Score −1
21. Are employees able to constructively voice their concerns or support?	Score +1
22. Is conflict dealt with openly, with a focus on resolution?	Score +1
23. Is conflict suppressed and smoothed over?	Score −1
24. Does the organization have a culture that is innovative and encourages innovative activities?	Score +1
25. Does the organization have communications' channels that work effectively in all directions?	Score +1

26. Will the proposed change be viewed as generally appropriate for the organization by those not in senior leadership roles?   Score +2

27. Will the proposed change be viewed as needed by those not in senior leadership roles?   Score +2

Rewards for Change

28. Does the reward system pay for innovation and change?   Score +1
29. Does the reward system focus exclusively on short-term results?   Score −1
30. Are people censured for attempting change and failing?   Score −1

Measures for Change and Accountability

31. Are there good measures available for assessing the need for change and tracking progress?   Score +1
32. Does the organization attend to the data that it collects?   Score +1
33. Does the organization measure and evaluate customer satisfaction?   Score +1
34. Is the organization able to carefully steward resources and successfully meet predetermined deadlines?   Score +1

The scores can range from −10 to +30.

The purpose of this tool is to raise awareness concerning readiness for change and is not meant to be used as a research tool.

If the organization scores below 10, it is not likely ready for change and change will be very difficult.

The higher the score, the more ready the organization is for change. Use the scores to focus your attention on areas that need strengthening in order to improve readiness.

Change is never "simple," but when organizational factors supportive of change are in place, the task of the change agent is manageable.

Table 4.1 is adapted from Stewart. (1994). Rate Your Readiness to Change scale. *Fortune*, 106–110; Holt, D. (2002). See also Readiness for change: The development of a scale. *Organization Development Abstracts, Academy of Management Proceedings*; and Judge, W., & Douglas, T. (2009). Organizational change capacity: The systematic development of a scale. *Journal of Organizational Change Management, 22*(6), 635–649.

departments and functions but be resistant to recognizing the need for change as it gets closer to home. If they see only the unraveling of what they've worked to accomplish and/or unpleasant alternatives ahead for them, they will be very reluctant to embrace change proposals. Even when the need for change is broadly recognized, action does not necessarily follow.

GARBAGE SERVICES IN NAPLES, ITALY

Naples, Italy, lived with a garbage problem for years. Poor management, organized crime and ineffective political leadership allowed the matter to fester and escalate. In 2008, worldwide coverage of the problem drew attention and political promises for action, as 55,000 tons of uncollected garbage filled city streets, and 110,000 to 120,000 tons awaited treatment in municipal storage sites. Though the streets are now cleaner, resolution has been slow and suspect. Untold tons of irresponsibly (some would argue criminally) handled waste continue to reside in illegal landfills that dot the countryside, or they were shipped elsewhere for "disposal." The results have fouled the environment, endangered health, and seriously harmed Naples' economy.[39]

In the story above, the need for change seems obvious. However, the politicians of the city were reluctant to take the difficult steps to deal with the problems. Clearly, Naples and her citizens were not ready for the type of change needed.

Once change leaders understand the need for change, they can take **different approaches to heighten the awareness of the need throughout the organization.** Change leaders can:

1. Create a crisis, increase awareness that crisis conditions exist, or communicate that a crisis is on the horizon.

2. Develop a vision that creates dissatisfaction with the status quo in the organization.

3. Find a champion-of-change leader who will build awareness of the need for change and articulate the vision for change.

4. Focus on common or superordinate goals.

5. Create dissatisfaction with the status quo through education, information, and exposure to superior practices and processes of both competitors and noncompetitors. This can include research on effective organizations.

The first method is a form of shock treatment and involves either **making the organization aware that it is in or near a crisis or creating a crisis that needs to be solved.** Many of the dramatic turnaround stories that are reported are successful because the actions of people were galvanized and focused by the necessity for action. In the face of crisis, people find it difficult to deny the need to change and to change **NOW.** When the crisis is real, the issue will be one of showing others a way out that they will follow if they have any confidence in its viability, given that the alternatives are far from attractive.[40]

At times, managers will be tempted to generate a crisis, to create a sense of urgency to change and mobilize staff around a change initiative that may or may not be fully justified. Creating a sense of crisis when one does not really exist must be approached with care.[41] If mishandled, it may be viewed as manipulative and result in heightened cynicism and reduced commitment. The change leader's personal credibility and trustworthiness are then at stake. The reputation developed in and around change initiatives casts a long shadow, for better or worse. The currencies that change agents use are credibility and trustworthiness. These take a long time to develop and can be quickly squandered.[42]

An extension of the crisis is the "burn or sink your boats approach." In this case, the change leader takes the process one step further and cuts off any avenue of retreat. That is, there is no going back. This approach is based on the belief that this will lead to increased commitment to the selected course of action. While it may aid in focusing attention, this approach can increase many of the risks outlined above. In particular, individuals may resent being forced into a situation against their will. It may produce compliant and even energized behavior in the short term due to the absence of alternatives, but it can give rise to undesirable long-term consequences if the actions come to be viewed as being inappropriate or unfair. Consequences can include elevated levels of mistrust, reduced commitment, and poor performance.[43]

CREATING URGENCY AT PHILIPS

Shortly after becoming CEO at Philips in 1990, Jan Timmer met off-site with his top 100 executives. He explained that the company's survival was in jeopardy and distributed a simulated press release of Philips' bankruptcy. Timmer used this dramatic approach to change managerial mindsets and create a process that would focus managers' attention on new goals. His approach was hardnosed and explicit: Become part of the change or leave. The launch of Operation Centurion marked the end of organizational life as previously experienced by those senior managers.[44]

The crisis Timmer inherited in 1990 was real and he knew that tough decisions were needed. He subsequently ended Philips' involvement in the telecommunications equipment business, eliminated 50,000 jobs, and in the process inherited the nickname "the Butcher of Eindhoven." While the company did avoid bankruptcy, the product and service areas that were targeted as the future did not perform well and revenues sagged, resulting in his replacement in 1996.[45]

A second approach to enhancing the need for change is by **identifying a transformational vision based on higher-order values**, such as the delivery of superb service and responsiveness. Transformational visions tap into the need for individuals to go beyond themselves, to make a contribution, to do something worthwhile and meaningful, and to serve a cause greater than themselves. These appeals can provide powerful mechanisms to unfreeze an organization and create conditions for change. In addition, transformational visions pull people toward an idealized future and a positive approach to needed change.

Cynics in an organization may reject these vision appeals for several reasons. They may see them as superficial, naive, ill-advised, off-target, or designed simply to serve the interests of those making the pronouncements. If organizational members have previously heard visionary pronouncements, only to see them ignored or discarded, they may believe the most recent iteration is simply the current "flavor of the week" approach to change.

Change agents need to ask themselves if they are really serious about following through on the values and action orientation that underlie their visionary appeals. If they are not, then they should stop rather than contribute to the buildup of organizational cynicism and alienation that accompanies unmet expectations. Nevertheless, the power of truly transformational visions should not be underestimated. How else do we understand the response to change leaders such as Mahatma Ghandi and Nelson Mandela?

A third approach to enhancing the need for change is through **transformational leadership**. Leadership in general and transformational leadership in particular continue to command attention in the change literature—not surprising, given its stature in western culture and mythology. [46] From George Washington to Adolf Hitler, from Nelson Mandela and Mother Teresa to Saddam Hussein, we've elevated the heroes and condemned the villains.

The same is true for the corporate world. Steve Jobs's resuscitation of Apple, Mukesh Ambani's leadership at Reliance, one of India's most valuable companies, Anne Mulcahy's transformation of Xerox, Thomas Tighe's work at Direct Relief International (a not-for-profit organization), Oprah Winfrey's growth of a media empire, Richard Branson's entrepreneurial initiatives at Virgin, and Frank Stronach's development of Magna's auto parts empire provide examples of the work of successful transformational leaders. The appeal of charismatic and transformational individuals is powerful. They have the capacity to create strong, positive responses and a willingness to change in followers that often overrides the followers' personal concerns. However, corporate scandals (e.g., Bernie Ebbers of WorldCom, Bernie Madoff of Madoff Investment Securities, and Angelo Mazilo of Countrywide Financial) remind people of the risks of idolizing CEO exemplars. Even Jack Welsh's image took a beating with published reports of his divorce battles and the size and nature of his retirement package. [47]

Caution is needed if you are relying on charisma to induce followers to change an organization. In an example cited earlier in this chapter, Nehru's concern over the impact of his charisma caused him to take public steps to rein it in. If the use of charisma is thought to be helpful, certain questions come to mind. First of all, do you have the necessary skills? Many people lack the capacities needed to create a charismatic response in others and they may also lack access to someone who supports the change and possesses those skills. More important is this the best approach to mobilizing people around a vision of change? Charismatic appeals can prove powerful and helpful (Barack Obama's successful 2008 presidential campaign attests to this), but there are good reasons for people to be suspicious of charismatic appeals because history demonstrates that personal magnetism is not always directed toward desirable outcomes.

It is important to note that many leaders are very effective change agents without being particularly charismatic. Some of those who have proven to be most influential in nurturing long-term organizational success have been much quieter in their approach.[48] Such a list would include Meg Whitman, former CEO, E-Bay, and Darwin Smith, CEO, Kimberly-Clarke.

A fourth way of stimulating awareness of a need for change is by **taking the time to identify common or shared goals and working out ways to achieve them.** Finding common areas of agreement is a very useful way to avoid and/or surmount resistance to change. Instead of focusing on what might be lost, an examination of the risks of not taking action and what will be gained by taking action can create momentum for change. This is often achieved by having people seriously consider their longer-term interests (rather than their immediate positions) and the higher-order and longer-term goals that they would like to see pursued. If the change leader can focus on the needs of resisting individuals or groups, new and interesting perspectives on change can emerge. Shared interest in and commitment to higher-order or superordinate goals can provide a powerful stimulus for commitment and mobilization.

Fifth, information and education can be used to raise awareness of the need for change. In many respects, this is the inverse of the "sink your boats" command-and-control approach to change, because it seeks to build awareness and support through information rather than edict. Reluctance to change may be a result of lack of information or confusion about multiple and sometimes conflicting sources of information. This can be overcome with a well-organized communications campaign that provides employees with the needed information (e.g., best practices, benchmark data about the practices and approaches of others, visits with others to see and hear about their practices, competitive data, and other research).[49] Research on effective organizations can provide a compare-and-contrast picture to an organization's current mode of operation and that process can stimulate discussion and facilitate change.

EDUCATING PROGRAMMERS AT GTECH

GTECH was an extremely successful gaming technology and services company. In 2002, however, Richard Koppel, VP of Advanced Technologies, knew change was needed. "Our systems were old, inflexible, and highly proprietary...Unless the company overhauled its technology platform, we wouldn't be able to innovate quickly or affordably enough to meet customers' needs." The executive at GTECH supported him, but there was stiff resistance from below. To create a sense of urgency, he and other executives repeatedly visited with the product developers to educate them about what was at risk. Discussions during regular staff meetings, dissemination of articles, and having GTECH's software developers talk about the issue with peers in other high-tech organizations further reinforced the message concerning the need for change.[50] Resistance was reduced as a result of these actions and the subsequent changes contributed to significant improvements to their financial performance over the next several years.

Once again, the change agent's credibility is crucial. If employees are suspicious of the motives of the change agent, the accuracy of the information, or there has been a history of difficult relationships, then the information will be examined with serious reservations. When employees accept information, the ground is fertile for the development of a shared sense of the need and the vision for change.

Factors That Block People From Recognizing the Need for Change

Giving voice to the need for change can create awareness in employees. However, future directions are not always obvious and an organization's history and culture can be strong impediments to creating awareness of the need for change. It took Robert Frey, the owner of Cin-Made Packaging Group, Cincinnati, Ohio, time to recognize that attempting to rectify matters by doing existing things faster or more cost effectively would not reverse the fortunes of his business. In his case, Frey and his partner first stumbled, and then Frey changed the company, realigning its strategy, corporate culture, and underlying systems and processes to make it successful.[51]

DEMANDING CHANGE AT CIN-MADE

Robert Frey's experience with turning around Cin-Made Packaging Group provides a graphic example of the choices senior managers face when their change management approach is not working. In 1984, Frey and a partner purchased the firm that had a paternalistic culture and a union that was pushing labor costs up as profits sank.[52] Frey and his partner's initial attempt to turn around the firm involved a confrontational, combative style that was viewed as mean and aggressive by many employees. Unhappy with the results of confrontation—it obtained little more than compliance and suspicion—Frey decided to alter his style to information sharing and empowerment. Because of Frey's previous autocratic management style and minimal credibility with employees, he created a paradoxical situation: Through autocratic and demanding means, he moved the organization to an empowered and involved environment. When an employee refused to engage in problem solving because it "wasn't his job," Frey threw a fit (his terminology). When confronted with a demanding boss and with major changes to the reward system, employees changed their mode of operation. As the changes took root and demonstrated their value to employees, the improvement initiatives developed a reinforcing momentum of their own that nurtured and sustained business-altering changes.[53]

To achieve market success, Frey initiated a business strategy of product leadership and superior customer service anchored in a revitalized organizational culture. Cin-Made invested in innovative products, revisited its relationship with its customers, and valued and empowered the employees who were delivering on the value proposition. Once he got their attention, Frey worked to provide employees with a heightened sense of purpose, rewards for success, and an improved climate within which to work. As all good strategic managers would, his team aligned the organization's structure, systems, and processes with the new strategy. A key ingredient was aligning relevant parts of the organization's culture, its value systems and norms, with the new strategy.[54]

All too often, strategists will introduce a new direction and seek to change the organizational culture without attending to the question of the impact of cultural artifacts on the desired change.[55] Cultural artifacts are the stories, rituals, and symbols that influence employees' attitudes and beliefs; they are important because they help to define and operationalize the culture. If change agents keep old artifacts, they may reinforce the old culture they wish to change. In 1994, Bethune and Brenneman faced this challenge when they tackled the turnaround of Continental Airlines, taking the firm from near bankruptcy and the worst customer service ratings in the industry to success on all fronts over the next decade.[56] One of the major reasons that they were successful in implementing a turnaround was their introduction of new cultural artifacts that reinforced service as a key value rather than keeping previous artifacts that signaled poor service.

CULTURAL CHANGE AT CONTINENTAL AIRLINES

A reward system was put into place (at Continental) for improved service. Performance-reward systems themselves are not necessarily cultural artifacts, but this reward system was tied directly to corporate performance, and the financial rewards were paid in a separate check to employees to draw attention to the relationship between performance and rewards. This reward system not only reinforced a new value at Continental, but it also became a symbol to employees of the importance of high levels of performance in the new Continental, as opposed to the acceptance of poor performance in the old Continental. In addition, stories were told throughout Continental about how the new CEO told jokes to employees, answered questions honestly, and was an all-around good guy to work for. These and numerous additional artifacts replaced old ones that had reinforced bureaucracy and the acceptability of poor performance and that had led to unbelievably low employee morale.[57]

Both Continental and Cin-Made show that the existing culture can impair organizational members' capacity to recognize the urgency of the need for change, even when things are going poorly. Even if organizational members recognize the need, culture can impede their ability to take appropriate actions until things occur that weaken the existing culture and open the way to new thinking about the organization, the current situation, and its leadership. When this occurred at Continental and Cin-Made, the door was opened to meaningful change. Actions that reinforced the development and strengthening of the new culture ensured that the organization would continue its journey of continuous improvement and wouldn't regress to old patterns.

Culture can get in the way of recognizing the need for change in poorly performing firms. However, it can represent an even more difficult barrier in successful firms. Consider Unilever, which had great brands and a long history in emerging markets and yet was falling behind competitors in those same markets. They knew they needed to change something but were mentally locked into the business practices that had become sources of disadvantage.[58] In 2004, they finally recognized the sources of the problem and by 2006 were reaping the benefits in terms of renewed growth and profitability. Sull argues that organizations trapped in their past successes often exhibit lots of activity (this was true for Unilever), but the outcome is "active inertia," because they remain essentially unchanged.[59] Even when organizations recognize that they need to change, they fail to take appropriate actions. He believes this occurs because:

- Strategic frames, those mental models or sets of assumptions of how the world works, become blinders to the changes that have occurred in the environment;
- Processes harden into routines and habits, becoming ends in themselves rather than means to an end;
- Relationships with employees, customers, suppliers, distributors, and shareholders become shackles that limit the degrees of freedom available to respond to the changed environment;
- Values, those deeply held beliefs that determine corporate culture, harden into dogma, and questioning them is seen as heresy.

During periods of financial difficulty or decline, senior management teams may become polarized in their positions, isolate themselves from data they need, and incorrectly assess the need for change. Senior management teams may prevent critical information from surfacing as they self-censor, avoid conflict, and/or are unwilling to solicit independent assessments as they attempt to preserve cohesion and commitment to a course of action.[60] These are conditions that lead to groupthink* and can result in disastrous decisions that flow from the flawed analysis.[61] Change agents need to be vigilant and take action to ensure that groupthink does not cloud a team's capacity to assess the need for change or impair the judgment of the teams with which they are working. If change agents are dealing with a cohesive team exhibiting the characteristics of groupthink, the agents need to take action with care, considering how to make the group aware of factors that may be clouding the group's judgment. Change agents who attempt to alert such teams to these realities are often dealt with harshly, since "shooting the messenger" is a

---

*Groupthink is "a mode of thinking that people engage in when they are deeply involved in a cohesive in-group, when the members' striving for unanimity overrides their motivation to realistically appraise alternative courses of action" (retrieved December 2010) from wps .prenhall.com/wps/media/objects/213/218150/glossary.html).

speedy way for teams to protect themselves from difficult data. Strategies for avoiding groupthink include:

- Have the leader play an impartial role, soliciting information and input before expressing an opinion.
- Actively seek dissenting views. Have group members play the role of devil's advocate, challenging the majority's opinion.
- Actively pursue the discussion and analysis of the costs, benefits, and risks of diverse alternatives.
- Establish a methodical decision-making process at the beginning.
- Ensure an open climate for discussion and decision making, and solicit input from informed outsiders and experts.
- Allow time for reflection and do not mistake silence for consent.[62]

Additional factors that obstruct managerial judgment over the need for change and the inability to develop constructive visions for future action have been highlighted in both the business and academic press. Ram Charan and Jerry Useem summarize such factors in their *Fortune* magazine article on the role executives play in organizational failure:

- They have been softened by past success.
- They see no problems or at least none that warrant serious change (internal and external blindness).
- They fear the CEO and his/her biases more than competitors.
- They overdose on risk and play too close to the edge. This is often tied to systems that reward excessive risk taking.
- Their acquisition lust clouds their judgment.
- They listen to Wall Street more than to employees and others who have valuable insights they should attend to.
- They employ the "strategy du jour"—the quick-fix flavor of the day.
- They possess a dangerous corporate culture—one that invites high-risk actions.
- They find themselves locked in a new economy death spiral—one that is sustained and accelerating.
- They have a dysfunctional board that fails in its duties around governance.[63]

Developing a well-grounded awareness of the need for change is a critical first step for change leaders when helping organizations overcome inertia, rein in high-risk propensities, address internal and external blind spots, disrupt patterns of groupthink, and view their environment in ways that open organizational members to change.

So far, this chapter has outlined the variety of perspectives that will exist regarding the need for change. It emphasizes that the perspective of the change leader may not be held by others and that often change leaders need to develop or strengthen the need for change before trying to make specific changes. (A Checklist for Change is shown in **Appendix 4.1** of this chapter.) One of the ways to enhance the perceived need for change and begin to create focused momentum for action is to develop a clear and compelling change vision.

Creating a Powerful Vision for Change

A vision for change clarifies the road ahead. It specifies the purpose of the change and provides guidance and direction for action. It can provide a powerful pull on employees to participate positively in the change process.[64] As Simons says, "Vision without task is dream world and task without vision is drudgery."[65]

Visions can be used to strengthen or transform existing cultures. At a micro level, visions are used to focus awareness, energy, and initiative around local issues, processes, and opportunities. At their best, change visions provide well-grounded, challenging reasons for hope and optimism. At their worst, they are trite bromides that accelerate organizational cynicism; hallucinations that are confusing or misguided; or specific directions that are simply inappropriate or counterproductive.

Change leaders use visions to create and advance the mental pictures people have of the future and to provide directional guidance for stakeholders whom change agents need to enlist in the enterprise. Creating the vision is a key part of defining a future state and, in turn, it is central to any gap analysis done by a change leader.

Storytelling is a technique employed by change leaders to communicate a vision and mobilize awareness and interest. Because people identify with and remember stories, change agents can use stories in several ways: to create contextual awareness of how an organization got to its problematic condition; to demystify data; to clarify a change initiative and why a particular course of action makes sense; to relieve or increase tension and awareness; and finally, to instill confidence.[66] The multiple uses of stories make storytelling a critical skill for change leaders.

Understanding the foundational components of **organizational vision** is important. In an ideal world, it is closely connected to the mission of the organization (its fundamental purpose or reason for existence) and informs the core philosophy and values of the institution. It addresses such questions as, "What does this organization stand for?" Vision identifies the desired ideal future. From this should flow the strategies, goals, and objectives.[67] When change leaders have fully developed a change process, the strategies, goals, and objectives flow from the vision and will address three essential questions for an enterprise: What business are we in? Who are our target customers and what is our value proposition to them? and How will we deliver on our value proposition?

Change agents often create change visions or "subvisions" in order to generate emotional energy, commitment, and directional clarity for the organizational change as the process proceeds from planning through to implementation in different departmental units. These allow the overall change vision to be adapted to reflect how it manifests itself within specific areas of the organization. If FedEx's overriding commitment to its customers for its express service is "absolutely, positively, overnight," then a change leader's vision concerning a logistics support initiative might deal with enhancing accuracy in package tracking to reduce error rates to below .00001%.

Beech states,

> Vision is an agenda of goals…vision is a dream about how the ideal future might be…it gives rise to and dictates the shape of plans…vision infuses the plan with energy because it gives it direction and defines objectives. Even the most unassuming vision constitutes a challenge to become something stronger, better, different."[68]

Approached properly, it can mobilize and motivate people[69] and have a positive impact on performance and attitudes.[70]

Change leaders need to know *how* to develop a vision. Jick outlines three methods for creating vision: leader-developed; leader–senior team-developed, and bottom-up visioning.[71] As the name suggests, **leader-developed vision** is done largely in isolation from others. Once it has been created, it is announced and shared with others in the organizations. **Leader–senior team-developed vision** casts a broader net. Members of the senior team are involved in the process of vision formation. Once completed, it is then shared with others. **Bottom-up visioning,** or an employee-centric approach, is time consuming, difficult, *and* valuable in facilitating the alignment of organizational members' vision with the overall vision for change. If a change leader can articulate a compelling vision that captures a broad spectrum of organizational members, then a leader-developed vision is likely appropriate. If, on the other hand, employees are diverse and have mixed feelings about the vision, then the change agent's job will be difficult and a bottom-up approach will be necessary. If employees both "get it" (i.e., the vision) and "want to get it," subsequent support for change will prove much easier to develop, leverage, and implement. This is particularly important when cultural changes are involved.[72]

What does it take to develop an effective change vision? According to Todd Jick, good change visions are:[73]

- Clear, concise, easily understood
- Memorable
- Exciting and inspiring
- Challenging
- Excellence centered
- Stable but flexible
- Implementable and tangible

The process of creating a vision statement encourages change agents to dream big. Paradoxically, when visions become too grand and abstract, they can cease to have much impact. Alternatively, they may provide guidance that energizes and mobilizes individuals to undertake initiatives that unintentionally work at cross purposes to other initiatives that have been embarked upon or that may even have the potential to put the organization at risk.[74]

> ## OPPORTUNITIES 2000
> ## "ELIMINATING POVERTY IN ORGANIZATIONS"
>
> The vision of Opportunities 2000, a community-based Canadian social service organization, was "Eliminating poverty in organizations."[75] This vision underpinned a specific change campaign to persuade organizations in the Waterloo Region to identify people working for them who were living below the poverty line. The initiative was launched in 1997 with a short-term goal of moving 2,000 families above the poverty line by the year 2000. The social service organization then worked with employees to help them move themselves out of poverty. The link between the transformational vision and concrete actions was fully developed by the social service organization, and by 2001, this successful initiative had evolved into a continuing antipoverty program in the local community.[76]
>
> **Exercise:** How well does this vision statement meet the criteria Jick specifies? Could it be improved? How?

Developing an effective change vision is easier said than done. To develop your skills in this area, **Toolkit Exercise 4.2** asks you to craft a vision statement for a change situation you are familiar with.

Lipton provides a pragmatic view of what makes for an effective vision statement. He argues that it needs to convey three key messages: (a) the mission or purpose, (b) the strategy for achieving the mission, and (c) the elements of the organizational culture that seemed necessary to achieving the mission and supporting the strategy.[77] He believes a vision will be more likely to fail when:

- Actions of senior managers are incongruent with the vision. They fail to walk the talk.
- It ignores the needs of those who will be putting it into practice.
- Unrealistic expectations develop around it that can't possibly be met.
- It is little more than limited strategies, lacking in a broader sense of what is possible.
- It lacks grounding in the reality of the present that can be reconciled.
- It is either too abstract or too concrete. It needs to stimulate and inspire, but there also needs to be the sense that it is achievable.
- It is not forged through an appropriately messy, iterative, creative process requiring a combination of "synthesis and imagination."
- It lacks sufficient participation and involvement of others to build a consensus concerning its appropriateness.
- Its implementation lacks "a sense of urgency…and measurable milestones."[78]

Lipton's list provides change leaders with a set of factors to consider when developing and operationalizing their vision for change. Are their actions aligned with the vision? Have they considered the needs of those who will be putting it into practice? If not, Lipton would argue that you are lowering the motivational and directional value the change vision can provide. Conversely, if they are present, the power of the change vision is enhanced.

Toolkit Exercise 4.3 asks you to review the vision for change you developed in Toolkit Exercise 4.2 and consider the factors raised by Lipton.

Change visions need to paint pictures that challenge the imagination and enrich the soul. Too many vision statements are insipid and dull. Too often they represent generic pap—right-sounding words but ones devoid of real meaning, designed for plaques and outside consumption and not rooted in the heart of the organization. Such visions focus on the lowest common denominator, something politically neutral that no one could object to. By trying to say everything or appeal to everyone, they say nothing and appeal to no one![79]

Table 4.2 contains the Handy-Dandy Vision Crafter, a cynical view of organizational vision statements and how they are developed. While many statements may end up containing words similar to those in the model, the Handy-Dandy Vision Crafter ignores the hard work and the difficult creative process and activities that organizations go through to develop a vision statement that works for them. In many ways, the process of developing the change vision is as important as the vision itself. However, too many vision statements read as if the Vision Crafter had been used to create them.

Table 4.2 The Handy Dandy Vision Crafter

Just fill in the blanks with the words that best suit your needs!

We strive to be the: _____

(Premier, Leading, Pre-eminent, World-class, Dominant, Best of Class ...)

Organization in our industry. We provide the best in: _____

(Committed, Caring, Innovative, Expert, Environmentally friendly, Reliable, Cost-effective, Focused, Diversified, High-quality, On-time, Ethical, High-value-added ...)

(Products, Services, Business Solutions, Customer-oriented Solutions ...)

To: _____

(Serve Our Global Marketplace; Create Customer, Employee and Shareholder Value; Fulfill Our Covenants to Our Stakeholders; Exceed our Customers' Needs; Delight Our Customers ...)

Through _____ employees

(Committed, Caring, Continuously Developed, Knowledgeable, Customer-focused ...)

In the Rapidly Changing and Dynamic: _____

(Industry, Society, World)

Sometimes a quick statement, a slogan, can serve as a vision proxy. The following slogans capture the essence of a vision message:

- Every life deserves world-class care (Cleveland Clinic)
- An Apple on every desk (Apple Computers)
- Saving people money so they can live better (Walmart)
- Inspire the world, create the future (Samsung)
- To organize the world's information and make it universally accessible and useful (Google)

These slogans are tied to statements of mission and vision, and they provide messages that are clear to employees and customers alike. They are meant to reflect underlying values that the organization holds dear.

The slogan "Quality is job #1" was used by Ford to symbolize its determination to improve quality in the 1980s. In the aftermath of quality and safety concerns that buffeted Ford, the automaker successfully used these words, with an accompanying concerted program of action, to refocus employee and public perceptions of the importance of quality to Ford and, ultimately, the excellence of its products. This major initiative spanned several years and was ultimately successful in taking root in the minds of employees and the public. However, the Ford Explorer/Firestone controversy in 2000[80] concerning vehicle stability in emergency situations reopened public questions of Ford's commitment to quality and safety and put extreme internal and external pressure on Ford and Bridgestone (Firestone's parent organization) to restore the public trust. The lesson to draw from Ford's experience is that an image built on a vision that took years to develop can be shattered quickly.

Johnson and Johnson's response to the Tylenol tampering scare[81] and Procter and Gamble's[82] response to inappropriate competitive intelligence activities related to hair care products provide two examples of how clear vision can help organizations respond effectively to potentially damaging events. In the case of Tylenol, this best-selling brand was pulled from store shelves until the company was confident it had effectively addressed the risk of product tampering, at the cost of tens of millions of dollars. In the Procter and Gamble situation, when the CEO found out, he fired those involved, informed P&G's competitor that it had been spied upon, took appropriate action with respect to knowledge that P&G had inappropriately gained, and negotiated a multimillion-dollar civil damage payment to the aggrieved competitor. The actions of these two firms demonstrated their commitment to their respective visions of how they should operate and reinforced public and employee confidence in the firms and what they stood for.[*]

---

[*]Johnson and Johnson's credo can be found at www.jnj.com/connect/about-jnj/jnj-credo/. Procter and Gamble's mission, vision, and values can be found at www.pg.com/en_US/downloads/media/PVP_brochure.pdf.

Compare Procter and Gamble's and Johnson and Johnson's responses with Toyota's initial reactions to safety concerns in 2009 and 2010. The Toyota vision is to become the most successful and respected car company in each market around the world by offering customers the best purchasing and ownership experience. However, one wonders if the desire to become the largest and most successful auto firm got in the way of the vision for respect that would be linked to quality and the willingness to put the needs of customers ahead of the company's own. The response to safety concerns was initially slow and defensive, and Toyota has paid a very heavy price in lost sales and damaged reputation and brand.[83] It was ranked the seventh most respected brand in the world by *Fortune* in 2010, but the data were collected before the bad news hit, and it is uncertain they will make the list in 2011.[84]

As noted earlier, companies can be trapped by the existing vision of their organization.[85] Goss, Pascale, and Athos argue that (a) narrow definitions of what the company is about, (b) failure to challenge the accepted boundaries and assumptions of the company, and (c) an inability to understand the context leads to inadequate or mediocre visions. They show the problems that can occur when a vision is achieved—now what? Once the vision is achieved, motivation is lost. It is a bit like a team whose vision was to "make it to the Super Bowl"—it is at a distinct disadvantage when playing against a team whose vision is to "win the Super Bowl."

Once the vision is clear, the issue becomes one of enactment by employees. Wheatley argues that one must "get the vision off the walls and into the halls"![86] She claims that people are often trapped by a mechanical view of vision, one that is limited to only a directional component of vision (vision as a vector). She argues that vision should be viewed as a field that touches every employee differently and is filled with eddies and flux and shifting patterns. This view emphasizes the need to understand how each individual "sees" or "feels" the vision. As Beach says, "Each member (of the organization) has his or her own vision"[87]. Somehow, these individual visions need to be combined into an overall sense of purpose for the organization. The active engagement and involvement of employees (or their representatives) in the development, communication, and enactment of the vision for change is a strategy that has been effectively used to advance the creation of a shared sense of purpose.[88] Twenty-six centuries ago, Lao Tzu observed that "the best change is what the people think they did themselves."

The Difference Between an Organizational Vision and a Change Vision

While the rules for crafting a vision remain the same, the focus of the vision shifts depending upon the level and position of the change leader. For example, Home Depot identifies at least four subvisions within an overall company framework (see Table 4.3).

Table 4.3 Home Depot Subvision Statements

The Home Depot strives to be the best corporate partner possible in our communities. We make positive contributions as a neighbor, an employer, a retailer, and as a profitable investment opportunity through successful and strategic operations of our company.

The Home Depot helps people fulfill their dreams by helping them:

- To live in a clean, safe, and caring community
- To be part of a challenging, diverse, and inclusive workplace
- To build and live in the house of their dreams
- To create wealth and financial security

What does it mean to be the Neighbor of Choice?

For The Home Depot, being a partner to our cities and towns is of paramount importance. Our business creates jobs and opportunities for other businesses in the community. We strive to purchase locally, therefore keeping local dollars in the community. We're committed to bettering our community through local and area volunteer projects. And by offering home solutions in your neighborhood, we help consumers to fulfill their dreams of turning a house into a home.

What does it mean to be the Employer of Choice?

To be the Employer of Choice means creating an inclusive and associate-centered culture. At The Home Depot, that means providing meaningful and challenging work for our associates that creates opportunity for growth and development. We also strive to provide economic opportunities through competitive wages and exceptional benefits packages to all associates. We recognize the contributions of our associates and reward their achievements, hard work, and dedication.

What does it mean to be the Retailer of Choice?

The Home Depot provides our customers with excellent service every time they come into our stores. We offer the right products, the right selection, the right prices, and a team of associates passionate about your needs. We build lasting relationships by helping customers realize their dreams and growing their trust through our products and services.

What does it mean to be the Investment of Choice?

Being an Investment of Choice means increasing economic growth through strategic marketing in stores and of products. It also means making decisions that reflect our policies surrounding social responsibility and considering the impact on our community. Being an Investment of Choice means continuing to gain on comparable store sales through innovative initiatives and growing adjacencies to meet the needs of the public to increase our economic bottom line and our corporate reputation.[89]

Source: Home Depot Inc.

Notice with the Home Depot example how its vision becomes more specific and defined as it develops these subvisions.

Change leaders' goals are advanced when they develop compelling messages that appeal to the particular groups of people critical to the change initiative.

However, in practice, there will be tensions between the changes proposed and what other parts of the organization are attempting to accomplish. For example, the sales force may be focused on how quickly it is able to respond to customers with the products they require, while manufacturing may be rewarded for how efficiently it is able to operate rather than how quickly it is able to respond to a customer order. These tensions need to be recognized and managed so that the change does not flounder, and various approaches for handling this will be addressed in the following chapters.

When change leaders develop their vision for change, they are challenged with the question of where to set the boundaries. A narrower, tighter focus will make it easier to meet the test of Jick's characteristics of effective vision for a specific target audience, but it may also reduce the prospects for building alliances and a broad base of support for change. As the need for change extends to the strategic and cultural areas of a firm, this issue of building a large constituency for the change becomes increasingly important. Two questions must be answered: First, where, if anywhere, do common interests among stakeholders lie? Second, can the vision for change be framed in terms of the common interest without diverting its purpose to the point where it no longer delivers a vision that will excite, inspire, and challenge?

This was a challenge that Dr. Martin Luther King met superbly. In 1963, King stood on the steps of the Lincoln Memorial and delivered his famous "I Have a Dream" speech on the 100th anniversary of the publishing of the Emancipation Proclamation by President Lincoln. This was a critical point in the Civil Rights movement, and Dr. King succeeded in seizing that moment by enunciating a compelling vision that embraced a large coalition. Attention to the coalition is apparent in his words:

> The marvelous new militancy which has engulfed the Negro community must not lead us to distrust all white people, for many of our white brothers, as evidenced by their presence here today, have come to realize that their destiny is tied up with our destiny and their freedom is inextricably bound to our freedom. We cannot walk alone.

Dr. King then went on to set out a vision in language all would understand: "I have a dream that one day this nation will rise up and live out the true meaning of its creed: We hold these truths to be self-evident: that all men are created equal."[90]

A broadly stated vision will potentially appeal to a range of people and engage diverse groups in a change process. For example, the National Campaign to Prevent Teen Pregnancy appealed to a very broad range of groups, from Catholics who opposed abortion to Planned Parenthood who accepted abortion.[91] Regardless of their specific positions, all groups wanted to prevent teen pregnancy. However, each of these groups had different ideas about the strategies for prevention. The risk of a broad vision is that the general appeal can break down when the vision gets translated into actions.

Coalitions that can develop around a common vision can be surprising. For example, the ability for environmentalists and conservative Republicans to forge a common cause around the reduction of fossil fuel consumption is not something many expected, but it now exists. Though their perceptions of the underlying rationale for the need for change are different, they have identified a common vision for change:

REDUCING FUEL CONSUMPTION AS A COMMON VISION

Environmentalists and groups of conservative Republicans are stepping up a campaign to promote alternative-fuel vehicles and wean the USA from dependence on foreign oil. While still skeptical about links between autos and global warming, the conservatives have concluded that cutting gasoline consumption is a matter of national security.

Right-leaning military hawks—including former CIA Director R. James Woolsey—have joined with other conservative Republicans and environmental advocates such as the Natural Resources Defense Council to lobby Congress to spend $12 billion to cut oil use in half by 2025. Their vision is to end America's dependence on foreign oil, build a sustainable energy system, and, in the process, create millions of jobs. The alliance highlights how popular sentiment is turning against the no-worries gas-guzzling culture and how alternative technologies such as gas–electric hybrids are finding increasingly widespread support.

"I think there are a number of things converging," said Gary L. Bauer, a former Republican presidential candidate and former head of the Family Research Council who has signed on to a strange-bedfellows coalition of conservatives and environmentalists called Set America Free. "I just think reasonable people are more inclined right now to start thinking about ways our country's future isn't dependent on...oil from a region where there are a lot of very bad actors."[92]

In the past, visions have generally been viewed as organization-level statements. However, change programs can benefit from a clear sense of direction and purpose that vision statements provide (see **Appendix 4.2** for Examples of Organizational Visions Change). The most powerful visions tap into people's need to be part of something transformative and meaningful. Mundane but important change programs involving restructuring or profit-focused issues need clear, concise targets.

Visions form the starting point for the chain of vision and mission —> objectives —> goals —> activities.* Change agents also need to specify measurable

---

*We use the following definitions. *Mission* means the overall purpose of the organization. *Vision* means the ultimate or ideal goal pursued. Thus, for a social service agency, the mission might be to look after the homeless. The vision would be to have no more homeless. An accounting firm's mission might be to provide excellent service in the provision and interpretation of financial information, while its vision might be to become the largest provider of such information in America.

goals for their change efforts. The research on goal setting has been quite clear on the benefits of **SMART** (specific, measurable, attainable, relevant, and time-bound) goals.[93] The provision of direction with measurable results for feedback galvanizes many people to pursue desired aims. This is easy to say, but defining the right measurable goals is not straightforward. Perhaps a critical task is to persuade a key stakeholder to view the change positively. How does one assess when such attitudes are beginning to change? Identifying interim goals for a change project that demonstrate progress toward the end goals is often a difficult task. These matters will be dealt with in subsequent chapters.

Summary

In summary, change occurs when there is an understanding of the need for change, the vision of where the organization should go, and a commitment to action. Change leaders need to address the question "Why change?" and develop both a sound rationale for the change and a compelling vision of a possible future. Unfreezing organizational members is advanced when these have been effectively executed.

The rationale for change emerges from a sound understanding of the situation: the external and internal data that point to a need for change, an understanding of the perspectives of critical stakeholders in the organization, internal data in the organization that affects any change, and the personal needs and abilities of the change leaders themselves. Critical in this is an understanding of the organization's readiness for change and the awareness of the need for change throughout the organization. Finally, the chapter discusses the creation of powerful visions and how to develop a specific change vision.

In addition to creating appealing visions of the future and demonstrating a compelling need for change, change agents need to understand the particular contexts of the major individuals in the change events. These stakeholders, or key players, will have an impact on the change situation, so their motives and interests need to be analyzed. The next chapter explores that topic.

Glossary of Terms

Need for Change

The need for change is the pressure for change in the situation. This need can be viewed as a "real" need, that demonstrated by data and facts, and a "perceived" need, that seen by participants in the change.

Developing a perspective on the need for change is aided by (a) seeking out external data, (b) seeking out the perspective, (c) seeking out data internal to the organization, and (d) reflecting upon personal concerns and perspectives of the change leader.

Perspective of the Stakeholder

The perspective of the stakeholder is the unique point of view of important participants in the change process. Understanding this perspective is critical to recognizing why this stakeholder supports or resists change.

Readiness for Change

Individual

Individual readiness for change is the degree to which the individual perceives the need for change and accepts it.

Organizational

Organizational readiness for change is the degree to which the organization as a whole perceives the need for change and accepts it.

Strategic Frame

A strategic frame is the mental model or set of assumptions held by change participants about how the world works.

Creating Readiness for Change

Readiness for change can be developed through the use of a variety of strategies, including (a) creating a crisis, (b) developing a vision that creates dissatisfaction with the status quo in the organization, (c) finding a champion-of-change leader who will build awareness of the need for change and articulate the vision for change, (d) focusing on common or superordinate goals, and (e) creating dissatisfaction with the status quo through education, information, and exposure to superior practices and processes of both competitors and noncompetitors. Different strategies have different strengths and weaknesses associated with them.

Factors That Block Recognition of the Need for Change

- Strategic frames, those mental models or sets of assumptions of how the world works, become blinders to the changes that have occurred in the environment;
- Processes harden into routines and habits, becoming ends in themselves rather than means to an end;
- Relationships with employees, customers, suppliers, distributors, and shareholders become shackles that limit the degrees of freedom available to respond to the changed environment;
- Values, those deeply held beliefs that determine corporate culture, harden into dogma, and questioning them is seen as heresy.

Change Vision

The change vision is the idealized view of the future that will be realized after the change occurs. The vision needs to be: (a) clear, concise, easily understood,

(b) memorable, (c) exciting and inspiring, (d) challenging, (e) excellence centered, (f) stable but flexible, and (g) implementable and tangible.

Leader-developed vision is developed directly by the change leader.

Leader–Senior-team-developed vision is developed by the senior management group in conjunction with the change leader.

Bottom-up visioning engages a broader spectrum of organizational members in the vision framing process. The change vision is developed through the active participation of those responsible for implementing the change, including those on the front line.

END-OF-CHAPTER EXERCISES

TOOLKIT EXERCISE 4.1

Developing the Background to Understand the Need for Change

As suggested earlier in this book, a careful diagnosis is essential for successful organizational change. Much of this diagnosis is needed to understand the need for change that the organization faces and then to engage and persuade organizational members concerning the need for change.

1. Consider an example of an organizational change that you are familiar with or are considering undertaking. What data could help you understand the need for change?

2. Have you:
   a. *Understood and made sense of external data? What else would you like to know?*
   b. *Understood and made sense of the perspectives of other stakeholders? What else would you like to know?*
   c. *Understood and assessed your personal concerns and perspectives and how they may be affecting your perspective on the situation?*
   d. *Understood and made sense of internal data? What else would you like to know?*

3. What does your analysis suggest to you about the need for change?

TOOLKIT EXERCISE 4.2

Writing a Vision Statement[94]

Think of an organization you are familiar with that is in need of change. If you were the change leader, what would be your vision statement for change?

1. Write your vision statement for the change you are striving for.

2. Check out this vision with others in the course. What is their response to it? Do they see it as:

   - Clear, concise, and easily understood?
   - Memorable?
   - Exciting and inspiring?
   - Challenging?
   - Excellence centered?
   - Stable and yet flexible?
   - Implementable and tangible?

3. Does the vision promote change and a sense of direction?

4. Does the vision provide the basis from which you can develop the implementation strategy and plan?

5. Does the vision provide focus and direction to those who must make ongoing decisions?

6. Does the vision embrace the critical performance factors that organizational members should be concerned about?

7. Does the vision engage and energize as well as clarify? What is the emotional impact of the vision?

8. Does the vision promote commitment? Are individuals likely to be opposed to the vision, passive (let it happen), moderately supportive (help it happen), or actively supportive (make it happen)?

TOOLKIT EXERCISE 4.3

Increasing the Value of the Change Vision

1. Return to the Change Vision you developed in Exercise 4.2. To the extent you can, assess it relative to the factors set out below.

   a. Actions of senior managers are congruent with the vision. They walk the talk.
   b. It pays attention to the needs of those who will be putting it into practice.
   c. Realistic expectations develop around it that are challenging but can be met.
   d. It communicates a broader sense of what is possible.
   e. It is grounded in the reality of the present and can be reconciled with it.
   f. It is neither too abstract nor too concrete. It has the potential to stimulate and inspire, but it also communicates the sense that it is achievable.
   g. It has been forged through an appropriately messy, iterative, creative process requiring a combination of "synthesis and imagination."
   h. It has sufficient participation and involvement of others to build a consensus concerning its appropriateness.
   i. Its implementation contains "a sense of urgency...and measurable milestones."[95]

2. Given your assessment of the above items, what would you recommend be done in order to strengthen the value of the change vision?

TOOLKIT EXERCISE 4.4

Putting the Need for Change and the Vision for Change Together

For any change to be successful, the need for change must be real and must be perceived as real. If the organization does not accept the need for change, the chances of anything substantive happening are negligible. Thus, developing the need for change is vital.

Understanding the **gap** between what is and what is desired is important in order to accurately describe the need for change.

Think of the situation you were considering in Exercise 4.2.

1. What is the **gap** between the present state and the desired future state?
2. How strong is the need for change?
3. What is the source of this need? Is it external to the organization?
4. Is there tangible evidence of the need for change in that there is concrete evidence of the need or a crisis situation that demonstrates the need for change?
5. If the change does not occur, what will be the impact on the organization in the next 2 to 6 years?
6. What is the objective, long-range need to change?

People can be motivated by higher-order purposes, things that relate to fundamental values. Change visions can be crucial in capturing support for change and in explaining the nature of change to others. Creating such a change vision is tricky. If one aims too high, it taps into higher values but often fails to link with the specific change project or program. If one aims too low, the vision fails to tap into values that motivate us above and beyond the ordinary. Such a change vision looks like and feels like an objective.

7. Return to the change vision you developed in Exercise 4.2. Does it capture a sense of higher-order purpose or values that underpin the change and communicate what the project is about?
8. Explain how the vision links the need for change.

Appendix 4.1: A Checklist for Change

Creating the Readiness for Change

1. What is the "objective" need for change? That is, what are the consequences to the organization of changing or not changing? Are people aware of these risks?

2. Are organizational members aware of the need for change? Do they feel the need for change or do they deny its need? Can they be informed?

3. Remember that individuals are motivated toward change only when they perceive the benefits as outweighing the costs. Do they see the benefits as outweighing the costs?

4. If individuals believe the benefits outweigh the costs, do they also believe the probability of success is great enough to warrant the risk taking, including the investment of time and energy that the change will require?

5. Are there other change alternatives that they are more predisposed to? What is it about their costs, benefits, and risks that make them more attractive? How should these alternatives be addressed by the change leader?

Appendix 4.2: Examples of Organizational Change Visions

Google's Implied Vision for Change in Telecommunications

Give carriers less control over what they can and cannot do with their networks through promoting net neutrality, developing Google's own mobile phone and operating system, and through forcing the carriers to build more high-speed networks through the threat that Google will do it if they don't.

Reed, B. (2010). How Google wants to change telecom: Google's foray into the telecom industry. *Network World*. Retrieved May 2010 from http://www.network world.com/news/2010/040110-google-telecom.html?page=3.

Xerox's Vision for Its India Affiliate

India Limited's strategic intent is to become the leader in the document market in India by helping improve customer work processes and positively impacting productivity and costs. In other words, "helping people find better ways to do great work." Retrieved May 2010 from http://www.xerox.com/go/xrx//template/009. jsp?view=About%20Xerox&Xcntry=IND&Xlang=en_IN.

IBM—Diversity 3.0

IBM has a long history of commitment to Diversity and has consistently taken the lead on Diversity policies long before it was required by law. It began in the mid-20th century, grounded in Equal Opportunity legislation and compliance (Diversity 1.0). We moved forward to Diversity 2.0 in the 1990s with a focus on eliminating barriers, and understanding regional constituencies and differences between the constituencies. As our demographics changed, we adapted our workplace to be more flexible and began our focus on work-life integration. In addition, over the past 5 years, we've introduced IBM's Values, which links to our diversity work.

This strong foundation brings us to where we are today—Diversity 3.0. This is the point where we can take best advantage of our differences—for innovation.

Our diversity is a competitive advantage and consciously building diverse teams helps us drive the best results for our clients. Retrieved May 2010 from http://www-03 .ibm.com/employment/us/diverse/index.shtml.

Ronald McDonald House Charities Vision

We believe that when you change a child's life, you change a family's, which can change a community, and ultimately the world.

We strive to be part of that change and part of the solution in improving the lives of children and their families. We extend our reach and impact by leveraging our 35 years of experience and strong relationships with local communities and people in the field to continually establish Chapters across the globe. We continually work to improve and expand our core programs, while also developing new services to address the unique needs of the communities we serve.

We don't do it alone. We rely on our Chapters to identify needs and carry out our mission on the ground. We rely on our strong relationships with the medical community to provide access to health care. We rely on strategic alliances with organizations that have the knowledge and infrastructure to extend our reach. We rely on you—our donors, volunteers, staff and friends. Retrieved May 2010 from http://rmhc.org/who-we-are/mission-and-vision/.

PepsiCo's Vision for a More Sustainable Future

At PepsiCo, Performance with Purpose means delivering sustainable growth by investing in a healthier future for people and our planet. As a global food and beverage company with brands that stand for quality and are respected household names—Quaker Oats, Tropicana, Gatorade, Lay's and Pepsi-Cola, to name a few— we will continue to build a portfolio of enjoyable and wholesome foods and beverages, find innovative ways to reduce the use of energy, water and packaging, and provide a great workplace for our associates. Additionally, we will respect, support and invest in the local communities where we operate, by hiring local people, creating products designed for local tastes and partnering with local farmers, governments and community groups. Because a healthier future for all people and our planet means a more successful future for PepsiCo. This is our promise.

Our Performance with Purpose agenda is comprised of three platforms:

1. Encourage people to live healthier by offering a portfolio of both enjoyable and wholesome foods and beverages.

2. Protect the Earth's natural resources through innovation and more efficient use of land, energy, water and packaging in our operations.

3. Invest in our associates to help them succeed and develop the skills needed to drive the company's growth, while creating employment opportunities in the communities we serve.

The people behind PepsiCo's brands are working hard to address these sustainability challenges, while partnering with key stakeholders to effect real change.

While we have taken significant strides on this journey, there is still more to learn and do. It is our intent to lead the way. Retrieved May 2010 from http://www .pepsico.com/Purpose/Sustainability/Performance-with-Purpose.html.

Tata's Vision for the Nano

Ratan Tata's 2003 Vision to his engineering team, led by 32-year-old star engineer Girish Wagh:

> Create a $2,000 "people's car." It has to be safe, affordable, all weather trans-portation for a family. It should adhere to regulatory requirements, and achieve performance targets such as fuel efficiency and acceleration.

The result of this vision is the **Tata Nano**. It gets 50 miles to the gallon, and seats up to five. And at $2,500 before taxes it is the most inexpensive car in the world.

Govindarajan, V. (2010). Vijay Govindarajan's Blog: Strategic Innovation, Indus-try Transformation and Global Leadership. Tuck School of Business at Dartmouth. Retrieved **May 2010** from http://www.vijaygovindarajan.com/2009/03/the_tata_ nano_product_or_socia.htm

World Wildlife Fund: Vision for its Community Action Initiative—Finding Sustainable Ways of Living

At WWF we protect wildlife, preserve habitats and empower people to conserve resources while improving their livelihoods. We understand the close relationship between humans and the environment, and incorporate elements of governance, gender relations, health and education into our conservation work. Our commu-nity conservation program links improving human lives with conserving biodiver-sity. Through WWF initiatives, communities are given the opportunity to reduce poverty, improve socio-economic conditions and become environmental stewards for the natural places WWF works to conserve.

Our vision: Build a sustainable balance between people and nature by empow-ering local communities to reduce poverty, enhance their opportunities and well-being, and strengthen their role as environmental decision makers. Retrieved May 2010 from http://www.worldwildlife.org/what/communityaction/index.html.

Save the Children—Vision for Its "Survive to 5" Program

We believe all children should live to celebrate their fifth birthday.

The Survive to 5 campaign supports Millennium Development Goal 4—to reduce child mortality by two thirds by 2015 and save the lives of over 5 million children under 5 who are dying of preventable and treatable diseases. Retrieved May 2010 from http://www.savethechildren.org/programs/health/child-survival/ survive-to-5/?WT.mc_id=1109_hp_tab_s25.

Notes

1. Wall Street Journal CEO council. (Producer). (2008). *Shaping the new agenda: Rahm Emanuel on the opportunities of crisis* [YouTube video]. Retrieved May 2010 from http://www.youtube.com/watch?v=_mzcbXi1Tkk.

2. Ten people who predicted the financial meltdown. (2008, October 12). *Times Online, Money.* Retrieved May 2010 from http://timesbusiness.typepad.com/money_weblog/2008/10/10-people-who-p/comments/page/2/.

3. Schmitt, R. B. (2008). FBI saw threat of loan crisis: A top official warned of widening mortgage fraud in 2004, but the agency focused its resources elsewhere. *Los Angeles Times.*

4. Critics say WHO overstated H1N1 threat. (2010, January 14). *China Daily Science and Health.*

5. Stoll, J. D., & Terlep, S. G. M. (2009, May 22). UAW reach crucial cost-cutting pact—agreement to modify work rules, trim cash obligation helps ease way for quick bankruptcy filing. *Wall Street Journal,* p. B1.

6. Lanes, W. J. III, & Logan, J. W. (2004, November). A technique for assessing an organization's ability to change. *IEEE Transactions in Engineering Management, (51)*4, 483.

7. Keeton, K. B., & Mengistu, B. (1992, Winter). The perception of organizational culture by management level: Implications for training and development. *Public Productivity & Management Review, 16*(2), 205–213.

8. Senge, P. M. (1994). *The fifth discipline: The art and practice of the learning organization.* New York: Currency Doubleday.

9. Sull, D. N. (1999, July–August). Why good companies go bad. *Harvard Business Review,* 42–52; Charan, R., & Useem, J. (2002). Why companies fail. *Fortune, 145*(11), 50–62; Schreiber, E. (2002). Why do many otherwise smart CEOs mismanage the reputation asset of their company? *Journal of Communication Management, 6*(3), 209–219.

10. Hamel, G. (2002). *Leading the revolution.* New York: Penguin.

11. Kotter, J. P. (2002). *The heart of change.* Boston, MA: Harvard Business School Press.

12. Mintzberg, H., & Westley, F. (1992). Cycles of organizational change. *Strategic Management Journal, 13,* 39–59.

13. Stapenhurst, T. (2009). *The benchmarking book: A how-to guide to best practice for managers and practitioners.* Oxford, UK: Elsevier.

14. Sull, D. N. (1999, July). Why good companies go bad. *Harvard Business Review,* 42–52.

15. Weisbord, M., & Janoff, S. (2005). Faster, shorter, cheaper may be simple; it's never easy. *Journal of Applied Behavioral Science, 41*(1), 70–82.

16. Gene Deszca, personal communication.

17. Sirkin, H., Keenan, P., & Jackson, A. (2005, October). The hard side of change management. *Harvard Business Review,* 4.

18. T. Cawsey, personal communication.

19. Collins, J. (2001). *Good to great.* New York: HarperCollins; Jennings, J. (2005). *Think big, act small.* New York: Penguin.

20. Corner office—Tony Hsieh of Zappos.com. (2010, January 10). *New York Times.*

21. Collins, J., & Porras, J. I. (1994). *Built to last* (p. 94). New York: HarperCollins.

22. Cited in Tunzelmann, A.V., (2007). *Indian summer* (p. 105). London: Simon and Schuster.

23. Spector, B. (1993). From bogged down to fired up. In T. D. Jick (Ed.), *Managing change: Cases and concepts* (pp. 121–128). Boston: Irwin/McGraw-Hill.

24. Wallace, E. (2009, May 5). Why Chrysler failed. *Bloomburg Businessweek.* Retrieved May 2010 from http://www.businessweek.com/lifestyle/content/may2009/bw2009055_922626.htm.

25. Lewis, K. (2003, November 10). Kmart's ten deadly sins. Book review in Forbes.com. Retrieved May 2010 from http://www.forbes.com/2003/10/10/1010kmartreview.html.

26. Fabrikant, G. (2004, January 5). Hollinger board accused of lax supervision. *New York Times.*

27. Thornhill, S., & Amit, R. (2003). *Learning from failure: Organizational mortality and the resource-based view.* Research Paper, Statistics Canada. Retrieved May 2010 from www.statcan.gc.ca/pub/11f0019m/11f0019m2003202-eng.pdf.

28. Verdú, A. J., & Gómez-Gras, J. M. (2009). Measuring the organizational responsiveness through managerial flexibility. *Journal of Organizational Change, 22*(6), 668–690; Santos, V., & García, T. (2007). The complexity of the organizational renewal decision: The managerial role. *Leadership and Organizational Development Journal, 28*(4), 336–355.

29. Trahant, B., & Burke, W. W. (1996). Creating a change reaction: How understanding organizational dynamics can ease reengineering. *National Productivity Review, 15*(4), 37–46; Lannes, W. J. III, & Logan, J. W. (2004). A technique for assessing an organization's ability to change. *IEEE Transactions in Engineering Management, 51*(4), 483.

30. Ratterty, A., & Simons, R. (2002). The influence of attitudes to change on adoption of an integrated IT system. *Organization Development Abstracts,* Academy of Management Proceedings; Mitchell, N., et al. Program commitment in the implementation of strategic change. *Organization Development Abstracts,* Academy of Management Proceedings.

31. Hyde, A., & Paterson, J. (2002). Leadership development as a vehicle for change during merger. *Journal of Change Management, 2*(3), 266–271.

32. Nevis, E. C., DiBella, A. J., & Gould, J. M. (1995). Understanding organizations as learning systems. *Sloan Management Review, 36*(2), 73–85.

33. Armenakis, A. A., Harris, S. G., & Field, H. S. (1999). Making change permanent: A model for institutionalizing change interventions. In W. Passmore & R. Woodman (Eds.), *Research in organizational change and development* (Vol. 12, pp. 289–319). Greenwich, CT: JAI Press.

34. Holt, D. (2002). Readiness for change: The development of a scale. *Organization Development Abstracts,* Academy of Management Proceedings.

35. Judge, W., & Douglas, T. (2009). Organizational change capacity: The systematic development of a scale. *Journal of Organizational Change Management, 22*(6), 635–649.

36. Stewart, T. A. (1994, February 7). Rate your readiness to change. *Fortune,* 106–110.

37. Woley, C., & Lawler, E. (2009). Building a change capability at Capital One Financial. *Organizational Dynamics, 38*(4), 245.

38. Klarner, P., Probst, G., & Soparnot, R. (2005). Organizational change capacity in the public service: The case of the World Health Organization. *Journal of Change Management, 8*(1), 57–72.

39. Willey, D. (2008, February 28). Naples battles with rubbish mountain. *BBC News.* Retrieved May 2010 from http://news.bbc.co.uk/2/hi/europe/7266755.stm; Quattrone, A. M. (2009, November 20). Garbage crisis and organized crime. *Naples Politics.* Retrieved May 2010 from http://naplespolitics.com/2009/11/20/garbage-crisis-and-organized-crime/; Italy Slammed by EU Court Over Naples Garbage. (2010, March 4). *Eubusiness.* Retrieved May 2010 from http://www.eubusiness.com/news-eu/court-italy-waste.3h2/.

40. Havman, H. A. (1992). Between a rock and a hard place: Organizational change and performance under conditions of fundamental environmental transformation. *Administrative Science Quarterly, 37*(1), 48–75.

41. Barnett, C. K., & Pratt, M. G. (2000). From threat-rigidity to flexibility: Toward a learning model of autogenic crisis in organizations. *Journal of Organizational Change Management, 13*(1), 74–88.

42. Simons, T. L. (1999). Behavioral integrity as a critical ingredient for transformational leadership. *Journal of Organizational Change Management, 12*(2), 89.

43. Hosmer, L. T., & Kiewitz, C. (2005). Organizational justice: A behavioral science concept with critical implications for business ethics and stakeholder theory. *Business Ethics Quarterly, 15*(1), 67.

44. Striebel, P. (1996, May–June). Why do employees resist change? *Harvard Business Review.*

45. Schenker, J. L. (2002). *Fine-tuning a fuzzy image.* Time Europe.com. Retrieved May 2010 from http://www.time.com/time/europe/digital/2002/03/stories/philips.html.

46. Tucker, B. A., & Russell, R. F. (2004). The influence of the transformational leader. *Journal of Leadership and Organizational Studies, 10*(4), 103–111.

47. Naughton, K. (2002). The perk wars. *Newsweek, 140*(14), 44.

48. Mintzberg, H., Simons, R., & Basu, K. (2002, Fall). Beyond selfishness. *Sloan Management Review,* 67–74; Collins, J. (2001). *From good to great: Why some companies make the leap...and others don't.* New York: HarperBusiness; De Geus, A. (1997). The living company. *Harvard Business Review, 75*(2), 51–59.

49. Wall, S. J. (2005). The protean organization: Learning to love change. *Organizational Dynamics, 34*(1), 37.

50. Editors, *Harvard Business Review.* (2005). *Managing change to reduce resistance* (pp. 143–150). Boston, MA: Harvard Business School Press.

51. Chakravarthy, B., & Lorange, P. (2007). Continuous renewal, and how Best Buy did it. *Strategy and Leadership, 35*(6), 4–11.

52. Callison, J. (2002, June 23). Vision rakes in profit, excitement for Cin-Made: Management overhaul, finding niche helped packaging firm survive. *Enquirer.* Retrieved May 2010 from http://www.enquirer.com/editions/2002/06/23/fin_vision_rakes_in.html.

53. Frey, R. (1993, September–October). Empowerment or else. *Harvard Business Review,* 80–94.

54. Callison, J. (2002, June 23). Vision rakes in profit, excitement for Cin-Made: Management overhaul, finding niche helped packaging firm survive. *Enquirer.* Retrieved May 2010 from http://www.enquirer.com/editions/2002/06/23/fin_vision_rakes_in.html.

55. Higgins, J. M., & McAllister, C. (2004). If you want strategic change, don't forget to change your culture artifacts. *Journal of Change Management, 4*(1), 63–73.

56. Helyar, J. (2004, October 4). Why is this man smiling? Continental's Gordon Bethune turned the airline around, guided it through 9/11, and became a great CEO. Now he's being forced out. How can this be? *Fortune.* Retrieved May 2010 from http://faculty.msb.edu/homak/homahelpsite/webhelp/Airlines_-_Why_s_Bethune_Smiling__Fortune_11-18-04.htm.

57. Higgins, J. M., & McAllister, C. (2004). If you want strategic change, don't forget to change your culture artifacts. *Journal of Change Management, 4*(1), 63–73.

58. The legacy that got left on the shelf—Unilever and emerging markets. (2008, February). *The Economist, 386*(8565), 76.

59. Sull, D. N. (1999, July–August). Why good companies go bad. *Harvard Business Review.*

60. Finkelstein, S. (2003). *Why smart executives fail: And what you can learn from their mistakes.* New York: Penguin.

61. Eaton, J. (2001). Management communication: The threat of groupthink. *Corporate Communications, 6*(4), 183–192.

62. Whyte, G. (1989). Groupthink reconsidered. *Academy of Management Review, 14,* 40–56; Neck, C. P., & Moorhead, G. (1992). Jury deliberations in the trial of *U.S. v. John DeLorean*: A case analysis of groupthink avoidance and enhanced framework. *Human Relations, 45*(10), 1077–1091.

63. Charan, R., & Useem, J. (2002, May 22). Why companies fail. *Fortune,* 50–62.

64. Cole, M. S., Harris, S. G., & Bernerth, J. B. (2006). Exploring the implications of vision, appropriateness, and execution of oganizational change. *Leadership and Organizational Development Journal, 27*(5), 352–369.

65. Simons, G. F., et al. (1998). In S. Komives, J. Lucas, & T. R. McMahon, *Exploring leadership* (p. 54). San Francisco: Jossey-Bass.

66. McKinnon, N.(2008). We've never done it this way before: Prompting organizational change through stories. *Global Business and Organizational Excellence, 27*(2), 16–25.

67. Thornberry, N. (1997). A view about vision. *European Management Journal, 15*(1), 28–34.

68. Beach, L. R. (1993). *Making the right decision* (p. 50). Englewood Cliffs, NJ: Prentice Hall.

69. Nanus, B. (1992). *Visionary leadership.* San Francisco: Jossey-Bass; Kirkpartick, S. A., & Locke, E. A. (1996). Direct and indirect effects of three core charismatic leadership components on performance and attitudes. *Journal of Applied Psychology, 81,* 36–51.

70. Baum, I. R., Locke, E. A., & Kirkpatrick, S. A. (1998). A longitudinal study of the relation of vision and vision communication to venture growth in entrepreneurial firms. *Journal of Applied Psychology, 83,* 43–54.

71. Jick, T. (2003). *Managing change* (pp. 98–100). Boston: Irwin.

72. Higgins, J. M., & McAllaster, C. (2004). If you want strategic change, don't forget to change your cultural artifacts. *Journal of Change Management, 4*(1), 63–73.

73. Jick, T. (1993). The vision thing (A). In T. Jick, *Managing change* (pp. 142–148). Homewood, IL: Irwin.

74. Langeler, G. H. (1992, March–April). The vision trap. *Harvard Business Review,* 46–55.

75. Personal experience of the authors.

76. Leviten-Reid, E. (2001, September 28). *Opportunities 2000: Multisectoral collaboration for poverty reduction final evaluation report.* Caledon Institute of Social Policy. Retrieved May 2010 from http://tamarackcommunity.ca/downloads/vc/OP_2000_Final_Eval.pdf.

77. Lipton, M. (1996, Summer). Demystifying the development of an organizational vision. *Sloan Management Review,* 86.

78. Lipton, M. (1996, Summer). Demystifying the development of an organizational vision. *Sloan Management Review,* 89–91.

79. Levin, I. M. (2000). Vision revisited. *Journal of Applied Behavioral Science, 36*(1), 91–107.

80. Kalogeridis, C. (2005). The Ford/Firestone fiasco: Coming to blows. *Radnor, 185*(1), 22–24.

81. The National Business Hall of Fame. (1990, March 12). *Fortune, 121*(6), 42.

82. Serwer, A. (2001, September 17). P&G's covert operation. *Fortune, 144*(5), 42.

83. *Searcey, D. (2010, April 19). Toyota agrees to $16.4 million fine.* Wall Street Journal Digital Network, *Auto Section.* Retrieved May 2010 from http://online.wsj.com/article/SB10 0014240527487045089045751928735543926804.html.

84. World's most admired companies. *Fortune.* Retrieved May 2010 from http://money .cnn.com/magazines/fortune/mostadmired/2010/index.html.

85. Goss, T., Pascale, R., & Athos, A. (1993, November–December). The reinvention roller coaster: Risking the present for a powerful future. *Harvard Business Review,* 97–108.

86. Wheatley, M. (1994). *Leadership and the new sciences.* San Francisco: Berrett-Koehler.

87. Beach, L. R. (1993). *Making the right decision* (p. 58). Englewood Cliffs, NJ: Prentice Hall.

88. Jørgensen, H., Owen, L., & Nues, A. (2008). *Making change work.* IBM Global Services. Retrieved May 2010 from http://www-935.ibm.com/services/us/gbs/bus/pdf/gbe03100-usen-03-making-change-work.pdf; Lockwood, N. R. (2007). Leveraging employee engagement for competitive advantage: HR's strategic role. *Society for Human Resource Management Research Quarterly.* Retrieved May 2010 from http://www.improvedexperience. com/doc/02_Leveraging_Employee_Engagement_for_Competitive_Advantage2.pdf; Morgan, D. E., & Zeffane, R. (2003). Employee involvement, organizational change and trust in management. *International Journal of Human Resource Management, 14*(1), 55–75.

89. HomeDepot.com [website]. Retrieved May 2010 from http://corporate.homedepot. com/wps/portal/!ut/p/.cmd/cs/.ce/7_0_A/.s/7_0_111/_s.7_0_A/7_0_111

90. Dr. Martin Luther King Jr.'s "I Have a Dream" Speech. *The Martin Luther King Jr. Papers Project* at Stanford University. Retrieved May 2010 from www.stanford.edu/group/King/publications/speeches/address_at_march_on_washington.pdf.

91. Sawhill, J. C., & Harmeling, S. S. National campaign to prevent teen pregnancy. (2000, March). *Harvard Business School Case Study,* 9–300–105.

92. Schneider, G. (2005, March 31). An unlikely meeting of the minds. *Washington Post,* p. E01.

93. Latham, G. P., & Locke, E. P. (1987). How to set goals. In R. W. Beatty (Ed.), *The performance management sourcebook.* Amherst, MA: Human Resource Development Press.

94. Drawn from Jick, T. (1993). The vision thing (A). In T. Jick, *Managing change.* Homewood, IL: Irwin; Lipton, M. (1996, Summer). Demystifying the development of an organizational vision. *Sloan Management Review,* 83–92.

95. Lipton, M. (1996, Summer). Demystifying the development of an organizational vision. *Sloan Management Review,* 89–91.

CHAPTER 5

Navigating Change Through Formal Structures and Systems

If you're going to sin, sin against God, not the bureaucracy; God will forgive you but the bureaucracy won't.

—H. G. Rickover, U.S. Admiral, quoted in the
New York Times, Nov. 3, 1986

We shape our buildings; thereafter they shape us.

—Winston Churchill from http://www.famousquotesandauthors
.com/authors/winston_churchill_quotes.html

CHAPTER OVERVIEW

- This chapter discusses the basics of how organizations structure themselves.
- It outlines how change leaders can diagnose the strengths and weakness of existing systems and structures.
- It examines how the formal structure and systems can foster, impair, and facilitate the acceptance of change initiatives.
- It lays out ways to manage systems and structures to gain approval for change initiatives. Formal, coalition-building, and renegade approaches are discussed.
- Finally, it reviews the ways to develop more adaptive systems and structures to increase the likelihood of continuous improvement.

Any discussion of organizational change needs to pay careful attention to the role of formal systems and structures. They influence what gets done, how it gets done, the outcomes that are achieved, and the experiences of the people who come into contact with the organization. While organizations define their systems and structures, the systems and structures shape the behavior of organizational members. Formal systems and structures play important coordination, communication, and control roles, and they influence how decisions are made about change. Sometimes systems and structures represent what needs to change.

An organization's formal structure is defined by how tasks are formally divided, grouped, and coordinated.[1] Formal structures are designed to support the strategic direction of the firm by enhancing order, efficiency, effectiveness, and accountability. They serve as guides and controls on decision-making authority; coordinate and integrate operations; provide direction to internal governance; and attempt to promote desired behavior and organizational outcomes.[2] The organization chart is the common document of organizational design.

Formal systems include planned routines and processes such as strategic planning, accounting and control systems, performance management, pay and reward systems, and the information system. Collectively, these set out how things are supposed to be done, the rules and procedures to be followed, how information is collected and disseminated, how individuals are to be compensated, and all the other formalized systems and processes that are used for coordination, integration, and control purposes. They provide the formal infrastructure that operationalizes the organization structure.

Organizations vary in their need for complexity in their structures and systems, but all require some degree of formalization to be sustainable. The corner grocer needs simple systems for accounting, staffing, and managing its suppliers, pricing, and inventory management. Walmart, on the other hand, requires sophisticated systems and structures to efficiently and profitably handle more than $400 billion in sales, processed by 2 million employees in 8,400 retail units that operate in 15 countries.[3] One reason that Walmart dominates the consumer retail market is its logistics systems that coordinate all aspects of inventory management, from ordering through to shipping, warehousing, shelving, and final disposition. Its knowledge-management system, Retail Link, provides Walmart and its suppliers with data that allow them to identify emerging opportunities for their products. Their systems are continuously improved in order to better drive business results. It is systems like this that allow Walmart to satisfy multiple stakeholders and maintain its competitive advantage in the industry.[4]

The purpose of this chapter is to describe the roles that formal systems and structures play in advancing change. It also provides guidance in identifying the gap between the existing structures and systems and what is needed to bring about alignment after the change. Figure 5.1 outlines where this chapter fits in the change management process. This chapter is the first of four that detail how change leaders can develop a sophisticated gap analysis. This chapter deals with formal systems and structures, and the chapters that follow will cover the informal aspects of organizations, change stakeholders and recipients, and change leaders themselves.

Change leaders need to develop a deep understanding of how existing structures and systems are currently influencing outcomes and how they are likely to facilitate or impede the proposed changes. Once that understanding is developed, change leaders need to put that system and structural awareness to use to promote and enact change. To advance this agenda, the chapter is divided into four sections:

1. Making sense of organizational structures and systems

2. Diagnosing the strengths and weakness of existing systems and structures

3. Understanding how structures and systems influence the approval process of a change initiative and how they then facilitate or hinder the acceptance of change

4. Designing adaptive structures and systems to enhance future change initiatives

Figure 5.1 outlines the change model and the key points for this chapter.

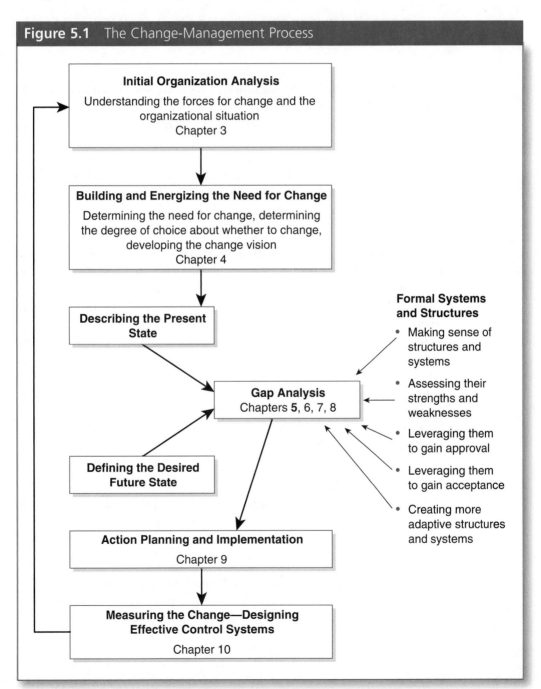

Figure 5.1 The Change-Management Process

Making Sense of Organizational Structures and Systems

The structural frame,[5] to use the language of Bolman and Deal, outlines an internal blueprint for how managers assign tasks, roles, and authority to produce products or services for the external marketplace. Wrapped around this structure are all the formal systems and processes that are designed to bring the structure to life and make it possible for the organization to deliver on its strategy and value proposition.

To make sense of structures, it is useful for change leaders to understand and be able to work with core concepts in this area. Some of the more common elements used include:[6]

1. **Differentiation: The degree to which tasks are subdivided into separate jobs or tasks.** This concept deals with who does what and asks about the degree to which jobs are specialized and distinctive from one another on both the horizontal and vertical organizational axes. The differentiation of tasks is an early step in the life of an entrepreneurial adventure as it grows from one to two and then three people, with further differentiation of tasks as the number of employees increases. As organizations grow and add more people, tasks are divided and subdivided. Large organizations, as a consequence, are often characterized by highly specialized jobs, leading to silos of similar and separate tasks and job categories.

2. **Integration: The coordination of the various tasks or jobs into a department or group.** This is the extent to which activities are combined into processes and systems, pulling together all the desperate pieces of tasks and jobs into a coherent whole. Small organizations are typically structured in a simple and straightforward manner, organized by functions such as production, accounting/finance, sales and marketing, and human resources. As they grow and become more complex, they look for more efficient and effective ways to group tasks and activities. Departments or divisions may be organized geographically or by product category, customer segment, or some other hybrid approach such as networks that seem to offer the best way to organize activities at that point in time. Sometimes they may even be spun off as separate, stand-alone entities. In large organizations, such as Boeing, there are integrative roles with people and teams who specialize in coordinating and communicating in order to bring together the disparate parts of the enterprise.

3. **Chain of command: The reporting architecture in a hierarchical organization.** This concept defines how individuals and/or units within an organization report to one another up and down the organizational ladder. It reflects the formal power structure and where decision responsibilities lie within the hierarchy.

4. **Span of control: The number of individuals who report to a manager.** This notion questions the optimal ratio of workers to managers in an organization. Since there is no one correct way to answer this question, part of the art of

organizational design is to figure this out, given the culture, strategy, and what needs to be done. An organization that gives managers too little span of control runs the risk of creating a costly and top-heavy administrative structure and encouraging its managers to micromanage too few employees. On the other hand, managers who have too many employees reporting to them run the risk of inadequate supervision, feedback, and employee development.

5. Centralization vs. decentralization: How and where decision making is distributed in an organizational structure. The more centralized the approach, the more the decision making gravitates to the top of the organization. Conversely, the more decentralized it is, the more the decision making is delegated to lower levels of employees. In general, organizations flatten their hierarchies when they adopt a more decentralized approach and vice versa.

6. Formal vs. informal: The degree to which organizational charts exist, are codified, and are followed. This is the extent to which structures and processes of the organization are set down in writing and expected to be followed.*

Impact of Uncertainty and Complexity on Formal Structures and Systems

Another way of thinking about structural alignment is to begin by reflecting on the environment they operate in. Beginning with the work of Thompson in the 1960s[7], researchers have explored the impact of uncertainty and complexity on why organizations structure their systems and processes as they do and the impact these configurations have on their capacity to successfully adapt to the environment over time.[8] When examining the structural dimensions, organizations have often been classified into two types: those that are (1) more formal, more differentiated, more centralized, and more standardized and those that are (2) less formal, less differentiated, more decentralized, and less standardized. The terms that are applied to this organization typology are *mechanistic* and *organic*. Table 5.1 outlines the characteristics of mechanistic and organic organizational forms as opposite ends of a continuum.[9]

Mechanistic organizations rely on formal hierarchies with centralized decision making and a clear division of labor. Rules and procedures are clearly defined and employees are expected to follow them. Work is specialized and routine. **Organic organizations** are more flexible. They have fewer rules and procedures, and there is less reliance on the hierarchy of authority for centralized decision making. The structure is flexible and not as well defined. Jobs are less specialized. Communication is more informal and lateral communications more accepted. While it may appear that one structural form is more appealing than the other, both can be effective depending upon their fit with its environment.

---

*For a detailed treatment of structural design dimensions, see Daft, R. L. (2007). *Organization theory and design* (9th ed.). Cincinnati, OH: South-Western College Publishing.

Table 5.1 Mechanistic and Organic Organization Forms	
More Mechanistic --- **More Organic**	
Tasks are broken down into separate parts and rigidly defined and assigned	Flexible tasks that are adjusted and redefined through teamwork and participation
High degree of formalization, strict hierarchy of authority and control, many rules	Relatively little formalization, less reliance on a hierarchy of authority and control, few rules, greater participation and decentralization
Narrow span of control with reliance on hierarchies of people in specialized roles	Wide span of control
Knowledge and control of tasks are centralized at the top of the organization, limited decision making at lower levels	Knowledge and control of tasks are decentralized and located throughout the organization. Highly decentralized decision making
Communication is vertical	Communication is horizontal and free flowing, with many integrating roles
Simple, straight-forward planning processes	Sophisticated environmental scanning, planning, and forecasting, including the use of scenarios and contingency thinking

Adapted from Daft, R. L. (2007). *Organization theory and design* (9th ed., p. 152). Cincinnati, OH: South-Western.

Formal Structures and Systems From an Information Perspective

A third way of thinking about the impact of systems and structures on how and why firms operate as they do is to look at how they formally manage information. One of the primary purposes of formal structures and systems is to place the right information in the hands of appropriate individuals in a timely fashion so that they can do what is needed. Information technology has been instrumental in allowing organizations to develop structures and systems that are more robust, dynamic, and flexible.

Supply chains, distributed manufacturing, flattened hierarchies with empowered workgroups, and networked organizations all owe their growth to improvements in this area. It has let organizations such as Dell move from mass-production models to mass customization, with little productivity loss.[10] By extension, technology has also allowed us to think differently about structures and systems when planning and managing organizational change.

Jay Galbraith defines this as the information-processing view of organizations.[11] If the organization is to perform effectively, there needs to be a fit between the organization's information-processing requirements and its capacity to process information through its structural design choices. The better the fit between these, the more effective the organization will be. As uncertainty increases, the amount of information that must be processed between decision makers during the transformation process increases. The organization must either increase its capacity to handle that information or restructure itself to reduce the need for information handling. Figure 5.2 outlines Galbraith's work.

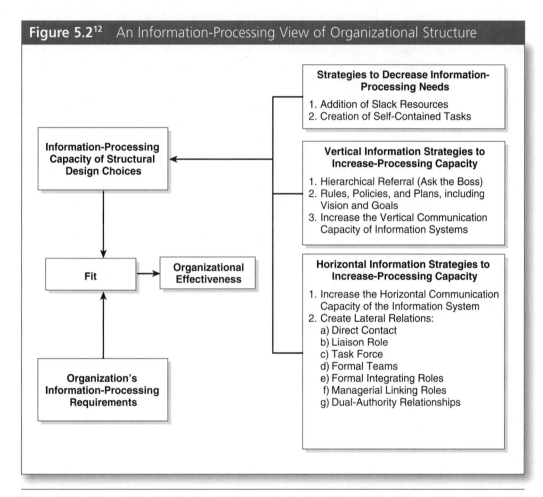

Figure 5.2[12] An Information-Processing View of Organizational Structure

Source: Adapted from Galbraith, J.R., *Organization Design.* Reading, MA: Addison-Wesley, 1977; and Daft, R.L., *Organization Theory and Design,* 8th Edition. Cincinnati, Ohio: South-Western, 2003.

As uncertainty increases, the traditional vertical information strategies for uncertainty reduction will prove increasingly less effective and the organization will require methods that either reduce the need for information processing or increase the capacity of the organization to process information.[13] Organizations can reduce their information-processing challenges by adding slack resources to act as buffers (e.g., extra people and inventory) and/or by creating self-contained tasks (e.g., divisions organized around product categories, geography, or customers). For example, extra inventory means that increased variation in demand for a product will be handled by drawing down or increasing inventory levels. Similarly, separating an organization into divisions operating as profit centers means that the divisions may not need to coordinate their activities as much. This reduces the information-processing requirements.

Initially, organizations attempt to increase their information-processing capacity by using the hierarchy. That is, if you are uncertain what to do, ask your boss. If the situation becomes repetitive, create a decision rule to guide the decision. If the subordinate knows more about the situation than the boss, they can agree on a set of objectives or goals or focus on the organizational vision, which allows the subordinate to act independently and handle the uncertainty. These represent what Galbraith calls vertical information strategies. A further vertical information strategy is when organizations increase their capacity to process information by investing in vertical information systems (e.g., computer-generated performance reports, decision support systems).

Organizations also can improve their information-processing ability by increasing their horizontal communication capacity (e.g., e-mail systems, intranets, and electronic bulletin boards). Finally, they can increase the capacity to process information horizontally by creating lateral relationships that vary in complexity for something as simple as direct, informal contact to complex, formal structures that facilitate the horizontal flow of information.

The role of the information systems is to develop needed information and get it to the individuals who most need it in timely manner for decision making. Interdepartmental and interdivisional boundaries and jurisdictional disputes can impede the flow of information (see the investigation of the 9/11 tragedy as an example of this[14]). Galbraith identified seven types of lateral relations that will help overcome such boundaries. These are:

- direct contact between affected individuals (e.g., a product designer and a manufacturing engineer)
- use of individuals in liaison roles to bridge groups
- multidepartment task forces
- formal teams
- integrating roles such as a product managers with cross-department authority
- managerial linking roles (similar to the integrating roles but with more formal decision authority)
- structures with dual-authority relationships such as are found in a matrix organization

If the organization is to perform effectively, this model points to the importance of congruence or fit between the firm's strategy, its information-processing requirements (e.g., market and competitive information, operational information), and the information-processing capacity that the firm's design choices have given rise to.

Change leaders need to be aware of the impact of vertical and horizontal information strategies on information flows and organizational performance when assessing what needs to change. Further, sensitivity to these issues needs to extend to the actual management of the change process. This is because even well-managed change will increase uncertainty in at least the short term, and major changes will significantly increase it for longer periods of time. This will give rise to information-processing needs that change leaders will need to manage. Otherwise the lack of fit may impair the effectiveness of the change initiative. Often multiple strategies are needed—extra resources to increase the capacity to process information, a focus on understanding the goals and purposes, and a significant increase in lateral relations.

Putting the Structural Concepts to Work

Aligning Systems and Structures With the Environment

The structural variables and models outlined above provide change leaders with an introduction to the multiple perspectives they can use when assessing structures and the formal systems that are developed to bring them to life. This can prove helpful when evaluating the internal consistency of structures and systems and their alignment with an organization's strategy, vision, culture, and environment. When cost strategies in a traditional manufacturing context are critical, a more mechanistic approach is often appropriate. When innovation is key, organic approaches provide a better fit with an organization's strategy.[15]

For change leaders, the importance of this material lies in the fact that organizations need to align their formal structures and systems with their environments. This led ITT to drop its organizationwide performance rating system when management realized it was having adverse impact on employees in different parts of the company's global operations and was not accomplishing its purpose.[16] In Nadler and Tushman's terminology, there needs to be congruence between the outside world, the strategy, and how the inside world is formally organized. By understanding the nature of the external environment and the organization's strategy, history, and resources, a change leader gains insight into the types of structures and systems that have the most to offer. By understanding the formal organizational arrangements, the leader gains insights on where and how decisions are made and how these can be leveraged to advance change.

Change leaders also need to be aware that even in a fairly mechanistic organization, different departments and divisions may face very different information-processing needs and will therefore need to be structured and managed differently. For example, a firm's R&D department's environment may be more dynamic and uncertain than that faced by the production department. As a result, R&D may need a more organic structure, whereas the production department will benefit from a more mechanistic one that leverages well-developed, standardized processes. Likewise, those involved with the launch of a new product or expansion into a new market will have to deal with higher levels of uncertainty and complexity than those responsible for mature markets, where concerns for structures and systems that enhance efficiency are likely the norm.

Structural Changes to Handle Increased Uncertainty

From a structural perspective, the quest for enhanced organizational effectiveness starts by looking at what needs to change in the organization and deciding how best to break things down and allocate the work. These differentiation approaches include aspects such as division of labor and departmentalization. If this has already been done, the challenge usually shifts to a discussion of how to integrate the components so that they can accomplish the intended results. The vertical and horizontal information linkage strategies identified by Galbraith in Figure 5.2 are examples of such integrating approaches.

Boeing's redesigned approach to the development and manufacturing of its aircraft provides an excellent example of the application of structural changes in a very complex business. The aircraft manufacturer realized that it had to change its approach to compete with Airbus, and it did so in its approach to the development of the 787.

BOEING RESTRUCTURES ITSELF

Before the 787, Boeing did all the engineering design work itself. The main reason to change, says Mike Bair, head of the 787 development team, was that the company realized it had to trawl the world and find the best suppliers in order to compete with its main rival in the market for commercial aircraft, the increasingly successful Airbus.

Airbus, a joint European venture involving French, German, British and Spanish partners, started from scratch. Almost by accident it stumbled on an organisational architecture that, along with generous subsidies, helped it overtake the giant of the business in less than two decades.

These days, Boeing is organising itself more like Airbus. It scoured the globe for new partners and found some in Europe, some in Japan and some not far from its home base in the United States. Whereas with the 777 aircraft the company worked with 500–700 suppliers, for the 787 it has chosen just under 100 "partners."

The difference is not just in the numbers, but in the relationship. Suppliers provide what they are asked for; partners share responsibility for a project. For over six months in 2005, teams of people from the various 787 partners met at Boeing's base in Everett, north of Seattle, to work together on the configuration of the plane—something that until then Boeing had always done by itself. Now the partners are back at their own bases, responsible for all aspects of their piece of the puzzle. The partners are building their own production facilities for their bits of the aircraft. The first flight is scheduled for 2007, and the 787 is due to come into service in 2008. As Mr Bair says, "it puts a high premium on the choice of partners in the first place."

It also puts a high premium on the management of that network of partners. Boeing holds a partners' "council meeting" every six weeks, and has set up a network to facilitate global collaboration which makes it possible for designers all over the world to work on the same up-to-the-minute database.

The company is also putting great faith in videoconferencing and has set up high-bandwidth facilities that are in constant use. People come into their offices in the middle of the night to have virtual meetings with colleagues in different time zones. Technically, the 787 will be an American plane; but in reality it will be a global one.[17] (From: *The Economist,* January 21, 2006.)

Source: "Partners in Wealth", The Economist Newspaper, Ltd., Vol.378, #8461, Jan 21, 2006, pg. 18. © The Economist Newspaper Limited, London 2006.

Boeing provides a graphic illustration of how structural approaches are changing in response to increasing complexity and ambiguity. In the aircraft maker's case, this included a radical reappraisal of where and how aircraft design and manufacturing should be undertaken, the role of suppliers and Boeing in the process, the treatment of intellectual property, and how the process should be managed. They recognized that their past approach was making them uncompetitive, and they have worked to break down silos and bring their suppliers into the design process as part of a dynamic network. This has necessitated a cultural shift toward treating their carefully selected suppliers as trusted contributing partners in the design and manufacturing challenges, and it has required the use of information-processing strategies to link it all together.

Boeing's structural and systemic transformation around the 787 has not been without its challenges and setbacks. It has logged record advanced orders, but its revolutionary use of composite materials to replace aluminum and its innovations on the global design and manufacturing front have resulted in more than a 2-year delay in the delivery of the first planes. There have been difficulties getting its global supply chain to work as expected, and a 2-month strike at Boeing exacerbated matters.[18] By April 2010, Boeing was more than halfway through its flight tests and on track to deliver the first 787 by the third quarter of 2011.[19]

Boeing has demonstrated a willingness to tackle fundamental questions of how best to deal with the structural challenges of differentiation and integration in order to enhance its performance. Wetzel and Buch[20] argue that organizations are more comfortable with increasing both differentiation and integrating mechanisms than with other approaches and tend to overuse these strategies. For example, a need for specialized response leads to a more structurally differentiated organization. This in turn leads to a need to coordinate or integrate more. An alternate strategy would be to decrease the need to differentiate, easing information-processing needs in Galbraith's terms.

Wetzel and Buch believe that it is useful to consider the benefits of such a reduction in the amount of structural differentiation in the organization, through such mechanisms as flattened structures, multiskilled workers, automated processes, and self-managed teams. By reducing their reliance on differentiating structural solutions, organizations can reduce their need for integrating mechanisms and increase the likelihood of developing congruent interventions. From an information-processing perspective, this falls into the category of strategies to ease information-processing linkage needs (see Figure 5.2).

Boeing provides an example of this approach at the enterprise level. At a more micro level, this approach was used by a medical regulatory body. By automating the certification-checking process and having physicians directly enter their professional certification data, the need for both differentiation and integrating mechanisms was reduced by the regulatory body, and efficiency and effectiveness were significantly enhanced, without a loss of control.[21]

Toolkit Exercise 5.1 asks you to examine the impact of structures and systems on an organizational change with which you are familiar.

Making Formal Structure and System Choices

An organization's design impacts the behavior of its members. In universities, faculty in the schools of management, government, and education may all teach courses on leadership, but these faculty may never speak with one another or teach one another's students. And yet these differentiated faculties may teach the same concepts and use the same textbooks. Similarly, in many large universities, each school or faculty often has its own specialized library and librarians, a costly arrangement. In fact, these diverse libraries might house the same books in different physical locations across a campus. Faced with significant budget cuts, the Harvard College Library took steps in 2009 to streamline services and foster collaboration with the sharing of research librarians across library facilities. Rather than only looking at cuts to fixed costs and personnel, the library administration chose to "encourage structural efficiency as a means of wringing savings from their ledgers".[22]

Every formal structure and system design has strengths and weaknesses associated with it. Bolman and Deal[23] argue that all organizational designs present structural dilemmas, or insolvable predicaments, that managers must deal with and reconcile. These fundamental design issues confront managers with enduring structural dilemmas: "tough trade-offs with no easy answers."[24] Bolman and Deal define, for example, the differentiation versus integration conundrum as:

> The tension between allocating work and coordinating sundry efforts creates a classic dilemma....The more complex a role structure (lots of people doing many different things), the harder it is to sustain a focused, tightly coupled enterprise....
> As complexity grows, organizations need more sophisticated—and more costly–coordination strategies. Rules, policies, and commands have to be augmented.[25]

Bolman and Deal identify other structural dilemmas. Another, for example, is the *gaps versus overlaps* dilemma. If tasks are not clearly assigned, then they can easily fall through the organizational cracks. If, on the other hand, managers overlap assignments, then they may create "conflict, wasted effort, and unintended redundancies."[26] The point is for change agents to understand these structural dilemmas, know the costs of mismanagement of these structural issues, and analyze if and how a gap has become an organizational liability that needs to change. Once a preferred structural option has been selected, weaknesses related to it can be alleviated and internal alignment improved through the design or modification of the formal policies, processes, structures, and systems.

Change leaders need to understand their organizations' strategy, how the formal structures and systems/processes are aligned with it, and the impact of those arrangements on the outcomes achieved. This is true at the macro or organizational level, and it is equally true down to the work-unit level. How can the formal structures and systems be modified to enhance the capacity of the organization to deliver on its strategy? If a change in strategy is needed, how do the formal structures and systems need to be realigned to contribute to the strategic change agenda? Wishnevsky and Damanpour found that sustained poor performance was likely to produce strategic change, and this in turn was likely to drive structural change.[27]

At the team or departmental level, change leaders have the option of creating several types of reporting structures depending upon the need under different conditions. For example, when new perspectives and ideas are sought, brainstorming sessions can be used to promote a free flow of ideas among all members of the group, with no hierarchical impediments. All ideas are equally welcomed. While brainstorming structures are good at generating ideas and engaging broad-scale participation, moving to the implementation stage typically requires the concentration of authority and decision making into fewer hands. This could take the form of a team or task force charged with making such decisions, or it could be delegated to a specific individual—more often than not, the manager responsible for the activity.

Mechanistic organizations can create structures and processes that allow them to either temporarily or permanently suspend hierarchical practices under certain conditions and constraints to advance creativity and innovation. The goal is to create spaces in which frank and open dialogue is encouraged and learning and organizational improvement advanced. Continuous-improvement teams within call centers, event-debriefing processes used by Special Forces units in the military, and innovation task forces within government are all examples of attempts to encourage reflection and innovation in more mechanistic structures. Decisions that lie beyond the authority and responsibilities of those who generate the analyses and insights can then be reviewed by the appropriate senior individuals. Approved initiatives can then be further developed and/or implemented on a broader scale where warranted. This is essentially what occurs at Parkland Memorial Hospital.

AN EFFICIENT HIERARCHY

In 2002, the Labor and Delivery (L&D) Ward at Parkland Memorial Hospital in Dallas, Texas, delivered 16,597 babies, more babies than any other maternity ward in the United States, at a neonatal death rate below the national average and at a cost lower than the national average. How does Parkland's L&D Ward provide such extraordinary care to indigent women? For some, it is a counterintuitive organization: There are 14 distinct levels of medical staff hierarchy with precise definitions of duties and authority at every level. Despite this hierarchical structure, the systems in place encourage everyone at all levels, doctors, nurses, and janitors, to "chip in" in order for the processes to run smoothly.[28]

The important points for change leaders to understand about formal structures and systems:

- There is no one best way to organize.
- Structural decisions should follow strategic decisions because the structure will then be there to support the strategy.
- All structures present leaders with dilemmas that they must manage. Today's trade-off may seem too costly in the future and will suggest a reorganization to fit tomorrow's external environment.
- Once structural choices are made, formal systems and processes need to be aligned so that weaknesses are addressed and the internal alignment with the strategy is supported.
- Organizational structures shape and impact people's behavior. A task force or committee, for example, that formally brings people together to analyze and report on a particular issue forces its members to cross organizational boundaries and to learn about and collaborate with people beyond their silo.

Using Structures and Systems to Influence the Approval and Implementation of Change

Using Formal Structures and Systems to Advance Change

Industrywide standard practices have inhibited change in the airline industry. At United, American, Air Canada, British Airways, and other traditionally organized air carriers, air routes were organized in what is called a "hub-and-spoke" design. That is, passengers were collected at many points and delivered to a central hub, where they changed planes and were sent out on a different spoke to their final destination. Different types of planes were purchased to service different routes, cabins were divided between business and economy class, and services were very similar across airlines. For many years, this strategy delivered cost savings to the airlines and served them well. Union agreements escalated labor costs over this period as employees sought to share in the success.

However, discount airlines, such as Southwest Air and West Jet, came along and opted for a different strategic approach. They adopted a single type of plane to ease maintenance challenges, offered a single no-frills service level in the cabin, and structured other aspects of their operations to lower labor and capital costs per passenger mile. Most importantly, they restructured their air routes to provide point-to-point service. The changes to the traditional airline practices evolved from cultural and strategic differences and were anchored in new structures, systems, and processes designed to support the new value proposition. Because of these changes, they were able to fly passengers directly to their destinations at a lower price and, in the case of Southwest and West Jet, become very profitable in the process. The traditional airlines' structures and systems that were designed to facilitate the efficient and effective delivery of services have become a problem and contributed to their recent financial challenges.

Poor financial performance has led to growing demands for major improvements from banks, shareholders, pension funds, and other stakeholders. Structural and system realignment to lower labor costs and cost drivers have been key targets of change. Those who have sought to resist the changes, such as the airline labor unions, have attempted to leverage existing structures and systems to advance their interests. The following example provides a fascinating but different look at the role that existing structures can play in organization change.

COMPETITIVE EFFICIENCY AT UNITED AIRLINES

One of the ways that the board at United Airlines responded to the competitive realities and the disastrous financial results was to use formal processes to replace a number of key executives[29] and charge senior management with responsibility for turning things around. Staffing arrangements, work rules, and labor costs were among the many areas that attracted the attention of senior management tasked with effecting change. Management analyzed and then used existing systems and structures (including formal judicial components) to advance and legitimize changes to their collective agreements and, by extension, changes to staffing levels, the organization of work, and related terms and conditions of work.

In response, employee groups enlisted formal (as well as informal) systems and structures to protect their interests—actions that airline executives saw as resisting needed changes. UAL's use of existing structures and systems to effect change was viewed by employee groups as adversarial, generating serious resentment in what was obviously a very difficult context. Despite the dissatisfaction of employees and their representatives with the imposed changes, they were enacted because the formal structures and rules that governed the situation allowed management to do so.

Similar hard-nose change tactics were employed at Air Canada in 2003 when it entered bankruptcy protection[30] and British Airways in 2010 as it responded to huge financial losses.[31] They show the use of existing structures and systems to advance change through the exercise of formal power and authority from the top of the organization and/or through the imposition of action by outside agents such as banks, courts, or regulators.

Approaches that leverage formal structures and systems to advance change do not have to result in a war with one's employees. Rather, their application can be undertaken in a manner that facilitates understanding, builds support (or lessens resistance), and legitimizes change among those who have serious reservations. Agilent had to downsize in 2002, laying off 8,000 employees.[32] Management was seen by its employees as having acted responsibly and humanely. Openness and honesty characterized how the financial and strategic issues were approached and how the appropriate systems and structures were applied by the executives. Employees believed all reasonable options were explored and that layoffs were undertaken as a last resort. Those exiting Agilent reported that they were treated with respect and dignity, while those remaining were left with hope for the future of the firm and confidence in the leadership. To go through this level of downsizing and still be ranked #31 on *Fortune*'s 100 Best Companies to Work For in the following period is no small accomplishment!

Using Systems and Structures to Obtain Formal Approval of a Change Project

Change is made easier when the change leader understands when and how to access and use existing systems to advance an initiative. In larger organizations, the formal approval processes for major initiatives are often well defined. For example, in universities, significant academic decisions usually require the approvals of department councils, faculty councils, and university senates in the form of formal motions and votes. The change agent's task is to engage in tactics and initiatives that will increase the likelihood of a positive vote for the proposed change through these various formal bodies.

Any significant change initiative will cost money. To maximize the chances of receiving resources for a change initiative, change leaders will need to understand the budget process and how to garner support for the proposed change through departments and individuals who approve the financial support. Timing is important. The likelihood of approval in the short term is less if the organization is in the middle of the budget cycle and available funds have already been allocated. Efforts to build interest and support should begin well in advance when significant funds are needed, building to coincide with key decision dates.

Earlier in this book, two dimensions of change were considered: the magnitude or size of the change and the proactive–reactive initiation dimension. Change projects that are incremental will normally require fewer resources and lower levels of organization approval. As the change increases in magnitude and strategic importance, change leaders will find that they need to pay more attention to formal approval processes, eliciting the support of more senior individuals prior to enacting the change. However, exceptions to this general pattern are often found in areas with safety and regulatory compliance implications. In these situations, significant change decisions (e.g., mandated changes to work practices) may be delegated to appropriate frontline staff due to the risk of not responding quickly enough. Once the urgency abates, decisions may be reviewed by more senior managers and other paths forward adopted. Reactive strategic changes tend to attract the greatest attention because of the risk, visibility, and criticality of such changes to the future of the organization.[33]

When senior decision makers believe the change initiative has significant strategic and/or financial implications and risks, the change will typically require the formal approval of the organization's senior executive team or its board of directors. A savvy change leader knows the approval levels and hurdles associated with different types of changes—that is, at what level does an issue become a board matter, a senior executive decision, or an issue that can be dealt with at a local level? What will they be looking for in the way of analysis and support?

No two organizations will be the same. Organizations in which there are significant negative consequences of failure (e.g., a nuclear power plant or a pharmaceutical manufacturer) will usually require more senior levels of approval for what may appear to be a relatively modest undertaking in a mission-critical area. Likewise, the hurdle levels are likely to be rigorous in organizations with senior managers and/or cultures that have a low tolerance for ambiguity.

Using Systems to Enhance the Prospects for Approval

Change leaders have a variety of factors they need to consider concerning the use of systems to increase the likelihood of approval.

First, they need to ask themselves if formal approval is required or if the change decision already rests within their span of control. If no approval is required, they may choose to make people aware of their intent and engage them in discussions to increase downstream acceptance. However, why initiate activities that trigger unnecessary formal approval systems and processes when they are not required? Figure 5.3 outlines the various considerations regarding positioning the approval of a change proposal.

In all cases:

a. When there is a decision maker, identify his or her attitude to the change and attempt to work with that person.

b. Demonstrate how the change project relates to the strategy or vision of the organization.

c. Use good process to legitimize the change proposal.

Figure 5.3   Positioning the Change for Formal Approval

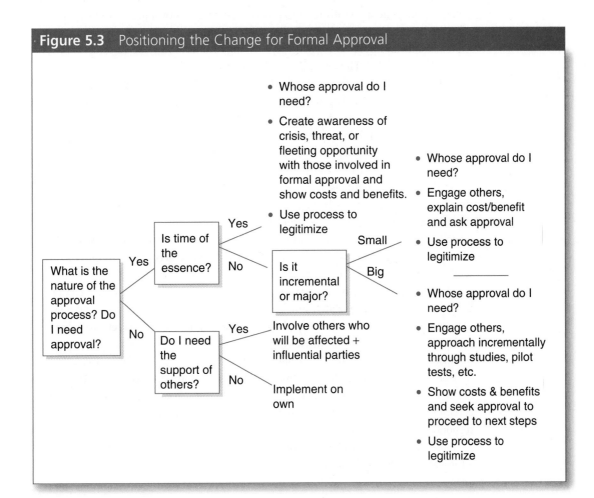

If formal approval is required, change leaders need to demonstrate that the initiative is aligned with the vision and strategy of the organization, advances the organization's agenda, and has benefits that exceed the costs. If the needed changes modify the vision, strategy, or key elements that make up the organization, the change leader will need to demonstrate how such changes will enhance organizational health and have downstream benefits that exceed the costs and risks associated with these significant organizational changes. Included in such a calculation should be the costs and risks of doing nothing.

If changes are more extreme and if there is sufficient time, leaders can frame and introduce the change in ways that increase management's familiarity and comfort with the proposal. They can do this incrementally, using vehicles such as staged agreements on the purpose and scope of the change (e.g., defining the scope of Stage 1, followed by defining the scope of Stage 2 once Stage 1 has been completed, etc.), preliminary studies, task force reviews, consultants' reports, and pilot projects prior to the request for formal approval. This, in turn, reduces perceived risks, enhances a sense of the benefits, and essentially conditions the organization to embrace (or at least not resist) more fundamental changes to the aligned systems.

If time is of the essence due to a crisis or emerging threats, the change leader can act with urgency and use the danger to focus attention, facilitate approval of the initiative, and generate motivation to proceed. Formal approval processes often have expedited processes available for dealing with imminent threats and emergencies.

When formal approval is required, a change leader will need to know whose agreement is needed. However, if broader acceptance is important before gaining formal approval, then those involved in approval discussions will need to be expanded accordingly. Approval and acceptance are generally enhanced when people are involved in the discussion and feel that they have been heard. They are also enhanced when there is the perception that the analysis and discussion around the alignment systems (e.g., vision, strategy, goals, balance scorecards, and strategy maps) have been discussed thoroughly.[34]

Acceptance is sometimes increased among the uncommitted and resistant when they believe that there has been a rigorous review process in place for the assessment of a change. That is, the procedures are thorough and complete. Further, when there is active involvement of those individuals or their representatives in the planning and approval processes, their understanding and acceptance of the change tend to rise. Some may see this as a cooption strategy.

Formal approval systems, therefore, can increase the perception that a change has been assessed appropriately and is worthy of support. However, those who are opposed to a proposal may usurp the process and intentionally erect procedural and approval barriers to an initiative. The oppositions' motives in doing this may be unsullied (the desire for due diligence, due process, and careful review), they may be firmly convinced that the change is not in the organizations best interests, or their motives may be to obstruct out of self-interest. Change leaders will need to carefully assess the motives of the opposition before deciding on how best to respond.

Table 5.2 sets out a checklist of questions to consider when seeking formal approval for a change initiative.

Table 5.2 Checklist for Change Initiative Approval

1. What does a review of documents related to relevant formal structures and systems reveal about the formal approval process and who has formal authority for approving the change initiative?

2. What are the key points in the process that a change leader needs to pay attention to: timing of meetings; getting on the agenda; cycle time; types of decisions made; and where decisions are made?
   a. How are the relevant systems and structures interconnected? How do they influence one another?

3. Develop a process map that tracks the change idea from start to finish.
   a. What role (and person) has formal authority and decision-making responsibility for this initiative?
   b. What are the decision parameters that are normally applied and are there zones of discretion available to decision makers?
   c. What are the power and influence patterns around particular systems and structures? Who has direct and indirect influence on how the systems and structures are applied?
   d. How should the change leader manage these formal systems and structures to reduce resistance? And how can they be managed to advance the change initiative?

Ways Around the Approval Process

Mastering the Formal Approval Process

Howell and Higgins[35] identified three different ways of approaching the formal approval process. The first involves the straightforward rational approach. Proposals are typically developed and brought forward for consideration, and they are reviewed for inclusion on the agenda. Once the proposal is presented and discussed, it is approved, rejected, or sent back for further study or rework. The likelihood of gaining approval is increased when change leaders:

- Have a well-placed sponsor
- Know their audience members and their preferences
- Understand the power and influence dynamics and the implications of the project for the organization and for those involved in the approval process
- Do their homework with respect to their detailed knowledge of the change project, its scope and objectives, its costs and benefits, and risk areas
- Informally obtain needed approval and support in advance
- Have the change project presented persuasively by an appropriate individual
- Have a good sense of timing concerning when best to bring it forward.[36]

The systems associated with obtaining formal approval for planned changes vary greatly. In organic or entrepreneurial organizations, the process may be loose and idiosyncratic. As organizations mature, even very entrepreneurial firms tend to systematize and formalize the approval processes in order to increase control.

The decision making associated with formal approval processes takes many forms (e.g., formal voting by an executive committee, consensus mechanisms, and go/no go decisions controlled by individual executives). While the exact approval process will be unique to the firm, the level of rigorousness and formality used to assess proposed changes usually varies with the magnitude of the change, the levels of perceived risk and uncertainty, the preferences of those involved with the decision, and the power dynamics at work in the organization.

When the proposed change lies in an area in which much is known, decision makers tend to focus on concrete information (e.g., benchmark data, industry patterns, and performance data). They then use this data to make a decision.[37] When the changes reside in areas that are inherently ambiguous, attention turns to an assessment of the quality of the analysis and the logic of the advocate for the proposal. In essence, the decision makers need to decide whether or not they trust the judgment of the change leader and the skills and abilities of the change team.[38]

As organizations mature, they often adopt a staged approval process for changes that are viewed as strategically significant, expensive, wide-reaching in their impact, and potentially disruptive. A staged approach establishes decision-approval steps that do not prematurely dismiss ideas worthy of further exploration while controlling the ever-increasing commitment of time and resources if the change were to progress to the next stage.[39] The goal is to provide focus through vision and strategic alignment; allow proposed initiatives to be explored and assessed in a rational manner; avoid unpleasant surprises; manage risk; and keep an eye on the portfolio of change initiatives to ensure the organization does not become overwhelmed with change initiatives.

As one proceeds through the approval stages, the assessment process becomes increasingly rigorous and the hurdles that must be met before proceeding to the next stage rise. When the process is working well, it should stimulate innovative thinking and initiatives, enhance the quality of assessment, reduce the cycle time from ideation to implementation, and reduce the likelihood of dysfunctional political behavior.

The formal approval process does more than ensure that the decision making concerning change is thorough and reasoned. If the process is viewed as legitimate by others in the organization, its decisions will lend legitimacy to what changes are pursued and enhance acceptance. When an incremental or staged approval process has been adopted to gain approval (e.g., commencing with concept and initial plan approval, followed by a field experiment or a pilot test, a departmental trial, and a final review prior to large-scale adoption), then the outcomes achieved and reactions to the results (e.g., the credibility of the data and the reaction of opinion leaders) will play an important part in building support for approval and downstream acceptance by others.

In addition to addressing the traditional hierarchical approach, Howell and Higgins identified two other ways to use system awareness to advance change: strategies based on creeping commitment and coalition building; and strategies involving simply forging ahead without formal approval.

Encouraging "Creeping Commitment" and Coalition Building

As an alternative to directly pursuing formal approval for a change initiative, change leaders can employ a strategy of creeping commitment (the foot-in-the-door approach[40]) and coalition building. Initiatives such as customer and employee surveys, benchmark data, pilot programs, and other incremental system-based approaches can be used to acclimate organizational members to the change ideas. Such initiatives can be used systematically to clarify the need for change, refine the initiative, address concerns, reduce resistance, and increase comfort levels. As well, they can create opportunities for direct involvement that will build interest and support for the change within key groups. This, in turn, will reduce resistance and increase the prospects for support if and when formal approval is sought.

Coalitions can be extremely important during a formal approval process. Change leaders need to understand key players to develop influential coalitions that will support the changes. Often in systems or technological changes, if key user groups want to adopt new software or systems, management will be more willing to accept the innovation. In other situations, developing the coalition provides the political clout to move the decision in a favorable direction.

The intent of this approach is to create the momentum needed to reach a tipping point[41] that significantly enhances the likelihood of approval. When formal approval is required, the support from key coalition members and stakeholders should make the process more manageable. If the change has been accepted by a sufficient number of key stakeholders, it may make the approval process all but automatic.

Developing coalitions for change often makes a great deal of sense when seeking formal approval. However, coalition building is not without its risks. This approach takes time and adds complexity (more fingers are in the pie) that may impede the approval process. It can also become quite political and divisive, with coalitions developing in opposition to the change that will need to be managed. Change leaders should avoid getting trapped in tactics that seriously harm relationships, diminish their integrity, and/or compromise long-term objectives.

Bypassing the Formal Approval Process: Just Do It!

The need to seek formal approval can sometimes be bypassed entirely. Peter Grant, a banker who changed the demographic of employees at his bank over a 30-year period, never sought formal permission. He understood the systems in his organization and used this awareness to quietly advance a change agenda over 30 years. Through this approach, he dramatically altered the nature of his organization. He would appear to have followed the classic change dictum, "Don't ask, just do it."

PETER GRANT'S "JUST DO IT" APPROACH

Peter Grant was a black manager, one of few in the firm when he joined. Over his career, he pursued his personal goal of bringing more women and minorities into the firm. Each time he had the opportunity, he hired a qualified minority. And he encouraged others to do the same. Over his career, he was instrumental in having 3,500 talented minority and female members join the organization.[42]

When the scope of the change is manageable, defensible, and arguably within their scope of authority, change leaders should seriously consider proceeding on their own without seeking formal approval. Key people such as supervisors should be kept sufficiently in the loop so that they are not unpleasantly surprised or left with the belief that someone acted in an underhanded fashion.

When the "just do it" strategy is effectively applied, the dynamics can be powerful. Those who might otherwise be predisposed to oppose the change may not notice it or be lulled into acquiescence as the change proceeds in a lower-key fashion during the initial phases (e.g. data gathering, preliminary experimentation). This approach allows for change refinement, the generation of supportive data, and the building of momentum for change that is difficult to stop.

Howell and Higgins refer to this as the renegade process.[43] It grows out of the premise that it is often easier to gain forgiveness than permission to do something in organizations. This tactic can prove helpful in the early stages of product innovation, but Frost and Egri[44] argue that securing permission is an important contributor to success when social innovations are involved. When using a renegade process, one must be careful not to create enemies unnecessarily or engage in tactics that create long-term damage to your reputation and credibility or the reputation of the firm.

The renegade method does not mean the chaotic introduction of disturbances merely to shake things up. Most organizations are already experiencing enough turbulence. Nor does it mean acting in organizationally naïve ways. Rather, this approach begins with a careful assessment of organizational and environmental factors, including the needs and preferences of key individuals who have the potential to harm or assist the change and the change leader. Finally, it asks change leaders to recognize the power and influence that they have to get things done through launching the initiative on their own and, when the situation is appropriate, to "just do it!"

Aligning Strategically, Starting Small, and "Morphing" Tactics

Gaining approval for change becomes less daunting when you are able to show how the change aligns with the organization's mission, vision, and strategy. When a change plan is being developed, questions of its relationship to these dimensions and its alignment with other existing systems need to be addressed.

If the case can be made that the change initiative adds value over other alternatives *and* fits within the context of the mission, vision, strategy, and significant downstream systems (e.g., information and reward systems, organization structure), the likelihood of acceptance and adoption of the change is enhanced. If the resources required for the change seem relatively minor relative to the benefits, approval is also more likely. For example, consider a proposed change in the level of customer service offered by call center personnel that has high potential to increase customer satisfaction and significantly reduce the need for call-backs. The likelihood of approval and acceptance is higher if the only required actions are an additional half day of training, the development of needed support materials, the modification of a couple of decision support screens, the presence of supervisory support, and the modification of performance metrics to reinforce the desired change. In effect, the change leader will have demonstrated that there is little to fear because the change is incremental, is not particularly disruptive in nature, and contains benefits that outweigh the costs.

Change leaders often find it is useful to frame changes in ways that reduce the sense of incongruence with existing structures and systems. In general, this approach makes it easier to gain approval because it reduces the sense of disruption and risk that the change will entail. For example, if the end state of a change were to move from mass marketing to relationship-focused, one-to-one marketing, this would be a huge change. The perceived risk can be reduced by breaking the change down into a number of smaller, manageable stages that begin with exploratory research and evaluation, followed by a pilot project, assessment of learning and system alignment challenges, extension to a customer group that was particularly well suited to the approach, and so forth. By starting small and minimizing the incongruence with existing systems, the change leader can move in a systematic fashion in the desired direction, learning and modifying systems and structures in ways that look incremental in the short term but have significant long-term effects.

As momentum and the critical mass of support build for a revolutionary change that is positioned as incremental, the change may take on a life of its own. When those smaller change elements are added together over time, the cumulative changes will look far more significant in retrospect than they did at any point along the way. The term "morphing" captures the sense of this approach to change because it depicts a slow and steady transformation of the organization over time.[45] Abrahamson refers to this as the "change without pain" approach, though not all recipients would share this sentiment.[46] The earlier example of Peter Grant, who was instrumental in the hiring of 3,500 women and visible minorities at his bank, falls into this category. The lesson is that approval can often be advanced by avoiding the depiction of the change as a marked departure of heroic proportions. An evolving series of ten 5% changes over the course of 3 years produces a total change of 50% in organizational performance, and that does not include the compounding effects!

The Interaction of Structures and Systems With Change During Implementation

Structures and systems not only have an impact on a change leader's ability to gain acceptance for a change project; they can also have a significant impact on the success of the implementation process. Sometimes there are existing systems and structures that change agents have to work with, while at other times they may represent aspects of the actual change. The transformation at MASkargo, a state-of-the-art Malaysian air cargo facility, provides an example of system-enabled changes. Tens of millions of dollars had been invested in the late 1990s in systems and technology designed to support the creation of a premier air cargo-handling center. However, performance fell far short of expectations. Rather than panic, MASkargo opted for a change path that began by working with and assessing existing systems and structures. It then used the learning from that assessment to modify and extend those systems and structures to improve existing services and develop new initiatives.

MASKARGO'S ADVANCED CARGO CENTER DELIVERS ON ITS PROMISE

Malaysia's state-of-the-art one-stop air cargo-handling facility had, in its first 2 years of operation, been plagued by system failures, bottlenecks, and misplaced shipments that proved extremely costly. However, MASkargo was able to correct these issues by fine-tuning the formal systems and processes and ensuring that employees developed their ability to work with the new structures and systems. Systemic cargo-handling glitches were identified and rectified. Workers developed greater familiarity with the fully automated operational process, and results improved. MASkargo recorded a RM52 million profit in the 2002/03 third quarter to sharply turn around from an RM242.86 million loss for the whole of 2001/02.

In the process, MASkargo has been nominated as Best Air Cargo Carrier (Asia), Best Air Cargo Terminal Operator (Asia), and Best Cargo Airport. "Our selling points are reliability and efficiency. All the sophisticated equipment will come to naught if we cannot deliver," says Mohd Yunus Idris (General Manager of Operations).

Among other things, they have established performance benchmarks for their key operations (e.g., cargo is processed in just 90 minutes for uploading to connecting aircraft to 100 destinations across six continents). More importantly, they take action when benchmarks aren't achieved. "If a process takes longer than specified, agents may immediately lodge a complaint and we will take action," says Yunus. Rising tonnage, their ability to handle very diverse cargo effectively and efficiently (from day-old chicks to elephants and Formula 1 cars), profitability, and high levels of customer satisfaction suggest their improvement changes are working.[47]

The change task at MASkargo was made easier by the fact that the facility was new, systems were well documented, and participants understood that refinement and improvement initiatives were to be expected and embraced. MASkargo recognized the value of aligning systems and structures with the vision and strategy and used this to promote the needed changes. Further, they avoided getting bogged down in finger pointing and other defensive tactics when things didn't pan out initially. Such actions can derail progress in even what appears to be a relatively straightforward problem.

Diagnosis of the nature and impact of structures and systems during implementation puts change leaders in a strong position to identify when and where these may present challenges that will need to be managed and where they can be used to facilitate change. The MASkargo and Peter Grant change examples involved approaches that refined and exploited existing systems in support of the desired changes.

Toolkit Exercise 5.2 asks you to engage in an assessment of the role that existing structures and systems are likely to play in an organizational change and how they might be managed and used to increase the likelihood of success.

Toolkit Exercise 5.3 asks you to consider a change project and think about how you might gain approval.

In summary, change agents need to understand the approval processes for their particular projects. They need to know the key players and how formal the process is. Does it require a vote? Will the go-ahead be authorized at a management or executive meeting? Alternatively, can the change agent act to develop a coalition first, or just act using available resources and power? In the next section, we will explore the role of systems in change approval, change acceptance, and change implementation.

Using Structures and Systems to Facilitate the Acceptance of Change

Change agents may be tempted to breathe a sigh of relief and relax once a change project is approved. However, gaining formal approval is not the same as gaining generalized acceptance of the change. Too often, the anticipated chorus of excitement fails to materialize and, in its stead, change agents experience begrudging cooperation, or covert or overt resistance. The assumption that approval will automatically lead to acceptance is a dangerous one.

Success rates in getting change acceptance are sometimes low. Consider the experience with customer relationship management programs:

CUSTOMER RELATIONSHIP MANAGEMENT

Complex implementations, failure to yield desired results, escalating maintenance costs have all marred the reputation of customer relationship management (CRM) programs...50% of CRM implementations generally fail...and almost 42% of CRM software licenses bought end up unused.... While some fault lies with the vendors, sometimes it is, unfortunately, the business that gets itself in a rut.[48]

Despite their best intentions, change leaders often have less-than-stellar success in bringing approved change to fruition. Lack of acceptance often plays a role in this. Systemic factors in an organization can be used to ease the legitimization and acceptance of a change initiative. However, they can also derail progress. The inappropriate delegation of sponsorship and the misapplication of systems are two of the most commonly cited mistakes made by top management in change initiatives.[49]

Paul Tsaparis of Hewlett-Packard did not make the mistake of underestimating the role that systems and structures can play.

SYSTEMS AND STRUCTURES AT HP (CAN)

In May of 2002, Paul Tsaparis, 42, president of Hewlett-Packard (Canada) Ltd., began managing the massive integration of Hewlett-Packard and Compaq in Canada. The new 6,800-person organization had annual revenues in excess of $3 billion (Canadian). As is often the case with organizational integration, staff reductions were involved.

Tsaparis approached the integration challenge by getting out and putting a human face on the challenges and changes. He needed to communicate the vision and corporate strategy and let people know what was happening to their employment situation as soon as possible. He needed to reassure other key stakeholders (customers, suppliers) that they would not be lost in the shuffle. Tsaparis knew he needed to develop organizational structures, systems, and processes that would support HP's strategy, reinforce the integration change initiative, and increase the likelihood of longer term organizational success. He created a team of individuals to facilitate the organizational changes. This, in turn, required structures, systems, and processes that would support the change team in the pursuit of its objectives.[50]

Tsaparis faced significant structural and systemic challenges to change. Each organization, HP and Compaq, had its own way of doing things. And many of those systems and structures would have explicit as well as implicit implications—ways of doing things that might not even be written down but were firmly embedded in the habits of organizational members. As a result, the conscious development of structures and systems that would support HP's strategy represented an important step in the building of an infrastructure that would support change and promote acceptance. Conflicting and misaligned structures and systems needed to be identified and addressed so that the resulting web of structures and systems were aligned.

Change agents need to understand the effects of structures and systems from the perspective of the person who is on the receiving end of the change—the actual person who will be asked to behave differently. If people do not accept the change (whether they like it or not), they are unlikely to modify their behavior in the desired direction, no matter how excellent the change project is.

Interestingly, acceptance or compliance does not necessarily mean attitude change. That is, attitude change need not come first. It may well evolve after the needed behavior is obtained. That is, if systems can be used to promote the desired behavior in individuals, (e.g., through having them live with new structural or systemic arrangements), their attitudes toward what they are doing may adjust over time in the desired direction as they live within the new context.[51]

The effective use of the formal communication, performance management, and reward systems can play useful roles in gaining acceptance and commitment. Clarity of purpose and direction, combined with employee involvement and rewards for desired behavior, can all be used to advance the engagement and involvement of employees in change-related initiatives. A top-down directive that orders change may lead to less information sharing, reduced risk taking, less acceptance of change, and greater employee turnover.[52] Unless the employees buy into the legitimate authority of executives and the legitimacy of the change, they may not accept it and instead may engage in actions that slow, disrupt or sabotage progress.

Much of the change leaders' difficulty in thinking through the impact of structure on acceptance flows from their assumptions. One sees clearly the need for change and the rationale underlying the change and believes the change is immensely logical. From that position, it is much too easy to assume that others will see and accept the logic of the change agent! But the logic falls flat for organizational members facing a reward system that works against the change or an organizational structure that emphasizes characteristics contrary to the desired change (e.g., cost controls rather than customer focus).

The passage of time, in conjunction with the use of formal systems, can also influence the acceptance of change. When a change initiative has been the subject of formal discussion and review for an appropriate interval, this gestation period may allow the idea to become more familiar and acceptable. Initiatives that are shocking at first may appear less threatening after a period of reflection. Alternatively, if approval has been granted and there seems to be little activity or visible progress, acceptability and support may diminish.

In summary, systems and structures, properly deployed, can play an important role in the speed and rate of acceptance of change. People don't resist all change. Lots of things have the potential to be seen as worth doing, and people tend to respond positively to change initiatives that they understand and believe are worth the effort and risk. The way that systems and processes are deployed will influence the perception of the change.[53]

Developing Adaptive Systems and Structures

The ability of organizations to adapt to change is aided by their ability to learn. Nevis suggests that organizations can be viewed as learning systems that acquire knowledge, disseminate it through the organization, and use that knowledge to accomplish their missions.[54] Learning is facilitated when organizational members do the following:

1. Systematically and deliberately scan their external environment and learn from it

2. Demonstrate the desire to question existing approaches and always improve

3. Have a concern for measurement of performance and shared perceptions of the gap between the current and desired levels of performance

4. Develop an experimental mindset where they try new things

5. Create an organizational climate of openness, accessibility, honesty, and active discussion and debate

6. Engage in continuous education at all organizational levels

7. Use a variety of methods, appreciate diversity, and take a pluralistic view of competencies

8. Have multiple individuals who act as advocates for new ideas and methods and who are also willing to exercise their critical judgment in the review of ideas

9. Have an involved, engaged leadership

10. Recognize the interdependence of units and have a systems perspective

Many of these learning actions are influenced by organizational structures and systems. The presence of early-warning systems and opportunity-finding systems advance the scanning capacity of the organization. The presence of a formal strategy and environmental review process, complete with performance metrics, will increase the likelihood that firms will systematically review where they are and where they want to go. Systems that reward innovation and information sharing will increase the prospects for openness and exploration. Systems that fund and reinforce development will open people to continuous education. Likewise, appropriately designed systems and processes can be used to advance diversity and the exploration of new ideas. Finally, systems can be used to increase the prospect that interdependencies are recognized and that a systems perspective is brought to problem solving.

Organizations that are flexible and adaptive have an easier time adjusting to incremental and upending changes than do bureaucratic ones.[55] As the complexity and turbulence of organizational environments increase, more flexible, adaptive systems will be required (this was discussed earlier in the chapter).[56] Essentially, they need to become more "change ready."[57]

In a study of strategic planning in an international nongovernmental development organization, the need for adaptive capacity manifested itself in an interesting way. Rather than opt for an unambiguous course of action, this organization tended to develop multiple strategies that were both ambiguous and ambitious. What looked like strategic drift to outsiders provided managers with flexibility in how they responded to changing conditions. Appropriate ambiguous strategies were used as metaphors to promote consensus and legitimacy with key stakeholder groups.[58]

To cope with turbulence and complexity, organizations are being designed in unconventional ways that include the use of formal and informal networks with external organizations. For example, designer, supplier, producer, and distributor capabilities are being brought together in ways that increase flexibility and adaptability. Thus, a product might be designed in Italy, built in Korea from Brazilian materials, and distributed in the United States by a Scandinavian firm. Think IKEA for this type of network.[59] The network partners are held together by market mechanisms such as contracts, just-in-time logistics, shared market intelligence and production systems, and customers' demands rather than by organizational charts and controls.[60]

One of the roles of the change agent is to help organizations learn from the past and evolve systems and structures that are likely to help them succeed in the future. Focusing on how organizations acquire knowledge and spread it throughout the organization can be a valuable diagnostic tool in this regard. By facilitating the development of adaptive systems and processes (keeping in mind the competitive realities and the need for congruence with the environment), change agents will succeed in enhancing the capacity of the organization to adjust to change in the future.

Summary

Formal systems and structures influence how change initiatives evolve and succeed. Change leaders need to understand them, how they operate, and how they influence the change process. In addition, change leaders need to know how to manage the approval process for initiatives so that they can work with, through, and/or around them in order to increase the prospects of the change being adopted. Formal systems and structures can be used to advance acceptance and implementation of the change in the organization. And finally, formal systems and structures increasingly need to be adaptive.

Glossary of Terms

Organizational Structure and Systems

The Organizational structure and systems are how the organization formally organizes itself to accomplish its mission. Structure is how the organization's tasks are formally divided, grouped, and coordinated. The structure would include the organization hierarchy, the structure of any manufacturing operation, and any formal procedures such as the performance appraisal system, as well as other structures. Systems are the formal processes of coordination within the organization.

Change Approval Process

The change approval process is the formal procedure that change agents must follow for organizational approval of a change project.

Acceptance of Change

The acceptance of change is the degree to which change participants accept or "buy into" the change that has been implemented.

Mechanistic Organization and Organic Organization

Organizations can be viewed metaphorically as machines or as organisms. A mechanistic organization is one that exhibits machinelike qualities. An organic organization is one that exhibits organism-like qualities.

Environmental Uncertainty

Environmental uncertainty measures the degree of variability of the environment. Duncan suggests two dimensions of uncertainty: degree of complexity of the environment and degree of dynamism.

Information-Processing View of Organizations

The information-processing view of organizations considers organizations as information-processing mechanisms. This view argues that the better the fit between the information-processing capabilities of the organization and its environment, the more effective the organization.

The Formal Approval Process

This is the traditional approach in which a person or persons develop a proposal and bring it forward for assessment and formal approval by the appropriate organizational members.

Creeping Commitment

Creeping commitment is the gradual increase in commitment by change participants toward the change project. Such an increase is often obtained by involving participants in decision making.

Coalition Building

Coalition building is the forming of partnerships to increase pressures for or against change.

Renegade Approach

Change is initiated without having first obtained formal approval. This is often done in conjunction with creeping commitment and coalition-building tactics. The intent of the approach is that the change is advanced to the point that it cannot easily be reversed by those with formal authority.

Adaptive Systems and Structures

Adaptive systems and structures are those that are relatively ready for change compared to others.

END-OF-CHAPTER EXERCISES

TOOLKIT EXERCISE 5.1

Impact of Existing Structures and Systems on the Change

Think of a change situation you are familiar with.

1. How did the organization use structures and systems to deal with uncertainty and complexity in its environment? Was this an appropriate response?

2. How did existing structures and systems affect the ability of the change leader to bring about desired change?

    a. What systems/structures were involved?
    b. How did these systems/structures influence what happened? Was this related to how they were formally designed? Or was this related to how they actually came to be used in practice?
    c. Who influenced how the systems/structures were used and how did this affect the outcomes that ensued?

TOOLKIT EXERCISE 5.2

Gaining Approval for the Change Project

1. Consider a change project in an organization with which you are familiar. What is the approval process for more minor change initiatives? For more major change initiatives? Can you describe the processes involved?

   a. If a project requires capital approval, are there existing capital budgeting processes?

   b. If the project needs dedicated staff allocated to it, or if it will lead to additions to staff complement, what are the processes for adding people permanently and selecting and developing staff?

   c. Does the project alter the way work is organized and performed? What are the systems and processes used for defining jobs and assessing performance?

   d. Can the project be approved by an individual? Who is that person? What approval power does he/she have?

2. Are there ways that the perceived risks of the change could have been reduced by the way the change leader staged the project and managed the approval process?

TOOLKIT EXERCISE 5.3

Using Existing Structures and Systems to Promote the Change

1. Look back at the questions raised in Toolkit Exercise 5.1. How could the existing structures and systems have been approached and used differently to advance the desired change?

2. What role could incremental strategies that were nested within existing systems and structures have played? Would they have really moved the process forward or simply avoided the real changes that needed to be addressed?

3. What role could more revolutionary strategies have played? Would they produce issues related to their alignment with existing systems and structures? How would you manage the challenges created by this?

Notes

1. Langton, N., Robbins, S. P., & Judge, T. A. (2010). *Organizational behaviour: Concepts, controversies, applications* (5th Canadian ed., p. 502). Toronto: Pearson Canada.

2. Daft, R. L. (2007). *Organization theory and design* (9th ed., p. 90). Cincinnati, OH: South-Western College.

3. Wal-Mart. (2010). *Annual report.* Retrieved May 2010 from http://walmartstores .com/sites/annualreport/2010/default.aspx.

4. Competitive advantage lies in systems efficiencies. (2002). *Chain Store Age, 78*(8), 74.

5. Bolman, L., & Deal, T. (2008). *Reframing organizations: Artistry, choice, and leadership* (4th ed., pp. 45–116). San Francisco: Jossey-Bass.

6. Langton, N., Robbins, S. P., & Judge, T. A. (2010). *Organizational behaviour: Concepts, controversies, applications* (5th Canadian ed., pp. 500–527). Toronto: Pearson Canada.

7. Thompson, J. D. (1967). *Organizations in action.* New York: McGraw-Hill.

8. Aragón-Correa, J. A., & Sharma, S. (2003). A contingent resource-based view of proactive corporate environmental strategy. *Academy of Management Review, 28*(1), 71–88; Moles, C., van der Gaag, A., & Fox, J. (2010). The practice of complexity: Review, change and service improvement in NHA department. *Journal of Health Organization and Management, 24*(2), 127–144; Davis, J. P., Eisenhardt, K. M., & Bingham, C. B. (2009). Optimal structure, market dynamism, and the strategy of simple rules. *Administrative Science Quarterly,* (3), 413–452.

9. Daft, R. L. (2007). *Organization theory and design* (9th ed., p. 152). Cincinnati, OH: South-Western College.

10. Tu, Q., Vonderembse, M. A., Ragu-Nathan, T. S., & Ragu-Nathan, B. (2004). Measuring modularity-based manufacturing practices and their impact on mass customization capability: A customer-driven perspective. *Decision Sciences, 35*(2), 147–168.

11. Galbraith, J. R. (1977). *Organization design.* Reading, MA: Addison-Wesley.

12. Adapted from Galbraith, J. R. (1977). *Organization design.* Reading, MA: Addison-Wesley; and Daft, R. L. (2003). *Organization theory and design* (6th ed.). Cincinnati, OH: South-Western College.

13. Daft, R. L. (2003). *Organization theory and design* (6th ed., pp. 204–211). Cincinnati, OH: South-Western College.

14. The 9–11 Commission. (2004). *9/11 Commission report: Final report of the National Commission on Terrorist Attacks upon the United States.* Washington, DC: Government Printing Office.

15. Langton, N., Robbins, S. P., & Judge, T. A. (2010). *Organizational behaviour: Concepts, controversies, applications* (5th Canadian ed., p. 512). Toronto: Pearson Canada.

16. McGregor, J. (2008, January 28). Case study: To adapt, ITT lets go of unpopular ratings. *Business Week, 4068,* 46.

17. Survey: Partners in wealth. (2006, January 21). *The Economist, 378*(8461), 18.

18. Boeing and the 787: Not so dreamy. (2009, June 24). *The Economist* online. Retrieved May 2010 from www.economist.com/businessfinance/displaystory.cfm?story_id=E1_TPRJQQDQ.

19. Paur, J. (2010, April 21). Boeing 787 passes critical step in flight test program. *Wired*. Retrieved May 2010 from www.wired.com/autopia/2010/04/boeing-787-passes critical-step-in-flight-test-program/.

20. Wetzel, D. K., & Buch, K. (2009, Winter). Using a structural model to diagnose organizations and develop congruent interventions. *Organization Development Journal, 18*(4), 9–19.

21. Hill, D. (2004). The case for standards. *Health Management Technology, 25*(10), 48–50.

22. Yi, E. I., & Zhu, P. F. (2009, February 24). Faced with budget cuts, Harvard College Library consolidates. *Harvard Crimson*. Retrieved December 2010 from http://www.thecrimson.com/article/2009/2/24/faced-with-budget-cuts-harvard-college/.

23. Bolman, L., & Deal, T. (2008). *Reframing organizations: Artistry, choice, and leadership* (4th ed.). San Francisco: Jossey-Bass.

24. Bolman, L., & Deal, T. (2008). *Reframing organizations: Artistry, choice, and leadership* (4th ed., p. 73). San Francisco: Jossey-Bass.

25. Bolman, L., & Deal, T. (2008). *Reframing organizations: Artistry, choice, and leadership* (4th ed., p. 73). San Francisco: Jossey-Bass.

26. Bolman, L., & Deal, T. (2008). *Reframing organizations: Artistry, choice, and leadership* (4th ed., p. 74). San Francisco: Jossey-Bass.

27. Wischnevsky, J., & Damanpour, F. (2009). Radical strategic and structural change: Occurrence, antecedents and consequences. *International Journal of Technology Management, 44*(1/2), 53.

28. Fishman, C. (2002, October). Miracle of birth. *Fast Company, 63,* 106–116.

29. Former ChevronTexaco executive tapped in special Labor Day board meeting. (2002, September 3). Retrieved May 2010 from money.cnn.com/2002/09/02/news/companies/ual/index.htm.

30. Air Canada seeking more labour concessions from unions. (2003, May 1). *CBC News*. Retrieved December 2010 from www.cbc.ca/money/story/2003/05/01/aircanada_030501.html.

31. Sackcloth and ashes: An entrenched dispute takes the shine off a proud airline. (2010, May 20). *The Economist*. Retrieved May 2010 from www.economist.com/node/16171321.

32. Roth, D. (2002, January 22). How to cut pay, lay off 8,000 people and still have workers who love you: It's easy: Just follow the Agilent way. *Fortune*. Retrieved December 2010 from http://www.danielroth.net/archive/2002/01/how_to_cut_pay_.html.

33. Nadler, D., Shaw, R. B., Walton, A. E., & Associates. (1994). *Discontinuous change: Leading organizational transformation*. San Francisco: Jossey-Bass.

34. Simons, R. (1995, March–April). Control in the age of empowerment. *Harvard Business Review,* 80–88; Simons, R. (1998, May–June). How risky is your company? *Harvard Business Review,* 85–94.

35. Howell, J., & Higgins, C. (1990). Champions of change: Identifying, understanding and supporting champions of technological innovations. *Organizational Dynamics, 19*(1), 40–55.

36. Tight, G. (1998). From experience: Securing sponsors and funding for new product development projects—the human side of enterprise. *Journal of Product Innovation Management, 15*(1), 75–81; Harrold, D. (1999). How to get control & automation projects approved. *Control Engineering, 46*(8), 34–37.

37. Harrold, D. (1999). How to get control & automation projects approved. *Control Engineering, 46*(8), 34–37.

38. Drew, S. A. W. (1996). Accelerating change: Financial industry experiences with BPR. *International Journal of Bank Marketing, 14*(6), 23–35.

39. Noori, H., Deszca, G., & Munro, H. (1997). Managing the P/SDI process: Best-in-class principles and leading practices. *International Journal of Technology Management*, 245–268.

40. Dillard, J., Hunter, J., & Burgoon, M. (1984). Sequential request persuasive strategies: Meta-analysis of foot-in-the-door and door-in-the-face. *Human Communication Research, 10*, 461–488.

41. Gladwell, M. (2000). *The tipping point: How little things can make a big difference.* New York: Little, Brown.

42. This example is drawn from Meyerson, D. E. (2001, October). Radical change, the quiet way. *Harvard Business Review*, 94–95.

43. Howell, J., & Higgins, C. (1990). Champions of change: Identifying, understanding and supporting champions of technological innovations. *Organizational Dynamics, 19*(1), 40–55.

44. Frost, P. J., & Egri, C. P. (1990). Influence of political action on innovation: Part II. *Leadership and Organizational Development Journal, 11*(2), 4–12.

45. Marshak, R. J. (2004). Morphing: The leading edge of organizational change in the twenty-first century. *Organizational Development Journal, 22*(3), 8–21.

46. Abrahamson, E. (2000, July–August). Change without pain. *Harvard Business Review*, 75–79.

47. Abdullah, M. (2003, March 24). *Business Times*, Kuala Lumpur, Malaysia.

48. Choy, J. (2003, March 17). The Cold Truth about CRM. *Asia Computer Weekly.*

49. Prosci Benchmarking Report. (2002). *Best Practices in Change Management.* Prosci 2000, 2.

50. Drawn from Pitts, G. (2002, September 30). *Globe and Mail*, p. B3.

51. Waldersee, R., & Griffiths, A. (2004). Implementing change: Matching implementation methods and change type. *Leadership and Development Journal, 25*(5), 424–434.

52. Mishra, K. E., Spreitzer, G. M., & Mishra, A. K. (1998, Winter). Preserving employee morale during downsizing. *Sloan Management Review*, 83–95.

53. Mishra, K. E., Spreitzer, G. M., & Mishra, A. K. (1998, Winter). Preserving employee morale during downsizing. *Sloan Management Review*, 83–95.

54. Nevis, E. C., DiBella, A. J., & Gould, J. M. (1995, Winter). Understanding organizations as learning systems. *Sloan Management Review, 36*(2), 73–85.

55. Beatty, R. W., & Ulrich, D. O. (1991, Summer). Re-energizing the mature organization. *Organizational Dynamics*, 16–31; Beer, M., & Nohria, N. (2000, May–June). Cracking the code of change. *Harvard Business Review*, 133–142.

56. Hoyte, D. S., & Greenwood, R. A. (2007). Journey to the North Face: A guide to business transformation. *Academy of Strategic Management Journal, 6*, 91–104; Hoogervorst, J. A. P., Koopman, P. L., & van der Flier, H. (2005). Total quality management: The need for an employee-centred, coherent approach. *TQM Magazine, 17*(1), 92–106.

57. Worley, C., & Lawler, E. (2009). Building a change capacity at Capital One Financial. *Organizational Dynamics, 38*(4), 245–251.

58. Harris, M., Dopson, S., & Fitzpatrick, R. (2009). Strategic drift in international non-governmental development organizations—putting strategy in the background of organizational change. *Public Administration and Development, 29*(5), 415–428.

59. Margonelli, L. (2002, October). How IKEA designs its sexy price tags. *Business 2.0*, 106.

60. Miles, R. E., & Snow, C. C. (1992, Summer). Causes of failure in network organizations. *California Management Review, 34*(4), 53–72.

CHAPTER 6

Navigating the Informal Organization

Power and Culture

People don't resist change; people resist being changed.

CHAPTER OVERVIEW

- Change leaders recognize the importance of understanding the informal components of an organization—culture and power—which are key forces at play within an organization, impacting important stakeholders in the change situation.
- Understanding the power dynamics in an organization is critical to a successful change process. Different sources of power are described so change leaders can gain leverage in their organizations.
- Force field analysis and stakeholder analysis are two key tools to use to advance the understanding of the informal organizational system and how to change it.

Change leaders' understanding of both the present and desired future state of organizations depends on an analysis of multiple dynamics within organizations. Chapter 5 looked at the formal structures and systems, noting how they impact change initiatives. Chapters 7 and 8 will examine the impact of key individuals in the organization on the change process. This chapter provides the background on the less tangible but no less real aspects of organizations—political dynamics and culture (see Figure 6.1).

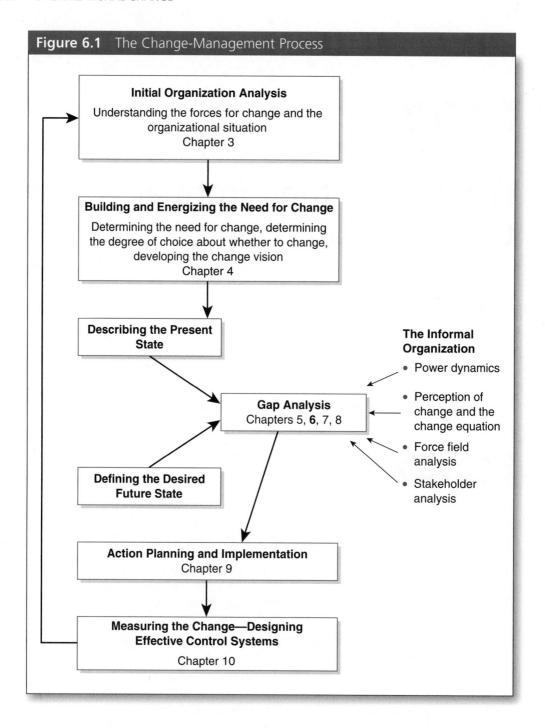

Figure 6.1   The Change-Management Process

To begin, two cases of significant organizational change—the merger of Daimler and Chrysler and the changes to 3M brought about by CEO McNerney—set the stage for this chapter.

The Daimler-Chrysler merger provides a classic example of the impact of organizational cultural clashes leading to "divorce." On May 7, 1998, the CEOs of

Daimler-Benz AG and Chrysler publicly announced that they had decided to "get together in a merger of equals,"[1] creating a colossus company of $132 billion in annual revenues and consummating the largest industrial merger the world had seen. Since the companies had complementary product lines (Daimler produced luxury cars and Chrysler mass-market vehicles) and geographical market coverage (Daimler primarily in Europe and Chrysler largely in the USA), the merger was hailed as having great potential for synergies. When the automotive industry had consolidated and globalized in the mid-1990s, Daimler-Benz AG, a valued brand by any standard, had found itself a "tiny player by global standards" (p. 2). As the number three auto manufacturer in the United States, Chrysler faced a similar problem in entering and succeeding in global markets. The merger seemed to make good business sense.

Quickly, however, the merger floundered on the different cultures of the two companies and different executive compensation systems, as well as poorly articulated and communicated goals. Reflecting their commitment to luxury products, Damiler-Benz executives flew first class and stayed in first-class hotels. In contrast, Chrysler executives generally flew coach class and stayed in inexpensive hotels to save money. The reverse marked their compensation systems: In 1996, Chrysler's CEO earned $9.8 million, and Daimler-Benz's entire management board earned $11 million that same year.[2] A shared vision failed to materialize, with Chrysler engineers predicting that German beer would be sold in their Detroit vending machines and Daimler engineers saying that over their dead bodies Mercedes would be built in Chrysler factories.[3]

DAIMLER-BENZ AND CHRYSLER

MERGER FAILURE

When Daimler-Benz and Chrysler Corp. announced their $36 billion "merger of equals" in 1998, it was hailed as a marriage made in heaven. At the time, Chrysler was the world's most profitable and cost-efficient carmaker, while Daimler was renowned as the planet's premier luxury carmaker. DaimlerChrysler became the new model for a global automotive powerhouse and its stock soared into triple digits, forcing rival automakers into mergers of their own. But in remarkably short order, the mass/class union has hit the skids, undermined by a transatlantic culture clash and a damaging exodus of talent. Virtually the entire "dream team" of Chrysler executives that built the hot models and big profits of the 1990s has departed, leaving behind a chaotic American operation where costs are spinning out of control.[4]

DaimlerChrysler executives officially announced the divorce on May 15, 2007. Cerberus Capital Management paid Daimler $7.4 billion for 80.1% of the Chrysler unit, ending "nine years of management agony and billions of dollars in losses."[5] Why did this marriage fail? Pundits observed different problems. One Merrill

Lynch auto analyst said: "The problem is not the concept of the partnership but the execution…This is a partnership where the two companies haven't partnered."[6] Another argued: "It (the merger) missed a basic building block from the start: honesty…the leaders of the two companies billed the so-called marriage as a merger of equals. That was a scam."[7]

If corporate mergers are the ultimate in change management challenges, then the arrival of a new CEO also challenges embedded power dynamics and cultural patterns. In December 2000, CEO Jim McNerney arrived at 3M's 28-building, 430-acre, suburban Maplewood (MN) campus. Interestingly, McNerney was the first outsider to lead 3M in all of its 98-year history. 3M's CEOs usually rise from within, after being steeped in the corporation's culture and philosophy. However, 3M employees found that the new CEO was able to work with those around him.

McNERNEY ENTERS 3M

McNerney's style has let employees feel that they, not McNerney, are driving the changes. He was able to introduce data-driven change without forcing his ideas from General Electric onto the organization.

McNerney was able to rely on existing 3M management rather than importing other GE executives. "I think the story here is rejuvenation of a talented group of people rather than replacement of a mediocre group of people," he says. As part of his change plan, he avoids giving orders and reinforces the 3M culture whenever he can. "This is a fundamentally strong company. The inventiveness of the people here is in contrast with any other place I've seen. Everybody wakes up in the morning trying to figure out how to grow. They really do." This diplomacy has generally played well with the 3M faithful. "He's delivered a very consistent message," says Althea Rupert, outgoing chair of Technical Forum, an internal society for all 3M technical people. "There's a sense of speed and a sense of urgency."[8]

In the 3M case, McNerney shows a clear understanding of the players, their perspectives, and their needs, and this made the implementation much easier to accomplish. Perhaps McNerney had no choice. But he did act in ways that involved people, focused their attention and interest, and brought them along rather than attempting to impose an outside set of views.

While the stories of the DaimlerChrysler merger-divorce and the installation of a new leader within a fully functional 3M are quite different, they demonstrate the impact of one aspect of the informal system, the organization's culture. How change leaders deal with norms and the difficult-to-define organizational culture will affect the speed and nature of the change.

When assessing possible responses to change initiatives, be it a merger, the installation of new CEOs, or a much more modest undertaking, leaders need to recognize the impact that individual and organizational history can have. Employees may have had significant experience with change that leads them to be wary. They may have also worked with the existing approaches and have their own perspectives on what is needed, so ambivalence and concern are natural—particularly in individuals who have demonstrated commitment to the organization and the quality of the outcomes achieved.[9] Many change projects that employees have been part of are downsizings in disguise and yet change leaders somehow expect employees to welcome such initiatives with open arms. Surely, such optimism is naïve!

Power Dynamics in Organizations

"In organizations, real power and energy is generated through relationships. The patterns of relationships and the capacities to form them are more important than tasks, functions, roles, and positions."

—Margaret Wheatley[10]

It is clear that if people have enough power, they get their way—on the surface, at least. Employees, citizens—in essence, everyone—responds to power and authority. While employees can reconcile themselves to power situations, unintended consequences often make the use of power riskier than change leaders think and intend. As an unknown author cynically stated, *"Reconciliation is where one side gets enough power and the other side gets reconciled."* The other parties often have options that the change leader is either unaware of or only vaguely aware of, and these can have a profound impact on the outcomes achieved. Ill-considered applications of power to influence outcomes can unnecessarily replace loyalty with passive resistance, active opposition, sabotage, or even exit from the firm. As mentioned in the DaimlerChrysler example, key senior Chrysler executives left soon after the announcement of the merger.* Such exits may, in some cases, be desirable due to interpersonal conflict or lack of fit with the organization's change. However, the unnecessary loss of important skills is never desirable, and in the DaimlerChrysler situation it was harmful.

When individuals express their reservations actively and use their voices to raise concerns about a change initiative, politically savvy managers pay attention. The use of voice may be self-serving and/or politically motivated, but in many situations it is the articulation of real apprehensions and concerns that deserve attention. People who feel that they are not listened to may shift their tactics. They may begin to work around the change agent in an attempt to build support for their perspective and influence more senior decision makers concerning the change.[11]

The power to do things in organizations is critical to achieving change. Power is a crucial resource used by change agents to influence the actions and reactions of others. The knowledgeable change agent asks multiple power-related questions,

---

*A useful way of thinking about this is given in Rusbult and Lowery's (1985) classic work, "When bureaucrats get the blues," *Journal of Applied Social Psychology, 15*(1), 83, where they classify the responses as active and constructive (Voice), passive and constructive (Loyalty), active and destructive (Exit), and passive and destructive (Neglect).

such as, What power do I have and what are the sources of my power? What formal power comes with my position? What signatory authority and what dollar limits of expenditure does my position have? And can I hire someone based on my signature alone, or do I need to obtain approval for the hiring? These questions help change agents to diagnose their formal authority and power.

While organizations confer specific authority and power on particular positions, change agents also need to articulate their own beliefs about power—and to be aware of others' perception of their power. There are both internal psychological and external, reality-based roadblocks to exercising power. Clearly, power can be real—one can influence people with knowledge and persuade them by strength of personality and integrity or the ability to reward and punish. But the perception of power is just as important as if not more important than the actual resources that one holds. If others do not believe that a person can be of influence, then the facts will have little influence until those perceptions are changed. The rookie manager has the same formal power as the experienced one. However, the perception of their power and influence are generally very different. Often the perception that an individual has power to act is all employees need. When individuals have the trust of their CEOs, they want to maintain that trust and are therefore not likely to use inappropriate influence tactics on their boss.[12]

The actions of the mediator who was working with Air Canada (Canada's largest national and international airline) and its unions demonstrate the impact of perception.[13] He ordered the senior executives of Air Canada to cancel their appointments for one evening and fly to Toronto to meet with union representatives (whom he had also ordered to come). Clearly the mediator had significant real power—he was appointed as a go-between and had the authority to demand serious negotiations. However, he did not have the formal authority to demand that both sides attend this meeting. But he took a position, exercised moral suasion, and gained the power once the executives and union representatives agreed to comply. Similarly, in the classic change case at AT&T Dallas, the change team often resorted to "if you don't like it, check with the general manager," and other managers (not wanting to bother the boss) went along with the proposed changes![14]

Power, regardless of its tainted image, is essential to making things happen. Robbins and Langton define power as the capacity to influence others to accept one's ideas or plans.[15] There is nothing inherently good or bad about power. Rather, it is the application and purposeful use of power and its consequences that will determine whether it is "good" or "bad." The mediator in the example above created power and used it to facilitate a labor settlement under very difficult conditions.

What gives people and organizations power? Individuals have power because of the position they hold, who they are (character and reputation), and who and what they know. These individual sources of power are classified in Table 6.1.[16]

In addition to personal or individual sources of power, departments within an organization have different levels of power. This power is dependent on the centrality of the work the department does, the availability of others to accomplish that task,

Table 6.1	Types of Power
Positional Power	• Resides in the legitimate authority of the position; includes access to resources and the ability to formally reward and punish. • In today's egalitarian world of flattened hierarchies and virtual organizations, this type of power is lessening in effectiveness as people demand to know the "why" of things. • This is most true in cultures where deference to positional power is lower[17]. Nevertheless, the formal right to make decisions often comes with position, and this is a major source of power.*
Knowledge Power	• Can be **expert** power, **information** power, or **connection** power. • Expert power is the possession of a body of knowledge essential to the organization. Credentials provide independent certification of expertise and increase one's ability to influence. • Information power is power gained through the flow of information: by creating, framing, redirecting, or distorting information and by controlling who receives the information. • Connection power arises because the informal network of connections of individuals permits them to access and pass on information.
Personality Power	• The ability to inspire trust and enthusiasm from others (charisma) provides many leaders with significant individual power. • Reputation, which comes from people's experiences with the person, including reports of success (or failure), influences personal power.

and the ability of the department to handle the organization's environment. These can be categorized as:

- **Ability to cope with environmental uncertainty:** Departments and individuals gain power if they are seen to make the environment appear certain. Thus, marketing and sales departments gain power by bringing in future orders, diminishing the impact of competitors' actions, and providing greater certainty about the organization's future vitality in the market-place. During times of economic turbulence, finance departments gain power through their ability to help the firm navigate its way. Likewise, other departments and functions either enhance or diminish their power based upon their ability to absorb uncertainty and make the world more predictable and manageable for the organization.
- **Low substitutability:** Whenever a function is essential and no one else can do it, the individual or department has power. Think, for example, of the power of human resources departments when no one else can authorize replacement

---

*Another way of looking at power is in terms of "yea-saying" or "nay-saying" power. Yea-saying means that a person can make it happen. For example, he or she could decide who would be hired. Nay-saying power means that a person could prevent something from happening. Thus, nay-saying power would mean that someone could prevent a particular person from being hired but could not decide who would be hired.

of positions or the power of data processing departments prior to the advent of the personal computer.

- **Centrality:** Power flows to those departments whose activities are central to the survival and strategy of the organization or when other departments depend on the department for the completion of work. In most large white-collar organizations, systems people have power because of our dependence on the computer and the information derived from it. Close the management information systems and you shut down the organization. Highly regarded and well-developed information systems anchor the success of firms such as Federal Express, Dell, Walmart, Statistics Canada, The Bank of Montreal, Scotland Yard, and BMW.

Hardy added to our understanding of the sources of power with her classification.[18] She described three dimensions of power:

1. **Resource power**—the access to valued resources in an organization. These include rewards, sanctions, coercion, authority, credibility, charisma, expertise, information, political affiliations, and group power. Resource power is very similar to the individual power listed above.

2. **Process power**—the control over formal decision-making arenas and agendas. Examples of process power would be the power to include or exclude an item on a discussion agenda. Nominating committees have significant process power as they determine who gets to sit on committees that make decisions.

3. **Meaning power**—the ability to define the meaning of things. Thus, the meaning of symbols and rituals and the use of language provide meaning power. For example, a shift from reserved parking and large corner offices for executives to first-come parking and common office space can symbolize a significant move away from the reliance on hierarchical power.

Hardy's introduction of process and meaning power adds significantly to the understanding of how one might influence a change situation. Anyone who has tried to get an item added to a busy agenda will understand the frustration of not having process power. And when one is told "we don't do things that way," one has run into meaning power.

While many sources of power exist, the type of power used by managers can have different effects. Some types of power or influence are used more frequently than others. One research study found that managers used different influence tactics depending on whether they were attempting to influence superiors or subordinates. Table 6.2 outlines the usage of these tactics. It shows that managers claim they use rational methods in persuading others. The use of overt power, either by referring something to a higher authority or by applying sanctions, is not a popular tactic.

Using power is often, by definition, political in nature and can involve the development of coalitions, the building and using of alliances, dealing with the personality of the decision maker, and using contacts and relationships to obtain vital information. Savvy change leaders do not underestimate the power of will, the determination to make something happen.

Table 6.2 Usage Frequency of Different Power Tactics[19]

	When Managers Influenced Superiors	When Managers Influenced Subordinates
Most Popular Tactic	Using and giving reasons	Using and giving reasons
	Developing coalitions	Being assertive
	Friendliness	Friendliness
	Bargaining	Developing coalitions
	Being assertive	Bargaining
Least Popular Tactic	Referring to higher authority	Referring to higher authority
		Applying sanctions

Source: Kipnis, D. et al. "Patterns of Managerial Influence: Shotgun Managers, Tacticians and Bystanders," *Organizational Dynamics.* Winter, 1984.

Toolkit Exercise 6.1 asks you to assess your personal power base. **Toolkit Exercise 6.2** then asks you to assess power in an organization you are familiar with and consider how it influences change.

Understanding the Perceptions of Change

Each individual chooses to consider and adopt a proposed organizational change—or chooses not to. Sometimes they do this willingly and other times they choose reluctantly, either feeling forced or mixed about their decision. This perspective is valuable when thinking about increasing the success of organizational change, for it is at the individual level that people choose—or don't choose. Their choice depends on their view of the situation and how it impacts their lives.

In the recent past, many change programs have been focused on cost cutting, including the downsizing of the number of employees in the organization. People are bright. They understand what is happening. And if a program will cost them their job, why would you expect them to be enthusiastic and positive? Such resistance demonstrates the point that individuals will choose to cooperate or not depending on their personal circumstances and their assessment of how the change will impact them personally. Individuals will adopt or accept change only when they think that their perceived personal benefits are greater than the perceived costs of change. This can be summarized as follows:

> ### CHANGE OCCURS WHEN:
>
> Perceived Benefits of Change > Perceived Cost of Change

This simple formula highlights several things. First, change agents have to deal with both the reality of change and its perceptions. Again, perception counts as much as reality. Second, in many situations, the costs of changing are more evident than the benefits of change. In most change situations, first the costs are incurred and then the benefits follow. The perceived benefits of change depend on whether people think the benefits are likely—that is, the probability of the change being successful in ways that count for them. As well, the benefits of change depend on the state of "happiness" or dissatisfaction with the status quo. Interestingly, people also tend to focus on the consequences of the change rather than the consequences of not changing and remaining the same. The more dissatisfied people are, the more they as individuals will be willing to change. The formula can be modified to capture this as follows:

CHANGE OCCURS WHEN:

Perception of Dissatisfaction with the Status Quo
X Perception of the Benefits of Change
X Perception of the Probability of Success
> Perceived Cost of Change

Thus, change agents need to build the case for change by increasing the dissatisfaction with the status quo by providing data that demonstrate that other options are better, demonstrating that the overall benefits are worth the effort of the change, and showing that the change effort is likely to succeed. Early successes become part of the change agent's toolkit.

It is important to differentiate between the costs and benefits to the organization and the costs and benefits to individuals. Too often, change leaders focus on the organizational benefits and miss the impact at the individual level. The earlier example highlighted this. If an individual sees that the change will increase profits and result in job loss, why would a manager expect support? It takes very secure people who feel they have alternatives and are being equitably treated to be positive under these circumstances even if they believe the change is needed for the organization.

Table 6.3 captures this. It contrasts the impact on individuals with the impact on the organization to predict the resulting support for a change initiative. The purpose of Table 6.3 is to encourage change leaders to avoid the trap of assuming that positive organizational outcomes will automatically be supported by individuals.

In addition to considering the direct impact of a change on a person, individuals will also think about and be influenced by the effects of the change on their coworkers and teammates. The strength of interpersonal bonds, including the shared values, goals, and norms within an organization, can have a significant impact on attitudes and actions. The traditions of how work is divided, how people and departments interact or do not, and simply the way of doing business create a culture within an organization. The desire to maintain the organization's traditions, even if there is a mutual understanding for a need to move on, can hinder the acceptance of changes. This challenge is greater if there are shifts in roles and

Table 6.3 Organizational and Individual Consequences and the Support for Change

Perceived Impact of the Change on the Organization	Perceived Impact of the Change on the Individual	Direction of Support of the Change
Positive consequences for the organization	Positive outcome for the individual (e.g., less work, better work)	Strong support for change
Positive consequences for the organization	Negative outcome for the individual (e.g., more work, worse work)	Indeterminate support for change but very possibly resistance
Neutral consequences for the organization	Positive outcome for the individual (e.g., less work, better work)	Positive support for change
Neutral consequences for the organization	Negative outcome for the individual (e.g., more work, worse work)	Resistance to change
Negative consequences for the organization	Positive outcome for the individual (e.g., less work, better work)	Indeterminate support for change
Negative consequences for the organization	Negative outcome for the individual (e.g., more work, worse work)	Resistance to change

responsibilities and therefore a shift in power. A change leader needs to understand and respect individuals' and organizational history and the individual members' perceptions of that history to effectively negotiate the change process and appropriately engage all stakeholders.

Toolkit Exercise 6.3 asks you to think through the perceived impact of change in an organization. Change agents need to think of the impact on individuals—particularly critical people. When doing so, consider also the people who will actually have to change and how they will view the change equation and assess the benefits, costs, and risks. A general manager may decide that new systems are needed, but it is the individual who will be operating the systems who will have to learn how to work with them and change his or her behavior.

Identifying the Organizational Dynamics at Play

Each of the organizational models introduced in Chapters 2 and 3 assumed that organizations consist of people, systems, and structures that interact according to the forces at play. In organizational change, the key is to understand the forces and how they respond to shifts in pressure. In system terms, the technical term is *homeostasis*, meaning a system in dynamic but relatively stable balance that tends to return to its original conditions. Organizations are as they are because the forces involved are in balance. If one force is changed, it could affect many things and may well be resisted. Alternatively, it may give rise to unanticipated support for the change.

Two tools are particularly useful in helping change leaders to understand such forces and why the organization changes (or doesn't).

1. **Force field analysis**—a process of identifying and analyzing the driving and restraining forces impacting an organization's objectives

2. **Stakeholder analysis**—a process of identifying the key individuals or groups in the organization who can influence or who are impacted by the proposed change and then of working with those individuals or groups to make them more positive to notions of change.

Once these tools have been deployed, it is important to integrate them. Stakeholders will show up in the force field analysis as forces that need to be considered, and an in-depth assessment of them in the stakeholder analysis will put the change agent in a stronger position to manage those forces in ways that will advance the change.

Force Field Analysis[20]

The force field analysis identifies the forces for and against change. In situations that are stable or in equilibrium, the forces for change (driving forces) and the forces opposing change (restraining forces) are balanced. To create change, the balance must be upset by adding new pressures for change; increasing the strength of some or all of the pressures for change; reducing or eliminating the pressures against change; or converting a restraining force into a driving force. Figure 6.2 depicts a force field analysis chart.

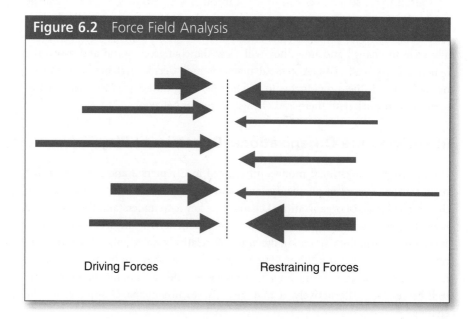

Figure 6.2 Force Field Analysis

Driving Forces   Restraining Forces

Pressures for change come in many shapes and include both internal and external sources. External factors often are the initial triggers that give rise to internal pressures. External driving forces could include benchmark data and various market forces that are putting pressure on senior management to improve their performance in the private sector. Politicians concerned about increased costs or declining service levels could generate driving forces in the public sector. Alternatively, external factors may involve opportunities for future growth or access to special incentives (e.g., tax relief) designed to promote certain activities. Internal pressures, such as the vision of a champion, work group attitudes and norms, and internal systems (e.g., the reward system) that are aligned with the change have the potential to act as driving forces.

Restraining forces for change might come from informal and formal organizational systems that are incongruent with the change. For example, if innovation is part of the desired change, control systems that focus on efficiency and minimize experimentation or variance from standard to reduce costs will act as a restraining force. Changes that are seen as threats to individuals will lead to resistance. Habits or patterns of behavior that could impede the change might be difficult to alter, even when individuals are supportive. The longer those habits have been in place, the more difficulty individuals will have in extricating themselves from those patterns. Work group norms, informal leadership patterns, and workplace culture may act as either driving or restraining forces, depending on the situation.

To do a force field analysis:

1. Identify the forces acting in the situation and estimate their strength. Both the immediate and the longer-term forces need to be considered. The immediate forces are the ones that are acting now and have a more immediate impact (e.g., quarterly sales targets). The longer-term forces are those that may have less immediate effect but whose impact may linger longer, such as customer satisfaction or employee morale.

2. Understand how the forces might be altered to produce a more hospitable climate for the change and develop strategies that will maximize your leverage on the driving and restraining forces with the minimum effort. Conserving your energy and resources is important because change management is a marathon, not a 100-yard dash.

3. Look beyond the immediate impact and identify ways to increase support and reduce resistance. Consider unanticipated consequences that may result from what is implemented. For example, you may be able to reduce resistance by throwing financial rewards at individuals, but in doing so you may inadvertently promote unethical behavior, reduce organizational commitment, and destroy your compensation system.

In the 3M example mentioned earlier, the appointment of McNerney created a new force in the organization. The Six Sigma system he introduced from GE was data based and thus appealed to the values of 3M employees. At the same time, he reduced defensiveness as a force by praising the 3M culture and showed how the employees could achieve more by focusing on the data and explicit goals. All of these things added to forces for change and reduced or eliminated forces against change. As positive outcomes began to ensue from these initiatives, the process provided sustaining reinforcement.

Strebel suggests looking at force field analysis graphically. That is, consider the forces for and against change separately—not necessarily opposing each other directly but operating orthogonally (at right angles).[21] Figure 6.3 shows this.

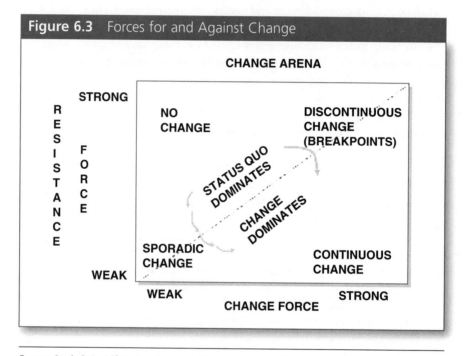

Figure 6.3   Forces for and Against Change

Source: Strebel, P., "Choosing the Right Change Path," *California Management Review. Winter,* 1994, 29–51.

Strebel's view of the change arena allows us to plot where forces for and against change are in balance. The change arena helps us to identify four areas with which many change agents are familiar: areas of constant change, areas of high resistance, areas of "breakpoint" change, and areas of "sporadic" or "flip-flop" change. With **breakpoint change**, pressures are significant and the resistance will be strong. Under these circumstances, resistance will prevent change until the driving forces strengthen to the point that the system snaps to a new configuration. For example, World War II was seen by many Americans to be someone else's battle until the attack on Pearl Harbor dramatically altered the status quo. When breakpoint change occurs, it will be radical and create significant upheaval because of the strength of the changes involved. The situations faced by General Motors and the UAW in 2006 and 2009 are classic breakpoint situations. The market pressures on General Motors were very strong. The UAW faced equally strong resistance forces from both active and retired members, who wished to protect their health benefits and their pension plans.[22] In 2006, this lead to significant concessions from the UAW, but these were a pale imitation of those obtained in 2009 after GM exercised breakpoint change through declaring bankruptcy and seeking court protection while it restructured.

In **flip-flop changes**, forces are weak and change events are not very important, and the situation could change only to reverse itself easily. Flip-flop changes tend to occur when participants have shifting preferences or are ambivalent concerning matters that are of only modest importance to them.

Force field analysis requires careful thinking about the dynamics of the situation and organization, including how people, structures, and systems affect and are affected by what is happening. How will these factors assist or prevent change?

Toolkit Exercise 6.4 asks you to do a force field analysis in order to develop your skills in this area.

Such analysis does lead individuals to think in relatively linear ways—forces are either for or against change. Their influence is linear and direct. However, a different, more nonlinear perspective is often needed. A tool called **stakeholder analysis** is valuable in gaining insights into a more nonlinear interactive view of organizations.

Stakeholder Analysis

Stakeholder analysis is the identification of those who can affect the change or who are affected by the change. Included in this is the analysis of the positions, the motives, and the power of all key stakeholders. Stakeholder management is the explicit influencing of critical participants in the change process. It is the identification of the "entanglements" in the organization, the formal and informal connections between people, structures, and systems.

The purpose of stakeholder analysis is to develop a clear understanding of the key individuals who can influence the outcome of a change and thus be in a better position to appreciate their positions and recognize how best to manage them and the context. A useful starting point is to think carefully about who has to change their behavior in order for the change to be successful. An obvious but often overlooked point is exactly that—someone or some people must change their behavior!* Once the key person or persons are identified, change leaders must focus on who influences those people and who has the resources and/or power to make the change happen or to prevent it from happening.

In doing a stakeholder analysis, the first step is to identify those people that need to be concentrated on. A change leader can identify those people by asking the following questions:

- Who has the authority to say "yes" or "no" to the change?
- Which areas or departments will be impacted by the change? Who leads and has influence in those departments?

---

*We are reminded of the old definition of insanity—"Doing the same things over and over, but expecting a different result!"

- Who has to change their behavior or act differently for the change to be successful? This is a key question—the change ultimately rests on having these people doing things differently.
- Who has the potential to particularly ease the path to change and who has the potential to be particularly disruptive?

Savage developed a model that plots stakeholders on two dimensions: their potential for threat and their potential for cooperation.[23] If a stakeholder has high potential for both threat and cooperation, Savage suggests that a collaborative approach should be developed. In this way, the stakeholder is brought on-side and his or her support obtained. If the stakeholder is supportive, that is, has high potential for cooperation and low potential for threat, Savage argues for a strategy of involvement where the change agent maximizes support from the stakeholder. A stakeholder who is nonsupportive, that is, has limited potential for cooperation but high potential for threat, should be defended against. Finally, a marginal stakeholder, one with limited potential for either cooperation or threat, should be monitored to ensure the assessment is correct.

Once these vested interests are mapped, the change leader can examine the effects of organization systems and structures. Only with this deep understanding can change be managed well.

Toolkit Exercise 6.5 provides a checklist for doing a stakeholder analysis.

The Stakeholder Map

Change agents need to know who the key participants are, their motivations, and the relationships between them. Creating a visual picture of the key participants and their interrelationships can be helpful to understanding the dynamics of the situation. A stakeholder map lays out the positions of people pictorially and allows the change agent to quickly see the interdependencies. In drawing stakeholder maps, some add complexity: Members of the same groups can be encircled; different thickness of lines can be used to signify the strength of the relationship; different colors can be used to signify different things (e.g., level of support or resistance); or arrows can be used to point to influence patterns, with their thickness often used to characterize the strength of the relationship. The only constraint on the construction of a stakeholder map is one's ability to translate data into a meaningful visual depiction of the key stakeholders and their interrelationships. It is also critical to not leave out stakeholders that are external to the organization. External stakeholders create and are a part of important dynamics, and understanding their connection to the organization as well as their power and influence will help the change agent in plotting the complete landscape.

Some of the factors that are useful to depict are:

- their wants and needs,
- their likely responses to the change,

- how they are linked,
- their sources and level of power and influence, and
- the actual influence patterns.

Figure 6.4 shows a hypothetical stakeholder map.

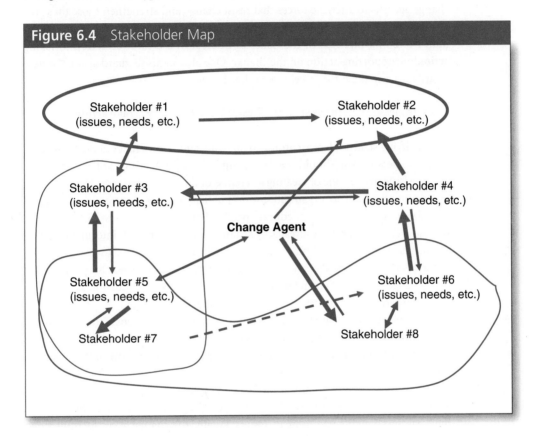

Figure 6.4   Stakeholder Map

Cross and Prusak classify organizational members as:

- **Central connectors**—people who link with one another. For example, Stakeholder 4 links Stakeholders 2, 3, and 6.
- **Boundary spanners**—people who connect the formal and/or informal networks to other parts of the organization. In the map, the Change Agent and Stakeholder 4 are both serving as boundary spanners.
- **Information brokers**—people who link various subgroups. In Figure 6.4, the change agent has the potential to play that role.
- **Peripheral specialists**—people who have specialized expertise in the network.[24]

Once the stakeholder map is developed, change agents can visually see groupings and influence patterns, levels of support and resistance, and the strength of existing groupings and relationships. They can use this map to assess their assumptions concerning the stakeholders by soliciting input and feedback from others. Action plans can be reviewed relative to the map and to see if the strategies and tactics are likely to produce stakeholder responses that will contribute to the desired results. These are just a few of the ways these maps can be applied.

Understanding the positions of key players or stakeholders is essential if a change agent is to alter the forces that resist change and strengthen those that promote change. One can think about moving each stakeholder on a change continuum from an **awareness** of the issues to **interest** to a **desire for action** to taking **action** or supporting action on the change. One also wants to guard against unnecessarily driving them to actively resist the change.

$$\text{Awareness} \longrightarrow \text{Interest} \longrightarrow \text{Desire for action} \longrightarrow \text{Take action}$$

Classifying stakeholders according to this continuum is useful because it can guide what change tools you should use. For example, in the initial stages of a change process, the issue may be one of creating awareness of the need for change. Here, one-on-one communication to organizationwide publicity counts. Articles in an internal organizational newspaper can educate people. Forums or open sessions discussing the issues can play a role. Addresses by senior executives can both inform and generate interest in a topic. Benchmark data can convince skeptics that change is necessary, and a special budgetary allocation or a pilot project can pave the way for people to try out a change program. Which tactic is used will depend on the situation as well as on the organization's culture and previous experiences with change.

As a general rule, change leaders should shift from low-intensity forms of communication to higher-intensity forms as individuals shift from awareness to interest and action. Impersonal but educational messages might inform, but persuasion often takes direct one-on-one action.

For example, in one organization, the CEO wanted independent sales agents to adopt a new and relatively expensive software program. Persuasion efforts about the costs and benefits had limited success. Finally, the change agent identified two things: First, the key influencers were the managers of the sales agents and second, these managers could be classed as supportive, neutral, or negative. The change agent had the CEO phone each manager directly, emphasize the strategic importance of the adoption of the software, query them about concerns they might have, and then directly ask them for their support. Clearly, this was a very powerful and persuasive technique, using all of the power and prestige of the president along with his considerable interpersonal skills.[25]

Stakeholders will vary not only in their readiness to change but also in their attitudes toward or predisposition to change. Some individuals tend to be inherently keener about change and fall into the categories of **innovators** and **early adopters**. Others will wait until the first results of the change are in—they follow the initial two groups of adopters and form the **early majority.** The **late majority** wait longer before adopting. They want more definitive data concerning the change and the reactions of others before they are prepared to commit. Finally, some will, by their nature, resist change until late in the process and can be classified as **laggards** or **late adopters** and **nonadopters**. Table 6.4 lists people's predisposition to change.

Table 6.4 Individual Predispositions to Change	
Innovators or early adopters	Individuals who seek change and want variety.
Early majority	Individuals who are receptive to change but are not first adopters.
Late majority	Individuals who follow others once the change has been introduced and tried.
Laggards or late adopters	Individuals who are reluctant to change and do so only after many others have adopted.
Nonadopters	Individuals who will not change or adapt under most circumstances.

In most organizations, we tend to know the innovators. They are constantly trying something new, including new products and services. Risk and novelty seem to provide the adrenalin they need to get through the day! Change comes easily and is sought. In contrast, we also know those who tend to be uncomfortable with new things. These individuals have a strong preference for order and routine. Change is to be avoided and when it must happen, it happens only after most others have shown the way and the status quo is no longer viable.

Change agents need to identify and work first with innovators and early adopters. There is no sense trying to shift someone whose personality resists change until others have adopted. It may be useful to keep certain stakeholders informed of your activities even though they are typically later adopters so as to avoid unnecessary backlash. However, the simple act of keeping people informed is not the same as working closely with innovators and early adopters to advance the initiative. Early in any change program, change agents must anticipate that they will lack support. Few people will know about the change, let alone support it. The process of adoption will often be gradual until a critical mass of support exists. This will be explored in greater detail in Chapter 9 when the topic of the tipping point is introduced.

While the willingness to change can be viewed as a personality variable, it is also dependent upon the degree to which someone understands the change and his or her commitment toward the change. Floyd and Wooldridge differentiated between understanding and commitment.[26] In their view, someone could have high or low understanding of the change and have high or low commitment to the change.* This provides a matrix of possibilities that helps us to think about stakeholders and their positions. Change agents need to consider those who actively oppose the change as well as those who are positive in their commitments. Being neutral or skeptical due to ambivalent feelings about the change is not the same as being an informed opponent of the change. See Table 6.5.

---

*Another way of looking at commitment is to categorize people as "Make it happen," "help it happen," and "let it happen."

Table 6.5 Stakeholder's Understanding and Commitment

	High understanding of the change	Low understanding of the change
High, positive commitment to the change	Strong consensus	Blind devotion
Low, positive commitment to the change	Informed skeptics	Weak consensus
Negative commitment to the change	Informed opponents	Fanatical opponents

Floyd and Wooldridge stress that change agents need to understand people's perspectives of the initiative and that there is no one "right" position. Often we assume that it is best to have people who both understand the change and are committed to it. This is the "strong consensus" cell in Table 6.5. Floyd and Wooldridge argue that at different times, blind devotion, informed skepticism, or a weak consensus is desirable. That is, at times we may need people to be blind devotees—if the change is a strategic secret, people need to accept the change and be committed to act and not ask questions because the change leaders are not in a position to answer them. On the other hand, when beginning a project and testing out ideas for action, change leaders may well want informed skeptics—people who understand the situation well and who are not too committed. These people may well give valuable advice regarding change tactics and strategies as well as contribute to the actual design of the change.

Table 6.6 provides a grid that allows each stakeholder's position and degree of resistance and awareness to be plotted. This form provides a systematic analysis of stakeholders. In the second column, each stakeholder's predisposition toward change can be noted. Is the person typically an innovator or an early adopter, or does that individual wait and see how others are reacting? If

Table 6.6 Analysis of Stakeholder's Readiness to Take Action

	Predisposition to Change: (innovator, early adopter, early majority, late majority, laggard)				
	Current Commitment Profile: (resistant, ambivalent, neutral, supportive or committed)	Aware	Interested	Wanting Change	Desiring Action
Stakeholder's Name					
Jones					
Smith					
Douglas					

the person waits, is he or she normally a part of the early majority of adopters or the late majority group, or does he or she tend to lag further (i.e., the laggards and nonadopters)?

The second column can also be used to assess the stakeholder's current commitment profile. Is this person currently resistant, ambivalent, neutral, somewhat predisposed, or supportive of the change, or is he or she already committed to the initiative? The change agent can then consider power and influence patterns and develop strategies and tactics that will move the individual stakeholders along the adoption continuum (aware, interested, desiring the change, and taking action). The movement of the stakeholders can be plotted in the appropriate columns, with attention given to learning (e.g., what was the impact of the action undertaken?) and the refining of strategies and tactics in the future. In the end, the objective is to move key stakeholders along the adoption continuum, or at minimum, prevent them from becoming significant obstacles to the success of the change initiative.

Summary

Change agents need to understand the power structures and informal dynamics in their organizations, including culture. They must recognize that resistance to change is likely and is not necessarily a bad thing—there is potential to use resistance in a positive way. It is important to know the forces impacting the organization and the individuals within them, as well as the internal and external stakeholders that will impact and will be impacted by the change process.

Two powerful tools to help us think through the organizational situation are force field analysis and stakeholder analysis. Force field analysis helps change agents to plot the major structural, systemic, and human forces at work in the situation and to anticipate ways to alter these forces. Stakeholder analysis helps us to understand the interactions between key individuals and the relationships and power dynamics that form the web of interactions between individuals.

Glossary of Terms

Resistance to change—the desire to *not* pursue the change. Resistance can stem from a variety of sources, including differences in information, perceptions, needs, and beliefs. In addition, existing informal and formal systems and processes have the potential to act as impediments to change.

Informal structures and systems—those structures, systems, and processes that emerge spontaneously from the interaction of people within the formal systems and structures that define the organizational context. They include: informal leadership, communication, and influence patterns; norms and informal roles; and, at a macro level, the culture of the organization that emerges and influences behavior.

Power—the capacity to influence others to accept one's ideas or plans. The chapter set out a number of sources from which power can be derived.

Power tactics—strategies and tactics deployed to influence others to accept one's ideas or plans.

The change equation—change occurs when the perception of dissatisfaction with the status quo times the perceived benefits of the change times the perceived probability of success is greater than the perceived cost of the change.

Force field analysis—a process of identifying and analyzing the force field in an organization and then altering those forces to accomplish your change. The force field is made up of driving and restraining forces.

Stakeholder analysis—the identification and assessment of those who can affect the change or who are affected by the change. Included in this is the analysis of the positions, motives, and power of all key stakeholders. It is the identification of the relationships in the organization, the formal and informal connections between people, structures, and systems. Stakeholder management is the explicit influencing of critical participants in the change process. As such, it is common to see stakeholders also reflected in the force field analysis.

Breakpoint change—change that occurs in a context defined by strong forces for change and strong sources of resistance. When things occur that heighten the change forces and/or weaken the resistance forces, the system is snapped into a new configuration.

Sporadic or flip-flop change—change that occurs within a context of weak change forces and resistance forces. Within this context, the change is not viewed as particularly important and as a result, change may occur, only to be easily reversed.

Continuous change—change occurs continuously because the forces for change are strong and the resistance forces are weak.

Stakeholder map—a visual representation of the key stakeholders, their interrelationships, influence patterns, wants, needs, issues, and predispositions toward the change.

Readiness to change—a person's predisposition toward change in general. Is the individual generally an innovator, an early adopter, a member of the early majority, a member of the late majority, or a laggard?

Commitment profile—a person's orientation toward the specific change in question. Is the individual resistant, ambivalent, neutral, supportive, or committed to the change?

END-OF-CHAPTER EXERCISES

TOOLKIT EXERCISE 6.1

Exercise: Assessing Your Power

1. What sources of power are you comfortable with and which ones do you have access to? Your personal style and comfort zone will affect your choice of tactics. Increasingly, reliance on positional power to effect change is becoming more limited in organizations.[27]

2. Consider a particular context in which you regularly find yourself (e.g., work, school, church, community group). What could you do to increase the power you have available to you in that context? What types of power are involved?

3. As it is important to know exactly the sources and limits to your power, it is also very important to understand the key players, structures, and systems in your situation. How do these influence the types and amount of power available to you? What could you do to change this?

TOOLKIT EXERCISE 6.2

Where Does the Power Lie in Your Organization?

1. Pick an organization you are quite familiar with. What were the perceptions around power in the organization? In particular, what factors led to the assumption of power? Which departments carried more weight and influence? What behaviors were associated with having power?

2. Think of a change situation in the organization. What types of power were at play? Who had position, knowledge, and personality power? What individuals and departments handled uncertainty, were central, and were not very substitutable?

3. In Hardy's terms, who controlled resources? Who had process power—that is, set the agendas, managed the nomination or appointment process to key committees, etc.? (Define what things meant and how important they were.)

4. Who had yea-saying power? On what issues? Who had nay-saying power?

5. If you examine Table 6.1, what types of power were used most often? What types are you most comfortable using when you are attempting to influence others? Where and how would you use them and why did you select them?

TOOLKIT EXERCISE 6.3

Perceived Impact of Change

1. Consider the impact of a change on an organization you are familiar with and then consider the impact on the individuals concerned. Were these impacts both positive? Are you certain they were perceived that way?

2. What were the perceived costs of change? Who perceived these? Were the perceptions accurate? How could they be influenced?

3. What were the perceived benefits of change? Were the perceptions accurate? What was the probability of achieving these benefits? Were the employees and managers dissatisfied with the present state? Why? What were the costs of not changing?

4. Did the organization incur the costs of change prior to the benefits? If so, why did the organization agree to this risk? (i.e., incurring rather definite costs but indefinite benefits?)

TOOLKIT EXERCISE 6.4

Understanding the Forces for and Against
Change: The Force Field Analysis

Consider a organizational change situation you are familiar with.

1. What are the forces for change? Include external forces as well as a consideration of key individuals or groups. Who is championing the change? How strong and committed are these forces? (Who will let it happen; who will help it happen; who will make it happen?)

2. How could these forces be augmented or increased? What forces could be added to those that exist?

3. What are the forces that oppose change? Include structural forces such as reward systems or formal processes in the organization. Consider as well the effect of informal processes and groups or the culture of the organization.

4. How could these forces be weakened or removed? What things might create major resentment in these forces?

5. Can you identify any points of leverage that you could employ to advance the change? For example, deploying key well-respected individuals who support the change or providing low-cost guarantees related to serious concerns.

TOOLKIT EXERCISE 6.5

Stakeholder Analysis Checklist

1. Who are the key stakeholders in this decision or change effort?

2. Is there a formal decision maker with the formal authority to authorize or deny the change project? Who is that person (or persons)? What are his/her attitudes to the project?

3. What is the commitment profile of stakeholders? Are they against the change, neutral (let it happen), supportive (help it happen), or committed champions of the change (make it happen)? Do a commitment analysis for each stakeholder.

4. Are they typically initiators, early adopters, early majority, late majority, or laggards when it comes to change?

5. Why do stakeholders respond as they do? Does the reward system drive them to support or oppose your proposal? What consequences does your change have on each stakeholder? Do the stakeholders perceive these as positive, neutral, or negative?

6. What would change the stakeholders' views? Can the reward system be altered? Would information or education help?

7. Who influences the stakeholders? Can you influence the influencers? How might this help?

8. What coalitions might be formed among stakeholders? What alliances might you form? What alliances might form to prevent the change you wish?

9. By altering your position, can you keep the essentials of your change and yet satisfy some of the needs of those opposing change?

10. Can you appeal to higher-order values and/or goals that will make others view their opposition to the change as petty or selfish?

Notes

1. Morosini, P., & Radler, G. (1999). DaimlerChrysler: The post-merger integration phase. *International Institute for Management Development, 121.*

2. Golden, B., & Nolan, N. (2002). *Crafting a vision at Daimler-Chrysler* (pp. 2–3). Richard Ivey School of Business, University of Western Ontario.

3. Golden, B., & Nolan, N. (2002). *Crafting a vision at Daimler-Chrysler* (p. 2). Richard Ivey School of Business, University of Western Ontario.

4. Naughton, K. (2000, December 11). A mess of a merger. *Newsweek.* Retrieved December 2010 from http://www.newsweek.com/2000/12/10/a-mess-of-a-merger.html.

5. Edmondson, G. (2007, May 15). Why Daimler gave Chrysler to Cerberus: After ponying up billions, German automaker pays buyout firm to take over. *Bloomberg BusinessWeek.* Retrieved December 2010 from http://www.msnbc.msn.com/id/18680299/ns/business-bloomberg_businessweek/.

6. Eisenstein, P. (2000, December 13). Signs of discontent. *Professional Engineering.*

7. Daimler-Chrysler: Why the marriage failed. (2007, May 17). *Auto Observer.* Retrieved December 2010 from http://www.autoobserver.com/2007/05/daimler-chrysler-why-the-marriage-failed.html.

8. Useem, J. (2002, August 12). 3M + GE = ?: Jim McNerney thinks he can turn 3M from a good company into a great one—with a little help from his former employer, General Electric. *Fortune.* Retrieved December 2010 from http://money.cnn.com/magazines/fortune/fortune_archive/2002/08/12/327038/index.htm.

9. Piderit, S. K. (2000). Rethinking resistance and recognizing ambivalence: A multidimensional view of attitudes toward an organizational change. *Academy of Management Review, 4*(25), 783–794.

10. Wheatley, M. J. (2006). *Leadership and the new science: Discovering order in a chaotic world.* San Francisco: Berrett-Koehler.

11. Carnall, C. A. (1986). Toward a theory for the evaluation of organizational change. *Human Relations, 39*(8), 745–766.

12. Ringer, R. C., & Boss, R. M. (2000). Hospital professionals' use of upward tactics. *Journal of Management Issues, 12*(1), 92–108.

13. (2003, June 2). *Globe and Mail,* June 2.

14. Jick, T. (1993). *AT&T: The Dallas works (B). Managing change.* Homewood, IL: Irwin.

15. Robbins, S. P., Langton, N., & Judge, T. A. (2010). *Organizational behaviour* (5th Canadian ed., p. 300). Toronto: Pearson.

16. Treatment of these power-related concepts can be found in: Whetten, D. A., & Cameron, K. S. (2010). *Developing management skills* (8th ed.). Englewood Cliffs, NJ: Prentice Hall.

17. Hoffstead identified and referred to this cultural variable as *power distance.* See Hofstede, G. (1993, February). Cultural constraints in management theories. *Academy of Management Executive,* 81–94.

18. Hardy, C. (1994, Winter). Power and organizational development: A framework for organizational change. *Journal of General Management, 20,* 20–42.

19. Kipnis, D., et al. (1984, Winter). Patterns of managerial influence: Shotgun managers, tacticians and bystanders. *Organizational Dynamics,* 58–68.

20. Lewin, K. (1951). *Field theory in social science.* New York: Harper and Row; Thomas, J. (1985). Force field analysis: A new way to evaluate your strategy. *Long Range Planning, 18*(6), 54–59.

21. Strebel, P. (1994, Winter). Choosing the right change path. *California Management Review,* 29–51.

22. More pain, waiting for the gain. (2006, February 11). *The Economist,* p. 58.

23. Savage, G. T., et al. (1991). Strategies for assessing and managing organizational stakeholders. *Academy of Management Executive, 5*(2), 61–75.

24. Cross, R., & Prusak, L. (2002, June). The people who make organizations go—or stop. *Harvard Business Review,* 5–12.

25. Luksha, P., personal communication to T. Cawsey.

26. Floyd, S., & Wooldridge, B. (1992). Managing the strategic consensus: The foundation of effective implementation. *Academy of Management Executive, 6*(4), 27–39.

27. Stewart, T. A. (1997). Get with the new power game. *Fortune, 135*(1), 58–63.

CHAPTER 7

Managing Recipients of Change and Influencing Internal Stakeholders

If there is any one secret of success, it lies in the ability to get the other person's point of view and see things from his angle, as well as from your own.

—Henry Ford

CHAPTER OVERVIEW

- People respond to change in many ways. Some embrace it. Others are ambivalent. Some view change negatively. Change leaders need to understand why people react to change as they do, gathering data to understand individuals' situations and their responses.
- When people are ambivalent to change, change leaders can use that period of mixed feelings to influence those individuals to see the positive aspects of the change.
- Change leaders need to rethink their assumptions about resistance to change. Employees often have good reasons for resisting the change leaders' proposals, and these reasons need to be understood and learned from.
- Change leaders can rethink the language that they use, naming employees and others "stakeholders." This new language implies a different stance toward power and the legitimacy of employees to voice their opinions during the change process.

(Continued)

(Continued)

- Change leaders need to be aware of the established psychological contract between the organization and its employees and to recognize that changes to the psychological contract need to be handled carefully.
- People usually respond emotionally to change directives, and leaders need to prepare themselves for the emotional upheaval, even though the need for change is often driven by rational factors.
- Although people's response to change is complex and driven by both internal and external factors, it is also somewhat predictable: pre-change anxiety, shock, defensiveness, depression, and alienation, a shift to acknowledgment of the change, and finally adaptation and acceptance.
- Stakeholders' views of change are influenced by their personalities, their prior experience with change, the attitudes and opinions of their peers, their roles and level in the organization's hierarchy, and the change leaders themselves.
- A present-day challenge is to make change the norm and encourage people to become change leaders or change implementers themselves. This capacity can be thought of as organizational agility and resilience.

It was 2003 and the women of Liberia changed their status and role from recipients of change to stakeholders in the national political process of their country. Charles Taylor, president of Liberia since 1997, controlled about one third of the country, and the Liberians United for Reconciliation and Democracy (LURD) and other rebel factions controlled the rest of the country. All groups were accused of a range of atrocities from creating child soldiers and the raping of women and young girls to painful maiming of enemies. No one was safe, and many were starving and homeless. In these desperate circumstances, the women of Liberia united. Christian and Muslin women, rather than seeing their differences and continuing their exclusive affiliation with their own religious and ethnic rebels, recognized that a change in political party from Taylor's National Patriotic Front of Liberia (NPFL) to LURD would not change their lives since violence was the permanent and lasting legacy of all the fighting factions.

The women's political slogan became PEACE. They dressed in white and sat in the fields in the sun, the rain. At first they were ignored. Then they were noted and President Taylor recognized the women. However, he did too little, too late. By the fall, 2003, Taylor was forced to resign and go into exile in Nigeria. (It should be noted that there were multiple forces, including but not limited to the Economic Community of West African States, ECOWAS, the United Nations, and the United States of America's government, that demanded Taylor's exile.) In 2005, Ellen Johnson-Sirleaf was elected president of Liberia with the support of the women's peace movement, Women of Liberia Mass Action for Peace. She took office in January 2006.

This remarkable story is told eloquently in *Pray the Devil Back to Hell*.[1] From the perspective of change leaders, it is important to note that these Liberian women upended their status as recipients of change and violence and established themselves as powerful stakeholders in the national political process. While most organizational change situations are not about physical violence, change leaders need to acknowledge that change can require people to modify their personal or professional identities, skill sets, and other deeply held beliefs and expectations. It is to legitimize these struggles of internal stakeholders that we use this language.

The reality of people's lives is that they are often on the receiving end of change, often called "the recipients of change." This chapter suggests how recipients of the change may react and how change agents can incorporate this understanding to improve their change plans. The chapter deals with the reality of those who find themselves on the receiving end of change. It will consider different reactions to change: support or enthusiasm; mixed feelings or ambivalence; and resistance or opposition to the change. While positive responses toward change are fairly common, depending upon the nature of the change and how it is introduced, the chapter focuses on people who are mixed or negative toward the change. The chapter helps managers understand the phases people as recipients of change go through. As well, the chapter considers the factors that influence how people respond to change: their personalities, their coworkers or teams, and their leaders or managers. It recognizes that both the **what** of change and the **how** of change matter. Change leaders need to ensure that what they do is based on excellent analysis and the process of change, the how, and allows and encourages the involvement of others. Finally, Chapter 7 looks at how change leaders can reduce the negative effects of change initiatives. Figure 7.1 summarizes the change model and highlights the key issues in dealing with recipients of change and influencing internal stakeholders.

Stakeholders Respond Variably to Change Initiatives

Not Everyone Sees Change as Negative

Many managers assume that resistance is inevitable in change situations.[*] It is time to dispel this myth. Employees do not always react negatively and in many situations will react quite positively. Will they raise questions and experience a sense of uncertainty or ambivalence when change is introduced? Of course they will. They are thinking individuals, trying to make sense out of the change and its impact. This questioning often is perceived as resistance but is not necessarily change resistance. Often if resistance arises, it does so after people resolve their mixed feelings. If they conclude that the benefits to them clearly outweigh the costs, have high personal

---

[*]Our tendency to focus on resistance is suggested by a Google search that recorded 788,000 hits for "resistance to change," but only 85,300 hits for "support for change" and 166,000 hits for "embracing change" (March 2006). The numbers shifted to 704,000 for "resistance to change," 2.56 million for "support for change," and 136,000 for "embracing change" (April 20, 2010). Our hypothesis is that the recession of the past 3 years caused this shift.

Figure 7.1   The Change-Management Process

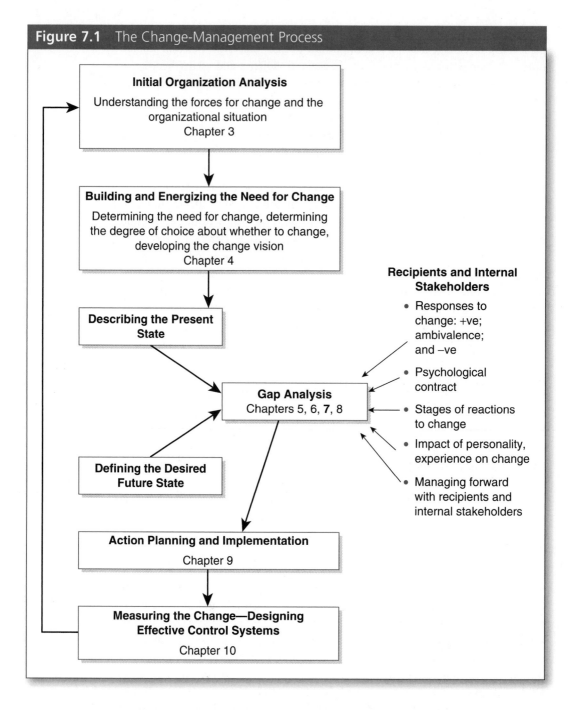

relevance, and are consistent with their attitudes and values, support for the change is highly likely.[2] As was noted in Chapter 6, negative reactions to change increase in frequency and intensity when people believe that the potential costs and consequences to them and the things they value outweigh the benefits.

Some researchers have suggested that "resistance to change" is a term that has lost its usefulness, because it oversimplifies the matter and becomes a self-fulfilling prophecy. We agree. That is, if change leaders assume resistance will occur, it becomes more likely. Change leaders should focus on trying to understand why people react to the change as they do and how those reactions are likely to evolve over time.[3]

When changes are introduced, people often find themselves pulled in different directions. Family, friends, relatives, coworkers, and subordinates may hold divergent views concerning the proposed change, and organizational leaders and managers may deliver ambiguous or conflicting messages concerning its rationale and implications. If things become polarized around the change, people who have come to a decision may view those who are of a different opinion with suspicion and disapproval. All of these pressures can lead stakeholders to feel ambivalent about the change.

These mixed feelings that many people feel can be magnified by concerns about their jobs and the impact of the change on (a) their relationships with others, (b) their ability to do what is being asked of them, (c) the fit with their needs and values, and (d) their future prospects. These concerns are further intensified when people lack confidence that matters will be resolved positively or produce results in alignment with their values. When employees see themselves as relatively powerless, a variety of undesirable coping responses, including alienation, passivity, sabotage, absenteeism, and turnover, may result.[4]

The perceptions of costs and benefits of change depend on what people are concerned about, what they have experienced in the past, and what they think they know. Sometimes relatively small changes will produce strong responses in one group due to the perceived consequences. In another group, more significant changes might produce mild reactions because of perceptions that the impact on them will not be significant.[5] Consider the reactions of employees of Home Depot to the hiring of a new CEO from outside of the company in 2000.[6]

ROBERT NARDELLI AND HOME DEPOT

With no retailing experience, Robert Nardelli arrived to a company that had experienced 20 years of growth but also faced financial and operational problems that would interfere with future growth and profitability if not managed through significant change. Home Depot had a strong, customer-oriented culture and had been very successful at generating top-line revenue. However, growth was flattening as the company matured as a large organization; it lacked needed systems and processes to manage the cost side of the equation, and invidious comparisons were being made with the rates of growth in sales and profitability at Lowe's, its younger and smaller competitor. In particular, supply chain management and inventory skills were lacking, stock-outs were all too common, and other areas related to internal control were weak.

The autonomous and close-knit culture of Home Depot came face to face with something quite unfamiliar when Nardelli entered with his more rigorous and thorough approach to systems and processes he learned at

(Continued)

(Continued)

General Electric. What did his change in leadership style and immediate efforts to shift the culture of the company mean for thousands of Home Depot employees? The way of doing business would no longer look the same, but Nardelli needed to be aware of a valid concern of employees that this outsider was coming in to "GE-ize" their company and culture. Processes, expectations, communication, and structure would all need to change. Some managers voiced strong resistance, and many top executives left. Others stayed, as they saw promise for the company's future with change. Through engagement of employees, Nardelli allowed everyone in the organization to see the need for change themselves.

Nardelli understood the need to recognize what worked and could continue to work and then built on that. The passionate commitment to the customer and the company that characterized the heart of the Home Depot culture needed to be embraced. Yet there needed to be more than simply intuition guiding decision making and attention to more than just sales growth as a measure of business performance and profitability. Using tools including metrics, processes, programs, and structure, Nardelli sought to bring greater discipline to the firm through the greater use of data and accountability to the culture of the company. Systems and processes were introduced to enhance their ability to manage control costs through more effective sourcing, logistics, inventory management, and performance management.

Employees were expected to embrace the changes and demonstrate more disciplined decision processes in how they managed the business, but satisfaction suffered and employee turnover rose during this period. Many employees recognized the need for stronger systems and processes, but they found the cultural shift very jarring and difficult to adjust to. One former official reported that Nardelli came across as warm and intelligent when you met with him individually, but he was not able to translate this to group situations. Critics amplified Nadelli's mistakes, and particular concerns were expressed for what was viewed as a deterioration of the customer-oriented culture.

From a financial perspective, the results of these efforts proved successful. Home Depot doubled its size during the 6 years of his leadership, becoming the second largest retailer after Walmart by 2006. During that period, revenue rose by 100% and profitability by 129%. Despite these improvements, Lowe's rates of growth outstripped Home Depot's performance during the 6-year period. This provided fuel for the fire from those pressuring for a leadership change—in particular certain shareholder groups and other critics who saw him as gruff and unresponsive. Home Depot's board responded to this pressure and replaced Nardelli with his long-term protégé in 2006. Blake was charged with revving up growth and earnings, but most analysts saw this as coming about through a continued commitment to what they viewed as a sound strategy and a much improved set of internal processes.[7]

How employees perceive changes will depend upon their assessment of the situation. If they see themselves **and** the organization benefiting from the change, they are more likely to embrace the change. If they see themselves as involved and participating in the initiative, they are more likely to be supportive.[8] If the outcomes are viewed as likely to be negative for the organization and the individuals, they will be unsupportive of the change. If their views are mixed, they will experience ambivalence concerning the change.[9] The financial successes achieved at Home Depot under Nardelli's leadership were due to his engagement of people around the improved systems and processes. Nardelli brought the challenges to the employees to create an understanding for the need to change and to think through what change could look like. He also used change tools, helping to shift and ingrain a new culture and continue to involve the employees in the process. He managed to convert many resistors and skeptics to partners in change. As the new head of human resources, Dennis Donovan, said, "Large-scale organizational change is not a spectator sport, and it's easy to be a cynic when you're in the stands. It's tough to be a cynic when you're on the playing field."[10]

The range of possible perceptions and responses is complex, as people assess the change against their interests, attitudes, and values. What Nardelli and Donovan were able to accomplish can be attributed to their engagement of both new recruits and the recipients of the change in helping to define the problem, design solutions, and implement them. This was aided by their use of hard data that all could understand, institutionalizing the change through individual projects, systems, and processes, and sustaining the change by creating a structure to promote collaboration and accountability. It was critical that the company's internal systems and processes catch up with its past growth, and the proof lies in its improved financial performance.

However, even in the face of improved financial performance, not all ambivalence concerning the changes disappeared, and pockets of resistance grew. A number of employees and customers remained concerned that too high a price was paid in the form of the deterioration in the culture of employee commitment to customer service, while shareholders worried about slowing growth and flat share price. The fact that many also failed to warm to Nardelli's management style and resented his approach provided enough momentum for a leadership change, even though the major elements of those changes were now viewed as critical to the long-term health of the organization.

Recipients' understanding and responses to the change will evolve over time as the change unfolds. As a result, the approaches used by change leaders will need to vary over the course of the change process. Whereas factual information delivered in a speech or a consultant's report may be useful when dealing with beliefs concerning the need for change and developing initial awareness, informal discussions and social support may be much more useful when ambivalence is stemming from conflicting emotions.[11] If downsizing or relocation is required, it will take more than the rational presentation of data or delivery of equitable relocation packages or early retirement provisions to alleviate distress. Often, executives have had months to consider the changes, and employees need time to adjust.

If resistance occurs, it may stem from those in middle and/or more senior roles, since they often have the most to lose, which happened at Home Depot. They may be seeking to maintain power and influence, sustain their capacity to perform, or avoid what they perceive to be a worsening of their position.[12] Change leaders need to be aware of this. Finally, attribution errors may cause change leaders to fixate on individual resistance rather than probe more deeply for causal factors. For example, behavior that is being categorized as individual resistance may be due to misaligned structures and systems rather than individual opposition.[13] As well, many managers are predisposed to expect resistance in subordinates. Care needs to be taken that a self-fulfilling prophecy is not created.

Responding to Positive Feelings in Stakeholders: Channeling Their Energy

As noted earlier, many individuals welcome change. A change initiative can represent a chance for personal growth or promotion. Some people enjoy variety and seek opportunities to create. Others want the challenge of new situations. Still others imagine a change is needed to improve the situation. When people are feeling positive, engaged, and hopeful, these emotions can be harnessed in support of the change.[14]

It is important, however, to anticipate the risks that may accompany the positive feelings in some stakeholders while others remain uncertain. Blind acceptance by some employees may lead to a lack of reflection in both them and others. Strong positive support of organizational initiatives from respected individuals may cause others to censor their doubts and give rise to the risk of groupthink. This potential tyranny of the minority or majority may lead to a stereotyping of those ambivalent to or opposing the change as "the enemy." This could lead to infighting rather than thoughtful analysis and the productive pursuit of organizational benefits.

Change leaders need to:

- Channel the energy in positive ways, not letting the enthusiasm for change overwhelm legitimate concerns
- "Name" the problem of mixed feelings and the need to understand the different reactions to change
- Appoint highly respected, positively oriented stakeholders to chair significant committees or other change initiative structures, but ensure they have the skills and resources required to fill these roles in ways that don't stifle needed discussions and debate
- Manage the dilemma and remember that going too slow can lose enthusiastic support of change enthusiasts and going too fast will choke those who are doubtful

Ambivalent Feelings in Stakeholders: They Can Be Useful[15]

It comes as no surprise that employees are likely to have mixed feelings about change, as it often gives rise to perceptions of increased complexity, uncertainty, and higher risk, particularly in the short run. People's beliefs about a change and its potential impact can be both positive and negative and can vary in intensity. To illustrate this, consider the example of an industrial paint manufacturer that changed how it handled its major customers by moving key technical service representatives from the head office to the customers' plants. The change provided staff with desired opportunities for increased responsibility, autonomy, and pay, but it required their relocation to a new workplace and the disruption of their cohesive work group. Naturally, their feelings were mixed. Some were excited and others anxious about their new responsibilities. Some were sad about leaving close friends behind.[16] This also created change in role definition, as the new duties required service representatives to play a much more active client-management role. These were activities that customer service representatives had viewed as belonging to sales personnel.

When ambivalence is prevalent, change leaders should expect to hear people voice concerns and need to create an environment that welcomes feedback. Piderit states that people are more likely to speak up when the ambivalence stems from conflicting beliefs. When conflicting emotions are involved, though, she notes that individuals often have more difficulty giving voice to negative emotional responses. She hypothesizes that "they would be more likely to wrestle with their ambivalence alone or to avoid the subject entirely."[17]

Ambivalence generates discomfort for people, causing them to seek resolution of the feeling. Once this resolution occurs, subsequent changes to attitudes become more difficult. People protect their attitudes by employing a variety of strategies:

- Turn to habits and approaches that have served us well in the past;[18]
- Engage in selective perception (actively seeking out confirming information and avoiding disconfirming data);[19]
- Selectively recall (we are more likely to remember attitude-consistent rather than inconsistent data);[20]
- Deny in the form of counterarguments geared to support and strengthen one's position.[21]

More extreme defensive responses can include sarcasm, anger, aggression, and withdrawal. Since attitudes become much more difficult to change once they solidify, there is all the more reason to invest the time needed at the front end of the change in order to effectively process people's reactions to change.

Rather than interpreting mixed feelings as resistance, change leaders are better served by:

- focusing on helping people make sense of the proposed changes;
- listening for information that may be helpful in achieving the change;
- constructively reconciling their ambivalence; and
- sorting out what actions are now needed.

It is almost always in the best interest of change agents to actively **engage** people in meaningful discussions early in the change process and help to **align** their interpretations with the process. Employees' input can prove invaluable in identifying potential problems and risk points.[22] Their engagement and involvement can allow concerns to be addressed.[23] Meaningful engagement can increase the likelihood of the formation of supportive attitudes toward the change and perceptions of fairness as they attempt to make sense of what they are being asked to do.[24] Home Depot's organizational change was largely effective, as can be seen by the shift in the behavior and decision-making processes now part of the routine. However, it never fully reconciled with employee concerns related to the preservation of the customer service culture—one of the drivers that led to Nardelli's departure.

Balogun and Johnson note that once the blueprint for more complex change is set out, it is brought to life through the interpretations and responses of employees. As a result, these authors argue that "managing change is less about directing and controlling and more about facilitating recipients' sense-making processes to achieve an alignment of interpretation."[25] As this evolves, so too does the change that subsequently unfolds.

Negative Reactions to Change by Stakeholders: These Too Can Be Useful

Change leaders undertake an initiative because they believe the benefits outweigh the costs. However, anticipate that stakeholders may have a range of different perspectives, from feeling imposed upon and unprepared to feeling anger and rage. Table 7.1 outlines the causes of negative reactions to change.

Table 7.1   Causes of Negative Reactions to Change
1. Negative consequences clearly outweigh the benefits.
2. The communication process is flawed, leading to confusion and doubt.
3. There is concern that the change has been ill conceived, insufficiently tested, or may have adverse consequences that are not anticipated.
4. The recipients lack experience with change and its implications or have habituated approaches that they rely upon and remain committed to.
5. The recipients have had prior negative experience with a similar change.
6. The recipients have had prior negative experience with those advocating the change.
7. The negative reactions of peers, subordinates, and/or supervisors whom you trust and respect and with whom you will have to work in the future influence your views.
8. The change process is seen to be lacking procedural justice and/or distributive justice

Concerns and negative reactions toward change develop for a variety of reasons:

- **Perception of negative consequences of the change may be a reality.** The change may be fundamentally incongruent with things the people deeply value about their jobs (e.g., autonomy, significance, feedback, identity, and variety[26]) or the workplace (e.g., pay, job security). The loss of work is likely the most extreme form of this. When significant job losses are involved, such as when the major employer in a town decides its plant needs to be closed for the good of the corporation, the costs are all too real for the recipients. In such situations, it is difficult, if not impossible, for people to see positive consequences ensuing from the change.[27] The closing of the Fishery Products International plant provides an example of employment loss.

JOB LOSS AT FISHERY PRODUCTS INTERNATIONAL

The closing of the Fishery Products International (FPI) processing plant in Harbour Breton, Newfoundland, is "devastating," says Earle McCurdy, president of the Fish, Food and Allied Workers Union. "This closing has put 350 people out of work in a community of 2,100. You don't have to be a Ph.D. to determine the size of the impact," he says. "And it's not only Harbour Breton; it's the entire peninsula."

FPI officials blame the closing on an independent report that claims "the plant has major structural problems and is no longer safe for occupancy." However, FPI spokesman Russ Carrigan released a statement saying, "The entry of China into the market for headed and gutted cod has driven the commodity price up dramatically—well beyond the point of our commercial viability."[28]

In this example, recipients would have difficulty accepting the corporate perspective.

- **Communication processes may be flawed,** and people may be left feeling ill informed or misled.[29] Support for management is less likely when people feel they lack the information they need to make an informed judgment. The prospects for support diminish further and faster when employees feel that information has been intentionally and arbitrarily withheld or manipulated. In our FPI example, there appears to be confusion over the reasons for the closure. Is it the structural problems or the entry of Chinese competition to the marketplace?

- **People may have serious doubts about the impact and effectiveness of the change.** They may be concerned that the change initiative has not been sufficiently studied and tested, or they may believe that the change will have adverse consequences that have not been thought through.[30] For example, a move by a head office to consolidate warehouse operations and trim inventory levels may be seen as a surefire way to increase efficiency, but it could cause serious concerns in sales and marketing about the firm's ability to effectively service its customers.

- **People may lack experience with change and be unsure about its implications or their capacity to adjust.** When conditions in an organization have been stable for long periods, even modest changes can seem threatening. During extended periods of stability, people tend to develop well-engrained habits, and the patterned behavior can result in negative reactions to change. Habituated approaches represent strategies that we believe have served us well in the past and that we are often not even conscious of. The Home Depot example earlier in the chapter demonstrates this, as the entrepreneurial culture led to store autonomy and a lack of attention to the company's need for internal systems, processes, and controls. Ignoring headquarters had become a norm.

- **People may have had negative experiences with change initiatives or approaches that seem similar to the one being advocated.** To use an old adage, once burned, twice shy. If stakeholders have learned that change initiatives lead to layoffs or that the initiatives begin with great fanfare but are never completed, people will be more negative. They have learned that they should be skeptical about change and its consequences.[31]

- **They may have had a negative experience with those advocating the change.** They may mistrust the judgment of those promoting the change, their ability to deliver on promises, their access to resources, their implementation skills, or their integrity.

- **People may be influenced by the negative reactions of peers, subordinates, or supervisors** whom they trust and respect and/or whom they have to work with in the future. These opinion leaders can have a significant impact.

- **Last but not least, there may be justice-related concerns.** People may see the process as lacking in procedural justice (i.e., was the process fair? did people have an opportunity to question change leaders, voice opinions, and suggest options?). For example, an absence of participation and involvement may leave employees feeling ignored and relatively powerless.[32] In addition to concerns about procedural fairness and the trustworthiness of leaders[33], they may also believe that distributive justice was lacking (i.e., the final decision was fundamentally unfair).[34]

When things do not unfold as planned, resistance is often flagged as the cause. Rather than assess the situation carefully and objectively, managers responsible for change are quick to lay the blame at the feet of those thought to be acting as obstacles.[35] The dynamics of this likely increases resistance as each blames the other and tensions rise. When managers and employees point fingers at each other as the cause of change difficulties, the focus is not on advancing the agenda for change. **The key question is not who is to blame, but rather what is happening, why is it happening, and what does this tell us about what we should do now?**

Kotter notes that impediments to change are much more likely to come from problems related to the misalignment of structures and systems than from individuals engaged in resistance.[36] For example, if existing systems continue to reward competitive behavior, why would you expect employees to behave in a cooperative manner?[37] Likewise, if critical information or resources are not available, how can individuals implement the change program? Change leaders need to be aware of the tendency to focus on individuals and not systems or processes.

For successful change management and implementation, there needs to be engagement and open conversation, especially in the face of resistance. Alignment also needs to exist between what is communicated and the systems and structures of the organization. Resistance is one of the responses to a change initiative. If resistance is based on different definitions of the issues, then leaders need to return to the underlying problems and data that surface from it. If the resistance is based on differing views of the consequences, the reasons need to be understood and change plans modified if appropriate.

Toolkit Exercise 7.1, at the end of the chapter, asks you to explore your experiences as a change recipient.

Make the Change of the Psychological Contract Explicit and Transparent

The organizational context plays a role in determining reactions of people to change. The **psychological contract** that people have with the organization can be a critical contextual variable.[38] The psychological contract represents the sum of the implicit and explicit agreements we believe we have with our organization. It defines our perceptions of the terms of our employment relationship and includes our expectations for ourselves and for the organization, including organizational norms, rights, rewards, and obligations. As such, they both influence and are influenced by the culture of the organization.[39]

Much of the psychological contract is implicit. Because of this, change initiators may be unaware of it when they alter existing arrangements. In effect, leaders often don't recognize the impact such changes may have on the psychological contract. They fail to realize that employees may have a very different view than they do of what constitutes "their deal," their employment contract, including what they have a right to expect and what is fair and equitable. The perceptions of sudden and arbitrary changes to the psychological contract of employees can lead to trouble. While most people recognize that psychological contracts will have to adapt to changing conditions, they don't react well to surprises and unilateral actions that fail to consider their input or that of their representatives. Changes that threaten our sense of security and control will produce a loss of trust, fear, resentment, and/or anger.[40] People need to devote time and effort to absorbing the change and its implications. Even unilateral changes that will have a positive impact on employees may be resisted because of factors such as suspicion over the "real agenda" and concerns about a reduced sense of control or the capacity to perform.

THE WASHINGTON SUBURBAN SANITARY COMMISSION

In 2002, Washington Suburban Sanitary Commission (WSSC)'s new general manager John Griffin was brought in to implement change given the threat of privatization that the organization faced. As an outsider hired into this role, he engaged in open and honest communication immediately, asking questions and being transparent with all stakeholders. Griffin led the organizational change with structural reorganization. As a manager working closely with Griffin, Steve Gerwin told his employees: "Don't worry, when the change comes, there will be a job for you and even a better one than you have now. But if you think the job you used to have is going to be there, you're wrong."[41]

Gerwin explicitly communicated that there was going to be a significant change in the psychological contract. "If you want to come to work and read the newspaper, talk to your friends and fill up space and get your paycheck, that job is gone. But if you want a challenge and something to do, there may be an opportunity there." He used language the people could understand and remember: They could not have their old jobs after the reorganization, but they could have a challenging job.[42]

Toolkit Exercise 7.2 asks you to reflect on the psychological contract and consider what happens when an organizational change causes key terms to be altered.

Predictable Stages in the Reaction to Change

Change is inevitable—growth is optional

—from a bumper sticker

Change can be thought of as occurring in three phases: before the change, during the change, and at the end of the change. Reaction to change typically begins in advance of the actual change initiative as individuals worry about what will happen and what their personal consequences will be. The reaction can continue until long after the change initiative has been completed as people work through the feelings created by the change. When experiencing traumatic changes and transitions, people tend to go through a predictable sequence of stages similar to those outlined by Elizabeth Kübler-Ross in her work on grieving.[43] The model suggests that emotionally healthy people will work through issues until they accept the change. From a change agent's perspective, this is sometimes referred to as helping others work through the "valley of despair." Table 7.2 integrates her insights with those of Fink,[44] Jick,[45] and Perlman and Takacs.[46]

Before the change: People who are anticipating significant change may experience **prechange anxiety**. At this stage, people think something is in the wind, but they don't know exactly what it is or how it will show itself. Uncertainty escalates and people often find themselves agonizing over the impact it could have on them as well as its impact on others. For many, the anticipation phase

Table 7.2 Stages of Reactions to Change		
Before the Change	*During the Change*	*After the Change*
Anticipation and anxiety phase	Shock, denial, and retreat phase	Acceptance phase
Issues: Coping with uncertainty and rumors about what may or may not happen	**Issues:** Coping with the change announcement and associated fallout; coping with uncertainty and rumors; reacting to the new "reality"	**Issues:** Putting residual traumatic effects of change behind you, acknowledging the change, achieving closure, and moving on to new beginnings—adaptation and change
1. **Prechange anxiety—** Worrying about what might happen, confusion, and perhaps significant denial of what change is needed or likely	2. **Shock—**Perceived threat, immobilization, no risk taking 3. **Defensive retreat—** Anger, rejection and denial, compliance; sense of loss, risk taking unsafe 4. **Bargaining** 5. **Depression and guilt, alienation**	6. **Acknowledgment—** Resignation, mourning, letting go, energy for risk taking begins to build 7. **Adaptation and change—**Comfort with change, greater openness and readiness, growing potential for risk taking

can be debilitating. In their desire to reduce uncertainty and anxiety, many will search for signs of what might be on the horizon. Rumors may abound. Others will deny the signs and signals of change, finding it too threatening to think about. During this phase, the organizational rumor mill often moves into high gear and increases anxiety levels. The confusion and uncertainty created often continue long after the change has been announced and may be coupled with fear, anger, alienation, defensiveness, and a variety of other responses that have strong attitudinal and performance implications. Ambivalent feelings described earlier are often generated at this point and are evident in comments and actions. As noted earlier in this chapter, people are more likely to speak up when the mixed emotions stem from conflicting beliefs. When conflicting emotions are involved, though, individuals often have more difficulty giving voice to negative emotional responses.[47]

Once change is announced: Even though people know that change is coming, many are still **shocked**. Individuals at this stage may feel overwhelmed by events to the point of immobilization. Some people will engage in **defensive retreat**, holding onto the past and experiencing anger over the changes. Insecurity and a sense of loss and unfairness are common reactions. People will often try to avoid dealing with the real issues and try to reduce their risk by lowering their exposure and relying on habituated responses that have worked in the past. The sense of betrayal will be strongest for those who placed their greatest trust in the firm and who feel their psychological contract with the organization has been violated. Their trust in the leadership will typically decline. Some individuals may agree outwardly, announcing their willingness to cooperate ("We're behind you all the way!"), only to act in a noncompliant manner when they are out of sight of those advocating the change. This behavior can sometimes extend to sabotage. Some people will engage in **bargaining** behavior, negotiating to make the change go away or to minimize its negative impact on them. **Depression and guilt,** stress and fatigue, and reduced risk taking and motivation have been regularly reported to follow such unsuccessful attempts to reverse the tide. **Alienation** can result.

At the end: Finally, people begin to accept the change and **acknowledge** what they have lost. They begin to let go of the past and start to behave in more constructive ways. At this point, they can again take risks—not those associated with getting even, but rather those associated with liberation from the past and moving on. As risks are rewarded with success, confidence builds in the change. During the **adaptation and change** stage, people become more comfortable with or accepting of the change, internalize it, and move on.

People need to work their way through their reactions to the change phases in a systematic fashion to avoid becoming stalled. The same is true for the change process itself, which needs to happen in the appropriate order, according to Kotter. As the subtitle of his article *Leading Change: Why Transformation Efforts Fail* says, "Leaders who successfully transform businesses do eight things right (and they do them in the right order)." This order is as follows: establishing a sense of urgency; forming a change team; creating a vision for change; communicating the vision of change; empowering others to act; planning for and creating short-term wins; consolidating wins to reinvigorate the process; and institutionalizing the change. Skipping steps, Kotter says, only creates an illusion of speed and never produces a satisfying result.[48] Both what you do and how you do it are important.

Even when people recognize the need for difficult decisions, they may have difficulty emotionally accepting and adapting to consequences of change decisions.[49] This emotional distress can be true regardless of the consequences. For example, even those who are retained after organizational downsizing will be upset. The *survivor syndrome* is a term that refers to the reaction of those who survive a poorly handled, traumatic change such as a downsizing.[50] Survivor syndrome effects include lower levels of job satisfaction, motivation, and organizational loyalty, greater stress, greater ambiguity, vulnerability about one's future position, a sense of entrapment in a negative situation, and guilt about being retained while others have been let go.[*]

As Jick points out, the above sequence provides a prescriptive, optimistic, and simplistic view of how individuals adjust to disruptive change.[51] Some will move through the stages quickly, others will move more slowly, some will get stuck, and some will move more quickly than they should, taking unresolved issues with them.

---

[*]For a detailed treatment of dealing with the survivor syndrome, see Noer, D. M. (1993). *Healing the wounds.* San Francisco: Jossey-Bass.

As an example, consider the actions of a senior executive who lost his job as the result of a merger. During the 8 months it took him to find a new position, he focused on maintaining a very positive attitude. Friends marveled at his resilience, though some questioned whether he was living in denial. Upon joining a new firm as a vice president, he became increasingly critical and bitter about his new employer. His hostility had little to do with the organization he had joined or his new position. It was unresolved anger and other baggage related to his earlier dismissal. His inability to recognize and deal with this ultimately cost him the new position.[52] When individuals get "stuck" in the early and middle stages, extricating themselves can prove very difficult.

Individual reactions to organizational change will be related to perceptions of the potential outcomes, and most changes will not be as severe and disruptive as those envisioned above. In the next section, the chapter explores three specific factors that have an influence on how people adapt to change:

- Personality and experience with the rate of change
- The reactions of coworkers and teammates
- Experience with and trust in leaders

Stakeholders' Personalities Influence Their Reactions to Change

Some individuals, innovators, early adopters, and early majority are generally predisposed to change (see our discussion in Chapter 6). Others tend to review carefully the experience of others and commit later in the process (the late majority and late adopters). Finally, there are those who resist adopting change until the bitter end (the resistors).[53] These predispositions are influenced by individual factors such as susceptibility to the social influence of others, tolerance for risk and ambiguity, and self-image (e.g., innovator versus cautious adopter).

Individuals' perceptions of the change experience and the risk of change will also be influenced by their personalities.[54] People who have a low tolerance for turbulence and uncertainty tend to be comfortable in stable environments.[55] As the rate of change accelerates, they will experience increased stress as they attempt to cope and adjust. At low to moderate levels, though, this increased stress may also lead to increased job satisfaction if people experience success with change. However, as change becomes more radical, the resulting stress and strain will tend to produce elevated levels of anxiety and fear, defensiveness, fatigue, alienation, and resignation. As a result, elevated levels of absenteeism and turnover, errors and accidents, and depressed levels of work satisfaction are commonly observed.[56]

People who have a high tolerance for turbulence and uncertainty will find stable and unchanging environments unsatisfying after a period of time. When they find novelty and challenge lacking, concerns grow that their careers have stalled[57], and they experience increasing levels of boredom, frustration, absenteeism, and turnover.[58] As the rate of change increases to moderate levels, so will their levels of satisfaction and interest, particularly if they become directly engaged with the change initiative. As the rate of change intensifies, effects similar to those seen in low-tolerance individuals are observed, although the effects occur later at higher rates of change.

Take a few moments to revisit the question of how you react to change and reflect on your experience. What is your predisposition to accept change? You can also use this to help understand your stakeholders and help them understand themselves as well (see **Toolkit Exercise 7.3**).

Prior Experience Impacts a Person's and Organization's Perspective on Change

Previous experience with change will affect a person's view and behavior. Long periods of stability and minimal change will lead to people seeing change as more unsettling and risky than those with more frequent encounters with change.[59] Even those who are thinking "thank goodness, we're finally doing something!" may experience elevated levels of risk and stress from exposure to even moderate levels of change.

A sustained period of continued success can cause individuals and organizations to be trapped by those strategies and tactics that have served them well. The tendency to rely on competencies and strategies that have worked in the past is referred to as a **competency or a complacency trap**.[60] Faced with the need for change, they rely on those approaches that have worked well in the past, even though the old strategies are not effective. These organizations are then incongruent with their environments. Breaking out of these traps is not easy.

If organizations and their employees have adapted successfully to moderate levels of change, then those employees are likely to be open and flexible. The organizations' change "muscles" are toned and ready for more change exercise. Those who have regular, ongoing exposure to moderate amounts of positive change (e.g., through continuous improvement) tend to find change to be less unsettling and hence less risky because they become accustomed to believing that tomorrow will likely be different from today and that this is not something that needs to be avoided.[61]

However, when organizations and employees live in an environment with extended periods of major upheavals and uncertainty, the sense of personal risk escalates and remains high. Under these conditions, employees may become exhausted and feel increasingly vulnerable to the next wave of change. They become jaded and alienated if earlier promises and hopes for improvement have gone unmet. Those who have not exited the firm may resign themselves to adopting a strategy of keeping their heads down to avoid personal risk. Under these extreme conditions, the perceived risk attached to a particular change initiative may actually diminish. Like those in danger of being swept overboard in a storm, individuals may be prepared to grasp onto any plausible change initiative that looks like it could serve as a lifeline unless their alienation is such that they have effectively given up.

Figure 7.2 depicts a hypothetical connection between past rates of change experienced by people in an organization and the degree of perceived risk with an anticipated change. It illustrates the adaptability and resilience individuals do or do not have as a result of the previous rates and types of change within an organization. For example, if people have experienced long periods of minimal change, they will likely perceive higher risks with the proposed change. The perceived risk of the proposed change declines if there has been a moderate rate of change within the organization and a general normalization and level of comfort associated with past changes. As the normal rate of change increases in intensity and/or becomes drawn out, the perception of risk associated with the new change begins to rise again. When the rate and level of intensity of change reach a certain point, those involved will be ready to grasp at anything with the potential of offering a way out (see drop-off line in Figure 7.2). This pattern can be seen when participants recognize that the organization is in a crisis state and they become unfrozen and ready to change. In a crisis situation, one can expect initial defensiveness followed by openness to change.[62]

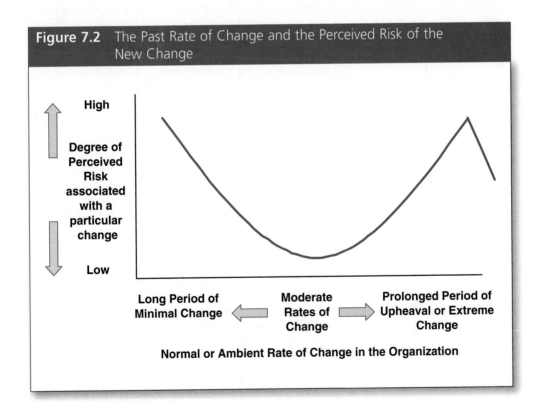

Figure 7.2 The Past Rate of Change and the Perceived Risk of the New Change

As has been discussed, both personality and experience with change affect how people view proposed changes. Table 7.3 outlines the hypothesized interactions between an individual's need for change, tolerance for ambiguity, and the frequency and magnitude of the change experience.

Table 7.3	The Interaction of Personality With the Experience of Change			
Individual Difference	*Change Experience*			
	Low	**Some**	**Frequent**	**Chaotic**
	No change experience for an extended period, a belief that this job will last indefinitely	Some change experience that demonstrates both the difficulties and survivability of change	Frequent change experience, nothing static, major upheavals and uncertainty	Chaotic environment characterized by temporary systems, fluid environments, and constant change
Individuals who have higher tolerance for ambiguity, novelty, and change	Restlessness; boredom, attempts to create change or to disrupt routines	Grappling with change issues; feelings of invigoration and new meaning in the job, expectation of improvement	Stress showing, coping strategies being developed, energy still present but fatigue starting, voicing of concerns; the desire to exit increases	Stress effects, fear, and fatigue as they attempt to cope; voicing of concerns exists, but the likelihood of resignation, alienation rises; and/or a willingness to grasp onto a plausible course of action as a way to reduce the chaos
Individuals who have a lower tolerance for ambiguity, novelty, and change	Acceptance of the situation, buy-in to the steady state, no preparation or anticipation of change	Stress effects present, concerns voiced, but a willingness to adjust to moderate amount of change present	Significant coping difficulties; stress effects, including fear, fatigue, and alienation often present; increased willingness to grasp on to a plausible course of action to reduce the chaos	Severe coping difficulties and resultant stress and strain, alienation, resignation and/or exit at high levels and/or elevated willingness to grasp at plausible courses of action to reduce the chaos

Toolkit Exercise 7.4 asks you to reflect on Figure 7.2 and Table 7.3. What is your personal response to change?

Coworkers Influence Stakeholders' Views

Our views are influenced by the comments and actions of those around us—particularly those whose opinions and relationships we value (see Table 7.4). Trusted mentors, managers, and friends can be particularly influential. If those we trust are positively predisposed toward a change initiative, we may be influenced in that direction. Similarly, if they are experiencing serious concerns about the change or are opposed to it, they will influence us to consider factors that may move us in the opposite direction.[63]

Coworkers and work groups play a critical role in how people sort out their own reactions to change, because these individuals live in a similar organizational world and their relationships are bound together by norms, roles, and shared obligations and experiences. When coworkers are ambivalent on the desirability of a particular change, one can expect to see skepticism in others as they sort out their own feelings about the matter. The importance of coworkers' reactions increases as the strength of relational ties rises. The more coworkers see themselves as part of a cohesive team, the greater will be their influence.[64] Even groups that seem to be in conflict will often become cohesive and turn on the "outsider" who is seen to be threatening group members. Change leaders who ignore cohesion, norms, and varying levels of ambivalence do so at their own peril.

Table 7.4 Impact of Trusted Peers on Recipients		
Opinions of Those Trusted by Recipients	*Recipients' Initial Attitude to the Change*	*Possible Implication*
Positive toward the change	Positive toward the change	Very motivated to support and predisposed to get involved
	Negative toward the change	Opposed to the change but potentially open to other perspectives because of new information and peer pressure
Negative toward the change	Positive toward the change	Support of the change may become more tempered due to information and the perspectives offered by trusted peers. Will often experience pressure to reconsider their support or perhaps be silenced by peer pressure
	Negative toward the change	Opposed to the change and reinforced in those views by trusted peers and the peer group

Feelings About Change Leaders Make a Difference

How employees view and react to change is influenced by their perceptions of the change leaders. If people believe their perspectives and interests are recognized and they trust these leaders, then they are likely to respond positively to the suggestions for change.

When change leaders talk about significant change, they often focus on the rationale, including the costs and benefits of changing. They may pay some attention to the costs of *not* changing, but usually little focus is given to the benefits of the status quo. Followers, on the other hand, assessing change at a personal level, will often reflect on the benefits of not changing and discount the costs of staying with the status quo. The followers may prefer the devil they know to the unknown one. They can estimate, and sometimes inflate, the costs of changing but may feel far less certain about the benefits. As a result, change leaders and followers' estimates of the benefits and costs can differ dramatically.

If change leaders recognize and deal with the issues factually, constructively, and sensitively, they will help people interpret the context in a more predictable manner and concerns can be brought to the surface and addressed.[65] From a procedural justice and a personal efficacy point of view, people want their voices to be heard, even if it doesn't result in a change in the decision. When the president of Continental Airways told employees that he was closing their airport's operations, his candor, combined with his positive reputation as a leader, resulted in an acceptance of the change.

CANDOR AT CONTINENTAL AIRWAYS

I met with the employees and their families—about 600 people in all. Along with explaining the details of the closing and relocation plans (the company had doubled the financial aspects of the relocation package over what was required by the contract), I also shared with them my vision for Continental and how far we had come. I then opened the floor to questions and answers.

For about five minutes, employees expressed appreciation that I had personally come to give them the news and had developed a financial package to meet their needs. But then the pilots walked in—in full uniform—with their families. They surrounded the room and refused to sit down. A pilot came to the microphone to express how incompetent he felt management was and how Continental was once again making the wrong decision. The rest of the pilots applauded.

Do you know what happened? The rest of the employees, led by a baggage handler who was also being relocated, stood up and defended me, one after another, for 20 minutes. They told the pilots that they should feel lucky that Continental finally had a senior management team that treated them with enough respect to deliver the bad news—as well as the good relocation package—in person. I left to a standing ovation.[66]

How change leaders handle the perceptions and the alterations to the psychological contract will matter to employees. The president of Continental was more successful in managing the shift in psychological contract with the employees than with the pilots. Perceptions of his promises may have been influenced by the employees' views that they were being treated reasonably under the circumstances—procedural and distributive justice was upheld.[67] When people feel steamrollered by the pressure exerted on them rather than reasonably engaged, resistance may go underground and resurface at a later date in the form of resentment for the change leader.[68]

Integrity is One Antidote to Skepticism and Cynicism

Some people believe change leaders when they promise a bright future or state that there is no alternative except what is offered. However, others are more skeptical—often for good reasons. Followers may believe that the promises are suspect, particularly if the leader is relatively unknown or untested. If followers have received promises before and found them wanting, then people will be skeptical. Followers sometimes report that change leaders have said the right things but acted in ways that advanced their own self-interest, ignoring what was good for most employees and the organization.

Skepticism can shift to cynicism (a real loss of faith) and heightened pessimism when people whose opinions we value share a similar negative belief.[69] The price of such cynicism includes reduced satisfaction, organizational commitment, and motivation to work hard. It results in an increase in accidents and errors, a lessened desire and will to engage in future change initiatives, and decreased leader credibility. As Reichers, Wanous, and Austin say, "People do not deliberately become cynical, pessimistic and blaming. Rather these attitudes result from experience, and are sustained because they serve useful purposes. Cynicism persists because it is selectively validated by the organization's mixed record of successful change, and by other people in the organization who hold and express similar views."[70]

The perceived trustworthiness and integrity of the change leader play important roles in the judgments made by the recipients. When change leaders are viewed as credible and trustworthy, their vision of the future reduces the sense of uncertainty and risk in recipients as the people put their faith in the leader's judgment. People often turn to credible leaders and colleagues to help them absorb uncertainty and make sense of confusion.[71] Leader efforts to actively involve recipients in the change initiative further reduce the chances of cynicism developing.[72]

Periods of transition represent a time when the ethical and reputational risks for leaders are particularly high. The "best course of action" is far from clear. Offering hope and direction without misleading or overstating the case is the narrow path that change leaders must navigate. As one CEO noted, the difference between a visionary leader and a huckster is the thin edge that is integrity.[73]

Table 7.5 outlines ways in which change leaders can minimize cynicism about change and eliminate many of the negative aspects resulting from such cynicism.

Table 7.5 Ways to Manage and Minimize Cynicism About Change[74]

1. Keep people involved in making decisions that affect them.

2. Emphasize and reward supervisors who foster two-way communications and good working relationships and show consideration and respect for employees.

3. Keep people informed about ongoing change—when, why, and how—and include honest appraisals of risks, costs, benefits, and consequences.

4. Keep surprises to a minimum through regular communications about changes, anticipating questions and concerns.

5. Enhance credibility by:
   a. using credible spokespersons who are liked and trusted
   b. using positive messages that appeal to logic and consistency
   c. using multiple channels and repetition.

6. Acknowledge mistakes, accept responsibility, apologize, and make amends.

7. Publicize successful changes and progress.

8. Use two-way communications in order to see change from the employees' perspectives and use this awareness to help with planning and future communications related to change.

9. Provide opportunities for employees to express feelings and receive validation and reassurance. Ensure you address the concerns raised.

Source: Adapted from Reicher, A.E., et al. (1997). Understanding and managing cynicism about organizational change. *Academy of Management Executive, 11*(1), 53.

Avoiding Coercion but Pushing Hard: The Sweet Spot?

Change leaders may find that they have to resort to the use of coercion. Kramer argues that under certain circumstances, intimidating leaders apply their political intelligence to creatively push followers to higher levels of performance than would otherwise have been achieved.[75] Importantly, Kramer specifically notes that while such individuals are tough and demanding, they are not simply bullies. Their initial coercion is to unfreeze the situation and achieve initial shifts in position. However, leaders who rely primarily on the application of fear and force to gain commitment to change are taking significant risks.[76] While it may be true that "if you have them by their throats, their hearts and minds will follow"[77], any release of the throat risks resistance and revolt. Effective change must be about more than the leader's power.

Nardelli at Home Depot pushed the employees, but he did so with a mix of encouragement, ultimatums, and modeling the desired change through his own behavior. Using metrics, he made the business challenges visible to everyone in a way they could understand and relate back to their work and the company they were deeply committed to. The institution of common metrics to produce companywide data was not only to help senior management understand the business and underlying problems. The metrics had a psychological effect as well, demonstrating the challenges the company faced to the employees and reinforcing the changes Nardelli wanted to see around collaboration, accountability, and performance assessment.

At times, employees respond to leaders out of fear of what will happen if they don't comply. While fear can motivate, leaders who rely primarily on fear or coercion are following a risky path—both ethically and pragmatically (i.e., will the support be there when the stick or threat is no longer present?).[78] In his book *From Good to Great*, Collins refers to this "doom loop" as the enemy of effective leadership.[79]

Leaders, frustrated by a lack of progress, are attracted to the use of punishment and fear, because these tools are available, are immediate in their short-term effects, and carry the illusion of control through obedience and compliant behavior.[80] However, we do *not recommend* the use of such strategies in most situations. Years ago, Deming noted that the move to total quality could not be achieved through fear, and evidence in the intervening years continues to demonstrate the lack of effectiveness of fear.[81] While activity controls like fear may produce compliance in the short run, they have proven to be ineffective over the intermediate to longer term.[82] Further, such techniques can create undesirable side effects (e.g., frustration, withdrawal in the form of absenteeism and turnover, aggression, and sabotage). A much more desirable and less risky course of action is through the positive engagement of people through initiatives that enhance the recipients' capabilities to deal effectively with the change.[83] At the same time, managers can use their power to make expectations and standards explicit in order to challenge employees.

Creating Consistent Signals From Systems and Processes

While the leader's words and deeds are important, so too are other parts of the organizational context. A leader's credibility will be either enhanced or diminished by the extent to which organizational systems and processes send a consistent message or are themselves the focus of changes that will bring them into alignment with the change vision.

Credibility and trust are diminished when the leader's words say one thing (e.g., quality is critical) but the systems and processes signal something else (e.g., ship now, fix later). In *Built to Last*, Collins and Porras found that firms with staying power possess resilient cultures that have the capacity to adjust and realign their systems and processes in response to changing conditions. This resilience was made functional by the underlying value set and supportive systems and processes that were installed by leaders.[84] As such, they provided continuity for organizational members while at the same time contributing to the adaptability and change of existing systems and processes. This reflects an interesting and important paradox for the change leader. The successful management of change is enhanced by giving voice to factors that develop the sense of continuity, the connection between the past and the future, as well as by giving voice to the need for and nature of the change.[85]

See **Toolkit Exercise 7.5** to examine how your leadership experiences have affected your views of change.

Steps to Minimize the Negative Effects of Change

Those who have been involved in significant changes know that how people view the change will have a profound impact on the ultimate success or failure of a change initiative.[86] Change recipients need to become willing change implementers. Therefore, the effects on the people need to be approached with care during the initial planning phases and throughout the change process, including the post-change period.

Engagement

Trust is increased and rumors are reduced when leaders share story after story after story about the problems that are driving the need for change, what is known and not known, process, action plans, and timelines. When coupled with the personal involvement of engaged leaders and executives and a meaningful degree of employee involvement in decisions that affect them (at minimum, the ability to ask questions, voice concerns, and receive answers that reduce uncertainty), individual adaptation and acceptance are advanced.[87] People want to know where things are going, why, and what the implications are on the organization, their parts of the operation, and on them personally. When change leaders don't know the answers to questions that are raised, people should be given a timetable detailing what they will hear and when.

Timeliness

Employees often want to vent their concerns and frustrations, and, at times, grieve what has been lost. No one benefits when recipients first hear about a particular change on the evening news or in the local coffee shop. When this happens, the information needs to be quickly and credibly dealt with through internal communication channels. Otherwise the rumor mill will shift into overdrive as people attempt to make sense of new and potentially conflicting information.[88]

Two-Way Communication

Change communication needs to be two way, as change leaders need to learn as much from exchanges as followers. A variety of communication channels are available to change leaders, and multiple channels are best. Redundancy is clearly preferable to gaps. Communicating through executive-staff briefings, teams, task forces, recipient representatives, advisory groups, video, newsletters, hotlines, and the creative use of the intranet (including bulletin boards, blogs, and e-mail to monitor concerns and expedite the delivery of answers) all have a role in helping people adapt to change. When coupled with transparency, authenticity, and minimal levels of executive defensiveness, these communication approaches advance recipient engagement and adaptation to change.

Exposure to employees' feedback and reactions allows change leaders to adapt strategies and approaches in an informed and sensitive manner, making it possible to enhance further the prospects for successful employee adaptation. For example, tracking themes from e-mails, postings on bulletin boards, and survey results can provide insights into how followers are interpreting and responding to the change. The importance of such feedback proves the adage that leaders who think they know it all have a fool as their advisor. To quote the movie director Blake Edwards, "Every time I think I know 'where it's at,' it's usually somewhere else."

Jick and Peiperl have identified a number of strategies that can assist both the recipients and their managers in coping with different stages of the change (See Table 7.6).

Table 7.6 Strategies for Coping With Change[89]	
Recipients	*Change Leaders*
Accepting Feelings as Natural	**Rethinking Resistance**
• Self-permission to feel and mourn • Taking time to work through feelings • Tolerating ambiguity	• As natural as self-protection • As a positive step toward change • As energy to work with • As information critical to the change process
Managing Stress	**Giving First Aid**
• Maintaining physical well-being • Seeking information about the change • Limiting extraneous stressors • Taking regular breaks • Seeking support	• Accepting emotions • Listening • Providing safety • Marking endings • Providing resources and support
Exercising Responsibility	**Creating Capability for Change**
• Identifying options and gains • Learning from losses • Participating in the change • Inventorying strengths • Learning new skills • Diversifying emotional investing	• Making organizational support of risks clear • Providing a continuing safety net • Emphasizing continuities, gains of change • Helping employees explore risks, options • Suspending judgment • Involving people in decision making • Teamwork • Providing opportunities for individual growth

Source: Adapted from Jick, T., & Peiperl, M. A. (2003). *Managing change, cases and concepts* (2nd ed.). New York: McGraw-Hill, p. 307.

Change recipients can develop support networks to facilitate letting go and moving on if they know and understand the stages of change. Change leaders need to develop an understanding of the dynamics around change and recognize the need to work through the change-management process in a systemic and supportive fashion. Often, followers' understanding for the need for change lags behind that of change leaders. By definition, those leading change have diagnosed the need for change, mourned the loss of the old, understood and embraced the new vision, and moved to action. Those impacted by the change need to work through the same process—but are lagging behind their leaders and lack their direct involvement. As change leaders, we need to give them time to adapt and catch up!

Toolkit Exercise 7.6 asks you to think about the change from the perspectives of recipients. Their receptivity will depend, in large measure, upon their perceptions of various factors and their personal predispositions.

Make Continuous Improvement the Norm

One way that organizations can reduce the perceived threat of changes is to adopt managerial approaches that challenge everyone to regularly question the status quo and seek to improve existing practices as part of their ongoing activities. If organizational members routinely question and initiate continuous improvement projects, then shifts in the environment will not be seen as threatening events. Leaders generate an atmosphere in which change is experienced as a naturally occurring condition by creating an organizational climate in which incremental changes are sought out and embraced. The fact that tomorrow is unlikely to be exactly the same as today becomes the expected norm as opposed to an unexpected shock.[90]

One benefit of continuous improvement approaches such as Six Sigma is the legitimization of ongoing changes in ways that provide continuity with the past. Rather than searching for the silver bullet that will produce the cure for current organizational ills, these approaches seek to advance less heroic, ongoing initiatives that will enhance organizational health in incremental ways.[91] In so doing, these approaches make revolutionary changes less likely and threatening because the real and perceived magnitude of the change is reduced.

If the organizational culture promotes an ongoing and constructive embrace of change, perceptions of the threat related to change are bound to be reduced. Abrahamson refers to this as dynamic stability and points to firms like GE as exemplars of the approach.[92] The experience tells organizational members that changes are normal and tend to work out for the best.

Even when the news is bad, an approach of ongoing employee engagement with change can lead to lower levels of uncertainty, quicker response times (people know what they are facing), improved outcomes (e.g., less undesirable employee turnover), and higher levels of satisfaction than likely would otherwise have occurred. If people (or their representatives) have participated in the analysis, planning, and/or implementation efforts, this tends to further reduce the fear and uncertainty.[93]

Creating organizational agility and resiliency enables organizations to be more prepared for change. Agility allows an organization to be more open to change while resiliency strengthens the core—common purpose, shared beliefs, and identity—to thoughtfully and strategically guide a change process. This requires the establishment of a knowledge-sharing system, commitment from top leadership, and cross-training of employees. In addition, there needs to be a commitment to organizationwide reevaluation and the use of all successes and failures as learning opportunities.[94] Today's and future organizations need to be designed to institutionalize change. This can be done through the promotion of organizational modularity, quick anticipation and response to external forces, construction of conflict-management processes, and building of organizational coherence around values and culture rather than structure.[95]

A final approach to reducing the perceived threat of change is to use approaches that do not cause people to believe they have to bet the farm. One can do this through encouraging the use of experimentation and pilot programs and through ensuring that the perceived rewards and punishments associated with success and failure are not excessive. Again, experience has demonstrated that a series of smaller, interrelated changes by dedicated change agents over time can produce substantial, even revolutionary changes in the organization—sometimes without the organization even knowing they were underway.[96]

Encourage People to Be Change Agents and Avoid the Recipient Trap

It is clear from this chapter that being a change recipient is not as energizing or exciting as being a change agent! Change agents are active and involved. Change recipients find themselves on the receiving end and may experience a lack of power and control. One way to reduce the negative effects of change is to take risks, get more involved, and become a change agent.

When people attempt to influence the events swirling about them, they are, in effect, acting as their own change agents. Since they are often in subordinate roles and dependent, to varying degrees, on the actions of others, skilled people manage the influence process by recognizing whom they are dependent on[97] and engaging in appropriate stakeholder analysis. By taking action, presenting ideas, and attempting to make a difference, potential change recipients can gain power in real or perceived terms. And they will be viewed differently in the organization.

Summary

This chapter has dealt with how people react and why they respond positively, negatively, or with ambivalence to change initiatives. It suggests that change leaders use feelings of ambivalence as opportunities to influence stakeholders. Change agents need to understand resistance to change and use such resistance to understand the change environment better.

The chapter outlines the prescriptive model of change phases that people go through when disruptive changes are involved. Knowing the model may provide useful insights as to how to act. The chapter deals with the factors that affect how people view change: their personalities, their experiences with change, their coworkers, the organization, and the change leaders themselves. Finally, the chapter ends by considering what change agents and leaders can do to manage the process and minimize the negative impact of change.

Toolkit Exercise 7.7 assesses recipients' readiness for change. Implicit in the scoring is advice for change leaders concerning things they can do to increase recipients' receptiveness to change.

Glossary of Terms

Recipients of Change

Those individuals who find themselves on the receiving end of a change initiative and who have little power to alter the direction or content of a change initiative.

Resistance to Change

Actions that are intended to slow or prevent change from happening. Resistance arises when an individual comes to believe that the costs outweigh the benefits and that opposition is warranted. Actions can vary from the expression of concern and "go slow" responses through to more active forms of resistance, including coalition building, formal protests, and even sabotage. Too often managers expect resistance and it becomes a self-fulfilling prophecy.

Ambivalence to Change

The mixed emotions that a change initiative can trigger. Ambivalence arises from uncertainty and occurs when we are asked to act in ways that are inconsistent with our existing attitudes. These mixed emotions generate discomfort that we seek to resolve. There is evidence that suggests we have an easier time giving voice to mixed feelings involving conflicting beliefs than we do when negative emotional responses are involved. Once the individual has resolved his or her ambivalence, subsequent changes to those attitudes become much more difficult until a new sense of ambivalence arises.

Psychological Contract

The psychological contract represents the sum of the implicit and explicit agreements we believe we have with key individuals and the organization concerning our employment relationship. These ground our expectations concerning ourselves and the organization, concerning terms and conditions, norms, rights, rewards, and obligations.

Stages in the Reaction to Change

The three primary stages that individuals typically must progress through when coping with a more traumatic change are the **anticipation and anxiety phase**, the **shock, denial, and retreat phase**, and the **acceptance phase**.

Transition Stages Perspective

The transition stage perspective begins with the **ending phase**, which involves letting go of your former situation, and is often characterized by fear, confusion, and anger. The **neutral zone** is the phase in which individuals feel lost and confused. The **new beginnings stage** occurs when individuals begin to explore new possibilities and start to align their actions with a new vision.

Tolerance for Turbulence and Ambiguity

Tolerance for turbulence and ambiguity involves our comfort level with these conditions. Individuals who have higher tolerance levels generally will be more comfortable and open to change, while those who have lower tolerance levels will prefer more stable and predictable environments.

Predisposition to Change

Relates to our general inclination toward change. Are we typically innovators, early adopters, members of the early majority of adopters, members of the late majority, or in the group of individuals who are very late adopters or nonadopters?

Skepticism and Cynicism Toward Change

Skepticism relates to doubts and concerns we may have concerning the capacity of the change to deliver the promised results. These may be rooted in the change itself, the adoption process, concerns about the change leadership, or unease about the organization's and other key stakeholders' responses to the change.

Cynicism occurs when we fundamentally lose faith in the change, the adoption process, the key individuals involved, or the organization.

END-OF-CHAPTER EXERCISES

TOOLKIT EXERCISE 7.1

Personal Reactions to Change

1. Think through your organizational experiences at school and at work when you have been a recipient of change. How have you typically responded to these changes? What were the factors that led to those responses?

    To help you think about these questions, ask yourself the following concerning three to four such changes:

    a. What was the change and how was it introduced?
    b. What was the impact on you?
    c. What was your initial reaction? Enthusiasm? "Wait and see" attitude? Ambivalence, due to conflicting reactions? Cynicism?
    d. Did your attitudes change over time? Why or why not?

2. Was there a pattern to your response?

    a. Under what circumstances did you support the change? When did you resist? What can you generalize from these experiences?
    b. If you experienced ambivalence, how did you resolve it and what happened to your attitudes toward the change once the ambivalent feelings were resolved?

3. Overall, have your earlier experiences with change been largely positive, largely negative, or mixed? Have these experiences colored your expectations and feelings toward change in the future?

TOOLKIT EXERCISE 7.2

Disruption of the Psychological Contract

Think about a change initiative that you are aware of. What happened or will likely happen to the psychological contracts of recipients?

1. What is the existing psychological contract? (If in the past, what was the contract?)

2. In what ways did the change disrupt the existing psychological contract? To what extent was this perception real? (If in the past, in what ways did the change actually disrupt the psychological contract?)

3. Given the individuals and the context, what reactions to these disruptions to the psychological contract do you anticipate? (If in the past, what were the reactions?)

4. Are there steps that could be taken to reduce the negative effects stemming from the disruption? (If in the past, could anything have been done?)

5. How should a new psychological contract be developed with affected individuals? (If this is in the past, how could this have been done?)

6. If you are the recipient of change, what steps could you take to better manage your way through the development of a new contract? (If this is in the past, what could you have done?)

TOOLKIT EXERCISE 7.3

Your Normal Reaction to Innovation and Change

When you find yourself dealing with matters of innovation and change, how do you typically react?

1. Do you find that you fall into the category of innovator or early adopter, readily considering and often adopting new approaches, well in advance of most people?

2. Or do you generally fall into the category of the early majority? If the initial responses and experiences of the early adopters are generally positive, you are willing to take the risk and adopt the new approach.

3. Or are you generally in the category of the late majority? You wait until the innovation or new approach has been tried and tested by many people before you commit to adopt.

4. Or are you a person who typically does not adopt the innovation or new approach until the vast majority of people have done so? In other words, are you a late adopter or even a nonadopter until forced to do so?

TOOLKIT EXERCISE 7.4

Your Tolerance for Change

1. What is your tolerance for change? What level of turbulence and ambiguity in a work situation do you find most stimulating and satisfying?

2. How do you react when the rate of change is quite low and is likely to remain there?

3. How do you react when the rate of change is at a moderate level? What constitutes a moderate level for you? Are your tolerance levels lower or higher than those of others you know?

4. What price do you find you pay personally when the rate of turbulence and ambiguity exceeds what you are comfortable with? When it is either too low or too high?

5. Have you had to cope with prolonged periods of serious upheaval or periods of extreme turbulence? Have these experiences affected your acceptance of change?

TOOLKIT EXERCISE 7.5

Leadership and Change Recipients

Think more specifically about an example of change leadership that you know.

1. What was the nature of that leadership?

2. Was the leader trusted?

3. Did he/she deserve the trust given?

4. What kind of power did the leader use?

5. How were the messages about the change conveyed? Were they believable messages?

6. Did organizational systems and processes support, or at minimum, not impair the change leader's messages?

7. Was there a sense of continuity between the past and the anticipated future? How was that sense of continuity developed and communicated? What was the impact?

8. What can you learn about the impact of the leader on people and stakeholders as a result of your responses to the above questions?

9. What can you learn about the impact of organizational systems and processes on the people and stakeholders?

10. Talk to others about their experiences. Can you generalize? In what way? What cannot be generalized?

TOOLKIT EXERCISE 7.6

Working Through the Phases of Change

1. Consider a significant and disruptive change situation that you know about (or talk to a friend or relative about such a change situation). Can you identify the different phases of change? What phases are you aware of?

2. Can you identify strategies that people used or could have used to help them work their way through the different phases?

3. Can you identify strategies that change leaders used or could have used to help people work their way through the different phases?

	Awareness Yes/No recipients	Strategies people can use to help them work through stage	Strategies change leaders can use to help recipients work through stage
• Prechange anxiety			
• Shock			
• Defensive retreat			
• Bargaining			
• Depression, guilt, and alienation			
• Acknowledgment			
• Adaptation and change			

Does the model hold? Why or why not?

What other consequences of change can you identify?

TOOLKIT EXERCISE 7.7

Assessing Recipient Openness to Change

In the previous sections, we have discussed the impact of the recipients' personalities, their sense of their psychological contract, and their coworkers, supervisors, and leaders on their reaction to change. Toolkit Exercise 7.7 will provide you with a general sense of the openness of the recipients of change to a specific undertaking.* Likewise, it can be used to evaluate your own openness to the change. If your scores are in the +50 or greater range, you will likely be quite open to change and ready to cope. Negative scores would suggest the opposite, while scores in the middle range (+50 to −50) point to increasing ambivalence. What do the scores tell you about what might be done to increase the openness of the recipient to the change?

Think about a change situation you know of or are involved with. How are the recipients of change likely to rate the following factors?	Score
1. Past experience with change, particularly changes similar to that advocated	Very Negative −10 −5 0 +5 +10 Very ___ Positive
2. Normal rate of change that has been experienced by the organization	Very Low −10 −5 0 +5 +10 Moderate ___ to High
3. Recipients' general predisposition to change as reflected in their personalities	Late Adopter −10 −5 0 +5 +10 Early ___ Adopter
4. People believe they understand the nature of the proposed change and the reasons for it (i.e., the need for change)	Low −10 −5 0 +5 +10 High ___
5. Recipients' personal beliefs about the need for this particular change	Very Negative −10 −5 0 +5 +10 Very ___ Positive
6a. Reactions of coworkers to the change	Very Negative −10 −5 0 +5 +10 Very ___ Positive
6b. Strength of coworker relations (norms)	**Multiply #6a by #6b** Weak 0.1 0.3 0.5 0.7 1.0 Strong ___

---

*This index is not the product of empirical testing. It was created to provide you with food for thought concerning openness to change and what may be facilitating and impairing the receptiveness that you are experiencing.

7. Leader credibility	Low −10 −5 0 +5 +10 High ___
8. Leader gains compliance through fear versus gains commitment through understanding and empathy	Fear −10 −5 0 +5 +10 Support ___
9. Organizational credibility (i.e., will it follow through on commitments related to change)	Low −10 −5 0 +5 +10 High ___
10. Congruence of systems and processes with the proposed change (or confidence that they will be brought into congruence)	Very −10 −5 0 +5 +10 Very___ Incongruent Congruent
Predisposition to Change Index: **Scores can range from −100 to +100**	Overall Score ___

Notes

1. Disney, A. (Producer), & Reticker, G. (Director). (2008). *Pray the devil back to hell* [Motion picture]. New York: Fork Films.

2. Frijda, N. H., & Mesquita, B. (2000). Beliefs though emotions. In N. H. Frijda, A. S. R. Manstead, & S. Bem (Eds.), *Emotions and beliefs: How feelings influence thoughts* (pp. 43–54). Paris: Oxford University Press.

3. Dent, E. B., & Goldberg, S. G. (1999). Challenging resistance to change. *Journal of Applied Behavioral Science, 35*(1), 25–41.

4. Withey, M. J., & Cooper, W. H. (1989). Predicting exit, voice, loyalty, and neglect. *Administrative Science Quarterly, 34,* 521–539.

5. Lines, R. (2004). Influence of participation in strategic change: Resistance, organizational commitment and change goal achievement. *Journal of Change Management, 4*(3), 193–215.

6. Charan, R. (2006, April). Home Depot's blueprint for culture change. *Harvard Business Review, 84*(4), 60–70.

7. Dell, J., & Krantz, M. (2007, January 4). Home Depot boots CEO Nardelli. *USA Today.* Retrieved December 2010 from http://www.usatoday.com/money/industries/retail/2007-01-03-hd-nardelli_x.htm; Kavilanz, P. B. (2007, January 3). Nardelli out at Home Depot. CNN Money.com.money.

8. Lines, R. (2004). Influence of participation in strategic change: Resistance, organizational commitment and change goal achievement. *Journal of Change Management, 4*(3), 193–215.

9. Piderit, S. K. (2000). Rethinking resistance and recognizing ambivalence: A multidimensional view of attitudes toward an organizational change. *Academy of Management Review, 25*(4), 783–794.

10. Charan, R. (2006, April). Home Depot's blueprint for culture change. *Harvard Business Review, 84*(4), 60–70.

11. Piderit, S. K. (2000). Rethinking resistance and recognizing ambivalence: A multidimensional view of attitudes toward an organizational change. *Academy of Management Review, 25*(4), 783–794.

12. Smith, K. K. (1982). *Groups in conflict: Prisons in disguise.* Dubuque, IA: Kendall/Hunt; Spreitzer, G. M., & Quinn, R. E. (1996). Empowering middle managers to be transformational leaders. *Journal of Applied Behavioral Science, 32*(3), 237–261.

13. Piderit, S. K. (2000). Rethinking resistance and recognizing ambivalence: A multidimensional view of attitudes toward an organizational change. *Academy of Management Review, 25*(4), 783–794.

14. Avery, J. B., Wernsing, T. S., & Luthans, F. (2008). Can positive employees help positive organizational change? Impact of psychological capital and emotions on relevant attitudes and behaviors. *Journal of Applied Behavioral Science, 44*(1), 48–70.

15. Much of the material on ambivalence and change management is drawn from two excellent articles: Lines, R. (2005). The structure and function of attitudes toward organizational change. *Human Resource Development Review, 4*(1), 8–32; and Piderit, S. K. (2000). Rethinking resistance and recognizing ambivalence: A multidimensional view of attitudes toward an organizational change. *Academy of Management Review, 25*(4), 783–794.

16. Lines, R. (2004). Influence of participation in strategic change: Resistance, organizational commitment and change goal achievement. *Journal of Change Management, 4*(3), 193–215.

17. Piderit, S. K. (2000). Rethinking resistance and recognizing ambivalence: A multidimensional view of attitudes toward an organizational change. *Academy of Management Review, 25*(4), 783–794.

18. Sull, D. N. (1999, July–August). Why good companies go bad. *Harvard Business Review, 42–51.*

19. Festinger, L. (1957). *A theory of cognitive dissonance.* Stanford, CA: Stanford University Press.

20. Hymes, R. W. (1986). Political attitudes as social categories: A new look at selective memory. *Journal of Personality and Social Psychology, 51,* 233–241.

21. Lines, R. (2004). Influence of participation in strategic change: Resistance, organizational commitment and change goal achievement. *Journal of Change Management, 4*(3), 193–215.

22. Barr, P. S., Stimpert, J. L., & Huff, A. S. (1992). Cognitive change, strategic action, and organizational renewal. *Strategic Management Journal, 13,* 15–36; Floyd, S. W., & Wooldridge, B. (1996). *The strategic middle manager.* San Francisco: Jossey-Bass.

23. Lines, R. (2004). Influence of participation in strategic change: Resistance, organizational commitment and change goal achievement. *Journal of Change Management, 4*(3), 193–215.

24. Peus, C., Frey, D., Gerkhardt, M., Fischer, P., & Traut-Mattausch, E. (2009). Leading and managing organizational change initiatives. *Management Review, 20*(2), 158–175; Giora, D. A., & Thomas, J. B. (1996). Identity, image, and issue interpretation: Sensemaking during strategic change in academia. *Administrative Science Quarterly, 41,* 370–403; Labianca, G., Gray, B., & Brass, D. J. (2000). A grounded model of organizational schema change during empowerment. *Organizational Science, 11*(2), 235–257; Lines, R. (2004). Influence of participation in strategic change: Resistance, organizational commitment and change goal achievement. *Journal of Change Management, 4*(3), 193–215; and Sagie, A., & Koslowsky, M. (1994). Organizational attitudes and behaviors as a function of participation in strategic and tactical decisions: An application of path–goal theory. *Journal of Organizational Behavior, 15*(1), 37–47.

25. Balogun, J., & Johnson, G. (2005). From intended strategies to unintended outcomes: The impact of change recipient sensemaking. *Organizational Studies, 26*(11), 1596.

26. Hackman, J. R., & Oldham, G. R. (1980). *Work redesign.* Reading, MA: Addison-Wesley.

27. Gustafson, B. (2005). Plant closure "devastates" Newfoundland community. *National Fisherman, 85*(10), 11–12.

28. Gustafson, B. (2005). Plant closure "devastates" Newfoundland community. *National Fisherman, 85*(10), 11–12.

29. Gopinath, C., & Becker, T. E. (2000). Communication, procedural justice, and employee attitudes: Relationships under conditions of divestiture. *Journal of Management, 26,* 63–83.

30. Piderit, S. K. (2000). Rethinking resistance and recognizing ambivalence: A multidimensional view of attitudes toward an organizational change. *Academy of Management Review, 25*(4), 783–794.

31. Reicher, A. E., Wanous, J. P., & Austin, J. T. (1997). Understanding and managing cynicism about organizational change. *Academy of Management Executive, 11*(1), 48–60.

32. Lines, R. (2004). Influence of participation in strategic change: Resistance, organizational commitment and change goal achievement. *Journal of Change Management, 4*(3), 193–215.

33. Peus, C., Frey, D., Gerkhardt, M., Fischer, P., & Traut-Mattausch, E. (2009). Leading and managing organizational change initiatives. *Management Review, 20*(2), 158–175.

34. Kickul, J., Lester, S. W., & Finkl, J. (2002). Promise breaking during organizational change: Do justice interventions make a difference? *Journal of Organizational Behavior, 23*, 469–488.

35. Watson, T. J. (1982). Group ideologies and organizational change. *Journal of Management Studies, 19*, 259–275.

36. Kotter, J. P. (1995). Leading change: Why transformation efforts fail. *Harvard Business Review, 73*(2), 59–67.

37. Kerr, S. (1995). On the folly of rewarding A, while hoping for B. *Academy of Management Executive, 9*(1), 7–14.

38. Turnley, W. H., & Feldman, D. C. (1999). The impact of psychological contract violations on exit, voice, loyalty, and neglect. *Human Relations, 52*(7), 895–922; Rousseau, D. M. (1995). *Promises in action: Psychological contracts in organizations.* Thousand Oaks, CA: Sage.

39. Matthijs Bal, P., Chiaburu, D. S., & Jansen, P. G. W. (2010). Psychological contract breach and work performance; Is social exchange a buffer or an intensifier? *Journal of Managerial Psychology, 25*(3), 252–273; Richard, O. C., McMillan-Capehart, A., Bhuian, S. N., & Taylor, E. C. (2009). Antecedents and consequences of psychological contracts: Does organizational culture really matter? *Journal of Business Research, 62*(8), 818–825.

40. Deery, S. J., Iverson, R. D., & Walsh, J. T. (2006). Toward a better understanding of psychological contract breach: A study of customer service employees. *Journal of Applied Psychology, 91*(1), 13; Suazo, M. M., Turnley, W. H., & Mai-Dalton, R. R. (2005). The role of perceived violation in determining employees' reactions to psychological contract breach. *Journal of Leadership and Organizational Studies, 12*(1), 24–36.

41. Edmondson, A. C. (2003). Large-scale change at the WSSC. *Harvard Business School,* 9–603–056.

42. Edmondson, A. C. (2003). Large-scale change at the WSSC. *Harvard Business School,* 9–603–056.

43. Kübler-Ross, E. (1969). *On death and dying.* New York: Macmillan.

44. Fink, S. L. (1967). Crisis and motivation: A theoretical model. *Archives of Physical Medicine and Rehabilitation, 48*(11), 592–597.

45. Jick, T. (2003). The recipients of change In T. Jick & M. A. Peiperl, *Managing change, cases and concepts* (2nd ed., pp. 299–311). New York: McGraw-Hill Higher Education.

46. Perlman, D., & Takacs, G. J. (1990). The ten stages of change. *Nursing Management, 21*(4), 33–38.

47. Piderit, S. K. (2000). Rethinking resistance and recognizing ambivalence: A multidimensional view of attitudes toward an organizational change. *Academy of Management Review, 25*(4), 783–794.

48. Kotter, J. P. (2007, January). Leading change: Why transformation efforts fail. *Harvard Business Review,* 96–103.

49. Doherty, N., Banks, J., & Vinnicombe, S. (1996). Managing survivors: The experience of survivors in British Telecom and the British financial services sector. *Journal of Managerial Psychology, 11*(7), 51–60.

50. Bedeian, A. G., & Armenakis, A. A. (1998, February). The cesspool syndrome: How dreck floats to the top of declining organizations. *Academy of Management Executive,* 58–67; Mishra, K. E., Spreitzer, G. M., & Mishra, A. K. (1998). Preserving employee morale during downsizing. *Sloan Management Review, 39*(2), 83–95.

51. Jick, T., & Peiperl, M. A. (2002). *Managing change, cases and concepts* (2nd ed.). New York: McGraw-Hill Higher Education.

52. Personal conversation with the author.

53. Rogers, E. M. (1995). *Diffusion of innovations* (4th ed.). New York: Free Press.

54. Deckop, J. R., Merriman, K. K., & Blau, G. (2004). Impact of variable risk preferences on the effectiveness of control of pay. *Journal of Occupational and Organizational Psychology, 77*(1), 63–80.

55. Oreg, S., Bayazıt, M., Vakola, M., Arciniega, L., Armenakis, A., Barkauskiene, R., Bozionelos, N., Fujimoto, Y., González, L., Han, J., Hřebíčková, M., Jimmieson, N., Kordačová, J., Mitsuhashi, H., Mlačić, B., Ferić, I., Topić, M. K., Pilar, I., Ohly, S., Saksvik, P. Ø., Hetland, H., Saksvik, I., & van Dam, K. (2008). Dispositional resistance to change: Measurement equivalence and the link to personal values across 17 nations. *Journal of Applied Psychology, 93*(4), 935–944.

56. Probst, T. M. (2003). Exploring employee outcomes of organizational restructuring: A Solomon four-group study. *Group & Organization Management, 28*(3), 416–439.

57. Tremblay, M., & Roger, A. (2004). Career plateauing reactions: The moderating role of job scope, role ambiguity and participation among Canadian managers. *International Journal of Human Resource Management, 15*(6), 996–1017.

58. Kass, S. J., Vodanovich, S. J., & Callender, A. (2001). State-trait boredom: Relationship to absenteeism, tenure, and job satisfaction. *Journal of Business and Psychology, 16*(2), 317–326.

59. Park, D., & Krishnan, H. A. (2003). Understanding the stability-change paradox: Insights for the evolutionary, adaptation, and institutional perspectives. *International Journal of Management, 20*(3), 265–270.

60. Barnett, W. P., & Sorenson, O. (2002). The Red Queen in organizational creation. *Industrial and Corporate Change, 11*(2), 289–325.

61. Kelly, P., & Amburgey, T. (1991). Organizational inertia and momentum: A dynamic model of strategic change. *Academy of Management Journal, 34,* 591–612; Huff, J., Huff, J., & Thomas, H. (1992). Strategic renewal and the interaction of cumulative stress and inertia. *Strategic Management Journal, 13,* 55–75.

62. Kovoor-Misra, S., & Nathan, M. (2000). Timing is everything: The optimal time to learn from crises. *Review of Business, 21*(3/4), 31–36.

63. Geller, E. S. (2002). Leadership to overcome resistance to change: It takes more than consequence control. *Journal of Organizational Behavior Management, 22*(3), 29; and Brown, J., & Quarter, J. (1994). Resistance to change: The influence of social networks on the conversion of a privately-owned unionized business to a worker cooperative. *Economic and Industrial Democracy, 15*(2), 259–283.

64. Bettenhausen, K. L. (1991). Five years of groups research: What we have learned and what needs to be addressed. *Journal of Management, 17*(2), 345–381.

65. Johnson, L. (2008). Helping employees cope with change in an anxious era. *Harvard Management Update, 13*(12), 1–5.

66. Brenneman, G. (1998). Right away and all at once: How we saved Continental. *Harvard Business Review, 76*(5), 162–173.

67. Tyler, T. R., & De Cremer, D. (2005). Process-based leadership: Fair procedures and reactions to organizational change. *Leadership Quarterly*, *16*(4), 529–545.

68. Sherman, W. S., & Garland, G. E. (2007). Where to bury the survivors? Exploring possible ex post effects of resistance to change. *S. A. M. Advanced Management Journal*, *72*(1), 52–63.

69. Reichers, A. E., Wanous, J. P., & Austin, J. T. (1997). Understanding and managing cynicism about organizational change. *Academy of Management Executive*, *11*(1), 48–60.

70. Reichers, A. E., Wanous, J. P., & Austin, J. T. (1997). Understanding and managing cynicism about organizational change. *Academy of Management Executive*, *11*(1), 50–51.

71. Munduate, L., & Bennebroek Gravenhorst, K. M. (2003). Power dynamics and organisational change: An introduction. *Applied Psychology: An International Review*, *52*(1), 1–13; Weick, K. E., & Quinn, R. E. (1999). Organizational change and development. *Annual Review of Psychology*, *50*, 361–386; Peus, C., Frey, D., Gerkhardt, M., Fischer, P., & Traut-Mattausch, E. (2009). Leading and managing organizational change initiatives. *Management Review*, *20*(2), 158–175.

72. Brown, M., & Cregan, C. (2008). Organizational change cynicism: The role of employee involvement. *Human Resource Management*, *47*(4), 667–686.

73. Personal communication, 2004.

74. Reichers, A. E., Wanous, J. P., & Austin, J. T. (1997). Understanding and managing cynicism about organizational change. *Academy of Management Executive*, *11*(1), 53.

75. Kramer, R. M. (2006). The great intimidators. *Harvard Business Review*, *84*(2), 88–96.

76. Sherman, W. S., & Garland, G. E. (2007). Where to bury the survivors? Exploring possible ex post effects of resistance to change. *S. A. M. Advanced Management Journal*, *72*(1), 52–63.

77. Source unknown.

78. Stimson, W. A. (2005). A Deming inspired management code of ethics. *Quality Progress*, *38*(2), 67–75; Farson, R., & Keyes, R. (2002). The failure-tolerant leader. *Harvard Business Review*, *80*(8), 64; Casio, J. (2002). Scare tactics. *Incentive*, *176*(9), 56–62.

79. Collins, J. C. (2001). *From good to great: Why some companies make the leap…and others don't.* New York: Harper Business.

80. Werther, W. B., Jr. (1987). Loyalty: Cross-organizational comparisons and patterns. *Leadership and Organization Development Journal*, *8*(2), 3–6.

81. Deming, W. E. (1986). *Drastic changes for western management.* Madison, WI: Center for Quality and Productivity Improvement.

82. Challagalla, G. N., & Shervgani, T. A. (1996). Dimensions and types of supervisory control: Effects on salesperson performance and satisfaction. *Journal of Marketing*, *60*, 89–105.

83. Appelbaum, S. H., Bregman, M., & Moroz, P. (1998). Fear as a strategy: Effects and impact within the organization. *Journal of European Industrial Training*, *22*(3), 113–127.

84. Collins, J. C., & Porras, J. I. (1994). *Built to last: Successful habits of visionary companies.* New York: HarperCollins.

85. Kolb, D. G. (2002). Continuity, not change: The next organizational challenge. *University of Auckland Business Review*, *4*(2), 1–11.

86. Balogun, J., & Johnson, G. (2005). From intended strategies to unintended outcomes: The impact of change recipient sensemaking. *Organizational Studies*, *26*(11), 1573–1601.

87. Evans, C., Hammersley, G. O., & Robertson, M. (2001). Assessing the role and efficacy of communication strategies in times of crisis. *Journal of European Industrial Training*, *25*(6), 297–309; Ashkenas, R. N., DeMonaco, L. J., & Francis, S. C. (1998). Making the deal real: How GE Capital integrates acquisitions. *Harvard Business Review*, *76*(1), 165–176.

88. Difonzo, N., & Bordia, P. (1998). A tale of two corporations: Managing uncertainty during organizational change. *Human Resource Management, 37*(3–4), 295–304.

89. Jick, T., & Peiperl, M. A. (2002). *Managing change, cases and concepts* (2nd ed.). New York: McGraw-Hill Higher Education.

90. Tersine, R., Harvey, M., & Buckley, M. (1997). Shifting organizational paradigms: Transitional management. *European Management Journal, 15*(1), 45–57.

91. Schneider, B., Brief, A. P., & Guzzo, R. A. (1996). Creating a climate and culture for sustainable organizational change. *Organizational Dynamics, 24*(4), 6–18.

92. Abrahamson, E. (2000, July–August). Change without pain. *Harvard Business Review*, 75–79.

93. Burke, R. J. (2002). The ripple effect. *Nursing Management, 33*(2), 41–43; Weakland, J. H. (2001). Human resources holistic approach to healing downsizing survivors. *Organizational Development Journal, 19*(2), 59–69; Mishra, K. E., Spreitzer, G. M., & Mishra, A. K. (1998). Preserving employee morale during downsizing. *Sloan Management Review, 39*(2), 83–95.

94. McCann, J., Selsky, J., & Lee, J. (2009). Building agility, resilience and performance in turbulent environments. *People and Strategy, 32*(3), 44–51.

95. Nadler, D. A., & Tushman, M. T. (1999). The organization of the future: Strategic imperatives and core competencies for the 21st century. *Organizational Dynamics, 28*(1), 45–60.

96. Meyerson, D. E. (2001, October). Radical change, the quiet way. *Harvard Business Review*, 92–100.

97. Cohen, A. R., & Bradford, D. L. (1990). *Influence without authority*. New York: Wiley; Keys, B., & Case, T. (1990). How to become an influential manager. *Academy of Management Executive, 4*, 38–49.

CHAPTER 8

Becoming a Master Change Agent

"Never doubt that a small group of thoughtful, committed individuals can change the world. Indeed, it's the only thing that ever has."[1]

—Margaret Mead

CHAPTER OVERVIEW

- The success of a change agent involves interplay among the **person, the situation, and a vision.**
- Successful change agents have a set of skills and personal characteristics: interpersonal, communication, and political skills; emotional resilience and tolerance for ambiguity and ethical conflicts; persistence, pragmatism, and dissatisfaction with the status quo; and openness to information, flexibility, and adaptability. They act in a manner likely to build trust. Change agents develop their skills with experiences in change situations.
- This chapter describes four change-agent types: the emotional champion, the intuitive adapter, the developmental strategist, and the continuous improver. Each has a different preference for his or her method of persuasion (vision versus analytic) and orientation to change (strategic versus incremental).
- This chapter considers two situational factors related to being a change agent: being an internal or external change agent and defining the dynamics and value of a change team.

C hange agents are critical to the entire change process, from initial diagnoses to implementation. They are sources of energy and intellect that help organizational members recognize the need for change, see what the future may look like, build support, and mobilize the troops to move toward the vision, then assess where and how to proceed next.

This chapter examines what makes a change agent. It looks at change agents' individual characteristics and how these interact with a situation and a powerful vision. The chapter contrasts change managers and change leaders and examines how change leaders develop through stages to become effective. Four types of change leaders are identified: the strategist (particularly important for a transformational change), the intuitive adapter, the continuous improver, and the emotional champion. The skills of these internal change agents are examined, the role of the external change agent discussed, and the usefulness of change teams is highlighted. The chapter ends with rules of thumb for change agents from the wisdom of organizational development and change-agent experts. Figure 8.1 highlights this chapter's place in the change management process.

The role of change agent is a double-edged sword. While it can prove exciting, educational, enriching, and career enhancing, it can also be hazardous to your career, frustrating, and demoralizing when risks escalate and failure looms. In general, people who become change agents will improve their understanding of organizations, develop special skills, and increase their networks of contacts and visibility in the organization.[2] Those who choose not to respond to the challenge of leading change, on the other hand, run the risk of becoming less central and relevant to the operation of their organizations.

When changes fail, there is the sense that the change agent's career has ended. However, this is seldom the case. While failure experiences are painful, change agents are resilient. For example, when Jacques Nasser left Ford in 2001, many thought he was a spent force. However, about a year after leaving Ford, he took over as chairman of Polaroid after it was acquired by One Equity Partners in a bankruptcy auction. In 2½ years, Nasser turned it around and its resale resulted in a $250 million dollar gain for One Equity.[3] In August 2009, Nasser again hit the business press news when he was nominated chairman of BHP Billiton, the world's largest mining company, and took office in early 2010.[4] The skills and personal attributes that Nasser developed at Ford have served him well since he left in 2001.

Many individuals find it difficult to identify where and how they fit into the change process. They believe that they cannot ignite change with their low- or mid-level roles and titles and minimal experiences in organizations. Years of autocratic or risk-averse bosses and top-down organizational cultures make it hard to believe that this time the organization wants change and innovation. Critics of present-day educational systems have suggested that schools encourage dependent rather than change-agent thinking. If teachers and professors see the students' role as absorbing and applying within prescribed boundaries rather than raising troubling questions, independent and innovative thinking will not be advanced.[5]

In the turbulent years of the 2010s, however, individuals will find themselves living in organizations that challenge them to take up one of the roles of change

Figure 8.1 The Change-Management Process

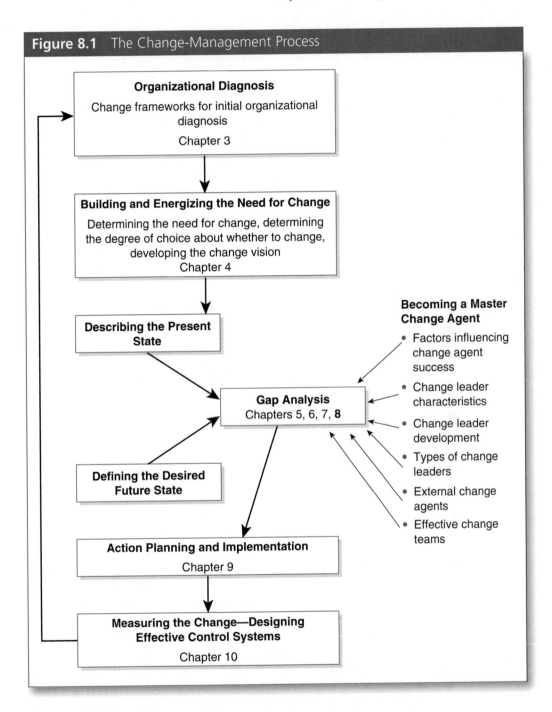

agency: initiator, implementer, facilitator, and/or task force team member. Leaders in organizations are asking people to step forward and make a difference. While the specific roles will vary over time and context, moving to an active role is critical. Simply providing information or offering armchair solutions seldom produces meaningful change. To disrupt inertia and drift, some individuals must move from an observer status to active. Those who wish to add value to their organizations and make a difference will challenge themselves to take on change leadership roles.

For many, their implicit model of change assumes that they must have the involvement and support of the CEO or some other senior sponsor before they can create meaningful change. There is no question that if a change initiative has the commitment and budget of a senior change champion, the job is immeasurably easier. However, for many individuals acting from subordinate organizational roles (e.g., technical professionals, first-line and middle managers, front-line staff), the changes they want require them to question existing systems and processes, with little top-level, visible support when they begin.

In *Leading the Revolution*, Hamel argues that every "company needs a band of insurrectionists" who challenge and break the rules and take risks.[6] One teacher provides an example.

REFLECTIONS ON A TEACHER

The teacher that influenced me the most was concerned with our learning and not with the power and influence of the administration. For example, when *Catcher in the Rye* was deemed unfit for our youthful eyes, he informed the class that this book was classed as unsuitable. This teacher reported that the book by J. D. Salinger should be avoided and while it was recognizable because of its red cover with yellow print and found in most bookstores, libraries and magazine stores, we should not seek it out. Later, the same teacher was instructed to black out certain risqué phrases from one of the assigned books for class. Of course, he marched into the class, described that the phrases on p. 138, lines 7 and 8, that were to be blacked out and that he was enlisting the class's help to do the work for him.

Anonymous caller, CBC Radio, January 2004.

Testing orthodoxies will become critical in the drive to keep pace with environmental demands.[7] The individuals wanting to remove student exposure to the perceived immorality in the books likely thought they were change agents as well. However, by doing so, they were limiting student access to information and the opportunity to think about common realities. For the teacher in the example, this was viewed as violating the prime purposes of a school system—educating the students and instilling a desire for learning. It drove him to action.

With the ever-increasing need for innovation and change in organizations, there is the recognition that change management is an essential part of every good manager's skill set.[8] Change agency has shifted from notions of "lone ranger," top-down heroic leadership to ones involving leaders who enable change teams and empower workers to envision change and make it happen.[9] As Jick points out, "implementing their own changes as well as others."[10] While we might think that change is led from the top, Jick and others dispute this. "Most well-known change initiatives (*that are*) perceived as being 'top-down' or led by a senior executive or the CEO, probably started at the bottom or the middle, years earlier."[11]

As Rosabeth Moss Kanter states, real change is for the long haul. It "requires people to adjust their behavior and that behavior is often beyond the direct control of top management."[12] Bold strokes taken by top management likely do not build the long-term capabilities of the organization unless they are buttressed by a concerted commitment to an underlying vision. Bold strokes can reduce, reorganize, and merge organizations, but each of these takes a toll on the organization. Unfortunately, the long-term benefits can prove to be illusory if the initiative fails to sustainably embrace the hearts as well as the heads of organizational members in ways that generate internal and external environmental congruence.

Factors That Influence Change Agent Success

The Interplay of Personal Attributes, Situation, and Vision

Images of organizational change agents often revolve around personalities that appear to be bigger than life: Jack Welch, former CEO of GE; Bill Gates, former CEO of Microsoft; and Meg Whitman, former CEO of eBay. If such grand standards are the benchmarks employed to assess personal qualities and potential as a change agent, most people will inevitably fall far short of the mark.

However, history suggests that leading change is about more than just the person. In the 1930s, Winston Churchill was a politician in decline. When World War II began, suddenly his skills and personality matched what was needed, and the British public believed he was uniquely qualified to be prime minister. Churchill did not change who he was, but the situation changed dramatically and, as prime minister, Churchill projected a vision of victory and took actions that changed history and his reputation. This match of person and situation is further highlighted by the fact that Churchill experienced electoral defeat in the postwar environment despite his enormous popularity during the war.

In other words, it was the person *and* it was more than the person. It was also the situation, the vision the person had, and the actions he took. A robust model for change considers the interaction between personality, vision, and situation. Michael J. Fox exemplifies a person who became a change agent extraordinaire in the fight against Parkinson's disease.

MICHAEL J. FOX BECOMES A CHANGE AGENT

Most people get Parkinson's disease late in life. Michael J. Fox, a television/movie star, contracted it when he was 30. Before his disease, Fox was focused on his career. Within a year, Fox had created the Fox Foundation that has become an exceptionally effective organization in fundraising and in shaping the research agenda for Parkinson's disease.[13]

Fox's basic personality didn't change with the onset of Parkinson's. But suddenly he was faced with a situation that generated a sense of purpose and vision that both transcended his self-interest and captured the attention and emotions of others. This powerful vision was crucial to Fox's transformation from movie star to change agent. He deployed his energy, interpersonal skills, creativity, and decision-making skills to pursue this vision. His contacts, profile, and reputation gave him access to an influential board of directors. In record time, he recruited a key executive director and created a foundation that became a funding force. Most importantly, he chose to act. He articulated values that resonated with key stakeholders and raised awareness and interest through his strategies and tactics. The ability to create alignment among stakeholders on the values front has been shown to be very valuable in reducing resistance and advancing change.[14] His is far from an isolated incident. From Paul Newman's social entrepreneurship and philanthropy with salad dressing[15] to Andrea Ivory's initiative to bring early breast cancer detection to uninsured women in Florida*, individuals from all walks of life are choosing not to accept the status quo and are making a difference.

In the above cases, the interaction of the person, situation, and powerful vision transformed a person into a change agent. This can be summarized in the following equation:

> **Being a Change Agent = Person × Vision × Situation**

Situations play a crucial part in this three-way interchange. Some situations invigorate and energize the change agent. Enthusiasm builds as coalitions form and the proposed change gains momentum and seems likely to succeed. Other situations suck energy out of the change agent and seem to lead to a neverending series of meetings, obstacles, and issues that prevent a sense of progress. Borrowing from the language of chemical reactions, Dickout calls the former situations **exothermic** change situations. Here energy is liberated by actions.[16] Conversely, the latter situations he calls **endothermic**. Here the change program consumes energy and arouses opposition—which in turn requires more energy from the change agent.

Change agents need exothermic situations that "liberate the energy to drive the change."[17] However, they will experience both exothermic and endothermic periods in a change process. Initial excitement and discovery are followed by snail-paced progress, setbacks, dead ends, and perhaps a small victory. The question is: Do the agents have the staying power and the ability to manage their energy flows and reserves during this ultramarathon? Do they have a team to

---

*CNN's Heroes Project seeks to inspire people to take action by annually recognizing the change initiatives of everyday people in their communities and celebrating the impact they are having. Their initiatives are highlighted on http://www.cnn.com/SPECIALS/cnn.heroes/?iref=allsearch.

help replenish their energy and keep them going? Or do they run out of energy and give up? Colleagues who serve as close confidantes can play an important role in sustaining energy. They help to keep things in perspective, enabling the change leader to face future challenges and pitfalls. While action taking is the defining visible characteristic of change, discussion and reflection play important and often undervalued roles in the development and maintenance of change leaders.[18] Reflection as a critical practice of change leaders is discussed later in this chapter.

Change Leaders and Their Essential Characteristics

An examination of the literature on the personal characteristics of change leaders yields a daunting list of personal attributes ranging from emotional intelligence to general intelligence, determination, openness to experience, and so forth.[19] Textbook treatments of leadership provide lists of the traits and behaviors that prove difficult to reconcile. While most of the literature is inconclusive about attributes that matter and can be generalized, six stand out as particularly relevant for change leaders.

1. Commitment to Improvement

The essential characteristic of change leaders is that they are people who seek opportunities to take action in order to bring about improvement. They possess restlessness with the way things are currently done, inquisitive minds as to what alternatives are possible, and the desire to take informed risks to make things better. Katzenbach argues that change leaders are significantly different in their orientation from traditional managers.[20] For Katzenbach, the basic mindset of a "real change leader" is someone who does it, fixes it, tries it, changes it, and does it again—*a trial-and-error approach* rather than an attempt to optimize and get it perfect the first time.

2. Communication and Interpersonal Skills

Doyle talks about potential change agents and argues that they need sophisticated levels of interpersonal and communication skills to be effective.[21] He describes change agents as requiring emotional resilience, tolerance for ethical conflicts and ambiguities, and political savvy. Conflict goes with the territory when stakeholders believe the changes will negatively impact them, and researchers have noted the importance of conflict-facilitation skills in change agents, including skills related to constructive confrontation and the development of new agreements through dialogue and negotiation.[22] Barack Obama's soaring oratorical skills allowed him to speak directly to the American people and bypass much of the Washington establishment when he was pushing for changes to the American health system in 2009. This set the stage for the difficult discussions, negotiations, and tactical maneuvers that followed and resulted in new health care legislation. Kramer maintains that this political awareness about what needs to be done may lead, in certain situations, to abrasive, confronting, intimidating behavior.[23] Such challenging behavior may be what is needed to "unfreeze" a complacent organization. Stories of Churchill's arrogant behavior, appropriate in wartime, cost him the prime ministry in the postwar election.

The communications and interpersonal skills needed to navigate the political environment and awaken the organization to needed action receive a lot of attention. However, this more muscular image of the transformational communications skills of change leaders is but a subset of the range of approaches they may deploy in this area. Not all change leaders have a gift for rhetoric and many are not charismatic in the traditional sense of the term.* In his book *From Good to Great,* Jim Collins[24] explores the skill sets of change leaders who successfully transformed their average organizations into great ones. He highlights the quiet, humble, grounded, and committed way in which many of these change leaders interacted with others on a day-to-day basis and the influence this had on the outcomes their organizations were able to achieve. Their positive energy was clearly visible, and frustration didn't give rise to the communication of cynicism that can taint the perspectives of others and derail a change.[25]

McCall and Lombardo identified a number of other characteristics that derail change leaders when they are communicated to others: being cold and aloof, lacking in critical skills, displaying insensitivity to others, being arrogant, being burned out, lacking trustworthiness, and being overly ambitious from a personal perspective.[26] When Malcolm Higgs looked at the question of bad leadership, he identified four recurring themes: abuse of power, inflicting damage on others, overexercise of control to satisfy personal needs, and rule breaking to serve the individual's own purposes. He saw these actions as caused by narcissism in the leader—a view of oneself as superior, entitled, and central to all that happens.[27]

3. Determination

Change agents need a dogged determination to succeed in the face of significant odds and the resilience to respond to setbacks in a reasoned and appropriate manner. After all, in the middle of change, everything can look like a failure. Change agents need to be able to persist when it looks like things have gone wrong and success appears unlikely.

4. Eyes on the Prize and Flexibility

Change agents also need to focus on the practical—getting it done. They must be ready to take informed risks, modify their plans to pursue new options, or divert

---

*Charisma is defined as a trait found in persons whose personalities are characterized by a personal charm and magnetism/attractiveness along with innate and powerfully sophisticated abilities of interpersonal communication and persuasion (http://en.wikipedia.org/wiki/Charisma).

their energies to different avenues as the change landscape shifts—sometimes because of their actions and sometimes because of the actions of others or shifts in other factors in the environment. Doggedness is balanced by flexibility and adaptability, and impatience is balanced by patience. Time for dialogue and reflection on the change process is needed to give perspective and make informed judgments.[28]

5. Experience and Networks

Given their desire to make things happen, it is not surprising to find that experience with change is an attribute common to many successful change agents. These individuals embrace change rather than avoiding it and seeing it as "the enemy." They are constantly scanning the environment, picking up clues and cues that allow them to develop a rich understanding of their organization's situation and the need for change. As the situation shifts, they are aware of those shifts and respond appropriately to them. They make this easier for themselves by ensuring that they are part of networks that will tell them what they need to hear—not what they want to hear. They build these networks over time through their trustworthiness, credibility, and interpersonal skills and through the value other members of these networks derive from them. Networks don't work for long if others don't feel they are getting value from them. To ensure that members of the networks and others continue to communicate with them, change leaders are well advised to remember to never be seen as shooting the messenger. If messengers believe the act of communicating will put them at risk, they will alter their behavior accordingly.[29]

6. Intelligence

Intelligence is needed to engage in needed analysis, to assess possible courses of action, and to create confidence in a proposed plan.[30] In general, one has more confidence in a proposal developed by a bright individual than one brought forward by a dullard. However, traditionally defined intelligence is not enough. Interpersonal and communications skills are needed to frame proposals effectively and implement them. This social dimension is why emotional intelligence is often highlighted in discussions of change agent characteristics.[31]

In his investigation of the characteristics of change leaders, Caldwell differentiates the attributes of change leaders from those he calls change managers.[32] Table 8.1 outlines his view of the differences. Caldwell argues that change leaders operate from a visionary, adaptable perspective while change managers are much more hands on and work with people. Of course, there is nothing that says a change agent cannot possess the attributes of both change leaders and change managers (as defined by Caldwell). In fact, they will need access to both, depending upon their role(s) and the change challenges they are addressing.

Table 8.1 Attributes of Change Leaders and Change Managers

Attributes of Change Leaders	Attributes of Change Managers
• Inspiring vision	• Empowering others
• Entrepreneurship	• Team building
• Integrity and honesty	• Learning from others
• Learning from others	• Adaptability and flexibility
• Openness to new ideas	• Openness to new ideas
• Risk taking	• Managing resistance
• Adaptability and flexibility	• Conflict resolution
• Creativity	• Networking
• Experimentation	• Knowledge of the business
• Using power	• Problem solving

*Adapted from Caldwell, R. (2003). Change leaders and change managers: Different or complementary? *Leadership & Organization Development Journal, 24*(5), 285–293. The attributes were ranked by experts. The most highly ranked are at the top of the list, with the others following in order. Note that Table 8.1 identifies attributes not specifically mentioned in the preceding pages.

Another way to think about the various attributes of change agents is to consider the sorts of behaviors they give rise to. The following three categories of change behaviors are a helpful way of grouping their actions:[33]

- **Framing behaviors:** behaviors oriented toward changing the sense of the situation, establishing starting points for change, designing the change journey, and communicating principles
- **Capacity-creating behaviors:** behaviors focused on creating the capacity for change by increasing individual and organizational capabilities and creating and communicating connections in the organization
- **Shaping behaviors:** actions that attempt to shape what people do by acting as a role model, holding others accountable, thinking about change, and focusing on individuals in the change process

Higgs and Roland examined such behaviors in a recent study and discovered that "framing change and building capacity are more successful than...shaping behavior."[34] They suggested that change leaders should shift from a leader-centric, directive approach to a more facilitating, enabling style in today's organizations.

Finally, James Kouzes and Barry Posner provide interesting thinking about the characteristics of effective change leaders in behavioral terms. In their book, they argue that leaders who are adept at getting extraordinary things done know how to: (1) challenge the process or the status quo, (2) inspire a shared sense of vision, (3) enable others to act, (4) model the way, and (5) encourage the heart of those involved with the change.[35] The authors do an excellent job setting out how to accomplish these things, and their book is recommended reading for those interested in pursuing these ideas further.

Toolkit Exercise 8.2 asks you to reflect on your personal attributes.

Developing Into a Change Leader

Intention, Education, Self-Discipline, and Experience

Many change leadership skills can be learned, which means that they can be taught.* The acquisition of concepts and language establishes mental frameworks for want-to-be change leaders. Reading about best practices and landmines can alert novices to predictable success paths and mistakes. The Center for Creative Leadership[36] is one of a number of organizations that produce publications about relevant leadership challenges and practices. In a 2007 article, Corey Criswell and Andre Martin identified a number of trends that future leaders need to be aware of that are creating change to the way business is done. They include (a) more complex challenges, (b) a focus on innovation, (c) an increase in virtual communication and leadership, (d) the importance of authenticity, and (e) leading for long-term survival.[37] The awareness of these macrolevel changes will help change agents within organizations better understand the environment and use and develop necessary skills to lead change internally.

Change leaders also need to understand and embrace the notion of experiential learning. It is rare that someone is a change agent only once. Change leadership capacities are a sought-out skill set. These skills are developed similarly to the way individuals strengthen their physical skills. Once you start toning a muscle set, it feels good and you strive to continue to maintain or develop that muscle. But performance typically is tied to our capacity to have our muscles act interdependently. So when one set of muscle responses is where you want it to be, you find others that need the work and commitment you put into the first in order to improve your overall capacity to perform. Similarly within an organization, change agents seek opportunities to continuously improve both themselves and their organizations as a whole. They may have great interpersonal skills, but they need expertise in crafting financial arguments, or vice versa. Over time, this process of development becomes part of one's professional identity. The journey never ends.

As part of this process, self-discovery, discipline, and reflection are critical to ongoing success and growth. Jeanie Daniel Duck argues that an organization will not change if the individuals within that organization do not change themselves. As a change leader, if you intentionally model reflective behavior, you will encourage others to do the same. The key questions to ask, according to Duck, are:

- Which of your behaviors will you stop/start or change? Identify this behavior and replace it with something else.
- What, specifically, are you willing to do? Brainstorm different actions and how you might measure them.
- How will others know? Help yourself by engaging others to hold you accountable.
- How might you sabotage yourself? Identify ways in which you might hold yourself back.
- What's the payoff in this for you? Construct a reward and motivate yourself.[38]

---

*Like many fields, formal study and education play their role in developing change leaders—thus this book!

Bennis describes four rules that he believes change leaders should accept to enhance their self development:

1. You are your own best teacher.

2. You accept responsibility and blame no one.

3. You can learn anything you want to learn.

4. True understanding comes from reflection on your experience.[39]

Bennis's fundamental message is to take responsibility for your own learning and development as a change leader. This requires reflection. Of course, reflection implies something to reflect on—thus, the role of experience. It is through reflection that a change leader hones existing skills and abilities, becomes open to new ideas, and begins to think broadly, widening the lens through which he or she looks at the situation at hand. In a disciplined manner, a would-be change leader needs to establish personal change goals and write them down. This calls for intentional reflection and continuous learning, which are important for both the individual level, as described by Duck, as well as the organizational level, in developing the ability to change.

What Does *Reflection* Mean?

Organizations are able to change more effectively when individuals and change leaders within the organization shift their mental maps and frameworks, and this requires openness and reflection. The skill of communication mentioned earlier is essential here, as it is through conversation and open dialogue that change occurs. Therefore, there is a need to be willing to think *with* others in a reflective way to see change happen. In order to do this, an individual needs to first and foremost understand what the group thinks and why. The group then needs to identify its shared assumptions and develop a mutual understanding of the current reality. This involves open and honest communication in a space where no one is wrong and there is a commitment to finding that common ground—for the present situation and the vision for the future. Change leaders are in the position to create safe spaces for reflection where members of the organization have a voice that is listened to and valued.

Appreciative inquiry (AI), a concept introduced by Dr. David L. Cooperrider at Case Western Reserve University, is critical in these conversations of reflection. AI is the engagement of individuals in an organizational system in its renewal. If you can find the best in the organization and individuals—that is, appreciate it—Cooperrider argues that growth will occur and renewal will result. Through AI, people seek to find and understand the best in people, organizations, and the world by reflecting on past positive experiences and performance. In doing so, the positive energy and commitment to improvement is embraced.[40] By framing positively, a different type of energy is found within the organization to move forward in the direction of change.

AI illustrates one of many ways that organizations, change agents, and consultants need to reframe how to approach and lead change and the value of ongoing individual and collective reflection. In order for reflection to add value, there can't be a "wrong" understanding. Everyone must strive to fully understand people's perceptions, assumptions, and visions through disagreement and challenging one another's views. In a global society with relationships developing and changing at all levels, organizations operate in an ever-changing context.

Developmental Stages of Change Leaders

Miller argues that there are developmental stages of change leaders. He believes that individuals progress through stages of beliefs about change, increasing in their complexity and sophistication.[41] (See Table 8.2 for an outline of his belief stages.) He believes that movement from Stage 1, Novice, to Stage 2, Junior, to Stage 3, Experienced might be learned vicariously—by observing others or by studying change. However, movement to Stage 4, Expert, requires living with a change project and suffering the frustrations, surprises, and resistance that come with the territory. (See Table 8.2 for an explanation of the different developmental stages of change leaders.)

Table 8.2	Miller's Stages of Change Beliefs
Stage	*Description*
Stage 1 Novice	Beliefs: People will change once they understand the logic of the change. People can be told to change. As a result, clear communication is key. Underlying is the assumption that people are rational and will follow their self-interest once it is revealed to them. Alternately, power and sanctions will ensure compliance.
Stage 2 Junior	Beliefs: People change through powerful communication and symbolism. Change planning will include the use of symbols and group meetings. Underlying is the assumption that people will change if they are "sold" on the beliefs. Again, failing this, the organization can use power and/or sanctions.
Stage 3 Experienced	Beliefs: People may not be willing or able or ready to change. As a result, change leaders will enlist specialists to design a change plan and the leaders will work at change but resist modifying their own vision. Underlying is the assumption that the ideal state is where people will become committed to change. Otherwise, power and sanctions must be used.
Stage 4 Expert	Beliefs: People have a limited capacity to absorb change and may not be as willing, able, or ready to change as you wish. Thinking through how to change the people is central to the implementation of change. Underlying is the assumption that commitment for change must be built and that power or sanctions have major limitations in achieving change and building organizational capacity.

Source: Adapted from Miller, D. (2002). Successful change leaders: What makes them? What do they do that is different? *Journal of Change Management, 2*(4), 383.

There is evidence that these change agent skills and competencies can be acquired through the systematic use of developmental assignments.[42] **Toolkit Exercise 8.3** will help you assess your maturity level as a change agent.

Four Types of Change Leaders

Regardless of their skill sets, change agents' ability to sense and interpret significant environmental shifts is of particular importance to their capacity to respond. Part of such an ability comes from the deep study of a field or industry. As well, some might have the intuition to understand significant changes in the environment by their ability to detect and interpret underlying patterns.[43] Take, for example, Glegg of Glegg Water Treatment Services.

GLEGG WATER SYSTEMS[44]

Glegg Water Treatment Services was an entrepreneurial organization that grew at a compound growth rate of 20 to 25% per year for more than 15 years. The executives of this organization had developed a clear and strong vision for their organization ("pure water for the world"). They used this vision to pull the organization in the direction they wanted. At the same time, they were tough, realistic analyzers of their situation. They used whatever data they could find to provide a sophisticated understanding of the organization's situation. They used this analysis to convince others and push them into accepting the needed changes. They were truly committed to growing their company. Also striking were the alternative periods of continuous growth and change and strategic leaps into new areas. Three times in their history, the leadership of the organization forecasted a decline in growth rates in what the organization was doing—so they shifted into completely new but related areas. For example, the organization delivered water treatment systems for power industries. As that market matured, the organization shifted to producing higher-quality water systems for computer makers. Eight years later, it shifted to a new membrane technology, which permitted integrated systems to be sold.*

What is significant in the Glegg example is the change leaders' ability to anticipate strategic shifts, manage that order of change, *and* continuously improve and grow between these significant changes. The levels of skill required to manage in all of these different situations are of a high order. Maintaining this is difficult.

At Glegg Water Systems, change leaders understood the strategic shifts in the industry and what that implied for their organization. Between these major disruptions, they worked incrementally to improve operations and to change the organization for the better. To do this, they motivated people by reinforcing their belief in the importance of what they were doing—providing the purest water possible. However, they did not just use these visionary or emotional appeals, they also used

---

*The company has since been sold to GE and its operations closed.

data to persuade. Hard, calculated numbers pushed their perspectives forward and provided convincing evidence of the need for change and the value of the vision.

Much of the change literature differentiates between the types of change that Glegg experienced: strategic or episodic change followed by incremental or continuous change.[45] Episodic change is change that is "infrequent, discontinuous, and intentional." Continuous change is change that is "ongoing, evolving and cumulative." Weick and Quinn suggest that the appropriate model here is "freeze, rebalance and unfreeze." That is, change agents need to capture the underlying patterns and dynamics (freeze the conceptual understanding); reinterpret, relabel (reframe and rebalance those understandings); and resume improvisation and learning (unfreeze).[46] Further, Weick and Quinn suggest that the role of change agents shifts depending on the type of change. Episodic change needs a prime mover change agent—one who creates change. Continuous change needs a change agent who is a sense maker and able to redirect the organization.

The Glegg Water example also shows that change agents and their agendas can act in "pull" or "push" ways. *Pull actions* by change agents create attractions or goals that draw willing organizational members to change and are characterized by organizational visions or higher-order purposes and strategies. *Push actions,* on the other hand, are data based and factual and are communicated in ways that advance analytical thinking and reasoning and that push recipients' thinking in new directions. Change agents who rely on push actions can also use legitimate, positional, and reward-and-punishment power in ways that change the dynamics of situations.[47] At Glegg Water, markets were assessed and plans were created and implemented based on the best data available. Similarly, at Home Depot, Nardelli and Donovan gained legitimate power by engaging employees and used their positional power to create significant structural and systemic changes to the company.[48] The reasons for the change were rooted in facts and figures regarding the competitive landscape and the company's performance. This created an understanding among the employees of the reasons for change and the need to measure the impact of that change as well.

As a further example of both push and pull tactics, the School of Management (SOM) faculty at Simmons College in Boston evolved its work patterns and foci over a 7-year period with the intention of achieving the Association to Advance Collegiate Schools of Business (AACSB) International accreditation. In spring 2009, the SOM reached its goal because a diverse faculty was united in its purpose and met the multiple standards set by AACSB. While facts and analytical thinking allowed the faculty to figure out its tactics and strategies to reach its goal, it was the strategic importance of the goal, that vision, that pulled people together.

Table 8.3 outlines a model that relates the motivational approaches of the change agent (analytical push versus emotional pull) to the degree of change needed by the organization (strategic versus incremental). The model identifies four change agent types: the emotional champion, the intuitive adapter, the developmental strategist, and the continuous improver. Some change agents will tend to act true to their type due to the nature of their personalities, predispositions, and situations. Others will move beyond their preferences and develop greater flexibility in the range of approaches at their disposal. The latter will therefore adopt a more flexible approach to change, modifying their approach to reflect the specific situation and the people involved.

Table 8.3   Change Agent Types

**Strategic Change and Incremental Change *versus*
Vision Pull and Analysis/Power Push**

Strategic Change

Emotional Champion	***Developmental Strategist***

Vision Pull | Analysis Push

Intuitive Adapter	***Continuous Improver***

Incremental Change

The Emotional Champion has a clear and powerful vision of what the organization needs and uses that vision to capture the hearts and motivations of the organization's members. An organization often needs an emotional champion when there is a dramatic shift in the environment and the organization's structures, systems, and sense of direction are inadequate. To be an emotional champion means that the change agent foresees a new future, understands the deep gap between the organization and its future, can articulate a powerful vision that gives hope that the gap can be overcome, and has a high order of persuasion skills. When Glegg Water Systems was faced with declining growth and needed to find new growth markets, it needed the visionary who could picture the strategic shift and create an appealing vision of that future.

An Emotional Champion:

- is comfortable with ambiguity and risk;
- thinks tangentially and challenges accepted ways of doing things;
- has strong intuitive abilities; and
- relies on feelings and emotions to influence others.

The Developmental Strategist applies rational analysis to understanding the competitive logic of the organization and how it no longer fits with the organization's existing strategy. S/he sees how to alter structures and processes to shift the organization to the new alignment and eliminate the major gap between the organization and the environment's demands. Again, in Glegg Water, the strategic shifts resulted not only from the capturing of a new vision but also from market intelligence and analysis. Hard-nosed thinking enabled Glegg to see how to take its company to a new level by finding a new market focus.

A Developmental Strategist:

- engages in big-picture thinking about strategic change and the fit between the environment and the organization;
- sees organizations in terms of systems and structures fitting into logical, integrated components that fit (or don't) with environmental demands; and
- is comfortable with assessing risk and taking significant chances based on a thorough assessment of the situation.

The Intuitive Adapter has the clear vision for the organization and uses that vision to reinforce a culture of learning and adaptation. Often the vision will seem less dramatic or powerful because the organization is aligned with its environment and the change agent's role is to ensure the organization stays on track. The change agent develops a culture of learning and continuous improvement where employees constantly test their actions against the vision. At Glegg Water, continuous improvement was a byword. Central to this were the people who understood the pure water vision and what it meant to customers. Efficiency was not allowed to overrule a focus on quality.

An Intuitive Adapter:

- embraces more moderate risks;
- engages in a more limited search for solutions;
- is comfortable with the current direction that the vision offers; and
- relies on intuition and emotion to persuade others to propel the organization forward through incremental changes.

The Continuous Improver analyzes micro environments and seeks changes such as re-engineering systems and processes. The organization in this category is reasonably well aligned with its environment and is in an industry where complex systems and processes provide for improvement opportunities. At Glegg Water, information systems captured data on productivity and processes. These data were used to improve efficiency and profits.

A Continuous Improver:

- thinks logically and carefully about detailed processes and how they can be improved;
- aims for possible gains and small wins rather than great leaps; and
- is systematic in his or her thinking while making careful gains.

The purpose of this model is to marry types of change with methods of persuasion. Each change agent will have personal preferences. Some will craft visions that could sweep employees onto the change team. Others will carefully and deliberately build a data-based case that would convince the most rational finance expert. Change agents will have their preferred styles but, as noted earlier, some will be more able to adapt their approach and credibly use other styles as the situation demands it. By knowing your own level of flexibility, you can undertake initiatives that will develop your capacity to adapt your approach as a change agent in a given situation. Alternatively, if you're concerned about your own capacity to respond, you can ally with others who possess the style that a particular situation demands.

In Chapter 1, we briefly discussed the preferences of adaptors (those with an orientation toward incremental change) and innovators (those who prefer more radical or transformational change).[49] Kirton's work with these two orientations points out that individuals tend to have clear preferences in their orientation and sometimes fail to recognize the value present in the alternative approach to change as they focus on what they are most comfortable with. When this occurs, there may be an inappropriate fit of approach with the situation or the people involved. Alternatively, when individuals with both preferences are present, this can lead to disagreement and conflict concerning how best to proceed. While constructive disagreement and debate concerning alternatives is valuable, managers need to avoid dysfunctional personal attacks and defensive behavior. This points again to the importance of developing greater awareness of the different change styles and the benefits of personal flexibility. When managers lack the needed orientation and style, they need access to allies with the requisite skills.

Toolkit Exercise 8.4 asks you to consider your preferences and helps you to determine your change agent style.

Many organizations expect their managers to develop skills as change agents. As a result, those managers need to improve their understanding of internal change agent roles and strategies. Internal organization members need to learn the team-building, negotiating, influencing, and other change-management skills to become effective facilitators. They need to move beyond technical skills, from being the person with the answer to being the person with process-management change skills; the person who helps the organization find the answers and handle the complex and multivariate nature of the reality it faces.[50]

Internal change agents involved with leading projects often have line responsibilities for the initiative. However, larger organizations also advance change through the use of individuals who are in internal consulting roles. Organization-development specialists, project-management specialists, lean or Six Sigma experts, and specialists from other staff functions such as accounting and IT are examples of this. When internal change agents are operating from a consulting role, Christopher Wright found that they manage the ambiguity and communicate the value associated with such roles by developing a professional persona that highlights their distinctive competencies as well as reinforces their internal knowledge and linkages.[51]

Hunsaker identified four different internal roles a change agent can play: catalyst, solution giver, process helper, and resource linker.[52] The **catalyst** is needed to overcome inertia and focus the organization on the problems faced. The **solution giver** knows how to respond and can solve the problem. The key here, of course, is having your ideas accepted. The **process helper** facilitates the "how to" of change, playing the role of third-party intervener often. Finally, the **resource linker** brings people and resources together in ways that aid in the solution of issues. All four roles are important, and knowing them provides a checklist of optional strategies for the internal change agent.

External Change Agents/Consultants

Internal change agents are critical to the process because they know the systems, norms, and subtleties of how things get done, and they have existing relationships that can prove helpful. However, they may not possess needed specialized knowledge or skills, lack (or be seen to be lacking) objectivity or independence, have difficulty reframing existing relationships with organizational members, or lack an adequate power base. When there are concerns that these gaps cannot be sufficiently addressed by pulling in other organizational members to assist with the process, it may be necessary to bring in external change agents or consultants to assist with the project. Sometimes the external consultants are sought out by the internal change agents, while at other times they are thrust upon them.

Provide Subject-Matter Expertise

Consultants may be used to provide subject-matter expertise, facilitate the analysis, and provide guidance to the path forward. As a result, they are often used to promote change through the technical expertise and credibility they bring to the internal change team. This was the case at Simmons College.

USING EXTERNAL CONSULTANTS AT SIMMONS COLLEGE[53]

The School of Management, Simmons College, turned to an external consultant when working to gain AACSB accreditation. The faculty had floundered for several years about how to assess students' learning of the overall management curriculum. Required by the AACSB's Standards to illustrate that its graduating students have learned a program's curriculum, some schools institute standardized tests to assess students' learning. However, the school wanted a customized approach to evaluate the unique aspects of its management curriculum. The faculty struggled to envision methodologies and content to reach its goals. Finally, Katherine Martell, an assessment guru, was hired, bringing with her knowledge of how 50 other business schools conducted their assessment processes. When she left the school after 2 days of working with the faculty, the assessment processes and plans were in place and readily implemented in the following months.

Katherine Martell, the external consultant, was able to help faculty solve the "assessment of learning" problem that had stalled their progress in attaining AACSB accreditation for years. She did so by helping them work their way through the issues and find a solution. In addition to her technical skills and professional credibility, she was also retained because she possessed well-developed team-process skills that were instrumental in helping them work their way through the problem. When internal change agents or their teams feel they lack the technical skills needed in these areas, they often turn to external expertise.

Bring Fresh Perspectives Through Exposure to Ideas That Have Worked Elsewhere

Too often, insiders find themselves tied to their experience, and outside consultants can be used to help them extricate themselves from these mental traps.[54] Much can be learned from the systems and procedures that others have used elsewhere. In the following example, the leadership team at Knox Presbyterian Church (Waterloo) recognized it had a problem with how to approach fundraising and turned to RSI Consulting, who had helped many other churches address similar challenges through the use of established procedures. Once it had examined RSI's approach, the church's leadership team retained Craig Miller's services and was able to successfully adopt the approach.

EXTERNAL CONSULTANTS AS PROCESS EXPERTS[55]

When Knox Presbyterian Church, Waterloo, was planning a new church building, church leaders decided they needed a capital campaign to bring life to their change initiative. However, the coordinating team knew that their view of fundraising was tied to past approaches and they recognized that these would not be able to raise the funds required. They searched out and hired RSI Consulting, specialists in church campaigns, with more than 9,000 conducted in 38 years. Craig Miller of RSI brought standard templates, which he used to guide church volunteers in framing the campaign and organizing their fundraising work. Knox had the vision and the manpower but lacked the expertise and structure in how to handle the fundraising. By hiring RSI, they did not have to design the structure for a capital campaign; they borrowed it. As a result, Knox raised more than $2.3 million in pledges, in the 90th percentile of results for that size of church, and they did so very economically.

Provide Independent, Trustworthy Support

To help them manage the change process, internal change agents may find they need access to outside consultants who are viewed as independent, credible, competent, and (most importantly) trustworthy by others in the organization. In addition to guidance, they may be able to lend external credibility and support for analyses or actions that advance the change initiative. Such consultants can prove extremely helpful with internal and external data gathering and the communication of the findings and their implications. Organizational members may feel more comfortable sharing their thoughts and concerns with the consultants than they would with internal staff. Finally, the external validation their analyses and conclusions provide may be the nudge needed to generate higher levels of support for the change and action.

External consultants can be instrumental in helping foster an atmosphere conducive to change by leveraging their reputations and skill sets through the way they manage the process. However, they have their limitations. They lack the deep knowledge of the political environment and culture of the organization that the inside change agents should have, and in the end it is the organization that needs to take responsibility for the change, not the external consultant. As a result, external change consultants may be able to assist internal agents, but they cannot replace them. Final decision making needs to reside with the internal change leader and the organization. To balance access to needed perspectives, change leaders are moving toward the use of change teams that embody both internal and external change agent perspectives.

How an internal change leader selects, introduces, and uses external consultants will have a lot to do with the ultimate success or failure of a change initiative. Consultants come in many forms, with different backgrounds, expertise, price tags, and ambitions. They often come with prescribed methodologies and offer prepackaged solutions. As a result, some consultants are insensitive to the organization's culture or needs. The provision of ready-made answers not based in specific organization research can be frustrating, and prescription without diagnosis is arguably malpractice.[56] Responsibility for this failure will fall back on the manager who retained the consultant, since he or she is accountable for managing this relationship.

Another risk factor is that consultants may receive signals that they are expected to unquestioningly support the position of the leader of the organization that brought them in, even when the external consultants have serious concerns with the course of action being undertaken. When external consultants lose their ability to provide independent judgment, their value and credibility are seriously reduced and their reputations may suffer irreparable harm if they succumb to pressure and the change subsequently fails in a very public manner.[57]

In spite of these and other risks, many organizations continue to use external consultants to advance their change agendas and mitigate the risks of failure. One study reports that 83% of organizations that used consultants said they would use them again.[58] To increase the chances of success, consider the following advice on how to select an external consultant.

HOW SHOULD YOU SELECT A CONSULTANT?[59]

Since the appropriate consultant or consulting team will either advance or detract from the success of your change initiative, selecting a suitable one is a critical step. The following process is recommended for complex organizational change situations:

(Continued)

(Continued)

1. **Ensure that you have a clear understanding of what you want from the consultants.** Too often organizations hire consultants without thinking through exactly what value they can and will bring. Know who they will report to, what roles they will play, and how much you are willing to pay for their services.

2. **Talk with multiple (up to five) consultants and/or consulting organizations.** Internal change leaders will learn a great deal about the organization's problems and how they might be solved by talking with multiple vendors. They will also be able to compare and contrast the consultants' working styles, allowing them to gauge the chemistry between the change leader/change team and the consultant. The internal change leader needs to ask: Do we have complementary or similar skills and outlook? Does this consultant bring skills and knowledge that I lack internally? Does the organization have the budget that is needed to engage this consultant?

3. **Issue a request for proposals (RFP).** Only ask those consultants with whom you would like to work, since writing and responding to RFPs is a time-consuming and labor-intensive process. Ask the internal leaders of the change process to objectively review the RFPs and provide you with feedback.

4. **Make your decision and communicate expectations.** Indicate clearly to the internal change leaders, the consultant(s), and all stakeholders the timeline, roles, expectations, deliverables, and reporting relationships.

Change Teams

Change initiatives that are larger require the efforts of more than one change agent. Outside consultants may be able to help, but as was noted earlier, they may lack credibility and often lack the deep knowledge of the political environment and culture of an organization. As a result, change agents look to extend their reach by using change teams. Worren suggests that teams are important because "employees learn new behaviours and attitudes by participating in ad-hoc teams solving real business problems."[60] Further, as change agents become immersed in the change, the volume of work increases and the roles and skills required of them vary. A cross-functional change team can be used to bring different perspectives, expertise, and credibility to bear on the change challenge inherent in those different roles.[61]

Organizational downsizing and increasing interest in the use of self-managed teams as an organizing approach for flattened hierarchies and cross-functional change initiatives have spurred awareness of the value of such teams.[62] Involvement in self-managed teams gives people space and time to adjust their views and/or influence the change process. It moves them out of the role of recipient and makes them an active and engaged stakeholders.

In a benchmarking study focused on the best practices in change management, Prosci describes a good change management team member as:

- Being knowledgeable about the business and enthusiastic about the change
- Possessing excellent oral and written communications skills and a willingness to listen and share
- Having total commitment to the project, the process, and the results
- Being able to remain open minded and visionary
- Being respected within the organization as an apolitical catalyst for strategic change.[63]

Some of these characteristics of a good change team member appear contradictory. For example, it is tricky to be simultaneously totally committed and open minded. Nevertheless, skilled change leaders often exhibit paradoxical or apparently contradictory characteristics. For example, the need to both be joined with and yet separate from other members of the change team in order to maintain independence of perspective and judgment is a difficult balance to maintain.[64]

Working with and in teams and task forces is a baseline skill for change leaders. They must not only achieve the change, but they must also bring the change team along so that it accepts and is enthusiastic about the change initiative. Many might believe that this requires individuals who are adept at reducing stress and strain in the team, but once again, this is not always the case. The most effective response will depend upon the needs of the situation. Bill Gates, for example, developed high-performance change teams in spite of a dominating personality and awkward social skills because of his abilities in the areas of vision and his capacity to attract and motivate highly talented individuals.

BILL GATES: TEAM LEADER

Gates rarely indulges in water-cooler bantering and social niceties that put people at ease. But while Microsoft's chairman and chief software architect is not considered a warm, affable person, he is an effective hands-on manager, says one former employee. "Bill is an exceptional motivator. For as much as he does not like small talk, he loves working with people on matters of substance," says Scott Langmack, a former Microsoft marketing manager.[65]

In the summer of 2008, Gates announced that he would cease full-time work at Microsoft to focus on his charitable foundations.[66] With this announcement, change agents and teams within Microsoft faced a new set of challenges related to managing this transition. Teams are essential components in making change happen.

Organizing the Change Team

Champions transform visions into realities, but a committed small group of individuals can win wars and transform society.[67]

Many years ago, a group of students at Case Western Reserve University decided that there had to be better ways of teaching organization change and development. This small group dedicated itself to changing the system. In 2 years, they transformed parts of Case Western and created the first doctoral program in organization development with themselves as potential graduates. They planned and plotted. They identified key stakeholders and assigned team members to each stakeholder with the responsibility of bringing that stakeholder on side—or at least neutralizing their opposition. It was the team that made the change happen. They put into practice what they were learning as students.[68]

Creating the conditions for successful change is more than having an excellent change project plan. Equally important is recognizing the different change roles that need to be played and then developing a strong change team. This section covers the different change roles that team members play and how you design an excellent change team.

Toolkit Exercise 8.5 provides an exercise on how to organize a change team for effectiveness.

Possible Roles Within Change Teams*

Many change examples point out the need for a **champion** within the team who will fight for the change under trying circumstances and will continue to persevere when others would have checked out and given up. These change champions represent the visionary, the immovable force for change who will continue to push for the change regardless of the opposition and the resistance to change. Senior managers need to ensure that those to whom the change is delegated possess (and are seen to possess) the energy, drive, skills, resilience, credibility, and commitment needed to make it happen. If these are lacking, steps need to be taken to ensure that they are either developed or appropriate team members need to be found to champion the implementation of the change.

Change champions should consider two further organizing roles that are often better operationalized through the use of two separate teams: a **steering team** and a **design and implementation team.** The steering team provides advice to the champion and the implementation team regarding the direction of the change in light of other events and priorities in the organization. As suggested by the name, it plays an advisory and navigational function for the change project. It is also involved in determining and providing direction to the team's mandate, resourcing requirements, higher-order policies, and major go/no go decisions.

---

*In Chapter 1, we discussed the roles that an individual can play: change recipient, initiator, facilitator, and implementer. These same roles are looked at here in relation to change teams.

The design and implementation team plans the change, deals with the stake-holders, and has primary responsibility for the implementation. The responsibilities of the different team members will vary over time, depending upon what is needed and their skill sets. The team will often have a **change project manager** who will coordinate planning, manage logistics, track the team's progress toward change targets, and manage the adjustments needed along the way.

Senior executives who act as **sponsors** of change foster commitment to the change and assist those charged with making the change happen.[69] Sponsors can act visibly, can share information and knowledge, and can give protection. *Visible sponsorship* means the senior manager advocates for the change and shows support through actions (i.e., use of influence and time) as well as words. *Information sharing and knowledge development* has the sponsor providing useful information about change and working with the team to ensure that the plans are sound. Finally, sponsors can *provide protection* or cover for those to whom the change has been delegated. Without such protection, the individuals in the organization will tend to become more risk averse and less willing to champion the change.[70]

Developing a Change Team

Developing the team is an important task for the change leaders because the ability to build teams, motivate, and communicate are all predictors of successful change implementation.[71] If change teams can be developed that are self-regulating or self-managed, change can often be facilitated because teams leverage the change leader's reach. The engagement and involvement of team members tends to heighten their commitment and support for the initiative,[72] and because they operate independently, self-managed teams can reduce the amount of time senior managers must commit to implementation-related activities. Self-managed teams share an understanding of the change goals and objectives, sort out the differentiation and execution of tasks, and have control over the decision quality.

Wageman has identified the following seven factors as critical to team success with self-managed teams:

- clear, engaging direction
- a real team task
- rewards for team excellence
- the availability of basic material resources to do the job, including the abilities of individual team members
- authority vested in the team to manage the work
- team goals
- the development of team norms that promote strategic thinking[73]

A similar list was developed by the Change Institute and is given in Table 8.4.[74]

The dedication and willingness to give it their "all" is the most obvious characteristic of highly committed change teams. The dogged determination to make changes regardless of personal consequences because of a deep-rooted belief in a

Table 8.4 Design Rules for Top Teams

1. Keep it small: 10 or fewer members.

2. Meet a minimum of biweekly and demand full attendance—less often breaks the rhythm of cooperation. How the team meets is less important—it may be face to face or through virtual means.

3. Everything is your business. That is, no information is off-limits.

4. Each of you is accountable for your business.

5. No secrets and no surprises within the team.

6. Straight talk, modeled by the leader.

7. Fast decisions, modeled by the leader.

8. Everyone's paid partly on the total results.

vision creates both the conditions for victory and the possibilities of organizational suicide. In the earlier example at Case Western Reserve University, if the change were not successful, the individuals involved would have sacrificed several years of their lives to no organizational effect. In the case of Lou Gerstner's turnaround at IBM,[75] there was a distinct possibility that the firm would not survive and members of his inner circle would be forever known as the individuals who oversaw the collapse of this American corporate icon. Many individuals don't have the fire to commit to such a degree. They lack the intensity of vision, the dedication to a cause, and the willingness to sacrifice everything to achieve change. Fortunately, most change situations do not demand that level of personal commitment and sacrifice.

In forming a change team, the **personalities and skills of the members** will play a significant role in the team's success. The change process demands a paradoxical set of skills: the ability to create a vision and the intuition to see the connections between that vision and all of the things that will need to be done. This includes identifying who will need to be influenced; thinking positively about stakeholders while recognizing what will influence them and why they may resist you; caring passionately for an initiative yet not interpreting criticism and opposition as a personal attack; and translating broad strategy or vision into concrete change plans. Having the capacity to deal with these paradoxes requires comfort and skill in dealing with ambiguity and complexity.

While those tasks around change demand the paradoxical expertise explained above, functional and technical competencies play a very important role. It is difficult to imagine a team establishing credibility if it lacks such basics. However, the personalities present in the team will influence how the team interacts and performs, including its ability to manage the inherent paradoxes. While it is usually not necessary for the team to be highly cohesive, cohesion, rooted in a shared sense of purpose, will lend strength to the change effort and focus the team's activities.

Toolkit Exercise 8.6 asks you to reflect on your experience with change teams.

The boxed insert below describes how Federal Express systematically develops a team approach to change.

> ## DEVELOPING CHANGE TEAMS AT FEDERAL EXPRESS[76]
>
> Federal Express has developed a checklist for using change teams.
>
> 1. Ensure that everybody who has a contribution to make is fully involved, and those who will have to make any change are identified and included.
>
> 2. Convince people that their involvement is serious and not a management ploy—present all ideas from management as "rough" ideas.
>
> 3. Ensure commitment to making any change work—the team members identify and develop "what is in it for them" when they move to make the idea work.
>
> 4. Increase the success rate for new ideas—potential and actual problems that have to be solved are identified in a problem-solving, not blame-fixing, culture.
>
> 5. Deliver the best solutions—problem-solving teams self-select to find answers to the barriers to successful implementation.
>
> 6. Maintain momentum and enthusiasm—the remainder of the team continues to work on refining the basic idea.
>
> 7. Present problem solutions, improve where necessary, approve, and implement immediately.
>
> 8. Refine idea, agree upon, and plan the implementation process.
>
> Adapted from Lamber, T. (2006). Insight. MENAFN.com. Retrieved May 2010 from http://www.menafn.com/qn_print.asp?StroyID=129531&subl=true.

Change From the Middle—Everyone Needs to Be a Change Agent

Increasingly, successful organization members will find that they need to act as change agents in their organizations. As Katzenbach suggests, the real change leader will take action—do things, try them out and then do it again while getting better.[77] While this book applauds this type of initiative, remember the first rule for change agents: *Stay alive.*

When managers find themselves involved with change, most will be operating from the middle of the organization. At times, they will have those above them attempting to direct or influence change while they are trying to influence those superiors about what needs to be initiated and how best to proceed. At other times, those middle managers will need to deal with subordinates and peers, those who will be on the receiving end of the change or who are themselves trying to initiate activities.

Oshry recognized the feelings of powerlessness that many feel when operating in the "middle" and outlined strategies for increasing one's power in these situations.[78] Problem ownership is one of the key issues. Far too often, managers insert themselves in the middle of a dispute and take on others' issues as their own when, in fact, intervention is not helpful. As well, when the issue is the managers, they may refuse to use their power. They need to take responsibility, make a decision, and move on. Or they need to refuse to accept unreasonable demands from above and attempt to work matters out rather than simply acquiesce and create greater problems below.

Oshry's advice to those in the middle is to:

1. "Be top when you can and take responsibility for being top."

2. "Be bottom when you should." Don't let problems just flow through you to subordinates.

3. "Be coach" to help others solve their own problems so they don't become yours.

4. "Facilitate" rather than simply carry messages when you find yourself running back and forth between two parties who are in conflict.

5. "Integrate with one another" so that you develop a strong peer group that you can turn to for advice, guidance, and support.

Whether a manager acts using logic or participation, or on his/her own,[79] the message is clear: Managers are increasingly being held accountable for either taking action or helping to make change happen. Scanning the environment, figuring out what will make things better, and creating initiatives are the new responsibilities today's managers carry. This text argues that any change agent role—initiator, implementer, facilitator, or team member—is preferable to constantly finding yourself only on the receiving end of change. A strategy of passively keeping one's head down and avoiding change increases a person's career risk because he or she will be less likely to be perceived as adding value.

Rules of Thumb for Change Agents

How should managers act as change agents? Several authors have proposed useful insights and wisdom from their experiences and analysis of change leaders. These guidelines, which have been integrated, combined, and added to, are listed below:[80]

- **Stay alive**—"Dead" change agents are of no use to the organization. The notion that you should sacrifice yourself at the altar of change is absurd unless you truly wish it. At the same time, the invocation to "stay alive" says you need to be in touch with those things that energize you and give you purpose.

- **Start where the system is**—Immature change agents start where they are. Experienced change agents diagnose the system, understand it, and begin with the system.
- **Work downhill**—Work with people in the system in a collaborative fashion. Confront and challenge resisters in useful ways. Don't alienate people if at all possible. Work in promising areas and make progress.
- **Organize, but don't overorganize**—Plans will change. If you are too organized, you risk becoming committed to your plan in ways that don't permit the inclusion and involvement of others.
- **Pick your battles carefully**—Don't argue if you can't win. A win/lose strategy deepens conflict and should be avoided wherever possible. The maxim "If you strike a king, strike to kill" fits here. If you can't complete the job, you may not survive.
- **Load experiments for success**—If you can, set up the situation and position it as positively as possible. Change is difficult at the best of times—if you can improve the odds, you should!
- **Light many fires**—High-visibility projects often attract both attention and opposition. Work within the organizational subsystems to create opportunities for change in many places, not just a major initiative.
- **Just enough is good enough**—Don't wait for perfection. Beta test your ideas. Get them out there to see how they work and how people react.
- **You can't make a difference without doing things differently**—Remember that definition of insanity—"doing things the same way but expecting different results"! You have to act and behave differently to have things change. Hope is not an action.
- **Reflect**—As individuals, as change teams, and as organizations, a commitment to learning from each experience and creating space for reflection on both positive and challenging moments is essential to effective and productive change.
- **Want to change; focus on important results and get them**—Not only does success breed success, but getting important results brings resources, influence, and credibility.
- **Think and act fast**—Speed and flexibility are critical. Sensing the situation and reacting quickly will make a difference. Acting first means others will have to act second and will always be responding to your initiatives.
- **Create a coalition**—Lone ranger operatives are easy to dismiss. As Gary Hamel says, an "army of like-minded activists cannot be ignored."

FROM A CHANGE EXPERT

Greg Brenneman has made a career out of turning large companies around and encourages people to work with sick organizations. "If you have a chance of working for a healthy or a sick one, choose the sick one. The sickest ones need the best doctors and it's a lot easier to stand out in a company

(Continued)

> (Continued)
>
> that needs help," he said to MBA students in 2008.[81] These companies are the ones where you really get into the work and help a company truly succeed. The successful ingredients in turnarounds, according to Brenneman, are: healthy financials; developing and sticking to a clear strategy, especially in a time of crisis; identifying new leaders from the industry to lead the company; and plain hard work.

Summary

This chapter describes how anyone, from any position in the organization, can potentially instigate and lead change. Assuming a change agent role is a matter of personal attributes, a function of the situation and the vision of the change agent. Four types of change leaders are described: the emotional champion, the intuitive adapter, the continuous improver, and the developmental strategist. Finally, the use of change teams was discussed and advice was provided to managers on how to handle the middle role they find themselves in when dealing with change.

The management of change is an essential part of the role of those who want to manage and lead. It will tax your skills, energize and challenge, exhaust, depress, occasionally exhilarate, and leave you, at times, with a profound sense of accomplishment. What it will not do is leave you the same.

The demands of organizations are clear—managers are expected to play an increasingly significant role in the management of change. Earlier, this book advised managers to know themselves, assess the situation carefully, and then **take action**. The next chapter outlines action planning to assist leaders of change.

Glossary of Terms

Change Agent Effectiveness

The effectiveness of a change agent is a function of the person, his or her vision, and the characteristics of the situation.

Change Leader

A **change leader** pulls people to change through the use of a powerful change vision.

Change Manager

A **change manager** creates change by working with others, overcoming resistance, and problem solving situations.

Developmental Stages of a Change Agent

Change agents can develop their change skills from a novice stage to an expert stage through successful experiences with increasingly complex, sophisticated change situations.

Types of Change Leaders

Four types of change leaders (**emotional champion, intuitive adapter, developmental strategist,** and **continuous improver**) can be identified through (1) their use of vision (pull) methods versus analytical (push) methods and (2) their orientation to change: strategic versus incremental.

Internal Change Agent

An **internal change agent** is an employee of the organization who knows the organization intimately and is attempting to create change.

External Change Agent

An **external change agent** is a person from outside the organization trying to make changes. Often this person is an outside expert and consultant.

Change Team

The **change team** is the group of employees, usually from a cross-section of the organization, that is charged with a change task.

Steering team—Steering teams play an advisory and guidance role to change leaders and design and implementation teams.

Design and implementation team—These teams are responsible for the actual design and implementation of the change initiatives.

Middle powerlessness—the feeling of a lack of power and influence that those in middle-level organizational roles often experience when organizational changes are being implemented. Pressure comes from above and below and they see themselves as ill-equipped to respond.

Rules of thumb for change agents—things for change agents to keep in mind to ensure their survival and success over the long term.

END-OF-CHAPTER EXERCISES

TOOLKIT EXERCISE 8.1

The Interaction of Vision and Situation With Who You Are

Later in this chapter, we will explore the behaviors and attributes common to many change agents. This exercise is to have you think of your personal situation to consider why, where, and when you might become more of a change agent.

1. What purposes do you consider vital? That is, what visions do you follow for which you would make significant personal sacrifices? Review your understanding of vision from Chapter 3.

2. For many of us, there are no visions that are as powerful as we describe above. What would be a vision that could catapult you into persistent, committed, and even sacrificial (by normal standards) action?

3. How does the situation you find yourself in affect your desire to become a change agent? Think through the understanding of organizational change that you developed in Chapters 4, 5, and 6.

TOOLKIT EXERCISE 8.2

Myself as Change Agent

1. The following list of change agent attributes and skills represents an amalgam drawn from the previous section. Rate yourself on the following dimensions:

Attributes of Change Leaders From Caldwell

Low 1 2 3 4 5 6 7 High

- Inspiring vision — 1 2 3 4 5 6 7
- Entrepreneurship — 1 2 3 4 5 6 7
- Integrity and honesty — 1 2 3 4 5 6 7
- Learning from others — 1 2 3 4 5 6 7
- Openness to new ideas — 1 2 3 4 5 6 7
- Risk taking — 1 2 3 4 5 6 7
- Adaptability and flexibility — 1 2 3 4 5 6 7
- Creativity — 1 2 3 4 5 6 7
- Experimentation — 1 2 3 4 5 6 7
- Using power — 1 2 3 4 5 6 7

Attributes of Change Managers From Caldwell

- Empowering others — 1 2 3 4 5 6 7
- Team building — 1 2 3 4 5 6 7
- Learning from others — 1 2 3 4 5 6 7
- Adaptability and flexibility — 1 2 3 4 5 6 7
- Openness to new ideas — 1 2 3 4 5 6 7
- Managing resistance — 1 2 3 4 5 6 7
- Conflict resolution — 1 2 3 4 5 6 7
- Networking skills — 1 2 3 4 5 6 7
- Knowledge of the business — 1 2 3 4 5 6 7
- Problem solving — 1 2 3 4 5 6 7

Change Agent Attributes Suggested by Others

- Interpersonal skills — 1 2 3 4 5 6 7
- Communication skills — 1 2 3 4 5 6 7
- Emotional resilience — 1 2 3 4 5 6 7
- Tolerance for ambiguity — 1 2 3 4 5 6 7
- Tolerance for ethical conflict — 1 2 3 4 5 6 7
- Political skill — 1 2 3 4 5 6 7
- Persistence — 1 2 3 4 5 6 7
- Determination — 1 2 3 4 5 6 7
- Pragmatism — 1 2 3 4 5 6 7
- Dissatisfaction with the status quo — 1 2 3 4 5 6 7
- Openness to information — 1 2 3 4 5 6 7
- Flexibility — 1 2 3 4 5 6 7

- Capacity to build trust   *1 2 3 4 5 6 7*
- Intelligence   *1 2 3 4 5 6 7*
- Emotional intelligence   *1 2 3 4 5 6 7*

2. Do you see yourself as scoring high on those items compared to others? If so, you are more likely to be comfortable in a change agent role. Lack of these attributes and skills does not mean you could not be a change agent—it just means that it will be more difficult and it may suggest areas for development.

3. Are you more likely to be comfortable in a change leadership role at this time, or does the role of change manager or implementer seem more suited to who you are?

4. Ask a mentor or friend to provide you feedback on the same dimensions. Does the feedback confirm your self-assessment? If not, why not?

TOOLKIT EXERCISE 8.3

Your Development as a Change Agent

Novice change leaders often picture themselves as being in the right and those that oppose them as somehow wrong. This certainty gives them energy and the will to persist in the face of such opposition. It sets up a dynamic of opposition—the more they resist, the more I must try to change them, and so I persuade them more, put more pressure on them, and perhaps resort to whatever power I have to force change.

1. Think of a situation where someone held a different viewpoint than yours. What were your assumptions about that person? Did you believe they just didn't get it, were wrong headed, perhaps a bit stupid?

   Or did you ask yourself, why would they hold the position they have? If you assume they are as rational and as competent as you are, why would they think as they do? Think back to Table 8.2. Are you at stage one, two, three, or four?

2. Are you able to put yourself into the shoes of the resister? Ask yourself: What forces play on that person? What beliefs does he or she have? What criteria is he or she using to evaluate the situation?

   (You might wish to refer to our chapter on stakeholder analysis to explore this further.)

3. What are the implications of your self-assessment with respect to what you need to do to develop yourself as a change agent?

TOOLKIT EXERCISE 8.4

What Is Your Change Agent Preference?

1. How comfortable are you with risk and ambiguity? Do you seek order and stability or change and uncertainty? Think of your level of comfort in higher-risk situations. Think of your degree of restlessness with routine, predictable situations.

2. How intuitive are you? Do you use feelings and emotion to influence others? Or are you logical and systematic? Do you persuade through facts and arguments?

3. Ask a significant other to reflect on your preferences and style. Does that person's judgment agree or disagree with yours? Why? What data do each have?

4. Given your responses to the above, how would you classify yourself? Are you:

   - An emotional champion
   - An intuitive adapter
   - A developmental strategist
   - A continuous improver

5. How flexible or adaptive are you with respect to the approach you use? Do you always adopt the same type, or do you use other approaches, depending on the needs of the situation? Which ones do you feel comfortable and competent in using? Again, check out your self-assessment by asking a significant other for comments.

TOOLKIT EXERCISE 8.5

Creating Structures for Team Projects

Whenever you create a change team, ensure you carry out this exercise. At individual and team levels, a shorthand designation, BART, is a useful way to structure tasks among a working group. Talking about BART in the context of a newly forming team can make the roles and responsibilities among people clear and decrease conflict among group members.

To be a useful tool, start with *Tasks* and end with *Boundaries*. It is wise to have a conversation about these issues, put the agreed-upon concepts in writing, and then revisit the structure at a designated time.

a) **Tasks:** This is the work that needs to be completed in a particular situation. Make a comprehensive list of tasks; next, assign the tasks to specific roles; then decide how much authority an individual has in the role; and, finally, describe how one role interfaces with another.

b) **Authority:** This is the scope of decision making that a particular person has in her or his role.

c) **Role:** This is a part that an individual has been explicitly assigned to be responsible for the execution of specific tasks.

d) **Boundary:** The edge where one person's responsibilities ends and another's begins. Sometimes managers blur boundaries, purposefully setting up a competitive situation.

TOOLKIT EXERCISE 8.6

Your Skills as a Change Team Member

1. Think of a time when you participated in a team. How well did the team perform? Were the results positive? Why or why not?

2. Review the list developed by Prosci. Did the team members exhibit the characteristics listed by Prosci? Did you? Why or why not?

3. What personal focus do you have? Do you tend to concentrate on getting the job done—a task focus? Or do you worry about bringing people along—a process focus?

4. How could you improve your skills in this area? Who might help you develop such skills?

Notes

1. Mead, M. Quote reported in *Webster's online dictionary—The Rosetta edition*, www .websters-online-dictionary.org.

2. Dover, P. A. (2003). Change agents at work: Lessons from Siemens Nixdorf. *Journal of Change Management, 3*(3), 243–257.

3. Lattman, P. (2005). Rebound. *Forbes, 175*(6), 58.

4. Jac the Knife new chairman of BHP. Retrieved May 2010 from http://www.smh.com .au/business/jac-the-knife-new-chairman-of-bhp-20090804-e8mx.html.

6. Hamel, G. (2002). *Leading the revolution: How to thrive in turbulent times by making innovation a way of life*. Boston, MA: Harvard Business School Press.

7. Mass, J. (2000). Leading the revolution. *MIT Sloan Management Review, 42*(1), 95.

8. Zaccaro, S. J., & Banks, D. (2004). Leader visioning and adaptability: Bridging the gap between research and practice on developing the ability to manage change. *Human Resource Management, 43*(4), 367–380.

9. Huey, J. (1994). The new post-heroic leadership. *Fortune, 129*(4), 42. Retrieved December 2010 from http://money.cnn.com/magazines/fortune/fortune_archive/1994/02/21/ 78995/index.htm.

10. Jick, T., & Peiperl, M. (2003). *Managing change: Cases and concepts* (p. 362). New York: McGraw-Hill/Irwin.

11. Tandon, N. (2003). The young change agents. In T. Jick & M. Peiperl, *Managing change: Cases and concepts* (p. 428). New York: McGraw-Hill/Irwin.

12. Kanter, R. M. (2003). The enduring skills of change leaders. In T. Jick & M. Peiperl, *Managing change: Cases and concepts* (p. 429). New York: McGraw-Hill/Irwin.

13. Hammonds, K. (2001, November). Change agents: Michael J. Fox & Deborah Brooks. *Fast Company*, (52), 106.

14. Branson, C. M. (2009). Achieving organizational change through values alignment. *Journal of Educational Administration, 46*(3), 376–395.

15. Frank, J. N. (2004). Newman's Own serves up a down-home public image. *PRweek, 7*(5), 10.

16. Dickout, R. (1997). All I ever needed to know about change management I learned at engineering school. *McKinsey Quarterly, 2*, 114–121.

17. Dickout, R. (1997). All I ever needed to know about change management I learned at engineering school. *McKinsey Quarterly, 2*, 114–121.

18. Francis, H. (2003). Teamworking and change: Managing the contradictions. *Human Resource Management Journal, 13*(3), 71–90.

19. Chilton, S. (2004). Book review of *Creating leaderful organisations: How to bring out leadership in everyone. Journal of Organizational Change Management, 17*(1), 110.

20. Katzenbach, J. R. (1996). Real change. *McKinsey Quarterly, 1*, 148–163.

21. Doyle, M. (2003). From change novice to change expert. *Personnel Review, 31*(4), 465–481.

22. Appelbaum, S., Bethune, M., & Tannenbaum, R. (1999). Downsizing and the emergence of self-managed teams. *Participation and Empowerment: An International Journal, 7*(5), 109–130.

23. Kramer, R. M. (2006, February). The great intimidators. *Harvard Business Review*, 88–96.

24. Collins, J. (2001). *From good to great.* New York: HarperCollins.

25. Rubin, R., Dierdorff, E., Boomer, W., & Baldwin, T. (2009). Do leaders reap what they sow? Leader and employee outcomes of leader organizational cynicism about change. *Leadership Quarterly, 20*(5), 680–688.

26. McCall, M., & Lombardo, M. (1983). *Off the track: Why and how successful executives get derailed.* Greensboro, NC: Center for Creative Leadership.

27. Higgs, M. (2009). The good, the bad and the ugly: Leadership and narcissism. *Journal of Change Management, 9*(2), 165–178.

28. Francis, H. (2003). Teamworking and change: Managing the contradictions. *Human Resource Management Journal, 13*(3), 71–90.

29. Much of this is drawn from Jick, T., & Peiperl, M. (2003). *Managing change: Cases and concepts* (p. 362). New York: McGraw-Hill/Irwin.

30. Ilies, R., Gerhardt, M. W., & Le, H. (2004). Individual differences in leadership emergence: Integrating meta-analytic findings and behavioral genetics estimates. *International Journal of Selection and Assessment, 12*(3), 207.

31. Leban, W., & Zulauf, C. (2004). Linking emotional intelligence abilities and transformational leadership styles. *Leadership and Organization Development Journal, 25*(7/8), 554.

32. Caldwell, R. (2003). Change leaders and change managers: Different or complementary? *Leadership & Organization Development Journal, 24*(5), 285–293.

33. Higgs, M., & Rowland, D. (2005). All changes great and small: Exploring approaches to change and its leadership. *Journal of Change Management, 5*(2), 121–151.

34. Higgs, M., & Rowland, D. (2005). All changes great and small: Exploring approaches to change and its leadership. *Journal of Change Management, 5*(2), 147.

35. Kouzes, J. M., & Posner, B. Z. (2007). *The leadership challenge* (4th ed.). San Francisco: Jossey-Bass.

36. Retrieved May 2010 from http://www.ccl.org/leadership/index.aspx.

37. Criswell, C., & Martin, A. (2007). 10 trends: A study of senior executives' views on the future. Center for Creative Leadership. Retrieved December 10 from http://www.ccl.org/leadership/pdf/research/TenTrends.pdf.

38. Duck, J. D. (2001). *The change monster: The human forces that fuel or foil corporate transformation & change.* New York: Crown Business.

39. Bennis (1989), as reported in Komives, S., et al. (1998). *Exploring leadership* (p. 109). San Francisco: Jossey-Bass.

40. Cooperrider, D. L., & Whitney, D. (1998). *Collaborating for change: Appreciative Inquiry.* San Francisco: Berrett-Koehler Communications.

41. Miller, D. (2002). Successful change leaders: What makes them? What do they do that is different? *Journal of Change Management, 2*(4), 383.

42. Zaccaro, S. J., & Banks, D. (2004). Leader visioning and adaptability: Bridging the gap between research and practice on developing the ability to manage change. *Human Resource Management, 43*(4), 367–380.

43. Patton, J. R. (2003). Intuition in decisions. *Management Decision, 41*(10), 989–996.

44. Personal communication with the authors.

45. Nadler, D., & Tushman, M. (1989). Organizational frame bending. *Academy of Management Executive, 3*(3), 194–204.

46. Weick, K., & Quinn, R. (1999). Organizational change and development. *Annual Review of Psychology, 50,* 366.

47. McAdam, R., McLean, J., & Henderson, J. (2003). The strategic "pull" and operational "push" of total quality management in UK regional electricity service companies. *International Journal of Quality & Reliability Management, 20*(4/5), 436–457.

48. Charan, R. (2006). Home Depot's blueprint for culture change. *Harvard Business Review, 84*(4), 60–70.

49. Kirton, M. J. (1984). Adaptors and innovators—Why new initiatives get blocked. *Long Range Planning, 17*(2), 137–143; Tushman, M. L., & O'Reilly, C. A. III. (1996). Ambidextrous organizations: Managing evolutionary and revolutionary change. *California Management Review, 38*(4), 8–30.

50. Saka, A. (2003). Internal change agents' view of the management of change problem. *Journal of Organizational Change Management, 16*(5), 480–497.

51. Wright, C. (2009). Inside out? Organizational membership, ambiguity and the ambivalent identity of the internal consultant. *British Journal of Management, 20*(3), 309–322.

52. Hunsaker, P. (1982, September–October). Strategies for organizational change: The role of the inside change agent. *Personnel,* 18–28.

53. Personal experience of the authors.

54. Saka, A. (2003). Internal change agents' view of the management of change problem. *Journal of Organizational Change Management, 16*(5), 489.

55. Personal experience of the authors.

56. Pitts, G. (2010, January 4). The fine art of managing change. *Globe and Mail.*

57. Jarrett, M. (2004). Tuning into the emotional drama of change: Extending the consultant's bandwidth. *Journal of Change Management, 4*(3), 247–258; Kilman, R. H. (1979, Spring). Problem defining and the consulting/intervention process. *California Management Review,* 26–33; Simon, A., & Kumar, V. (2001). Client's view on strategic capabilities which lead to management consulting success. *Management Decisions, 39*(5/6), 362–373.

58. Prosci Benchmarking Report. Best Practices in Change Management. (2000).

59. Prosci Benchmarking Report. Best Practices in Change Management. (2000).

60. Worren, N. et al. (1999, September). From organizational development to change management: The emergence of a new profession. *Journal of Applied Behavioral Science,* 277.

61. Worren, N. et al. (1999, September). From organizational development to change management: The emergence of a new profession. *Journal of Applied Behavioral Science,* 277, Table 2.

62. Appelbaum, S., Bethune, M., & Tannenbaum, R. (1999). Downsizing and the emergence of self-managed teams. *Participation and Empowerment: An International Journal, 7*(5), 109–130.

63. Prosci Benchmarking Report. Best Practices in Change Management. (2000).

64. Kahn, W. A. (2004). Facilitating and undermining organizational change: A case study. *Journal of Applied Behvioral Science, 40*(1), 7–30.

65. Rooney, P. (2001, November 12). Bill Gates, chairman and chief software architect. Microsoft. *CNR.*

66. Retrieved May 2010 from http://www. newswire.ca/en/releases/archive/June2006/15/ c4768. html.

67. Source unknown.

68. H. Sheppard, personal communication with T. Cawsey.

69. Webber, A. M. (1999). Learning for change (an interview with Peter Senge). *Fast Company, 24.* Retrieved December 2010 from http://www.fastcompany.com/magazine/24/senge.html.

70. Senge, P. M. (1996). The leader's new work: Building learning organizations. In K. Starkey (Ed.), *How organisations learn* (pp. 288–315). London: International Thompson Business Press.

71. Gilley, A., McMillan, H., & Gilley, J. (2009). Organizational change and characteristics of leadership effectiveness. *Journal of Leadership and Organizational Studies, 16*(1), 38–47.

72. Banutu-Gomez, M. B., & Banutu-Gomez, S. M. T. (2007). Leadership and organizational change in a competitive environment. *Business Renaissance Quarterly, 2*(2), 69–90.

73. Wageman, R. (1997, Summer). Critical success factors for creating superb self-managing teams. *Organizational Dynamics,* 49–61.

74. Johnston Smith International (2000, November 22). 2000 Change Management Conference, The Change Institute, Toronto.

75. Gerstner, L. (2002). *Who says elephants can't dance?: Inside IBM's historic turnaround.* New York: HarperCollins.

76. Lambert, T. (2006). Insight. MENAFN.com. Retrieved May 2010 from http://www.menafn.com/qn_print.asp?StroyID=129531&subl=true.

77. Katzenbach, J. (1996, July/August). From middle manager to real change leader. *Strategy and Leadership,* 34.

78. Oshry, B. (1993). Converting middle powerlessness to middle power: A systems approach. In T. Jick, *Managing change: Cases and concepts.* Homewood, IL: Irwin.

79. Howell, J., & Higgins, C. (1990, Summer). Champions of change. *Organizational Dynamics,* 40–55. Retrieved May 2010 from http://www.deloitte.com/view/en_US/us/Insights/Browse-by-Content-Type/Case-Studies/index.htm.

80. Shepard, H. (1975, November). Rules of thumb for change agents. *Organization Development Practitioner,* 1–5; Ransdell, E. (1997). Rules for Radicals. *Fast Company,* 11, 190–191; Hamel, G. (2000, July). How to start an insurrection. *Ideas@Work,* Harvard Business Review Press.

81. The sage of Quiznos: The skills of Greg Brenneman, a corporate-turnaround specialist, are in demand. (2008, August 28). *Economist,* Retrieved December 2010 from http://www.economist.com/node/12001911.

CHAPTER 9

Action Planning and Implementation

CHAPTER OVERVIEW

- Change leaders recognize the usefulness of plans and the imperative of action. Prepare, take action, and learn from the results. Change initiators have a "do it" attitude.
- Action planning involves planning the work and working the plan. "Right" decisions mean approximately "right" as change agents obtain feedback from action and make adjustments as they act.
- Change agents learn to specify who does what, when, and how to monitor and track their change initiatives. Agents use a variety of management tools, such as responsibility and project planning charts, surveys and survey feedback, critical path methods, and so forth, to successfully plan and implement their change programs.
- Successful change agents develop detailed communications plans and understand how to manage transitions from the present to a future desired state.

This book has a philosophical bias for taking action. Rather than passively waiting or complaining from the sidelines, change agents get engaged. However, the goal is not action simply for novelty and excitement. Action must increase the likelihood of positive change. Great ideas don't generate value until they are effectively executed. One of the ways to improve the quality of action is to use proven tools to execute a change agenda.

Tools in Chapter 9 translate plans to action. If this were a political campaign, these tools would be steps that are deployed after the candidate has been selected, the platform finalized, and the election called. The chapter provides advice on implementation tactics and project management tools. It addresses communication and influence tactics during the change process. And finally, the management of transition, or the process of keeping the organization operating while implementing the change, is detailed. In terms of the model in Figure 9.1, these are the issues of "getting from here to there"—assessing the present in terms of the future, determining the work that needs to be done, and implementing the change.

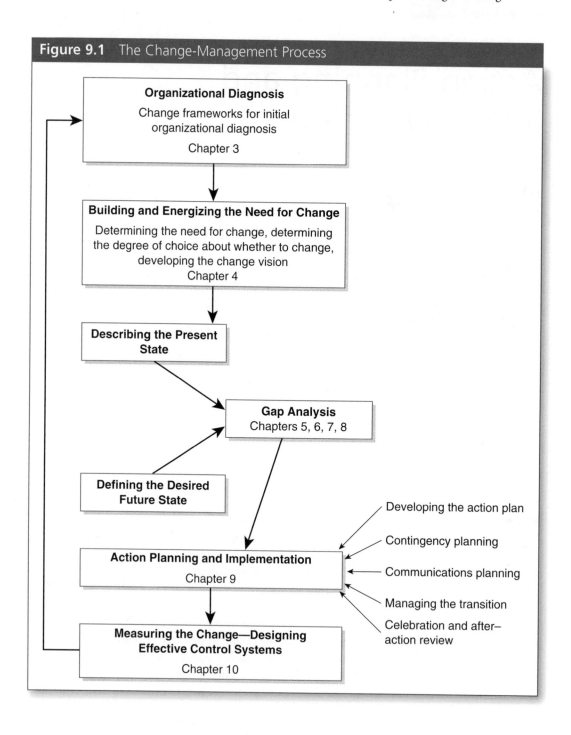

Figure 9.1 The Change-Management Process

Organizational Diagnosis

Change frameworks for initial organizational diagnosis

Chapter 3

Building and Energizing the Need for Change

Determining the need for change, determining the degree of choice about whether to change, developing the change vision
Chapter 4

Describing the Present State

Gap Analysis
Chapters 5, 6, 7, 8

Defining the Desired Future State

Developing the action plan

Contingency planning

Action Planning and Implementation

Chapter 9

Communications planning

Managing the transition

Celebration and after– action review

Measuring the Change—Designing Effective Control Systems

Chapter 10

Without a "Do It" Orientation, Things Won't Happen

In an ideal world, change agents will find they have ready access to supportive executives who provide directional clarity, ensure their organizations are ready for change, approve needed resources, cultivate employee commitment for change, and offer other needed support. Typically, this is not the case. Many or most executives will have little or no knowledge of the initiative or its value and implications. If they have heard of the idea, they may lack interest because of other priorities and political realities; some may have heard of it and have concerns, while others will simply want to distance themselves from the change in the event it doesn't work out. Some will fail to understand the important role they have to play in nurturing innovation from within the organization; others will not see it as their role.

The absence of senior management awareness and support is normal during the early stages of change. If senior managers represent 5% of the organization, there's a 95% chance that internally generated ideas for change will have been developed elsewhere. Organizations are complex systems, and their prospects for successful adaptation are advanced when they can also learn and grow from the bottom up. This is one of the reasons that firms such as 3M, Procter & Gamble, and Deloitte have demonstrated such staying power: They grow from within and from the bottom up. Wise senior managers know how to nurture and leverage employees' adaptive energy. Wise change agents know how to save short-sighted senior managers from themselves.

INNOVATION AND CHANGE AT 3M

Front-line freedom to innovate and senior-level support have been critical ingredients to 3M's success. Technical and marketing employees commit 15% of their time to work on projects of their own choosing, without supervision. The environment is open and informal; input from customers and lead users is sought; and collaboration and inquisitiveness are valued. Social media facilitates front-line collaboration and helps to overcome the communication barriers that organizational size and complexity bring. At the same time, 3M's culture is demanding, and the process for funding new ideas is highly structured.

The degree of management scrutiny and oversight increases as new ideas evolve to require significant resources. Products that are eventually successful in the marketplace are typically rejected several times in management's funding process before receiving funds, requiring persistence from innovators. Management and employees embrace and learn from failures because innovation won't happen otherwise. George Buckley, 3M's CEO and a Ph.D. in engineering, is deeply interested in innovation. He regularly visits the labs to find out what people are exploring, believing that "creativity comes from freedom, not control."[1] This commitment to innovation allows new products and services to percolate and develop from the ground up.[2]

If senior-level support for change is unlikely to develop in the near future, change initiators may feel that abiding by formal organizational protocols and waiting for official support will slow progress unduly. Faced with this situation, change agents may choose to follow the advice of Rear Admiral Grace Hopper, a pioneering female software engineer in the U.S. Navy, who said "it is easier to seek forgiveness than permission."[3]

Several approaches to action planning and implementation were introduced in Chapter 5, such as creeping commitment, coalition building, and the bypassing of the formal approval process. As noted, a "do it" approach does not suggest precipitous action that gets one into trouble. Rather, the action should be based on savvy experiments. In *The Leadership Challenge*, Kouzes and Posner argue that "challenging the process"[4] is one of the five fundamental leadership skills. They dare managers to look outward and search for opportunities to innovate and improve. They also advocate experimenting and learning from those trials.

Pfeffer states that "actions count more than elegant plans or concepts" and that "there is no doing without mistakes." He asks, however, a crucial question: "What is the company's response?"[5] If the organization's response to reasoned initiatives and honest mistakes is to scapegoat and blame, people quickly learn not to take risks that might lead to mistakes. Or they learn to cover up mistakes. Either way, the organization suffers.* However, beliefs about likely organizational responses can also become a convenient excuse for inaction and the avoidance of risk taking (e.g., What if my idea really won't work or what will I do if it does work?). If such beliefs are never challenged, their stability will produce self-fulfilling prophecies.

Effective managers of change are aware of the consequences of their actions and intuitively test their organizational assumptions by engaging in an action—learning—reaction cycle.[6] Sayles recognized this when he wrote, "...working leaders...instead of simply waiting for and evaluating results...seek to intervene. And the interventions they undertake require a more intimate knowledge of operations, and more involvement in the work than those of traditional middle managers."[7]

TESTING LIMITS

"Traditional thought says that nothing happens without top management's approval (but) change need not be something that is 'done to you.' Here is another way to think of it: empowerment is something you grasp until you find its limits. I tell people that they can constantly test the limits of their empowerment, carefully reading internal politics to see when they are pushing up against a boundary...Too many people think they are not empowered, but actually they have failed to test their limits."

Dr. Ross Wirth, Chair of Business, Franklin University, reflecting on his 32-year career at Citgo Petroleum.[8]

---

*This does lead to an accountability paradox. Accountability is a needed and useful attribute. However, there needs to be a fine balance between holding change leaders accountable for what they do and encouraging the risk-taking behavior that leads to needed learning and change.

The reality of much organizational life is somewhere between an environment that punishes those who dare to challenge the status quo and one in which all such initiatives are unconditionally embraced and rewarded. Organizational members who choose not to wait on formal permission and undertake reasonable self-initiated change initiatives may experience some chastisement for not first seeking approval, particularly if the initiative runs into difficulty. However, in many organizations, they are also commended for showing initiative and having a positive impact. The organization's culture and the personality of a boss (e.g., managerial style and tolerance for ambiguity) will obviously influence what response the initiator receives, but most managers value initiative.

What can be done to increase the likelihood that taking action will produce desired results? The following sections address this question by exploring a variety of planning and implementing tools. The purpose of these tools is to assist change leaders in designing and then managing their initiatives in ways that increase their prospects for success.

Prelude to Action: Selecting the Correct Path

Any action plan for change needs to be rooted in a sophisticated understanding of how the organization works and what needs to be achieved. Since there are a variety of action paths available, how do you decide which to take? Henry Mintzberg provides guidance in this matter by setting out three generic approaches: thinking first, seeing first, and doing first:[9]

- **Thinking first** works best when the issue is clear, data are reliable, context is structured, thoughts can be pinned down, and discipline can be established as in many routine production processes. The introduction of an initiative such as Six Sigma is an example where management needs to think first.
- **Seeing first** works best when many elements have to be combined into creative solutions, commitment to those solutions is key, and communication across boundaries is essential. New product development is an example of the need to see first.
- **Doing first** works best when the situation is novel and confusing, complicated specifications would get in the way, and a few simple relationship rules can help people move forward. For example, if a manager is testing an approach to customer service and wants feedback about what works, then doing first is appropriate.

As complexity and ambiguity rise, Mintzberg argues that the preferred approach to action shifts. **Thinking first** fits when the situation is well structured, a manager has the needed data, and there is not much confusion about how to proceed. As ambiguity and complexity rise, though, certainty over how best to proceed becomes less clear. **Seeing first** approaches the challenge by experimentation, prototyping, and pilot programs so that commitment can be gained by having others see and experience an initiative. **Doing first** is a response to even more ambiguous situations and takes the process of exploration further in the search for new paths forward. As these paths begin to emerge, the approach can then be altered to **seeing first** or **doing first**, depending on what is suitable for the next stage.

Nitin Nohria offers a slightly different assessment of the generic change strategies available.[10] He identified three strategies, defined their characteristics, explained the typical implementation, and highlighted their risk points. **Programmatic change** (similar to Mintzberg's thinking first change) involves the implementation of straightforward, well-structured solutions. It is best suited to contexts that are clear and well defined and where the magnitude of the change is incremental in nature. Risks with this approach lie in potential problems with inflexibility, over-reliance on a "one size fits all" solution, and a lack of focus on behavior.

Discontinuous change involves a major break from the past. If the environment is shifting dramatically and a continuation of activities based on existing assumptions will not work, then discontinuous, top-down change may be fitting. Organizational restructuring due to downsizing, rapid growth, or the realignment of markets is an example of this category. Risks with this approach come from political coalitions that may form and derail the change, a lack of sufficient control to enforce the change, and the loss of talented people who become frustrated and quit.

Emergent change (similar to Mintzberg's doing first change) grows out of incremental initiatives and can create ambiguity and challenge for staff members. An employee-centered change initiative to modify the culture of the organization that emerges from customers' and staff's feedback would be an example. If the organization has a talented, knowledgeable workforce that understands the risks and possibilities, utilizing an emergent change approach may be appropriate. Risks with this approach come in the form of confusion over direction, uncertainty as to the impact of the change, and slow progress (See Table 9.1).

To counteract the pitfalls of programmatic or "thinking first" change, consider using employee engagement and feedback to connect with those on the receiving end, learn from their experiences, and decentralize decision making to allow for

Table 9.1 Three Generic Change Strategies[11]

Change Type	Characteristic	Implementation	Issues or Concerns
Programmatic change	Missions, plans, objectives	Training, timelines, steering committees	Lack of focus on behavior, one solution for all, inflexible solutions
Discontinuous change	Initiated from top, clear break, reorientation	Decrees, structural change, concurrent implementation	Political coalitions derail change, weak controls, stress from the loss of people
Emergent change	Ambiguous, incremental, challenging	Use of metaphors, experimentation, and risk taking	Confusion over direction, uncertainty and possible slow results

Source: Adapted from Nohria, N. & R. Khurana, "Executing Change: Three Generic Strategies," Harvard Business School Note. 494–039.

adaptation to local conditions. The pitfalls from discontinuous change will be lessened by processes that reduce ambiguity and build support by enhancing member understanding of the change and why it was undertaken.

The issues related to emergent or "doing first" change may be managed through the use of field experiments and task forces to provide engagement and feedback. These can be used to create clarity concerning what is emerging and build understanding and support for the next steps in the change process. In metaphorical terms, this points to a move from "ready—aim—fire" to "ready—fire—aim— re-fire—re-aim…."* for an emergent approach to planning. In fast-moving contexts, it is likely that a traditional planning process will be too lengthy and that by the time the planning is finished, the opportunity may have been missed. This metaphor recognizes that significant information can be obtained from action feedback. When a change leader initiates action, reactions will occur that can provide insight into how to respond and take corrective actions.

A third approach to thinking about change strategies is found in the **unilateral** versus **participative** approaches to change. Advocates of **unilateral** approaches to change believe that if one first changes systems and structures, forcing behavioral changes, that action will in turn produce changes in attitudes and beliefs over time. Those who promote a **participative** approach believe the opposite. They argue that you first need to engage and change attitudes and gain acceptance of an initiative before restructuring systems and organizational structures.

Waldersee and Griffiths note that change initiatives have been traditionally grouped into two broad categories. Techno-structural changes refer to those that are based in structures, systems, and technology. Behavioral-social changes are focused on altering established social relationships. After investigating 408 change episodes, they concluded that the **unilateral** approach was perceived to be more appropriate for techno-structural change, while **participative** approaches were seen as more appropriate when behavioral-social changes such as cultural change were involved.[12] When Australian managers were asked about the perceived effectiveness of these two change approaches, they saw unilateral methods as more effective in bringing about successful change, regardless of the type of change. What does all of this mean for action planning? Waldersee and Griffiths concluded that:

> Concrete actions taken by change managers are often superior to the traditional prescriptions of participation (Beer et al., 1990[13]). Forcing change through top-down actions such as redeploying staff or redesigning jobs may effectively shift employee behavior. With the context and behavior changed, interventions targeting attitudes may then follow. (p. 432)

---

*The managerial use of this metaphor is usually credited to T. Peters and R. H. Waterman, Jr., *In Search of Excellence* (New York: Harper & Row, 1982). Our understanding is that its presence in its modified form has its roots in missile defense. If you are defending against incoming missiles, you don't have time to wait and plan a response. You do need to fire before you aim your missile. Then once you have things in motion, you can re-aim your missile based on new, current information.

While a unilateral approach may have appeal for those who want to ensure that things are done, such an approach can be risky and needs to be managed with care. When implementation lacks sensitivity, stakeholders may feel that their perspectives and concerns have been ignored. As noted in Chapter 7, this can result in fallout that could have been avoided, resistance, and missed opportunities for valuable input.

What conclusions can be drawn from this material on a "do it" orientation and change strategies? Start a change process rather than waiting to get things perfect. Be willing to take informed risks and learn as you go. Finally, pick your change strategy with care and remember to take steps to manage the risks associated with the adopted approach. Regardless of how difficult change appears to be, Confucius was right—"a journey of a thousand miles begins with a single step."[14] You need to **plan your work and work the plan.**

Toolkit Exercise 9.1 asks you to consider the type of change and then begin to build your work plan.

Plan the Work

If the change leader's approach to planned change has followed what this book suggests, then much planning will have already been done. In addition, Michael Beer[15] offers a prescriptive list of "steps to effective change." (**Appendix 9.1** contains a table that compares Beer's steps with the prescriptions of others.[16]) Beer's steps are:

1. Mobilize commitment to change through joint diagnosis of business problems.

2. Develop a shared vision of how to organize and manage for competitiveness.

3. Foster consensus for the new vision, competence to enact it, and cohesion to move it along.

4. Spread revitalization to all departments without pushing it from the top.

5. Institutionalize revitalization through formal policies, systems, and structures.

6. Monitor and adjust strategies in response to problems in the revitalization process.

For many change situations, this checklist provides valuable guidance in the development of an action plan. However, assuming a "one-size fits all" approach to change is risky. For example, the above list assumes a fundamental cooperative orientation. That is, there is sufficient commonality of goals that a shared vision is possible. The list also suggests that change should evolve and not be pushed down by top management. However, change agents will need approaches that allow them to face situations in which cooperation and commonality of goals is weak or absent and where changes are being pushed from the top.

As well, the need for contingent thinking needs to be addressed. That is, an action plan depends significantly upon the action-planning context. In complex and ambiguous situations, plans and tactics must be able to adapt as events unfold. Plans need to be able to adapt! As such, it is useful to remember the old saying: "**No plan survives first contact.**"[17]

In summary, while careful planning is critical, change leaders must also recognize that planning is a means—not an end in itself. Don't ignore vital emerging information just because it does not fit with carefully conceived plans. The abilities to think contingently, consider alternative paths forward, and adapt are important contributors to enhanced adaptive capacity.[18]

Engage Others in Action Planning

Occasionally, change planning must be undertaken under a cloak of secrecy, such as when a merger is in the works and the premature release of information would significantly affect the price and the level of competitive risk. In general, though, the active involvement of others and information sharing enhances the quality of action planning for most change strategies. Consider one of the experiences of Barbara Waugh, who spent 25 years as a change agent at Hewlett-Packard:

CHANGE AT HP LABS

Waugh's campaign for change at HP Labs began when its director asked her, "Why does no one out there consider HP Labs to be the best industrial research lab in the world?" Rather than propose answers, she and the director began by asking questions through a survey. The inquiry generated 800 single-spaced pages of feedback related to programs (e.g., too many projects and too few priorities); people: (e.g., poor performers are not removed quickly enough and researchers lack sufficient freedom to do their jobs well); and processes (e.g., the information infrastructure is inadequate).

The feedback, says Waugh, was "800 pages of frustrations, dreams, and insights." But how could she capture and communicate what she learned? She drew on her experience with street theater and created a play about HP Labs. She worked passages from the surveys into dialogue and then recruited executives to act as staff members and junior people to act as executives. The troupe performed for 30 senior managers. "At the end of the play, the managers were very quiet," Waugh remembers. "Then they started clapping. It was exciting. They really got it."[19]

Waugh's approach is instructive because it illustrates the power of presenting potentially boring data in an engaging and compelling manner. This was not the first time she nurtured change in an emergent, grass-roots fashion. Her approach leveraged listening and questioning, built networks with individuals with complementary ideas, and when needed, arranged for access to financial resources for worthy endeavours.*

---

*In planning the work, the use of interviews, surveys, survey feedback, and appreciative inquiry (a rigorous commitment to active listening, feedback, mutual development, and renewal) are powerful action planning tools. They come from the Organizational Development (OD) approach to change. For more information, two good sources are: Cooperrider, D. L., Whitney, D., & Stavros, J. M. (2008). *Appreciative inquiry handbook: For leaders of change.* Brunswick, OH: Crown; and Cummings, T. G., & Worley, C. G. (2009). *Organization development and change.* Mason, OH: South-Western.

Underlying planning-through-engagement strategies are assumptions regarding top-down (unilateral) versus bottom-up (participative) methods of change. Although Waldersee and Griffiths[20]'s study showed that unilateral implementation methods have much to offer, the success of a change is enhanced when people understand what it entails, why it is being undertaken, what the consequences of success and failure are, and why their help is needed and valued. All too often, techno-structural changes have floundered because of design problems getting tangled up with acceptance and implementation issues that never get sorted out.

Regardless of the change strategy preferred, the plan needs to be examined carefully for logic and consistency. The next section outlines a series of questions to improve change agents' abilities in this area.

Ensure Alignment in Your Action Planning

Change agents often understand what needs to be done but get the sequence of activities wrong. They might leave a meeting after a productive discussion but fail to sort out who is responsible for what. Sometimes critical steps in the plan are risky and alternative strategies need to be considered in case things do not go as planned. At other times, change agents may over- or underestimate the available resources and constraints or their own power and competence. Table 9.2 provides a checklist

---

Table 9.2   Action Planning Checklist[21]

1. Is the action plan consistent with the analysis?

2. Is the plan time-sequenced in logical order?

3. Is it clear who will do what, when, where, and how?

4. What is the probability of success at each step?

5. Have you developed contingencies for major possible but nondesirable occurrences?

6. Have you anticipated secondary consequences of your actions?

7. Is the plan realistic given your influence (both formal and informal) and the resources likely to be available to you?

8. Do you have the competence to implement the action steps? If not, who on your team does?

9. Who does your plan rely on? Are they "on-side"? If not, what will it take to bring them "on-side"?

10. Who (and what) could seriously obstruct the change? How will you manage them?

Source: Adapted from Gabarro, J., & Schlesinger, L. (1983). Some preliminary thoughts on action planning and implementation. *Managing Behaviour in Organizations* (pp. 342–343). New York: McGraw-Hill.

of questions to use when reviewing an action plan. This checklist tests the viability of the plan and asks for a rethinking of the connections between the analysis of the situation and the plan itself. Tough-minded thinking can improve the coherence and thoughtfulness of action plans.

Action Planning Tools

This section explores a selection of action planning tools that change agents find particularly useful (see Table 9.3). Selecting the appropriate tool is both an art and science: An art as the story of Waugh at HP illustrated (see above), and a science as one analyzes data carefully and makes an appropriate selection.

Table 9.3 Tools for Action Planning

1. To-do list—a checklist of things to do

2. Responsibility charting—who will do what, when, where, why, and how

3. Contingency planning—consideration of what should be done when things do not work as planned on critical issues

4. Surveys and survey feedback—capturing people's opinions and tracking them over time to assist in identifying what needs changing or in tracking a change project

5. Project planning and critical path methods—operations research techniques for scheduling work. These methods provide deadlines and insight as to which activities cannot be delayed to meet those deadlines.

6. Force field and stakeholder analysis—examination of the forces for and against change and the positions of the major players and why they behave as they do
   a. Commitment charts—an evaluation of the level of commitment of major players (against, neutral, let it happen, help it happen, make it happen)
   b. The adoption continuum or awareness, interest, desire, adoption (AIDA) analysis— examination of major players and their position on the AIDA continuum related to the proposed changes

7. Leverage analysis—determination of methods of influencing major groups or players regarding the proposed changes

---

1. To-Do Lists

When managers engage in action planning, they often begin by outlining in detail the sequence of steps they will take initially to achieve their goals. That is, they make a list. A **to-do list**, a checklist of things to do, is the simplest and most common planning tool. Sometimes this is all the situation requires. As the action planning becomes more sophisticated, simple to-do lists will not suffice and responsibility charting provides more control.

2. Responsibility Charting

Responsibility charting can be a valuable tool to detail who should do what, when, and how. As well, it can be used to help keep projects on track and provide a basis for record keeping and accountability. Table 9.4 provides an example responsibility chart. The process begins by defining the list of decisions or actions to be taken. Then individuals are assigned responsibility for achieving specific actions at specified deadlines.

Table 9.4 Example Responsibility Chart[22]				
Decisions or Actions to Be Taken			*Responsibilities*	
	Susan	Ted	Sonja	Relevant Dates
Action 1	R	A	I	For meeting on Jan. 14
Action 2		R	I	May 24
Action 3	S	A	A	Draft Plan by Feb. 17; action by July 22
Etc.				

Coding:

R = Responsibility (not necessarily authority)

A = Approval (right to veto)

S = Support (put resources toward)

I = Inform (to be consulted before action)

Note that if there are a large number of *A*s on your chart, implementation will be difficult. Care must be taken to assign *A*s only when appropriate. Likewise, if there are not enough *R*s and *S*s, you will need to think about changes needed here and how to bring them about.

Source: Adapted from Beckhard, R. (1987). *Organizational transitions* (p. 104). Reading, MA: Addison-Wesley.

3. Contingency Planning

The importance of thinking through possible contingencies should events not go as planned was discussed earlier. Two tools that aid in contingency planning are decision tree analysis and scenario planning.*

Decision tree analysis asks change agents to consider the major choices and the possible consequences of those alternatives. Analysts are then asked to plan for the possible next actions and consider what the consequences of those actions might be. Such alternating action–consequence sequences can be extended as far as reasonable. As well, probabilities can be assigned as to the likelihood of each consequence. For many applications, a simple scale (*very likely, likely, possible, unlikely,* or *very unlikely*)

---

*Readers are encouraged to consult standard operations research texts for further information on these tools.

is sufficient. This approach helps model the possible consequences to change decisions and assess the benefits and risks associated with the different pathways.

A second tool that helps managers with contingency planning is scenario planning. Here a change strategy is formed by first developing a limited number of scenarios or stories about how the future may unfold and then assessing what the implications of each of these would be to the organization.[23] Change leaders typically frame these around an issue of strategic and/or tactical importance. For example, if a firm producing paper forms is concerned about the long-term viability of its business model, then management could develop scenarios of what a paperless form producer would look like. Once the scenarios were developed, managers would ask themselves: how likely is this scenario? What would need to happen to make the scenario a reality? And what contingencies might arise that would need to be addressed? If one or more of these future scenarios seemed worth investing in, then management would develop its plans accordingly. To open people's minds to possibilities and avoid blind spots, external parties are often brought into the process to offer data and insights (often from other perspectives), challenge assumptions, and stimulate thinking, discussion, and informed analysis.

Scenario planning is different from forecasting. Forecasting starts in the present and uses trend lines and probability estimates to make projections about the future. Scenario planning starts by painting a picture of the future and works backward, asking what would have to happen to make this future scenario a reality and what could be done.[24]

While most uses of scenario planning are at a strategy level, the principles can be applied to frame possible visions for change and develop the action pathways that will increase the likelihood that the vision will be achieved. Royal Dutch Shell[25] was one of the first users of scenario planning. The firm used it as a way to link future uncertainties to today's decisions.

4. Surveys and Survey Feedback

Change agents may find it is helpful to use surveys to capture people's attitudes, opinions, and experiences at a particular point in time and then possibly track those attitudes over time. Tools in this area can provide anonymity to the respondents and make it possible to capture the opinions of a larger proportion of the participants than might otherwise be possible. Political agendas don't disappear with the use of a survey, but they may make it possible for people to say things that they would not feel comfortable stating publically. Services such as **SurveyMonkey.com** and **EmployeeSurveys.com** have made the design, delivery, and analysis easy to manage.

Surveys are used to access the opinions of internal and external stakeholders and assess attitudes and beliefs of relevance to the change. For example, how do customers view the firm's service levels, innovativeness, and product performance? What ideas do they have concerning new product offerings or service improvements? Employees can be sampled to assess the organization's readiness for change, the culture or work climate, their satisfaction and commitment levels, or what is helping or hindering their ability to do their jobs. Sometimes surveys are deployed to develop options and assess opinions on their viability. Later in the change process, surveys may sample understanding and knowledge levels, emerging attitudes and issues, and levels of acceptance and satisfaction with the change. The possible applications are restricted only by imagination, people's willingness to respond, and legal and ethical considerations.

Ready-made surveys are available on virtually any topic. Some are publically available at no cost, while others are proprietary and have charges attached to their use. Costs can vary from a few dollars per survey to thousands of dollars when outside consultants are used to design, administer, assess, and report the findings. When it comes to scoring and interpretation, some are straightforward and easy to interpret, while others require the assistance of a skilled practitioner. Some of these instruments have been carefully assessed for reliability and validity, while others have nothing more than face validity.

The bottom line with respect to surveys is that they can prove very helpful to change agents but need to be approached with care. Their design, administration, and analysis require the assistance of someone well trained in survey research. Even when a change agent is sampling opinions, the ability to frame good questions is a prerequisite to getting useful information. The same holds true for analysis and interpretation.*

A powerful use of surveys is an approach called **survey feedback**.[26] It is an action research method developed by organizational development (OD) practitioners as a way to stimulate and advance conversations and insights concerning what is going on in the organization, how members are feeling, and how things could be improved. As the name suggests, it involves the sharing of survey results with the individuals affected by the findings. Those involved in the discussion will have responded to the survey. Skilled facilitators guide work groups through the discussion of the findings. They use this as an opportunity to enrich the assessment of the data and their interpretation and explore the implications for action. The process is used to raise awareness and understanding, advance the analysis, and build support and commitment for actions that will benefit both the individuals and the organization.

5. Project Planning and Critical Path Methods

Project planning and critical path methods can provide valuable assistance to change managers as they think about what action steps to take.** These methods have been developed into sophisticated operations research techniques to aid the planning of major projects. Critical path methods ask planners to identify when the project should be completed and to work backward from that point, scheduling all tasks that will require time, effort, and resources. These are arranged in time sequence such that tasks that can occur simultaneously can be identified. These

---

*For further information on survey research: Rea, L. M., & Parker, R. A. (2005). *Designing and conducting survey research*. San Francisco: Jossey-Bass.

Software packages are available in this area. A commonly used one, **Microsoft Office Project (http://www.microsoft.com/project/en/us/default.aspx), allows you to track steps, resource requirements, and costs, see the impact of possible changes, trace the source of issues, visually communicate project information to others, and collaborate with them on the plans. Colleges, universities, and organizations such as the Project Management Institute (http://www.pmi.org/Pages/default.aspx) offer professional training in project management.

tasks are then plotted on a timeline. Sequential tasks are plotted to determine the needed time to complete the project.

With this done, managers can assess bottlenecks, resource requirements, slack at particular points in the process (i.e., more time or resources than the minimum required), and progression paths. The critical path, the path with the least slack time, can be identified and special attention can be paid to it. If there are concerns about the time to completion, the project manager can add resources to speed up the project, revisit the specifications, look for viable alterations to the implementation path, or increase the amount of time required to complete the project. Likewise, if there are concerns over the cost of the project, the project manager can explore alternatives on this front.

The critical path method introduces the notion of parallel initiatives. That is, it recognizes that different things may be able to be worked on simultaneously if the work is properly organized. Phase 1 tasks don't have to be totally completed before beginning work on Phase 2 tasks. Care and sophistication are required with this approach because it carries the risk of increasing confusion and redundant effort. When properly applied, though, it can shrink the time required to complete the change. This is readily visible in areas such as new product development. Figure 9.2 gives an example of a sequential and a parallel plan for new product development. In the upper half of the figure, the tasks are plotted sequentially. In the lower half of the figure, the tasks overlap. Concept development begins before opportunity identification ends and the cycle time to completion is reduced.

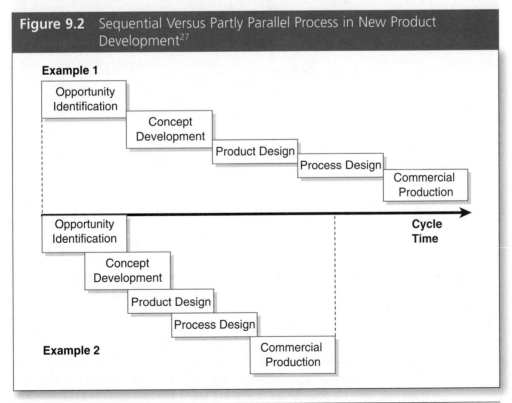

Figure 9.2 Sequential Versus Partly Parallel Process in New Product Development[27]

Source: Shilling, M.A., & W.L. Hill, "Managing the New Product Development Process: Strategic Imperatives," *Academy of Management Executive,* Vol.12, #3,1998, 67–81.

6. Force Field and Stakeholder Analysis

Chapter 6 of this book explored force field and stakeholder analysis. Force field analysis asks change agents to specify the forces for and against change. Stakeholder analysis and stakeholder maps ask that the key players be identified and the relationships among players be examined. Two additional tools that are helpful when planning actions related to stakeholders are commitment charts and AIDA charts.

A. Commitment Analysis Charts

Managers can use commitment charts to analyze the commitment of each stakeholder. Stakeholders can be thought of as being weakly to strongly opposed (**against**) to your change project, "neutral" (**let it happen**), slightly positive (**help it happen**), or strongly positive (**make it happen**). Change leaders also need to consider the level of understanding that underpins stakeholders' commitment level. Identifying the existing level of commitment is the first step in planning tactics designed to alter those pre-existing patterns. Table 9.5 provides an example commitment chart. (Note that the "X" in the table shows where the person is and the "O" shows where a change agent wants them to be.)

Table 9.5 An Example Commitment Chart[28]						
	Level of Commitment					Level of Understanding (high, med, low)
Key Players	Opposed Strongly to Weakly	Neutral	Let it Happen	Help it Happen	Make it Happen	
Person 1		X	→O			Med
Person 2				X	→O	High
Person 3		X	→	→O		Low
Etc.						

B. The Adoption Continuum

Stakeholder analysis will have identified the people who are critical to the change process. With this information in hand, change agents need to consider how they propose to encourage those individuals to move along the **adoption continuum** until the needed stakeholders are aligned with the change, or at least their opposition has been minimized.

As noted in Chapter 6, change agents can think of the process of getting people on-side with change as one of first creating awareness and then encouraging them to move from **awareness** of the issues to **interest** in the change to **desiring** action and, finally, to **action** or adopting the change. This is called the **AIDA** or adoption continuum. Table 9.6 provides an example of how a change agent might map people on to the adoption continuum as a method of tracking their change attitudes.

Table 9.6 Mapping People on the Adoption Continuum

Persons or Stakeholder Groups	Awareness	Interest	Desiring Action	Moving to Action or Adopting the Change
Person 1				
Person 2				
Person 3				
. . .				

Different individuals will be at different points on the AIDA continuum, which makes change strategies complex. For each stage, change agents need to use different tactics. For example, to raise initial awareness, well-designed general communication vehicles such as newsletters, reports, and videos can be used. The messages will be used to raise awareness of the need for change, set out the vision for the change, and provide access to thought-provoking information and images that support the initiative. However, if most people are already aware of what is being proposed, managers shouldn't waste efforts on general-information communications.

To move people to the interest phase, managers need to outline how the change will affect stakeholders personally and/or why this change should be of interest to them. Discussion groups on the issue, benchmark data, simulations, and test runs showing results can be effective in stimulating interest. Once interest is aroused, specific tactics to demonstrate and reinforce the benefits and build commitment are needed. Change agents might use one-on-one meetings to influence stakeholders, to persuade them to get directly involved with the change, or to connect them with influential supporters of the change. Change agents might reallocate resources or designate rewards in ways that reinforce adoption. Influencing people one at a time or in small groups can be valuable if influential individuals are identified and the right message is communicated to them.

7. Leverage Analysis

In Chapter 6, we stated that people's position on the adoption continuum is influenced by their general orientation to change—whether they tend to be an innovator, early adopter, early majority, late majority, or laggard in matters related to change. One of the action planning challenges for the change leaders is to sort out people's overall predisposition to change in general and the proposed change in particular.

Moving individuals on the adoption continuum is aided by engaging in **leverage analysis.** Leverage analysis seeks to identify those actions that will create the greatest change with the least effort. For example, if opinion leaders of a key group of individuals can be identified and persuaded to back the proposed organization change, the job of the change leader is easier. Likewise, if the task is to persuade senior management, one needs to identify influential individuals in this group. Identifying high-leverage methods will depend on the quality of your knowledge of the participants and your analysis of the organization and its environment. (One successful change agent ensured the adoption of a new software system by persuading the CEO to personally call every regional manager, key stakeholders in the change, and ask for their support!)[29]

Gladwell presents an excellent example of the notion of leverage in his book *The Tipping Point*.[30] Gladwell points out how little things can have large consequences if they occur at the right moment and are contagious. If things catch on and momentum builds, eventually a tipping point is reached. This is the point where a critical level of support is reached, the change becomes more firmly rooted, and the rate of acceptance accelerates. As Burke puts it, change agents need to find the critical few individuals that can connect with others in ways that change the context and tip things into a new reality. The vision needs to be sticky (i.e., cast as a story so that it will stay in people's minds), and change agents need to understand the connectors in the organization to get this message out.[31] Moore notes that one of the biggest challenges to reaching the tipping point is to build sufficient support to allow the acceptance of the change to cross the "chasm" between the early adopters and visionaries and the early majority.[32] Once this gap has been bridged, the rate of progress accelerates. As things accelerate, new challenges emerge, such as how to scale your efforts so that momentum is maintained and enthusiasm is not soured due to implementation failures or stalled progress.

TIPPING POINTS AND THE MOMENTUM FOR CHANGE IN THE OBAMA ELECTION

Barack Obama's path to the presidency was dotted with several tipping points during the state primaries and the federal campaign. Some were related to specific things done by the candidate; some related to the actions of others; and some tied to specific situations (e.g., the mortgage/banking crisis). His creative use of social media (e.g., Facebook) is particularly noteworthy. It allowed him to reach out virally to groups of electors and move them along the commitment continuum at speeds not seen before. This generated grass-roots financial support and media buzz that legitimized his candidacy very early on.

During the primaries, Representative James E. Clyburn, a prominent uncommitted South Carolina Democrat, felt the tipping point occurred around midnight on Tuesday, May 6th. "I could tell the next day, when I got up to the Capitol that this thing were going to start a slide toward Obama." I don't believe that there is any way that she (Hillary Clinton) can win the nomination." Contentious remarks by former President Bill Clinton created a

> rift with African-Americans, Obama's 14-point North Carolina victory exceeded expectations, and Hillary Clinton's weaker-than-expected win in the Indiana primary all conspired to take the wind out of her campaign while energizing Obama's.
>
> Super-delegates were still not committing in large numbers to Obama in early May. Clyburn saw this as "the long shadow of the Clintons in the Democratic Party stretching back more than a decade and the reservoir of goodwill." However, he expected to see a steady and significant movement in the days ahead. "That's pretty much where everybody knows it's going to end up." Representative Rahm Emanuel, the Democratic conference chairman, went further and labeled Obama the presumptive nominee.[33]

This discussion of Obama's campaign points to the value that the Internet and social media can play in raising awareness and advancing commitment levels. Blogs, Facebook pages, Second Life…the terrain continues to evolve, and change agents need to pay attention to how these technologies can be used to leverage their plans.

8. Other Change-Management Tools

The operations management area provides useful planning tools and diagnostic aids: Pareto diagrams (which classify problems according to relative importance), cause–effect diagrams, histograms, approaches to the development of benchmark and normative data, control charts (to show abnormal trends), and scatter diagrams are some of the tools that can be used to manage change initiative.[34] The selection of which of these tools to use depends upon the nature of the change challenge, the needs of the change agents, and the resources available to them. In general, the value of these tools lies in focusing attention, sorting out patterns and underlying effects, and assessing progress.

The variety of techniques and tools in the popular business press continues to grow. Over the years, Darrell Rigby and Barbara Bilodeau have tracked management's use of 25 different change tools on a global basis and assessed managerial satisfaction with them (see **Appendix 9.2**).[35] By tracking usage patterns by region and types of firms, differences in the sorts of change issues seen as most needing attention become apparent. This generic listing of change approaches provides a useful touchpoint for change leaders when they are considering how to proceed given the needs for change that they have identified.

In summary, planning the work asks change leaders to translate the change vision into specific actions that people can take. The plan outlines targets and dates and considers contingencies—what might go wrong (or right), how managers can anticipate those things, and how they can respond. Further, it examines how realistic the chances are for success and how a change agent increases the probabilities for success. Table 9.7 outlines a checklist for developing action plans.

Table 9.7 A Checklist for Change: Developing an Action Plan
1. Given your vision statement, what is your overall objective? When must it be accomplished?
2. What would be the first step in accomplishing your goal?
3. What would be milestones along the way that will allow you to determine if you are making progress?
4. What is your action plan? Who will do what, when, where, why, and how? Can you do a responsibility chart?
5. What is the probability of success at each step?
6. Do you have a contingency plan when things go wrong? What things are most likely to go wrong? What things can you not afford to have go wrong? How can you prevent such things from happening?
7. Is your action plan realistic given your influence both formal and informal?
8. Who does your plan rely on? Are they on-side? What would it take to bring them onside?
9. Does your action plan take into account the concerns of stakeholders and the possible coalitions they might form?

Working the Plan Ethically and Adaptively

Working the plan requires change agents to focus, develop support and delivery capacity, test their thinking, see things as opportunities, adapt to changes in the environment, and take appropriate risks. At the same time, change agents need to proceed ethically. Otherwise they risk destroying credibility and the trust others have in them. Relationships can and do recover from strong disagreements, but recovery is less likely if people feel they have been lied to or otherwise ethically abused. A permanent sense of betrayal tends to ensue when you have been dealt with unethically.

Working the plan recognizes the importance of being able to roll with the punches and learn as you go. Chris Argyris warns, "people who rarely experience (and learn from) failure end up not knowing how to deal with it."[36] De Bono echoes this sentiment, saying, "success is an affirmation but not a learning process"[37] Post hoc memories of what led to success (or failure) tend to be selective; valuable learning will be lost if steps aren't taken to actively and objectively reflect on the process as you go. There will be missteps and failures along the way, and a key attribute of a "do it" orientation to working the plan is the capacity to learn and adapt the paths to change along the way.

When working the plan, generating stakeholder and decision-maker confidence in the viability of the initiative is critical. However, it is also important not to be deluded by your own rhetoric. Russo and Shoemaker provide us with guidelines for managing under- and overconfidence; in particular, they differentiate the need for confidence when one is an implementer as opposed to a decision maker. Decision makers need to be realistic; implementers can afford to be somewhat overconfident if it provides others with the courage to change.[38]

Developing a Communication Plan

When implementing a change program, change leaders often find that misinformation and rumors are rampant in their organization. The reasons for change are not clear to employees, and the impact on employees is frequently exaggerated, both positively and negatively. In all organizations, the challenge is to persuade employees to move in a common direction. Good communication programs are essential to minimize the effects of rumors, to mobilize support for the change, and to sustain enthusiasm and commitment.[39] In a study on the effectiveness of communications in organizations, Goodman found that only 27% of employees felt that management was in touch with employees' concerns, regardless of the fact that the company had a carefully crafted communications strategy.[40]

RUMORS AND REALITY IN ORGANIZATION CHANGE

In an inbound call center of an insurance firm, employees became convinced that the real purpose of an organizational change initiative was to get rid of staff. Management made public announcement and assurances that the reorganization was designed to align processes and improve service levels, not reduce headcount. However, staff turnover escalated to more than 20% before leaders convinced employees that the rumors were false.

Often, much of the confusion over change can be attributed to the different levels of understanding held by different parties. Change agents and senior management may have been considering the change issues for months and have developed a shared understanding of the need for change and what must happen. However, frontline staff and middle managers may not have been focused on the matter. Even if they have been considering these issues, their vantage points will be quite different from those leading the change.

Communication plans need to be developed for four major reasons: (1) to infuse the need for change throughout the organization; (2) to enable individuals to understand the impact that the change will have on them; (3) to communicate any structural and job changes that will influence how things are done; and (4) to keep people informed about progress along the way. As the change unfolds, the focus of the communication plan shifts.

Timing and Focus of Communications

A communication plan has four phases: (a) prechange approval, (b) creating the need for change, (c) midstream change and milestone communication, and (d) confirming/celebrating the change success. The messages and methods of communication will vary depending upon which phase your change is in. Table 9.8 outlines the communication needs of each phase.

Table 9.8 Communication Needs for Different Phases in the Change Process

Preapproval Phase	Developing the Need for Change Phase	Midstream Change Phase	Confirming the Change Phase
Communication plans to sell top management	Communication plans to explain the need for change, provide a rationale, reassure employees, and clarify the steps in the change process	Communication plans to inform people of progress and to obtain feedback on attitudes and issues, to challenge any misconceptions, and to clarify new organizational roles, structures, and systems	Communication plans to inform employees of the success, to celebrate the change, and to prepare the organization for the next change

This chart is based on Klein, S. N. (1996). A management communications strategy for change. *Journal of Organizational Change*, 9(2), 32–46.

In the prechange phase, change agents need to convince top management and others that the change is needed. They will target individuals with the influence and/or authority to approve a needed change. Dutton and her colleagues suggest that packaging the change proposal into smaller change steps helps success. She found that timing was crucial in that persistence, opportunism, and involvement of others at the right time were positively related to the successful selling of projects. Finally, linking the change to the organization's goals, plans, and priorities was critical.[41]

When creating awareness of the need for change, communication programs need to explain the issues and provide a clear, compelling rationale for the change. If a strong and credible sense of urgency and enthusiasm for the initiative isn't conveyed, the initiative will not move forward. There are simply too many other priorities available to capture people's attention.[42] Increasing awareness of the need for change can also be aided by the communication of comparative data. For example, concrete benchmark data that demonstrate how competitors are moving ahead can shake up complacent perspectives. Spector demonstrates how sharing of competitive information can overcome potential conflicting views between senior management and other employees.[43] The vision for the change needs to be articulated and the specific steps of the plan that will be undertaken need to be clarified. People need to be reassured that they will be treated fairly and with respect.[44]

As the change unfolds, people will want to have specific information communicated to them about future plans and how things will operate. If the organization is being reorganized, employees will want to understand how this reorganization will affect their jobs. If new systems are being put into place, training needs to happen in order to help employees understand and use the systems properly. If reporting relationships are altered, employees need to know who will do what in the organization. Thus, intentional strategies are needed to communicate this information.

In the middle phases of change, people need to understand the progress made in the change program. Management needs to obtain feedback regarding the acceptance of the changes and the attitudes of employees. Change leaders need to understand any misconceptions that are developing and have the means to combat such misconceptions. During this phase, extensive communications on the content of the change will be important as management and employees begin to understand new roles, structures, and systems.[45] As the newness of the initiative wears off, sustaining interest and enthusiasm and remaining sensitive to the personal impact of the change continue to be important. Change leaders need to remain excited about the change and communicate that enthusiasm often. Recognizing and celebrating progress, achievements, and milestones all help in this regard.[46]

Rumors, gossip, and horror stories will compete with the messages from the change leaders, and their frequency rises when the change leader's credibility declines or ambiguity increases. Employees tend to believe friends more than they do supervisors and tend to turn to supervisors before relying on the comments of senior executives and outsiders. Change agents have a choice: They can communicate clear, timely, and candid messages about the nature and impact of the change or they can let the rumors fill the void. An effective communications campaign can reduce the number of rumors by lowering uncertainty, lessening ambivalence and resistance to change, and increasing the involvement and commitment of employees.[47]

Change websites, electronic bulletin boards, online surveys to sample awareness and opinions, and change blogs can all play useful roles in the communications strategy. However, when uncertainty rises on things of importance, don't forget the power of face-to-face communications. Positive reactions tend to increase and negative reactions are lessened when people have an opportunity to hear from those in authority and ask them questions about the change and its impact.[48]

The final phase of a change program needs to communicate and celebrate the success of the program. Celebration is an undervalued activity. As noted earlier, celebrations are needed along the way to mark progress, reinforce commitment, and reduce stress, and they are certainly warranted at the conclusion. The final phase also marks the point at which the change experience as a whole needs to be discussed (more will be said about this in the next section on transition management) and unfinished tasks identified. The organization needs to be positioned for the next change. Change is not over—only this particular program or phase is.

While change agents attend to the different phases in the change process, they need to match the communications challenge with the communications channel selected.[49] Channel richness ranges from standard reports and general information e-mails at one end through to personalized letters and e-mails, telephone conversations, video conferencing, and face-to-face communications at the other end. When the information is routine, memos and blanket e-mails can work well. However, when things become more complex, ambiguous, and personally relevant to the recipient, the richness of the communication channel needs to increase. A change agent can follow up with a document that provides detailed information, but face-to-face approaches are valuable when matters are emotionally loaded for stakeholders or when you want to get the recipients' attention.

Goodman and Truss suggest using line managers and opinion leaders as lynchpins in the communications strategy, but this requires that they be properly briefed and engaged in the change process. They also stress that change agents need to recognize communication as a two-way strategy.[50] That is, the gathering of information might be as important as delivering the message.

Key Principles in Communicating for Change

Klein suggests six principles that should underlie a communications strategy:

1. Message and media redundancy are key for message retention. That is, multiple messages using multiple media will increase the chance of people obtaining and retaining the message. Too often, management believes that since the message was sent, their work is done. It is the employee's fault for not getting the message! As one author pointed out, it takes time for people to hear, understand, and believe a message, especially when they don't like what they hear.[51] Some change agents believe that it takes 15 to 20 repetitions before a message gets communicated effectively.

2. Face-to-face communication is most effective. While the impact of face-to-face is highest, the cost is also higher. Face-to-face permits two-way communication, which increases the chance of involvement of both parties and decreases the probability of miscommunication.

3. Line authority is effective in communications. Regardless of the level of participative involvement, most employees look to their management for direction and guidance. If the CEO says it, the message packs a punch and gets attention.

4. The immediate supervisor is key. The level of trust and understanding between an employee and his or her supervisor can make the supervisor a valuable part of a communications strategy. People expect to hear important organizational messages from their bosses.

5. Opinion leaders need to be identified and used. These individuals can be critical in persuading employees to a particular view.

6. Employees pick up and retain personally relevant information more easily than other types of information. Thus, communication plans should take care to relate general information in terms that resonate with employees.[52]

The importance of communications in helping recipients deal with change was discussed in Chapter 7. Creating a sense of fairness, trust, and confidence in the leadership and interest and enthusiasm for the initiative is important to the success of change initiatives. Well-executed communications strategies play an important role here.[53] However, change leaders seldom give enough attention to this topic. They intuitively understand the importance of the timely communication of candid, credible change-related information through multiple channels, but they get busy with other matters. As communication shortcomings escalate, so too do downstream implementation difficulties.[54]

Influence Strategies

Influencing others is a key concern for change leaders when working the plan. It involves consideration of how they can bring various stakeholders on-side with the change. The sooner this is addressed, the better. When implementing change, there is a tendency to give insufficient attention to the constructive steps needed to foster employee support and alleviate dysfunctional resistance.

Kotter and Schlesinger outline six general change strategies for influencing individuals and groups in the organization.[55] These are:

1. **Education and communication**: This strategy involves using education and communication to help others develop an understanding of the change initiative, what is required of them, and why it is important. Often people need to see the need for and the logic of the change. Change leaders may fail to adequately communicate their message through the organization because they are under significant time pressure and the rationale "is so obvious" to them they don't understand why others don't get it.

2. **Participation and involvement**: Getting others involved can bring new energy and ideas and cause people to believe they can be part of the change. This strategy works best when the change agent has time and needs voluntary compliance and active support to bring about the change. Participation fits with many of the norms of today's flattened organizations, but some managers often feel that it just slows everything down, compromising what needs to be done quickly.

3. **Facilitation and support**: Here change agents provide access to guidance and other forms of support to aid in adaptation to change. This strategy works best when the issues are related to anxiety and fear of change, or where there are concerns over insufficient access to needed resources.

4. **Negotiation and agreement**: At times, change leaders can make explicit deals with individuals and groups affected by the change. This strategy can help deal with contexts where the resistance is organized, "what's in it for me" is unclear, and power is at play. The problem with this strategy is that it may lead to compliance rather than wholehearted support of the change.

5. **Manipulation and co-optation**: While managers don't like to admit to applying this tactic, covert attempts to influence others are very common. Engaging those who are neutral or opposed to the change in discussions and engaging in ingratiating behavior will sometimes alter perspectives and cause resistors to change their position on the change. However, trust levels will drop and resistance will increase if people believe they are being manipulated in ways not consistent with their best interests.

6. **Explicit and implicit coercion**: With this strategy, as with the previous one, there is a negative image associated with it. Nevertheless, managers often have the legitimate right and responsibility to insist that changes be done. This strategy tends to be used when time is of the essence, compliant actions are not forthcoming, and change agents believe other options have been exhausted. Change leaders need to recognize the potential for residual negative feelings and consider how to manage these.

In addition to the six strategies noted above, open systems analysis points to a seventh change strategy—**systemic or system adjustments**. At times, adjustments can be made to formal systems and processes that reduce resistance while advancing the desired changes. For example, if employee resistance has coalesced in a group of employees who are employed in a particular function, organizational restructuring or the reassignment of group members to other areas may reduce resistance markedly. However, if it is mishandled, it can mobilize and escalate resistance in others.

SYSTEM ADJUSTMENTS AT WAL-MART

Wal-Mart has used systemic adjustments over the years as a change tool to assist in maintaining managerial discretion in employment practices by retaining their nonunion status. In 2005, 200 employees at the store in Jonquiere, Quebec, Canada, were attempting to negotiate the first-ever union contract with the firm. However, after 9 days of meetings, over 3 months, Wal-Mart announced it was closing the store because of concerns over its profitability. In 2008, the same approach was adopted when six employees in Gatineau, Quebec, won the right to unionize their small operation within Wal-Mart. The only other time a unionization drive had been close to succeeding was in 2000. Eleven meat cutters in their Jacksonville, Texas, store voted to join the UFCW. Wal-Mart responded by eliminating the meat cutting job companywide.[56]

Toolkit Exercise 9.2 asks you to examine the methods you've seen used to influence reactions to change.

Another way to think about influence strategies is to consider whether they attempt to push people in the desired direction or pull them. **Push tactics** attempt to move people toward acceptance of change through rational persuasion (the use of facts and logic in a nonemotional way) and/or pressure (the use of guilt or threats). The risk with the use of push tactics is that they can lead to resistance and defensiveness. Recipients may oppose the pressure simply because it is pressure and they feel a need to defend their positions.

Alternatively, change leaders can rely on **pull tactics**: inspirational appeals and consultation. Inspirational appeals can arouse enthusiasm based on shared values or ideals. *Consultation* (as it is used here) refers to when you seek the participation of others through appeals to the individuals' self-worth and positive self-concept. Both these approaches are designed to pull individuals in the desired direction.*

Falbe and Yukl examined the effectiveness of nine different influence tactics. The **most effective** strategies were two pull tactics: (1) inspirational appeals and (2) consultation (seeking the participation of others).

The strategies of **intermediate effectiveness** were a combination of push and pull strategies: (3) rationale persuasion (facts, data, logic), (4) ingratiation (praise, flattery, friendliness), (5) personal appeals (friendship and loyalty), and (6) exchange tactics (negotiation and other forms of reciprocity).

The three strategies that were **least effective** were push strategies: (7) direct pressure, (8) legitimating tactics (framing of the request as consistent with policy and/or the influencer's authority), and (9) coalition building (creation of subgroups or linkages with other groups to exert pressure).[57]

Nutt categorizes four influence tactics used during implementation: (1) intervention, (2) participation, (3) persuasion, and (4) edict. **Intervention** is where key executives justify the need for change and provide new norms to judge performance. **Participation** involves engaging stakeholders in the change process. **Persuasion** is the use of experts to sell a change. And **edict** is the issuing of directives. Table 9.9 summarizes Nutt's data on the frequency of use, initial and ultimate adoption rate, and the time to install for each of these tactics.

This table demonstrates the value of a well-respected sponsor who acts as a lightning rod and energizes and justifies the need for change. The frequency of the use of participation as a strategy is somewhat higher than intervention and may reflect the challenge of managing change from the middle of the organization. Adoption takes longer, but it has the second best success rate. Persuasion is attempted more frequently than the other three tactics, but its success rate is significantly lower than participation and the time to adoption slightly longer. Finally, it is difficult to understand the frequency of use of edict as a tactic, given its poor adoption rate and length of time to install.

Toolkit Exercise 9.3 asks you to continue the assessment of influence tactics that you began in Toolkit Exercise 9.2 and reflect on their use in change situations.

This section has outlined a variety of influence tactics that can be used to build awareness, reduce ambivalence and resistance, and move people to acceptance and

Table 9.9 Implementation Tactics and Success[58]

Tactic	Percentage Use	Initial Adoption Rate	Ultimate Adoption Rate	Time to Adopt (Months)
Intervention	16%	100%	82%	11.2
Participation	20	80.6	71	19
Persuasion	35	65	49	20.0
Edict	29	51	35	21.5

---

*These styles are described more fully in Chapter 8.

adoption of the initiative. In general, it is wise to move as slowly as is practical. This permits people to become accustomed to the idea of the change, adopt the change program, learn new skills, and see the positive sides. It also permits change leaders to adjust their processes, refine the change, improve congruence, and learn as they go. However, if time is of the essence or if going slowly means that resisters will be able to organize in ways that will make change highly unlikely, then change leaders should plan carefully, move quickly, and overwhelm resistance where possible. Just remember, though, that it is far easier to get into a war than it is to build a lasting peace after the fighting ends. Don't let your impatience and commitment to moving the change forward get the better of your judgment concerning how best to proceed.

Transition Management

Change management is about keeping the plane flying while you rebuild it.[59]

When dealing with an ongoing operation, you typically don't have the luxury to put everything on hold while making a major change happen. You can't say "sorry, we aren't able to deliver the product we promised because we are making improvements." Most organizations have many change projects underway simultaneously. One part of the organization may be re-engineering itself. Another might be introducing a quality program while another part focuses on employee empowerment. All of these must be managed concurrently while continuing to produce products and services.

Morris and Raben argue for a transition manager (a change agent in the language of this book) who has transition resources, structures, and plans.[60] The transition manager has the power and authority to facilitate the transition and is linked to the CEO or other senior executive. Transition resources are the people, money, training, and consulting expertise needed to be successful. Transition structures are structures outside the regular organizational ones—temporary structures that allow normal activities to take place as well as change activities. The transition plan is the change plan with clear benchmarks, standards, and responsibilities for the change. Table 9.10 outlines a checklist for transition management.

Transition management is making certain that both the change project and the continuing operations are successful. The change leader and the team in charge of the transition are responsible for making sure that both occur. The change leader is visibly involved in articulating both the need for change and the new vision, while others involved in implementing the change manage the organization's structural and system changes and the individuals' emotional and behavioral issues so that neither is compromised to a danger point.[61] Ackerman described the application of a transition management model at Sun Petroleum.[62] She addressed the question, "How can these changes be put into place without seriously straining the organization?" Her solution was to create a transition manager who handled the social

Table 9.10 A Checklist for Change: Transition Management

The following questions can be useful when planning transition management systems and structures.

1. How will the organization continue to operate as it shifts from one state to the next?

2. Who will answer questions about the proposed change? What decision power will this person or team have? Will they provide information only or will they be able to make decisions (such as individual pay levels after the change)?

3. Do the people in charge of the transition have the appropriate amount of authority to make decisions necessary to ease the change?

4. Have people developed ways to reduce the anxiety created by the change and increase the positive excitement over it?

5. Have people worked on developing a problem-solving climate around the change process?

6. Have people thought through the need to communicate the change? Who needs to be seen individually? Which groups need to be seen together? What formal announcement should be made?

7. Have the people handling the transition thought about how they will capture learning throughout the change process and share it?

8. Have they thought about how they will measure and celebrate progress along the way and how they will bring about closure to the project at its end and capture the learning so it is not lost (after-action review)?

system requirements. Ackerman also argued for the use of a transition team to create a transition structure that would enable the organization to carry on operating effectively while the major changes take place.

Beckhard and Harris focus on the transition details in organizational change.[63] They reinforce the importance of specifying midpoint goals and milestones, which help motivate the members of the organization. The longer the span of time required for a change initiative, the more important these midcourse goals become. The goals need to be far enough away to provide direction but close enough to provide a sense of progress and accomplishment and an opportunity for midcourse changes in plans.

A second component of transition management is keeping people informed and reducing anxiety. During major reorganizations, many employees are assigned to new roles, new bosses, new departments, or new tasks. Those individuals have a right to know their new work terms and conditions. Transition managers will put systems in place to ensure that answers to questions (such as "Will my pay be affected?," "Who is my new boss?," or "What is my new job description?") can be provided in a timely manner. An example of this need occurred in the Ontario (Canada) Ministry of Agriculture, Food and Rural Development. As the designer of a major change in that organization, Bill Allen commented that the Ministry "underestimated the importance of a well thought out transition structure and plan." Employees of the Ministry had hundreds of questions about the organization change and there was no formal structure to handle these in a consistent and professional manner."[64] The transition team needs to be authorized and given the capacity to do this.

The final phase in transition management occurs in and around the same time as the celebrations are occurring in recognition of what has been accomplished. Project completion can be a bittersweet time for participants because they may not be working directly with one another in the future. They've worked hard, developed close friendships, and shared emotional highs and lows along the way. The experience can be extremely influential to their future development, and it needs to be processed and brought to closure in ways that do it justice. One way to approach closure (in addition to the celebration) and maximize the learning for all is to conduct an **after-action review**.[65]

An after-action review involves reviewing the change experience as a whole and learning from what transpired along the way. There needs to be a candid assessment from multiple perspectives of the change process and the strengths and weakness of the various approaches used along the way. It asks: (a) What were the intended results, (b) what were the actual results, (c) why did the actual results happen, and (d) what can be done better, next time? As the participants explore these questions, the approaches, tools, sources of information, and insights that have the potential to improve performance in the future need to be identified, and the knowledge must codified in ways that will allow others to access and learn from it. This knowledge is potentially the most significant legacy that those involved with the change can leave for themselves and others who will follow.

Summary

"Doing it" demands a good plan and a willingness to work that plan. To advance a "do it" orientation, the chapter assesses several generic strategies for approaching the change and planning the work. The chapter examines various action planning tools and considers how to handle the communications challenges that arise during a change initiative. Finally, transition management is considered, because the delivery of services and products typically needs to continue while the "doing it" is underway.

Glossary of Terms

"Do it" orientation—a willingness to engage in organizational analysis, see what needs to be done, and take the initiative to move the change forward

Generic change strategies—Eight generic change strategies were introduced:

1. **Thinking first strategy**—an approach used when the issue is clear, data are reliable, the context is well structured, thoughts can be pinned down, and discipline can be established, as in many production processes

2. **Seeing first strategy**—an approach that works best when many elements have to be combined into creative solutions, commitment to those solutions is key, and communication across boundaries is essential, as in new product development. People need to see the whole before becoming committed.

3. **Doing first strategy**—an approach that works best when the situation is novel and confusing, complicated specifications would get in the way, and a few simple relationship rules can help people move forward. An example would be when a manager is testing an approach and wants feedback about what works.

4. **Programmatic change strategy**—traditional approach to planned change; starts with mission, plans, and objectives; sets out specific implementation steps, responsibilities, and timelines

5. **Discontinuous change strategy**—an approach adopted for a major change that represents a clear break from the previous approach, often involving revolutionary ideas

6. **Emergent change strategy**—change that grows out of incremental change initiatives. It often evolves through the active involvement of internal participants. As it emerges, it can come to challenge existing organizational beliefs about what should be done

7. **Unilateral change strategy**—top-down change. Change requirements are specified and implemented—required behavioral changes are spelled out and it is anticipated that attitude changes will follow once people acclimatize themselves to the change.

8. **Participative change strategy**—bottom-up participation in the change initiative focuses on attitudinal changes that will support the needed behavioral changes required by the organizational change.

Focus of the Change

Techno-structural change—change initiatives focused on the formal structures, systems, and technologies employed by the organization

Behavioral-social change—change initiatives focused on altering established social relationships within the organization

Alternative for Influencing Reactions to Change

1. Six alternatives to reducing negative reactions to change and building support were developed by Kotter and Schlesinger: (1) **education and communication**, (2) **participation and involvement**, (3) **facilitation and**

support, (4) **negotiation and agreement**, (5) **manipulation and coopera-tion**, and (6) **explicit and implicit coercion.**

2. A seventh approach to reducing negative reactions to change was identified—(7) **systematic adjustments**—adjustments made to formal systems and processes that reduce resistance while advancing the desired changes.

3. Push tactics attempt to move people in the desired direction through rational persuasion (e.g., the use of facts and logic) and/or direct or indirect pressure (e.g., guilt, threats). Pull tactics attempt to draw people in the desired direc-tion through arousing interests and enthusiasm through inspirational appeals, consultation and their active participation.

4. Four strategies of influence were identified by Nutt:

   a. **Intervention** involves key executives justifying the need for change and providing new norms to judge performance.
   b. **Participation** involves engaging stakeholders in the change process.
   c. **Persuasion** involves the use of experts to sell a change.
   d. **Edict** is the issuing of directives.

Action Planning Tools

1. **To-do list**—a checklist of things to do

2. **Responsibility charting**—who will do what, when, where, why, and how

3. **Contingency planning**—consideration of what should be done when things do not work as planned on critical issues

4. **Surveys**—involve the use of structures questions to collect information from individuals and groups in a systematic fashion. **Survey feedback** is an orga-nization development technique that involves participants in the review and discussion of survey results. The goal is to actively engage them in the inter-pretation of the findings, the discussion of their implication, and the identi-fication of how best to proceed.

5. **Project planning and critical path methods**—operations research tech-niques for scheduling work. These methods provide deadlines and insight as to which activities cannot be delayed to meet those deadlines.

6. **Force field and stakeholder analysis**—examination of the forces for and against change and the positions of the major players and why they behave as they do

7. **Commitment charts**—an evaluation of the level of commitment of major players (against, neutral, let it happen, help it happen, make it happen)

8. **The adoption continuum or AIDA analysis**—examination of major players and their position on the awareness, interest, desire, and adoption contin-uum related to the proposed changes

9. **Leverage analysis**—determination of methods of influencing major groups or players regarding the proposed changes

Phases in the Communications Process

Four phases in the communications process during change are outlined: (1) **the preapproval phase**, (2) **developing the need for change phase**, (3) **the midstream phase**, and (4) **confirming the change phase.**

Purpose of the communication plan for change—(1) to infuse the need for change throughout the organization, (2) to enable individuals to understand the impact that the change will have on them, (3) to communicate any structural and job changes that will influence how things are done, and (4) to keep people informed about progress along the way

Richness of the communication channel—Different channels vary in the richness of the information they can carry. Standard reports and general-information e-mails represent the lean end of the continuum. Richness increases as one moves to personalized letters and e-mails, telephone conversations, video conferencing, and face-to-face communications (the richest channel).

Transition management—Transition management is the process of ensuring that the organization continues to operate effectively while undergoing change.

After-action review—This is a final phase of the transition-management process. It seeks to bring closure to the experience and engage participants in a process that will allow the learning gained through the change process to be extracted and codified in some manner for future use.

END-OF-CHAPTER EXERCISES

TOOLKIT EXERCISE 9.1

Working Your Plan

Think of a change situation you are attempting to implement or one that you are familiar with. Return to Table 9.1 and consider whether it is a programmatic, discontinuous, or an emergent change.

Then look at the implementation guidelines outlined in the table and begin to build a work plan for the change.

TOOLKIT EXERCISE 9.2

Action Plans for Influencing Reactions to Change

1. What methods have you seen used in organizations to influence people's reactions to a specific change? Think specifically about a change instance and what was done.

   a. Education and communication
   b. Participation and involvement
   c. Facilitation and support
   d. Negotiation and agreement
   e. Manipulation and co-optation
   f. Explicit and implicit coercion
   g. Systemic adjustments

2. What were the consequences of each of the methods used? What worked and what did not work? Why?

3. What personal preferences do you have regarding these techniques? That is, which ones do you have the skills to manage and the personality to match?

TOOLKIT EXERCISE 9.3

Influence Tactics

1. Think specifically of change situations in an organization you are familiar with. What influence tactics did people use?

   a. Inspirational appeals
   b. Consultation (seeking the participation of others)
   c. Relying on the informal system (existing norms and relationships)
   d. Personal appeals (appeals to friendship and loyalty)
   e. Ingratiation
   f. Rational persuasion (use of facts, data, logic)
   g. Exchange or reciprocity
   h. Coalition building (creation of subgroups or links with other groups to exert pressure)
   i. Using organizational rules or legitimating tactics (framing of the request as consistent with policy and/or your authority
   j. Direct pressure
   k. Appeals to higher authority and dealing directly with decision makers

2. How successful were each of the tactics? Why did they work or not work?

3. How comfortable are you with each tactic? Which could you use?

Appendix 9.1

A Comparison of Four Models of Change*			
Beer's Six Steps for Change (1990)	*Kanter et al.'s Ten Commandments for Change (1992)*	*Kotter's Eight-Stage Process for Successful Organizational Transformation (1996)*	*Lueck's Seven Steps for Change (2003)*
Mobilize commitment to change through joint diagnosis of problems.	Analyze the organization and its need for change.	Establish a sense of urgency.	Mobilize energy, commitment through joint identification of business problems and their solutions.
Develop a shared vision of how to organize and manage for competitiveness.	Create a vision and a common direction.	Create a guiding coalition.	Develop a shared vision of how to organize and manage for competitiveness.
Foster consensus for the new vision, competence to enact it, and cohesion to move it along.	Separate from the past.	Develop a vision and strategy.	Identify the leadership.
Spread revitalization to all departments without pushing it from the top.	Create a sense of urgency.	Empower broad-based action.	Focus on results, not activities.
Institutionalize revitalization through formal policies, systems, and structures.	Support a strong leader role.	Communicate the change vision.	Start change at the periphery, then let it spread to other units, pushing it from the top.
Monitor and adjust strategies in response to problems in the revitalization process.	Line up political sponsorship.	Generate short-term wins.	Institutionalize success through formal policies, systems, and structures.

(Continued)

(Continued)			
Beer's Six Steps for Change (1990)	*Kanter et al.'s Ten Commandments for Change (1992)*	*Kotter's Eight-Stage Process for Successful Organizational Transformation (1996)*	*Lueck's Seven Steps for Change (2003)*
	Craft an implementation plan.	Consolidate gains and produce more change.	Monitor and adjust strategies in response to problems in the change process.
	Develop enabling structures.	Anchor new approaches in the culture.	
	Communicate, involve people, and be honest.		
	Reinforce and institutionalize change.		

*This table is based on articles by: Todnem, R. (2005). Organisational change management: A critical review. *Journal of Change Management, 5*(4), 369–381; and Beer, M., Eisenstat, R., & Spector, B. (1990, November–December). Why change programs don't produce change. *Harvard Business Review, 1000,* 158–166.

Appendix 9.2

Rigby's List of the Best Tools for the Job[66]					
	Impact of the Change Tool				
Type of Tool	*Financial Results*	*Customer Equity*	*Performance Capabilities*	*Competitive Positioning*	*Organizational Integration*
Customer Retention		++		+	
Customer Satisfaction Measures		++		++	
Customer Segmenting		++			
Cycle Time Reduction	++		+	+	
Growth Strategies	+		+		
Merger Integration Teams					+
Mission and Vision Statements					++
One-to-One Marketing	++	++	++	++	++
Pay for Performance	+				
Strategic Alliances		+		+	
Strategic Planning		+	++	++	++
Supply Chain Integration	++			++	
Total Quality Management		++			
Virtual Teams					++
+ Significantly above the mean in 1 year ++ Significantly above the mean in every year (over 10 years)					

Management Tool Usage Rate and Satisfaction Level, 2008[67]		
Change Tool	*Usage*	*Satisfaction Level*
Benchmarking	76%*	3.82
Strategic Planning	67%*	4.01*
Mission and Vision Statements	65%*	3.91*
Customer Relationship Management	63%*	3.83
Outsourcing	63%*	3.79
Balanced Scorecard	53%*	3.83
Customer Segmentation	53%*	3.95*
Business Process Reengineering	50%*	3.85
Core Competencies	48%*	3.82
Mergers and Acquisitions	46%*	3.83
Strategic Alliances	44%	3.82
Supply Chain Management	43%	3.81
Scenario and Contingency Planning	42%	3.83
Knowledge Management	41%	3.66**
Shared Service Centers	41%	3.68**
Growth Strategy Tools	38%**	3.87
Total Quality Management	34%**	3.80
Downsizing	34%**	3.59**
Lean Six Sigma	31%**	3.87
Voice of the Customer Innovation	27%**	3.88
Online Communities	26%**	3.69**
Collaborative Innovation	24%**	3.71**
Price Optimization Models	24%**	3.75
Loyalty Management Tools	17%**	3.79
Decision Rights Tools	10%**	3.68

*Significantly above the overall mean

**Significantly below the overall mean (usage = 42%, satisfaction = 3.82)

Source: Rigby, D., "Management Tools and Techniques: A Survey", California Management Review, Vol. 43, No. 2, Winter, 2001.

Notes

1. Mattioli, D., & Maher, K. (2010, March 1). At 3M, innovation comes in tweaks and snips. *Wall Street Journal* (Digital Network). Retrieved May 2010 from http://online.wsj.com/article/SB10001424052748703787304575075590963046162.html.

2. Swanborg, R. (2010, April 30). Social networks in the enterprise: 3M's innovation process. *CIO*. Retrieved May 2010 from http://www.cio.com.au/article/344909/social_networks_enterprise_3m_innovation_process/; From Post-its to Face-bras: How 3M puts innovation into practice. (2010, April 1). *Knowledge@SMU*. Retrieved May 2010 from http://knowledge.smu.edu.sg/article.cfm?articleid=1281.

3. Retrieved May 2010 from www.chips.navy.mil/links/grace_hopper/file2.htm; or www.ideafinder.com/history/inventors/hopper.htm; or www.inventors.about.com/library/inventors/bl_Grace_Hopper.htm.

4. Kouzes, J., & Posner, B. (1995). *The leadership challenge.* San Francisco: Jossey-Bass.

5. Pfeffer, J., & Sutton, R. (1999). Knowing "what" to do is not enough: Turning knowledge into action. *California Management Review, 42*(1), 83–110.

6. O'Hara, S., Murphy, L., & Reeve, S. (2007). Action learning as leverage for strategic transformation: A case study reflection. *Strategic Change, 16*(4), 177–190.

7. Sayles, L. (1993, Spring). Doing things right: A new imperative for middle managers. *Organizational Dynamics*, 10.

8. Kahan, S. (2008, October 13). Personal empowerment in difficult times. *Fast Company*. Retrieved May 2010 from http://www.fastcompany.com/blog/seth-kahan/leading-change/personal-empowerment-difficult-times.

9. Mintzberg, H., & Westley, F. (2001). Decision making: It's not what you think. *Sloan Management Review, 42*, 89–93.

10. Nohria, N. (1993). Executing change: Three generic strategies. *Harvard Business School Press #9–494–039.*

11. Nohria, N., & Khurana, R. (1993). Executing change: Three generic strategies. *Harvard Business School Note 494–039.*

12. Waldersee, R., & Griffiths, A. (2004). Implementing change: Matching implementation methods and change type. *Leadership and Organization Development Journal, 25*(5), 424–434.

13. Beer, M., Eisenstat, R., & Spector, B. (1990, November–December). Why change programs don't produce change. *Harvard Business Review*, 158–166.

14. Retrieved May 2010 from http://www.everyday-taichi.com/confucius-saying.html.

15. Beer, M., Eisenstat, R., & Spector, B. (1990, November–December). Why change programs don't produce change. *Harvard Business Review*, 158–166.

16. Rune, T. (2005). Organisational change management: A critical review. *Journal of Change Management, 5*(4), 375.

17. Source unknown.

18. Welbourne, T. M. (2009). Extreme strategy. *Leader to Leader, 2009*(2), 42–48.

19. Mieszkowski, K. (1998). Change—Barbara Waugh. *Fast Company, 20,* 146.

20. Waldersee, R., & Griffiths, A. (2004). Implementing change: Matching implementation methods and change type. *Leadership and Organization Development Journal, 25*(5), 424–434.

21. This table is modified from Gabarro, J., & Schlesinger, L. (1983). Some preliminary thoughts on action planning and implementation. *Managing Behaviour in Organizations* (pp. 342–343). New York: McGraw-Hill.

22. Refer to Beckhard, R. (1987). *Organizational transitions* (p. 104). Reading, MA: Addison-Wesley for a further discussion on responsibility charting.

23. Retrieved May 2010 from http://www.valuebasedmanagement.net/methods_scenario_planning.html.

24. Noori, H., Munro, H., Deszca, G., & McWilliams, B. (1999). Developing the right breakthrough product/service: An application of the umbrella methodology. Parts A & B. *International Journal of Technology Management, 17,* 544–579.

25. Wylie, I. (2002, July). There is no alternative to… *Fast Company,* 106–110.

26. Cummings, T. G., & Worley, C. G. (2009). *Organization development and change.* Mason, OH: South-Western.

27. Shilling, M. A., & Hill, W. L. (1998). Managing the new product development process: Strategic imperatives. *Academy of Management Executive, 12*(3), 67–81.

28. Beckhard, R., & Harris, R. (1987). *Organizational transitions* (p. 95). Reading, MA: Addison-Wesley.

29. Personal communication with author.

30. Gladwell, M. (2002). *The tipping point.* New York: First Back Bay.

31. Burke, W. (2002). *Organization change: Theory and practice* (pp. 274–280). London: Sage.

32. Moore, G. (1999). *Crossing the chasm.* New York: HarperBusiness.

33. Lui, M. (2008, May 9). Clyburn sees "tipping point" to Obama. *New York Times.* Retrieved May 2010 from http://thecaucus.blogs.nytimes.com/2008/05/09/clyburn-sees-tipping-point-to-obama/; Balz, D. (2008, January 8). Obama's tipping point. *Washington Post.* Retrieved May 2010 from http://voices.washingtonpost.com/44/2008/01/obamas-tipping-point-1.html; Stanton, J. (2009, April 20). The man behind Obama's online election campaign. Web 2.0 Convergence Blogs. Retrieved May 2010 from http://www.digitalcommunitiesblogs.com/web_20_convergence/2009/04/the-man-behind-obamas-online-e.php.

34. Imai, M. (1986). *Kaizen: The key to Japan's competitive success* (p. 239). New York: Random House.

35. Rigby, D. (2001). Management tools and techniques: A survey. *California Management Review, 43*(2); Rigby, D., & Bilodeau, B. (2009). Management tools and trends, 2009. *Bain and Company.* Retrieved May 2010 from http://www.bain.com/management_tools/Management_Tools_and_Trends_2009_Global_Results.pdf.

36. Argyris, C. (1991, May–June). Teaching smart people how to learn. *Harvard Business Review,* 104.

37. De Bono, E. (1984). *Tactics: The art and science of success* (p. 41). Toronto: Little, Brown.

38. Russo, J. E., & Schoemaker, P. J. H. (1992, Winter). Managing overconfidence. *Sloan Management Review,* 7–17.

39. Isern, J., & Pung, C. (2007). Harnessing energy to drive organizational change. *McKinsey Quarterly, 1,* 16–19.

40. Goodman, J., & Truss, C. (2004). The medium and the message: Communicating effectively during a major change initiative. *Journal of Change Management, 4*(3), 234.

41. Dutton, J. et al. (2001). Moves that matter: Issue selling and organizational change. *Academy of Management Journal, 44*(4), 716–736.

42. Kotter, J. P. (1995). Leading change: Why transformation efforts fail. *Harvard Business Review, 73*(2), 59–67.

43. Spector, B. (1989, Summer). From bogged down to fired up: Inspiring organizational change. *Sloan Management Review,* 29–34.

44. Klein, S. (1996). A management communication strategy for change. *Journal of Organizational Change Management, 9*(2), 37.

45. Klein, S. (1996). A management communication strategy for change. *Journal of Organizational Change Management, 9*(2), 37.

46. Welch, J., & Welch, S. (2007). How to really shake things up: Transforming a company requires total commitment and serious stamina. *Business Week, 4061*(84), 84.

47. Goodman, J., & Truss, C. (2004). The medium and the message: Communicating effectively during a major change initiative. *Journal of Change Management, 4*(3), 234; Nelissen, P., & van Selm, M. (2008). Surviving organizational change: How management communication helps balance mixed feelings. *Corporate Communications, 13*(3), 306–318.

48. Daft, D., & Lengel, R. H. (1984). Information richness: A new approach to managerial behavior and organizational design. In B. Staw & R. Cummings, *Research in Organizational Behavior* (Vol. 6, pp. 191–233). Greenwich, CT: JAI Press.

49. Daft, D., & Lengel, R. H. (1984). Information richness: A new approach to managerial behavior and organizational design. In B. Staw & R. Cummings, *Research in organizational behavior* (Vol. 6, pp. 191–233). Greenwich, CT: JAI Press.

50. Goodman, J., & Truss, C. (2004). The medium and the message: Communicating effectively during a major change initiative. *Journal of Change Management, 4*(3), 218.

51. Duck, J. D. (1993, November–December). Managing change: The art of balancing. *Harvard Business Review,* 4.

52. Klein, S. (1996). A management communication strategy for change. *Journal of Organizational Change Management, 9*(2), 34.

53. Peus, C., Frey, D., Gerkhardt, M., Fishcher, P., & Traut-Mattausch, E. (2009). Leading and managing organizational change initiatives. *Management Review, 20*(2), 158–175.

54. Kotter, J. P. (1995). Leading change: Why transformation efforts fail. *Harvard Business Review, 73*(2), 59–67.

55. Kotter, J., & Schlesinger, L. (1982). Choosing strategies for change. *Harvard Business Review, 57*(2), 106–114.

56. Geller, A. (2005, February 10). As union nears win, Wal-Mart closes store. *Associated Press.* Retrieved May 2010 from http://www.commondreams.org/headlines05/0210–13.htm; Wal-Mart shutters Quebec auto shop after union win. (2008, October 16). *Montreal Gazette.* http://www.commondreams.org/headlines05/0210–13.htm   http://www.canada.com/montreal/story.html?id=01e454a4-b613–47d6-b0fa-ead56e06ec1d.

57. Falbe, C., & Yukl, G. (1992). Consequences for managers of using single influence tactics and combinations of tactics. *Academy of Management Journal, 35*(3), 638–652.

58. Nutt, P. (1992). *Managing planned change* (p. 153). Toronto: Maxwell Macmillan Canada.

59. Source unknown.

60. Morris, K. F., & Raben, C. S. (1999). The fundamentals of change management. In D. Nadler et al., *Discontinuous change* (pp. 57–58). San Francisco: Jossey-Bass.

61. Duck, J. D. (1993, November–December). Managing change: The art of balancing. *Harvard Business Review,* 9.

62. Ackerman, L. (1982, Summer). Transition management: An in-depth look at managing complex change. *Organizational Dynamics,* 46–66.

63. Beckhard, R. (1987). *Organizational transitions* (p. 47). Reading, MA: Addison-Wesley.

64. Personal correspondence with W. Allen, Ministry of Agriculture, Food and Rural Affairs, Ontario Government.

65. For information on how to conduct an After-Action Review, see *After-action review technical guidance.* (2006). Washington, DC: U.S Agency for International Development, PN-ADF-360. Electronic version available at http://pdf.usaid.gov/pdf_docs/PNADF360.pdf.

66. Rigby, D. (2001). Management tools and techniques: A survey. *California Management Review, 43*(2), 139–161.

67. Rigby, D., & Bilodeau, B. (2009). Management tools and trends, 2009. *Bain and Company,* 31. Retrieved May 2010 from http://www.bain.com/management_tools/ Management_Tools_and_Trends_2009_Global_Results.pdf.

CHAPTER 10

Measuring Change

Designing Effective Control Systems

What gets measured is what gets done.

CHAPTER OVERVIEW

- Measurement and control processes can play a critical role in guiding change and integrating the initiatives and efforts of various parties.
- Four types of control processes exist: diagnostic/steering controls, belief systems, boundary systems, and interactive controls. Different types of controls are needed as the change project shifts from the planning to implementation phases.
- The use of strategy maps as an alignment tool is explored.
- Three measurement tools are presented: the balanced scorecard, the risk exposure calculator, and the duration, integrity, commitment, and effort (DICE) model.

Measurements matter. What gets measured affects the direction, content, and outcomes achieved by a change initiative. Measurements influence what people pay attention to and what they do.[1] When organizational members see particular quantifications as legitimate, believe their actions will affect the outcomes achieved, and think those actions will positively affect them personally, the motivational impact increases. But when the legitimacy or impact of the measures is questioned or when people believe they can't affect the outcomes, the measurements are seen as interference and can result in cynicism and alienation. Change agents know that measurement is important, but sometimes they need to understand more fully how measures will be used to help frame and guide the change.[2]

Measurement is given little attention for many reasons. The change is complex, requiring multidimensional measurements tools; numbers do not measure what is important; the evolution of change initiatives makes end-point measures difficult to quantify; or end-point measures suggest a line in the sand that is difficult to modify to match changing conditions.[3] In addition, change leaders often explain that they lack time to assess outcomes, that they were too busy making the change happen, and/or that they did not get around to thinking fully about measurement of outcomes.

The reality is that measurement and control systems can clarify expected outcomes and enhance accountability. This leaves some change agents feeling vulnerable. They worry that critics will use the assessment to second-guess an initiative and even undermine both the change and the change agent.

In spite of these concerns, well-thought-out measurement and control processes provide change leaders with valuable tools. Information from these measurement systems enables change managers to: (1) frame the implications of the vision in terms of expected outcomes; (2) monitor the environment; (3) guide the change, gauge progress, and make midcourse corrections; and (4) bring the change to a successful conclusion.[4] Key change leadership skills include identifying assessment measures, building them into the change process, adapting them as needed, and using them as tools to aid in decision making, communication, and action taking.[5] At RE/MAX (described below), the measurement system supported a change to the employment relationship, allowing the firm to attract and retain superior agents.

MEASUREMENT SYSTEMS AT RE/MAX

For RE/MAX, the Denver, Colorado-based real estate franchise network, a redefinition of customers away from industry norms was crucial. Cofounder and chairman David Liniger noted that the firm's success came from the simple idea that RE/MAX customers were the real estate agents themselves, not the buyers and sellers of real estate. More specifically, RE/MAX targeted high-performing agents who represented just 20% of the entire pool of real estate agents but accounted for approximately 80% of all sales.

RE/MAX's focus on high-performing agents originally consisted of changing the industry's traditional 50–50 fee split between broker and agent to a franchise system in which agents kept all commissions after payment of a management fee and expenses. In some cases, that shift changed retention rates of real estate agents as much as 85%. RE/MAX followed the change in the reward system with additional services, including national

> marketing campaigns, training of agents in sales techniques by satellite, and coordinated administrative support.
>
> The results were impressive: According to CEO Liniger, in 2003, the average RE/MAX agent earned $120,000 per year on 24 transactions versus an industry average of $25,000 on seven transactions. "The customer comes second," he says, but hastens to add, "If our emphasis is on having the best employees, we're going to have the best customer service."[6]

At RE/MAX, management's strategic realignment was anchored in a change to the reward system from fee-splitting the sales commission to one based on a franchise model. This example demonstrates that what is measured and rewarded will have a major impact on what outcomes are achieved. Sometimes measures are a matter of personal goal setting, as in the case of an athlete who links training metrics to performance goals and then celebrates small steps that lead to the accomplishment of a major milestone. In other situations, assessment grows out of expectations and/or requirements established by others, such as just-in-time measurement systems imposed on suppliers by automobile firms.

Employees' acceptance or rejection of measurements of a change initiative's outcomes is important. When employees' acceptance of organizational measurements increases, people experience less work stress, more job satisfaction, improved job performance, better work/family balance, less absenteeism, less job burnout, and more organizational commitment.[7] Because RE/MAX's executives structured a win–win strategy for the firm and for agents, agents accepted the firm's measures and, in turn, the firm attracted and retained above-average real estate agents.[8]

This chapter looks at the role of measurement in change management and how assessment influences people's behavior. Issues over the development, use, and impact of measures are examined. The role of measurement and control in risk management is discussed, as is the question of what to measure at different stages in the life cycle of the change. Finally, strategy maps and balanced scorecards are introduced to demonstrate how to address the alignment of action with the change vision and strategy. Throughout this chapter, the goal remains the same: to learn how to use measurement and control mechanisms to increase the prospects for successful change.

Figure 10.1 suggests that measurement and control occur at the end of the change process. In fact, change leaders should analyze these processes to help define the need for change, quantify what is expected from a change initiative, assess progress at specified intervals, and, at the end of the process, demonstrate the change initiative's impact. Measures can help change agents in five ways: clarify expectations; make mid-course corrections; assess the extent to which initiatives are being internalized and institutionalized; assess what has been ultimately achieved; and set the stage for future change initiatives.[9]

Figure 10.1 The Change-Management Process

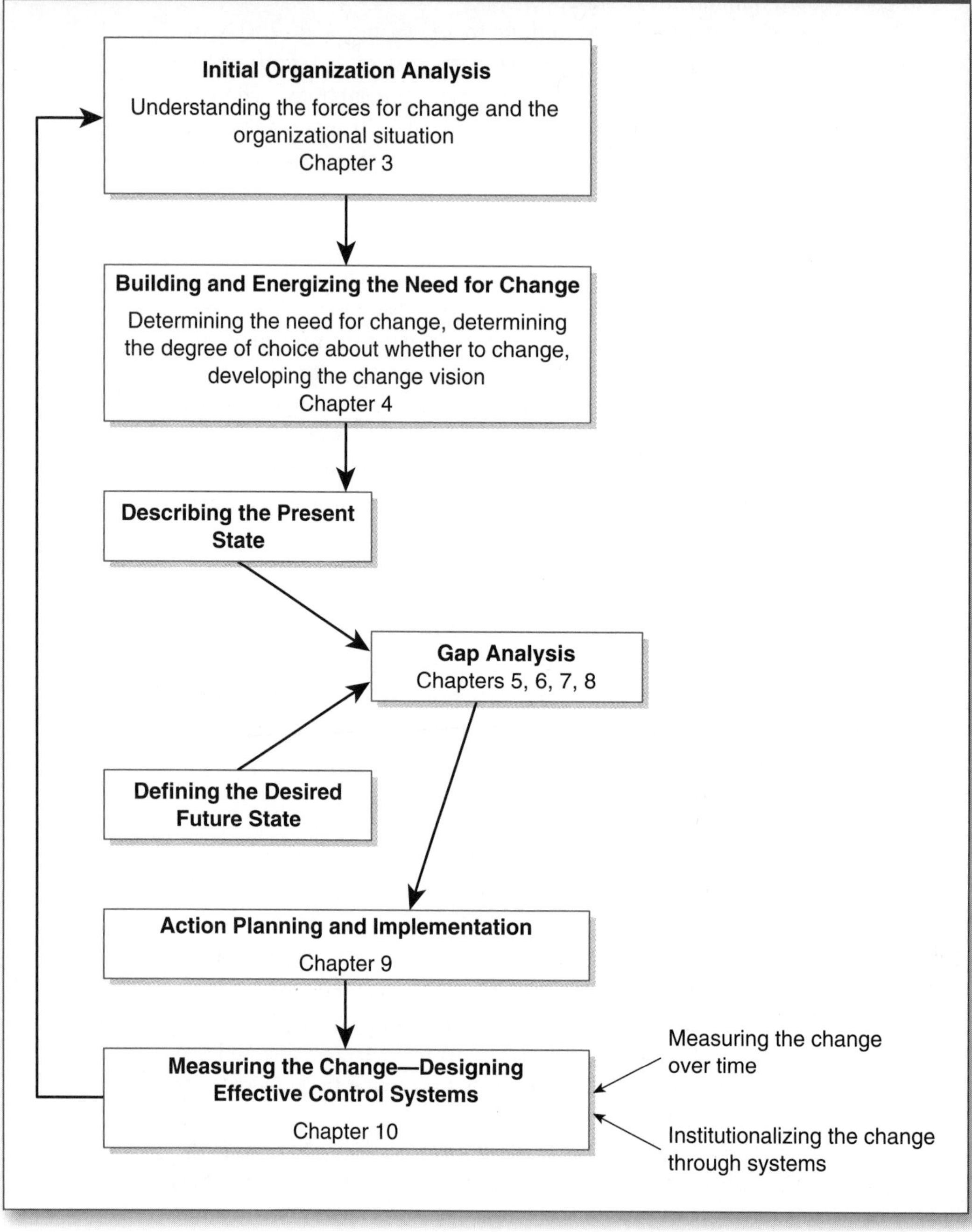

```
┌─────────────────────────────────────┐
│     Initial Organization Analysis     │
│                                       │
│  Understanding the forces for change  │
│        and the organizational         │
│              situation                │
│              Chapter 3                │
└─────────────────────────────────────┘
                  │
                  ▼
┌─────────────────────────────────────┐
│  Building and Energizing the Need     │
│            for Change                 │
│                                       │
│  Determining the need for change,     │
│  determining the degree of choice     │
│  about whether to change,             │
│  developing the change vision         │
│              Chapter 4                │
└─────────────────────────────────────┘
                  │
                  ▼
┌──────────────────────────┐
│  Describing the Present   │
│          State            │
└──────────────────────────┘
                   ╲
                    ▼
              ┌──────────────────────┐
              │     Gap Analysis      │
              │  Chapters 5, 6, 7, 8  │
              └──────────────────────┘
                   ╱            ╲
┌──────────────────────────┐     ╲
│  Defining the Desired     │      ▼
│      Future State         │
└──────────────────────────┘
                          ┌─────────────────────────────────────┐
                          │  Action Planning and Implementation  │
                          │              Chapter 9                │
                          └─────────────────────────────────────┘
                                        │
                                        ▼
┌─────────────────────────────────────┐          Measuring the change
│  Measuring the Change—Designing       │◄─────── over time
│     Effective Control Systems         │
│                                       │          Institutionalizing the change
│              Chapter 10               │◄─────── through systems
└─────────────────────────────────────┘
```

Using Control Processes to Facilitate Change

Many managerial discussions of measurement systems and control processes focus on how they impede progress.[10] Though measurement systems can get in the way, well-designed and -deployed systems have the potential to overcome organizational barriers and contribute to successful change.

The following case example outlines how change agents at Control Production Systems (CPS) approached their deteriorating market position. The example shows how change agents benefited from consultation with key participants[11] and collaboration with diverse groups[12] and how they used measurement and control processes to frame and reinforce the needed changes.

A CASE STUDY IN THE VALUE OF REALIGNING MEASURES

Control Production Systems (CPS)[*], a mid-sized firm that designs, manufactures, sells, and services customized production control systems, had noticed an erosion of its market share to competitors. Declining customer loyalty, greater difficulty selling product and service updates, and an increased reliance on price to win the business were shrinking margins and making competitive life difficult, even though product and service offerings were innovative and of a high quality. The firm possessed a strong, positive culture that reflected the values of innovation, quality, and open communications, but recent setbacks had shaken people's confidence.

As a result of a town hall meeting called to discuss the corporation's situation, the CEO acted on a suggestion to form a cross-functional change team to assess the firm's circumstances and recommend a course of action. The team included sales agents and customer support staff and was led by the director of sales and service. The director reported to the senior management team on a monthly basis, and the team was expected to diagnose and analyze the problem and frame recommendations for change within 2 months, which would be followed by implementation activities. An intranet website facilitated communications about the change, and transparency, candor, and no reprisals were the watchwords for the change team's approach. As well, the team received sufficient resources to allow it to get on with its task.

Prior to the change, sales agents were organized geographically and paid on a salary-plus-commission basis. After a sale, agents handed off responsibility to customer support staff to address order fulfillment and postsales servicing. The customer support staff was rewarded on the basis of cost control and throughput. If customers never contacted the firm for help, that was considered good because no contact generated no cost and suggested customer satisfaction. Short calls were seen as better than long ones due to cost implications, and standardized responses and online help were preferred over trouble-shooting phone calls for the same cost reasons. The firm kept no systematic record of customer calls and responded to customers was on a first-come, first-served basis.

---

[*]Firm's name is disguised.

(Continued)

(Continued)

Analysis by the change team showed that customers who had minimal contact with the customer support staff were less likely to develop a relationship with the firm, were likely deriving less value from their purchases, and were less likely to be aware of product and service innovations and applications that could benefit them. In other words, the activities that kept short-term costs low hurt customer loyalty and long-term profitability. Benchmark data concerning service models, customer satisfaction, and purchase decisions confirmed that CPS was falling behind key competitors.

After the diagnosis, the team concluded that there was a need to change the way the firm dealt with and serviced its major customers. The team determined that the way to increase sales and profitability was to ensure that customers saw CPS as a trusted partner who could find ways to enhance customers' productivity and quality through improvements in CPS's control systems.

The company realigned how it managed its relationships with customers. The firm integrated sales and customer support services, created subteams with portfolios of customer accounts by industry, and assigned the subteams to manage customers as ongoing relationships. The vision was a customer-focused partnership in which one-stop shopping, customer intimacy, service excellence, and solution finding would frame the relationship rather than simply selling and servicing in the traditional manner.

During the change, the change team measured employees' understanding and commitment to the new service model, employees' skill acquisition, and results of pilot projects. Further, the team measured service failures in areas of delivery, response time, quality, and relationship management to identify and deal with problems quickly if they occurred during the transition period. The team searched for systemic problems, developed remedies, encouraged openness and experimentation, and avoided finger pointing. Milestones for the change were established and small victories along the transition path were identified, monitored, and celebrated.

Once the team initiated the changes, it aligned performance measures by focusing on customers' satisfaction with the breadth and depth of services, response time, customers' referrals, repeat sales, and margins. The reward system shifted from a commission base for sales personnel and salary plus small bonus for customer service staff to a salary-plus-team-based performance incentive that included customers' satisfaction and retention, share of the customers' business in their product and service area, and customers' profitability over time. In the 3 years since implementation, there have been significant improvements in all the targeted measures, and feedback from customer service has become an important influencer of product refinement and development.

The case above demonstrates how measurements can support a change initiative at each stage of the process. At the beginning, change leaders used measurements in problem identification, in root cause analysis, and in the development of awareness for a new vision and structure. The leaders recognized the misalignment between measures that reinforced cost reductions in servicing clients (first-order effects) and the desired but unrealized long-term outcome of customer loyalty and profitability (second-order or lag effects). As the change leaders and team continued to diagnose their organization's structure and systems, at each step data were collected, analyzed, and used to fine tune plans. Employees came to trust using data to make savvy decisions. In the end, clients' satisfaction with CPS's products and services (first-order effects) gave rise to customer loyalty and follow-up purchases and profitability (second-order effects) that management had not previously measured or achieved.

To make the question of the impact of measures and control processes all the more real, consider a change you are familiar with and complete **Toolkit Exercise 10.1**.

Selecting and Deploying Measures

There is no shortage of possible measurement indicators: cycle time, machine efficiency, waste, sales per call, employee satisfaction, waiting time, market share, profitability per sale, cost of sale, and customer retention, to name a few. If change agents try to measure everything concurrently, they are likely to lose focus. To focus attention, agents need to be clear about the stage of the change process and what dimensions are important to monitor at a particular stage given the desired end results. Here is a list of criteria to help change leaders determine which measures to adopt.

Focus on Key Factors

An accurate analysis of the change challenges will mean that change leaders will know which factors are key and what levers will move people in the direction of the desired change. Measures influence what people pay attention to and how they act, even when they believe those actions are ill advised.[13] Consider the all-too-common practice of trade loading, the inefficient and expensive practice of pushing excess inventory onto distributors and retailers in order to make the manufacturer's numbers look better in the short term.[14] For years, staff at Gillette knew that the practice of trade loading was having a negative effect on pricing, production efficiencies, customer relationships, and profitability. Trade loading meant unsold inventory was hidden from Gillette's eyes in the distribution channels and price discounting was eroding margins (distributors quickly learned how to time purchases to take advantage of such discounts). In spite of the widespread awareness that this practice was ill advised, it continued until new leadership realigned key measures and practices to support the desired changes and finally brought an end to an unhealthy practice.[15]

Knowing the critical measures to develop, deploy, and monitor at the different stages of the change process is a complex issue. In the Gillette case, this involved measures that demonstrated the negative consequences of trade loading, showed the positive consequences of the change vision, and assessed performance in ways that aligned with the change vision and targeted outcomes.

Use Measures That Lead to Challenging but Achievable Goals

Employees need to believe that they can achieve challenging goals. Measurements that note small steps to the larger goal and measures within an individual's control will tap into desired motivations.

Use Measures and Controls That Are Perceived as Fair and Appropriate

Employees' perception of the appropriateness and fairness of the measures and control processes is driven as much by the process used to develop and legitimize them as by the outcomes they deliver.[16] Even reasonable measures may not be acceptable if people feel the measures were forced on them. Good processes will reduce resistance through communication, as communication provides opportunities for input and feedback while building trust and support. Avoid applying measures in ways that punish people who take reasonable actions based on their understanding of the change goals and what is expected of them.

Measurement and control processes are more likely to be accepted if the process used in developing them is seen as reasonable and fair, even if those measures lead to negative outcomes for those being measured. (This matter of fair process was discussed earlier and in more detail in Chapter 7.) It is very beneficial if individuals who are responsible for delivering on measures see them as relevant.

Avoid Sending Mixed Signals

Measurement systems related to change often send conflicting signals, and it is not unusual for change leaders to say one thing but signal another through what they measure and reward. For example, an organization may initiate changes aimed at enhancing quality and customer satisfaction but then "wink at" the shipment of flawed products to meet just-in-time delivery metrics and avoid exceeding its internal scrap and rework targets. Managers do this even though they know that substandard products will increase warranty work, require customers to do rework, and put the firm's reputation with the customer at risk. The fundamental problem in this example is that measures are not aligned with goals.

Aligning measurements and avoiding mixed signals is tricky because there are always tradeoffs. For example, employees' acceptance of a particular step (as measured by survey results) and the achievement of a particular performance milestone (e.g., going "live" with a new customer service module) may end up conflicting. Change leaders need to address this matter by providing advice on how these tradeoffs should be handled. If this isn't done, change initiatives will flounder.

The Canadian division of a U.S. auto parts firm initiated a quality program and reinforced it with a gigantic display board preaching "Quality is important because General Motors demands it!" However, next to this sign sat pallets of completed parts with supervisory tags that approved shipment, overriding quality control inspection reports that had ordered rework prior to shipment. The firm's management had not addressed how to resolve conflicts between the quality initiative and their just-in-time obligations. Supervisors looked at how they were measured and concluded that delivery trumped quality. Employees looked at how their supervisors reversed decisions on substandard quality and concluded the new quality program was a joke and a waste of money. The inability to reconcile the handling of the quality problems with their delivery obligations led to the loss of the GM contract and the closure of the plant approximately 18 months after the display board was first unveiled.[17]

Employees are very aware of such conflicting messages. Confusion, frustration, sarcasm, and eventually alienation are the natural consequences. When such inconsistencies are built into a change initiative and go undetected or unaddressed by the change leader, cynicism about the change and its supporters increases, and the change process falters. Kerr's well-known paper, "On the Folly of Rewarding A, While Hoping for B" explores many of the issues around measurement and the production of unintended consequences.[18]

Ensure Accurate Data

Employees, customers, and others are likely to supply accurate and timely data when they trust the measurement system and believe that data will not be used to harm them. Excessive rewards for success, undue sanctions for missed targets, or a very stressful work environment can lead to flawed information from carefully designed sets of measures.[19] These pressures create incentives for individuals to report inaccurately or to shade the reality of the situation. To ensure accurate and timely data from the measurement system, those supplying the data need to trust who it is going to and believe that it is their responsibility to comply fully and honestly. Keep pressure at reasonable levels and avoid excessive rewards for success or excessive consequences for not achieving targets.

Match the Precision of the Measure
With the Ability to Measure

A measurement motto might read, "Better to be approximately right than precisely wrong!" Change leaders need to match the measures to the environment. If the change is significant, clearly structured, and predictable, leaders can devote time and resources to developing precise, sophisticated measures. However, if the change environment is turbulent and ambiguous, approximate measures are more appropriate.[20] Change agents need to make their choices based upon (a) how quickly they need the information; (b) how accurate the information needs to be; and (c) how much it will cost. Information economics point to the fact that designing the needed information for a change initiative inevitably involves trade-offs among these three components.[21]

The general rule of thumb is to keep the measures as simple and understandable as possible, and make sure that they attend to the important elements of the change in a balanced way. Table 10.1 looks at the nature of the change context and considers what types of measures will be appropriate.

Regardless of the measures chosen, change leaders need to be seen as "walking the talk." When leaders treat the measures as relevant and appropriate,

Table 10.1 The Change Context and the Choice of Measures

Change Context	Choose More Precise, Explicit, Goal-Focused Measures	Choose More Approximate Measures, Focus on Vision and Milestones, and Learn as You Go
When complexity and ambiguity are:	Low	High
When time to completion is:	Short	Long

employees will see that they are serious about what they are espousing. Use sound communication practices when dealing with questions related to what to measure, who to engage in discussions about measurement and control, how to deploy the measures, and how to interpret and use the data effectively to manage the change. Change leaders' behaviors that reinforce perceptions of the fairness and appropriateness of the measures and instill confidence in their proper application are very important in legitimizing measurement as a powerful tool in the change process.[22]

Control Systems and Change Management

Robert Simon, an expert in the area of management control systems, believes that managers focus too much on traditional diagnostic control systems developed from management accounting. He argues that managers need to think about four types of control levers as constituting the internal control systems.[23]

- **Diagnostic/steering controls**—the traditional managerial control systems that focus on key performance variables. For example, sales data based on changed selling efforts.
- **Belief systems**—the fundamental values and beliefs of organizational employees that underpin the culture and influence organizational decisions. For example, the stated organization values that often accompany the vision and mission.
- **Boundary systems**—the systems that set the limits of authority and action and determine acceptable and unacceptable behavior. For example, limits to spending authority placed on managerial levels. These focus on what is unacceptable and identify both what is prohibited and what is sanctioned.
- **Interactive controls**—the systems that sense environmental changes crucial to the organization's strategic concerns. For example, market intelligence data that helps firms better understand and anticipate competitor actions.

Each of these systems can help in promoting the change. A well-developed **diagnostic control system** means that change agents will understand critical performance variables and can modify systems to encourage new, desired behaviors while discouraging dysfunctional ones. An understanding of the **belief system** allows the change leader to appeal to higher-order values of individuals and the core values of the organization and helps to motivate behavior and overcome resistance to change. Understanding the **boundary system** means that change leaders know their limits and the risks and actions to be avoided. If they choose, change leaders can test those boundaries explicitly to push in new directions. Finally, change leaders will need to be sensitized to environmental shifts and strategic uncertainties and the impact of these on the change project by the **interactive control system**. This will allow them to modify change plans in the face of environmental factors (see Figure 10.2).

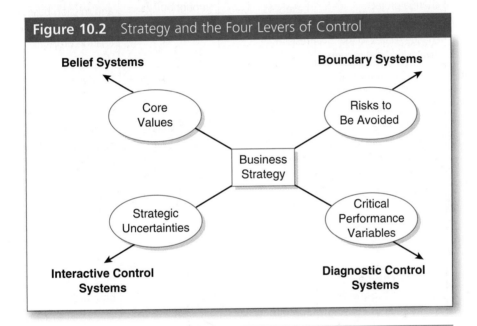

Figure 10.2   Strategy and the Four Levers of Control

Source: Simons, R., "Control in the Age of Empowerment," **Harvard Business Review**, March-April 1995, p. 85.

Table 10.2 sets out the different elements of the control system and relates them to the measures used at different stages of the change process. As the change progresses from initial planning to wrap-up and review, the control challenges and measurement issues also shift. The key is to align the controls and measures to the challenges posed at each stage of the change and prepare for the next. This helps to ensure that change leaders have the information and guidance they need to assess matters, make decisions, and manage their way forward.

Controls During Design and Early Stages of the Change Project

At the commencement of a major change, mission and vision (i.e., belief systems), interactive control systems (e.g., environmental assessment), and boundary systems play particularly important roles in clarifying overall direction as options and

Table 10.2 Control Systems, Measures, and the Stage of the Change

	Controls When Designing and Planning the Change	Controls in Beginning Stages of the Change Project	Controls in Middle Stages of the Change Project	Controls Toward the End of the Change Project
Belief System (What are our beliefs and values? What is our purpose?)	Assess congruence between core values of the firm, its mission, and the purpose of the change project. Communicate how the change relates to the core values and mission.	Congruence assessment. Appeal to fundamental beliefs to overcome resistance.	Congruence assessment. Reaffirm core values throughout the change project.	Congruence assessment. Reassess and potentially reaffirm the core values and mission based on learning during the change project.
Diagnostic and Steering Controls (Focusing resources on targets; measuring progress; taking corrective action and learning as we go)	Assess the impact of existing controls on the change project. Consider what diagnostic systems will have to be developed and/or altered under the change.	Develop milestones, diagnostic measures, and steering controls. Develop tactics to alter control systems as needed.	Evaluate progress against milestones. Assess whether systems and processes are working as they should. Modify milestones and measures as needed.	Determine when the project has been completed. Confirm that new systems, processes, and behaviors established by the change are working appropriately. Evaluate project and pursue learning on how to improve the change process.
Boundary System (What behaviors are *not* OK?)	Limit the change options to those within the boundary conditions. Test the limits of what is acceptable.	Go/no go guidance as to appropriateness of actions.	Go/no go guidance as to appropriateness of actions. Reassess risks. Re-establish boundaries if needed. Test new boundaries where appropriate.	Re-evaluate the boundary limits.
Interactive Controls (Environmental scanning; assessing possible paths and targets)	Assess opportunities and threats; consider possibilities. Test the viability of existing vision, mission, and strategy given the environmental situation.	Affirm that the change project is aligned with environmental trends. Assess how to use environmental trends to increase the chances of change success.	Ongoing monitoring. Confirm that environmental assessment continues to support the change.	Obtain feedback regarding the success of change initiative relative to the environmental factors. Ongoing environmental scanning and assessment of organizational strengths, weaknesses, opportunities, and threats (SWOT).

potential courses of action are explored. Data from secondary research, exploratory discussions, preliminary organizational assessments, and initial experimentation are helpful at this stage because they allow projects and alternatives to be considered in a grounded manner. The organization's readiness for change (discussed in Chapter 4) can be assessed and steps taken to enhance readiness. Information from multiple sources is used to sort out options, assess what should be done next, and make an initial "go/no go" decision on whether to proceed in the development of the initiative.

In the early stages, change leaders need to have systems that will identify who to talk to and who will tell them what they need to hear, not what they want to hear. Enthusiasm and commitment on the part of change leaders are beneficial to the change but can create serious blind spots if not tempered by the reality checks that control systems can provide. As go/no go decisions are made, change agents need to develop and refine the directional and steering control measures and specify important milestones. Project planning tools, such as the critical path method, can play a useful role (see Chapter 9).

Controls in the Middle of the Change Project

Indicators that define the overall purpose, direction, and boundary conditions (what actions are acceptable and unacceptable) for the change are still important in clarifying what change is intended. However, diagnostic and steering controls (e.g., budgets and variance reports, project and activity schedules, and tracking of content from e-mails and phone conversations) play an increasingly important role in the middle of the change project. At this point, change leaders want quick feedback on progress. Change leaders need to recognize whether the information produced leads or lags the desired outcomes. As in the example of CPS discussed earlier in this chapter, customer satisfaction was a lead indicator of an improved sales climate, while repeat sales and profitability were lag indicators of the improved situation. If this had not been recognized, initiatives undertaken to improve customer satisfaction may have been discontinued because there was no immediate improvement in sales.

Milestones and road markers need to be developed through project planning and goal- and objective-setting activities. These markers can then be used to track progress and reinforce the initiative of others by recognizing their achievement. For example, if a firm were implementing a new performance management system, the completion and signoff on the design of the system, the completion of a training schedule, the achievement of needed levels of understanding and acceptance of the system (as assessed by measures of comprehension and satisfaction with the system), and the completion of the first cycle of performance reviews (with system evaluation data from those using the system) are possible road markers.

At important milestones, go/no go controls once again enter the picture, with conscious decisions made about refinements to the change initiative. Change leaders need to make decisions about the appropriateness and desirability of proceeding to the next stage. If milestones are not being achieved, change leaders need to consider what sorts of actions, if any, should be undertaken or they may need to revisit the timeline or refine the measures used to track progress. In that respect, change leaders also need to consider how measures can help them think about contingencies and adapt to unforeseen situations.

Controls Toward the End of the Change Project

As the end of a planned change approaches, diagnostic and steering measures are replaced by concrete outcome measures. What was accomplished and what has been the impact? How do the results compare with what change agents expected at the beginning? What can be learned from the change experience? Change leaders need to capture the observations and insights from those who have been involved in the change, as it will help them prepare for future initiatives.

Toolkit Exercise 10.2 asks you to apply Simon's control systems model to a change initiative.

Other Measurement Tools

Four tools that can assist in planning, deploying, and managing change are discussed in the next section. These are the strategy map, the balanced scorecard, the risk exposure calculator, and the DICE model. They can enhance internal consistency and alignment and aid in assessing risk.

Strategy Maps

Once change leaders have framed their vision and strategy for the change, they can develop a visual representation of the end state and the action paths that will get them there. The tool was developed by Robert Kaplan and David Norton and is called a strategy map.[24] As can be seen from Figure 10.3, financial outcomes are driven by customer results. These customer results come from corporate strategies and tactics, which in turn rest on the organization's resources (human, informational, and capital).[25]

Once the change vision and strategy are defined, Kaplan and Norton recommend starting with financial goals and objectives and then setting out the objectives, initiatives, and paths needed to generate those outcomes.

- If the vision for change is achieved, how will it look from the perspective of the financial results achieved?
- To accomplish these financial outcomes, what initiatives have to be undertaken from a customer perspective to deliver on the value proposition in ways that generate the desired financial results?
- To accomplish these customer outcomes and/or contributions directly to the financial outcomes through efficiencies, what changes must be tackled from an internal business process perspective?
- Finally, to attain the internal process goals and objectives, what must be undertaken from a learning and growth perspective to increase the organization's capacity to do what is needed with the internal processes and customers?

The learning and growth perspective embodies people, information, and organizational capital (e.g., culture, intellectual property, leadership, internal alignment, and teamwork).*

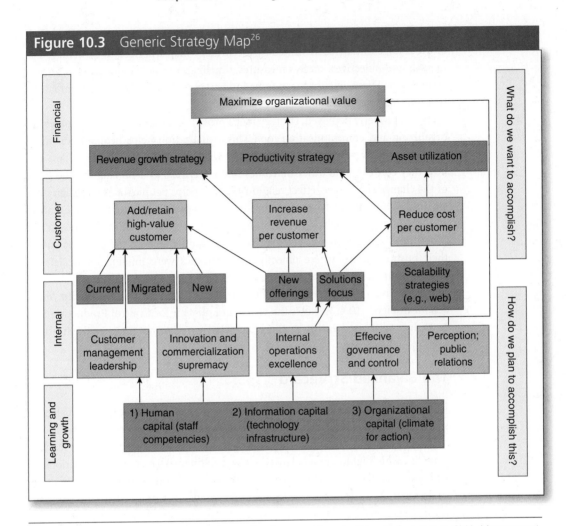

Figure 10.3 Generic Strategy Map[26]

Source: From Armitage, H.M. & C. Scholey, "Using Strategy Maps to Drive Performance," CMA Management, Vol. 80, #9, 2007, pg. 24.

The assumption underlying strategy maps is that financial outcomes are the end goals that for-profit organizations are striving for and that other objectives within the change program should be aligned to produce and support those desired outcomes. If particular activities and the objectives don't support the changes, they

---

*For not-for-profit organizations, many recommend placing the customer perspective (relabeled by some as the stakeholder perspective) at the top, since this is the reason for the organization's existence. Some place the financial perspective parallel with the customer or stakeholder perspective, while others place it below learning and growth or elsewhere. Others have added levels or change labels on the strategy map. However, the goal remains the same—develop a coherent picture that aligns your change strategy with the organization's purpose so it generates the desired outcomes. It is all about translating the change vision into action, communicating with key constituents, integrating and aligning the specific action plans, implementing, and learning and refining as you go.

should be seriously questioned and either dropped or reduced in importance. Each of the change initiatives identified by the strategy map will need to be managed as to goals and objectives, success measures, timelines, resource requirements, and an action plan. These, in turn, need to be integrated with the other change initiatives that are embodied in the strategy map.

When properly deployed, strategy maps provide change leaders with a powerful organizing and communication tool. This visualization helps people understand what is being proposed and why. It clarifies why certain actions are important and how they contribute to other outcomes that are critical to achieving the end goals of the change (i.e., cause–effect relationships). It helps people focus and align their efforts and appropriately measure and report progress. It can assist change leaders to identify gaps in their logic, including missing objectives and measures. When Mobil used strategy maps, it helped them to identify gaps in the plans of one of their business units, where objectives and metrics were missing for dealers—a critical component for a strategy map focused on selling more gasoline.[27]

To give you a concrete example of how a strategy map can be used to help, one is set out in Figure 10.4. It shows the vision and mission for Control Production Systems, Inc. (discussed earlier in this chapter). Then it shows the specific measures used in each category.

The Balanced Scorecard

If the strategy map links capabilities, change strategies, and outcomes, the balanced scorecard integrates measures into a relatively simple way of tracking the critical success factors. Kaplan and Norton argue that four categories of goals and measures need to be highlighted in a balanced scorecard: financial, a company's relationship with its customers, its key internal processes, and its learning and growth. In doing so, management can achieve a balanced, integrated, and aligned perspective concerning what needs to be done to produce the desired strategic outcomes.[28]

Figure 10.4 Strategy Map for Control Production Systems

Mission for CPS:

Design, manufacture, service, and support industry-leading production control systems that enable CPS to enhance the efficiency and effectiveness of its production processes beyond what is possible through other means. Customer loyalty and long-term profitability are built on a foundation of excellence in these areas.

Vision for the Change in Customer Orientation:

Our valued industrial partners will experience service and performance that delight. We will exceed all our competitors' standards through superbly designed and expertly installed and supported control equipment and software.

We will support our customers through technically competent account representatives who are focused on the challenges and needs of specific industries and customers and committed to ensuring that their success is significantly enhanced through the value derived from the production control systems. Our product leadership combined with superb customer care and excellent technical support will result in highly loyal and committed customers who look to CPS for all their more sophisticated control system needs.

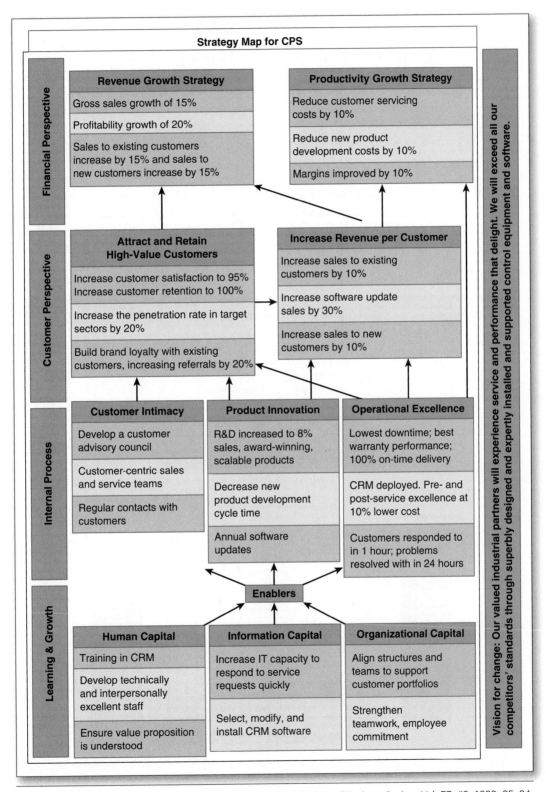

Strategy Map for CPS

Financial Perspective

Revenue Growth Strategy
- Gross sales growth of 15%
- Profitability growth of 20%
- Sales to existing customers increase by 15% and sales to new customers increase by 15%

Productivity Growth Strategy
- Reduce customer servicing costs by 10%
- Reduce new product development costs by 10%
- Margins improved by 10%

Customer Perspective

Attract and Retain High-Value Customers
- Increase customer satisfaction to 95% Increase customer retention to 100%
- Increase the penetration rate in target sectors by 20%
- Build brand loyalty with existing customers, increasing referrals by 20%

Increase Revenue per Customer
- Increase sales to existing customers by 10%
- Increase software update sales by 30%
- Increase sales to new customers by 10%

Internal Process

Customer Intimacy
- Develop a customer advisory council
- Customer-centric sales and service teams
- Regular contacts with customers

Product Innovation
- R&D increased to 8% sales, award-winning, scalable products
- Decrease new product development cycle time
- Annual software updates

Operational Excellence
- Lowest downtime; best warranty performance; 100% on-time delivery
- CRM deployed. Pre- and post-service excellence at 10% lower cost
- Customers responded to in 1 hour; problems resolved with in 24 hours

Learning & Growth

Enablers

Human Capital
- Training in CRM
- Develop technically and interpersonally excellent staff
- Ensure value proposition is understood

Information Capital
- Increase IT capacity to respond to service requests quickly
- Select, modify, and install CRM software

Organizational Capital
- Align structures and teams to support customer portfolios
- Strengthen teamwork, employee commitment

Vision for change: Our valued industrial partners will experience service and performance that delight. We will exceed all our competitors' standards through superbly designed and expertly installed and supported control equipment and software.

Source: Adapted from: Simon, t. " How Risky is Your Company?", Harvard Business Review, Vol. 77, #3, 1999, 85–94.

Among these indicators, some will lead while others will lag. For example, improvements in service levels such as the response time to a customer's inquiry could be lead indicators of improvements in customer satisfaction. However, this may not immediately translate into new sales and increased profitability. Improvements in such measures will often be lag indicators of improvements in service levels because of the nature of the purchase cycle involved. The balanced scorecard recognizes that not all effects are immediate. By setting out assumptions concerning what leads to what, it makes it easier for the change leader to test assumptions, track progress, and make appropriate alternations as necessary.

When developing a balanced scorecard for a change initiative, remember that the relevant customers may be employees in other departments of the organization. Kaplan and Norton argue that the likelihood that multiple measures will mislead change leaders at the same time and in the same direction is much less than if they rely on a single indicator. Figure 10.5 outlines a generic balanced scorecard for a change project. Figure 10.6 outlines the scorecard for Control Production Systems.

Figure 10.5   Generic Balanced Scorecard for Change

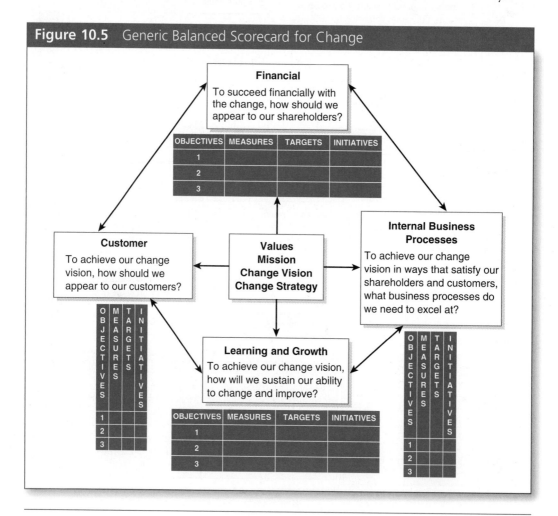

Source: Adapted from: Kaplan, R.S. & D.P. Norton, "Using the Balanced Scorecard as a Strategic Management System," Harvard Business Review, Vol. 74, #1,1996, pg. 76.

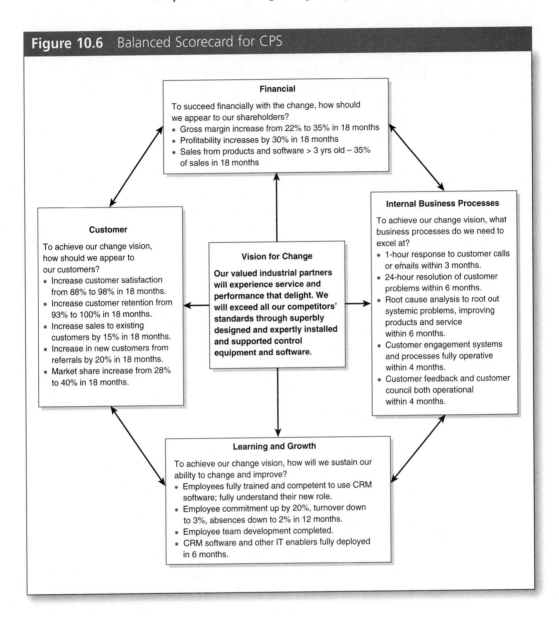

Figure 10.6   Balanced Scorecard for CPS

Financial

To succeed financially with the change, how should we appear to our shareholders?
- Gross margin increase from 22% to 35% in 18 months
- Profitability increases by 30% in 18 months
- Sales from products and software > 3 yrs old – 35% of sales in 18 months

Customer

To achieve our change vision, how should we appear to our customers?
- Increase customer satisfaction from 88% to 98% in 18 months.
- Increase customer retention from 93% to 100% in 18 months.
- Increase sales to existing customers by 15% in 18 months.
- Increase in new customers from referrals by 20% in 18 months.
- Market share increase from 28% to 40% in 18 months.

Vision for Change

Our valued industrial partners will experience service and performance that delight. We will exceed all our competitors' standards through superbly designed and expertly installed and supported control equipment and software.

Internal Business Processes

To achieve our change vision, what business processes do we need to excel at?
- 1-hour response to customer calls or emails within 3 months.
- 24-hour resolution of customer problems within 6 months.
- Root cause analysis to root out systemic problems, improving products and service within 6 months.
- Customer engagement systems and processes fully operative within 4 months.
- Customer feedback and customer council both operational within 4 months.

Learning and Growth

To achieve our change vision, how will we sustain our ability to change and improve?
- Employees fully trained and competent to use CRM software; fully understand their new role.
- Employee commitment up by 20%, turnover down to 3%, absences down to 2% in 12 months.
- Employee team development completed.
- CRM software and other IT enablers fully deployed in 6 months.

Toolkit Exercise 10.3 asks you to construct a strategy map and balanced scorecard for an organization that you know. Remember that customers can be internal or external to the firm.

Risk Exposure Calculator

Robert Simon has developed a risk exposure calculator for use in assessing the level of risk associated with a company's actions.[29] Simon argues that risk is related to the rate of growth of the company, its culture, and how information is managed. The tool focuses primarily on internal rather than external environmental risks. Though it was designed for use on the overall organization, it has been modified to assess the risk exposure related to a particular change initiative as well as maintaining the status quo.

The first three risk drivers are grouped under **Change Pressure**. When the change leader is (a) under significant pressure to produce, (b) there is a great deal of ambiguity, or (c) employees are inexperienced in change, then the risks associated with the change initiative will be higher than if those three conditions were less present.

Change Culture identifies the second set of risk drivers. If (a) the culture pushes risk taking, (b) executives resist hearing bad news, or (c) there is internal competition, then risks will be further elevated.

The final set of risk drivers is grouped under **Information Management**. When (a) the change situation is complex and fast changing, (b) there are gaps in diagnostic change measures, and (c) decision making regarding change is decentralized, then risks will rise once again. These risk factors are cumulative in nature. The overall level of change risk rises as the total number of significant risk factors rises.

If Simon's risk calculator had been applied to Enron or Lehman Brothers by those knowledgeable about their internal operations, scores indicating extreme risk would have been recorded. The environment at both organizations was complex, fast moving, and highly ambiguous. Many senior managers lacked knowledge and experience with the high-risk products and services they were responsible for, risk taking and competition were pushed to the extreme, and the bearers of concern and bad news put themselves at risk of being fired.

There are also dangers for the organization when risk levels get too low. Little positive change will occur if there is no pressure for change, little cultural support for risk taking, and very stable and predictable information. With lower risk, the capacity of the organization to be flexible and adapt will atrophy over time. When they are then faced with change that can no longer be ignored, their ability to respond will be compromised.

There is no optimal risk score that fits all organizations. These vary, depending on the nature of the environment, the upside and downside consequences of risk taking (and the probabilities associated with these), and the ability to take steps to alleviate risks. The risk appetites of change leaders should prudently reflect the needs and opportunities for innovation and change balanced by the needs for appropriate levels of caution and oversight. Of course, the organization's resources and capabilities will also determine the degree of risk that is sustainable.

Change leaders can take advantage of the risk calculator by using the information from it to make the risks manageable during the planning and deployment stages. For example, ambiguity can be reduced by emphasizing the change vision or by creating explicit milestones. Risks related to inexperience can be moderated by adding experienced managers to the change team. Further, it can be used to monitor risk levels as the change proceeds, with steps taken along the way to moderate levels up or down, depending on the situation.

Toolkit Exercise 10.4 sets out a risk calculator based on Simon's work and allows you to calculate a risk score indicating whether the project is in a safety zone or not.

The DICE Model

A process-oriented approach to assessing and managing the risks associated with change projects is offered by Sirkin, Keenan, and Jackson. Based upon empirical data, they have developed a four-factor model for predicting the success of a change initiative. They refer to this as the DICE framework.[30]

Duration asks about how frequently the change project is formally reviewed. If the frequency of formal review is less than every 2 months, it receives a score of 1. A score of 2 is awarded when the frequency is from 2 to 4 months; a 3 for a frequency of between 4 and 8 months; and a 4 for time intervals in excess of 8 months. The message is that the risk of failure increases as the time between formal reviews rises.

Integrity asks about the team leader's skills and credibility and the skills, motivation, and focus of members of the change team. A score of 1 is recorded if: the team leader has the skills needed and the respect of coworkers, if the team members have the skills and motivation to complete the project on time, and if at least 50% of the team members' time has been assigned to the initiative. If the change team and leader are lacking on all dimensions, a score of 4 is recorded. If the factors lie somewhere in between, scores of 2 or 3 are allocated.

Commitment is a two-stage measure. The first part assesses the commitment of senior management. If the words and deeds of senior managers regularly reinforce the need for change and the importance of the initiative, a score of 1 is given. If senior managers are fairly neutral, scores of 2 or 3 are recorded. When senior managers are perceived to be less than supportive, a score of 4 is applied.

Secondly, the employee or "local level" commitment is evaluated. If employees are very supportive, a score of 1 is given. If they are willing but not overly eager, the score shifts to 2. As reluctance builds, scores shift to 3 and 4.

Effort is the final factor in the DICE model and refers to the level of increased effort that employees must make to implement the change. If the incremental effort is less than 10%, it is given a score of 1. Incremental effort of 10% to 20% raises the score to 2. At 20% to 40%, the score moves to 3, while additional effort in excess of 40% raises the score to 4.

The overall DICE score is calculated in the following fashion: The Integrity and Senior Management Commitment scores are weighted more heavily in the model, with each being multiplied by 2. This is because the scores on these factors have been found to be more significant drivers of risk. Then the scores of all factors are added together.

> Overall Dice Score = Duration + (2 × Integrity of Performance) + (2 × Senior Management Commitment) + Local Level Commitment + Effort
>
> The research shows the following about scores:
>
> 7–14: high likelihood of success
>
> 15–17: worry zone
>
> 17+: extremely risky, woe zone, with higher than 19 very unlikely to succeed

This model is useful in assessing risk and also in pointing to concrete things that can be done to make the risks manageable during the planning and deployment phases. For example, risks can be reduced by having frequent formal project reviews and by the staffing of change initiatives with competent and credible team leaders and members. Likewise, increasing local and senior-level commitment and allocating sufficient time to change leaders will also help in reducing risks.

Toolkit Exercise 10.5 asks you to apply the DICE model to a change you are familiar with.

Summary

Care taken in the selection of measures and control processes helps focus energy and effort. It also saves change managers a great deal of time later on because it enhances the efficiency and effectiveness of the change process, provides an early warning system of problems, and thus leads to faster attention to needed areas and appropriate midcourse corrections. It also forces change leaders to be honest with themselves and others about what will be accomplished and what it will take to bring these things to reality. There is an old management adage that makes a lot of sense—it is far better to underpromise and overdeliver than to overpromise and underdeliver.

The careful selection and use of metrics can be used to enhance ownership of the change through how the measures are selected (i.e., who participates in their selection) and through ensuring that those involved receive the credit for what is accomplished.

Glossary of Terms

Control and measurement systems—the measures and control processes developed to focus, monitor, and manage what is going on in the organization

Control Systems

Diagnostic/steering controls—the traditional managerial control systems that focus on key performance variables, for example, sales data responding to changed selling efforts

Belief systems—the structure of fundamental values that underpin organizational decisions, for example, the stated organization values that often accompany the vision and mission

Boundary systems—the systems that set the limits of authority and action and determine acceptable and unacceptable behavior, for example, limits to spending authority placed on managerial levels. These tend to focus on what is unacceptable and identify not only what is prohibited but also the sanction.

Interactive controls—the systems that sense environmental changes crucial to the organization's strategic concerns, for example, market intelligence that will determine competitor actions

Strategy map—the visualization of how the vision and strategy can be systematically brought to fruition. Strategy Maps begin by defining the vision and strategy for change. They then turn to the **financial perspective** and identify the financial outcomes that the change will give rise to and define the paths that will produce those outcomes. To achieve the financial objectives, what objectives have to be accomplished from the **customer perspective**? To achieve these customer objectives and financial efficiency objectives, what must be accomplished from an **internal business process perspective**? Finally, to accomplish the internal process objectives, what must occur from the **learning and growth perspective**? The assumption underlying strategy maps is that financial outcomes are the end points the organization is focused on and that other objectives support and lead to financial outcomes.

Balanced scorecard—an integrated set of measures built around the mission, vision, and strategy. Measures address the financial perspective, customer perspective, internal business process perspective, and learning and growth perspective. As such, they provide a balanced perspective on what is required to enact the strategy.

Simon's risk calculator—an assessment tool that considers the impact that specific factors may have on the risk levels faced by the firm:

Change pressure—When change leaders feel significant pressures to produce and accomplish the change, when there are high levels of ambiguity and the leaders have little experience with change, risk is increased.

Change culture—When the rewards for risk taking are high, when senior executives resist hearing bad news, and when there is internal competition between units, risk is increased.

Information management—When the situation is complex and fast changing, when gaps in diagnosis exist, and if decision making is decentralized, risk is increased.

DICE method of assessing risk—a process-oriented approach to assessing and managing the risks associated with change projects:

Duration measures how frequently the change project is formally reviewed. As duration increases, risk increases.

Integrity of performance is a two-part measure. The first part asks about the team leader's skills and credibility and the second part asks about the skills, motivation, and focus of members of the change team. As skills, credibility, and motivation decrease, risk levels increase.

Commitment is a two-stage measure. The first part assesses senior management commitment. The second part evaluates employee or "local level" commitment. As commitment decreases, risk levels increase.

Effort measures the level of increased exertion that employees must make to implement the change. As the amount of incremental effort increases beyond 10%, risk levels increase.

END-OF-CHAPTER EXERCISES

TOOLKIT EXERCISE 10.1

Reflecting on the Impact of Measures and Control Processes on Change

Think of a change initiative that you are familiar with.

1. What measures and control processes were employed in tracking and guiding the change initiative? Were they consistent with the vision and strategy of the change? Were they viewed as legitimate by those who would be using them?

2. How was the measurement information captured and fed back to those who needed to use it? Was it a user-friendly process and did the information arrive in a useful and timely form?

3. Did the change managers consider how the measures might need to evolve over the life of the change initiative? How was this evolution managed? By whom?

4. Were steps taken to ensure that the measures used during the change would be put to proper use? Were there risks and potential consequences arising from their use that would need to be managed?

5. Were goals and milestones established to plot progress along the way and used to make midcourse corrections if needed? Were the smaller victories celebrated to reinforce the efforts of others when milestones were achieved?

6. What were the end-state measures that were developed for the change? Were they consistent with the vision and strategy? Were they viewed as legitimate by those who would be using them?

7. How was the end-state measurement information captured and fed back to those who would need to use it? Was it a user-friendly process?

8. Were steps taken to ensure that the measures would be put to proper use? Were there risks and potential consequences arising from their use that would need to be managed?

TOOLKIT EXERCISE 10.2

Application of Simon's Control Systems Model

Consider a change you are familiar with.

1. Describe the control processes and measures that were used with the change (i.e., the belief, interactive, boundary, and diagnostic controls). When and how were they used and what was their impact?

   a. During the earlier stages of the change initiative
   b. During the middle stages of the change initiative
   c. During the latter stages of the change initiative

2. Were there forbidden topics in the organization, such as questions related to strategy or core values? Were those limits appropriate and did anyone test those limits by raising controversial questions or concerns? Were small successes celebrated along the way?

3. What changes could have been made with the control processes and measures that would have assisted in advancing the interests of the change?

TOOLKIT EXERCISE 10.3

Aligning the Change With Systems
and Building the Balanced Scorecard for the Change

Think about a change you are familiar with.

1. State the mission, vision, and strategy for the change.

2. Consider the mission, vision, and strategy of the organization:

   • Is the proposed change consistent with these?
   • If not, what needs to be done with the change or the existing mission, vision, and strategy to bring them into line?

3. Financial component of scorecard: If you succeed with the change vision, how will it appear to the shareholders or those responsible for funding the change? How will you know (objectives and metrics)? Are some of these leading indicators while others are lagging indicators?

4. Customer component of scorecard: If you succeed with the change, how will it appear to your customers? How will you know (objectives and metrics)? Are there leading and lagging indicators here?

5. Internal business processes component of scorecard: If you succeed with the change, how will it appear in your business processes? How will you know (objectives and metrics)? Are there leading and lagging indicators here?

6. Learning and growth component of scorecard: If you succeed with the change, how will it appear to your employees and demonstrate itself in their actions? What about the information and organizational capital? How will you and they know (objectives and metrics)? Are there leading and lagging indicators here?

7. Lay out the scorecard you've designed for your change and seek feedback from a classmate.

8. Can you show how the different components are connected to each other by developing a strategy map for the change?

TOOLKIT EXERCISE 10.4

Using the Risk Exposure Calculator

Consider a change initiative that you know is currently being considered for adoption and apply the risk exposure calculator to it.

				Score
Change Pressure	Pressure to produce Low High 1 2 3 4 5 Score:	Level of ambiguity Low High 1 2 3 4 5 Score:	Experience with change High* Low 1 2 3 4 5 Score: *Note: High and Low anchors are reversed for this item.	Out of 15 ___
Change Culture	Degree to which individuals are rewarded for risk taking Low High 1 2 3 4 5 Score:	Degree to which executives resist hearing bad news Low High 1 2 3 4 5 Score:	Level of internal competition Low High 1 2 3 4 5 Score:	Out of 15 ___
Information Situation	Degree to which situation is complex and fast changing Low High 1 2 3 4 5 Score:	Level of gaps that exist in diagnostic measures Low High 1 2 3 4 5 Score:	Degree to which change decision making is decentralized Low High 1 2 3 4 5 Score:	Out of 15 ___
				Total Score =

Using scoring criteria consistent with that developed by Simon:

- If your score is between 9 and 20, you are in the safety zone.
- Between 21 and 34, you are in the cautionary zone.
- Between 35 to 45, you are in a danger zone.

1. Does the organization have an appropriate level of risk taking given the nature of the business it is in? Does it play it too safe, about right, or does it take excessive risks?

2. Does the approach help you in thinking about risk and what factors may be contributing to the overall risk levels?

3. Do the findings help you to think about what can be done to make the levels of risk more manageable?

Source: Adapted from: Simon, R. (1999). How risky is your company? *Harvard Business Review,* 77(3), 85–94.

TOOLKIT EXERCISE 10.5

Applying the DICE Model

Consider a change initiative that you know is currently being considered for adoption and apply the DICE model to it.

- **Duration:** How frequently is the project formally reviewed?

    a) Time between project reviews is less than 2 months—1 point
    b) Time between project reviews is 2–4 months—2 points
    c) Time between project reviews is 4–8 months—3 points
    d) Time between project reviews is more than 8 months—4 points

- Duration Score = _____

- **Integrity:** How capable is the project team leader? How capable and motivated are team members? Do they have the sufficient time to devote to the change?

    a. Leader is respected, team is capable and motivated, and members have sufficient time to commit to the project—1 point
    b. If leader or team is lacking on all these dimensions—4 points
    c. If leader and team are partially lacking on these dimensions—2 to 3 points

- Integrity of Performance Score: (Your Initial Score × 2) = _____

- **Commitment of Senior Management:** How committed is senior management to the project? Do they regularly communicate the reasons for the initiative and its importance? Do they convincingly communicate the message and their commitment? Is the commitment to the project shared by senior management? Have they committed sufficient resources to the project?

    a. If senior management clearly and consistently communicated the need for change and their support—1 point
    b. If senior management appears neutral—2 to 3 points
    c. If senior management is reluctant to support the change—4 points

- Senior Management Commitment Score: (Your Initial Score × 2) = _____

- **Local Level Commitment:** Do those employees most affected by the change understand the need and believe the change is needed? Are they enthusiastic and eager to get involved or concerned and resistant?

    a. If employees are eager to be engaged in the change initiative—1 point
    b. If they are willing but not overly keen—2 points
    c. If they are moderately to strongly reluctant to be engaged in the change—3 to 4 points

- Local level Commitment Score = _____

- **Effort:** What incremental effort is required of employees to implement the change? Will it be added on to an already heavy workload? Have employees expressed strong resistance to additional demands on them in the past?
  a. If incremental effort is less than 10%–1 point
  b. If incremental effort is 10% to 20%–2 points
  c. If incremental effort is 20% to 40%–3 points
  d. If incremental effort is greater than 40%–4 points

- Effort Score = _____

To calculate your overall DICE score: Add the scores from the above:___

1. What score did the change project receive? Was it in the low-risk category (7 to 14), the worry zone (between 14 and 17), or the high-risk area (over 17)?

2. Do the findings help you to think about important sources of risk to the success of the project?

3. Do the findings help you to think about what can be done to make the levels of risk more manageable?

Source: Adapted from Sirkin, H. L., Keenan, P., & Jackson, A. The hard side of change management. *Harvard Business Review, 91*(9), 108–118.

Notes

1. Fred, E. (2004). Transition in the workplace. *Journal of Management Development, 23*(10), 962–964.

2. Ford, M. W., & Greer, B. M. (2005). The relationship between management control system usage and planner change achievement: An exploratory study. *Journal of Change Management, 5*(1), 29–46.

3. Ford, M. W., & Greer, B. M. (2005). The relationship between management control system usage and planner change achievement: An exploratory study. *Journal of Change Management, 5*(1), 29–46; Schreyogg, G., & Steinmann, H. (1987). Strategic control: A new perspective. *Academy of Management Review, 12*(1), 91–103; Preble, J. F. (1992). Towards a comprehensive system of strategic control. *Journal of Management Studies, 29*(4), 391–409.

4. Kotter, J. P., & Schlesinger, L. A. (2008). Choosing strategies for change. *Harvard Business Review, 86*(7–8), 130–139; Lorange, P. M., Morton, S., & Goshal, S. (1986). *Strategic control.* St. Paul, MN: West; Simons, R. (1995). Control in the age of empowerment. *Harvard Business Review, 73*(2), 80–88.

5. Kennerley, M., Neely, A., & Adams, C. (2003). Survival of the fittest: Measuring performance in a changing business environment. *Measuring Business Excellence, 7*(4), 37–43.

6. Brant, J. R. (2003). Dare to be different. *Chief Executive, 188,* 36.

7. Szamosi, L. T., & Duxbury, L. (2002). Development of a measure to assess organizational change. *Journal of Organizational Change Management, 15*(2), 184–201.

8. Harkins, P., & Hollihan, K. (2004). *Everybody wins: The story and lessons behind RE/MAX.* New York: Wiley.

9. Miller, D. (2002). Successful change leaders: What makes them? What do they do that is different? *Journal of Change Management, 2*(4), 356–368.

10. Grasso, L. P. (2006). Barriers to lean accounting. *Cost Management, 20*(2), 6–19.

11. Weber, P. S., & Weber, J. E. (2001). Changes in employee perceptions during organizational change. *Leadership and Organizational Development Journal, 22*(5/6), 291–300.

12. Nauta, A., & Sanders, K. (2001). Causes and consequences of perceived goal differences between departments within manufacturing organizations. *Journal of Occupational and Organizational Psychology, 74*(Pt. 3), 321–342; Cooke, J. A. (2003). Want real collaboration? Change your measures. *Logistics Management, 42*(1), 37–41.

13. Denton, D. K. (2002). Learning how to keep score. *Industrial Management, 44*(2), 28–33; Anonymous. (2002). Materials management benchmarks easy to find, but often measure wrong things. *Hospital Materials Management, 27*(3), 3–4.

14. Sellers, P. (1992). The dumbest marketing ploy. *Fortune, 126*(7), 88–92.

15. Kanter, R. M. (2003). Leadership and the psychology of turnarounds. *Harvard Business Review, 81*(6), 58–67.

16. Kim, W. C., & Mauborgne, R. (2003). Fair process: Management in the knowledge economy. *Harvard Business Review, 81*(1), 127–139.

17. Cawsey, T., & Deszca, G. Personal experience.

18. Kerr, S. (1995). On the folly of rewarding A, while hoping for B. *Academy of Management Executive, 9*(1), 7–14.

19. Higgins, J. M., & Currie, D. M. (2004). It's time to rebalance the scorecard. *Business and Society Review, 109*(3), 297–309.

20. Eisenhardt, K. M., & Sull, D. N. (2001). Strategy as simple rules. *Harvard Business Review, 79*(1), 106–116.

21. Stiglitz, J. E. (2000). The contributions of the economics of information to twentieth century economics. *Quarterly Journal of Economics, 115*(4), 1441–1478.

22. Lawson, E., & Price, C. (2003). The psychology of change management. *McKinsey Quarterly, Special Edition: Organization, 2003.*

23. Simons, R. (1995). Control in the age of empowerment. *Harvard Business Review, 73*(2), 80–88.

24. Kaplan, R. S., & Norton, D. P. (2000). Having trouble with your strategy? Then map it. *Harvard Business Review, 78*(5), 167–176.

25. Kaplan, R. S., & Norton, D. P. (2004). The strategy map: Guide to aligning intangible assets. *Strategy and Leadership, 32*(5), 10–17.

26. Armitage, H. M., & Scholey, C. (2007). Using strategy maps to drive performance. *CMA Management, 80*(9), 24.

27. Kaplan, R. S., & Norton, D. P. (2000). Having trouble with your strategy? Then map it. *Harvard Business Review, 78*(5), 167–176.

28. Kaplan, R. S., & Norton, D. P. (1996). Using the balanced scorecard as a strategic management system. *Harvard Business Review, 74*(1), 75–85.

29. Simon, R. (1999). How risky is your company? *Harvard Business Review, 77*(3), 85–94.

30. Sirkin, H. L., Keenan, P., & Jackson, A. The hard side of change management. *Harvard Business Review, 91*(9), 108–118.

CHAPTER 11

Summary Thoughts on Organizational Change

Once you fall in a river, you're no longer a fisherman, you're a swimmer.

—Gene Hill

CHAPTER OVERVIEW

- This chapter presents an expanded summary model of organization change and applies the model to a case situation.
- The future of organizational change and organizational change agents is discussed.
- Individuals wishing to become organizational change agents need to recognize that two main routes exist: sophisticated technical specialists and strategic generalists.
- Several paradoxes in the field of organization change are summarized.
- The chapter ends with questions on how to orient yourself to organization change and what questions do change agents need to ask.

Writing a concluding chapter on organizational change is paradoxical. How does one conclude something one sees as ongoing? In some ways, a conclusion violates the orientation of this book. We see change as normal, pervasive, everyone's responsibility, and a necessary skill for all managers. Change is not something you deal with and move on. Rather, it is a continuing process of learning and accomplishment. Nevertheless, in this chapter we present two major sections: a summary of the key concepts as applied to a case situation and concluding thoughts about how organization change will evolve. We end with key questions for change agents.

A Summary Organizational Change Model

Throughout this book, we have argued for the use of an explicit model for change. Figure 11.1 outlines our summary model. This model suggests that

Figure 11.1 A Summary Model of Organizational Change

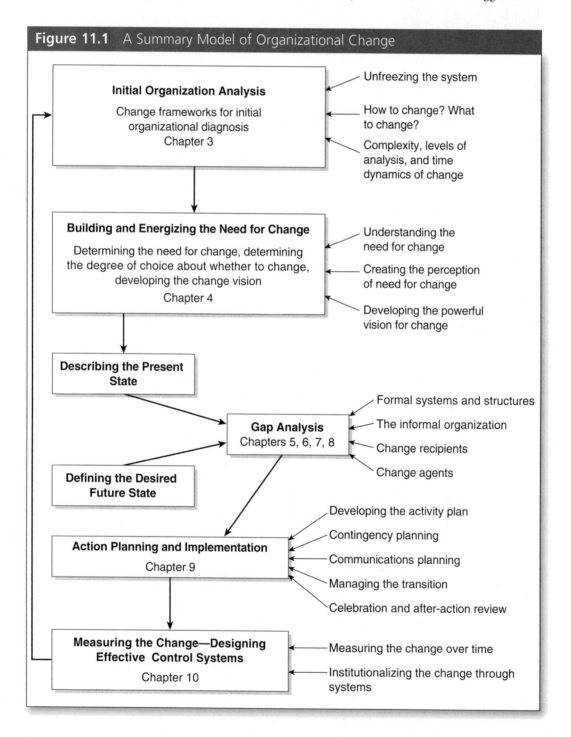

- Initial Organization Analysis
  - Change frameworks for initial organizational diagnosis
  - Chapter 3
  - Unfreezing the system
  - How to change? What to change?
  - Complexity, levels of analysis, and time dynamics of change

- Building and Energizing the Need for Change
  - Determining the need for change, determining the degree of choice about whether to change, developing the change vision
  - Chapter 4
  - Understanding the need for change
  - Creating the perception of need for change
  - Developing the powerful vision for change

- Describing the Present State

- Gap Analysis
  - Chapters 5, 6, 7, 8
  - Formal systems and structures
  - The informal organization
  - Change recipients
  - Change agents

- Defining the Desired Future State

- Action Planning and Implementation
  - Chapter 9
  - Developing the activity plan
  - Contingency planning
  - Communications planning
  - Managing the transition
  - Celebration and after-action review

- Measuring the Change—Designing Effective Control Systems
  - Chapter 10
  - Measuring the change over time
  - Institutionalizing the change through systems

change agents move systematically from awareness of the need for change through initiation, planning, and implementing the change to the measuring and confirming the change. A summary Checklist for Change is given in Appendix 11.1 at the end of this chapter. (Note: This checklist is also given in Chapter 1.)

A review of this model is given below using the case of Harry and the Company Takeover.[*] Each of the concepts—Initial Organization Analysis, Why Change?, Gap Analysis, Action Planning and Implementation, and Measuring the Change—is evident in Harry's actions. The purpose of the analysis is to demonstrate the usefulness of the explicit model on which this book is based.

HARRY AND THE COMPANY TAKEOVER

When Harry decided to help his cousin turn around his business, he had no idea things were in as bad shape as they were. He knew that the banks had called their demand notes, which would put the company into receivership, but he was shocked at the number of problematic issues. In his mind, the company's business model was straightforward: renting out specialized heavy equipment (either with or without operators) to a relatively easily identified set of customers. Straightforward, maybe, but there was no question that things were a mess.

Harry's cousin had founded the firm 15 years ago. He had grown it steadily through the first 10 years, followed by accelerated growth over the past 5 years. The bankruptcy of a key competitor and unprecedented growth in the area had resulted in a robust market opportunity. Staff levels had more than doubled during the past 5 years to 57 employees. Fifteen employees were located in the office area, handling administrative, accounting/finance, and sales functions. The remainder were in the repair shop, in the yard, or on the road, dealing with maintenance, delivery, and equipment operation roles.

In the past year, sales had flattened and moved to a modest decline. Other financial indicators showed worrying trends. For 2 years, operating expenses had risen significantly. While Harry wasn't certain why, he thought that equipment purchases had led to higher interest charges and that labor costs had risen dramatically. It was as if the firm had lost its capacity to manage the growth.

Things had gone from difficult to worse in the past 2 years. The company's bank was demanding repayment of loans. His cousin had varied his management approach from requesting to pleading and finally to avoiding issues at work. Employees referred to him as Waldo (from the children's book *Where's Waldo?*), because he was usually impossible to find when guidance was sought or a decision needed to be made.

(Continued)

---

[*]This case is based on personal experience of the authors.

(Continued)

Harry agreed that he would try to turn things around in return for his cousin consenting to turn over decision-making power and control while focusing on what he knew best—things related to operations and the equipment. His cousin had grown up with a love for heavy equipment and family members said that the only reason he was in business was so that he had newer and bigger toys to play with. He had specialized knowledge about which equipment was suitable for which jobs and, prior to the past 2 years, had been adept at developing relationships with customers that generated repeat business.

Their terms were agreed to, but Harry's arrival did not reverse his cousin's disappearing act. He continued to appear depressed and distant, with little appetite for assuming a more active operational role in the business.

Harry believed that the business had solid prospects and should sustain an adequate return on the investment. However, it certainly was not doing so now. He met with the bank and presented a turnaround plan. Based on his reputation as a successful entrepreneur and his willingness to make a significant investment to improve liquidity, the bank agreed to renegotiate the operating loan and line of credit. This would provide the firm with the breathing space needed to execute the turnaround.

Harry moved into his cousin's office and began to take control of the management of the firm. He was shocked to find a culture of permissiveness, waste, and tolerance for corruption. As he walked through the parts and maintenance areas, he found parts, tools, and equipment scattered about. Grease on the floor made walking a risky proposition. Pizza boxes, pop tins, and bottles were littered around. He thought he smelled liquor on some employees. He observed that lateness and absenteeism were problems. No one seemed to be doing anything about these problems because the labor market for mechanics and operators was tight and supervisors were afraid that people might quit.

The housekeeping within the office/administrative area was somewhat better than other parts of the operation, but it still left much to be desired. Some employees smoked in work areas despite no-smoking rules. While the accounting and finance area appeared to be better organized, they often had difficulty providing the managerial data Harry requested.

After reviewing sales information, Harry also found himself wondering about the source of orders. Most orders came from brokers rather than directly from users of the equipment. He wondered why and guessed that the brokers were taking 15% to 25% off the top for the orders.

In an inspection of the operations shortly after his arrival, Harry found seven brand new tires and rims stashed behind a building. When he checked purchasing invoices, he learned that nine had been bought the week before. On further investigation, he was told that no new tires had been mounted on any equipment. Harry could not locate two tires and rims worth more than $1,500 each.

One of the first things that Harry did was to walk around the operation and talk to people. He would look them in the eye and say, "I want to make money here. What do you want?" At the same time, he started insisting that if people came to him with problems, they should also come with what they wanted out of the situation—a solution to the issue. When they did, he would listen intently, take time to discuss things thoroughly, voice appreciation and support and approve action, when appropriate, with the words, "Great—let's get on with it. Let me know if you need anything and keep me in the loop with how it goes." The consistent message from Harry was that this operation will be a success and everyone will win—if we exercise more discipline and if everyone shows initiative and contributes to improvements needed to make this operation a winner.

Harry realized that many members of the firm probably wanted to do a good job. That was the sense he got as he visited departments, talked with individuals one on one, and heard about their frustrations. Some employees seemed to come and go as they wished—three even brought their dogs to work. He had listened to one customer complaint about late delivery of equipment and learned that the person delivering the machinery had stopped for 3 hours on route. The driver's excuse was lunch and engine problems that had miraculously resolved themselves. Employees' morale was in the toilet, but turnover had yet to become a problem.

Harry called the employees together during his first week to introduce himself, address the need for improvement, solicit their cooperation, ideas, and effort, and let them know that he planned to be around regularly. Harry also put up flip-chart sheets in the office during the first week and began listing every issue or problem that he or others identified. His list contained 93 items by the end of the third week. However, by the third week, he had also approved four employee-initiated improvement plans.

During his first week, Harry smelled alcohol on the breath of an employee who appeared to be under the influence. He fired him on the spot. He told employees that new rules on attendance would be enforced.

During the third week, Harry called people together for a second plant meeting and summarized some of the problem areas that had been identified that needed attention. He also announced the initial change recommendations that employees had advanced and publicly thanked the initiators. He stated that new rules on work scheduling would be implemented. He stated that housekeeping in both the plant and office had to improve. He said that the business had the potential to be a first-class operation, and it was time for it to quit looking like a pigsty. The shop floors would be degreased, the walls would be repainted, and tools and equipment should be properly stored. If people wanted pizza or anything other than a donut or muffin with their coffee, they would be expected to eat it in the lunchroom or not at all. Major cleanup activities were undertaken over a 3-week period, with floor degreasing and painting occurring during the weekends.

During his third week, Harry went into the workspace of the people with dogs and said, "What are these? Employees or pets?" They vanished from the

(Continued)

(Continued)

workplace. After further investigation of the tires he had found stashed, Harry concluded that the person who had signed the purchase order for the nine tires was selling them out the back door, and on the Wednesday of week three, he escorted him off the premises.

During the fourth week, Harry had an opportunity to follow up on his hunch that the company was losing money by relying on brokers. He phoned one of their customers who regularly used their equipment but who went through a broker and asked why they were not placing orders directly. "Because you never called us before" was the answer. Before he ended the conversation, he had a $50,000 work order placed directly. When Harry relayed this conversation and its results to the sales staff, they were at first defensive. Further conversation, combined with his now standard question ("We want to make money—do you want to be part of it?"), elicited affirmative responses, though they still seemed unsure as to how they should change their sales approach. Harry made a note to himself that they would need further training and guidance or they would need to be replaced.

Harry recalled similar conversations with other employees. For example, in a conversation with a truck driver, Harry said, "We make money when you are delivering equipment to clients. If you stand around when orders are pending, we don't make money. People who work hard and get more equipment to clients are going to make more money. Do you want to be part of this or not?" "I'm in" was the response.

During the fourth week, Harry noticed that certain pieces of equipment that had been in for repair in week one were still inoperable. He asked why and was told that the maintenance supervisor was in a dispute with the field service foreman and sales staff over the allocation of repair and maintenance charges, and as a result, needed repairs had not been undertaken. This resulted in lost rental sales. The argument had been going on for more than a month, and he was told this was not the first time. Harry reacted with frustration. He called an immediate meeting of those involved, ordered the equipment repaired as soon as possible, and stated that this was no way to resolve conflicts. He added "unclear responsibilities" to his list of issues on the flipchart.

During Harry's sixth week on the job, he announced that he wanted a system that would give him a profit-and-loss statement for each piece of equipment. "Why do you want that?" was the response. When he explained why to the employees in accounting, they understood, but operational employees saw it as more paperwork that might get in the way of sales and servicing.

When he began to explore equipment repair invoices during week 6, he noted that many expensive repairs had been done on-site at their clients' premises. Much of the work looked routine but was made much more expensive because of the location and because the company had to negotiate with the client over operating losses while the machine was down. Harry wondered why that equipment hadn't been serviced prior to leaving the shop. When he inquired further, he discovered that there was no formal preventive maintenance program established for the equipment.

By week 7, the cleaning and painting of the office area and workplace had been completed and it helped to spruce up the environment. Employees were reacting positively to the improved workplace, as reflected in comments Harry received during his weekly walks through the work areas. Little additional action seemed to be needed from Harry to maintain the improvements. Even the paperwork in the office area seemed to be better organized now, but Harry wondered whether it was simply being put in boxes and hidden from view. When he told employees in the plant that he thought that swearing was unprofessional conduct at work, they just looked at him.

Things seemed to be getting better, but much more needed to be done. He went down his list, noting some of the most pressing items:

1. No formalized preventive maintenance systems

2. Questionable inventory management system, missing parts in some areas, excess inventory in others, and a significant volume of obsolete parts that were held in inventory

3. Missing tools and equipment, including some big-ticket items, such as a $35,000 loader and a $25,000 compressor

4. Sales relationships not actively managed, clients not phoned in a timely manner, customer complaints not acted upon until threats were invoked

5. Logistics/scheduling, customer delivery and pickups, on-site servicing of equipment not handled well. Customers complained about downtime and their ability to predict when things would be done

6. Lags between order fulfillment and client billing, slow payment of accounts payable

7. Poor relations with suppliers of parts and equipment, due in part to slow payment, disagreements over terms and conditions, and lack of supplier responsiveness to emergency requests

8. Finally, and importantly, there was the lingering question: What role would his cousin play after the company had been revitalized?

As one can surmise from the case, Harry's *initial organizational analysis* provided extensive evidence of **what** needed to change. The list was long: employees drinking on the job; sloppy shop conditions; potential theft of valuable equipment; low performance expectations; a lack of systems and processes in critical areas such as equipment maintenance; and the absence of a disciplined approach to interpersonal conduct and dispute resolution. How to change was not as clear, as the culture of the organization reinforced the negative dynamics. Clearly, Harry needed to change the systems and culture to get things back on track—assuming, of course, that the bank would give him the time to turn the operation around.

The question (see Figure 11.1) of *"why change?"* was evident to Harry and to the bank but was not evident to all the employees. Harry needed to "unfreeze the situation." The initial behavior of some employees indicated complacency, resignation, and in some cases, a desire to milk the company for as long as it lasted. He dealt with the bank by giving them a plan and putting in his own money. This and his reputation as a skilled owner-manager persuaded the bank to work with him. Harry tackled the culture of permissiveness by making his expectations clear to employees (Are the dogs "employees or pets"?). While some of this was unorthodox, the communication was clear. As well, Harry understood that actions counted. By firing people who were abusing the organization, he was making the strongest statements possible about what was not acceptable. Because he was in charge of the operation, he had the power to do this. Note that Harry's cousin also had the formal authority to take such actions, but he had chosen not to act. Over time, Harry's cousin had come to be perceived as powerless.

Harry's *vision for change* was clear and simple: "I want to make money. This will take individual initiative, discipline, and systems and processes that can support our work. What do you want?" The strategy was to service clients with the rental equipment they needed in a timely and profitable manner. One could argue over the nature of the appeal, but the vision was clear and appropriate to the company situation. At the same time, Harry seemed to have an implicit vision for the longer term. His actions to clean up the workplace, stop employees from swearing and smoking, empower employees to engage in active problem solving, become more customer, cost, and performance focused, and act on their improvement ideas all suggest a new vision for the workplace.

The list of 93 issues was his *gap analysis*. In his view, there would be employees who would want to work and who would welcome being part of a successful company. Those he appealed to directly by outlining how they could make money by helping the company succeed. Those who resisted strongly were fired if their behavior was illegal or unethical or if they failed to meet standards. Harry recognized and reinforced employees who began to embrace the change. Implicitly, the message was that they could be viewed as change agents working in the employee group. Harry recognized that there was an absence of formal structures. The reporting lines and procedures were unclear, as shown by the dispute between the maintenance supervisor and the general foreman and sales staff. Formal systems either were faulty or didn't exist. For example, the accounting system could not track usage and profitability by machine and there was no preventive maintenance system. Harry dealt with key stakeholders in priority: the bank, the employees, and key clients. The aftermath of these contacts created initiatives that raised expectations, began to improve performance, and helped to generate hope for the future.

The case demonstrates nicely the *dynamics of action planning and implementation*. The operation was relatively simple and his plan consisted explicitly of dealing with the list of issues needing attention. He discussed specific problems with employees and demanded that others take action to deal with the issues. As he learned about the ambitions and competencies of employees, he encouraged them. He also fired those who were engaged in inappropriate behavior or who failed to meet reasonable performance standards. His communications plan was personal, constant, and direct.

Because of the size of the operation, Harry was able to *measure the changes* directly. Some changes he could see. The plant was cleaner. The dogs were gone. Others he could track by looking at sales figures and profit margins. At the same time, he knew that the systems he wanted, such as a system to track profits per piece of rental equipment and a preventative maintenance program, would take longer to install.

Finally, the change initiatives that Harry took were just the beginning. He recognized and rewarded those who joined him in turning the company around. He learned a great deal about the operation and what were critical factors in a successful operation. And finally, he developed a new list of change initiatives that would take the organization to the next level of development.

Harry exemplifies what this book is about. He was very action oriented. Importantly, his actions were based on a thorough understanding of the key success factors and the levers that needed pulling to achieve change. He insulated the organization from the environment long enough for the change processes to work and he recognized that both short- and long-term changes were needed. In summary, he was an expert change leader.

The case illustrates the change process outlined in Figure 11.1. Toolkit Exercise 11.1 provides a detailed step-by-step summary for planning a change project. While change agents need a model for change, they also need to understand how organization change will develop in the future. The chapter now considers these shifts.

The Future of Organizations and Organizational Change Processes

In Chapter 1, we presented Barkema's views on the changes organizations face and how they need to adapt.[1] In his view, all organizations will need to be global in orientation. Small and medium-sized firms will access global markets through the Internet in low-cost/high-information-transmission ways. Others will form organizational networks, partnering with others to complete the value chain. Some will be large, focused global firms with worldwide activities.

Barkema states that organizations will have autonomous, dislocated teams. That is, organizations, large or small, will require motivated teams to coordinate their activities across borders and cultures. At the same time, structures will be "digitally enabled." They will have the electronic systems to facilitate coordination. Scanning systems will transmit sales data from stores and warehouses anywhere to manufacturing facilities in real time and will be used to determine future production levels. Personal communications devices such as the Blackberry and other smartphones will mean that people can communicate any time, all the time. Such dispersed systems facilitated by almost instantaneous communications will make it easy for competitors to respond to each other's actions. The world will move faster.

Such changes will mean that organizations will need tight/loose controls both within and between firms. Within organizations, critical strategic variables will be closely monitored and controlled. Visions will be articulated and adhered to. At the same time, rapid environmental shifts will demand local responses that will vary by region as well as responses that are broad in their geographic reach. What works in one country won't necessarily work in another. Think of the regional differences in the formulation of branded products such as Coke and McDonald's, and this reality becomes clear. Consequently, managers will need to have the autonomy and loose controls to respond to local needs within the critical boundaries of the firm.

Between organizations, networks of firms will be linked to allow for needed information exchange. What is shared will vary from the purely transactional to the strategic, depending on the levels of trust and intimacy existing between firms. At the same time, these firms will maintain their independence on key strategic dimensions viewed as proprietary and/or sources of competitive advantage critical to their long-term success.

Galbraith suggests that strategy and structure of organizations will continue to be closely tied.[2] Organizations will come in an enormous variety of forms and complexities. Straightforward work that is repetitive and easily understood will disappear and companies will organize around opportunities and resources. The key management tasks will involve innovation and the mastering of complexity. Galbraith classifies potential strategies and suggests matching structures.

According to Galbraith, organizations in the 21st century will become increasingly customer oriented and focused. In the customer-oriented organization, organizations will have three major organizational parts: business units, international regions, and customer accounts. These parts will be linked with lateral processes: teams and networks. Focused organizations will have subunits focused on different key criteria: costs, products, or customers.

Malone argues that tomorrow's organizations will have the benefits of both large and small organizations.[3] Digital technologies will enable economics of scale and knowledge while preserving the freedom, creativity, motivation, and flexibility of small organizations. There will be a shift from traditional centralized hierarchies to organizations of loose hierarchies, democracies, and markets—like organizations.

- *Loose hierarchy example:* Wikipedia, a free online encyclopedia that anybody can edit and when errors occur, others will spot and correct them
- *Democracy examples:* W. L. Gore, where you become a manager by finding people who want to work for you, or Mondragon, where employees elect a board of directors to make decisions
- *Market example:* An Intel proposal where plant managers propose to sell futures on what they produce and salespeople buy futures for products they want to sell. Prices fluctuate and will determine what products get produced at what plants and who gets to sell the products.

The above is not comprehensive but is suggestive of how organizations will evolve in the future. As a result of these and other trends, organizational change and change agents will need to shift as well. Table 11.1 is based on the forecasts in Chapter 1 and summarizes these potential changes. The table suggests that change agents will have a set of generalist capabilities providing basic competencies. As well, specific change skills of pattern finder, organization analyst, mobilizer, empowerer, enabler, enactor, disintegrator, and integrator need to be developed. Finally, specialist roles for change agents will continue to develop. For example, change skills in information technology and mergers/acquisitions are two specialist areas.

Table 11.1 The Impact of Organizational Trends on Organizational Change and Change Agents

Organizational Trend	Organizational Change	Change Agent
Globalization—be big, or be specialized & excellent, or be acquired, squeezed, or eliminated	Strategic global perspective for both large firms and niche SMEs	Pattern finder
Virtual and networked organizations	Knowledge of networks and emergent organizational forms	Vision framer
Loose/tight controls	Knowledge and risk management	Organizational analyst and aligner
24/7 response requirements	Web-enabled communication, change-related blogs, fast response capacity with a human face	Mobilizer, empowerer, enabler, enactor
Cost & quality focus, outsourcing & supply chain rationalization	Negotiation & network development, quality, cost leadership, and/or customer focus	Disintegrator and integrator
Shortening product life cycles & increasing customer expectations	Creativity, innovation, and deployment	Corporate gadfly & trend surfer
Increasing focus on integrated customer services and knowledge management	Empowerment, teams, and process focus	Generalist capacities: facilitation, influencing, negotiating and visioning skills; project management expertise
Technological change fundamentally alters industry structures, in terms of both the "what" and the "how"		Specialist roles, related to expertise needed for specific change initatives. For example, software system integration, customer relationship management, flexible manufacturing, organizational integration following acquisition
Changing demographic, social, and cultural environment		
Political changes are realigning alliances and the competitive environment		Capacity to develop and sustain the trust and confidence of mutiple stakeholders
Political changes are realigning alliances and the competitive environment		

In summary, those involved with organization change, if they have not already done so, need to develop:

- A strong strategic and global perspective
- Knowledge of networks and emergent organizational forms and how they work
- Skills in risk management and knowledge management
- Understanding of the impact of Web-enabled communication, change-related blogs, and fast response capacity
- The ability to communicate worldwide while maintaining a human face
- Perceptiveness of different cultures and norms and how these factors affect organizational change
- The capacity to deploy empowered but bounded teams operating with a focused vision. The boundaries come from the vision and agreed-to expectations concerning performance, modes of operation, and other predefined standards and shared commitments.

As the environment evolves, the role of the change agent will shift. All change agents will continue to need basic skills in facilitation, influencing, negotiation, and visioning. They will need to understand project management and to be able to implement projects. In addition to the generalists, some change agents will specialize and add value through their intimate knowledge of a particular industry, sector, or change target. Specializations, such as those listed below, will evolve further:

- Merger and acquisition specialist
- Joint venture and alliance specialist
- Organizational integration specialist
- Business stage specialists: early stage growth, maturity, decline, and/or renewal
- Large-scale or disruptive change specialist
- Crisis management specialist
- Information technology system integrator
- Organization structure specialist
- Supply change integrator
- Cross-cultural specialist by specific cultures
- Interorganization specialist including government or industry relations
- Multiparty negotiation specialist

In addition to specialist areas, new "generalist" skills will be needed. Skilled change agents will be increasingly sensitive to what is happening in the organization's environment—"trend surfers," perhaps, who recognize and give voice to factors that represent potential opportunities and threats. They will help manage the complexity of organization change by developing skills in recognizing and understanding patterns within organizations. They will understand how to mold disparate perspectives into a compelling vision and know which actions provide significant leverage within the organization. Their abilities to mobilize others will be grounded in empowerment and enabling skills. They will be able to both disaggregate and integrate parts of the organization as needed. That is, they will know both how to separate organizational units into self-directed entities and how to link disparate parts into an integrated whole. Finally, they will need to manage their activities and actions with integrity so that they will be able to develop and sustain the trust and confidence of multiple stakeholders.

Many would argue that these represent skill areas that have always been important. While this is true, the pace of change and the speed of competitive responses have made these skills even more critical to sustained organizational success. As a result, the value to both the change agent and the firm has increased.

Becoming an Organizational Change Agent

For many change agents, their initial involvement with the design and/or implementation of change typically begins when they are asked (or volunteer) to join a team or task force or otherwise assist with a change initiative. Invitations arise for a variety of reasons. Individuals may have been noticed because they exhibited interest in a project, or someone may believe they would be helpful because of their skills or perspective.

Change skills tend to fall into two broad categories. First, there are the technical skills that develop from functional training and experience. Change implementation often requires the involvement of individuals who possess specific technical skills and abilities in order to advance a project. If the change involves the deployment of new software or a new approach to customer relationship management, individuals with appropriate technical competencies will need to be involved with the implementation. Second, there are the more broadly applicable general management skills that grow out of experience with the framing, approving, and implementing of change initiatives and include the development of interpersonal competences that facilitate change.

Some change agents will choose to remain more focused on particular technical/ functional areas, with those skills becoming increasingly more sophisticated with the passage of time. Their initial involvement could be the provision of computer training to support a system upgrade. Gradually, these change agents could be involved in more sophisticated technical changes. Their expertise would grow and they might become expert in an area such as large scale software system integration. Likewise, the person who begins doing job design and group development work might develop, over time, into an organizational integration specialist. Technically oriented change specialists will require some competence in more general change management skill areas (e.g., interpersonal communications). However, it will be their technical expertise that will be sought after when the initiative lies within their domain.

Those who choose to orient their development around general change management skills may initially start their careers in technical/functional change management. However, these individuals may develop more sophisticated general change management competencies such as organizational analysis, leadership, interpersonal communication and influence, negotiation, project management, and implementation skills. The management of complex change initiatives benefits from those who possess these broadly applicable change management skills.

When managers first become involved with change, their skills are usually at an early stage of development. Their competencies become increasingly sophisticated and well honed in either a technical/specialist stream or a broader generalist stream as the result of the change challenges they experience over time. Some will choose to specialize, while others will migrate between these two streams at different points in their career. Each stream will provide interesting and useful career opportunities. (Figure 11.2 outlines these streams.)

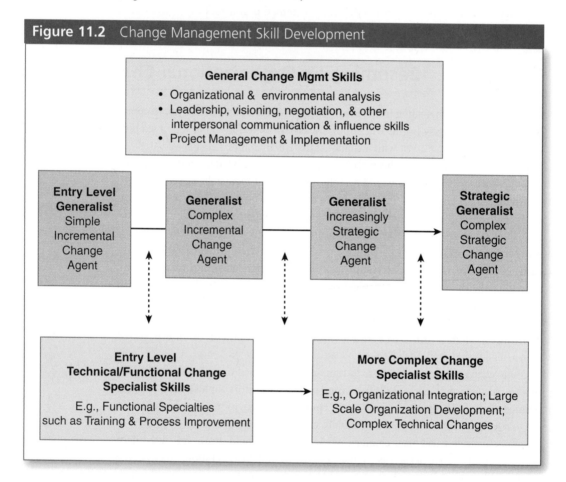

Figure 11.2   Change Management Skill Development

Paradoxes in Organization Change

The field of organization change has a set of underlying paradoxes that change agents struggle with. Just as quantum physics considers an electron as both a particle and a wave,* some aspects of organization change have two perspectives. Both aspects are important and neither should be rejected. Several of these paradoxes are outlined below.

---

*Under certain circumstances, the electron looks like a particle and has the characteristics of a particle (mass, solidity, etc.). Under other circumstances, the electron seems to be a wave. It has a frequency and other wave characteristics. This paradox is only resolved by accepting an electron as both.

First, example, the management of organizations will become more complex as the strategic focus of organizations develops a global perspective. Organization change will need tools and processes that encourage the systematic management of a wide number of elements (organization systems, structures, cultures, leadership, technology, etc.) while maintaining the speed of change. Clearly a challenge will be to handle complexity without being overwhelmed and frozen by it. Organization change as a field needs to handle the paradox of how to maintain the momentum of change (something that may require simplification) while not dismissing the complexity of an organization's environment.

A second paradox involves an organization's need to be simultaneously centralized and decentralized. Organization change needs to learn how to help organizations understand this paradox and to evolve better mechanisms of handling this tension.

As organizational leaders become skilled in promoting decentralized initiatives, they will face the challenge of handling multiple change initiatives simultaneously. Change agents need to consider which change initiatives will block or run counter to others and which ones will support and facilitate others. Interaction effects are not always self-apparent, and sometimes initiatives that look like they are supportive of other activities in the short run may have adverse consequences over the long term. How can change leaders help an organization institutionalize or finish one project while continuing multiple other ones, and how can they assist in identifying unintended side effects?

Organization change involves both incremental/continuous and radical/discontinuous change. Depending on how rapidly the environment is changing, organizations may need to engage in both kinds of change. The challenge for change agents will be to develop adaptive, flexible organizations while simultaneously engaging in radical organization change when it is needed. Organization change as a field needs to develop insights into this paradox.

Finally, the digital world and the rise of the knowledge worker shift the territory of organization change from a hierarchical frame to a democratic, participative one. But the essence of many change projects is a new direction that, in the end, is mandated, nondemocratically, from above. Most change projects need input from rank-and-file employees but also need some degree of central direction and management. The tension between participative involvement of many and the pressure to drive change from the top and center of an organization creates potential paradoxes.[*]

Given these paradoxes, change agents must develop a positive orientation to change that permits them to deal with inherent contradictions.

Orienting Yourself to Organization Change

Everyone who is a member of an organization will participate in organization change. As the environment shifts, organizations mature, grow, and die. Change is just part of

---

[*]Organizational change will need to be prepared for blogs that discuss openly the issues surrounding change initiatives. Can change leaders accept and deal positively with open criticism that may show up on such blogs?

living and opportunities will emerge that will allow you to act as a change leader or agent. Given this, several lessons stand out that may provide a useful orientation:

1. Gain perspective and insight by recognizing the dynamism and complexity of your organization. What connections exist between parts and how do they work?

2. Recognize that people's perceptions are critical. The perception of benefits and costs determines a person's reaction to a change proposal.

3. Understand that your perception is only one of many. Your view is neither right nor wrong. It is just your point of view of how things are.

4. Gather people as you go. There are multiple ways to achieve your change, but the ways that bring friends with you are easier and more fun. And remember, people can't rock the boat when they are busy rowing.

5. Pull people toward you with a powerful change vision. Push people through argument and rewards when you need to, but gain support through their hearts.

6. Get active in pursuit of your vision. If you do something, you will get responses, and you can learn from those. Not doing anything cuts you off from learning.

7. Have a plan oriented around your change vision. Having an explicit plan means your thinking can be discussed and challenged. Know that your plan won't last and will require modification when you start implementing it, but it will certainly be useful in starting a discussion and gaining commitment.

8. Do things that are positive. Actions that suck energy from you and the system are difficult to sustain. Growing your energy as change agent is important.

9. To start meaningful change, you need only a few believers. To continue, you need to develop momentum until a critical mass of key participants is on-side. Some will never join in, and that's OK unless they attempt to sabotage or otherwise disrupt agreed-to initiatives.

10. There are many routes to your goal. Find the ones with the least resistance that still allow you to proceed with integrity.

Revisiting the Critical Questions

We ended Chapter 1 by examining critical questions for change. We wish to end this book by highlighting those critical questions.

1. What is the environment telling you prior to, at the beginning of, during, and following the implementation of the change? In particular:
   a. What is the broad environment communicating to you about future economic, social, and technological conditions and trends?

  b. What are your customers or clients (both inside and outside the organization) telling you?

  c. What are your competitors doing, how are they responding to you, and how are you responding to them?

  d. What are the partners within your network doing and how are they responding to you?

  e. What do the people who will potentially be the leaders, managers, and recipients of change want and need?

2. Why is change needed? Who sees this need?

3. What is your purpose and agenda? How does that purpose project to a worthwhile vision that goes to the heart of the matter?

4. How will you implement and manage the change?
  a. How will you resource the change initiative?
  b. How will you select and work with your change team?
  c. How will you work with the broader organization?
  d. How will you monitor progress so that you can steer and alter speed and course if necessary?
  e. How will you ensure that you act (and are seen to act) ethically and with integrity?

5. What have you learned about change and how can you remember it for the future? How can you pass on what you learned?

6. Once the change is completed, what comes next? The completion of one change simply serves as the start point for the next.

That's it. It's an evolving list and its further development is up to you. You've been reading and thinking about how to develop your skills as an agent of change. It's time to deploy those ideas, see what works when, where, why, and how, and learn as you go. No excuses. If you want to make things happen, you will have to learn to live with the frustration, excitement, uncertainty, loneliness, and personal development that come with being a change agent. The learning lies in the journey, while joy, a sense of accomplishment, and feelings of fulfillment accompany the completion of milestones and the realization of changes that have a positive impact on the lives of others.

> *And the day came when the risk it took to remain tight in a bud was more painful than the risk it took to blossom.*
>
>   —Anaïs Nin

END-OF-CHAPTER EXERCISE

TOOLKIT EXERCISE 11.1

Developing Your Change Plan

This Toolkit Exercise applies the tools from all chapters and asks you to develop a complete change plan for a change you want to make happen.

As a first step, reflect back on Toolkit Exercises 4.1–4.4 and develop your statement of the need for change and your vision for the change.

Once the need for change and vision have been articulated, your assignment is to begin the development of an action plan for the change. This will be broken into four parts:

a. The development of a sequence of action steps and the arrangement of them into a critical path with a clearly defined end goal, intermediate targets, and specific first step.
b. The consideration of contingencies—what might go wrong? How will these things be handled?
c. A responsibility chart. That is, who will do what, where, when, and how?
d. A transition plan including a communications plan. How will the transition be managed? Who will make the innumerable decisions required to handle the details? Who will provide information to those affected? As well, how will the change be communicated to organizational members?

The Action Plan

Begin the development of an action plan. What are the critical steps that must be accomplished?

In what sequence should these occur? Can some be done simultaneously?

Who needs to become committed to the project? Where are key players at on the adoption continuum? Are they even aware of the change? If aware, are they interested or have they moved beyond that stage to either desiring action or having already adopted?

What will it take to move them along the continuum in the direction of adoption?

The AIDA Continuum

Key Player Name	Aware?	Interested?	Desires Action?	Adopter?

What is the commitment to the adoption of those who have reached the adopter stage? That is, are they at the "let it happen" stage, the "help it happen" stage, or the "make it happen" stage?

How can the commitment levels of key stakeholders be increased?

The Measurement of Change

How will you know that your goal or change project is successfully implemented? (At times, success will be obvious—e.g., a new system in place. At other times, success will be more difficult to measure—e.g., attitudes toward the adoption and acceptance of a new system.)

What intermediate signals will indicate that you are making progress? What is the first step or sequence of steps?

Your end goal is:

You can measure it by:

Intermediate measures and milestones are:

The first step is:

The Critical Path

Arrange your action steps in sequence. What should go first, second, and so forth? What activities cannot begin or should not start until others are completed? What timelines should you observe? Often it is useful to begin at the end of the project and work backward to now.

Contingency Planning

Remember O'Brien's Law[*]? Well, it holds, and things will not go as planned. But you can plan for the unexpected.

What are the critical decision points? Who makes those decisions?

What will you do if the decision or event does not go as planned? What plans can you make to account for these contingencies? If you can, draw a decision tree of the action plan and lay out the decision–event sequence.

Responsibility Charting[4]

Who will do what, where, when, and how? Often a responsibility chart can be useful to track these things.

Actions or Decisions	Person #1	Person #2	Person #3	Person #?
Action #1				
Action #2				
Decision #1				
Action #3				
. . . . .				

---

[*]O'Brien's Law states: *Murphy was an optimist.*

Coding:

R = Responsibility (not necessarily authority)
A = Approval (right to veto)
S = Support (put resources toward)
I = Inform (to be consulted before action)

Note that if there are a great number of As on your chart, implementation will be difficult. Care must be taken to assign As only when appropriate. Likewise, if there are not enough Rs and Ss, you will need to think about changes needed here and how to bring them about.

Appendix 11.1: A Summary Checklist for Change

Initiating Change

- Understanding the need for change
- Creating the perception of need for change
- Developing the powerful vision for change

Planning Change

- Having an organization model
- Differentiating HOW to change and WHAT to change
- Structures and systems: approval of change, facilitating and hindering change, developing adaptive structures for change
- Informal systems: resistance to change, power dynamics, the role of perceived impact, force fields, stakeholders (commitment, adaptiveness)
- Recipients: reactions (negative, ambivalent, positive), recipients' adaptation (anticipation, denial, anger, acceptance)
- Change agents: leading and managing, change agent types, change teams

Doing the Change

- Engaging others
- Developing the activity plan
- Contingency planning
- Commitment planning
- Communicating the change
- Managing the transition

Measuring and Confirming the Change

- Measuring the change
- Changing the measures over the life of the change project

Celebrating Success and Preparing for the Next Change

- Recognizing achievements and enjoying the successes
- Review of the change process and developing new learnings
- Anticipating and planning for the next wave of change

Notes

1. Barkema, H. G., et al. (2002). Management challenges in a new time. *Academy of Management Journal, 45*(5), 916.

2. Galbraith, J. R. (2005, August). Organizing for the future: Designing the 21st-century organization. *Strategy and structure. The process will continue.* Academy of Management, Hawaii. Retrieved May 2010 from http://www.aom.pace.edu/odc/2005/galbraith.pdf.

3. Malone, T. (2005, August). *Inventing organizations.* Academy of Management. Hawaii. Retrieved February 2010from http://www.aom.pace.edu/odc/2005.html.

4. Refer to Beckhard, R. (1987). *Organizational transitions* (p. 104). Reading, MA: Addison-Wesley, for a further discussion on responsibility charting.

Case Studies

The following teaching cases examine different aspects of leading organizational change. Consequently, the authors suggest that colleagues teach the cases in conjunction with particular chapters, as noted below. Please go to this book's website (**http://www.sagepub.com/cawsey2e/**) to find extensive teaching notes for each case.

Chapter 4: Building and Energizing the Need for Change

Case Study 1: Radio Station WEAA: Leading in a Challenging Situation

Corin Fiske, Director of News and Public Affairs at WEAA, a public radio station, needs to convince multiple constituents—from top-level university administrators to volunteer radio staffers—that organizational change is essential for this station to grow and thrive. The immediate question is this: What and how does Fiske begin?

Chapter 5: Navigating Change Through Formal Structures and Systems

Case Study 2: FOX Relocation Management Corp.

Gretchen Fox, President of the company that she founded, needs to decide if another layer of management and changes in the compensation and incentive plans are needed for her company to continue its trajectory of growth. These possible changes in organizational structure represent a change in vision, as Fox fears that more hierarchy might ruin the carefully constructed culture of independent thinkers at her company.

Chapter 7: Managing the Recipients of Change and Influencing Internal Stakeholders

Case Study 3: Travelink Solutions

William, a young staff member of Travelink Solutions Canada, sees multiple problems within this 24/7 travel assistance business. As a low-level, sixteen-month employee, William has documented and discussed the situation with his friend, Robert, a marketing manager who has three years experience with the firm. William and/or Robert must decide if and how he might bring the organizational problems, and possible solutions, to the attention of management.

Chapter 10: Measuring Change: Designing Effective Control Systems

Case Study 4: Ellen Zane—Leading Change at Tufts/NEMC

By summer, 2006, Ellen Zane, CEO of Tufts/New England Medical Center, has brought about a dramatic turnaround of one of America's oldest hospitals through meeting a series of efficiency goals, by aggressively recruiting doctors, and by tough negotiations with Massachusetts' health insurance providers. Zane must now take the hospital to the next level of sustainability in a highly competitive healthcare marketplace: How should she do this?

Case Study 1

Radio Station WEAA: Leading in a Challenging Situation[1]

Mary Foster

Corin Fiske, Director of News and Public Affairs at WEAA, a public radio station licensed and owned by Morgan State University (MSU) in Baltimore, Maryland, felt like she'd just had the wind knocked out of her. She'd just gotten off the phone with Micah Razan, host of the "Women Today" program, for the past 14 years. Razan was calling to let Fiske know that she was resigning from her volunteer on-air host position and that she would be taking the show's name and concept with her. As Fiske collected her thoughts, she realized that not only did she need to find a replacement host and new program concept quickly, but she also needed to deal with her staffing situation.

In August of 2006, Fiske was recruited by the Chair of the Communication Studies Department to be a change agent, to help the organization achieve its full potential. She planned and delivered 15 hours of world-class news and community affairs programming every week through a staff of 30 direct reports, 29 of whom were volunteers. In the two months Fiske had been at WEAA, she felt like some of her staff

weren't fully supporting her or the organization's goals. As she reflected on the situation, she realized she needed to figure out what to do and quickly. She'd have to tell her new boss, Jabari Owens, the station General Manager, about the resignation, the loss of the show concept, and the resistance from her staff. He would surely expect her to have a plan to deal with these urgent short- and long-term issues.

WEAA Background

WEAA, a non-profit, National Public Radio (NPR) affiliated station, served the Baltimore market. It was licensed and owned by Morgan State University. The station began operating on January 10, 1977, and operated at 12,600 watts, 24 hours a day, 365 days a year. WEAA, a community-oriented radio station, reached out to its multicultural audience with social, political, and multicultural programs and music. The station was committed to academic excellence and

---

[1]This case is intended to stimulate classroom discussion rather than to illustrate the effective or ineffective handling of a managerial situation. All events and individuals are real, but the names are disguised. Unlike most NPR-affiliated radio stations, WEAA did not run the full roster of NPR programming; most of WEAA's programming was original.

the professional development and training of students interested in careers in broadcasting. In 1999, *Gavin Magazine* named WEAA the Jazz Station of the Year. In 2000, 2002, and 2005, *Citypaper* newspaper named WEAA the best radio station in Baltimore. The average WEAA listener was an affluent, educated, community-active, professional African American in the 25–54 age group (64 percent males, 36 percent females).

According to the Music Director, Narius Coleman, the station started as a "refreshing, new African American perspective, playing jazz and R&B and having great talk shows. We were the voice of the community. Our call letters[2] stood for 'We educate African Americans.'" As the station evolved in the 1980s, he said "they played less R&B and more jazz; talk shows remained an important part of the format." Coleman noted that in the 1990s the station became a "straight ahead" jazz station (i.e., focused on jazz without R&B) with talk shows. Now he says the station has evolved to be "a blend of contemporary and traditional jazz with some soul and R&B classics and talk shows, closer to its original format." According to Coleman, the definition of the call sign has been expanded to signify: "we educate African Americans and all who listen, whether they are Latino, Caucasian, or African . . . we speak to many different cultures."

The station competed in the Baltimore market, the 21st largest radio market in the United States with a population of about 2.3 million people. There were 24 other radio stations that also competed in the market. Three were public radio stations—WYPR, previously affiliated with Johns Hopkins University; WTMD affiliated with Towson University; and WBJC affiliated with Baltimore City Community College. As well, a number of radio stations in the market also competed with news/talk, jazz, or mixed music formats.

Fiske and Jabari Owens, the station General Manager, admired WAMU, the leading public radio station for NPR news and information in the Washington DC area. They cited it as a role model for their station and what they hoped to achieve. WAMU was in the 9th largest radio market in the country with a population of 4.2 million people. On air since 1961, the station was member supported, professionally staffed, and licensed to American University. The station had about 580,000 unique listeners in 2006. In that same year, the station generated revenue of $11.4 million, expenses of $10.3 million, and a profit of about $1.1 million.

In comparison, WEAA had about 90,000 unique listeners in 2006. The station had annual revenue of $563,000, annual operating expenses of $770,500, and an annual loss of $207,500 in that same year. (See Table 1 for Profit and Loss Statements for WEAA.)

Like WAMU, their role model, and other public, non-profit radio stations (e.g., WTMD, WBJC), WEAA was licensed under and owned by a higher education institution. WEAA was part of Morgan State University's College of Liberal Arts, Communications Studies Department, Telecommunications Program. The College of Liberal Arts, the largest academic division of the University, served over 30 percent of the University's 6,000 enrolled students. Twenty-five percent of the College's students were telecommunications majors, the most popular major. In the Telecommunication Program, students learned about telecommunications theory and practices, through on-campus media laboratory experiences, and with workshops and internships. In 2006, a new, $21 million building was completed to house the Communications Studies Department, the Media Center, the Journalism and Writing programs of the College of Liberal Arts, and the WEAA radio

---

[2]Letters assigned to broadcast stations by the Federal Communications Commission (FCC), by which stations identify themselves. In general, stations east of the Mississippi River have call letters beginning with W; those west of the Mississippi have call letters beginning with K.

Table 1 WEAA Profit and Loss Statement

	2004	2005	2006	2007 est.
Revenue				
Underwriting/membership (fund raising)	$234,000	$250,000	$113,000	$135,000
Studio rental				$5,000
Grants	$200,000	$200,000	$200,000	$200,000
University Funds	$186,000	$300,000	$250,000	$200,000
Total	$620,000	$750,000	$563,000	$540,000
Expenses	$770,500	$770,500	$770,500	$770,500
Profit/Loss	−$150,500	−$20,500	−$207,500	−$230,500

Sources: 2004 Audited Financial Statement, General Manager estimates, 2007.

station. The station moved into their state-of-the-art broadcasting facility, including modern offices and studios in the fall of 2006. According to Jabari Owens, the station "has a 'great stick.'"[3]

The radio station was organized as outlined in Figure 1. Jabari Owens was the fourth general manager hired by WEAA in the past four years. Volunteers typically have had little interaction with station management. Jabari Owens, the new General Manager, noted that "turnover has hurt the organization, stalling growth and development." The Membership Director position, responsible for leading fund raising, had been open for over a year and consequently the station had not had a formal fund raising drive in at least two years. As he became familiar with the organization, Owens noticed that there were some unconventional aspects of the organization in terms of titles, reporting relationships, and business processes (e.g., directors reporting to directors, people reporting to whomever they wanted to, tasks allocated in inefficient ways).

Corin Fiske's Perspective

Fiske was attracted to the position at WEAA because she saw an opportunity to be part of building a radio station, transforming it from a small station to a larger, profitable, highly regarded station like WAMU. "I have an entrepreneurial spirit. Themes that have emerged over the course of my career are change and learning. I am a change agent. I also love to learn. So, I found the opportunity at WEAA very attractive. I think they were looking for a leader to make things happen, to lead change. That's me."

Fiske had 10 years of experience in the broadcasting industry. She started her career as a radio personality and entertainment reporter for radio station WAFL-FM in Dover, Delaware, the

---

[3]A very powerful broadcast antenna for a public radio station.

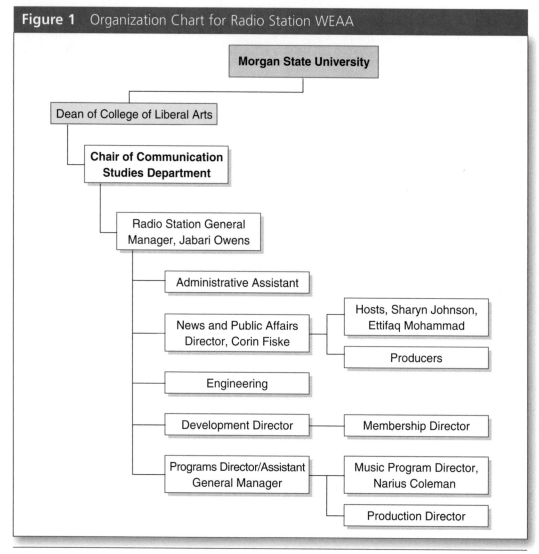

Figure 1 Organization Chart for Radio Station WEAA

Source: General Manager, 2007; www.morgan.edu, 2007.

75th largest radio market in the United States. After two years, she became a TV reporter at the NBC affiliate KWES-TV in Midland, Texas (a market with a population of just under 100,000 people), for a year. Next she jumped to Philadelphia, the 5th largest city in the United States based on population, where she spent a year as a TV reporter and photographer for the number 4 ranked station, a 24-hour news station. Then she moved to Youngstown, Ohio (a market with a population of just under 100,000 people), where she was a TV reporter for CBS/Fox for two years. While at CBS/Fox she was recruited to be a reporter for a new station launch, a 24-hour news Time/Warner TV station in Houston, the 4th largest market in the United States based on population. She spent two years there, before she moved to Atlanta and helped build a broadcast school, the Connecticut School of Broadcasting (CSB). For two years she developed their TV curriculum, which was adopted at all their campuses. "Then I was wooed to Morgan to be part of building a radio station. I have industry experience, I am a teacher. I joined WEAA to develop curriculum, to leverage the radio station in the community, to develop and file content[4] locally and nationally, to grow," she explained.

The call from Micah Razan, resigning, was one of many incidents that contributed to Fiske's growing feeling that there were significant issues she needed to address, if she wanted to be successful in her new position. During the call, Razan said she had just gotten a promotion in her full-time job and would be moving. Razan told Fiske that she had come up with the original idea for the show and had been hosting the show for 14 years, and she planned to take the name and concept with her, so that she could use it when she relocated. Fiske said, "I believe that the question of ownership of the intellectual property of the show is debatable." However, because of the turnover, turmoil, and the laissez-faire management approach at the station any history or documentation about the intellectual property rights (e.g., evidence of a work for hire policy or contract) would be very difficult to find. She decided not to fight Razan; but to Fiske the situation illustrated the vulnerability of the station when policies and expectations were unclear. She viewed the lack of commitment to and agreement on operating policies and standards as a serious issue. She also thought some of her staff were resistant to change, disengaged, and lacking motivation.

She recalled, "Shortly after I started this job, I was in my office, we were in two buildings then, I still hadn't moved to the new building. A young woman came in to be a guest on a show. She'd come to the wrong building (the old building). I knew the show started at 6:00 p.m., so I decided to speed-walk her to the other building where the show was being produced live. When we got there, just after 6:00, the show hadn't started yet. The theme song was playing; it played for 10 minutes. Finally, the host runs in, says 'Oh !@%&, I know you're going to be upset,' then starts the show."

"Later, I called him in for a meeting. I explained that the next time he was late, even if it was by one minute, we would air an encore presentation[5]. . . . Over the years we have had a history of this. Some volunteers who serve as hosts and are not working at a high effort, they undermine the quality of the programming." She explained that sometimes hosts do not have the skills, experience, or motivation to deliver high-quality, timely programming. For example, she noted that not all hosts called in if they were going to be late or miss the show. This resulted in shows not starting on time or having to substitute an encore presentation at the last minute instead of airing a live show as scheduled.

She recalled another situation during the fall of 2006: "This one was a nightmare. Ed Zeigler, a college professor from a local community college, hosted one of the shows, a political talk show. Zeigler and his producer couldn't understand the importance of balance in reporting on the show. A very strict balance is required to maintain credibility and have high journalistic integrity. As journalists we should investigate, report, and cover the story. We are not actors/actresses; we should not create the story. On one show, Zeigler talked about an individual, a prominent public figure, not doing his job. I explained that you are the host; you can't just present your opinion or even just one side of the story. Your job as host is to present both sides of the story, a balanced view. Zeigler said: 'Well, what about Rush Limbaugh, he presents his opinion. He doesn't present all sides of an issue.' I said, 'Rush Limbaugh isn't on a public radio station.' I spent over an hour going back and forth with him about balance and our responsibility as a public radio station to offer listeners an opportunity to discover opposing views in a way that respects differences and our listeners. We should not be featuring shouting matches. If we want to criticize a public official for something, we need to invite him to explain

---

[4]Radio programming content

[5]A repeat of a previously aired program.

his perspective or at least be able to say we asked the official for his response and he declined. It was a frustrating conversation."

As Fiske reviewed the situation, she noted, "Of the 20 volunteer talk show hosts that I'm responsible for, many have never been trained. Many do not understand public radio standards and some are resisting and/or putting in a low effort. Some have never been oriented; some have never been evaluated. Most shows don't have a producer.[6] We have an issue of lack of consistency of programming standards across the board. And we don't have enough key personnel to facilitate the production of solid news."

Fiske experienced some resistance from her staff in terms of communicating and reporting. Volunteer staff members did not have offices (i.e., a room with a phone and a computer) at the radio station. Most worked out of their homes or offices and only came into the station to work on their shows. When she was introduced to her staff at a meeting in September, she asked them to meet with her individually, on a regular basis, so they could get to know each other and work together on programming. Some staff members have never followed up on this request. Some did not return her phone calls or emails. Every quarter she needed to compile programming information for mandatory reporting to the FCC. It had been a struggle to get complete information from her staff on a timely basis. Recently, she tried a new approach. After explaining the importance of the information to her staff, she sent them, via email, a schedule of the due dates; she also sent them a reminder a few weeks before the deadline, and gave them a template

document to fill in. This helped, Fiske explained, and she got a great improvement in the response rate and got reports from half her staff.

"One of the challenges in my position has been the staffing philosophy of using mostly or all volunteer staff versus paid staff. I applaud volunteers working at a high effort level. I've been a volunteer; I was an executive on loan to the United Way for over a year. I was personally in charge of raising $8 million. I exceeded the goal. I was very committed. All the volunteers were very committed. I knew they valued me. I knew they appreciated my skills. It was one of the best experiences of my life. They really worked hard to show their appreciation. They had a volunteer appreciation dinner. Every month they had one or two events honoring volunteers. So I know what it is to be a volunteer and to be committed. The United Way was an important part of my development and I want to bring that emphasis on commitment and recognition to WEAA."

Fiske felt an urgent need to address the issues she faced; they could jeopardize her success and the success of WEAA. But, she had many other duties also: "I have been writing grants, developing curriculum, and recruiting, training, and managing volunteers. I am working long hours, 12–13 hour days. I return phone calls, respond to emails, and deal with operating priorities as they pop up. I have had to turn down opportunities to develop community relations, simply because I don't have time for it."

Fiske reviewed a list of priorities she had drafted when she first arrived. (See Table 2.) She wondered if they still made sense.

Table 2   Ideas for Change Within Department of News and Public Affairs
• Establish core values and standards
• Strengthen content
• Underwriting for all news and public affairs programming
• Discontinue and reposition all first Sunday and fifth week Tuesday, Wednesday, and Thursday shows

---

[6]A producer for a radio show is responsible for generating and researching ideas for show content, identifying and booking resources/guests, overseeing production, evaluating performance, and providing feedback and direction for performance improvement.

- Diversify programming
- Develop volunteer curriculum and career development workshops
- Produce vignette, modules, and segment
- Purchase field reporting equipment for expansion
- Feature reporting
- Strengthen relationship with University
- Develop more versatile approach to programming (interactive via web, pod casting, etc., TV)
- Establish ownership of programs
- Explore syndication opportunities
- Establish relationship with NPR to file content nationally
- Develop volunteer appreciation awards ceremony

Source: Corin Fiske, 2007.

To provide additional insight about the situation at WEAA, Fiske's boss, a peer, and two volunteer subordinates shared their perspectives.

Jabari Owens's Perspective

Jabari Owens, General Manager of WEAA since October 2006, was a third-generation radio broadcaster and Fiske's boss. He had 10 years of experience in the radio business. He started in college radio at the University of Miami and just left a satellite radio firm to join WEAA. He was attracted to WEAA by the "turn around" opportunity and the chance to build a profitable, competitive public radio station from the ground up. His mission was to "run the station as a business . . . and to make the station financially self sufficient in five years so that it does not rely on the roughly $350,000 the university provides in yearly financial support. He saw WAMU as a role model from which WEAA could learn.

Owens thought that the station's strong community connection was both a strength and a weakness. "Featuring members of the community on-air results in a high level of buy-in and ownership. However, over reliance on volunteer community members has made the station vulnerable (sometimes unable to operate independently). One of my roles as the General Manager is to protect the station's license. The lack of direction, lack of structure, and lack of understanding can be dangerous."

He said, "Radio is an art and a science. We have the art down. But being opinionated and articulate is not enough. We need to get the science part of it down. Producing news, talk, and public affairs programming is the most difficult type of programming to create and we are doing it mostly with volunteers. We need qualified producers to manage the complete lifecycle of every show. Some folks will welcome these changes and the opportunity to take it to the next level. Others will say 'I don't need any help, I want to do my own thing.' Some will think 'this is just a way of trying to control me' versus trying to improve my show." Owens said, "As a management team we must set expectations, provide the tools and resources, and establish regular evaluations. Fiske will need to tackle the challenges of motivating a volunteer staff, reigning in the types of programs on-air, and creating a culture of commitment.

Owens believed Fiske had a wealth of experience, and a desire to build, and that she would be instrumental in developing the station's mission and programming philosophy. "She instantly conveys an air of professionalism, she can and has established a higher level of professionalism. She has an ability to build relationships with students, with other departments, and within the University and the community. One opportunity for her to become even more effective is to develop a more fluid working relationship with the Program Director/ Assistant General Manager." Owens said, "The only thing holding us back is us, the infrastructure is here. We have the art down. We have the passion, the stuff you can't teach. We need to teach the science."

Narius Coleman's Perspective

Narius Coleman, Assistant Program Director, Music Director, and "In the Groove" host, had been in the radio business for 14 years and was a colleague/peer of Fiske's. He started working at WEAA as a student, after graduation he left to work in commercial radio, and he had now been back at the station for two years. Coleman saw the station "as a very small team (five full-time employees, a few part-time employees, and 30 plus volunteers). The advantage is that we are a small, close-knit group; the disadvantage is that the amount of work can be overwhelming at times. I'd love to see more full-time employees; unfortunately we just don't have the money. We have so many opportunities, if we had free rein; but we have to abide by the rules and regulations of the Communications Department. There is a lot of red tape."

Coleman said, "You can only expect so much from volunteers. Sometimes they don't put their all into it. If talk show hosts can't make it, they just don't come in. Then we have to run an encore presentation. If they were paid, they'd be here, because time is money. One of our biggest challenges is to get folks to take ownership as if it was a paid job."

"Corin has a vision, she has the background. She's put together curriculum. She's trained students. She's making a difference. She is 'on point' on so many things. My only suggestion for her is to pick up her phone," he said with a smile. "She is so busy, she's hard to get on the phone."

Sharyn Johnson's Perspective

Sharyn Johnson, "Real Money" volunteer host for eight years, was a 20-year veteran of the financial services industry and one of Fiske's direct reports. When she had children, Johnson said she "downshifted" (i.e., tried to work less and to achieve a better balance between work and family life), starting her own consulting business, Johnson's Media Group. Her firm specialized in consulting on how to sell financial services and the financial empowerment and education to consumers. Volunteering as a radio show host made a lot of sense to Johnson because she got a lot of return in terms of publicity and awareness for herself and ultimately her business.

Johnson noted that for many years WEAA had been considered a community service of the University, not a business. Johnson said, "Five years ago this was a little radio station, hosts said what they wanted to say, there was no rigor, most hosts were winging it." Johnson saw the station as a "diamond in the rough." She saw the value and potential of the station and believes that Fiske and the other managers needed to help the university administration see that potential also—"get the leadership to see what's sitting in front of them." Johnson liked the fact that Fiske was introducing NPR standards and a higher level of expectations for the staff. She thought that Fiske should try to communicate more frequently with the staff. "People need to hear her voice, we need to hear praise when we're on track, and we need her to let us know when we're off track."

Johnson talked about the challenges of delivering quality programming with an all-volunteer staff: "As soon as a volunteer intern is trained and ramped up, they're moving on. A show needs a producer to come up with story ideas, do research, book guests—'feed the beast.' It is very difficult to produce quality programming with an all-volunteer staff. If people add value, you have to pay them. I think it would be much better to hire hosts versus have volunteers. Then we could set standards."

Ettifaq Mohammad's Perspective

Ettifaq Mohammad, "Listen Up" volunteer host for three years and one of Fiske's direct reports, was the 27-year-old co-founder and president of New Light Leadership Coalition, Inc., a nonprofit organization devoted to leadership development among youth, by youth. Mohammad said, "I am very grateful to be part of WEAA. I feel like the organization has always been very supportive, giving me a platform to communicate with an audience of 100,000 at a young age with relatively little radio experience. If I could get paid it would be great, but I'm just so happy to be on air, I'm grateful for the opportunity."

Mohammad had seen a lot of changes and transitions at the station and he thought they were generally positive; however, they hadn't really affected him. He noted that the station had different types of General Managers, from Zack Johnson who had been outgoing and emphasized getting Hollywood-style entertainment on air, to more introverted, "hands off" educators.

He noted that the culture had been one where most hosts don't have journalism or radio backgrounds. Mohammad believed the staff supported Fiske—she had good interpersonal skills—"It is comforting to know the News Director and to know that she knows my name, she listens to my show and will give me feedback."

According to Mohammad, one of Fiske's biggest challenges was to get the support of the University administration. "Sometimes Morgan (MSU) suffers from administrative and management problems, so it can be a challenge to work through the red tape and politics. Fiske comes from a fast paced TV environment; she may need to balance her passion and urgency with the level of passion and urgency of other people. She needs to work through the culture, helping to regain the trust and support of students and the administration that has been lost due to prior poor management."

Mohammad noted the challenges of a volunteer staff: "You can't put too many expectations on them. I just lost a student intern producer, her grades were falling, so she just couldn't do the show." In closing, he said, "We all want to see WEAA thrive . . . we want to see WEAA get to the top of its game."

Conclusion

As Fiske reflected on her relatively short time at WEAA, she realized she faced some urgent issues and she had concerns about the level of support and motivation among her staff for her and for the station's goals. She had a lot on her plate. The call from Razan, resigning, was still fresh on her mind, as was the frustrating conversation with Zeigler and his producer. She'd heard rumors Zeigler was thinking of making their disagreements public (possibly talking to reporters). She was still excited about the opportunities at WEAA. What could she do to ensure her success and the success of the organization? A serious strategy meeting with Owens, her boss, was urgently needed. She needed to share her ideas and concerns and get his ideas and advice about how to resolve these issues. Then she could develop a plan of action and focus on implementing it.

References

Best of Baltimore. 2008, from www.citypaper.com/bob/story.asp?id=12612

WEAA. 2007, from www.weaa.org/index.html

Arbitron radio stations. 2008, from www.arbitron.com/radio_stations/home.htm

List of radio stations in Maryland. 2007, from http://en.wikipedia.org/wiki/List_of_radio_stations_in_Maryland

On the radio dot.net. 2008, from www.ontheradio.net/states/maryland.aspx

WAMU. 2007, from http://wamu.org/

Morgan State University. 2007, from www.morgan.edu

Dash, J. (2008). Whose public radio?, from http://baltimore.bizjournals.com/baltimore/stories/2008/03/10/focus1.html

Case Study 2

FOX Relocation Management Corp.

Cynthia Ingols and Lisa Brem, Simmons College

Gretchen Fox smiled as she drove back to her office one afternoon in June 1999. She had just attended an awards banquet for the New England Women Business Owners Association, where she was named Business Woman of the Year.

As she drove, Fox reflected on all that had transpired in her career since she earned her MBA from the Simmons School of Management in 1987. She had started her business, FOX Relocation Management Corp., a year after graduation. Over the next 11 years, the business, which specialized in moving offices, branches, or entire companies to new locations, had grown from a one-person consultancy to a successful private company employing 40 people. Fox wholly owned the subchapter S corporation, and had thus far avoided taking out loans to grow the company, other than the use of an occasional line of credit.

Fox had reason to feel that she had "made it." But she also felt that she could not simply sit back and savor her success. Her business continued to have opportunities for growth. For Fox, change was not only inevitable, it was preferable. As she explained:

> The real joy for me comes from founding and growing a business. We are a growing company, and we need sparks of excitement that come from change, from going to the next level. Opening new offices, going national or international, expanding the services we offer, going public—all these things would give us as a company more reasons to be proud. People here are invested in the future. We can't get to the future by standing still.

This growth showed the business was prospering, but it also posed urgent problems. For the first time, Fox felt she needed to add another layer of management to her organization. Fox wasn't sure that the compensation and incentive plans currently in place were appropriate for this new layer. She also worried that more hierarchy would ruin the carefully constructed culture of independent thinkers at her company.

Fox had built her business by maintaining close contact with both employees and clients. Her vivacious personality, intelligence, and "can do" attitude set the tone for her company. Fox's personal touch was one of the major motivators for her staff and one of the selling points for the company's services. The central question in Fox's mind was how to grow the business without losing the hands-on style that had made the company successful. As Fox explained:

So much of what we do and who we are is attributable to our small size. We are more like a family than a company. We've always been fairly informal with our employees. Conventional wisdom would say that now we are getting too big to do business that way any more. We have put some formal procedures in place, but will they be enough as we move forward?

An Easy Way to Start a Consulting Company

For Gretchen Fox running a relocation company was a perfect fit. She had moved several times throughout the United States and internationally with her late husband, who was an officer in the U.S. Air Force. In 1983, she settled in the Boston area. She earned her MBA part time while holding down a job and raising two children. Throughout the 1980s she held administrative management positions at a variety of Boston law and consulting firms. As it happened, a common denominator of all her jobs was moving the office. As Fox recalled:

All the firms I worked for made major moves, and I ended up managing them. I became something of an expert at it. I preferred the project management aspect of moving rather than the day-to-day maintenance tasks.

In August 1987, at the end of her third year of her part-time MBA program, Fox was ready for a change. She felt restless at her job and wanted to try her hand at an entrepreneurial venture.

Fox had become increasingly impatient with the rigid hierarchies she saw in the legal firms where she worked. She felt it took too long to make decisions and that steep hierarchies promoted a lack of accountability. Fox explained:

One reason I really don't like hierarchies is their lack of immediate decision-making.

One example that had serious repercussions was when I worked at a law firm and we had a bad snow storm. I wanted to send people home early, but my boss had to go to his boss and on up the chain. By the time I got out of there, I ended up with a seven hour drive home.

The other part of it for me, is that I don't automatically respect someone with a title or position; I'm more interested in a meritocracy. That's personal bias I suppose. The law firms couldn't give underlings decision-making authority because they weren't lawyers. Conversely, I remember a time I was lugging huge water bottles to the cooler and the big, strapping, male lawyers walked right by me, not one stopped to help. Being a partner took precedence over being a person. Those kinds of separations don't make for a cohesive team. I wanted to create a place where I didn't have to live by those rules anymore.

She felt she could be successful if she put all her experience with corporate relocation to work in a consulting business. Fox, however, was not sure how to get started—would companies actually pay her to be a "move expert"?

In 1988, she had the answer to her question. An office manager from a large Boston law firm called Fox to see if she'd be interested in organizing their upcoming move. The call came as a result of a networking group that Fox had started while she was working for a law firm in Washington DC. Fox explained the connections that led to her first consulting job:

I was working for the DC satellite office of a large Boston law firm. There was one other Boston firm that also had a satellite office, so I started a lunch group that brought together managers from both companies. I felt as though we probably dealt with similar issues and could benefit from sharing experiences. I got to know the office manager of the other firm pretty well. A couple of years later, after I'd moved back to Boston, the office manager from the Boston firm happened to be talking to the DC office manager. The Boston office manager was looking for someone to manage the firm's move, and my DC friend immediately recommended me.

I interviewed for the job along with about eight other people. The hiring manager told me later that even though he'd interviewed people with a lot more experience—one was a very senior architect—he said my interpersonal skills were so strong that they decided to offer the job to me.

The company offered Fox a full-time one-year contract to move its 950-member workforce, giving her the choice of being on payroll or acting as an independent contractor. As Fox recalled:

There I was—wondering how to start consulting and this job dropped in my lap. I decided to go in as an independent contractor. I remember thinking—what easier way to start a consulting company? Of course, I didn't think then of what being a consultant meant. Later, I realized that, in addition to delivering services, I would have to send out invoices, set up a book-keeping system, and find more clients.

Fox set up shop in her Lexington home and worked independently on small projects until 1992, when she accepted a large job at Harvard Business School that eventually developed into a two-year commitment. She hired several temporary employees to help coordinate the move, but realized in August 1992 that she would need permanent help. Fox hired Lori Coletti, a facility management specialist from a large telecommunications company. Coletti had a degree in interior design and experience with business furnishings that complemented Fox's business degree and relocation skills. Although Fox was happy to gain an employee with Coletti's background, hiring a full-time employee was unsettling. As Fox explained:

Hiring Lori, my first permanent employee, was the first big milestone for the business. It was the hardest thing I have ever had to do. I was suddenly responsible for someone else—for her family—for her livelihood. It was a combination of worrying about not having enough work for her and having to pay her even if the work wasn't coming in. We sort of got around that. We negotiated an hourly wage, figuring that if I didn't need 40 hours per week consistently, I wouldn't have to pay for it. But in reality, Lori ended up working 50 hours a week from the start and that has never really changed. She is still here—and is vice president of the company.

A Loose Collection of Consultants

In the fall of 1992, when a large regional bank hired Fox to move its Massachusetts headquarters, Fox hired two more employees. From September 1992 through May 1993, FOX Relocation moved 1,500 people for the bank. From that time on, Fox continued to augment the bank's project management staff, managing various aspects of employee relocation on a permanent basis.

By 1994, the company had seven hourly employees. The base of operations was still Fox's home, although most of the work was done on-site at client facilities. One long-time employee, Jane Menton, described the start-up phase:

I started working for Gretchen in 1992. At the time, Fox Relocation wasn't so much a company as a loose collection of consultants. She had one employee—Lori. Mostly, though, Gretchen would hire consultants to get the jobs done. Eventually, she hired me as the second employee.

It was interesting working out of someone's house. I feel fortunate to have started that way because I was able to work directly with Gretchen. I got to really understand what she expected and how she worked with clients. At the time she was a project manager running projects instead of the more administrative role she plays now as president of the company. I enjoyed those early days. I felt we were all learning at the same time.

The energy of starting something new and operating on a shoestring was exciting, but Fox felt the need to become established in a Boston location closer to her client base. "People were trying to do business out of phone booths," she recalled. "It was time we moved downtown."

In October 1994 the company's five employees were working with two large clients and managing four smaller projects. Fox decided to sublease space from a Boston real estate management firm. For $500 a month, Fox and her employees shared a small office and had use of the real estate firm's equipment and conference room. Fox felt that this arrangement was a good way to test the waters without incurring significant financial risk. It wasn't long, however, before the company outgrew the space. "We were getting in the way. We were using the conference room more than the company we were subleasing from," Fox explained.

By December 1995, FOX Relocation had doubled in size, with enough work to keep 10 full-time employees busy. The company moved to 2,200 square feet of space on the 11th floor of a downtown Boston office building. Six months later, it increased its office size by another 2,200 square feet. Fox explained the financial risk the company took that year:

Instead of paying $6,000 a year on rent, we were now paying more than 10 times that amount. It was daunting. But the up side was that our business was expanding as well. By the end of 1996, we had over 20 employees. We had doubled in size in two years.

Relocation Consultants—A Niche Within the Facility Management Industry

Before 1980, the term *move consultants* was not in Corporate America's vocabulary. Most—if not all—moves were performed by employees. Office managers in small to medium-sized firms and facility management teams in large firms typically had the dubious honor of managing and executing a move. In the 1980s, however, as the tidal wave of downsizing swept away administrative personnel and departments, corporate executives found that there was no one left with the expertise and the time to plan a large move. The facility management outsourcing industry gave birth to a small subset of firms that chose to specialize in the high-stress world of corporate relocations.

Another trend in facilities management, called *workforce churn*, also fueled the growth of relocation consultants. *Churn* was the term used to describe the continual movement of employees as a result of expansion, downsizing, redeployment, or a project-oriented workforce. *The Boston Globe* reported in 1998 that the average churn rate (the percentage of employees who took part in some type of organizational move) was 44% nationwide, with the Boston area's rate much higher, at 60 to 70 percent.[1] As one facility management industry magazine wrote:

American businesses are changing at an ever-increasing rate. Churn rates of 55 to

---

[1] Valigra, Lori, "Helping Firms on the Move," *The Boston Globe,* November 25, 1998.

60 percent are now common compared to 25 to 30 percent just a few years ago. And churn rates of 100 percent are no longer shocking. A Texas computer manufacturer reports moving more than 12,000 people in one city over a one-year period to accommodate a one-third growth in employment and a 100 percent churn rate. An energy company moves more than 800 people, 40 percent of its employees, over a four-month period.[2]

The reasons for the high level of churn rates were increases in industry consolidations and corporate mergers, and the rapid expansion of high-tech firms that used fluid teams to perform projects. As the article described:

It's not unusual for companies to form teams involving up to 300 people, and then as the project nears completion, ramp-down to 20 people. This trend is particularly prevalent among software and computer manufacturers. [. . .] About 15 percent of this activity involves moves into new facilities, consuming more than $10 billion each year in goods and services to do so.[3]

In addition to offering an experienced, cost-efficient team to manage moves, relocation consultants also took the heat of a stressful move off an employee or department. Since two-thirds of employees in charge of a move are either fired or quit soon after the move, hiring a move consultant saved companies the cost of hiring and training new personnel.[4] Fox pointed out that consultants were, for the most part, protected from office politics and made space assignments and other decisions objectively.

The FOX Way

Throughout the early 1990s, Fox experienced growth in number and scope of assignments. She continued to hire project managers in response to the increasing demands of both new and existing clients. In 1995, Fox promoted Lori, her first employee and right arm, to the position of Vice President. This marked a departure from Fox's "loose collection of consultants" and the installation of a rudimentary hierarchy. The bulk of the staff, the project managers, remained on the same level.

The company prided itself on its lack of formal titles and status symbols. As Fox explained:

We are not departmentalized. I didn't set up the company to operate that way. I didn't personally do all that well in hierarchical organizations that typically operated under the more traditional business model. I didn't like it, and I chose not to subject other people to it.

That's not to say we don't have *any* hierarchy or that we have a totally flat organization. Of course we do have some hierarchy—we have hierarchy of experience. We have some people who have been in this business for 25 years and some who have been in it for one. The one with 25 years of experience is much more likely to be managing a project than the person with little experience. But we don't use titles, except for Lori and myself. It's not something that's needed internally.

Despite the lack of titles, it was always clear to the client who to contact if there was a problem or issue. In the beginning

---

[2]Fischer, Glenn, "Four Elements of a Successful Move," *Buildings,* March 1998, p. 1.

[3]Ibid.

[4]Valigra.

they always talked to me, then after I made Lori Vice President, she talked to her clients and I kept mine. There was perhaps more internal than external confusion.

Although most of the staff at FOX Relocation were female, Fox asserted that she didn't set out to build an all-female company. The fact was the overwhelming majority of applicants happened to be female. Fox believed the reason for this was that the work lent itself to a traditionally "female" approach to tasks and problem solving. As she explained:

The way we work is very hands-on. Of course, not all relocation companies work this way. One of our competitors is almost entirely male, and they don't offer the same level of hands-on attention to detail that we do. It's really a different business model.

We are widely known for our incredible ability to coordinate and manage all the details of a move. One of our employees said to me at lunch the other day that a lot of what we do is handholding and giving pats on the back. And that really is important. People are traumatized by moves. Even if they are moving to a different floor in the same building, there is something very unsettling about it. We help communicate with people and listen to their concerns. At the same time we handle a zillion details, from selecting voice/data networks to making sure there are coat hangers in every closet.

Employees at FOX Relocation expressed a strong sense of shared values and prided themselves on their customer-service orientation. As Project Manager Robin Dorogusker explained:

At FOX, we have a style of working that is tightly focused on customer service. We want the customer to be happy and we want to do a good job. Everyone here is willing to get down and dirty and do whatever it takes to get the job done—whether it's designing

office space or crawling around on the floor looking for phone jacks.

The culture at FOX Relocation was expressed in its code of ethics and mission statement, written in the spring of 1997:

Code of Ethics

- We are a community and our clients are part of that community
- We treat our employees and clients with utmost respect
- We seek continuous improvement
- We have as much fun as our work allows

Mission Statement

Our mission is to provide a full range of corporate real estate program and project management services in a way that supports our clients' culture and fulfills their unique needs so as to ensure that the clients' business operations and revenue stream are not disrupted.

The culture at Fox was communicated to new employees in a variety of ways. One employee told of how, the first day on the job, he[she] was added to the company-wide email distribution list. One of the first emails is below:

As you all know, our good friend Bob will be retiring this Spring. The good news is that he has already sold his house. The bad news is that he has to be out of it by the week of January 12—yikes!

We are looking for volunteers to help pack his (4,400sf!) house on the following dates:

Saturday 1/3/03

Saturday 1/10/03

Sunday 1/11/03

Any and all help will be appreciated. Bob will offer snacks, beverages, and even a little pool playing during the breaks! Also—who knows what he will decide not to take? There may be a few cool items to raffle off to helpers! In any case, we will make it fun.

Please understand that this is not a FOX project (not billable) . . . it is merely helping out a fellow FOX (builds good karma)! Please let me know if you are able to help on any of these dates. I will be happy to provide directions as well as coordinating any carpooling if necessary.

Thanks!

—Ginny

Workflow at FOX Relocation

Client projects at FOX Relocation generally fell into two categories: one-time moves and on-going facility management. FOX Relocation employees were primarily coordinators. They did not actually pick up and move boxes; rather, they set schedules and coordinated the moving company's activities with the activities of other sub-contractors such as security, electricians, and environmental systems. One-time moves involved anything from a small group relocating to another floor, to 2,500 employees moving to a new building over the course of a single weekend. Teams were formed for each job and were disbanded when a job was completed. **Exhibit 1** is a representation of responsibility areas involved in a typical one-time move. It was created as a guideline for a move, a reminder of what should be completed, but the actual implementation was up to the individual assigned the move. It also served as an agenda for the kick off meeting with the client. It made it clear what responsibility areas Fox was willing to take on.

The on-going facility work usually entailed at least two people working full-time, or nearly full-time, on-site at a client's facility. On-going work included space planning; inventorying, refurbishment, or procurement of furniture and art; coordinating new construction and building maintenance; and moving and installing technology. Employees at FOX either worked for several clients and projects at once or were stationed full-time on-site as part of the client's facility management team. Clients included Harvard University Law School, Fleet Bank, BankBoston, and Bell Atlantic.

Fox and Coletti conducted most of the company's marketing, which took the form of networking, nurturing client relationships, following leads, and the occasional write-up in the local press media. Approximately 30% of new jobs came from repeat customers, and most new clients came to FOX Relocation through word-of-mouth. Once a new client or job was identified, Fox or Coletti wrote proposals and conducted negotiations.

Coletti maintained a two-month workflow projection based on current jobs and what she and Fox judged to be "in the pipeline." Jobs were assigned to project managers based on their availability and expertise. Employee preferences were taken into account whenever possible. Generally, jobs were given to teams of two or three people. Although one person usually functioned as the primary client contact and maintained a budget and schedule for the project, that person did not have authority over others in the team and did not act as team leader. When the job was completed, members of the team moved on to form new teams around a new project. In large or complex moves, the teams were bigger and Fox or Coletti appointed a team leader to manage the overall move. Fox explained the fluid nature of the project manager roles:

> People are given projects based mainly on availability. They could be managing a large project this month and put on another project that someone else is running next month. So a person is not always in charge, nor is he or she always in the position of underling. This structure really makes a difference to how people see their roles.

Exhibit 1

One-Time Move: Areas of Responsibility

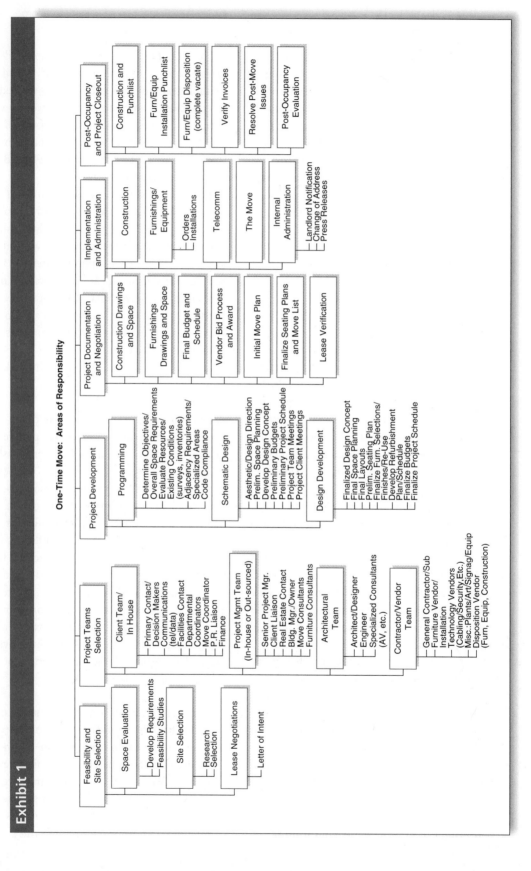

As Robin Dorogusker explained:

We don't have politics at FOX. People don't have to vie for position. There's no real hierarchy. People aren't trying to get to the next level, because there is no next level. So there isn't a sense of competition—just a feeling that we want to do a good job on our projects. We enjoy each other's successes and help out from job to job. There is a lot of camaraderie.

Since most clients wanted to minimize the downtime associated with relocation, the actual moving was done over a short and convenient period of time—usually at night or over a weekend. The team in charge of the move often needed more people to get the job completed on schedule. In particularly large or complex moves, the entire company could be mobilized. As Project Manager Jane Menton explained:

We think of ourselves as a team—one that needs to work together. Everyone is very good about that. Because even if you're on a two-person team, you may have a large move and you'll need extra help. I've never seen an instance when someone's needed help and no one has come forward. Sure, there are lots of times when you don't know what people are working on, but there are also the times when everyone— even Gretchen—will pitch in and help with a move. One great example of that was the Suffolk County Courthouse. We had to conduct a huge records inventory for that move. Everyone in the company had to contribute to get it done and they were all willing to help.

Human Resources

New employees came to FOX Relocation almost exclusively through word-of-mouth. Even in the low unemployment job market of the late 1990s,

the company had never needed to place a help-wanted advertisement. The company received several unsolicited resumes almost every week. Fox and Coletti conducted interviews on an on-going basis. Most of the resumes came from people with art, architecture, interior design, space planning, or facility management backgrounds. Many had experience as project managers for larger companies. Some FOX Relocation employees had previously been downsized as their corporations out-sourced their facility management divisions. Fox felt that despite the word-of-mouth method of hiring, she was as or more diverse in her hiring practices than most companies in her industry.

Project Manager Steven Smith recalled why he was attracted to FOX Relocation:

I wanted to work for a small company. I like to keep a balance between my work life and personal life and be able, for the most part, to maintain a 40-hour work week. I talked to some people who work for big companies and they had war stories about how many hours they put in. One of the benefits of working at FOX Relocation is that Gretchen and Lori recognize that people have a life outside the office, and empower us to manage our own workload and hours.

In the early years of the company, all employees interviewed and approved each new hire. Since the company was so small, Fox wanted to ensure that personalities meshed and that every employee understood and fit into the culture. Project Manager Larry Ellsworth, who was stationed full-time at a client site, described a typical FOX Relocation employee:

We are generally people who can fit in with other people. I like fitting in—I like understanding my client's needs, understanding their organization, and becoming part of it. I keep a reasonable distance while actively taking part in the job and acting in my client's interest. I think most of us here at

FOX have that ability. We're chameleons. We can pick up the color of our surrounding environment. It helps to get the job done when you are able to think the way your client thinks.

As the company grew, it was no longer feasible for all employees to be involved in hiring decisions. Instead, new hires met with an ad hoc committee of veteran employees. Jane Menton described the hiring process and what she looked for in an applicant:

Nervous people don't do well here. This is a high stress job. We are usually the last people brought in—after the architect, the builders, and so on. We are also the last people standing there after the move is completed, and we end up taking responsibility for decisions we didn't make. It's also our job to stay on a bit after the move to make sure everyone is settled. Sometime this takes a lot of diplomacy. Lots of people hate their job or hate their company, and the way they express that is to say "I hate my chair." People will try to gain control over whatever they can. So we change the chair, the employees are happy, and the project is a success.

Employees here also need to be comfortable with the lack of formal structure. People come from all kinds of backgrounds. Some, who've come from large organizations with a lot more structure, have a hard time adjusting to the flexibility we have at FOX. We have to work odd hours. We don't have defined roles. And we don't get a lot of formal feedback.

Other than annual reviews conducted by either Fox or Coletti, employees were given feedback and direction on a situational basis. Project managers had considerable autonomy over their projects. Menton explained the review process:

There is a form Gretchen uses for employee reviews, but she just uses it as a guide.

I haven't seen her actually fill it out. We are not managed very closely at all. Basically, Gretchen and Lori look at whether we bring our projects in on budget and on time. At the beginning of a job, they give us a not-to-exceed price based on a scope of work, and then it is up to us to manage the job. We occasionally get feedback from clients through letters or telephone calls. Most times we will ask the client if we can use them as a reference. We get a lot of our jobs through word-of-mouth, so it's important to have a good on-going relationship with our clients.

As Steven Smith described his feelings about the way employees were managed:

One thing I like more than anything else about this job is that, as far as the client is concerned, I *am* FOX Relocation. Lori, my boss—who I immediately report to—does not check in with us on a regular basis. We manage ourselves and we represent our own company. I think it's great that I'm a reflection of our company. I've never fully had that feeling before in any other job. It's very satisfying. I have a feeling of ownership without all the liability that true ownership would bring.

However, Smith, also saw drawbacks to the lack of formal structure:

I have three people on my team. We are stationed full-time at one of our large corporate clients. I am considered the senior person of that team, there is also another project manager and what I'd call a junior person on the team. To the client I am considered the team leader, but at FOX we're all considered to be on the same level. That's where I think there is something lacking in the organization. There is some lack of clarity on our part; our internal roles don't always correspond with our external roles. Most people here seem comfortable with this ambiguity, so I have not made an issue of it.

As one would expect in a service business, payroll and related expenses comprised the largest percentage of expenses (see **Exhibit 2, % Income Statements**[5]). All the project managers at FOX Relocation had the choice of being paid on an hourly or salaried basis. Hourly wages and salaries were negotiated individually, with the applicant naming a preferred rate, which Fox compared to other employees in the company with similar experience. Occasionally, Fox researched architectural and design firm employee pay rates. However, Fox was more concerned with maintaining internal wage parity than comparing with other firms. Most employees chose to be paid hourly. As Coletti explained:

In the early days of the company, people were paid hourly because we weren't sure we could guarantee full-time employment. It was fine with the other employees and me—we didn't need the guarantee of a 40-hour salary. Now, paying hourly wages serves as a motivator for people. It's similar to being on a sales force. The employees have some control over how much they make because, in most situations, they can set their schedules. We certainly don't want people working significantly more than 40 hours per week on a regular basis. People know, however, that if they do need to put in that kind of time, they will be paid for it. In certain cases, individuals who are paid hourly make out better on an annual basis than those same individuals would have on salary, so I encourage some people to opt for hourly pay. A few of the people who started out as salaried have eventually asked to go hourly, I have never seen anyone go the other way.

Growing Pains

As the company grew, one way that Fox kept abreast of employee attitudes and morale was to conduct a workplace satisfaction survey. Fox explained the differences in responses over the last several years:

Every year, I've sent out a survey to people asking: "What three things do you value in your workplace that you do have here?" and "What three things do you value that you don't have here?" At first the answer to the second question was health and dental benefits. So we added that. Then the answers were more in the vein of profit sharing and 401(k) plans, so we added that. Now we have what I consider a generous and complete benefits package (see **Exhibit 3, Benefit Compensation Package**). In every year we have had the 401(k) plan, we have added the maximum amount. Most employees were matched 100%. The profit sharing plan was simple. All employees, excepting me, took an equal share in profits of the company, after an amount was set aside for future growth. I found that satisfaction in incentive plans fell along gender lines. The males seemed to want more to strive for, that they needed a goal. I disagree with that. When one big accounting firm was falling apart, the chairman went to the board to ask for more money, arguing that he needed more pay to get quality work. I have to ask: What are you paying them for now? I don't really believe in incentive pay. I don't think getting more money at the end of the year makes one person work harder than another.

In 1998, 100% of the respondents said they valued most about FOX was the flexibility and number two was the teamwork aspect. One

---

[5]Since Fox Relocation is a privately held company, no financial statements were available for publication.

Exhibit 2   % Income Statements

	Jan–Dec 1997	Jan–Dec 1998	Jan–Dec 1999
Revenues	100.0%	100.0%	100.0%
Total Revenues	100.0%	100.0%	100.0%
Expenses			
401(k) Employer Contrib.	2.4%	2.4%	2.4%
Automobile Expense	0.2%	0.4%	0.4%
Dues and Subscriptions	0.1%	0.1%	0.1%
Equipment Rental	0.2%	0.3%	0.3%
Freelancer Expense	7.0%	4.0%	3.8%
Insurance	1.0%	1.0%	1.0%
Interest Expense		0.1%	0.3%
Marketing and Advertising	2.0%	1.1%	1.9%
Medical Insurance	1.0%	1.5%	1.5%
Moving and Storage	0.0%	0.5%	0.2%
Office Supplies	1.2%	1.1%	1.2%
Payroll Expenses			
Salaries and Wages	51.2%	55.0%	54.1%
Payroll Taxes	5.0%	4.5%	4.5%
Postage and Delivery	0.2%	0.2%	0.3%
Printing and Reproduction	0.2%	0.9%	0.3%
Professional Development	0.5%	0.2%	0.2%
Professional Fees	0.5%	0.5%	0.5%
Recruiting	0.2%		0.2%
Rent	3.1%	2.7%	2.2%
Repairs	0.3%	0.9%	0.3%
Taxes	0.2%	0.1%	0.3%
Telephone	1.1%	1.5%	1.3%
Travel and Entertainment	1.8%	2.5%	2.0%
Utilities	0.2%	0.2%	0.2%
Total Expenses	79.6%	81.7%	79.5%
Net Income	**20.4%**	**18.3%**	**20.5%**

Exhibit 3 Benefit Compensation Package

Benefit Compensation Package
As of July 1999

FOX provides the following employment benefits:

Tufts Associated Health Plan HMO	Employer pays 100% individual premium
Delta Dental Plan	Employer pays 50% individual premium
UNUM life insurance equal to annual Salary	Employer pays 100% premium
UNUM long-term disability policy	***Employees voted to pay 100% premium*** to preserve right to tax-free benefit
Maternity and Family Leave	In accordance with Maternity and Family Leave Act
401(k) Profit Sharing Plan	25% employer matching contribution (Note: Since plan inception, FOX has matched 100% of contributions)
Year-end Profit-Sharing	For past 5 years, FOX has paid every employee an equal amount from profits
Paid vacation	1 week in year 1 3 weeks in years 2–5 4 weeks in years 6–10
Paid holidays	8 plus 1 floating at employee discretion

Source: Company records.

thing they would like to see added now is the ability to have a greater role in firm management.

One Fox employee, Steven Smith, described how he saw incentives at Fox:

> You have to find ways to continually challenge yourself. After being at one client site for several years, I was able to move around a lot. I managed nine different clients the following year. That was a big change. It's a great incentive for me to be given autonomy to meet and exceed client expectations, to personally represent your entire company, and to be held responsible to stay within a set budget of billable hours. Hourly pay can be an incentive to work longer hours, but I don't abuse it. It does compensate me, though, when I'm working

a lot. Salary is just not discussed here. It is a closely guarded secret. No one knows what another person makes.

In 1997 and 1998 many of FOX Relocation's bank clients experienced mergers, leading the company to double in size from 20 to 40 employees to meet their clients' relocation needs. Up until this point, the company had enjoyed steady, manageable expansion. Robin Dorogusker explained the impact of this growth spurt:

> There was a rough period when we were growing rapidly. It was very difficult. We had some growing pains. We just weren't prepared for the pace at which we grew. We went to 40 employees before we had the

infrastructure or the technology to support them. So many people were getting hired so quickly. People felt they were thrown into the lion's den without any training. We didn't have time to train, and we weren't able to communicate with each other. Its hard working in an organization with 38 people when you don't know who some of the new people are.

By 1998, Fox realized that the company needed to change the way it trained new employees:

It became clear that we could no longer train people just by osmosis. We had to institute a more formal training program, which is basically a mentoring system. New people, regardless of how much work experience they have, are partnered with someone more senior on projects until such time as they can go out on their own. There is no rule as to how long the mentoring will last—it depends on the person.

Dorogusker agreed that the worst of the transition times seemed past:

As things slowed down a little, we started making time for meetings, and Gretchen and Lori have made an effort to get people to know each other. They tried to shift around the teams to allow people to work with others they hadn't gotten to know yet. Gretchen started picking names out of a hat and having those people go to lunch with each other. Through all of this rapid growth, Gretchen and Lori have tried to keep up the family atmosphere. For example, they are very tolerant of people's personal lives. Some bring their children to the office now and then. Gretchen and Lori try to understand what is going on with everyone and how their personal lives may or may not interfere with their work.

In late 1997, Fox felt the time had come to replace their outdated equipment and second-hand office furniture. She established an employee committee to redesign the office layout, purchase new furniture, and research computer networks. The committee came up with a "partial hoteling" solution, where employees, such as Coletti, Fox, and the administrative personnel had permanent desks and offices. The rest of the space was assigned and reassigned based on how much time each employee spent at the office. Employees that were based in the office, but were often at client sites, had a desk and file cabinet. The employees that were stationed full-time on client sites had temporary use of desks, drafting tables, and phones when they visited the office. The new office furniture the committee chose was designed to be lightweight and flexible to allow for easy movement as employee needs changed.

In 1998, the company completed the installation of a computer network and in 1999 was in the process of designing a website. The network made it much easier for Fox to communicate to employees and for employees to communicate with each other. Employees were also given cell phones and beepers, and the company maintained an updated list of all phone numbers, beeper numbers, and employee email addresses to make it easier for employees to keep in touch with the company.

Another way Fox communicated with her growing workforce was a two-hour bi-weekly staff luncheon. All employees attended the meetings—even those stationed off-site. At the meetings, people had a chance to apprise others of particular issues or staffing needs they may have on a project. The company also invited vendors or other experts to give presentations as a way to keep staff up to date on industry issues and new products. The company always paid for lunch, and each meeting concluded with a cake and celebration of staff birthdays and distribution of paychecks.

Growth at FOX Relocation was not only measured in the increased number of client projects and employees. The company was also expanding its capabilities. New employees brought with them a range of skills that FOX Relocation added to its capacities. In 1994, the company acquired a small interior design firm that had expertise in computer-aided design and computer-aided facilities management. FOX Relocation also developed expertise in art collection management. In addition, the company was handling bigger and more complex moving projects that required larger teams of people and a more formal hierarchy to execute. Dorogusker described the team put in place to conduct the Federal Courthouse move:

> The project was different in that it was much more massive than anything I had experienced before. It was the first time we designated an actual team leader, feeling that one point person would be most efficient. I was the project leader, and I had all the direct client contact. I directed three project managers who worked with the individual courts. I had to keep the project managers focused, maintain the schedules and budgets, and keep a view of the big picture. It was difficult at first. We had never worked in that kind of a structured team. It caused some tension because previously we'd been equals. But we talked it out and came to an understanding that our roles had to be different for this project. In the end we learned that sometimes we need that kind of structure to get the job done.

For Fox, growth also meant she was forced to step away from project management and the day-to-day oversight of her company. She refocused her role on marketing and public relations. As the company grew, Coletti shouldered more and more of the daily responsibility of running the company and supervising employees. As Dorogusker described:

> Gretchen and Lori play different roles. Gretchen has become a personality—winning

the award and being written about in the paper and that kind of thing. She is now more externally focused and involved in the marketing of the company. Lori is more hands-on. She keeps tabs on staffing and the status of projects. Lori also works with us and is connected to us on a more regular basis. Right now, I report to Lori. I used to work with Gretchen, and I'm fortunate in that respect. Most people here have not worked with Gretchen directly on a project.

As Coletti's and Fox's roles evolved, some employees expressed a sense of ambiguity concerning reporting relationships and authority. As Larry Ellsworth described:

> It's a little hard to say exactly what the reporting structure is here. Clearly Gretchen is the president of the company. I think about her as the overall strategic "big picture" person. Lori I think of more as the general manager/operations director. But I don't feel I have to go to only one of them about a specific problem. They are more like twin managers.

Coletti described the way she saw the reporting process:

> Some employees will come to me, while others go to Gretchen. There is some ambiguity about who makes certain decisions. Sometimes an employee will email both of us with a question. It gets a little sticky when we come back with different answers, but we work it out.

The Future

As Fox sat at her desk, looking out over Boston's teeming business district, she felt satisfied that she had built a reputable company, had a great team of people who were happy to work for her, and had a client base that would continue to expand. She knew that some key questions had to be answered in order to meet the future proactively. In what direction should she take the company? What will be the impact of growing from 50 to 100 people? How much longer could she pay people on an hourly basis? She was sure that soon, she would have to move to a conventional salary model. How would that impact her incentive structure? Fox also felt that she needed to create another layer of management. But should she? What impact would such changes have on teams and leadership of teams?

As Fox became more focused externally, how should she change her role and what should that new role be? Are isolated tensions and ambiguities indicative of systemic problems that could be exacerbated as the company grows? Can FOX Relocation maintain its culture, structure, and ability to respond quickly and effectively to client needs throughout this period of rapid growth?

Case Study 3

Travelink Solutions

Gene Deszca and Noah Deszca

Sixteen months had passed since William had joined Travelink Solutions' call center. It had been a fulfilling and, at times, frustrating employment experience. Now he was facing a decision concerning what to do next. Should he remain and try to make a difference or should he follow through on his plans to leave? Rather than letting the experience simply fade or become the subject of selective recall, he had followed through on an old teacher's advice and documented the work experience, hoping it might be helpful to him and maybe even to the firm.

Rather than keeping the documentation to himself, he decided to share it with Robert, a close friend and a marketing manager at Travelink. Discussing his observations with Robert would help him test the accuracy of his perceptions and sort out what he should do next. When William had joined the firm he had signed a non-disclosure agreement; consequently when he documented the experience he decided to disguise the firm. William didn't want to put individuals, the organization, or himself at risk.

Robert had been with Travelink for three years. His first job had been in the call center and he remained keenly interested in its operation, due to its impact on customer relations. He had been eager to see what his friend William had written. However, Robert found himself wincing as he read. All too clearly, the writing captured what had been happening and left him pondering what he ought to do with the concerns it raised. Change was needed but raising awareness and generating solutions that would be agreed to and implemented would not be easy. He turned to William and shook his head. "Fascinating—let me read this once again and think about it a little before we talk." Robert hoped that the answers would become clearer to him after another review of the matter.

William's Background

William was enthusiastic about his new job at Travelink Solutions Canada: a service company that provided travel assistance to global travelers on a 24/7 basis. Its core product had been emergency roadside automobile assistance, but over the years Travelink had expanded into other areas of travel help, such as legal assistance and emergency travel arrangements. The company did this for both its own individual customers and for other firms that offered related services but who had outsourced the product design and/or post sale customer service function to Travelink.

William had successfully completed his final university course requirements while working full time as a baker on the midnight shift at Tim Horton's. After eight months of beginning his workday at 11 pm, it would be nice to reintegrate himself into the realm of daylight. He knew that there would be occasional night and weekend shifts (no more than one week or weekend per month) to work at the call center, but that would be fine. He hoped that the challenge of a new job working within a call center would prove more satisfying than slinging dough at four in the morning.

The application process had been an intensive experience. At the age of 24, William had never applied for a position that demanded a lengthy series of interviews, references that were verified and tests designed to document his computer literacy, interpersonal and problem solving skills. While these procedures had been stressful, William felt positive about the process. Surviving such a careful system of selection left him feeling good about himself. It suggested to him that this firm must be serious about the quality of the people it hired.

Call Centers: How They Operated

Several call centers were located in William's home town. The presence of universities and the ethnic diversity of the area provided call centers with access to a literate and multilingual labor pool. Further, office rental costs and labor rates were moderate by provincial standards and there was an excellent telecommunications infrastructure. As a result, many of William's friends had worked or were working for other call centers. Their experiences, however, had generally been negative—particularly for those working in outbound call centers, those that make unrequested solicitations for everything from rug cleaning services to cell phones and charitable

donations. Friends who had worked in this type of call center told him that there were attractive sales related performance bonuses but that the base pay of between \$10–\$12.00 per hour was what most had to rely upon to pay the rent. In addition, his friends reported that there seemed to be few employment benefits (e.g., dental plans) available in many of these firms and that some positions were structured as permanent part-time positions, in order to fit the need for labor in the late afternoon and early evening period and reduce benefit obligations. They were almost unanimous in their descriptions of their outward bound call center jobs as quite stressful, characterized by hang-ups, call recipient abuse, and performance pressure.

Travelink, however, was an inbound call center that responded to customer requests for help with services they had already purchased. Furthermore, the people William knew who had worked for the firm spoke very positively about the work atmosphere. Robert, for example, had started on the phones but had been promoted to a marketing management position. He commented on the supportiveness of co-workers and his boss, as well as the satisfaction derived from helping a customer sort through a difficult situation.

William's new position came with comprehensive health benefits, paid holidays that exceeded legislated standards, and special rates for things such as local gym memberships, theme park passes, and concerts—discounts that the human resources department had negotiated for Travelink employees. It seemed to William that his new employer had thought about how to make the firm an appealing company to work for. *Wow*, William thought. A living wage combined with such benefits represented a pleasant change (see Exhibit 1 for compensation and benefit details).

Building a Business

Travelink was founded in 1987, in Jackson, Mississippi, to provide roadside assistance to car

Exhibit 1	Travelink Solutions Compensation Package for Full-Time Customer Service Representatives
Salary	$13 per hour or $27,040 to start, progressing to $18 per hour or $37,440 after 2 years (performance reviewed every 6 months)
Performance Bonus	Up to a 5% bonus is available to individual representatives, on an annual basis, based upon individual and corporate performance
Salary Review	Every 6 months until staff reaches the maximum for their pay category. After that, salary is reviewed annually
Benefits	A comprehensive benefit package, including dental, eye care, drugs, extended health, and insurance
Pension	Firm contributes 3% of employee's annual salary, employee can elect to contribute up to an additional 5% of his or her salary, with the firm matching this at a 50% level
Vacation	2 weeks of vacation for the first year of employment; 3 weeks after 5 years, 4 weeks after 15 years
Sick Days	5 paid sick days per year
Personal Obligation Days	Up to 2 paid personal obligation days per year
Education and Development	100% reimbursement for courses pre-approved by the manager

owners. It had grown from a tiny office space of 15 employees to a billion dollar, global service firm with offices based in Europe, Asia, and Australia. In 1992, a Canadian office of 20 employees was established in William's home town. Thirteen years later, Travelink Solutions Canada had grown to 200 employees, occupying two stories of a 10-story office building. Travelink's offerings had been extended over the years to include insurance policies that provided emergency support for national and international travelers facing a variety of perils, including the theft of personal property, automobile break-downs, accidents, legal assistance, travel interruptions, and emergency travel related concierge services. Policies were modular in nature and were designed for the traveler who wanted to avoid unpleasant surprises.

Travelink's Canadian call center was located on the lower of the two floors it occupied and involved approximately 150 of its 200 employees. A reception area on the upper story led into office space for underwriting and marketing employees, the human resources and training department, IT, accounting, supervisory personnel, and the senior administration (see Exhibit 2 for a partial organization chart of the Canadian Division). Call center activities were supported by a website that provided customers with valuable travel-related information, advice, and links to other relevant websites.

New Employee Orientation and Training

Training for William commenced December 1 and lasted one month. On his first day, William joined 11 other new employees, all of whom were university arts graduates. Some (William included) had been referred to the company through friends that worked for the firm. As a recruitment incentive, a bonus of $500 was offered to any employee who referred a potential employee who was hired and successfully

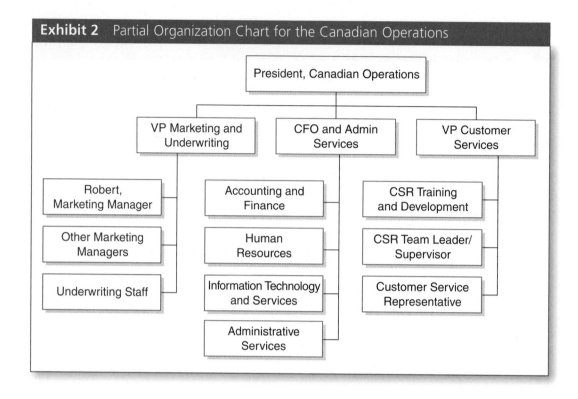

Exhibit 2 Partial Organization Chart for the Canadian Operations

completed the training. Travelink Solutions tried to coordinate its hiring so that a group of 6 to 12 began training at the same time.

William's trainers, Luther and Marie, seemed approachable and knowledgeable. They worked diligently to accommodate any questions that were asked about work procedures, customer service, company policies, or the call center industry. William found himself quickly integrated into a comfortable training environment, where dialogue occurred openly and people seemed to be genuinely helpful. The training program was quite structured and occurred in a classroom environment. The first two weeks focused on industry and firm specific information that would be relevant to those who would be addressing customer questions and concerns. It included information related to specific products and services, what associates could expect from the customer and their employer, and what was expected of them. The second two weeks included additional content related to products, corporate policies, and workflow procedures, as well as call

center simulations and role plays. These latter activities were designed to develop employee competence with the firm's customer service strategies and effective work practices.

At one of the first training sessions, Marie explained that the Travelink Solutions call center offered uniquely satisfying service opportunities. The services that associates provided, as she explained, acted as an island of sanity amid an ocean of uncertainty and panic. As Marie said: "You are not merely the voice on the end of the line. You are the line. You are someone's lifeline during an inherently unstable, frustrating, and, at times, frightening situation. If a customer's car breaks down in Mexico, or they get mugged, arrested, or stranded in a foreign land, you are the person they turn to for help."

Luther told William's training group that the average cost of recruiting and training a new call center employee was approximately $14,500. William learned that Travelink Solutions employed approximately 200 people in the Canadian office, 2/3 of whom were directly involved with the phones in the call center. Direct sales of Travelink's services were done through brokers, agencies, and the Internet. Travelink Solutions had a team of underwriters and marketers who crafted and promoted automobile and travel-related service policies throughout Canada, via its distribution systems. This group was also heavily involved in the design and delivery of similar services for other firms (e.g., banks and insurance companies), under their clients' brand names. This accounted for approximately 75% of Travelink's gross billings, profitability, and call center volumes. Trainees were told that Travelink was considered a leader in customer service quality. Industry benchmark data rated them in the top 10% in customer satisfaction and quality and it was reported that they had almost never lost a corporate account, once the business was won. Business volumes and profitability had been growing by more than 20% per year since 1998, with the exception of the 12-month period following September 11, 2001.

At the end of the month long training period, each new employee was required to write a three hour comprehensive exam, dealing with the information that they had been exposed to. If a grade of 90 percent was not achieved then an employee was required to rewrite the test before being permitted to field calls. Although he was nervous, William believed that his training sessions had been effective in transferring the needed knowledge, and he passed the exam with flying colors. Out of his training group of 12, two people needed to rewrite the exam before receiving a desk within the call center, one week later.

The Work Began

When he was initially assigned to the phones, William was apprehensive. He often consulted on-line and paper manuals, to ensure that he was providing callers with the proper information and advice. For the first few weeks, Luther and Marie were available on the floor to answer trainee questions that arose. Beyond the presence of the trainers, team leaders encouraged new employees to discuss any questions or concerns with experienced associates. William was directed to Yolanda, a senior associate who said that she would be happy to help. She had been working at Travelink Solutions for more than three years and the supervisors allowed Yolanda to log off her phone whenever new associates approached her with questions. Overall, it seemed to William that the call center was a smooth and efficient operation. The friendly and helpful environment gave him confidence that he would be able to effectively assist callers. Initial supervisory checks and feedback during his first month on the phones further honed his competence and reinforced his confidence.

Marie's comments during the training session concerning the importance of the services that call center employees provided to customers proved true. Offering assistance to distressed travelers was quite satisfying. William deepened his familiarity with policy details and advisory support materials to ensure that he was providing callers with the correct information, useful advice, and effective service. Of course, there were occasional complaints and angry callers who vented their unhappiness with the quality of service (e.g., tow truck operators who were slow to respond or rude) or the answers they received concerning whether or not they were eligible for the requested coverage. William quickly learned that it was not helpful to dwell on such calls. Instead, through the guidance of the trainers and Yolanda, he developed techniques that calmed customers and helped to defuse difficult situations. By and large, William received positive feedback from the callers and this increased in frequency over his first three months on the phones.

William's experience within the call center was not an anomaly. Comments from fellow trainees echoed his reactions. He noticed that there was less turnover and absenteeism than what friends at other call centers had led him to believe were the norms in the places they worked.

Employees at Travelink voluntarily participated in and seemed to enjoy company events, such as potluck lunches. Friends employed at other call centers typically told him that this was not the case within their firms. One person reported that her firm had made participation mandatory at its corporate social events, leading someone to post an email stating that management had decided the floggings would continue until morale improved.

The Changes

After about five months of employment, William began to notice changes in his workplace. For example, senior managers were voicing concerns related to the need for greater efficiency and new business at the monthly company meetings and team leaders seemed more stressed than had been the case earlier. Robert, the marketing manager and William's friend, explained to William that Travelink had ramped up its staff levels within the call center in anticipation of obtaining new business that had not materialized. As a result, management was under pressure from the head office to improve its financial performance. "I've been working 60 hour weeks for the past several weeks, exploring new market opportunities and drafting proposals related to potential contract bids. There have been rumors that senior management is talking about layoffs if new contracts do not materialize," Robert explained.

William was shocked by Robert's candid comments. Sure, the phones had been unusually quiet lately, but this was also May, a month in which clients were no longer faced with the harsh winter elements that breed traffic accidents and mechanical breakdown. May was also a month in which vacation travel was typically down, resulting in fewer travel-related emergencies. Was this not a time when the phones were supposed to be quieter, allowing staff to follow up on the claims that had arisen earlier?

Within the next four weeks, four of the people who had trained with William left the firm. In their places were empty cubicles. Every time an employee was laid off or quit, the human resources department would send an email to all employees, notifying them of the person's departure. For example, one day William came into work to find that Linda, a friendly woman who sat in the cubicle next to him, was no longer there. Within two hours, he received a company memo that read: "We regret to inform you that, as of today, Linda Jameson is leaving Travelink Solutions. Please join us in wishing Linda all of the best in her future endeavors." Within another hour, William received a second email that read: "Please be advised that the door security codes have been changed to 25678. Thank you for your cooperation." Over the next several weeks the number of empty cubicles grew. He was surprised that the departures were almost never discussed on the floor. It was as if the employees who had once filled the unused space had never been there in the first place. However, the loss of people did seem to be associated with rising tension levels. People's willingness to help one another declined, as did the overall friendliness of the workplace. William began to save his money to ensure that he would have something to carry him through in the event that he too "went missing."

A New Assignment

But William did not go missing. One afternoon in June, he was surprised to find that his employment situation was about to change for the better. He was invited by his team leader and the Director of Information Technology to participate in the "Datasmart" project, as the individual who would be in charge of drafting and editing the standardized company correspondence forms that would be used by employees in Canada. He would be entering these documents into a new corporate database that was under development. He was excited over the opportunity to advance within the company and use some of the writing skills he'd developed at university. As part of his new assignment, William was offered a pay increase that would kick in after his next performance review, which he anticipated would be held within a few weeks. He was given a quiet workspace away from the call center where he could concentrate on his writing and editing tasks.

The company correspondence project was part of a larger organizational undertaking that involved the revamping of their information systems. In order to pave the way for a new database called Datasmart, all company information, standardized documents, reports, and work flows were being charted and reviewed. While working on the project, William was to report to the Datasmart project manager and was involved in weekly meetings with the IT department, who was overseeing the implementation.

William reacted positively to his new assignment. Within two weeks, he was sent on his first business trip to attend a training seminar at the parent company's headquarters. However, supervisory guidance in Canada was quite limited. It seemed as if his new supervisor was always very busy with more pressing tasks and had minimal time to discuss questions that William had regarding the content of specific documents or due dates. "Sorry, but I can't meet with you this week. I'm drowning in work. Can we reschedule? Just use your judgment—you seem to be making good progress," was the usual response he received from his supervisor.

All members of the 10-person Datasmart project team seemed to be very busy with the components that they were individually responsible for. However, William could not help but feel somewhat out on a limb as he revised and rewrote company correspondence and related required documentation. People were using his revisions, but had he understood the implications of the wording and made the right changes? He was concerned that one day, he would be terminated as the result of something he had written that opened the firm to unanticipated liabilities or created serious difficulties with one of the firms for whom Travelink supplied services. Since everyone else on the implementation team was focused on the technical aspects of the project, no one was available to provide specific guidance to William concerning the correspondence and documentation component of the project. The formal processes related to approving document changes had become informal over the years, with the individuals processing the claims handling theses elements largely on their own.

A number of other events over the next three months caused William additional concerns about his future prospects at Travelink. William knew that the firm had invested a lot of time and money trying to implement Datasmart. However, the launch date for this software solution had come and gone on at least three separate occasions. Each time that Travelink appeared ready to go live with the new software, an email would come out, advising that the launch would be postponed to a later time. The emails that William received, as a member of the project team, suggested that both the U.S. and Canadian offices were confused about implementation problems and what the firm now needed to do to fix them. Eventually, no new emails concerning the release date for Datasmart were sent out. It seemed as if the entire Datasmart initiative had disappeared.

By mid-September, William was stunned to notice that there was a new topic on the embargo list. No one within the company was discussing the new software at all. All employees had received two hours of training on the basic functions of the new software and staff had been told that detailed training related to the use of the software would follow. Luther, the trainer, had led a half-day workshop about adapting to technical change and everyone in the company, including the managers and directors, had attended. In the beginning there had been a lot of excitement circulating around the office concerning what the new system would be able to do for the firm. T-shirts had been printed to commemorate the launch of the project and a potluck lunch and information session had been held to celebrate its anticipated benefits. William wondered if other employees felt the same way that he did: Were they wondering what had happened to Datasmart but were afraid to ask such questions for fear of the answers? William heard from Robert that the plug was going to be pulled on the project because of persistent problems associated with integrating it with existing applications and data bases. It was somewhat reassuring, though, to find that his rewritten documents were being put to use on a daily basis.

Frustrations Deepen

William had still not received his performance review and promised raise by the middle of September. The Travelink Solutions employee handbook stated that each call center associate would receive an appraisal review after six months of continuous employment. Once a successful review was completed, an employee would be entitled to a pay increase. William had checked with the remaining members of his training group and none had been approached yet regarding their six month reviews, despite the fact that they were now into their 10th month of employment.

The initial feelings of frustration that William experienced concerning this were slowly turning into anger. After all, he believed that he had done an exceptional job. He had taken the initiative to learn about the office structure, the policy and procedure intricacies underlying different types of services, and different service techniques that went well beyond the competence required of a phone operator. He had worked long and hard to improve corporate correspondence and documentation and done so under minimal supervision. Yet, 10 months had passed and still William had received no recognition, no review, and no raise, despite his attempts to remind his supervisors that such a review was long overdue. There had been consistent supervisory comments that he was doing a terrific job and that the performance review would be looked after soon. However, managers were very busy and nothing was ever scheduled.

By October, William's correspondence and documents project was three quarters of the way to completion, but the phones in the call center were busy again . . . very busy! Robert told William that Travelink had been successful in winning two new major contracts. While management was thrilled to have obtained the new business, Robert was apprehensive. As a marketing manager, he was delighted that his hard work had contributed toward obtaining these new accounts. As a former employee in the call center, however, Robert was frightened that the additional call volume would greatly exceed the current resources available. Robert told William that he had argued to have new employees hired and trained in advance of the start dates for the new contracts. "What happened? Well, senior management said no. The word from upstairs is that budgetary pressures mean that they cannot afford to bring on new employees until the new revenue begins to flow. Even crazier, a couple of senior managers seem to believe that fewer new employees will be required if the call center is properly organized and staffed to respond to volume patterns. All that I can tell you is that I sure wouldn't want to be in the call center right now," Robert said.

Robert's prophecy became a nightmare for the employees within the call center over the next few months. The phones started ringing and there were simply not enough hands to pick them up (see Exhibit 3 for call center volumes). In addition to the spikes in call volume generated from the new contracts, Travelink was now entering its busier season. Just a few months ago, the phones had been relatively quiet—to the extent that employees often found time in between calls to provide extra service steps for their clients, such as arranging billing for insured expenses or expediting alternative hotel and flight arrangements. Now, there was no time between calls. From his new workspace, William overheard managers discussing that it was not uncommon for clients to be placed on hold for up to five minutes while waiting for an available agent. Travelink provided a contractual guarantee that clients would only be on hold for a maximum of three minutes, and Robert told William that account managers were finding themselves having to explain to their contract representatives why individual customers were forced to hold for extended periods of time.

One day in early November, William was asked to move back down to the call center. The increase in call volume necessitated his reassignment to his old position, without even a formal "thank you" for the work he had been doing. With the lack of available trained employees to service the high volume of incoming calls, the customer service managers were scrambling to ensure that the hold time was eased as much as possible. The following Monday morning, William entered the call center and noticed that Luther, the trainer, was sitting beside him in the empty desk that Linda used to occupy. Marie was sitting directly behind him. As he looked around the office, William realized that other staff members were also in the call center, answering calls. When asked why he was there, Luther simply shook his head in disgust and said: "I worked here and earned my way to a training position. Now, I'm back where I started." Marie overheard the conversation with Luther and simply threw her arms up in frustration when William nodded to her. All available hands were now busy answering calls rather than providing their usual support services.

William noted that there were also a diminishing number of company events being organized by the human resources department. Social events such as potlucks, staff birthday celebrations, and theme days were cut from the schedule due to work pressures and the monthly company noon hour meetings became bimonthly affairs. When an event did occur, added pressure was placed on employees to partake. It seemed to William that senior managers desperately needed to give the impression that employees were enjoying their work and feeling good about the firm, in spite of the workload.

By mid-February, customers' hold times had increased from five minutes to, at times, 30 minutes or more. As Robert confided, it was not uncommon to have customers waiting on hold for an hour. On one occasion, William talked to a man who had been on hold for two hours, waiting for someone to arrange for a tow truck. Team leaders sent out emails that reminded agents to apologize to customers who were required to wait for periods of 20 minutes or longer. "Please apologize profusely," the messages read. At this point, William was so frustrated that he would often forget to apologize. After all, it was not his fault that the company he worked for had not made the proper arrangements to service their clients. Why should he apologize when he and his coworkers were suffering too? William found himself making less use of some of the techniques that contributed to customer service excellence, such as empathy, friendliness, and attention to detail.

The lack of appropriate planning and implementation related to heightened call volumes was having a visible, negative impact on the performance of all call center associates. For example, any time that an agent logged off the phone to document a call, they were required to go on "not ready" status. This status was employed in order to write the required case notes into the Travelink database. According to the employee manual, agents were allowed to go on "not ready" for an hour each day, in addition to scheduled break times. With so many calls flowing into the call center, however, acceptable "not ready" time had disappeared. Team leaders were able to see agents who were not taking calls and they began sending out emails that read: "Please log in. Several calls are waiting." Out of frustration, William began counting the number of emails he had received that were entitled "Please log in." Within one week, the tallied amount was 32.

Eventually, team leaders stopped using emails to ask agents to log in and began phoning their direct extensions every time they were not

Exhibit 3 Call Center Call Volumes by Month

Assumptions:

- Call staff answering norms are 15 minutes per call or 26 calls per 8 hour shift (1 hour is allocated for post call documentation and follow-up work + two 15 minute breaks).
- It takes approximately 2 months (1 month of training and 1 month on the phones) before an operator is fully able to operate at capacity, handling both direct customer contact and call documentation with < 1% error rate.
- One full-time, trained employee equates to approximately 18 availing working days per month. Absenteeism is estimated at 5%. Since all non-statutory holidays are taken in the July–August period, available days during the winter remains at 18 days.
- Further capacity could be created by scheduling overtime and statutory holiday work.
- A maximum of 80 call cubicles are available, leading to a maximum shift capacity of 2,080 calls per 8 hour shift.
- At a staffing level of 140 full-time employees on the phones, total call volume capacity per month = 65,520.

	Jan	Feb	Mar	Apr	May	June	July	Aug	Sept	Oct	Nov	Dec	Jan	Feb	Mar
Call	48.6	48.6	47	44.3	40	36.2	35	33.2	33	40.7	42.9	46.7	52.9	56.5	57.2
Volume	000	000	000	000	000	000	000	000	000	000	000	000	000	000	000
Wait	<2	<3	<2	<1	<1	<1	<1	<1	<1	6	6	9	10	11	12
Time	min	min	min	min	min	min	min	min	min	min	min	min	min	min	min
Avg															
Lost Calls	<1%	<1%	<1%	<1%	<1%	<1%	<1%	<1%	<1%	2%	6%	6%	8%	10%	10%

434

prepared to take a call. On one occasion, William received a call from his team leader asking him to log in while he was documenting a call that he had received from an elderly couple that had been in an automobile accident in Mexico. From that point on, he attempted to type his notes for one case while he was on the phone with the next client. He questioned the efficacy of the new shortcuts that he was employing, but there was nothing that could be done. Every time that William or any of the other operators tried to log off of his phone to document a call, they were bombarded with messages telling them to log back in. Every other agent that William talked to was utilizing the same tactics to deal with their inability to go on "not ready." Essentially, everyone was short-changing documentation in an attempt to meet the incoming demands. To make matters worse, the claims department, which was in charge of reviewing the documented cases, was growing increasingly frustrated with the customer service agents over the large number of mistakes that were occurring within the documentation. The load of case corrections related to errors had essentially quadrupled.

Travelink began to actively recruit new phone agents in January, with the first ones arriving in the call center on February 1. Melanie, a new agent, moved into the empty desk in front of William. She was friendly and a hard worker, but she noted that she was feeling overwhelmed and ill prepared. She explained that some of the new employees were being hired on a contractual basis and that her contract was for a period of three months. William could not understand the rationale behind hiring new employees on a contractual basis. After all, call center employees had just been informed that they would now be taking all of the incoming complaints calls—a queue that naturally became busy in the aftermath of the busy season. Who would be there to take all of the calls that would surely come in regarding long hold times and inadequate service? Furthermore, the fact that the new hires had only received two weeks of

training made them unaware of several elements, including workflows and basic policy terms and conditions that were essential to the proper documentation of cases. Essentially they were being left to figure it out for themselves, and William believed that the impact in errors, added costs (e.g., authorizing services the customer was not entitled to), and service failures would become all too apparent. By this point, employee turnover and absenteeism had risen markedly (see Exhibit 4).

Marketing Manager Robert was distressed by the fallout that had occurred from the growing call volume and lack of properly trained customer service agents. As he explained to William, some of the companies that had placed their customer service contracts with Travelink Solutions call center were now threatening to pull their contracts because Travelink was not honoring its service delivery promises. The operations department noted that 10% of all calls were now being lost due to the lengthy response time. In other words, 10% of all customers were not getting through to a representative, even though this might be a time of great need.

Considering His Alternatives

One evening in early April, William sat down to consider his future with Travelink Solutions. He was thankful for the training and job experience that he had received—competencies that would undoubtedly be useful in many other positions—but he was unsure how much more turmoil he could endure. He had saved enough money to, at the very least, pull himself through until a better opportunity came along. One thing seemed certain: Travelink Solutions no longer fit well with William's goals.

William submitted his resignation in the second week of April, to take effect on April 30, 16 months after he had commenced employment. Ironically, on the week that he submitted his resignation, William received an email reminding him that he had now been with the firm for over a year and was long overdue for his first

Exhibit 4 Turnover Data by Quarter and With the Year End Total

	Jan–Mar 04	Mar–May 04	June–Aug 04	Sept–Dec 04	Year 04 12 Month Summary	Jan–Mar 05
Absenteeism	3%	2%	3%	6%	3.6%	8.3%
a) Quits	0	2	5	10	17	19
b) Layoffs	0	0	16	0	16	0
c) Dismissals	0	1	1	2	4	0
Total (a+b+c)	0	3	22	12	37	19
New Hires	24	9	0	13	46	20 Full-time + 19 Contract Employees
Total Call Center Staff (excluding trainers and team leaders)	140	146	124	125		145 Full-time + Contract Employees

performance appraisal interview. His team leader immediately found an hour to meet with him, applauded his performance, rated his potential as excellent in all categories, and ask what it would take to get him to reconsider and stay. As William thought about the offer, the words that came to mind were: too little, too late.

William, however, bit his tongue and paused: Should he ask his team leader to read William's documentation of the call center's problems? Might William ask his friend Robert, in his role as Marketing Manager, to join the conversation with his team leader and himself and devise a plan to improve the situation in the call center and the larger office? How might they bring about significant change in a company's branch office? Did the branch office need the leadership, approval, and guidance of top-level executives in the headquarters office?

As his team leader waited, William knew that he needed to decide quickly.

Case Study 4

Ellen Zane—Leading Change at Tufts/NEMC

Cynthia Ingols and Lisa Brem, Simmons College

It was a difficult decision to take this job. But there was something about the history of Tufts-NEMC and its importance to so many stakeholders that really grabbed me as the epitome of what one could do in one's career. I'd also learned not to be adverse to risk. You have to take risk, not stupid risk, but you have to take risk.

—Ellen Zane, CEO, Tufts/NEMC

Ellen Zane brought a cup of coffee into her home office. It was 4:30 a.m. and she was, as usual, starting the day early. She fired off a few emails to her senior staff and looked over the *Women's Business* magazine on her desk. Her photograph was on the cover, highlighting the article on the turn around she was attempting to execute at Tufts/New England Medical Center (Tufts-NEMC). It was the summer of 2006 and it had been an incredibly

rough two and a half years since she accepted the CEO position at the ailing Boston hospital. Since then the hospital had survived the worst of its financial troubles—they were meeting efficiency goals and for the first time in years, more doctors joined the hospital than left it. Tufts-NEMC posted an $18 million gain in 2005, after losing nearly $60 million since 2001 (see **Exhibit 1** on page 459 for financial statements). People were smiling and thanking Zane in the corridors.

But that was a piece of the problem. This was the tricky part, she thought, in one of her rare moments of quiet as the pre dawn light slowly infused the room. Zane realized that she was still deeply worried about the future:

This place was just so fragile and I still consider it fragile. It's one month forward and one month back. This market is unforgiving and tough—I swim with the sharks and nobody glad-hands us. I tell the staff all the time—not a minute do we take our foot off the gas.

Zane struggled with how to maintain the solidarity that the financial crisis had created

---

Source: From Linda E. Swayne, W. Jack Duncan & Peter M. Ginter. *Strategic Management of Health Care Organizations.* Jossey-Bass. 2008.

[1]Tufts/NEMC employed roughly 5,000 people, who accounted for 3,000 full-time equivalent (FTE) positions in 2006.

among Tufts-NEMC's 5,000 employees.[1] She knew from her 30 years of experience in hospital management that sustaining change in Boston's cutthroat medical industry was the hardest part of any turn around. She had been successful before with Quincy Hospital, but Quincy had been a much smaller player. Tufts-NEMC was a 450-bed Academic Medical Center (AMC) that was the primary teaching site for Tufts University School of Medicine, and conducted over $50 million in research each year. It had 17,000 admissions in 2005 and generated $600 million in revenue. Unfortunately, while Boston's other AMCs merged, built networks, and grew stronger, Tufts-NEMC had for years floundered directionless in Boston's rough seas. As Zane headed to her office overlooking Boston's Chinatown she wondered: How could she create and sustain true and lasting change for Tufts-NEMC?

The Health Care Industry in Boston

"Health care, together with education and computer technology, is what Massachusetts is known for throughout the world."[2]

Home to several high-profile Academic Medical Centers, the Boston area was a world-renowned destination for health care services. Massachusetts General Hospital (MGH), Brigham and Women's Hospital (BWH), and Beth Israel/Deaconess Medical Center were affiliated with Harvard Medical School, Boston University Medical Center with Boston University, and Tufts-New England Medical Center with Tufts. These large AMCs led the way in capturing $2.3 billion in

National Institutes of Health (NIH) research grant money, second only to California. Massachusetts hospitals employed 12.2% of the total labor pool and accounted for a whopping 11.7% of the gross state product. Health care expenditures per capita were between 27% and 29% higher than the national average from 1990 to 2000 (see **Exhibits 2–9** on pages 462–467 for Massachusetts health care statistics). Consumers, health plans, and governing bodies tended to accept that health care in Boston cost more in accordance with the high quality and cutting edge services the region provided.

Nationally, however, years of under-funding by federal and state governments and rising enrollment left Medicare and Medicaid payments lagging behind surging medical costs. Hospitals in Massachusetts and the rest of the nation amassed significant debt in the 1970s and 1980s as they refurbished older facilities, expanded services, and purchased expensive new technologies. While reimbursements fell behind rising costs, hospital discharges declined sharply in the 1980s, as did the average length of stay. In Massachusetts, a decrease in hospital births and non-resident discharges[3] led to an overall decline of 24% in total hospital discharges from 1991 to 1996. The increase in outpatient surgeries also affected hospitalizations.[4]

Throughout the 1990s, Massachusetts health care insurance plans followed nationwide trends when they merged into three large competitors: Harvard Pilgrim Health Care, Blue Cross/Blue Shield of Massachusetts, and Tufts Health Plan. These "big three" plans wielded increasing power in the marketplace, and their movement to managed health (HMO) plans resulted in lower payments to providers[5] and more oversight

---

[2]Ferguson, Christine C. "Massachusetts Health Care Trends: 1990–2004," Massachusetts Division of Health Care Finance and Policy, March 2003, page 5. Accessed from www.state.ma.us/dhcfp

[3]Non-resident discharges refer to number of patients from out of state.

[4]"Analysis in Brief—Massachusetts Inpatient Hospital Trends," Massachusetts Division of Health Care Finance and Policy, Number 6, April 2004, page 1. Accessed from www.state.ma.us/dhcfp

[5]Provider refers to any hospital, AMC, or ancillary service that provided medical care.

on costs and medical services. All three expanded regionally to entice large regional and national companies to offer their plans to employees. HMOs used capitated payments, meaning they reimbursed providers based on number of "covered lives" in the provider system. Thus, providers of health care services such as hospitals and doctors believed volume and efficiency of services to be the most important factors in future financial success.

In 1991 Massachusetts deregulated hospitals for the first time in 10 years. These conditions succeeded in making an impact—threatening the financial viability of hospitals and moving them toward more efficient and cost effective management practices. Boston's health care leaders struggled for a strategy to survive in the new environment. Mergers, closures, and conversions loomed.

The leaders of MGH and BWH made the first decisive move. Managers at both hospitals believed they needed additional leverage to hold their own in negotiations with the ever more powerful health insurance plans. They also envisioned building a network of community primary care and specialist providers who would refer tertiary[6] patients to the member hospitals, thus bolstering volume. In 1994, when the news of the merger of these two behemoths—forming Partners Healthcare System, Inc. (Partners)— became public, it was a seismic change in the landscape of the New England medical industry. Others quickly followed suit. From 1990 to 2000, there were 47 acquisitions and mergers and 19 acute care hospital closures, not including the formation of 10 major hospital systems in Massachusetts.[7]

Following the market consolidations in the 1990s, the turn of the twenty-first-century years were difficult ones for Boston's hospitals and insurers. Both Harvard Pilgrim and Tufts Health Plans were hindered by regional over-expansion. In 1999, Harvard Pilgrim went into receivership after posting a $226 million loss, while Tufts Health Plan lost $42 million. Community hospitals also continued to struggle from high debt, inadequate reimbursements, high labor and pharmaceutical costs, and failed merger or network integration attempts. In Massachusetts particularly, consumers began to migrate to the more expensive AMCs from the smaller regional or community hospitals, seeking what they perceived to be higher quality of care. Cuts in payments from Medicaid, Medicare, and private insurance plans continued to plague many providers. To encourage more efficient management and cost containment practices among its providers, HMOs started to move away from capitated care and toward pay-for-performance plans.

Even some AMCs felt the pressure on their organizations. CareGroup—another Massachusetts-based hospital umbrella organization—posted a loss of $215 million over 1999 and 2000 and lost market share and network physicians. Partners, however, grew and remained strong, reaching 5,600 doctors in its Partners Healthcare System, Inc. (PCHI) network. In a seminal flexing of its market strength, Partners negotiated up to 30% increases from all three major health plans, at one point refusing to continue a contract with Tufts Health Plan until it agreed to higher payments.[8]

By 2005, the provider market was dominated by four major hospital systems: Partners reporting a surplus of $30 million, Caritas Christi, CareGroup (which had decentralized most of its operations back to its member hospitals), and Boston Medical Center. See **Exhibit 10** on page 468 for provider descriptions. When the dust settled on the consolidation activity, there were approximately 25 acute care,

---

[6]Those patients who needed high levels of care, such as surgery.

[7]Ferguson, Christine C. "Massachusetts Health Care Trends: 1990–2001," appendix iii–vi.

[8]Community Report—Boston, Mass. Third Visit 2000–2001. Center of Studying Health System Change, Report 11 of 12, summer 2001. www.hschange.org

five psychiatric, and five rehabilitation hospitals in the metropolitan Boston area, with Partners leading in market share.[9] On the insurer's side, the major health plans recovered, with Blue Cross/Blue Shield of Massachusetts coming out on top, Harvard Pilgrim regaining strength, and Tufts maintaining a third position.

According to one survey of the Boston health care industry, trends through 2005 were:

- AMCs faced lack of capacity from years of merging and downsizing, while admissions moved to AMCs from community hospitals;
- pay-for-performance (quality incentive) programs were gaining in popularity, using measures such as cost, efficiency, IT capacity, admission rates, and patient satisfaction to bolster reimbursements;
- hospitals struggled to recruit new doctors and nurses—with AMCs poaching from each other;
- nationally, the growing number of uninsured and underinsured people increased the amount of bad debt hospitals carried. Although mitigated in Massachusetts by strong safety net programs, collections were still a rising concern.[10]

History of Tufts/NEMC[11]

New England Medical Center, originally the Boston Dispensary, was one of the oldest hospitals in the United States. Started in 1796 by the philanthropic activities of historical Boston figures Samuel Adams and Paul Revere, the Boston Dispensary was the first permanent medical facility in New England. First envisioned as a community medical service for the poor, the hospital quickly gained a reputation for innovation. It was the first U.S. hospital to assign nurses to patients, to form a visiting nurse association, and establish dental, rehabilitation, venereal disease, lung, food and nutrition, and evening pay clinics. It pioneered employer-paid clinic treatment, well-child services, and moving X-rays. The first modern test for syphilis, the first group psychotherapy experiment, the first human growth hormone and immuno-suppression therapies were developed at the Boston Dispensary. In 1929 New England Medical Center was formed by the merger of the Dispensary and Tufts College Medical and Dental Schools. By 1965, it added the Floating Hospital and the Pratt Diagnostic Clinic–New England Center Hospital.[12]

In recent years, the tradition of innovation continued, with strong programs in cancer treatment, transplants, and neurosurgery. In 1992, with the addition of a maternity service, Tufts-NEMC became the first full-service, private teaching hospital in Boston. The Neely House, opened in 1997, was a unique bed and breakfast style home located within the hospital for cancer patients and their families. And in 2001, Tufts-NEMC opened a transplant exchange program, the first of its kind in the United States, which allowed family members of transplant patients to donate kidneys to patients on the global waiting list, thus increasing the number of organs available for transplant.

---

[9]The Boston metropolitan area was generally described as being inside Interstate 495. Statistics provided by Massachusetts Health and Educational Facilities Authority, Revenue Bonds, Partners HealthCare System Issue, Series F (2005). Accessed from www.mehfa.org

[10]Community Report—Boston, Mass. Center of Studying Health System Change, Report 11 of 12, December 2005. www.hschange.org

[11]Information in this section derived from www.nemc.org and www.bostonhistory.org/mchina.php accessed June 7, 2006.

[12]The Boston Dispensary archived records. A summary available online at simmons.edu/resources/libraries/archives/char_coll/char_coll_027.htm

Financially, however, Tufts-NEMC was struggling. Although in the 1990s the hospital had posted gains, it was largely due to a write-down in assets and not improved efficiency or an enhanced revenue cycle. The hospital had fallen prey to the same negative market forces that had taken their toll on other non-affiliated hospitals in the 1990s. By 1996, it was $240 million in debt (up from $130 million in 1990) and was losing physicians, market share, and hospital acquisitions to Partners and CareGroup. Like many AMCs, Tufts-NEMC was slow to react to market pressures and ineffective in improving processes and cash flow. In a particularly devastating blow to the hospital, Harvard Pilgrim Health Care discontinued coverage to Tufts-NEMC in 1995, citing high costs. As Zane explained:

> Harvard Pilgrim HC had taken Tufts-NEMC out of their network and it had almost killed the place. A doctor in Hyannis wants to send a patient to Boston. He or she has to ask "does this patient have Harvard Pilgrim?" The situation caused doctors to have to think too much about insurance. It was just easier to send everybody to the Brigham. So, for Tufts-NEMC, not being in that contract was incredibly hurtful.

The Lifespan Merger

In the mid-1990s, Tufts-NEMC began to actively look for a partner to remedy its fiscal dilemmas. It needed more clout against the health plans, more referrals from community hospitals, and a partner with deep enough pockets to help pay for growth to compete with Partners, CareGroup, and the other Boston systems. It was in talks with Columbia/HCA, a for-profit hospital chain from Tennessee that wanted to expand its presence in New England.

If the merger went through, it would be the first AMC owned by a for-profit company in New England. This did not sit well with some of the board members, faculty, and community, who strongly wanted to preserve Tufts-NEMC's non-profit nature.

In late 1996, the hospital was treating a high-ranking official from the Lifespan Corporation, a regional non-profit hospital system formed in 1994 with a merger of the Miriam and Rhode Island hospitals.[13] One of Tufts-NEMC's physicians explained the hospital's dilemma and talks began between Lifespan and Tufts-NEMC to merge. Tufts-NEMC leadership saw benefits to joining with Lifespan, such as needed capital, a chance to gain back the Harvard Pilgrim Health Care contract, and the potential referrals from the Rhode Island system. On Lifespan's side, Tufts-NEMC was enticing for its status as an AMC, its base in Boston, and its expertise in high-level care. The merger would create, as one journal wrote, "a $1.5 billion, 14,500-employee health care giant with the ability to serve 70 percent of the entire New England market" and would rival the $1.8 billion Partners system and $1.1 billion CareGroup.[14] In January 1997, Tufts-NEMC and Lifespan officially announced the merger, which became effective in November of that year. Ed Schottland, Senior Vice President—System Integration at Lifespan and appointed COO at Tufts-NEMC at the time of the merger, explained:

> Lifespan was interested in Tufts-NEMC because it gave them instant access into Boston and made them the regional system they wanted to be. The plan was to create Lifespan of Rhode Island and Lifespan of Massachusetts—of which Tufts-NEMC would be the hub—both overseen by an overarching corporation.

---

[13]The Miriam and Rhode Island hospitals were the two largest hospitals in Rhode Island and affiliated with Brown Medical School.

[14]"NEMCs bold move," *Boston Business Journal,* January 17, 1997, and Van Voorhis, Scott. "NEMC discusses hospital network," *Boston Business Journal,* January 24, 1997. Accessed online at http://boston.bixjournals.com

Tufts-NEMC is a tertiary and quaternary[15] medical center, we do bone marrow, solid organ transplants, and we have a neo natal intensive care unit. They didn't do any of those things in Rhode Island. The only BMT[16] program allowed in Rhode Island was at Roger Williams Hospital. So Lifespan got instant access to highest levels of care. The merger filled out the service complement with a high class, well respected organization with great outcomes and great medical care. Everyone assumed that we would be able to direct our patients here from Rhode Island. We would have a system of care, just as Partners was trying to do with their North Shore hospitals.

The marriage was not a happy one, however—the hoped-for synergies never materialized. Rhode Island regulators objected to large amounts of capital migrating to Boston and required Lifespan to reduce the amount Tufts-NEMC was to receive to $8.7 million a year for 10 years, down from 30 years as originally planned. Although Harvard Pilgrim did eventually re-contract with Tufts-NEMC, some in the industry believed that legislation or litigation would have forced that outcome regardless. The referrals also did not pan out. As Schottland explained:

Physicians make their own decisions about where they refer. Physicians like to refer primarily based on personal and professional relationships. A secondary reason they didn't refer to Tufts-NEMC was they felt that if they started to support a program here they might never get approval within the Lifespan system to get that program down in Rhode Island.

This was a unique system since there were two medical schools—Brown and Tufts. The Brown faculty wanted to have the programs, like bone marrow transplants, in Rhode Island. So there was a certain reluctance to cooperate at times.

Another problem with the merger was the "brain drain." Lifespan took many of the administrative and support functions out of Tufts-NEMC and centralized them in Rhode Island. Tufts-NEMC lost their human resource, finance, purchasing/supply chain, and IT, an area where Tufts-NEMC had been ground breaking in the past. The anticipated growth in acquisitions also failed to take place. Hospitals that had previously affiliated with Tufts-NEMC, such as Faulkner, another Tufts Medical School teaching site, joined Partners instead, while Tufts-NEMC was busy finalizing its merger with Lifespan. In 2000, Lifespan/Tufts-NEMC also lost Hallmark Health System in Malden. As one industry journal wrote:

Every time a decision had to be made, Tufts-NEMC President and Chief Executive Officer Tom O'Donnell, M.D., traveled 55 miles across the state line to Providence, R.I. There he conferred with the 21-member board of his parent system, Lifespan Corp. He would return to meet with his own 21-member board, then respond to Hallmark. [. . .] The extra corporate layer proved to be too much. Hallmark, at the time a four-hospital system, walked away from the deal.[17]

Adding insult to injury, Quincy (Mass.) Medical Center and MetroWest Medical Center spurned Tufts-NEMC, citing that the "local hospitals did not think of Tufts-NEMC as a Massachusetts hospital."[18]

---

[15]Quaternary refers to most advanced level of care, such as bone marrow and organ transplants.

[16]Bone marrow transplant

[17]Duff, Susanna, and Becker, Cinda. "Here we go again," *Modern Healthcare,* Chicago: Sep 9. 2002, pg. 8. Accessed online at http://proquest.umi.com

[18]Ibid.

But perhaps the worst thing about the merger was that insurance contracting was done in Rhode Island. Lifespan did not understand the cost of doing business in the Boston market and therefore settled for reimbursement rates far below the average for an AMC in Boston. Lifespan, struggling to keep control of five acute-care hospitals, suffered an operational loss of $34.1 million on total revenue of $1.3 billion ending fiscal year 2001. Zane explained her take on the Lifespan merger:

> When Partners came together it freaked out the whole market and everybody was looking for a partner. Long story short, Tufts-NEMC hooked up with the Lifespan system in Rhode Island. I could not understand why they did it. It was an ill fated, ill conceived, ill constructed, and ill-implemented merger and it had no meat on the bone. The health care market in Rhode Island might as well have been Siberia it was so different from eastern Mass.

In the summer of 2002, five years after they merged, both Lifespan and Tufts-NEMC agreed to separate at a cost of $30 million to Tufts-NEMC. Financial results for Tufts-NEMC for fiscal year 2002 were dismal—a loss of $12.3 million on revenue of $476 million; and 2003 was looking worse—a loss of $38.5 million on revenue of $582 million. The Massachusetts Attorney General's office stepped in to ensure that the hospital would meet bond covenants. O'Donnell and the chairman of Tufts-NEMCs board called Ed Schottland and enticed him to come back as COO. Schottland took the job and set about re-creating the administrative departments lost in the merger. He also started initiatives to stem the millions of dollars that Tufts-NEMC was losing monthly. Schottland targeted improvements of $30 million in cost savings in the supply chain and human resources. He began a year of initiatives designed to improve the bottom line. In the first nine months of 2003, Tufts-NEMC reduced staffing levels by 200 FTEs through attrition and consolidation and made improvements in supplier contracts. The hospital also began to look at selling some of its 1.5 million square feet of prime real estate to gain needed capital. The Board, meanwhile, set about looking for a leader who could take Tufts-NEMC out of the shadow of Lifespan and orchestrate a true turn around.

Ellen Zane

Ellen Zane was educated at Waltham Public Schools, and later graduated from George Washington University and Catholic University in Washington, DC with master's degrees in both audiology and speech-language pathology. She spent her entire career in health care, starting in 1975 as a speech language pathologist at Lawrence (Massachusetts) General Hospital. In 1979 she took a job as director of speech and language pathology and audiology at Morton Hospital in Taunton. Under the mentorship of the COO of Morton, Zane worked her way up to vice president of professional services until taking the COO job at Quincy (Mass.) Hospital in 1987. When Quincy's CEO left in 1990, both Quincy's board and the city's mayor convinced Zane to take on the task of turning around the hospital, which was on the brink of closure. Like many community hospitals, Quincy had taken out bonds to renovate its ailing facilities. When the Medicaid/Medicare and HMO reimbursement rates lowered drastically, Quincy found it almost impossible to meet payroll and other expenses. Hampered by years of nepotistic and political hiring practices and high competition in the surrounding area, the hospital was in danger of defaulting on its bonds. Zane recalled her decision to take the job at Quincy as the most difficult in her career:

> It was the hardest decision I ever had to make, since I really felt that failure was not an option. Closing a hospital as the result of my first CEO job would have been awful.

However, at the same time, women weren't getting CEO jobs. I needed an underdog job to try to prove myself, since it wasn't likely that a woman was going to get a job at what I called a "Bloomingdale hospital"— Mt. Auburn, Newton Wellesley, Beverly, or South Shore. Those weren't coming to women in those days. But the main reason I took the job was that I could see the steps it would take to fix it. When I had a very quiet, private conversation with myself, I knew that if I could figure out the road map of what to do, then I would just need the grit to do it. And I *could* see the way. So I jumped off a cliff and took the job. It was the best decision I ever made.

From a grass roots point of view the opportunity I got at Quincy was the bedrock foundation to my management prowess. And it was really hard. It taught me not only the value of risk, but it taught me that if you took a job that no one else wanted to do because it was too hard, then all the benefits accrue back to you. If you are successful at it, you are only better because it was harder. All these good old boys with the cushy jobs around me at richer hospitals—I believe—aren't as good at managing simply because they didn't have to be.

Quincy was unique in that it was managed by HCA, a for-profit hospital management chain that owned and managed hospitals across the United States. In addition, Quincy had a strong union and civil service workforce. Working for HCA honed her business acumen and decision-making abilities. Working with unions helped Zane understand the need for clear, open, and honest communication and financial transparency. As Zane recalled:

I sat down with stewards of all the unions and showed them the financial statements and highlighted all the things I wanted them to learn—like days cash on hand and

cash reserves. I taught them the meanings of those things and explained that we had no money and that I was worried about meeting payroll. One of the biggest joys of my career came when I left Quincy hospital and met with the stewards for the last time and one union steward said to me: "How many days cash on hand do we have?" The fact that they had learned that and appreciated it taught me the value of transparency, the value of admitting that I needed help and I couldn't do it alone.

She also learned the importance of reaching out to the community. As Zane explained:

I got in my car and drove out to community doctors who weren't referring many patients to us. I asked them: "What would it take for you to use Quincy Hospital?" They said simple things like parking. All the construction had closed the parking lots. It was not that intellectually complex. The doctors also complained that employee work ethic was dismal. The employees didn't smile or pick up a candy wrapper off the floor. They treated the hospital as though it existed solely for them and their paychecks. They didn't believe the day of reckoning was coming. Hearing that from the community doctors was incredibly valuable for me.

After a successful run at Quincy, she was tapped in late 1993 for a groundbreaking job with the nascent Partners organization. As Zane recalled:

I got a call from Dr. H Richard Nessen. He was the CEO of the Brigham and Women's Hospital. He told me they had just gotten permission from the Attorney General to merge the General [MGH] and the Brigham [BWH]. This was huge, giant, gargantuan news. He told me they wanted to build a vast network of physicians throughout eastern Mass. And that he wanted me to come run it.

I told him I had no idea how to do that job, but he said that no one did, it was completely new. He said he needed a leader. He told me that he had academic physicians who were lining up at his door to do this job, but that he didn't want to give it to any of them. He felt that academics wouldn't understand community doctors or community hospitals, and would turn them off. He was right about that.

Zane was successful at building what came to be called PCHI,[19] Partners Community Heathcare, Inc. At Partners, she gained expertise at negotiating affiliation agreements with physicians and contracts with health plans, and with building consensus with disparate groups. Zane recalled her time at PCHI:

> I went from this incredibly resource poor environment at Quincy, where I was plugging holes and trying to meet payroll, to this environment that was so resource rich. There were so many smart people around, but there was no trust between the Brigham [BWH] and the General [MGH] people, they were fierce competitors for years. So each committee had to have counterparts from each organization. Trying to develop a strategy in that environment was a challenge. The committees were made up of type A personalities who wanted me to build a network overnight. I felt this intense need to get the strategy going very, very quickly. So we spent the summer of 1994 building the strategy. The most incredible thing for me is, when I go and talk to investment bankers or health plans now, PCHI is all they talk about. PCHI was the most formidable market transforming activity other than the [MGH/BWH] merger itself. PCHI is the 800-pound gorilla in this market. And I

knew it and started it before it even had a name. It was very rewarding, and very hard.

As Partners grew, so did their clout in the marketplace. Zane was the lead negotiator in the famous clash between Partners and Tufts Health Plan, which culminated when Partners decided to no longer accept Tufts subscribers due to the plan's low reimbursement rates. Her bargaining skills and strategic planning won the day for Partners. In the end Tufts agreed to substantial rate increases. After that encounter, Zane's reputation as a tough and savvy negotiator became legendary.

Zane Moves to Tufts/NEMC

In late 2003, after 10 years with Partners, Zane was thinking of slowing down. Her husband had sold his successful business and had retired and Zane was hoping to do the same. She was getting ready to give her notice at Partners when she received a call from Lawrence Bacow, the President of Tufts University. Bacow was on the board of Tufts-NEMC, which had recently decided to dissolve the merger with Lifespan. He was looking for a new leader for Tufts-NEMC, and felt that Zane had the right mix of skills to build and implement a successful strategy for the hospital. Met by her initial reluctance, Bacow reminded Zane of the hospital's historical significance, its importance for its 5,000 employees, Tufts University, and Chinatown's economy. Zane recalled her reaction after the meeting with Bacow:

> There were two enormous feelings that came over me. One was on the positive side: wow this could really be important. To help this ailing organization means to really help a lot of people in their careers, their lives, the economy, and the University. The other feeling was: this is so daunting—I'm frozen. It was so scary.

---

[19] Pronounced "peachy."

In July 2003, O'Donnell announced his resignation, clearing the way for Zane, the first non-physician and female permanent CEO in Tufts-NEMC's history. Reaction from both industry pundits and employees at Tufts-NEMC was uniformly positive. As one expert wrote:

At this time and in this place, there is no one better for the top job than Ellen Zane. The first non-physician chief executive, she comes onboard at a time when tough decisions need to be made. Yes, she has the necessary management skills, but she also has demonstrated a passionate commitment to preserving the relationship that exists between physicians and patients and between this hospital and the community it serves.[20]

John Greenwood, VP of Finance, explained some of the things he felt Zane brought to Tufts-NEMC:

We lost our identity during the Lifespan merger. We also lost touch with the Mayor's office and Beacon Hill,[21] and making sure our concerns were being heard. So when Ellen came on board, for the first few months we spent a lot of time on Beacon Hill. She brought visibility and a very recognizable name in the market.

Accountability was also a big leadership trait that came on board with Ellen. She and the consultants she brought in assisted the leadership in diagnosing what the issues and root causes were, as well as prioritizing them. Then she held someone accountable for fixing it. We'd done a lot of diagnosis before, so we had an idea of what the problems were, but Ellen provided the leadership to drive the projects to completion.

She also provided unity to the physicians throughout the hospital. There used to be two autonomous physician corporations with faculty/staff physicians. Both groups were completely separate. The first year she came, Ellen pursued merging the two boards into one entity and eventually made it happen. So now there is input and a synergy between the faculty at the hospital. They speak with one voice.

Michael Burke, senior vice president and CFO, added:

Ellen is so acutely aware of what's going on in the market—she's been in this market her whole life, she built PCHI. She knows all the players. She knows whom to call and she has the personal relationships so that people are willing to work with her.

Ellen is also the kind of person who takes action. She gets 80%–90% of the information she needs and then she does something. Most academic medical centers have what I call "analysis paralysis." You can accept the status quo, but the reality is things never stay the same—they either get better or they get worse. And if you are not actively working to improve them, they will get worse. This place was constantly assessing what to do, but not doing anything. And things got worse, year after year after year. Now what we're doing is assessing the data, assessing the market, and acting, and doing, and getting things done.

Diagnosis: Critical (2004)

When Zane came on board, she brought in a consulting group called BDC Advisors, Inc. They gathered data to determine why Tufts-NEMC was

---

[20]Lutch Bender, Ellen. "A new chapter for the venerable Tufts-NEMC," *Boston Business Journal*, December 26, 2003. Accessed online at http://boston.bizjournals.com

[21]The Massachusetts legislature

losing an estimated $3 million a month. Zane sat down with Schottland who gave her the bad news: Tufts-NEMC was not losing $3 million a month; since the split with Lifespan the number was closer to $6 million. Zane recalled how the new reality changed her priorities:

> Although I had done a fair bit of due diligence before taking the job, I was still shocked to find out that we didn't have two years of cash on hand: we had 10 months. So it changed everything overnight. Because strategy was the last thing I could worry about—I had to worry about payroll. This place was hemorrhaging millions every month. It was incredibly important to begin to think about how to stabilize.

Zane and BDC conducted what she called a "rapid diagnostic" to quickly determine how to stem the losses. BDC concluded that, although Tufts-NEMC was on the right path with Schottland's initiatives, they were still behind industry benchmarks for many areas, such as days in accounts receivable, accounts payable, average length of stay, operating margin, and days cash on hand. There was also more savings to be had in the supply chain (see **Exhibit 11** on page 440 for BDC analysis). After reviewing the managed care contracts, Zane also realized that Tufts-NEMC was woefully underpaid.

Another challenge for Tufts-NEMC was its size. In any other market, Tufts-NEMC would be considered one of the biggest players. But in Boston, it was dwarfed by Partners, CareGroup, and Caritas. Tufts-NEMC fundraised $10 million in 2005, up from $5 million the year before but impossibly behind the $200 million Partners raised. Tufts-NEMC was the smallest teaching hospital in the Boston area, but it was the primary teaching site for Tufts Medical School and was the 11th highest paid in NIH research funding. Underwriting that research cost Tufts-NEMC $15 million a year. Maintaining the level of services and research required for a major medical center was extremely difficult for

an organization without the volume of cases or endowments enjoyed by its competitors. Zane realized early on that however difficult it may be, it was absolutely crucial for Tufts-NEMC to remain an AMC:

> We made a conscious decision to keep funding research because we are an AMC with a tripartite mission, which includes clinical excellence, research and teaching. If you take one of the legs off that stool we are no longer an AMC and I would venture to say that no fewer than 80% of the doctors who practice here would leave. They are here because they want to work in an AMC.

Treatment (2004–2006)

Zane set to work on building her management team and reopening the managed care contracts. Along with Schottland and BDC, she pushed hard on cost cutting and efficiency initiatives to bring Tufts-NEMC in line with industry best practices. Zane continued plans to sell real estate in order to get the hospital on some solid financial footing while giving these initiatives time to take hold. She also felt the need to re-establish Tufts-NEMC's brand in the Boston market place, to set about rebuilding affiliations and networks, to reverse the trend of hospitals poaching Tufts-NEMC's physicians, and to retain the talent it had.

Staff Changes

Once Zane assessed the mission, she set about evaluating the senior staff. She greatly appreciated the experience and expertise of people like Shottland and Deeb Salem, Tufts-NEMC's chief physician. But others she felt needed to be replaced. Within two weeks she replaced the senior vice president of strategy with Deborah Joelson, a network building expert who Zane recruited from Partners; and the vice president of fundraising and development with Deb Taft, who had been extremely successful at the Dana Farber/Jimmy Fund. In all, she replaced seven members—half of the senior management team. Zane shared her thoughts on the senior staff turnover:

One of the people I fired was a favorite of one of the board members. I spent a lot of time listening to that board member telling me that I had no right to fire his guy. But in the end he supported me. There was no question that I had to do it.

If you ask most people about me they will tell you I'm very good at picking people. I really do believe that is a skill I have—it's gut level for me. I'd like to get credit for picking good people, not for a brilliant turn around, strategies, or anything like that. I'm only as good as the people around me, and I do pick great people. I have a sixth sense. I can tell when I go into the waiting room for interviews whether they have a shot. For most of these characters here I knew it wasn't going to happen. There were a couple of other positions in the administrative round that I changed pretty fast. The COO Ed Schottland was very solid. He was only here about 9 months. He came from Lifespan and I am very grateful to this day that he was here and that he stayed. I would be toast without him.

Schottland added:

It was chaos here before. I think it's easy to disrupt the COO's role, especially in an organization this size. People used to go around the COO to the CEO—it doesn't take long before you are neutralized.

Ellen has been very supportive of my role. She'll either say: "you really have to talk to Ed about that" or she'll just have me in the room when they talk to her. Now, most people in the organization don't attempt to go around me. I appreciate that . . . that's important to me. Ellen's let me continue to run the operations in an

appropriate way. We understand our roles and we know when to ask each other for help and advice.

Deb Taft, the new vice president for fundraising and development, talked about why she joined Tufts-NEMC:

If I could be a part of creating a fundraising department that was vibrant and strong, this would be a career moment for me. I had people stopping me in the street saying "I can't believe you are taking this job." But what greater thing could there be than helping this place survive? It deserves to be here. Keeping this place alive was important enough for Ellen Zane not to retire. Ellen recognized that I had what she called fire in the belly. That was her number one criteria in bringing me in.

Communication and Outreach

Ellen is a remarkable communicator of good news and bad news. She was somehow able to be fully transparent about what was going on and have people appreciate that she was being honest with them about the situation. And no one felt that they had to bail out of here because the place was going down the tubes. I don't know how she did that.

—**Deborah Joelson,** senior vice president for market development and planning

Very early on, Zane led a series of "town meetings" where she presented financial facts, specifics on new initiatives, and areas targeted for growth. Because the hospital worked around the clock, Zane scheduled a series of meetings at various times throughout the day and night, to ensure that everyone had a chance to attend. The meetings worked so well to disseminate information that Zane continued to do them twice per year on all shifts. She also augmented them with regular emails updating the staff and physicians on finances and other topics. As Deeb Salem, Tufts-NEMC's chief physician, explained:

The things that she and Ed do are quite remarkable. Periodically they have town meetings for the entire staff. They go out of their way to talk to everybody, even the housekeeping staff. They have sessions in the middle of the night so they can talk to the night shift.

Taft agreed:

Ellen does the town meetings in every shift, and she wants the senior staff and VPs there because every shift matters. I've been at employee parties and holiday parties helping her serve dessert from midnight to two a.m., and we've brought desserts to the emergency department when they are so busy they can't get there. Ellen greets people and introduces herself and says "thanks for coming." That is a big thing for an employee who's never met the CEO. So the staff starts to feel like she belongs to them. She laughs and says she gets more emails from the staff than anybody. But the fact is, she does.

Zane explained what she saw as the benefits of the town meeting format:

I did a lot of town meetings. I was new—I had to get to know employees and I had to tell them what was going on. I put up this chart, which turned out to be a wonderful chart. It had all the losses this place experienced during the Lifespan era. The $40 million loss in '96, the $20 million loss in '97. Loss after loss after loss after loss. That adds up to $250 million. I threw the chart up at my first board meeting. I threw it up at the Board. And I said a lot of people have got egg on their face. That's what I said to my Board. I used the same chart with the employees.

Then after those town meetings—to my utter shock—I would come back to my office and I would have 20 emails from employees who had been sitting in the audience and they were saying thank you. It was so incredible. People would say: "I want to help. I knew something was wrong but no one was ever honest enough." It was really encouraging. And that was the pearl I learned—that you *can* tell people bad news. But you have to do it in such a way that you are viewed as being honest, open, credible, and consistent.

Zane explained that the culture of Tufts-NEMC made it easier for her to effect change:

The one thing about this place that is so fabulous—that I can take no credit for—is that it has a different, better, unique culture. I had been used to the Harvard culture where there was all this bravado and testiness. This culture is much warmer—much more collegial—much more cooperative. And I call it an "Avis—we try harder culture." I tell them: "Guys, we have to go left," and they say "ok." At Partners you'd need a committee and two years to get a decision. Maybe it's because this place is smaller, I don't know.

I've never, ever worked in a place, where employees who've been there for decades, physicians who've been here a long time, will spontaneously, unsolicited, come up to me and say "I love this place. And I'm sorry to see what's happened." Even physicians who have left—and it hemorrhaged doctors in the tough days—felt that way. I called up a lot of them and asked them to have a cup of coffee with me and tell me why they left. All of them—to a person said—I didn't want to leave.

Zane used a variety of mediums to get the word out and to manage the turnaround effort. She held weekly senior staff meetings with

Schottland, the general counsel, the CFO, the vice president of external affairs, the vice president of development, and the senior vice president for market development and planning. The focus of the meetings was mostly external, with Schottland providing updates on internal operations from his weekly meetings with the operational vice presidents, the CIO, the vice presidents of clinical services, and the vice president of human resources. Zane also met regularly with the board of trustees.

She reached out to physicians in an attempt to both spread her message for change and to retain them in the face of active poaching from other AMCs. She worked hard on both retention and recruitment. In 2005 she convinced three neurosurgeons to move from Beth Israel Deaconess Medical Center to expand Tufts-NEMC's minimally invasive neurosurgery department. Schottland described the outreach that he and Zane conducted to physicians:

When Ellen came, she came with the reputation, credibility, and ability to deliver a hopeful message that prompted people to change and gave them more hope.

One thing we've done since she came here—that I've never done anywhere else—is spend an incredible amount of time talking to physicians, both recruiting and retaining them. Ellen leads that charge, although I spend a lot of time with her on it. It's one of our challenges being in Boston—it's so hard to recruit from out of town—and everyone is stealing from everyone else.

The neurosurgery department was a great example of an Ellen coup. She led the negotiations on recruiting those new doctors. Our group, which was split between Beth Israel and Tufts-NEMC, announced that they wanted to consolidate to a single hospital. We gave them a better deal and they are doing a great job here. They are young and aggressive—great surgeons. Ellen is very good at recruitment

and retention. She knows it's important. You can't run a hospital without physicians and they are very expensive to replace. A lot of hospitals have recruitment and retention programs, but most times the doctors don't get to talk to the CEO. This is a smaller and friendlier place in a lot of ways. It's not hard to get to Ellen or me. For physicians, that's a big deal. To have access to Ellen in particular is enticing for them, and she's very good at talking to them.

Not only did Zane work with physician groups, she began a monthly tour of different wards in the hospital to get in touch with patients and nurses. Salem explained:

Once a month Ellen and I tour a ward together and she speaks to patients. She'll ask them: "How's Tufts-NEMC treating you? Why did you come here? What can we do better?" The patients who understand it are shocked that the CEO is talking to them. She also learns from the patients and the floor nurses. They see that she really cares because she'll walk around their floor. When she's done touring, she'll talk to the head nurse and say, "You guys are doing a great job."

When you talk to the patients yourself, you get a whole new feel for things. We found that a lot of people liked the intimacy at Tufts-NEMC as opposed to one of the larger hospitals like Children's. We're thinking about how to use that fact in our marketing. Another thing we learned was that a lot of people didn't like the food here. So now the food service is working to change the whole menu.

Agenda for Change

In 2004, Zane, Shottland, and BDC initiated a second round of cost cutting and efficiency plans designed to improve Tufts-NEMC's processes. It was called the Agenda for Change.

Along with improving the reimbursements, it included restructuring and basic "blocking and tackling" as Zane called it:

> Blocking and tackling means the day-to-day gritty operations. The eight areas we wanted to improve were: length of stay, managed care contracts, accounts receivable, FTEs, supply chain, real estate, ambulatory clinics, and research costs. We focused really hard on those things. I think a lot of people in my job like the limelight—they want to give speeches. But the fact is if your house isn't in order, the limelight is fleeting. My first year here I resigned from most of my boards, backed off from a lot of things. I had to stick to my knitting. At the very beginning, I really hunkered down, and then I slowly started to come up for air.

The latter half of 2004 Joelson and Schottland, along with the vice president of human resources and the director of business planning, developed a restructuring plan. The plan created eight product lines that were essentially business lines: cardiac, cancer, surgery, general medicine, transplant, OB/GYN, pediatrics, psychiatry, and neurosciences. Every service in the hospital was included in one of these product lines. This was different from the past, when some services were left out of the product lines. As Schottland explained:

> It's very hard to be all things to all people. That is one of our greatest challenges programmatically and financially. But, because we are committed to doing that, we really can't afford to have key constituents feeling they are unimportant. We can't deliver care in transplants, for example, without infectious disease or internal medicine. The product lines here give everyone an opportunity to have a forum to talk about their programs. It is also a way to drive decision-making down to the physicians and give people who deliver the service control of that service.

The chief of cardiology was the clinical head of the cardiac product line, for example. He partnered with a clinical vice president—an administrator. Together, they were responsible for developing and implementing annual business plans, with goals, objectives, and budgets for the product line. The CFO and COO approved the budgets every year and reviewed the business plans monthly. The business plans were the venues by which decisions were made on investments in staff, facilities, infrastructure, and technology. The plans directed decisions regarding whether, and how much, to grow and how to accomplish that growth. Some of the areas Tufts-NEMC hoped to grow were core services, such as cardiac and cancer programs, pediatrics and maternal health, psychiatry, bariatric/obesity surgery, and organ and bone marrow transplants.

Support services such as pharmacy, nursing units, and radiology, however, were outside the management structure of product lines. Schottland explained why:

> A lot of hospitals have tried product lines in different ways. One way is the matrix structure that we have and the other way is a purer structure. We weren't big enough to be pure. We can't have a free-standing heart hospital or cancer center. We can't afford to never put a medical patient on the cardiac unit. If we don't have a cardiac patient we need that bed to put someone else in. We have to have the flexibility. So that's why the product lines can't control the nursing units. The head of cardiac would want to keep those beds just for cardiac patients and we can't afford to do that.

Length of Stay

On the operations side, one of the most important cost saving initiatives was to reduce length of stay (LOS). The consultants that Zane brought in identified that Tufts-NEMC was keeping patients a day and a half too long, compared to other AMCs. David Fairchild, Tufts-NEMC's new chief of general medicine, chaired the 30-person Care Management Committee, which was charged with reducing LOS. Fairchild and his committee set about educating the staff about the importance of reducing LOS, changing attitudes about patient care, and attacking and identifying procedural failures called "unnecessary delays" in various ways:

- The team set up a special internal email address—*LOS delays*—where staff could send a complaint or description of an unnecessary delay that impacted length of stay. This delivered useful information directly to hospital leadership regarding causes of delays.
- The BDC consultants identified areas where Tufts-NEMC could improve, such as use of tracheotomies and blood transfusions.
- Use of data, which drilled down to individual physicians' LOS statistics year over year, and presenting that feedback to physicians frequently.

One major issue that the email address identified was the use of "PICC lines." PICC lines were more durable IV lines that allowed patients to continue their medication at home. Specially trained nurses had to insert the PICC lines, and many times the doctor discharged the patient too late in the day, and these nurses were not available. Another problem with PICC lines arose when the nurse was unable to insert the line and needed fluoroscopy to aid the insertion. In the old system, the nurse informed the doctor that the PICC line was unsuccessful, then the doctor arranged for the patient to go to the fluoroscopy suite. Doctors conducted teaching rounds between 10:30 a.m. and 1 p.m., so if the nurse was unable to insert the PICC line, the patient often had to wait until the next day for the fluoroscopy suite to become available.

Fairchild and his committee came up with new procedures to remedy the situation. They required doctors to make decisions on discharges before they went on teaching rounds and they gave the nurses who inserted PICC lines the authorization to send patients directly to fluoroscopy if the PICC line could not be inserted by the nurse. Within a year of raising awareness and using more efficient procedures, the committee was able to reduce LOS by a full day, saving Tufts-NEMC $2 million per year. Fairchild explained how Zane's leadership helped with the LOS project:

Ellen brought a sense of urgency. She and the consultants identified a few key initiatives. One was the contracting initiative that she was heading, and another was reduction in length of stay for hospitalized patients. Ellen brought a compelling vision supported by compelling data for where we needed to go. One of the most compelling pieces of data was a graph showing our LOS compared to all our competitor hospitals. We were an outlier, above the line by a day and half! A one-day reduction in the average length of stay across our hospital is worth millions of dollars. I took that graph around to every department meeting I attended. After that it was just a matter of identifying what was causing the delays. There was almost no resistance to changing procedures, since everyone understood that length of stay was crucial to financial turn around, and that financial improvement was the first step toward fulfilling the vision for the future of NEMC. That is where good leadership came in.

Contract Negotiations

The hospital had just completed a round of contract negotiations with insurers when Zane joined Tufts-NEMC. She realized how critical it would be to immediately increase rates, so she went to the major health plans and asked them to reopen negotiations. Zane discussed her talks with the insurance companies:

> Because I went toe-to-toe with the insurance companies when I was at Partners, I was afraid they would think "it's payback time" since I no longer had the same leverage. To my utter delight none of them did that. They all had the attitude that it wasn't personal, it was a business decision. My argument to them about why Tufts-NEMC should get higher rates was simple. I said to them—look if you guys want the strong to get stronger and the weak to get weaker, then don't open these contracts. But if you want competition in this market, you need to open these contracts. And they did. It wasn't a cakewalk, they didn't just write me a check. We fought about it. But the truth is they all stepped up to the plate and I will always be grateful to Blue Cross, Harvard Pilgrim and Tufts.

The improvements in the contracts were absolutely critical to the financial bottom line. As Shottland explained:

> After Ellen arrived, we discovered that we were getting paid really poorly. We improved our reimbursement by $20–$25 million. That was the missing piece. That's what brought us from where we were— which was a $10 million loss—to actually making some money last year. That was Ellen's guidance and leadership that did that.

Network Building

Zane went to work bringing back the affiliations and networks Tufts/NEMC had lost in the past. By October of 2004 the hospital announced

plans to affiliate with Children's Hospital in order to augment the services of the Floating Hospital for Children, which was fragile and had lost sufficient scale over many years of neglect and poor management. Zane was able to move quickly on affiliation agreements, not allowing deals to get bogged down in red tape. Deborah Joelson, senior vice president for market development and planning, related one example of this:

> One of the first things I had on my desk when I arrived here was an affiliation agreement with a community hospital. I finished negotiating the deal and went to Ellen and said, "Ok we have an agreement." She said "Great, let's do it." I said, "What, just sign it? No committees? No . . . nothing?" At Partners, an agreement like that would take months, if not years, if it were ever to get done, because of all the internal constituencies that needed to approve everything. It was just a lot more complicated. So I always laugh when I think that she said "just do it, trust your instincts and just go ahead." With the sense of urgency and lack of resources that we have here, we don't have the time to spend noodling over every little decision.

A year later, Tufts-NEMC won a major coup when they affiliated with Primary Care, LLC (PCLLC),[22] one of the state's oldest and largest primary care independent networks. The new network became part of Tufts-NEMC and was called New England Quality Care Alliance (NEQCA). Zane recruited Jeffrey Lasker, the former chairman of the Partners physician network to run it. PCLLC had for nine years negotiated contracts (a large percentage of which were Medicare risk products, such as Secure Horizons) for its 164 physicians, which served 500,000 patients. The group felt that they needed to become affiliated with an AMC and

---

[22]Pronounced "pickle"

sent out a proposal request to systems in the Boston area. Joelson recalled how Tufts-NEMC closed that deal, when every other hospital was vying for the practice:

> We had almost no network, and few people to manage the network we had. We didn't have the infrastructure here to deal with payer contracts. That had been done at Lifespan. The PCLLC physicians wanted a seat at the table—that was most important to them. We saw an opportunity to integrate PCLLCs infrastructure into Tufts-NEMC, and not only give them a place at the table, but *make* them a table. We created an organization—NEQCA—that they ran, that provided something to Tufts-NEMC that we didn't have.
>
> This is also an example of where Ellen is so good. If you need her at a meeting she goes. We literally met every week for two months with PCLLC and Ellen was there every week to meet with them. Quite frankly I don't think many CEOs would have sat down once a week to make this happen. She is willing to get her hands dirty, but she's a leader when she does. She doesn't micro manage the process, but she makes herself available and it's clear to everyone that this is important and that it matters to her.

Working With Tufts University

Zane cultivated a close working relationship with Bacow and Michael Rosenblatt, the new dean of Tufts Medical School. She recognized the importance of the hospital and the University to each other. She sat on the board of overseers for the medical school and worked to build joint initiatives in research and fundraising. As Zane described:

> It is very famous in AMC cultures that Deans and hospital CEOs don't get along. There is usually a tremendous amount of tension. One of the things I'm proudest of—and I think the Dean would say this too—is that we get along extremely well. He started his job three weeks before I started mine, neither of us own a lot of the problems here or at the medical school so we started with a clean slate. The relationship is so strong between us. We have now developed a joint fundraising plan. We're better together than apart. That gives Larry Bacow a great deal of pleasure. He really is vested in Mike's success and mine.

Taft explained the disconnect that Tufts-NEMC had with Tufts University in the past:

> Some years ago, Tufts-NEMC actually took the Tufts name off of its signs and logos. That was a big mistake. They were not building the Tufts name, or building that relationship. In a Harvard medical town, Tufts-NEMC was not leveraging one of the top trump cards they had: the terrific and growing reputation of Tufts University, their nutrition school, medical, dental, veterinary schools. So they had all of that at Tufts-NEMC, and it wasn't being leveraged.

In the real estate arena, Tufts-NEMC held many buildings on and around the Tufts University campus on Kneeland Street in Chinatown. When Tufts-NEMC decided to sell one building it made sense for the University to purchase it. In one local business journal, Zane explained her thinking:

> If you drive down Huntington Avenue, you know when you're at Northeastern University. When you're at Commonwealth Avenue, you know you're at Boston University. But if you drive down Kneeland Street into Chinatown, you don't know you're at Tufts. You don't get the feeling you're in an urban campus.[23]

---

[23]Hollmer, Mark. "Tufts-NEMC wants a more campus feel in Chinatown," *Boston Business Journal*, June 30, 2006. Accessed online at http://boston.bizjournals.com

The University and Tufts-NEMC were in the "preliminary stage of looking at how to make the area more like a traditional urban university campus. The university held 'town meetings' to discuss the issues and is hiring planners to develop possible scenarios," the magazine reported.[24]

Prognosis: Short- and Long-Term Outlook

Leadership is about what's next. A lot of initiatives were started before Ellen got here, but she added the extra "umph" to make it happen. Now it's about what is next. What is the strategy. We're still a small hospital, we're still challenged every day because of our size to meet the financial basics to succeed.

—Ed Schottland, COO

In 2006, with her leadership team established, the sale of a building to Tufts University for $28 million adding needed capital, cost savings initiatives in place and improved managed care contracts, Zane was starting to move to the next phase: building a strategy for the future. Zane and her team were working with the Board in a major strategic planning initiative. In addition, Joelson was doing marketing research, the first Tufts-NEMC had conducted in years. They were trying to answer questions such as:

- What scale should Tufts-NEMC be?
- How can we best market ourselves?
- How can we differentiate ourselves in the market place?
- What is the best way to work with community hospitals and physicians?

As Joelson explained:

We are trying to create an alternative. Our goal is to be big enough to have the scale we need to operate efficiently and to be able to provide sufficient sub specialties to be an academic medical center—the principle teaching hospital of Tufts University School of Medicine. We don't want to be as big or expensive as Partners. We have 3% market share; Partners has 25% market share. We're at best a 400-bed hospital; Partners has 2,000 beds. We see ourselves as a network of some physicians and some community hospitals, and as a lower cost alternative in the market. We can be effective with the new pay for performance contracts. It is more efficient and less expensive to keep the care local, so our strategy is to try to move the care that can be moved to community hospitals where we have relationships.

On the marketing side, we are implementing what we call an anti-invisibility advertising campaign. Our market research determined we had no identity in the market. We also learned that we were a house of individual brands—the doctors—rather than a brand in itself. As a result, we are building a physician-to-physician marketing campaign, using NEQCA as that the starting point. We also plan to grow NEQCA from 600 to 1,000 doctors by 2010.

Perhaps the biggest plan to come out of the strategic initiative was the partnership with New England Baptist Hospital, another Tufts Medical School affiliated teaching hospital, to build a new 190-bed hospital in the Boston suburbs. If the plan came to fruition, it would be the first hospital built in Massachusetts in 25 years. Although the site had not yet been selected, Zane was quoted as saying that

In the past, hospitals have asked people in the suburbs to come to them and pay more for parking than the co-pay on their health insurance. Our view is: Wouldn't it be a

[24]Ibid.

good idea to take sophisticated academic medicine and bring it to the people?[25]

This type of bold planning gave the employees at Tufts/NEMC confidence about the future. Deeb Salem gave his viewpoint on where the hospital stood in mid-2006:

> I've never been more optimistic. There are still a lot of problems. But the main source of anxiety is what happens if Ellen decides to leave. That's the problem having somebody that good. We've seen how well she runs things. But with her in charge I do have a lot of hope.

Zane finally saw the light at the end of the tunnel she had entered in January 2004, but she knew that her work had only just begun. She needed to find a way to keep the staff on track for the turn around. She needed improved efficiency and cash flows to keep wind in the sails in order to move the rudder in the right direction. She also knew that Tufts-NEMC was far from a safe harbor:

> I have lots of friends at Partners—but business is business—if they could steal my best bone marrow transplant surgeon they would. It's the way it is. That is the deal. I can't let down my guard for a minute.
>
> I am able, now, to spend much more of my time on strategy, on the future, on where this place is going. That is, frankly, why I took the job. I didn't come here to pull down accounts receivable, I came here to do something to position this place for the future.

---

[25]Rowland, Christopher, and Bailey, Steve, "Tufts Affiliates Plan Hospital in Suburbs," *The Boston Globe,* September 8, 2006, page A1 Section: Metro/Region. Accessed online at www.boston.com/news/bostonglo bearchives

Exhibit 1 Tufts/NEMC Income and Expense for Fiscal Years 1989–2005 (in thousands)

	1989	1990	1991	1992	1993	1994	1995	1996	1997	1998	1999	2000	2001	2002	2003	2004	2005
Revenue:																	
Net patient services revenue	218,820	230,616	272,108	297,351	314,445	301,385	309,938	281,791	287,076	299,930	318,145	341,894	371,273	397,212	473,012	452,786	495,005
Direct expenditures on grants, contracts, and other activities	21,063	21,423	23,083	25,608	28,467	33,302	60,805	52,059									
Recovery of indirect costs on grants and contracts	5,770	7,129	5,778	7,900	8,883	9,762			55,205								
Software including support and consulting			12,009	14,660	18,934	23,469	28,777	6,175									
Other revenue	22,340	23,949	16,788	14,443	14,801	13,961	13,690	17,917	22,797	24,045	22,561	26,228	36,055	33,790	51,686	42,853	48,232
Endowment earnings contributed toward community benefit										9,229	10,647	16,512	7,949	1,596			
Net assets released from restrictions used for operations										3,435	2,272	3,037	3,020	4,753	4,526	17,259	2,924
Net assets released from restrictions used for research										44,001	41,314	47,582	37,702	38,250	53,196	52,891	55,901
Total Operating Revenue	267,993	283,117	329,766	359,962	385,530	381,879	413,210	357,942	365,078	380,640	394,939	435,253	455,999	475,601	582,420	565,789	602,062

(Continued)

Exhibit 1 (Continued)

	1989	1990	1991	1992	1993	1994	1995	1996	1997	1998	1999	2000	2001	2002	2003	2004	2005
Net Investment income	5,151	698															
Unrestricted gifts, grants, and awards/ net assets released from restrictions	535	817					1,104	936									
Adjustments to prior year estimates with third party payors						12,600	11,342	11,800									
Total Revenue	273,679	284,632	329,766	359,962	385,530	394,479	425,656	370,678	365,078	380,640	394,939	435,253	455,999	475,601	582,420	565,789	602,062
Expenses:																	
Salaries and wages	104,574	113,557	128,739	143,124	158,511	160,183	167,380	146,900	184,746	191,629	180,206	203,449	222,489	227,706	297,827	295,645	308,057
Employee benefits	15,591	18,920	21,163	23,407	26,004	26,787	31,130	24,581	24,031	21,531	21,058	24,098	25,491	28,543	55,918	57,004	56,416
Purchased services of physician groups	23,033	24,579	29,648	31,236	35,354	32,051	39,620	37,176		34,021	35,875	36,416	40,201	43,075	49,461	40,303	47,627
Supplies and expenses	63,924	68,740	77,499	87,684	96,660	102,688	132,843	119,242	115,950	95,124	109,120	119,730	135,132	140,891	158,501	141,793	140,371
Interest	8,266	8,561	8,048	8,165	9,194	8,996	12,115	14,230	14,164	13,983	13,775	13,576	13,350	13,193	12,561	12,044	11,607
Depreciation and amortization	15,687	15,382	18,914	19,188	22,548	26,065	32,033	32,996	32,646	14,525	15,168	16,034	18,076	18,959	21,410	23,976	23,307
Direct expenditures on grants, contracts, and other activities	21,063	21,423	23,083	25,608	28,467	33,302											
Uncompensated care/provision for bad debts	16,433	7,911	12,171	18,878	14,087	12,796	16,187	17,175	18,853	18,344	19,492	21,309	17,099	15,747	15,934	21,184	12,541

	1989	1990	1991	1992	1993	1994	1995	1996	1997	1998	1999	2000	2001	2002	2003	2004	2005
Other Expenses							(6,250)		(138,500)						14,638		
Total operating expenses	268,571	279,073	319,265	357,290	390,825	402,868	425,058	392,300	390,390	389,157	394,694	434,612	471,838	488,114	626,250	591,949	599,926
Income (loss) from operations	5,108	5,559	10,501	2,672	(5,295)	(8,389)	598	(21,622)	(163,812)	(8,517)	245	641	(15,839)	(12,513)	(43,830)	(26,160)	2,136
Nonoperating Gains and Losses:																	
Net unrestricted investment income		8,611	9,748	6,090	5,242	2,995	805	5,461	4,561	7,974	4,421	9,226	4,040	2,277	2,102	2,041	2,838
Net realized gain on sale of investments	1,490	1,405	1,814	3,876	3,770	6,570	2,357	2,253	9,711	9,100	6,083	5,506	2,691	(2,150)	3,429	4,842	11,074
Gain on sale of TSI and other property								72,958		(245)						19,698	2,075
Other nonoperating losses									50	(1,063)	(28)				(196)	188	234
Total nonoperating gains, net	1,490	10,016	11,562	9,966	9,012	9,565	3,162	80,672	14,272	16,829	10,476	14,732	6,731	127	5,335	26,769	16,221
Excess (deficit) of revenues over expenses	6,598	15,575	22,063	12,638	3,717	1,176	3,760	59,050	(149,540)	8,312	10,721	15,373	(9,108)	(12,386)	(38,495)	609	18,357
Total other capital items						(11,814)	4,765	13,455	(3,070)						18,041	5,888	2,636
Excess (deficit) of revenues over expenses	6,598	15,575	22,063	12,638	3,717	(10,638)	8,525	72,505	(152,610)	8,312	10,721	15,373	(9,108)	(12,386)	(20,454)	6,497	20,993

Source: Company Records.

Exhibit 2 Boston Comparative Demographic and Health Care Indicators

	Demographics[a]		Health System Characteristics			Health Care Utilization[c]	
	Boston	Metropolitan Areas 200,000+ population		Boston	Metropolitan Areas 200,000+ population		Boston	Metropolitan Areas 200,000+ population

	Boston	Metropolitan Areas 200,000+ population		Boston	Metropolitan Areas 200,000+ population		Boston	Metropolitan Areas 200,000+ population
Population	4,579,137		Staffed Hospital Beds per 1,000 Population (2002)	2.2	3.1	Adjusted Inpatient Admissions per 1,000 Population	240	197
Persons Age 65 or Older	12.7%	10%	Physicians per 1,000 Population (2003)[b]	2.8	1.9	Persons With Any Emergency Room Visit in Past Year	20%	18%
Median Family Income	$39,182	$31,301	HMO Penetration (including Medicare/Medicaid)[c]	37%	29%	Persons With Any Doctor Visit in Past Year	86%	78%

Demographics[a]	Boston	Metropolitan Areas 200,000+ population
Unemployment Rate	5.2%	6.0%
Persons Living in Poverty	9%	13%
Persons Without Health Insurance	5%	14%

Health System Characteristics	Boston	Metropolitan Areas 200,000+ population
Medicare-Adjusted Average per Capita Cost Rate, 2005	$768	$718

Health Care Utilization[c]	Boston	Metropolitan Areas 200,000+ population
Persons Who Did Not Get Needed Medical Care During the Last 12 Months	3.6%	5.7%
Privately Insured People in Families With Annual Out-of-Pocket Costs of $500 or More	33%	44%

Source: Center for Studying Health System Change, Community Report Number 11 of 12, December 2005.

[a] Statistics for year ending 2003.

[b] Includes nonfederal, patient care physicians, except radiologists, pathologists, and anesthesiologists.

[c] Markets with population greater than 250,000.

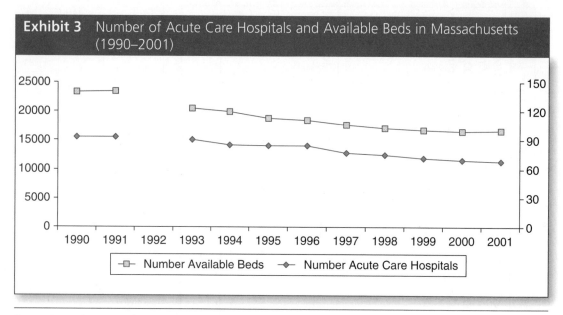

Exhibit 3 Number of Acute Care Hospitals and Available Beds in Massachusetts (1990–2001)

Source: Massachusetts Health Care Trends: 1990–2004.

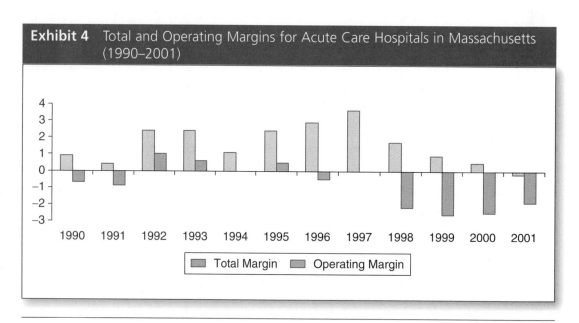

Exhibit 4 Total and Operating Margins for Acute Care Hospitals in Massachusetts (1990–2001)

Source: Massachusetts Health Care Trends: 1990–2004.

Exhibit 5   Distribution of Health Care Expenditures in Massachusetts (1990 and 1998)

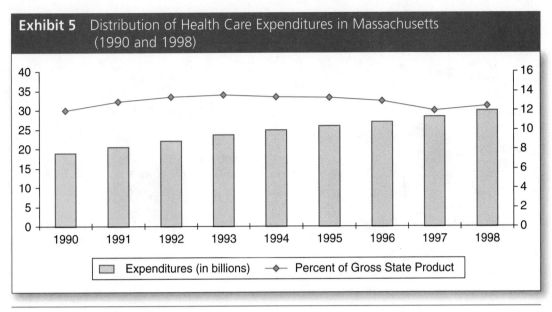

Source: Massachusetts Health Care Trends: 1990–2004.

Exhibit 6   Distribution of Acute Care Hospital Revenues by Payment Source in Massachusetts (1991 and 2001)

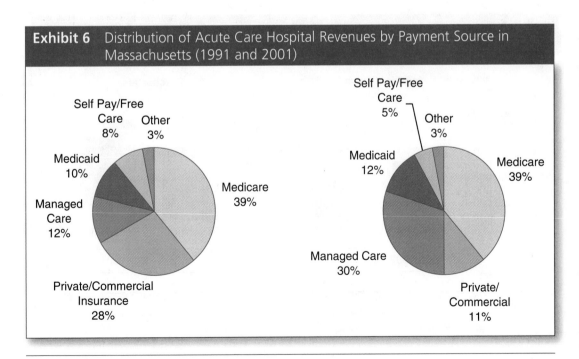

Source: Massachusetts Health Care Trends: 1990–2004.

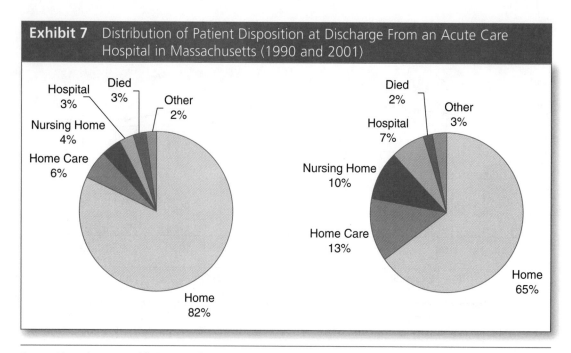

Exhibit 7 Distribution of Patient Disposition at Discharge From an Acute Care Hospital in Massachusetts (1990 and 2001)

Source: Massachusetts Health Care Trends: 1990–2004.

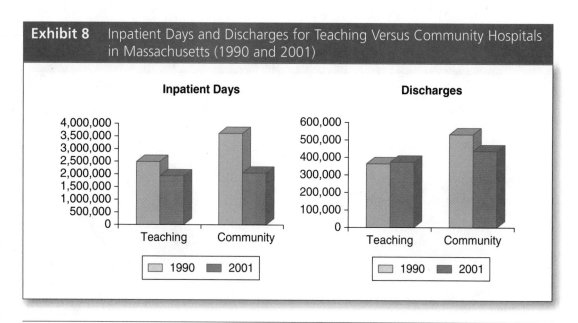

Exhibit 8 Inpatient Days and Discharges for Teaching Versus Community Hospitals in Massachusetts (1990 and 2001)

Source: Massachusetts Health Care Trends: 1990–2004.

Exhibit 9 Acute Care Hospital Discharges per 1,000 Population and Average Length of Stay in Massachusetts (1990–2001)

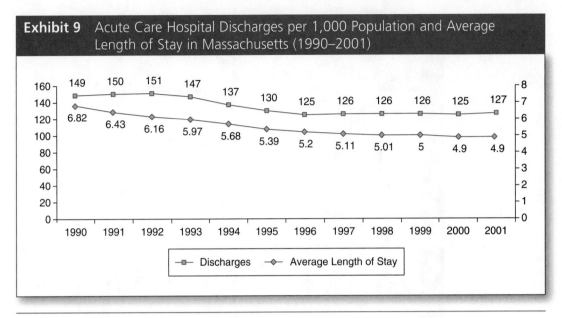

Source: Massachusetts Health Care Trends: 1990–2004.

Exhibit 10 Major Provider Networks and Other Care Institutions in the Greater Boston Market

Name	Acute Care Hospitals	Physician Networks	Other Facilities	Medical School Affiliation	Employees (FTE)	Revenues/ Net Assets*	Admissions (2004)/ Discharge % (2003)
Partners Health Care System	MGH, BWH, Faulkner, Newton-Wellesley, North Shore Medical Center (NSMC), McLean (mental health)	PCHI	Spaulding Shaughnessy-Kaplan, RHCI, Partners Home Care, 2 Skilled Nursing homes	Harvard Tufts (Faulkner & NSMC)	35,300	$395 million $1.5 billion	87,616 20.8%
Boston Medical Center (BMC)		Boston HealthNet Quincy Medical Center		Boston University	4,429	$752 million $1.06 billion	28,173 6.0%
CareGroup	Beth Israel Deaconess, Mt. Auburn Hospital, New England Baptist, Beth Israel Deaconess-Needham	Community Care Alliance	Joslin Diabetes Center	Harvard Medical School	5,000 (Beth Isreal Deaconess)	$24 million $95 million	33,640 9.0%

Name	Acute Care Hospitals	Physician Networks	Other Facilities	Medical School Affiliation	Employees (FTE)	Revenues/ Net Assets*	Admissions (2004)/ Discharge % (2003)
Caritas Christi Healthcare	Caritas St.Elizabeth's St. Anne's Fall River, Holy Family Hospital and Medical Center, Caritas Norwood, Caritas Carney Hospital Dorchester, Caritas Good Samaritan Medical Center Brockton	Caritas Physician	St. Joseph Nursing Care Center, Neponset Valley Nursing Association, Good Samaritan Hospice, St. Mary's Women & Infants Center of Dorchester	Tufts Medical School	12,000	$90 million $20 million	15,781 11.6%
New England Medical Center	Tufts-NEMC Floating Hospital For Children	NEQCA		Tufts	3,000	$487 million $389 million	17,000 2.7%
Hallmark Health System	Lawrence Memorial, Melrose-Wakefield Hospitals	Ell Pond Medical Association	Malden Medical Center, other long term care, home health and diagnostic services	Tufts (family practice), Hallmark School of Nursing		$225 million $180 million	2.7%

Source: Massachusetts Health and Educational Facilities Authority. Accessed from www.mehfa.org; WebMD Quality Services. Accessed from www.webmdqualityservices .com

*From IRS Form 990 fiscal year ending 2003. Available at www.guidestar.org/findocuments/2004

Exhibit 11 Tufts/NEMC Operational Indicators Versus Industry Benchmarks

	Industry Benchmark	NEMC (FY 2006)	Translated Impact on Budget	Impact on Cash
Days in Accounts Receivable	48.8	55.6	$775,416	$7,049,234
Accounts Payable Days	60.0	51.2	$1,203,061	$10,936,918
Average Length of Stay	5.5	5.79	$2,085,627	$2,085,627
Operating Margin	1.9%	0.4%	$10,169,579	$10,169,579
Days Cash on Hand	110.7	89.4	$609,468	$5,540,621
Commercial Insurance Contracts			$40,000,000	$40,000,000

Index

About the Authors

Tupper F. Cawsey is Professor Emeritus of Business, Wilfrid Laurier University. He is presently Editor, *Case Research* Journal, for the North American Case Research Association. He has served on several boards of directors and was Chair, Lutherwood Board from 2003–2008. Tupper was recognized nationally in 2001 as one of Canada's top five business professors by receiving the Leaders in Management Education award, sponsored by PricewaterhouseCoopers and the National Post. He is also the 1994 recipient of the David Bradford Educator Award, presented by the Organizational Behaviour Teaching Society, and the 1990 Wilfrid Laurier University "Outstanding Teacher Award."

Tupper created the Case Track for the Administrative Sciences Association of Canada, a peer review process for cases. He is author or co-author of over 6 books and monographs including, *Toolkit for Organizational Change—1st Edition, Canadian Cases in Human Resource Management, Cases in Organizational Behaviour,* and several monographs including *Control Systems in Excellent Canadian Companies* and the *Career Management Guide.* Tupper has over 50 refereed journal and conference publications. In 2005, he received the Christiansen Award from the Kaufman Foundation and the North American Case Research Association, and in 2007.his case, "Board Games at Lutherwood," won the Directors College Corporate Governance Award and the Bronze Case Award at the NACRA Conference. In 2009, his case, "NuComm International," won the Gold Case Award at the NACRA Conference.

Gene Deszca is Professor of Business Administration, a former MBA Director, and currently the Associate MBA Director in the School of Business and Economics at Wilfrid Laurier University. He has held a number of leadership roles at Laurier, including ones involving the development and launch of the full-time, one-year MBA program, the executive MBA program, and the international concentration. He was instrumental in the development of the Society of Management Accountants of Canada's post-university professional accreditation programs and is a member of their national Board of Directors.

Gene is the author or coauthor of over 100 journal, conference publications/ presentations, books, monographs, and technical papers. These include the books *Canadian Cases in Human Resource Management* and *Cases in Organizational*

Behaviour and the articles *Driving Loyalty Through Time-to-Value* and *Managing the New Product Development Process: Best-in-Class Principles and Leading Practices.* His current research and consulting activity focuses on organizational change and the development of high performance enterprises.

Cynthia Ingols is an Associate Professor, School of Management (SOM), Simmons College, Boston. At the SOM, she directs the internship program for undergraduate and MBA students and teaches courses in Organizational Change and Career Strategies to MBA students. Ingols leads Strategic Leadership for Women, an executive education program with a global reach that strengths the leadership skills and self-confidence of its participants. Early in her career, she received her doctorate from the Harvard Graduate School of Education in Organization Behavior and taught Management Communication at the Harvard Business School.

Cynthia focuses her consulting work in three areas: conducting diagnostic work to promote change in organizations; developing interactive executive education programs, particularly using cases and simulations; and coaching executives to enhance their leadership capacity and careers. Ingols's research and publications follow similar lines. Her research on executive education programs has been published in leading journals, such as *Harvard Business Review, Organizational Dynamics,* and *Training.* Her research work on creating innovative organizational structures and change was published in the *Design Management Journal.* She has published numerous articles about careers in journals such as the *Journal of Career Development* and *Human Resource Development Quarterly.* She co-authored two books on career management: *Take Charge of Your Career* (2005) and *A Smart, Easy Guide to Interviewing* (2003).

SAGE Research Methods Online

The essential tool for researchers